RODALE'S

GARDEN ANSWERS

VEGETABLES, FRUITS AND HERBS

At-a-Glance Solutions for Every Gardening Problem

Edited by Fern Marshall Bradley

CONTRIBUTORS: LINDA A. GILKESON, TERRY KRAUTWURST, LYNN MCGOWAN, PATRICIA S. MICHALAK, JEAN M. A. NICK, SARA PACHER, PAMELA K. PEIRCE

D1385016

Rodale Press, Emmaus, Pennsylvania

Rodale's Garden Answers
Editorial and Design Staff
Editor: Fern Marshall Bradley
Contributing Editors: Barbara W. Ellis, Jean M. A. Nick,
    and Nancy J. Ondra
Senior Research Associate: Heidi A. Stonehill
Copy Editors: Ann Snyder and Barbara Webb
Administrative Assistant: Susan Nickol
Cover and Book Designer: Linda Brightbill-Bossard
Book Layout: Peter A. Chiarelli
Front Cover Illustrator: Jean Emmons
Back Cover Illustrators: Robin Brickman,
    Rae D. Chambers, Julia S. Child, and Patti Rutman
Interior Illustrators: Robin Brickman,
    Pamela Carroll, Rae D. Chambers,
    Julia S. Child, and Patti Rutman
Indexer: Nanette Bendyna
Production Coordinator: Melinda Rizzo

Rodale Organic Gardening Books
Managing Editor: Fern Marshall Bradley
Executive Creative Director: Christin Gangi
Art Director: Patricia Field
Production Manager: Robert V. Anderson Jr.
Studio Manager: Leslie M. Keefe
Associate Copy Manager: Jennifer Hornsby
Manufacturing Manager: Mark Krahforst

We're always happy to hear from you. For questions
or comments concerning the editorial content of this
book, please write to:
    Rodale Book Readers' Service
    33 East Minor Street
    Emmaus, PA 18098
Look for other Rodale books wherever books are
sold. Or call us at (800) 848-4735.

For more information about Rodale Organic
Gardening magazine and books, visit us at
www.organicgardening.com

**Library of Congress
Cataloging-in-Publication Data**

Rodale's garden answers : vegetables, fruits and
herbs : at-a-glance solutions for every gardening
problem / edited by Fern Marshall Bradley ; contributors, Linda A. Gilkeson ... [et al. ; illustrators, Robin
Brickman ... et al.]
    p.   cm.
    Includes bibliographical references (p.   ) and
index.
    ISBN 0–87596–639–X   hardcover
    1. Vegetable gardening. 2. Fruit-culture. 3. Herb
gardening. 4. Organic gardening. I. Bradley, Fern
Marshall. II. Gilkeson, Linda A. III. Rodale Press.
IV. Title: Garden answers, vegetables, fruits and
herbs.
SB321.R63 1995
635'.0484—dc20   94–37770
                                            CIP

Distributed in the book trade by St. Martin's Press

12 14 16 18 20 19 17 15 13 11 hardcover
 2   4   6   8 10   9   7   5   3   1 paperback

*Gardening is more than
just digging, planting, pulling
weeds, and picking vegetables
and fruits.
It is also the savoring and
cultivation of life.*

❧

ROBERT RODALE
1930–1990

CONTENTS

GROWING FRUITS

PART 3

GROWING HERBS

PART 4

CONTROLLING PESTS AND DISEASES

PART 5

CREDITS

The Contributors

Linda A. Gilkeson, Ph.D., is coauthor of *Rodale's Successful Organic Gardening: Controlling Pests and Diseases.* She is the integrated pest management coordinator in the Ministry of Environment, Lands, and Parks for the Province of British Columbia.

Terry Krautwurst is a freelance garden and nature writer from North Carolina. He is a former senior editor of *Mother Earth News* magazine.

Lynn McGowan is a freelance writer from Pennsylvania. She is a former associate editor for *American Horticulturist* magazine.

Patricia S. Michalak is the author of *Rodale's Successful Organic Gardening: Herbs.* She has a master's degree in entomology from Michigan State University.

Jean M. A. Nick is an associate garden book editor at Rodale Press. She has a master's degree in horticulture from Rutgers University and grows vegetables and small fruits on her farm in eastern Pennsylvania.

Sara Pacher is a freelance garden writer and former senior editor for *Mother Earth News* magazine.

Pamela K. Peirce is a garden writer, horticultural photographer, and photo editor from San Francisco. She is the author of *Golden Gate Gardening.*

The Editors

Fern Marshall Bradley has a master's degree in horticulture from Rutgers University. She has managed an organic market garden, is an avid vegetable gardener, and is an editor of garden books at Rodale Press.

Barbara W. Ellis is a freelance garden writer and editor from Pennsylvania. She has a bachelor's degree from Kenyon College and a bachelor's degree in horticulture from the Ohio State University. She is a former managing editor at Rodale Press and a former publications director/editor for *American Horticulturist* magazine.

Nancy J. Ondra has a bachelor's degree in agronomy from Delaware Valley College and is an associate garden book editor at Rodale Press. Her special interest is collecting and propagating perennials.

The Experts

Many garden professionals took time to answer our questions and suggest new techniques and ideas. We especially want to thank Deborah Bertoldi, owner of Cedar Hill Gardens in Reading, Pennsylvania; Alan Kapuler, research director for Seeds of Change in Santa Fe, New Mexico; Calvin Lamborn, vegetable breeder for Rogers Seed Company in Twin Falls, Idaho; Mohammed Nuru, landscape architect and executive director of SLUG in San Francisco, California; and Barbara Pleasant, garden writer and editor in Huntsville, Alabama.

INTRODUCTION

Which would you rather do: Read a book or spend time in the garden? If you're like me, you'd rather be planting, or pruning, or just soaking up the beauty and freshness of plants and the outdoors.

I do love books. And in fact, I spend much more of my time thinking and reading about gardening than the average gardener. But, as a garden book editor, that's my job. My hobby, my relaxation, and one of my great joys is working with plants. That's why I love *this* new book, *Rodale's Garden Answers.* It's designed especially for gardeners who want to read a little so they can garden a lot. We've planned this book for quick reference—for finding instant answers to last-minute questions when you're heading out the door with seeds or plants in hand. We've filled it with practical illustrations that explain gardening techniques at a glance. We've designed special season-by-season schedules for crops so you'll always have an answer to that question, "What should I do today in my garden?" We matched crop-by-crop lists of common symptoms of problems with causes and organic remedies, to give you fast, accurate solutions when your cry is "What's wrong with my plants?"

Finding the Answers

This book has five parts: "Getting Started," "Growing Vegetables," "Growing Fruits," "Growing Herbs," and "Controlling Pests and Diseases." Turn to the contents for a list of topics covered in each part. You'll find each of your favorite crops, from Asparagus to Turnip, and Apple to Strawberry. Chances are, if you have a specific question about a crop, such as "How much carrot seed should I plant?" or "When should I prune peach trees?", you'll find the answer in the entry about that crop. You'll also find special coverage of practical topics like "Soil Testing," "Watering the Garden," and "Staking and Trellising." If you have general questions— "How can I tell when my garden needs watering?" or "What should I use to frame a raised bed?"—look for the related special topic, and turn to that page for answers.

Of course, you don't have to have a *specific* question to find useful information in *Garden Answers.* Perhaps you'd just like to know more about growing tomatoes. Turn to "Tomato," and you'll find concise, complete coverage of tomato culture, from choosing plants through harvesting and storage. Take note of the special feature "Season-by-Season Care." It summarizes what-to-do-when from spring through fall to get the best from your tomato crop. You can customize the information to suit your particular region and season. We've even included illustrations to help you link the timing of certain practices to the stage of development of your fruit trees and bushes.

Keep an eye out for "Green Thumb Tip" and "For Best Results" recommendations throughout the book. These cue you to special techniques you may want to try and to essential information for getting the most for your dollar or ensuring crop success.

And if ever you're in doubt about where to find information in *Garden Answers,* remember the index. It's a detailed summary of the book and should speed you on the way to finding answers and getting back out where you belong—in your garden.

Fern Marshall Bradley

Editor

PART 1

GETTING STARTED

STARTING YOUR FIRST GARDEN

You don't have to know everything about gardening to grow vegetables, fruits, and herbs successfully. Gardening is a learn-as-you-go endeavor. To get started, all you need is some basic information about your local growing conditions, a few tools, and a willingness to get your fingernails dirty.

Gather Essential Facts

Neighboring gardeners, garden clubs, and the Co-operative Extension Service are all excellent sources for information you'll need to begin gardening.

Know your climatic zone. A plant's ability to withstand a given climate is called its *hardiness*. The USDA has developed a Plant Hardiness Zone Map that divides North America into 10 numbered climatic zones. Zone 1 is the coldest, and Zone 10 the warmest. Knowing your zone enables you to choose plants appropriate for your location. You can check which zone you live in by looking at the map on page 357.

Seed and nursery catalogs often list hardiness zones in their descriptions of fruit trees and perennial plants. If

you live in Zone 6 (for example) and a plant is listed as "hardy in Zones 5–8" or "hardy to Zone 5," it will probably do well in your area. But if you live in Zone 4, you'll need to choose a more cold-hardy species or cultivar.

Learn your area's last and first frost dates. The last frost in spring and the first killing frost in fall mark the beginning and end, respectively, of the growing season. Knowing when frosts occur in your area helps you determine proper planting and harvest times. The instructions on a seed packet, for example, might read, "Sow seeds outdoors two weeks after the last spring frost" or "Start seeds in flats indoors four weeks before the last spring frost."

Determine your soil's pH and fertility. Soil acidity or alkalinity influences plant growth. It is commonly expressed as a pH number ranging from 1.0 (very acid) to 14.0 (very alkaline). Most vegetables and fruits prefer soil with a pH of 6.5 to 7.0. Soil fertility also affects the health and eventual yields of crops. A soil test measures pH as well as nutrient content. The results will reveal imbalances that you may need to correct. See "Soil

Testing" on page 10 to learn how to collect a sample of your soil and have it tested.

Go Easy on Yourself

Gardening should be a pleasant, rewarding pastime. For beginners, especially, keeping things simple is the best approach for success.

Start small. The most common mistake made by inexperienced gardeners is to plant too much in too large a space. A lot of garden is a lot of work. A small, compact garden gives you time to tend your crops carefully, practice skills, and learn about the garden environment. A 10- by 10-foot row plot or two 4- by 10-foot raised beds are plenty for a beginning gardener and can yield 75 to 100 pounds of vegetables.

Buy transplants. Starting every crop from seed can be daunting. Transplants bought from a nursery give your garden an instant start. Broccoli, cabbage, cauliflower, peppers, and tomatoes do well as transplants. Most herbs thrive when set out as transplants, too.

Grow foods that you like. There's no sense raising

spinach if nobody in your family will eat it. Choose foods that you'll really enjoy at the dinner table.

Start with easy crops. Some plants are easier to grow and produce larger harvests than others. Good vegetable crops for beginners include green beans, cabbage, cucumbers, leaf lettuce, summer squash, and tomatoes. Raspberries and strawberries are relatively easy to grow and produce a tasty harvest within a few months to a year after planting. Some easy herbs to try: basil, chives, dill, parsley, sage, and thyme.

Buy good-quality tools. Start with the basics, such as a garden spade, digging fork, hoe, trowel, garden rake, and pocketknife. See "Using Garden Tools" on page 34 for additional advice.

GARDEN STYLES

You can have a garden almost anywhere, whether in the city or country. Choose a garden layout that suits the space you have available. To learn more about how to plan a garden layout and make crop choices, refer to "Deciding What to Grow" on page 42.

Raised-bed garden. *Raised beds provide a space-efficient garden that produces higher yields for a given area than does a row garden.*

Container garden. *Salad greens and dwarf vegetables make good choices for pots or planters; also try strawberries, blueberries, and grapes.*

Minigarden. *Small yard? Try a miniature crop plot: Plant a few vegetables in a sunny spot along the driveway, or even in a flower bed.*

Row garden. *This traditional garden is easy to lay out and plant. However, it requires lots of space and may need frequent weeding.*

ORGANIC GARDENING BASICS

A backyard organic garden should be a bit of a wild place. Weeds poke up here and there among the crops. There's wildlife in the garden—birds, toads, and a wide variety of insects.

An organic garden is a balanced, natural environment in which plants can thrive without chemical fertilizers or pesticides. The plants, animals, insects, fungi, and even the microscopic soil organisms all play an important and necessary role. Rather than struggling to wipe out weeds and pests, the organic gardener uses natural controls—such as mulches and beneficial insects—to suppress them and minimize their effects on crops. Compost, cover crops, and natural amendments feed the soil and replenish the nutrients taken up by growing plants.

Is it difficult to establish this kind of diverse mini-ecosystem? The answer is No! You can easily take the first steps toward establishing an organic garden.

Start a Compost Pile

Compost is decomposed plant and animal material. To make compost, you encourage things like leaves, pulled weeds, and grass clippings to rot; the end result is a wonderful soil conditioner. Adding compost to your soil makes your garden easier to cultivate, helps to balance the pH, improves moisture retention and root penetration, and converts soil nutrients into a form more easily taken up by plants. What's more, compost virtually makes itself, at no cost, from yard and garden waste and kitchen scraps that you'd otherwise throw away. See "Making Compost" on page 22 for more information.

Enrich Your Soil

Nutrient-rich soil supports vigorous, healthy plants that resist insect pests and diseases naturally. Use the results of a soil test as a guide to creating a balanced soil that will foster robust crops.

Start now, but remember that building fertile soil the organic way is a gradual, ongoing process. Add compost regularly. Grow green manure crops and till them into the soil to add organic matter. Test your soil every few years to monitor its condition. Add organic soil amendments as needed to correct imbalances.

Encourage Beneficials

Only a relative handful of insects and other creatures actually damages crops. Most insect species are beneficial; they pollinate food plants and flowers, eat weeds, and prey on pest insects. Birds, toads, and bats also are efficient pest predators. A single bat will gobble up over 1,000 flying insects a night; just one toad will eat more than 100 insects, slugs, and cutworms a day.

Invite these natural allies into your garden by providing them with sources of food, shelter, and water. Build birdhouses and bat boxes. Provide grassy areas and weedy patches to encourage predatory beetles. Plant flowering herbs such as mint and dill to attract bees and parasitic wasps.

Grow Pest-Resistant Crops

With diligence and care, you can grow virtually any vegetable, fruit, or herb organically. Some crops, however, are less susceptible to disease and insect attack than others. Small fruits such as raspberries and strawberries, for instance, generally require less attention than tree fruits such as apples and cherries. Also, individual cultivars have been bred to resist specific diseases and pests. For example, 'Liberty' apple is known for its mildew resistance. 'Katahdin' and 'Sequoia' potatoes resist the Colorado potato beetle. Seed catalogs include resistance characteristics in their descriptions.

Study Your Garden

Spend time looking carefully at the creatures and plants that inhabit your garden. Examine the undersides of leaves and the soil around plant stems for crawling insects; look beneath mulch for spiders, beetles, and other ground dwellers. Learn to identify weed seedlings; tiny weeds are easier to control than big ones. Using a good field guide, learn to identify common pest and beneficial insects in their egg, larva, and adult stages. Handpicking insects is a great organic pest control method, but handpicking beneficial insects isn't!

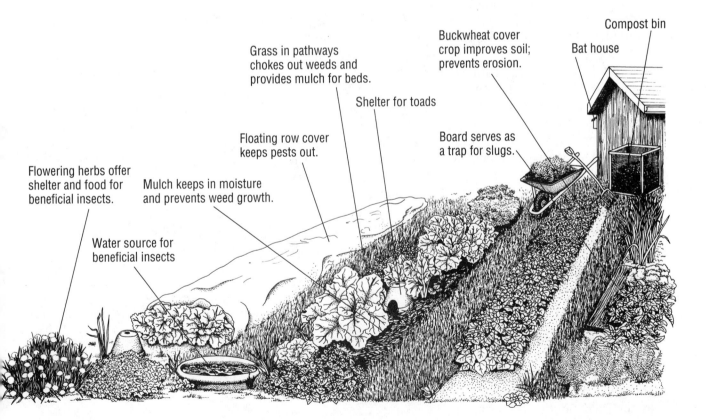

Grass in pathways chokes out weeds and provides mulch for beds.

Buckwheat cover crop improves soil; prevents erosion.

Compost bin

Bat house

Shelter for toads

Floating row cover keeps pests out.

Board serves as a trap for slugs.

Flowering herbs offer shelter and food for beneficial insects.

Mulch keeps in moisture and prevents weed growth.

Water source for beneficial insects

An ideal organic garden. *A carefully tended organic garden produces crops that thrive naturally. The keys to success are constant attention to soil building, careful management of plants, and an approach to pest control that mimics nature's own system of checks and balances.*

SELECTING A SITE

Search for the sun when you choose a site for vegetables, fruits, and herbs. Adequate sunlight is essential for growing good crops. While drainage and soil fertility can be improved, it may be impossible to turn a shady site into a sunny site (short of knocking down buildings).

Before you choose your site, observe how the sun hits your property at different times of the day. A site that's sunny in the morning may be shaded in the afternoon by your house.

Keep in mind that light exposure changes with the seasons. A location that seems open and sunny in winter, when trees are leafless, may be shaded in summer and fall.

Vegetables and Herbs

Look for the following conditions when choosing a site.

Daylong full sun. Most vegetables and herbs need a minimum of six hours of direct sun every day. A south- or southeast-facing site is ideal. In most areas, choose the sunniest available site. In very hot regions such as the Deep South, try to find a spot where high shade from overhanging trees will protect plants from midday heat.

Good air circulation. A free flow of air helps prevent disease and reduces damage from late-spring or early-fall frosts. Avoid sites closed in on all sides by buildings or dense vegetation.

Too much wind, however, can dehydrate plants. Look for a partial windbreak, such as a loose hedge or stand of trees, to protect your garden without completely blocking air flow.

Adequate drainage. Many vegetables and most herbs cannot tolerate wet soil. Before you settle on a site for your garden, wait for rain. Then grab your umbrella and visit the site. Is water puddling heavily there? Check the site after the rain to see how long it takes to dry out. Avoid sites that stay swampy. If you must deal with a wet site, build raised growing beds to improve drainage.

HIDDEN PITFALLS

Don't put your garden over buried water, septic, or utility lines. Avoid planting food crops near old buildings, where the soil may contain high levels of lead from chipped paint. In snowy regions, sites next to or downslope from highways may be contaminated with road salt.

No trees nearby. Keep your garden as far as possible from trees, which consume huge amounts of water through their widely spreading root systems. Allow clearance of at least one and one-half times the height of any black walnut (*Juglans nigra*) trees, which exude a substance that inhibits growth in many vegetables.

A water supply nearby. Your garden must be within

Choosing the right site. On hilly terrain, don't site your garden at the top of the slope. Also avoid the bottom of the slope, where water and cold air collect. Pick a warm, well-drained site on the face of the slope.

hose range of a reliable water source. Rainfall seldom provides all the water a garden needs during an entire growing season, and you'll tire of hauling water by hand.

Close to the house. The closer your garden is to your house, the easier it will be to tend regularly. There also should be a driveway or path to your garden wide enough for a tiller (if you use one) or for a garden cart. If you have the space, choose several small sites near your kitchen door for easy-to-pick salad and herb plantings.

Fruits

When selecting a site for fruit trees and bushes, you'll want to follow most of the criteria given above. Fruits need full sun, good air circulation, and good drainage. Also consider the following factors when choosing sites for fruit.

Cool early-spring conditions. Look for a site near the top of a gentle north-facing slope or about 15 feet from the north wall of a building. Cooler spring soil and air temperatures there delay flowering, reducing the possibility of damage to blooms from late frosts. Avoid warm south-facing slopes and light-colored buildings that reflect the sun's heat.

Protection from frost and wind. Avoid frost pockets at the bottoms of slopes and on the uphill sides of buildings and hedges, as well as excessively windy sites on hilltops and in open areas.

Sufficient space. For fruit trees, allow a distance of more than half a tree's anticipated mature diameter from buildings and fences, so branches won't end up rubbing against walls or extending past property lines. Also be sure you're allowing enough room between trees if you're planting more than one. See the individual fruit entries, beginning on page 228, for recommended spacings for specific crops.

GARDEN MICROCLIMATES

Terrain, air flow, the positions of fences and buildings, and a variety of other factors create *microclimates* in your yard—places where temperatures are several degrees higher or lower than the overall air temperature. Here are some suggestions for using microclimates to your advantage.

House blocks north winds and releases heat at night.

• Put early vegetables near the south wall of a house or outbuilding. The wall provides protection from northerly winds, and it absorbs solar heat and releases it to the plants at night.
• Coax summer harvests from cool-season vegetables such as lettuce and spinach by planting them in semishady areas.
• Locate crops near a lake or pond, where water reflects light and heat to plants, and moisture-laden air delays killing frost.
• Place early-spring and late-fall crops on a west-facing slope. They'll get the last of the sun's heat each day. If frost strikes overnight, they'll thaw more slowly, preventing tissue damage.

EVALUATING YOUR SOIL

Studying your soil can help you garden more effectively and can guide your efforts to improve your soil over time. Analyzing a soil's precise chemical composition is a job best left to specialized laboratories. (See "Soil Testing" on page 10 for instructions on taking a soil sample and choosing a lab.) You can, however, learn much about your soil by performing simple backyard tests.

Analyzing Texture

Soil *texture* refers to the relative size and proportion of mineral particles in a given soil. The particles are classified as clay, silt, and sand; clay is finest and sand is coarsest.

Clay. Clay soils drain poorly and tend to crust over, blocking air and water.

Silt. High-silt soils tend to compact, preventing deep root penetration.

Sand. Sandy soils drain well but lose nutrients quickly.

Loam is a term that refers to a soil containing about 40 percent sand, 40 percent silt, and 20 percent clay. Loam soil is considered the best type for gardens.

Texture Tests

There are two easy ways to evaluate your soil's texture. The most basic is to pick up a handful of soil and feel its texture. See "The Squeeze Test" on the opposite page for how to judge texture in this way.

Another way is to visually compare the proportions of sand, silt, and clay. To do so, fill a quart glass canning jar halfway with soil from your garden, then fill it to the top with water. Cover the jar and shake it until the water and soil are thoroughly mixed. Then let the contents settle for 24 hours. Look at the layers—sand on the bottom, silt in the middle, and clay on top—to get a rough idea of the proportions of particles in your soil.

Analyzing Soil Health

Soil *structure* refers to the way soil particles are bound together and to the proportion of solids and pore space. Healthy garden soil is roughly half solid material (mineral particles and organic matter) and half pore space (occupied by water, air, living creatures, and plant roots). Structure affects how easily roots can penetrate the soil, how well

water drains through the soil, and how available air and nutrients are in the soil. Maintaining organic matter content is essential for good soil structure and health. There are four tests that will help you decide whether your soil is healthy.

Sniff Test

Grab a loose handful of soil, rub it between your fingers, and smell it. Soil that contains lots of organic humus is dark, has a slightly spongy feel, and gives off a pleasing "earthy" aroma. If the soil smells sour or vinegary, it may indicate a pH problem. See "Analyzing Soil pH" on the opposite page.

Earthworm Survey

One measure of a soil's overall fertility and organic content is the amount of living organisms it supports. Earthworms serve as a general indicator of soil fauna.

Pick a day in late spring or early summer when the soil is fairly moist and has warmed to at least 50°F. Dig out a section of soil from your garden equivalent to a 1-cubic-foot block. Spread out the dug soil. Sift through it and count the earthworms (return each one to the hole as you find it and cover it with a bit of soil; worms can't tolerate exposure to the sun). A cubic foot of healthy soil will contain at least ten earthworms. Soil with fewer than ten worms needs additional organic matter.

Drainage Test

Dig a hole roughly 1 foot deep and 1 foot in diameter. Fill the hole with water, let it drain, then fill the hole again. The liquid should percolate gradually but completely into the surrounding soil within eight hours.

If you suspect your soil may be *too* well drained, thoroughly soak a small area of your garden with water, wait two days, then dig a 6-inch-deep hole. If the bottom of the hole is dry, the soil is losing water too rapidly for good plant growth.

Soil Profile

To assess your soil's general health and structure, find a spot in your garden where plants are growing and dig a trench 3 feet long and 2 feet deep. Take care to keep one side smooth and vertical.

Examine the straight side closely. The top 4 to 6 inches of soil should be dark and easily crumbled. Earthworms and other life should be evident. Plant roots should penetrate deeply and spread freely. Crusty or compacted upper soil, stunted or horizontal roots, and an absence of living organisms indicate neglected soil.

Analyzing Soil pH

Soil acidity or alkalinity is expressed as a pH number ranging from 1.0 (extremely acid) through 7.0 (neutral) to 14.0 (highly alkaline). Soil pH affects the chemical form of nutrients like phosphorus and iron. When soil pH is too high or low, some nutrients convert to a form that cannot be absorbed by plants. So even in nutrient-rich soil, if the pH is off balance, plants may suffer nutrient deficiencies.

Most plants do best in slightly acidic to neutral soil, with a pH between 6.5 and 7.0.

A laboratory soil analysis will include a precise pH reading. You can also check the pH with a home soil-test kit or with a handheld pH meter. Equipped with a probe that provides an instant reading, such meters are easy to use and are available through garden suppliers for about $20. See "Soil Testing" on page 10 for complete information on testing soil pH.

THE SQUEEZE TEST

Clay. Roll a handful of moist soil into a ball. Squeeze the ball lightly. If the soil feels slippery and your fingers leave an impression in the surface, it has a clayey texture.

Loam. If the soil crumbles into large particles or is difficult to roll into a ball, it has a well-balanced texture characteristic of loam. Loamy soils are excellent for gardening.

Sand or silt. If the soil feels gritty and forms a loose ball when you squeeze it, there's a significant sand content. But if the soil feels greasy, that indicates a high proportion of silt.

SOIL TESTING

When to Test

Having your soil tested makes good sense when you start a new garden or if your crops as a whole aren't growing well. It's not necessary to test garden or orchard soil routinely every year. If you add organic matter to your soil every year, a complete soil analysis every five years is sufficient.

If possible, test your soil before adding fertilizers or mineral amendments such as gypsum or rock phosphate. Then use the results to help you decide which, if any, amendments you need to add.

You can test soil at any time of the year. Most gardeners prefer to have samples analyzed in the fall so that if they need to improve the soil, they'll have time to take action before the next growing season.

Testing Options

Soil tests run the gamut from basic do-it-yourself kits available from garden supply catalogs to detailed and somewhat costly laboratory analysis. Choose a test appropriate to your needs and budget. If you are checking only for pH and major nutrients, a simple test may suffice. If you suspect your soil has a serious imbalance, a more expensive analysis may be justified.

Home soil-test kits. Commercial test kits are convenient to use and give you same-day readings on pH, nitrogen, phosphorus, and potassium. The results, however, are less accurate than those from a soil lab because they don't take into account regional soil composition differences. If you use a home test kit, follow the instructions precisely; the tiny quantities of soil and testing agents involved leave little margin for error. If the results suggest a deficiency or imbalance, confirm the readings with a lab test before making changes to your soil.

Cooperative Extension Service soil tests. County extension offices provide soil-testing services for only a few dollars (or in some states for free). You will receive instructions for collecting a soil sample and a container for shipping the soil to a regional lab for professional analysis. Soil is tested for pH, humus content, and major nutrients and trace minerals. The reports,

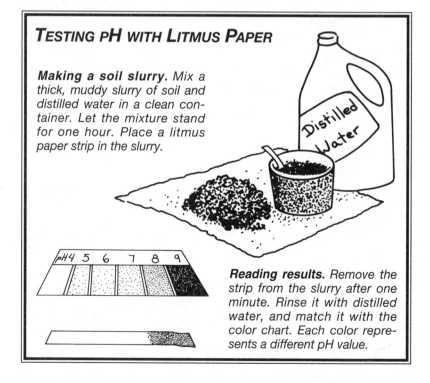

TESTING pH WITH LITMUS PAPER

Making a soil slurry. Mix a thick, muddy slurry of soil and distilled water in a clean container. Let the mixture stand for one hour. Place a litmus paper strip in the slurry.

Reading results. Remove the strip from the slurry after one minute. Rinse it with distilled water, and match it with the color chart. Each color represents a different pH value.

however, are geared to commercial chemical farming and can be difficult for organic gardeners to interpret.

Private laboratory soil tests. Private testing labs charge between $25 and $40 for a basic soil audit. Most ask you to send both a soil sample and a completed questionnaire concerning your soil and the kinds of crops you intend to grow. In return, you'll receive a comprehensive and generally user-friendly analysis of your soil's composition and characteristics, along with suggestions for improving its makeup. Several labs specialize in making recommendations tailored for organic growers. (For a listing of labs, refer to "Sources" on page 358.)

Test Results

When you mail your soil sample, be sure to request that the lab's report give recommendations for organic soil amendments. The lab will test your sample and send you a report with the results of their analysis and recommendations for improving the soil.

Some lab reports can be cryptic and confusing. If you don't understand part of the report or the recommendations made, contact the lab or your county extension agent for a clearer explanation.

HOW TO COLLECT A SOIL SAMPLE

1. If you've recently added compost, manure, or other materials to your soil, wait two weeks before collecting a sample. When you're ready to collect the sample, first clear away gravel, vegetation, or other surface litter from a small spot in the area you want to sample. Use a stainless steel trowel or large spoon to dig a small hole 4 to 5 inches deep.

2. Scrape 2 or 3 tablespoons of soil from the side of the hole. Keep roots, twigs, and other organic matter out of the sample. Be careful not to touch the soil with your hands. Put the soil in a clean stainless steel or plastic container.

3. Clear the soil surface, dig holes, and collect soil from 10 to 15 other spots in the area to be tested. Mix all the soil you've collected in a stainless steel or plastic container. This mixture is the sample for testing.

4. Pour the soil from the bowl into the bag or box provided by the testing service for shipment to the lab. Most labs require 1 to 2 cups of soil per sample.

IMPROVING YOUR SOIL

Taking care of your soil is your most important garden chore. Spend time improving your soil and your payoff will be less time spent watering, fertilizing, and fighting pests. Why? Because healthy soil will hold more water and feed your plants naturally. Plants will grow vigorously in healthy soil and be more resistant to attack by insects and infection by disease.

Add Organic Matter

Adding organic matter stimulates the natural cycles that enrich soil. Earthworms and soil microorganisms break down organic matter into forms that plants can use. As they do, they create humus. Humus is a stable form of decomposed organic matter that improves soil structure so roots can penetrate the soil easily. It also increases the soil's capacity to hold air and water.

You can add organic matter as mulches of straw, grass clippings, or shredded leaves. Or you can make compost—a mix of decomposed plant and animal materials—and work it into your soil. Good compost is by far the most beneficial and the most all-purpose amendment for soil. To learn how to make and use compost, see "Making Compost" on page 22.

Adjust Soil pH

Soil pH is a measure of the acidity or alkalinity of your soil. When you evaluate your soil, you will test its pH. (See "Analyzing Soil pH" on page 9 for more information.)

A pH less than 6.5 means your soil is too acid for best plant growth. To raise the pH, spread ground limestone on your soil and work it into the top few inches.

A pH more than 7.0 means your soil is alkaline. Sulfur is the amendment most often used to lower soil pH. Spread sulfur on your soil and work it into the top few inches.

Refer to "Correcting Soil pH" on this page to determine how much lime or sulfur to add to correct pH for your type of soil.

CORRECTING SOIL pH

The table below shows the pounds of limestone or sulfur needed per 100 square feet to change the pH to 6.5, based on initial soil pH. Soil pH changes more readily in sandy soil than in clay soil; the table recommends different quantities for different soil textures. It is highly unusual for loam soils to have alkaline pH; thus, for sulfur, recommendations are given for sandy and clayey soils only.

INITIAL SOIL pH	POUNDS OF LIMESTONE PER 100 SQUARE FEET		
	SAND	LOAM	CLAY
4.5	5.0	13.5	19.5
5.0	4.0	10.5	15.5
5.5	3.0	8.0	11.0
6.0	1.5	4.0	5.5

	POUNDS OF SULFUR PER 100 SQUARE FEET	
	SAND	CLAY
7.0	0.5	1.0
7.5	1.0	2.0
8.0	3.0	4.5
8.5	4.5	7.0

Add Amendments

Organic soil amendments release their nutrients slowly, over months or even years, as they are broken down by microorganisms. They can be made of natural plant or animal materials or of powdered minerals or rock.

Adding organic amendments to the upper few inches of soil mimics nature's process of feeding not only plants but the soil. This is in contrast to synthetic chemical fertilizers, which are water-soluble and produce a sudden flush of mineral salts that are taken up rapidly by plants. Such salts can produce good yields. But they also repel earthworms and other humus-making creatures. The eventual result is a lifeless soil, low in nutrients and humus, that can support crops only with additional doses of chemicals.

Test Before Applying

A good soil test will indicate existing levels of the three main plant nutrients—nitrogen, phosphorus, and potassium—as well as major trace elements and soil pH. (See "Soil Testing" on page 10 for full information on having your soil tested.) The report also will include recommendations for applying amendments, or fertilizers, to offset existing imbalances or to bring nutrients up to levels required for growing crops.

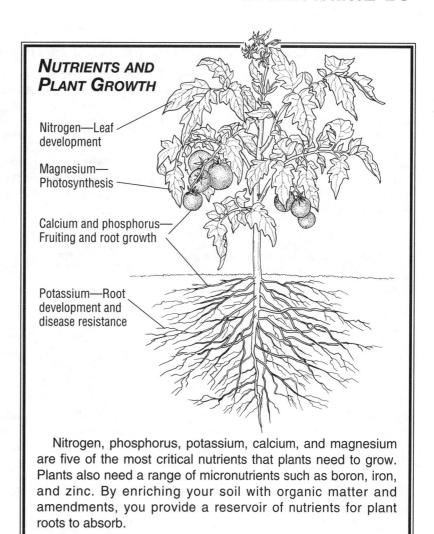

NUTRIENTS AND PLANT GROWTH

Nitrogen—Leaf development

Magnesium—Photosynthesis

Calcium and phosphorus—Fruiting and root growth

Potassium—Root development and disease resistance

Nitrogen, phosphorus, potassium, calcium, and magnesium are five of the most critical nutrients that plants need to grow. Plants also need a range of micronutrients such as boron, iron, and zinc. By enriching your soil with organic matter and amendments, you provide a reservoir of nutrients for plant roots to absorb.

Decide What to Apply

Some commercial test labs tailor their services for organic growers and will recommend specific quantities of natural amendments. Many labs, however, make recommendations in terms of common chemical fertilizers, such as 10-10-10 or 5-10-5. The three numbers indicate the N-P-K ratio, which is the percentage, by weight, of each major nutrient in the fertiliz-er. For example, a 10-pound bag of 5-10-5 contains ½ pound (5 percent) of nitrogen, 1 pound (10 percent) of phosphorus, and ½ pound (5 percent) of potassium.

"Common Organic Soil Amendments" on page 14 lists typical N-P-K ratios for common organic amendments as well as suggested application rates based on a soil's existing overall fertility. Use it as a guide to help select

(continued on page 16)

Common Organic Soil Amendments

This table lists the amendments most commonly used by organic gardeners. Use it both as a guide to help you select natural amendments and to determine the approximate quantities to add to your soil.

Note that the N-P-K ratios listed are only *typical* of the products available on the market and may not reflect the actual N-P-K ratio of a given brand. Always check the N-P-K ratio on the label to determine the nutrient content of that specific product. When selecting phosphorus sources such as rock phosphate or bonemeal, remember that many suppliers list the *total* phosphate content in the N-P-K ratio; the actual amount of phosphorus available to plants may be substantially less.

Application rates are provided for soils with low, medium, and adequate fertility. Use a soil test and your own observations of how well plants do in your garden to determine which fertility level is appropriate to your site.

ORGANIC AMENDMENT	PRIMARY NUTRIENT OR BENEFIT	TYPICAL N-P-K RATIO OR MINERAL CONTENT	AVERAGE APPLICATION RATE PER 100 SQUARE FEET	COMMENTS
Alfalfa meal	Nitrogen; organic matter	2.5-0.2-2.0	Low: 10 lb. Medium: 6 lb. Adequate: 3 lb.	Quick-acting. Contains triaconatol, a natural fatty-acid growth stimulant, plus trace minerals.
Blood meal	Nitrogen	11-0-0	Low: 3 lb. Medium: 2 lb. Adequate: 1 lb.	Use sparingly. Can burn plants.
Bonemeal (steamed)	Phosphorus	1-11-0; 20% total phosphate; 24% calcium	Low: 3 lb. Medium: 2 lb. Adequate: 1 lb.	More readily released to plants than rock or colloidal phosphate but also more expensive. Raw bonemeal products contain up to 6% nitrogen.
Colloidal (soft) phosphate	Phosphorus	0-2-0; 18–20% total phosphate; 23% calcium	Low: 10 lb. Medium: 3 lb. Adequate: 1 lb.	Somewhat quicker-releasing than rock phosphate. Best choice for alkaline soil.
Compost (dry)	Organic matter	1-1-1	Low: 30 lb. Medium: 20 lb. Adequate: 10 lb.	
Compost (homemade)	Organic matter	0.5-0.5-0.5 to 4-4-4; 25% organic matter	Low: 200 lb. Medium: 100 lb. Adequate: 50 lb.	
Cottonseed meal	Nitrogen	6-2-1	Low: 10 lb. Medium: 5 lb. Adequate: 2 lb.	Acidifies soil. May contain pesticide residues.
Fish meal	Nitrogen	10.5-6-0	Low: 5 lb. Medium: 2.5 lb. Adequate: 1 lb.	Releases gradually, over 6–8 months. Contains trace minerals.

ORGANIC AMENDMENT	PRIMARY NUTRIENT OR BENEFIT	TYPICAL N-P-K RATIO OR MINERAL CONTENT	AVERAGE APPLICATION RATE PER 100 SQUARE FEET	COMMENTS
Granite meal	Potassium	1–4% total potash	Low: 10 lb. Medium: 5 lb. Adequate: 2.5 lb.	Also contains 67% silicas (which aid soil fertility) and 19 trace minerals.
Greensand	Potassium	6–7% total potash	Low: 10 lb. Medium: 5 lb. Adequate: 2.5 lb.	Also contains some phosphorus, 50% silicas, and trace minerals.
Gypsum	Soil modifier; calcium	22% calcium; 17% sulfur	Low: 4 lb. Medium: 2 lb. Adequate: 0.5 lb.	Use only if soil test indicates excess magnesium and need for calcium. Do not apply if pH is below 5.8.
Hoof and horn meal	Nitrogen	12-0.5-0	Low: 4 lb. Medium: 2 lb. Adequate: 1 lb.	Slow-releasing. Application takes effect in 4–6 weeks; lasts at least 1 year.
Kelp meal	Potassium, iron, trace minerals	1.0-0.5-2.5	Low: 1 lb. Medium: 1 lb. Adequate: 1 lb.	Apply sparingly. Contains natural growth hormones and variety of trace minerals.
Limestone (calcitic or hi-cal)	Soil modifier; calcium	65–80% calcium carbonate; 3–15% magnesium carbonate	Low: 10 lb. Medium: 5 lb. Adequate: 2.5 lb.	Raises soil pH. Use where magnesium levels are adequate or excessive. Soil type affects application rate; use lab results as a guide. Do not overapply.
Limestone (dolomitic)	Soil modifier; calcium, magnesium	51% calcium carbonate; 40% magnesium carbonate	Low: 10 lb. Medium: 5 lb. Adequate: 2.5 lb.	Raises soil pH. Use only if soil test shows magnesium deficiency. Soil type affects application rate; use lab results as a guide. Do not overapply.
Rock phosphate	Phosphorus	0-3-0; 32% total phosphate; 32% calcium	Low: 6 lb. Medium: 2.5 lb. Adequate: 1 lb.	Long-lasting but very slow-releasing. Most effective in acid soil. Contains 11 trace minerals.
Soybean meal	Nitrogen	7.0-0.5-2.3	Low: 5 lb. Medium: 2.5 lb. Adequate: 1 lb.	Commonly sold in farm stores as livestock feed supplement. Releases gradually, over 3–5 months.
Wood ash	Potassium; soil modifier	0-1.5-8	Low: 1 lb. Medium: 0.5 lb. Adequate: 0.25 lb.	Raises soil pH. Nutrient content varies according to type of wood and type of soil in which it grew. Use in conjunction with lime to adjust pH. Do not apply to same area more than once every 2–3 years.

amendments and convert a testing lab's chemical fertilizer recommendations to quantities of natural amendments.

Be careful not to overdose your garden with amendments. Too much of any given supplement can be as detrimental to plant growth as too little and can take years to correct. Never make a major change in your soil based on "instinct" or the results of a home soil-test kit. Have a professional soil test conducted first.

Organic Fertilizer Blends

Most gardens—particularly new or neglected gardens—can benefit from a once-a-season application of a balanced organic fertilizer. Because most natural amendments are nonburning and won't harm delicate plant roots, you can also use balanced organic fertilizers to side-dress plants during the growing season or apply small amounts when setting out seedlings.

Commercial soil amendments can be particularly useful to gardeners who don't have access to much compost or the materials needed to make it. Commercial amendments are also important if you're working with poor soil that needs a more pronounced nutrient boost than compost alone can provide.

When buying commercial organic fertilizers, look for the words "All-Natural" or "100% Organic" and read the label carefully. The ingredients listed should be strictly natural ones, such as seaweeds, rock phosphate, granite dust, greensand, and bonemeal.

You can also make your own. To make enough for 100 square feet of growing space, mix 6 pounds of alfalfa meal, 3 pounds of bonemeal, 4 pounds of greensand, and 1 pound of kelp meal. For additional general-purpose fertilizer blends, see "Make Mix and Match Fertilizers" on this page.

Mix fertilizer blends outdoors, when winds are calm, on a concrete driveway or other dry, flat surface. Weigh the ingredients and pour them on top of one another in a heap. Add the smallest quantities last. Then mix the amendments with a shovel, scoop, or dustpan, pouring and turning materials from the bottom up to the top repeatedly until everything is thoroughly blended. (It's a good idea to wear a dust mask while you work with amendments.) Put the fertilizer in clean, tightly closed plastic or paper bags and store in a dry location.

When to Apply

Because most organic amendments are slow-acting, allow a few weeks between the time you apply amendments and the time you plant. For example, you can give your garden its main feeding in early spring, when preparing the soil for planting, or in fall, when working the soil after the season's harvest. For directions on how to work amendments into your soil, see "Digging In Amendments" on page 18.

MAKE MIX AND MATCH FERTILIZERS

To make your own general-purpose organic fertilizer blend, combine individual amendments in the proportions shown below. Just choose one ingredient from each nutrient column.

NITROGEN (N)	PHOSPHORUS (P)	POTASSIUM (K)
2 parts blood meal	3 parts bone-meal	1 part kelp meal
3 parts fish meal	6 parts rock phosphate or colloidal phosphate	6 parts greensand

WORKING THE SOIL

Cultivating your garden's soil can improve aeration and drainage and allow the roots of your crops to spread more freely. Working the soil before planting seeds is a must if the bed is weedy or compacted. Also, working the soil is important for thoroughly mixing compost and soil amendments into the upper soil layer.

However, there's a downside to working your soil. While cultivation can stimulate microbial activity and the release of nutrients, it can also overload the soil with oxygen. This may cause a population explosion of soil microbes, followed by a sharp downturn in their numbers. Tilling or digging also may kill earthworms and other soil organisms.

Working the soil when it is too wet can seriously damage its structure. Garden soil that's ready to work should be just dry enough to crumble easily in your hand and slide off your spade or fork without sticking. If the soil seems very dry and hard, water the area deeply, then wait two or three days before turning it. If the soil sticks to your tools, wait for a couple of fair days, and check moisture again.

If you till or dig your soil, do so in moderation. If you're interested in gardening techniques that don't require tilling, see "No-Dig Soil Improvement" on page 20.

Breaking Ground

Scythe or mow tall weeds and grass from the area (use the cuttings to make compost as long as they haven't set seed). If the patch was gardened previously, remove crop residues and destroy them if you suspect they might harbor diseases or pest insects. Pull out large rocks and rake away surface litter.

Areas that have been in sod for several years are the most difficult to prepare for planting. If you're planning a large garden, you may want to hire a tractor owner to plow and disk the plot initially. Then go back over it with a tiller to break up the clods. Most household-size gardens, however, can be entirely hand-dug or tilled. To make the job easier, cover the area with black plastic or a thick layer of leaves for several weeks to smother the turf and soften the soil.

Tilling

When using a rotary tiller to prepare a new garden, start with the machine at half throttle and the tines at the shallowest or next-shallowest depth setting. It will take several passes to turn over sod. Gradually increase the speed and depth on each pass. If the tiller bucks and pops out of the ground, you're trying to take too big a "bite."

Work the soil thoroughly to a depth of 4 to 6 inches. If you're planning a row garden, now is the time to spread and till in compost and soil amendments.

Plots checkered with perennial weeds or persistent grasses will need a second or even a third tilling. Water the plot and wait a week to give surviving weeds a chance to emerge; then retill.

GREEN THUMB TIP

Simplify the task of converting a lawn area into a garden space by leaving strips of sod as paths between beds. You'll have less sod to turn, and the strips left behind are instant planted pathways! Make the strips slightly less than twice the width of your lawn mower. During the season, mow the grass walkways, allowing the clippings to fall on the beds as mulch.

First pass
of tiller

Second pass
of tiller

Crisscross tilling. *Use an alternating crisscross pattern when you till a large area. Run your rotary tiller in one direction over the entire garden, then make the next pass at right angles to the previous one. This ensures good coverage of the entire plot.*

Avoid overtilling your garden. Frequent tillage at the same depth can destroy soil structure and deplete organic matter. A single tilling in the spring, and perhaps another tilling in the fall to turn under green manures or crop residues, should be sufficient.

Double Digging

Double digging is the classic method for creating raised garden beds. While there are easier ways to make raised beds (as explained in "Building Raised Beds" on page 30), double digging is well worth the effort if you need to improve sandy or heavy clay soil. It's also important to start beds by double digging if you plan to

practice intensive gardening. The double-dig technique loosens the soil to a depth of 2 feet, improving aeration and root penetration, and allows you to add large amounts of compost or other organic materials.

"How to Double Dig" on the opposite page provides a step-by-step guide to the technique. But before you get out your spade and digging fork, consider the following points about double digging.

• Double digging is difficult work. You'll be moving lots of heavy soil. Take frequent breaks. And spread the work over time: Give yourself several days to complete a bed.
• The best width for a bed is between 3 and 5 feet. While bed length can vary, it's best to start small. Don't try to dig a bed more than 30 feet long.
• Don't feel obliged to double dig your entire garden all at once. Many gardeners add just one or two double-dug beds to their gardens each year.
• If you plan to dig additional beds now or in the future, allow about 3 feet for pathways between them.
• It's not necessary to double dig beds more than once. At the most, a well-constructed bed should need only a light forking

each spring to prepare for planting.
• When you're digging the bed, keep the spade close to your body. Bend your knees and use your legs to help you lift soil from one trench to the next.
• After you finish digging the bed, use a hoe to shape the bed. The sides should angle gently downward; if they're too steep, the bed will erode during a hard rain.

DIGGING IN AMENDMENTS

Applying soil amendments is a final step after digging or tilling. Choose a calm day, because many amendments are powdery. Spread the amendments one at a time, close to the soil surface. Cover the soil as evenly as possible.

If you're not sure how much soil a measured amount of amendment will cover, spread it lightly over the entire area at first. Then go back a second time to use any remaining. If you're using several amendments, spread a light-colored powder first, then a dark-colored, then a light. This will help you see that each is distributed consistently. When you're done, till or fork the amendments into the upper 3 to 4 inches of soil.

HOW TO DOUBLE DIG

Rolled sod

Compost

Getting started. *Presoak the site with water. Several days later, slice under the existing sod just below the roots (left). Next, dig a trench across the full width of the cleared plot. Pile the soil onto a wheelbarrow or heavy tarp (above).*

Working the trenches. *Plunge a garden fork into the exposed subsoil and loosen, but don't turn, the soil (left). Then make a second trench alongside the first. This time, simply tip the soil into the first trench (right). Loosen the subsoil as before. Continue the trench-and-loosen process down the bed.*

Finishing up. *When you reach the end of the bed, use the top-soil from the first trench to fill in the last trench (left). Then work over the bed surface, breaking up large clods (right). Spread compost, lime, or other amendments and fork them into the top 4 inches of soil.*

No-Dig Soil Improvement

Many gardeners assume that they should till or cultivate their garden frequently to control weeds and keep the soil loose and friable. Cultivating soil can be important, particularly when breaking new ground or adding amendments. But working soil repeatedly can destroy its structure, cause a rapid loss of organic matter, and reduce earthworm populations.

Some gardeners have found simple ways to improve soil in established gardens without cultivating or digging. It's even possible to prepare a new site without turning the soil. Such methods not only nurture soil health but also save time and labor.

Grow "Compost Crops"

Traditionally, green manure or cover crops are tilled into the soil to add organic matter and nutrients. (See "Planting Cover Crops" on page 28 for more details.) You can gain the same benefits in a no-dig garden by growing and harvesting green manure crops specifically for compost.

To use a green manure as a "compost crop," sow the seed in the usual manner. Harvest the mature crop when it's con-venient. Either pull out the crop by hand or use a scythe or sickle to cut it off at the surface (the remaining roots will decompose in the soil, supplying organic matter). Chop the growth roughly with a mower or sharpened spade, then add the material to your compost pile.

Apply Organic Mulch

Keeping a layer of organic mulch on your garden not only hinders erosion and weed growth but also helps to fertilize and condition the soil. Mulched soil stays moist and friable, favorable to earthworms and other soil life.

Organic mulch materials for food gardens include:

- grass clippings
- compost
- straw
- leaves
- weed-free hay
- pulled weeds that have not set seed

If possible, use a combination of materials. A mixed mulch provides a good balance of nutrients and trace minerals. If you can, shred or chop materials to speed decomposition.

Apply mulch in a layer 2 to 4 inches thick (or more, if weeds are a problem). Cover the soil completely, but keep the material 1 inch away from plant stems and leaves. Add more mulch throughout the

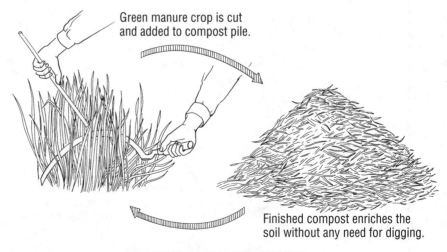

Green manure crop is cut and added to compost pile.

Finished compost enriches the soil without any need for digging.

GROWING "COMPOST CROPS"

year as it decays. In spring, pull the mulch back from beds or rows a week or two before planting to allow the soil to warm. Replace the mulch when crops begin to grow.

Use Root Power

Plant roots keep topsoil from eroding, create channels that loosen and aerate the soil, and reach deep into the earth to bring up minerals and trace elements. Try using root power to improve your soil's structure and fertility.

- In idle garden areas, let nonspreading annual weeds such as purslane, lamb's-quarters, ragweed, and chickweed serve as a cover crop. Just before they go to seed, cut the weeds down and add them to your compost pile.
- Allow a few taprooted weeds such as dandelion, nightshade, prickly lettuce, or Queen Anne's lace to grow in your garden. To reclaim the long-buried minerals they bring up, cut and compost the weeds before they go to seed.
- Plant deep-rooted green manure crops like alfalfa, annual rye, and sweet clover to help loosen poor garden soil.
- Rotate deep-rooted crops such as chard and cabbage throughout your garden to open up the soil.

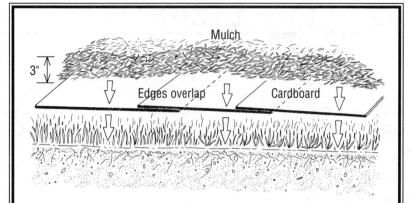

TRY NO-DIG GROUNDBREAKING

This technique is good for starting a small garden in persistent sod or on a very weedy site. It is also excellent for gardeners with back problems or other physical impairments that make it difficult to use a spade or tiller. With this no-dig method, you smother out plants and improve the soil at the same time.

To start, remove tall vegetation, twigs, branches, and other surface litter from the site. Then cover the ground completely with corrugated cardboard or heavy paper such as that from dog-food or chicken-feed bags. Or use newspaper layered a dozen sheets thick. Overlap the edges of the cardboard or paper by at least 3 inches.

Wet the cardboard or paper thoroughly. Spread a 4-inch layer of grass clippings or shredded leaves on top of the paper. Also moisten this mulch layer completely.

Make planting holes right through cardboard.

Let things sit undisturbed for at least two weeks (a month or more is better) so the grass and weeds can decompose.

At planting time, push a trowel through the mulch and paper into the softened soil, set a seedling in place, and arrange the mulch around (but not touching) the stem.

During the season, pull any weeds that emerge through the paper, and add more mulch as needed. By the second year the paper will have decomposed almost completely, and the soil will be sufficiently friable for most crops.

MAKING COMPOST

If you garden, you can make compost. Compost is nothing more than grass clippings, kitchen scraps, crop residues, weeds—or almost any other organic waste—that's been piled together long enough to decompose completely. You don't need manure or other hard-to-get ingredients. You don't need a lot of space or time either. With little effort, you can turn throw-away materials into the sweet-smelling, nutrient-rich, no-cost soil conditioner known as "gardener's gold." It is the single best thing you can do for your garden's soil.

How a Compost Pile Works

A compost pile is a smorgasbord for billions of hungry microscopic creatures—bacteria, fungi, actinomycetes, and other decay organisms that break down organic matter. Your goal is to provide those compost makers with the right foods in the right proportion, along with three other essentials: air, moisture, and warmth.

Compost Ingredients

The two vital ingredients in a decay organism's diet are carbon (for energy) and nitrogen (for building protein). Anything of living origin contains both, but some materials have more carbon than others, and some are higher in nitrogen. Carbon-rich compost makings (called "browns") are generally dry and dull colored—straw and dried leaves, for instance. Nitrogen-rich materials ("greens") are usually green or moist or messy. Manure, kitchen scraps, and fresh grass are "greens." See "Composting Materials" on this page for a list of recommended compost-pile ingredients. Do not put meat, grease, fat, or cheese in compost. Also avoid putting synthetic fabrics or plastic in your pile.

In order to produce compost efficiently, decay organisms need their carbon and nitrogen in a certain proportion, known as the C/N (for carbon/nitrogen) ratio. If the ratio is too high in carbon, the pile won't decompose completely. If the ratio is too low, the pile will lose the extra nitrogen to the air as a gas and smell bad. But if the ratio is just right, in the range of 25 or 30 parts carbon to 1 part nitrogen, the pile will heat up and "cook" and will yield rich compost.

You don't need to carefully weigh or measure compost ingredients in order to reach the optimum C/N ratio. In most cases, simply mixing carbon- and nitrogen-rich materials, using roughly two to three times as much "brown" material by bulk as

---

COMPOSTING MATERIALS

High-Carbon "Browns"

Dry leaves, weeds, cover crops
Straw
Hay
Chopped cornstalks
Aged sawdust
Nutshells
Paper (moderate amounts)

High-Nitrogen "Greens"

Vegetable scraps
Fruit scraps
Coffee grounds
Tea bags
Fresh grass clippings
Fresh leaves (avoid walnut and eucalyptus)
Weeds
Green manure crops
Hair (pet and human)
Milk
Manure (cow, fowl, horse, pig, sheep; *not* cat or dog droppings)
Seaweed

"green," will come reasonably close to the desired ratio.

Collect as great a variety of ingredients for your pile as possible. The more kinds of ingredients you add to your compost, the more sure you can be of creating a well-balanced soil conditioner.

Aeration

Most of the microbes in a compost pile are *aerobic:* they can survive only in the presence of oxygen. That's why it's important to be sure plenty of air gets to the pile, inside and out. The easiest way to accomplish this is to turn the pile from time to time. See the illustration on this page for tips on other ways to get air into your pile.

Moisture

The materials in a compost pile should be damp but not soggy. Give dry ingredients a sprinkling of water as you add them to the pile or top them with wet material such as table scraps or fresh manure. If you let the pile become either too wet or dry, decomposition will slow or stop. In dry areas, wet the pile occasionally.

Warmth

In an active compost pile, decay organisms will generate their own heat even in extreme cold. But to maintain that warmth, the pile has to

Aerating a compost pile. *Compost bins should have openings in the sides and/or bottom to provide ventilation. A PVC pipe with holes drilled through it stuck upright in the center of the pile will aerate it. You can put poles upright in the pile as you build it and pull them out when you're finished to create airways. Or just poke holes in the pile occasionally with a pry bar or the handle of a hoe or rake.*

be big enough. A freestanding compost pile should be at least 3 feet wide, high, and long. If you live where winters are very harsh, insulate the pile in late fall with an enclosure of hay bales or a 2- to 3-foot covering of leaves.

Building a Pile

Your compost pile should be close to the garden so you can easily add materials and transfer finished compost to the garden. Wetting the pile will be easier if it's within a hose length of an outside faucet. High shade from a deciduous tree will shelter the pile from heavy rain and summer sun but allow warming sunlight in fall and winter.

You can make compost in a freestanding heap or by piling the materials in an enclosure. See "Compost Bins" on page 26 for a range of compost bin styles.

Whether you use a bin or just make a heap, making a compost pile is roughly like mixing up a casserole or cake. Gather together your materials, and begin piling them in the bin or in a heap. You can make separate alternating layers of "greens" and "browns." Or, just dump or shovel on some of each, and mix them with a garden fork. Sprinkle the materials with water as you go. The more "mixed" your pile is, the faster it's likely to begin heating up.

Build the pile to any manageable width, but not more than 4 to 5 feet high. A taller pile is difficult to turn and compresses under its own weight, cutting off airflow.

After four or five days the decay organisms in your

Compost pile preparations. *Gather your materials and have the hose handy when you build a compost pile. If you're building the pile on bare ground, use a garden fork or spade to loosen the top few inches of soil. Then put down a 4- to 6-inch base layer of dry branches, brush, or stalks.*

compost pile should be generating heat. To check the pile's progress, push your arm into the mound up to your elbow. The temperature inside should be just tolerably hot.

Slow and Hot Compost

Once built, a pile will produce finished compost in about one year, with no further attention. You can speed things up, however, simply by turning the pile: Fork the materials from the inside to the outside and from the bottom to the top.

The more often you turn the pile, the faster its contents will decompose. Typically, turning a compost pile three or four weeks after you build it will cut the rotting time by about half. Turn it again a month later, and you should have good compost in another two to three months.

If you want to make compost faster than that, try hot composting. This method requires more time and attention, but it offers the advantage of temperatures high enough to kill weed seeds and disease organisms in the ingredients. See "Making Hot Compost" on the opposite page for instructions.

Using Compost

Before you use fresh compost, make sure that it is ready. Immature compost may contain substances that are toxic to plants. Finished, mature compost has the pleasant texture and aroma of freshly turned soil.

To test new compost, put a handful from the pile into a glass jar, close the lid, and place the container in a warm, sunny location. After three days, open the jar and sniff. If the compost smells sour or rotten, it isn't yet mature. Let the pile age another week, then test again.

Once your compost is ready, you'll have no trouble finding uses for it.

Preseason soil conditioner. In late fall or early spring in vegetable and herb gardens, work a 1-inch layer of compost into the top 2 or 3 inches of soil. You'll need about 8 cubic feet of finished compost (two 30-gallon garbage cans full or two standard wheelbarrow loads)

Protecting compost. *Unless you live in an arid climate, cover the top of the pile (but not the sides) with a tarp or a layer of straw to keep rain from waterlogging the pile and from washing nutrients away.*

for every 100 square feet of garden space. A newly constructed pile measuring 4 by 4 by 3 feet will eventually yield about 16 cubic feet of compost.

Mulch and side-dressing fertilizer. Apply compost as a mulch and slow-release organic fertilizer anytime during the season. A 1-inch layer is sufficient to suppress most annual weed seeds. In orchards, spread compost in a circle beginning 1 foot from

Preparing compost tea. *Put a shovelful of compost into a burlap bag or old pillowcase. Let it steep in water for three days. If necessary, dilute it to the color of weak tea. Remove the "tea bag," and spread its contents in your garden.*

the tree's trunk and extending outward as far as its branches reach. Compost tea is another good fertilizer, used as a soil drench or sprayed directly on plant leaves. See the illustration to the left for directions.

Cover crop decomposer. When turning under cover crops in late summer or fall, work a little compost into the soil at the same time. It will help the fresh green material decompose.

MAKING HOT COMPOST

The payoff for the labor of hot composting is its speed. You can make several batches every season. In addition, the high, constant temperature kills weed seeds and disease pathogens. One disadvantage of the process: More of the nitrogen in the pile is burned off during hot composting, so the final product contains less nitrogen than would slow compost made with the same ingredients. You can make finished compost in less than two months, or even in as little as three weeks. Here are the keys to making hot compost.

Turn the pile frequently. This is *the* essential element of hot composting. Turn the pile whenever its initial high temperature (120° to 160°F) begins to drop—about every three to five days. Monitor the temperature with a commercial compost thermometer, or simply stick your hand into the pile. You shouldn't be able to keep it there comfortably for much more than a minute.

Make the pile large enough. The minimum size for hot composting is a pile 3 feet high, wide, and long.

Use a commercial compost activator. These products contain millions of active bacteria and fungi that rapidly initiate the decay process.

Chop or shred coarse materials. This increases the surface area of materials such as cornstalks or dry leaves available to microbes and speeds up decomposition. Some dedicated composters shred everything in their piles *and* turn them every three or four days to get finished compost in less than a month.

Be sure the pile has enough moisture. If all other factors are right—the proper mix of high-carbon and high-nitrogen ingredients, shredded material, good aeration—and you still can't get a high temperature in your pile, it may be because it's too dry. Check the moisture; the materials should have the moistness of a wrung-out sponge.

COMPOST BINS

Homemade Bins

You can build a compost bin of almost any durable material, including cinder blocks, hay bales, chicken wire, snow fencing, or wood. Plant a border of flowers or herbs around the bin, or place it near a trellis with flowering vines, to help blend it into the landscape.

Here are a few simple do-it-yourself bin designs.

Welded-wire bin. Clip or wire together the ends of a 10-foot length of 48-inch 12½- or 14-gauge welded steel wire fencing. The result is a cylindrical compost bin 4 feet high and slightly more than 3 feet across. When the bin is half full, drive a stake into the pile. (Water will run

WOOD-AND-WIRE BIN

down the stake, helping to keep the center of the pile moist.)

To turn the pile, simply unfasten the bin's ends, slip the fencing from around the materials, and set the bin up again next to the heap. Then refill the empty bin, turning the materials from the top of the original pile to the bottom of the new pile and from the outside to the inside.

Wood-and-wire bin. Using 2 × 4 lumber, make four identical open frames measuring 3 by 3 feet or 4 by 4 feet. Staple ½-inch hardware cloth to one side of each frame. Nail three of the panels together to form a back and two sides. Use the remaining panel to make a door by hinging the edges at one corner and placing hooks and eyes on the opposite cor-

ner, as shown in the illustration to the left.

Barrel bin. Use a clean 55-gallon (or larger) drum with a tight-fitting lid. Drill six parallel rows of ½-inch-diameter holes around the barrel. Set it on blocks, and fill it about three-quarters to the top with compost makings. To mix and aerate the compost, fasten the lid, tip the barrel on its side, and roll it around the yard.

Cinder-block bin. Stack cinder blocks three or four high to form walls for an open U-shaped bin. Leave 1-inch spaces between the blocks to allow good airflow. You can add a middle wall to create a double bin. To turn the pile, simply fork the pile from one half of the bin to the other.

WELDED-WIRE BIN

CINDER-BLOCK BIN

Wooden-pallet bin. Simply nail four wooden shipping pallets together to form a sturdy holding bin. Or, to make a removable door, use wire to fasten one of the pallets to the bin at both sides. The pallets' open slats provide good ventilation and drainage.

Commercial Bins

Ready-made compost bins are more expensive than most do-it-yourself designs, but they are also quite attractive and durable. Most composters on the market fall into either of two categories.

Pen-type composters. These bins resemble square or rectangular homemade compost bins. Most are made of recycled plastic, which (unlike wood) won't warp or discolor or give the user splinters. Some models are covered and have slats in which you can insert a garden fork to turn the materials. Dark-colored bins catch and hold the sun's heat, making them a good choice for those who live in frigid climates. Prices range from about $75 to $110.

Tumbler or drum composters. These composters make it easy to produce compost quickly by eliminating much of the work of turning materials. Most designs feature a barrel-shaped bin mounted on an elevated frame. You simply add the proper mix of materials, moisten the contents, and close the bin's loading door. To aerate the compost, rotate the bin on its frame every few days. Some models have gear-driven turning mechanisms; others spin on ball bearings. Prices range from about $250 to $400.

Another type of tumbler composter resembles a boulder-size metal or plastic ball. To turn the contents, the user just rolls the sphere around on the ground. Prices range from $130 to $180.

Deciding What to Buy

Don't make your choice of a commercial composter based on cost alone. Also consider the following.

Portability. Some models, particularly tumblers, are too large or heavy to move easily. Be sure you have a good site for such a bin before you buy it. Portable bins allow you to make compost at several sites around the garden; they're especially good for gardeners who don't have a wheelbarrow or who grow crops over a large area.

Capacity. Choose a bin size appropriate to the amount of materials you expect to have for composting. Bigger is not necessarily better if you have only small quantities of waste to compost. If you compost a lot of material, two or three inexpensive pen or open-type bins may be a better choice for you than a single large bin.

Ease of assembly. Some of the more complicated bins are sold unassembled and have dozens of pieces to screw and bolt together.

Ease of use. If the bin has a loading door or lid, you should be able to lift or open and close it easily. The opening should be wide enough to accommodate bulky material. When considering a drum-type tumbler composter, check to see that there's enough room under the drum to park a wheelbarrow for unloading finished compost.

DRUM COMPOSTER

PLANTING COVER CROPS

Bare garden soil erodes easily, loses nutrients quickly, and soon sprouts a multitude of weeds—nature's own protective "cover crops." Avoid these problems by planting domesticated cover crops, also called green manures. Like weeds, a good cover crop grows rapidly to blanket and hold the soil. But unlike weeds, it is entirely controllable—*you* decide when and where to sow it and when to harvest it or till it under.

Cover crops aren't just for covering the garden over the winter. You can plant cover crops:

• Between plantings of food crops or between growing seasons.
• For a full year to rejuvenate poor soil. Plant a warm-season cover for the summer, and replace it with a winter-hardy type for winter.
• As a temporary living mulch between rows or beds and around plants.
• As a permanent mulch around fruit trees or bushes or between rows of perennial vegetables.

Crop Choices

Some cover crops are quick-growing, warm-season grasses; others are winter-hardy. Nonlegumes such as ryegrass do a superior job of holding soil and producing large amounts of organic matter, while legumes "fix" nitrogen in the soil, converting it into a form plants can use.

A good general-purpose approach is to plant a mixture containing both a nonlegume and a legume; the blend will result in plenty of organic matter as well as nitrogen. Also, the fast-growing grain serves as a protective "nurse crop" for the slow-growing legume, giving it time to become established.

Different types of legumes need specific strains of soil-dwelling bacteria, or rhizobia, to help them fix nitrogen efficiently. Most soils already contain these bacteria, but to guarantee good nitrogen fixation, plant rhizobium-treated seed. Check the label (or ask your supplier) to find out if the seed you're buying has already been treated, or inoculated. If not, buy a packet of the appropriate inoculant, and treat the seed according to the instructions before planting.

There are more than two dozen different kinds of cover crops. Ask your seed supplier or extension agent to recommend types and varieties adapted to your climate and soil.

The following cover crops are suited to most parts of the country and are widely used by home gardeners.

Buckwheat (*Fagopryum esculentum*). A summer cover crop that grows rapidly even in poor soil. Excellent for building organic matter. Can be tilled under four to six weeks from planting, and rots quickly. Good choice for planting between early and late vegetable crops or as a spring cover prior to planting warm-season vegetables. Plant in spring or summer, up to ten weeks before first fall frost. Sow 3 to 4 ounces per 100 square feet.

Annual ryegrass (*Lolium multiflorum*). A good winter or early-spring cover crop. Grows rapidly; roots hold soil well and prevent nutrients from leaching, even after tops die back. Till or dig into soil six weeks before planting vegetables. Sow in spring or in early fall at least four weeks before first frost. Sow 1½ to 2 ounces per 100 square feet. (Be sure not to plant *perennial* ryegrass by mistake.)

Winter rye or rye grain (*Secale cereale*). The hardiest and most commonly used winter cover crop. Since it

SOWING COVER CROPS

Step 1. *Till or rake the area lightly before spreading the seed.*

Step 2. *Distribute the measured seed lightly at first. Use leftover seed to fill gaps.*

Step 3. *Rake the seed into the soil, then water the area thoroughly, using a fine mist.*

germinates at 33°F, it can be planted even after frost; ideally, sow one month before frost. Overwinters and puts on lush new growth in spring. Can be difficult to work into soil; allow at least three weeks before planting food crops. Sow 4 ounces per 100 square feet.

Oats (*Avena sativa*). Thrives in cool, moist weather. Sow in early spring for a quick early-season cover crop. Sow in early fall as a winter cover. Overwinters in southern states. In other areas, it winter-kills; dead tops form a thick mulch that's easy to till under or rake off in spring. Sow 4 ounces per 100 square feet.

Hairy vetch (*Vicia villosa*). A versatile winter legume cover crop. Grows rapidly to smother out weed seeds. Hardy to 0°F. For best results, sow with a small grain such as buckwheat, oats, or rye. Plant in late summer or early fall; in spring, dig or till under after the vetch blooms but before it sets seed. Plant as soon as one week after tilling. Sow 4 ounces per 100 square feet.

Red clover (*Trifolium pratense*). This deep-rooted legume grows vigorously even in marginal soils. Sow in spring, summer, or early fall. For maximum nitrogen enrichment, leave the crop in place for a full year. Sow ³/₄ ounce per 100 square feet.

White (Dutch) clover (*Trifolium repens*). Plant any time during the growing season, up to six weeks before fall's first hard frost. This low-growing and shade-tolerant legume makes an excellent living mulch. Sow ¹/₄ to ¹/₂ ounce per 100 square feet.

Managing Cover Crops

If weeds outgrow your cover crop before it gets established, use a rotary mower on its highest setting to trim back the unwanted plants without harming the cover crop. In raised beds, use a sickle or pull the weeds by hand.

Always work cover crops back into the soil before they set seed. Grain-type crops are easiest to till or dig under when they are less than 6 inches tall. Mow or cut the growth down, then use a tiller or garden spade to work the fresh greenery into the upper 4 to 6 inches of soil.

BUILDING RAISED BEDS

Once built, raised beds are never walked on; you'll tend your plants from adjacent pathways. Keep this principle in mind as you lay out your beds. Allow enough space between them for ample pathways; 2 to 3 feet is enough room for a gardener and a wheelbarrow.

Limit bed width to between 3 and 5 feet, so you'll be able to reach comfortably into the bed's middle from either side. A raised bed can be any length, up to about 30 feet.

Consider different shapes too. A triangular raised bed may make the best use of an out-of-the-way corner. Planting corn in several small, adjacent square beds will help assure good pollination. An arc-shaped bed of herbs or salad greens makes an attractive minigarden near the kitchen door.

Build the Beds

Your first task is to clear the site and remove weeds or sod. (See the top left illustration on page 19 for sod removal instructions.) Then use one of the following techniques to build your beds.

Mounding. This is the quickest and easiest way to make a raised bed. Simply till or fork up the soil to loosen it, then heap compost, well-rotted manure, and other organic matter on top and rake it together to create a mounded growing bed. If your soil is very poor or rocky, use purchased topsoil mixed with compost and amendments to build the beds from the ground up.

Because a freshly built mounded bed is loose and full of air, it settles initially and can easily erode. Add more soil/compost if the bed loses height. Frame the bed if erosion is a problem.

Double digging. This traditional method is best if you are trying to improve sandy or heavy clay soil or if you will be practicing intensive gardening. (See the illustrations on page 19 for step-by-step double-digging instructions.)

Single digging. To use this method, follow the instructions for double digging, but

EDGING A BED WITH CINDER BLOCKS

4'

15'

Step 1. *Remove sod from the area and till lightly. Mark the bed edges with stakes and twine, then use a shovel or spade to cut out the perimeter of the bed 2 to 3 inches lower than ground level.*

Plastic lawn edging

Step 2. *Place plastic lawn edging along the inside of the perimeter to keep grass out of the bed.*

don't fork up and loosen the subsoil. Single digging is a little faster and less demanding than double digging. It works well for building small beds in soil that is naturally loose and well drained or that has been previously cultivated.

Tilling and hilling. This bed-building method prepares the soil almost as thoroughly as double digging but takes much less time.

1. With a rotary tiller, thoroughly till the entire garden area to a depth of 6 to 8 inches. (See "Tilling" on page 17 for more about tilling.)

2. Using stakes, twine, and a tape measure, lay out the perimeter of the beds. Be sure you're leaving adequate space for pathways. From this point on, walk only in those pathways, not on the marked beds.

3. Loosen the subsoil in the marked-off areas with a garden fork.

4. Next, using a spade, scoop up the top 2 to 3 inches of soil from the pathways around the beds, and add it to the beds to produce nicely raised beds.

Finish and Shape

To complete a freshly dug bed, break up any chunks of earth with a garden fork or hoe. Then spread 1 inch of compost over the surface, and add lime or other organic amendments as needed. Fork the materials thoroughly into the top 4 inches of soil.

Use a rake or hoe to shape the soil in an unframed bed. The sides should angle gently downward.

Framing

Frames, often made of wood, rocks, bricks, or cinder blocks, keep soil from eroding and create a tidier-looking raised-bed garden. If you build frames from wood, use naturally rot-resistant woods such as cypress or cedar. Avoid commercially pressure-treated wood because it contains arsenic-based compounds. Also avoid wood treated with penta (pentachlorophenol). Used railroad ties are acceptable, but new ties may ooze creosote, which is harmful to plants.

Use nuts and bolts to assemble wooden frames so that you can take each frame apart periodically to remove pests that may congregate. After dismantling the frame, dry the wood in the sun for a few hours to extend its life.

Step 3. *Use a hoe to backfill the edging with soil. Tamp the earth down and level it.*

Large holes in blocks face up.

Step 4. *Put blocks in place. Keep the blocks plumb with the outside twine.*

Step 5. *Fill the bed and the block cavities with a mix of soil, compost, and amendments.*

BUYING PLANTS AND SEEDS

Leggy, light-starved broccoli plants

Healthy tomato plant

Healthy broccoli plants

Sickly tomato plant

Check plant quality. *Seedlings should have short, thick, sturdy stems and deep green foliage. Avoid plants with leaves that are yellow, curled, mottled, or misshapen. Check undersides of leaves for insect eggs and insects such as aphids, whiteflies, and spider mites.*

Examine plants carefully. When picking plants, look for the most vigorous, problem-free plants you can find. The illustration on this page offers specific tips for finding good plants.

Buying Seeds

Freshness is the key to good seed; old, stale seed doesn't germinate reliably. Check the dates on seed packets sold in garden centers and supermarkets. If the seed isn't marked for the current season, don't buy it.

The best way to ensure you're buying fresh seed is to order it by mail, direct from the seed company. Most seed companies will deliver your order within two to three weeks. Seed catalogs also generally offer a much wider selection of cultivars than do retail outlets.

Reading Seed Catalogs

Learn how to translate seed-catalog jargon. Cultivar descriptions often contain special terms. Here are some you need to know.

Days to maturity. For seeds normally sown directly in the garden, such as carrots or corn, this is the average number of days from planting until harvest. For crops

Buying Plants

Vegetable and herb seedlings can give your garden an instant start. You'll have a narrower choice of cultivars than if you nurture your own plants from seed, so be sure to seek out a nursery that offers a good selection of plants.

Buy from local nurseries. Small commercial growers raise their own

stock on the premises. The plants are better cared for and better suited to local conditions than those that are shipped long-distance to chain stores.

Size up the nursery. Are plants and flats crowded together? Is there adequate airflow to prevent disease? Ask questions about the plants; at a good nursery, you'll get thorough, knowledgeable answers.

customarily started indoors and then transplanted outside, such as broccoli and tomatoes, this is the average number of days from *transplanting* to harvest.

F_1. An F_1 cultivar is a hybrid—a cross between two different parents to produce a plant with exceptional hardiness, vigor, or other trait.

OP. This stands for "open pollinated." Open-pollinated cultivars often cost less than hybrids.

Disease- or blight-resistant. Resistant cultivars are less susceptible to certain disease problems. Some catalogs indicate the specific diseases the cultivar resists as an abbreviation, such as "VFT," while others spell them out: "verticillium wilt, fusarium wilt, tobacco mosaic virus."

Read between the lines in catalogs. Sometimes what a description doesn't mention is as important as what it does. For example, a catalog may say a certain tomato cultivar produces "super-early, super-large fruit" without once mentioning flavor. There's a good chance that cultivar has been bred more for early harvest and size than for taste.

Making Your Order

Compare prices. When comparing prices, note the number of seeds per packet.

Seed quantity per packet varies widely from company to company. So do shipping charges; take them into account before choosing one supplier over another.

Order early. If you place your order in January, you'll have your seed by February and avoid delays caused by the customary early-spring rush. Keep the packets in an airtight container stored in a cool, dry place until you need them.

Save your seed catalogs for reference. Catalogs often contain better planting and care information than do the packets the seed come in.

Buying Fruit Trees

Fruit tree performance is affected by humidity, the growing season length, the harshness or mildness of winters, and the number of below-freezing days. So the most important consideration in buying fruit trees is choosing cultivars suited to local conditions. If possible, buy trees grafted and raised at a nearby nursery. Or buy from a mail-order nursery in your climatic zone or one that offers cultivars adapted to your region.

See the individual fruit entries, beginning on page 228, for more information on factors to consider when choosing specific fruit crops.

When buying by mail, be sure your order will be shipped at an appropriate planting time (spring in the North; spring or fall in the South). Also be sure a guarantee is offered. Most nurseries will refund your money or replace a tree that doesn't survive its first few weeks.

If you buy container trees at a nursery, examine the roots. Such trees may be bareroot stock that's been trimmed and potted up simply for better appearance and higher price. These trees are handicapped from the start. A true container-grown tree will have an extensive, well-developed root system.

Inspect roots. *Healthy roots should be white with no brown or black tissue. Some soil should be visible around the roots.*

USING GARDEN TOOLS

You don't need a lot of tools to garden, but you do need to choose them carefully. A good tool, well constructed and put to its intended use, can make hard work easier and time-consuming tasks shorter.

Given good care, quality hand tools and power equipment will serve you well for many years. So don't put those tools away dirty! It's worth the extra effort to make tool maintenance a day-to-day part of gardening.

If you're a beginning gardener, start your tool collection with the essentials listed in "Basic Garden Tools" on this page. Then add other equipment as the need arises.

Hand Tools

Hand tools get a lot of hard wear, so they must be sturdy and efficient. Unless you intend to use the tool only occasionally, buy the best you can afford.

Before buying a tool, try it on for "size." Heft it and go through the motions of using it. The tool should feel comfortable in your hands and shouldn't strain your neck or back. The handles of tools intended to be used standing up, such as rakes and hoes,

Spade

Digging fork

Metal collar surrounds handle.

Choosing tools. *The working end of digging and cultivating tools should be one solid piece of rust-proof or rust-resistant metal, such as carbon steel. Heavy digging tools should have solid-socket or solid-strapped construction.*

BASIC GARDEN TOOLS

Toolmania may strike if you go shopping for tools without deciding what you need beforehand.

Here's a rundown of standard garden tools and their uses. If you start with these, you should be prepared for most of your garden chores.

Garden spade. For general digging, turning soil, cutting sod.
Digging fork. For loosening soil, mixing in compost and soil amendments, harvesting root crops.
Hoe. Traditional blade or "push-pull" scuffle blade. For shallow weeding, aerating soil.
Garden rake. For smoothing and leveling soil, building raised beds, thinning seedlings, planting cover crops.
Trowel. For spot weeding, planting bulbs and seedlings.
Pocketknife. For harvesting, sharpening stakes, cutting twine.
Twine and wooden stakes. For marking and laying out rows and growing beds.

---

should be at least shoulder height. Many tools are available with extra-long handles for tall gardeners.

Digging fork. This is an essential tool for double digging, loosening soil, mixing in compost and other amendments, and harvesting root crops. A standard digging or garden fork has broad, flat tines; English-style forks have square tines.

Shovel. The familiar American shovel has a concave, pointed blade and a long handle. Shovels are good for general digging and scooping, chopping cover crops into the soil, and planting trees. Some models have a flat metal tread across the blade's shoulders to make pushing the tool into the soil with your foot easier.

Spade. The classic English garden spade has a short handle and a flat, square-cornered blade. It works well for double digging, trenching, removing sod, lifting soil from planting holes, and

Don't buy tools with painted handles—the paint may conceal weak wood.

Grain of wood should run straight up and down the handle, with no knots.

Choosing tool handles. Wooden handles have more "give" and absorb shock better than metal and fiberglass tool handles. Northern white ash is strong and durable and is not as heavy as hickory.

edging beds. Long-handled styles are also available.

Hoe. The classic American hoe, with a round-shouldered blade, is a favorite for cultivating around plants and creating furrows for sowing. It is sold in a variety of sizes; the bigger the blade, the heavier the work it is intended to do.

Both the Dutch scuffle hoe and the oscillating stirrup hoe are superb for weeding and light cultivating. Each has a blade that cuts weeds just below soil level with an easy push-pull action. The swan hoe, good for light weeding close to plants, has a small heart-shaped blade and a curved neck that allows you to work without stooping.

Garden rake. The rigid-toothed garden rake comes in a variety of widths and types of teeth. Choose a rake with widely spaced teeth for working heavy or rocky soil; closer spacing is best for average soil and for finer work such as smoothing seedbeds and planting cover crops.

Trowel. Trowels are handy for weeding, planting, and many other on-the-spot digging chores. They get frequent hard use and, as a result, are the most-often-broken of all garden tools. Never buy a cheap trowel. If you can't find a good forged-steel garden trowel, consider a pointed mason's trowel, built for heavy-duty work and available in most hardware stores.

1-piece trowel

Tang

Standard trowel

Choosing trowels. Trowels and other small hand tools should be socketed or have a tang that extends well up into the handle. Or trowels may be formed from a single piece of metal.

Garden cart or wheelbarrow. The boxlike garden cart, with oversized pneumatic tires, makes it easy to move compost and other bulky materials to and from the garden, even over bumpy terrain. A wheelbarrow requires more muscle to use but is less expensive and more maneuverable in tight spaces.

Push cultivator or wheel hoe. The traditional hand-pushed cultivator, with a large spoked wheel mounted ahead of cultivating tines or a furrower blade, is a good choice for aerating and weeding soil between closely spaced row crops. The modern wheel hoe has a smaller,

Straight, sharp blade closes down onto broad, flat-bottom blade.

Anvil pruners

Two sharp cutting blades move past one another, like scissor blades.

Bypass pruners

Pruning shears. *You can choose between anvil-type and bypass-type pruners.*

wider front wheel. It can be fitted with such attachments as an oscillating stirrup blade.

Pruners. *Anvil*-type pruners withstand heavy use and are good for removing dead branches or other dry woody material. *Bypass*-type pruners make a cleaner cut and are the tool of choice for pruning fruit trees and for all-around garden use. Long-handled pruning shears, also called loppers, give additional leverage and work well for reaching into crowded plants.

Pitchfork. Pitchforks have between three and six pointed tines and are for lifting and moving bulky materials. Use long-handled models for light work such as spreading straw mulch; short-handled forks are best for heavier chores such as turning compost piles.

Pocketknife. Choose a small model with a stainless steel locking blade for harvesting vegetables and herbs, sharpening stakes, and cutting twine.

Garden hose. Cheap plastic hose kinks up, has weak fittings, and seldom lasts more than a couple of seasons. Instead, buy two- or four-ply reinforced rubber or rubber and vinyl hose with well-built solid brass or snap-on fittings. Look for a manufacturer's warranty of at least five years.

Hand sickle or scythe. These old-fashioned tools are ideal for cutting down cover crops. Sickles and scythes are also used for clearing garden sites and removing cornstalks and other large debris at the end of the season.

Power Equipment

Most day-to-day garden work can be done efficiently with hand tools. If you need power equipment only once or twice a year, such as in the spring and fall to till your soil, renting the machinery for a day or two will be more cost-efficient than buying your own. Renting is also a good way to try out different models and brands of machinery before making a purchasing decision.

Two of the most common pieces of power equipment that home gardeners use are rotary tillers and chipper/shredders. Here are some basic facts about both of these tools.

Rotary tillers. Power tillers range in size from tiny 1½-horsepower between-row soil scratchers to full-fledged 12-horsepower walk-behind tractors. Most models under 4 horsepower have front-mounted tines; heavier-duty tillers have rear tines and powered front wheels. Tillers make fast work of breaking new ground and cultivating. But if used too frequently, tillers can pulverize soil, destroying its structure.

When shopping for a tiller, consider not only overall size and power but also maximum tilling depth. Check whether the tilling width can be adjusted, and ask about the length and conditions of the manufacturer's warranty. Sale offers are not uncommon and can save you $100 or more.

Chipper/shredders. These machines quickly convert yard

waste into mulch or material for composting. Electric models (1.75 to 4 hp) are light and quiet. They can easily handle leaves, cornstalks, and other garden debris, as well as branches up to 1½ inches in diameter. Because of the extension cord required, however, they're useful only on small properties.

Gas-powered models (3 to 10 hp) are more expensive but often have more features (such as a tilt-down chute that allows you to rake leaves directly into the shredder). Most units can handle limbs up to 3 inches in diameter.

Day-to-Day Tool Care

Take a few minutes to clean tools after each use.

Finding the bevel. *To determine the bevel on a hoe, hold it as you would when using it, then scrape the blade on a hard surface like concrete. File the edge where you see bright scratch marks.*

Knock or scrape soil off metal blades with a plastic or wooden spatula. Don't use the metal blade of one tool to clean another; you might damage both. Remove any remaining soil with a wire brush or by spraying with a hose. When the tool is completely clean and dry, wipe the metal with an oily cloth to prevent rust.

On power equipment, keep the engine's cooling fins clear of dirt and debris. Cut away tangled vegetation from tiller tines and around wheel axles.

Sharpening Tools

Most garden tools, including digging tools such as spades, hoes, and shovels, are far easier to use when kept sharp. Here are some basic tool-sharpening principles, which are also illustrated on this page and page 38.

• Use a flat file for flat-bladed tools and a half-round file for shovels and other tools with curved surfaces.
• Sharpen single-beveled tools such as hoes, spades, and pruning shears on the beveled (angled) side only. Sharpening the flat side can destroy the tool's effectiveness.
• File each tool at an angle that matches the blade's original bevel. Cutting and

Sharpening a spade. *Turn the blade upside down and rest it against a support. Hold file at a low angle while sharpening.*

slicing tools generally have a shallow-angled bevel and a keen edge. Digging tools have a steeper bevel to produce a thicker, longer-lasting edge.
• Look closely to find the bevel on well-worn tools. Most garden spades are beveled along the back edge.
• When sharpening, press the file down hard and push it forward and across the tool's edge at an angle, rather than straight into the blade. Use the full length of the file on each forward stroke, then lift the file up off the blade on the back stroke.
• Stop filing when you can feel a burr, or slight ridge of metal, along the full width of the blade's underside. Finish the

edge by drawing the file lightly over the burr, flush with the unbeveled surface, to remove it.

Storing Tools

Keep tools in a dry place; metal will rust in a damp garage or basement. Reserve an area solely for tool storage, and give each tool its own place. Hang long-handled tools upright, off the floor, on nails, pegs, or a commercial tool rack. You can also hang small tools, such as trowels and pruners, or store them in a cabinet.

Store all gas-powered machinery (and fuel and oil) in a shed away from other buildings. This minimizes the danger from fumes and flammable materials.

Sharpening a hoe. Press the file down hard and push forward and across the edge at an angle, not straight into the blade.

End-of-Season Tool Care

Spend an autumn afternoon preparing and storing your tools for the winter.

Hand Tools

Clean and polish. Use water and a wire brush to soften and remove caked-on mud from spades, forks, trowels, and other digging tools. Sharpen any tools that need it. Polish all metal parts with steel wool, then wipe with an oily rag or give the surface a coat of paste wax.

Disinfect pruning shears and loppers by soaking the cutters for a full minute in a 10 percent bleach solution (1 part chlorine bleach to 9 parts water). Then wipe the metal dry and oil it to prevent rust.

Lubricate. Lubricate pruners and other tools with moving parts using light oil.

Check handles. Inspect wooden handles for chips or splinters. Sand any rough areas. Rub all wooden handles with boiled linseed oil or tung oil. Be sure to get plenty of oil into the areas where wood and metal meet.

Clean up trellises and stakes. Brush off all soil from wooden trellises and stakes, and let them dry in the sun for a few hours before storing. If disease was a problem in your garden, wash the stakes and trellises

Sharpening a shovel. Sharpen the top edge of the shovel blade, using a half-round file.

with a 10 percent bleach solution. Be sure they dry thoroughly before you store them.

Drain and store watering equipment. Disconnect, drain, and put away all hoses and sprinklers before winter.

Power Equipment

Always disconnect the spark plug before servicing power equipment. Work outdoors or in a well-ventilated area. Follow these steps to thoroughly and safely prepare power equipment for storage.

1. Wipe or scrape accumulated soil and dust off all exposed metal parts. Use a rag soaked in kerosene to clean greasy or oily areas. Use a putty knife or paint scraper to remove matted vegetation from the under-

Use a wire brush to remove soil from tools.

Tung oil seals wooden handles and keeps out moisture.

Use rags to apply tung oil.

Lubricate moving parts of tools with light oil.

End-of-season cleanup. *As your garden winds down in the fall, gather all your tools for a thorough cleaning. Come spring, you'll be ready to start gardening again.*

sides of rotary tillers and chipper/shredders. A sharp knife will help you slice away vines and other fibrous materials from around tiller tines, engine shafts, and wheel axles.
2. Inspect machines carefully for loose or missing nuts, bolts, or screws. Tighten or replace as necessary.
3. Clean and oil the air filter. Change the oil in four-cycle engines.

4. Examine tiller tines and chipper blades for wear or breakage. Replace if necessary.
5. Lubricate moving parts according to the manufacturer's instructions.
6. For four-cycle engines (these have separate oil and gas systems), drain the gasoline from the tank, then run the engine until all the fuel in the line and carburetor is gone. Use the drained-off gasoline in

your car. For two-cycle engines (oil and gas mixed together), if you haven't used up all the fuel while doing end-of-season chores, add commercial gas stabilizer to the fuel in each tank. Run the engine for a minute or two to make sure the stabilized fuel is in the system.
7. Remove and clean (or replace) the spark plug. Reinstall the plug, but leave the wire disconnected.

GROWING VEGETABLES

PART 2

Preventing Problems 68
How to encourage beneficials, use insect barriers, make repellents, and handle pest outbreaks

Vegetables in Containers 72
Crop and container choices, a soil mix recipe, and care guidelines

Extending the Season 74
Shade devices, frost protectors, cold frames, hotbeds, and soil-warming techniques

Ending the Season 78
Garden cleanup, in-ground crop storage, and winter soil protection

Saving Seeds 80
How to collect, clean, and store seeds

Crop Entries

DECIDING WHAT TO GROW

Develop a Crop List

A great garden starts with a good plan. Thinking about the crops you want to grow next season is the first step to creating that plan.

Start by jotting down a list of the vegetables you most like to eat. Skim through seed catalogs to jog your memory, and write down the names of other crops you'd like to try.

Next, it's time to organize the list. Arrange your choices so the crops you want to grow most are at the top. For each crop, add notes on the important characteristics. You'll want to know:

• If the crop is annual or perennial.
• How much space it will take up.
• How much sun it needs.
• What kind of soil it prefers.
• How much moisture it requires.
• When to plant it.
• How long it will take from planting to harvest.

If you don't know the answers for some crops, refer to the vegetable crop entries, beginning on page 82.

Map the Garden

How much room is there in your garden for the crops on your list? To find out, you must go outside and measure your garden's dimensions and major features. Jot down rough notes as you measure.

Back indoors, transfer your measurements to graph paper. Choose a scale that lets you show details. For example, if you decide that one square on the graph

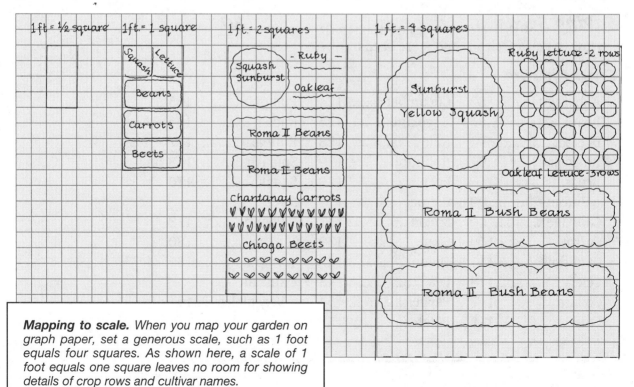

Mapping to scale. *When you map your garden on graph paper, set a generous scale, such as 1 foot equals four squares. As shown here, a scale of 1 foot equals one square leaves no room for showing details of crop rows and cultivar names.*

paper will equal 2 feet, and the squares are 1/5 inch on each side, then a 4- by 8-foot bed would occupy less than 1 square inch on your map—not much room for a planting plan.

The illustration on the opposite page shows that the more generous you are in choosing a scale, the more details you can show. To get the most detailed plan, have one square equal 3 inches.

For a very large garden, you may have to tape several sheets of graph paper together to fit everything in. Or map the whole garden on a small scale so it fits on one sheet; then map smaller sections on separate sheets at a larger scale to have room for notes.

Plan the Crop Layout

Now it's time to see how many of the crops on your list will realistically fit in the space you have. Using a sharpened pencil with a good eraser, start sketching the crops you want to grow onto your map. Use different symbols for small plants and large plants, as shown on the opposite page. Write each crop's name on the map by the row or in the block where it will grow.

Begin your layout with the crops at the top of your list, so you can allow enough room for the ones you want most. Try to group crops that have similar care needs; refer to the notes on your list for that information.

For help deciding how much of each crop you need to grow, refer to "Planting" in each of the vegetable entries that begin on page 82. Planting instructions in the entries will also tell you the optimum distance between rows and between the plants in a row.

If you will be planting a crop in a bed, use the recommended distance between plants in a row between all of the plants in the bed. For example, conventional rows of leeks should be planted 1 to 2 feet apart, with leeks 6 inches apart in the rows. But in a bed, you can set leeks in a grid pattern, 6 inches apart in each direction.

Narrow Down the List

When you don't have enough room to grow everything you want, resist the temptation to crowd everything in at close spacings. Go through your list and mark the crops that you feel you really must have; cross off anything you think you can live without.

If you won't have time to

check your garden every day or two, concentrate on growing crops that don't need frequent harvesting. Cabbage, collards, eggplants, kale, lettuce, peppers, pumpkins, root crops, winter squash, and tomatoes are good choices for weekend gardeners.

Experienced gardeners may want to grow only unusual crops that aren't easily found at the grocery store or farmers' market. 'Lemon' cucumber, 'Ruby' chard, and currant tomatoes are just a few of the uncommon crops that are fun to try at home.

PLANNING A PRACTICAL GARDEN

A key part of having a successful vegetable garden is planning an effective garden layout. You'll want to shape a layout that suits your needs and the amount of time you have to spend on the garden.

Choose a Garden Arrangement

One thing you need to consider is whether you'll plant in rows or beds. Use traditional row planting when:

- You have plenty of land.
- You plan to cultivate with machinery.
- You have ample amounts of organic matter and nutrients.

It's better to plan your garden in beds with paths in between when:

- Your space is limited.
- Your soil is poor.
- You plan to hand-cultivate.
- You have a limited supply of organic matter and fertilizer.

A system of beds and paths uses space more efficiently than rows and allows you to concentrate your soil preparation efforts. Build *raised* garden beds if you have poorly drained or shallow soil or if you have difficulty stooping. (For complete directions, see "Building Raised Beds" on page 30.)

For easy access, paths between garden beds should be at least 2 feet wide. Make some of the paths 3 to 4 feet wide so you'll be able to reach most areas of the garden with a wheelbarrow. Cover the path with some kind of material that will reduce weeds, allow moisture to enter the soil, and prevent muddiness in wet weather. This can be as simple as a mulch of straw or wood chips or as permanent as bricks set in sand.

Plan Planting Areas

As you map out your planting plan, place perennial plants in their own area to one side of the central garden space. That way you won't have to maneuver around them as you prepare the soil each year for annual crops.

Also, place taller crops on the north side of your garden so they won't shade shorter ones. If you will be planting in rows, keep in mind that rows oriented east to west shade each other least. In rows that run north to south, taller plants may shade shorter ones in morning or afternoon.

FAMILY MATTERS

If you plan to avoid planting related crops in the same spot year after year, you need to know which crops belong to the same botanical family. Here's a list of the most common families, along with some of their members.

Beet family: beet, chard, spinach
Cabbage family: broccoli, brussels sprouts, cabbage, cauliflower, collard, kale, kohlrabi, radish, turnip
Carrot family: carrot, celery, chervil, cilantro, dill, parsley, parsnip
Grass family: corn
Lettuce family: artichoke, chicory, endive, lettuce
Lily family: chives, garlic, leek, onion
Pea family: bean, cowpea, pea, peanut
Squash family: cucumber, melon, pumpkin, squash
Tomato family: eggplant, pepper, potato, tomato

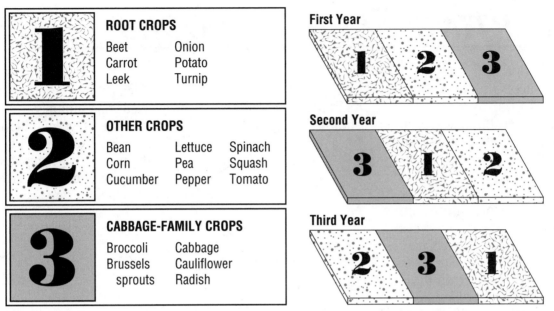

1 ROOT CROPS

Beet	Onion
Carrot	Potato
Leek	Turnip

2 OTHER CROPS

Bean	Lettuce	Spinach
Corn	Pea	Squash
Cucumber	Pepper	Tomato

3 CABBAGE-FAMILY CROPS

Broccoli	Cabbage
Brussels	Cauliflower
sprouts	Radish

First Year
1 2 3

Second Year
3 1 2

Third Year
2 3 1

A simple rotation system. This three-year crop rotation scheme separates cabbage-family crops and root crops from the rest of the common vegetable garden crops.

This shade can be welcome for cool-season crops, like peas or lettuce, that are maturing or germinating in warm weather. But sun-loving plants, like peppers and eggplant, can suffer if their light is blocked by taller plants.

Rotate Crops for Better Production

To get the most out of your soil—and minimize pest and disease problems as well—avoid planting the same annual crops in the same place each year. As you plan your layout, refer to your previous year's notes to see where each crop grew last year. Choose a different bed or area in which to grow it this year. This technique is known as *crop rotation.*

To reduce the buildup of soilborne pests and diseases, also avoid replanting where any of that crop's relatives grew last year. For example, tomatoes, peppers, and eggplants are in the same botanical family. So, you shouldn't plant tomatoes where peppers or eggplants grew last year. See "Family Matters" on the opposite page to learn how many common vegetable crops are related.

If soilborne pests and diseases aren't a big concern for you, consider trying a very simple rotation system, as diagrammed on this page. Divide your garden into three parts or three beds. To one bed, add a moderate amount of balanced organic fertilizer before planting. Plant root crops in this bed.

In the second bed, work in plenty of compost or aged manure but no fertilizer. Here, plant crops other than root and cabbage-family crops.

To the third bed, add a moderate amount of a balanced organic fertilizer plus compost or aged manure. Also add lime, if needed, so the soil pH is between 6.5 to 7.5. Here's where you'll grow your cabbage-family crops.

Next year, shift each crop group over to the next bed. The root crops move to the second bed, the "other" crops to the third bed, and the cabbage-family crops to the first bed. Prepare the soil as needed before planting.

STARTING SEEDS INDOORS

For successful seed starting, it's vital to start with healthy seed. Buy packets of fresh seed from a catalog or your local garden center. Look for the phrase "Packed for . . ." somewhere on the packet; the date should be the current year. Packets from mail-order catalogs may not be dated. Be sure to write the year of purchase on these packets for future reference.

Eventually, you'll end up with a pile of half-full packets from previous years' purchases. Before you buy new seed, inventory the leftovers to see which ones are still good. Try the plate germination test on the opposite page or this seed roll test to check seed viability.

Seed Roll Test

This method gives you an accurate reading of the percent of your seed that should germinate.

1. Fold a paper towel in half (if you're testing large seeds like squash) or thirds (for smaller seeds).

STEP 1

2. Space ten seeds evenly apart along one of the short edges, about 1 inch from the edge.

STEP 2

3. Roll up the paper towel, and secure it with two wire twist ties. Place the end without the seeds in a glass containing a little water.

STEP 3

4. Unroll the towel after the germination period for the kind of seed you are growing has passed (you should find this information on the seed packet).

Then count the germinated seeds and multiply by 10 to learn the germination rate. For example, if six of the ten seeds germinated, that would be a 60 percent germination rate.

STEP 4

If 90 percent or more germinate, the seeds are healthy. If less than 50 percent germinate, buy new seed. If 50 to 90 percent germinate, they are worth sowing, but more thickly than usual.

Prepare to Plant

Buy a commercial seed-starting mix, or make your own with equal parts of vermiculite, milled sphagnum moss (or screened compost), and perlite. If the mix is dry, put it in a plastic bucket or basin, add a bit of warm water, and stir. Keep adding water until the mix is evenly moist. Squeeze a handful tightly—

PLATE GERMINATION TEST

Step 1. *Arrange small groups of seeds on a double layer of paper towels. Mark the top of the arrangement with a pin.*

Step 2. *Top the seeds with a double layer of towels, moisten the towels, and cover the setup with plastic wrap or a plastic bag.*

Step 3. *After the seeds germinate, lift the towels and record on your notes how well each cultivar sprouted.*

only a few drops of water should ooze out. If the mix is too wet, add more dry mix.

Containers for seed starting should be 2½ to 3 inches tall. Use commercial seed-starting containers or recycled household items like milk cartons. Punch drainage holes in the bottoms of recycled containers.

You'll transplant most seedlings to individual pots after they have a few true leaves. Plant seeds of squash-family plants and other crops that don't transplant easily in pots from the start.

Plant Your Seeds

To plant seeds, fill a container to the top with moist mix, then tap it on a hard surface to settle it a bit. Use a pencil to poke holes for larger seeds like squash; scatter small seeds evenly over the surface. If the seed should be covered (according to the seed packet), use one finger to gently fill the holes, or scatter a little moist mix over the seed. Use the flat of your fingertips to

---

AVERAGE SEED LIFE

Don't throw away those half-full seed packets! Many crop seeds will stay viable for several years if you store them in a cool, dry place. The life expectancy of vegetable seeds ranges from only one year up to six years.

Bean: 3 years	**Eggplant:** 4 years
Beet: 4 years	**Lettuce:** 6 years
Broccoli: 3 years	**Onion:** 1 year
Cabbage: 4 years	**Pea:** 3 years
Carrot: 3 years	**Pepper:** 2 years
Cauliflower: 4 years	**Radish:** 5 years
Corn: 2 years	**Spinach:** 3 years
Cucumber: 5 years	**Squash:** 4 years

lightly press the mix down and level it. Add a label for each kind of seed. On the label, note the crop's name, the cultivar, and the date you planted it.

Don't plant too thickly; you'll have trouble thinning and transplanting later. But if you have the room, plant up to twice as many seeds as you want plants. If all of them thrive, you can pick the best ones for planting and share extra with friends.

Water newly sown seeds with a gentle mist from above until water runs out the bottom. Or set the container in a shallow pan filled with water for several hours, so it will absorb water from below. Lay a sheet of moistened newspaper over the planted container, and place the container in a waterproof saucer or tray.

Find the Right Spot

Vegetable seeds typically germinate best at soil temperatures somewhat warmer than the average home. You will probably need to locate a special warm spot for your seedling containers. This could be atop a refrigerator, water heater, television set, or a stove with a pilot light, or on a shelf above (not directly on) a radiator. The area doesn't have to be well lit; you can move the container to a brighter spot when the seeds sprout. If no warm place is available, consider buying a small heating coil or mat designed for seed starting.

Supervise Your Seedlings

Check under the newspaper cover daily for growth. Water

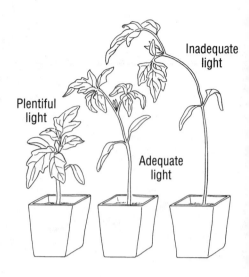

Growing healthy seedlings. *Seedlings that get lots of light and cool temperatures will be short and stocky.*

again if the mix begins to dry out. As soon as the first stems or seed leaves break through the soil, remove the newspaper covering.

As soon as seedlings break the surface of the mix, it's critical that they get plenty of light. A large window, preferably a south-

SEED-SOWING BASICS

Use a pencil to make holes for seeds.

Soak seeded containers in water.

Set saturated containers in empty pan to drain.

Sowing seeds in containers. *You can plant seeds in pots or commercial six-packs. You can also reuse milk cartons, aluminum pans, and other household items as seed flats and drainage trays.*

facing one, provides enough light for most seedlings. Turn them daily to keep the stems from developing a permanent bend toward the light. If window space is limited, set up plant growth lights; see "Raising Transplants" on page 50 for details.

Most vegetable seedlings will grow fine at normal room conditions. Many prefer an air temperature near 60°F at night. (You'll find the preferred growing temperatures of common crops in "Seed Starting at a Glance" on this page.) If your home tends to be warmer at night, look for a cooler location, such as an enclosed porch.

Seed Starting at a Glance

CROP	GROWING GUIDELINES
Broccoli	Sow seed 8 weeks before the last spring frost to 12 weeks before the first fall frost. Seeds sprout in 3 to 10 days at 70˚ to 80˚F. Grow seedlings at 60˚ to 70˚F.
Brussels sprouts	Sow seed 14 weeks before the first fall frost. Seeds sprout in 3 to 10 days at 70˚ to 80˚F. Grow seedlings at 60˚ to 70˚F.
Cabbage	Sow seed 8 weeks before the last spring frost to 14 weeks before the first fall frost. Seeds sprout in 4 to 10 days at 70˚ to 80˚F. Grow seedlings at 60˚ to 70˚F.
Cauliflower	Sow seed 6 weeks before the last spring frost to 14 weeks before the first fall frost. Seeds sprout in 4 to 10 days at 70˚ to 80˚F. Grow seedlings at 60˚ to 70˚F.
Cucumber	Sow seed 5 to 6 weeks before the last spring frost. Seeds sprout in 6 to 10 days at 70˚ to 95˚F. Grow seedlings at 70˚ to 80˚F.
Eggplant	Sow seed 6 to 8 weeks before the last spring frost. Seeds sprout in 7 to 14 days at 75˚ to 85˚F. Grow seedlings at 70˚ to 80˚F.
Leek	Sow seed 8 weeks before the last spring frost to 12 weeks before the first fall frost. Seeds sprout in 7 to 12 days at 65˚ to 80˚F. Grow seedlings at 60˚ to 70˚F.
Lettuce	Sow seed 8 weeks before the last spring frost to 9 weeks before the first fall frost. Seeds sprout in 4 to 10 days at 60˚ to 75˚F. Grow seedlings at 55˚ to 75˚F.
Muskmelon	Sow seed 5 to 6 weeks before the last spring frost. Seeds sprout in 4 to 8 days at 75˚ to 95˚F. Grow seedlings at 70˚ to 80˚F.
Onion	Sow seed 8 weeks before the last spring frost to 17 weeks before the first fall frost. Seeds sprout in 7 to 12 days at 65˚ to 80˚F. Grow seedlings at 60˚ to 70˚F.
Pepper	Sow seed 6 to 8 weeks before the last spring frost. Seeds sprout in 10 to 20 days at 75˚ to 85˚F. Grow seedlings at 65˚ to 80˚F.
Squash	Sow seed 5 to 6 weeks before the last spring frost. Seeds sprout in 3 to 10 days at 70˚ to 95˚F. Grow seedlings at 60˚ to 75˚F.
Tomato	Sow seed 5 to 7 weeks before the last spring frost. Seeds sprout in 6 to 14 days at 75˚ to 80˚F. Grow seedlings at 60˚ to 75˚F.
Watermelon	Sow seed 6 to 8 weeks before the last spring frost. Seeds sprout in 3 to 12 days at 75˚ to 95˚F. Grow seedlings at 70˚ to 80˚F.

RAISING TRANSPLANTS

Many gardeners have good luck starting seed, but sometimes they find it trickier to grow those tiny sprouts on into strong, healthy transplants. "Starting Seeds Indoors" on page 46 covers the basics of getting seedlings off to a good beginning. Here you'll learn how to follow through and raise great transplants.

Keep Conditions Right

As your seedlings grow, continue to keep the mix moist, the light bright, and the temperature appropriately

Provide high humidity. *Set pots on a tray of pebbles and water to keep humidity high around the leaves.*

cool (especially at night). If the containers are by a window, turn them daily so that the seedlings don't stay bent in one direction.

If the seeding mix does not contain compost or soil, water with a half-strength solution of fish emulsion as soon as the true leaves begin

to develop. If the mix does contain compost or soil, wait until you pot the seedlings before you fertilize.

Provide High Humidity

Most seedlings do best in an environment that has a 50 to 70 percent humidity range. Heated houses often have drier air. You can make a humidifying setup to keep plants healthy. Place a 1-inch layer of pebbles (pea gravel or aquarium gravel) in a large baking tray. Then add ½ inch of water. Set seedling containers on the pebbles. Add water when the water level drops.

Supply Lots of Light

As the seedlings get larger, they may outgrow your limited window space. Light-deficient seedlings will become pale and spindly.

One solution is a two-bulb, fluorescent shop-light fixture. You can buy special plant growth lights, although you'll

4"–6"

Raising transplants under lights. *Seedlings grow best when their growing tips are 4 to 6 inches from the light.*

get similar results with less expensive cool-white bulbs. Leave the lights on for 16 hours a day for maximum benefit. For extra convenience, plug the lights into a timer that will turn them on and off automatically.

Separate Crowded Seedlings

If your seedlings are growing close together, you'll need to decide whether to thin them or transplant them to separate containers. If you thin, keep the largest, best-formed seedlings.

Thinning Seedlings

Some seedlings, like cucumber and squash, just don't like their roots disturbed. It's best to thin these crops with scissors instead of

Thinning with scissors. *Cut unwanted seedlings off at soil level.*

transplanting. Use sharp scissors to snip off unwanted seedlings at the soil level.

Transplanting Seedlings

If you've decided to transplant your seedlings, you have two options. First, you can thin out the extra seedlings that you don't want to transplant (again, use scissors to do this). After thinning, prepare the seedlings for transplanting by using a knife to "block" the roots. About a week before you plan to transplant, cut the soil into blocks around the individual seedlings, much as you would cut up a sheet cake. Then it's a simple matter to separate the seedlings at transplanting time.

When you want to save as many seedlings as possible, try using your thumbs to separate individual seedlings and roots from one another. At transplanting time, remove a group of seedlings from an individual cell or pot. Place your thumbs at the soil level between two seedlings or two groups of seedlings; hold the root ball with your fingers. Use your thumbs to divide the root masses. Gently pull the two root masses apart, shaking them slightly as the roots separate. Discard any seedlings that lose too much root; transplant the rest.

Blocking roots. *Cutting the soil and roots between seedlings helps prepare the plants for transplanting.*

Pick the Right Mix

You can use a commercial potting mix or make one yourself. Good formulas for a homemade mix are half compost and half vermiculite, or 2 parts garden soil, 2 parts compost, and 1 part builder's sand. Mix the dry ingredients, then add enough water to lightly moisten the mixture.

Separating small seedlings. *Handle delicate seedlings gently. Use your thumbs to tease tangled roots apart with minimal damage.*

Move Transplants to Pots

Water your seedlings the day before you plan to transplant so the seed-starting mix will be moist and cling to the roots. Fill your containers (3 inches in diameter is a good size) half full of moistened potting mix. Then follow these simple steps for transplanting, as shown on this page.

1. Push seedlings from their containers, or use a small tool, such as a fork or Popsicle stick, to remove them from a flat. Separate seedlings if necessary.
2. Holding each seedling by its leaves, set the root ball on top of the potting mix. If the roots are long and hanging down, poke an ample hole in the mix and hold the seedling over it so that the roots fall into the hole.
3. While holding the seedling with one hand, fill in potting mix around the roots or root ball with the other hand, until the container is nearly full of potting mix. Plant the seedling so it is at the same level it was before. (If the stem is elongated, plant deeper, so the soil comes up to just below the seed leaves.) Use your fingertips to press the soil down, gently but firmly, around the seedling stem and level the soil.

Aftercare

Water newly settled transplants with a gentle trickle or by setting the containers in a deep basin of water for a few hours. Place the transplants out of direct sunlight for a day or two, then return them to a bright window or a fluorescent light setup.

If your seedlings begin to wilt after transplanting, put the containers in a clear plastic bag, out of direct sun, until the plants recover. Use a stick or wire support to keep the plastic off of the plants.

Adapt Plants to the Outdoors

When spring arrives, it's time for your seedlings to

STEP 1

STEP 2

STEP 3

Potting up transplants. *Handle seedlings gently when transplanting them. Be sure not to squeeze the stem, and preserve as many of the roots as possible. Do your best not to knock soil off the roots as well.*

move from their indoor shelter to the sunnier, cooler, windier conditions of the garden. To help them adjust, you need to gradually expose them to the tougher conditions of the outdoors. This process is called *hardening off*.

Begin by setting the plants outdoors in a shady, not-too-windy spot for a few hours in the afternoon. Bring them indoors at night. Gradually increase the time plants spend outdoors until, in a few days, they will be ready to stay out all day.

After a few more days, place them in part shade or even full sun on days that aren't extremely warm, and leave them out on nights that are not too cold. (If you work weekdays, begin this process when you get home from work on Thursday or Friday. You should be able to leave the plants out all day by Monday.)

Hold back on watering and fertilizing at this time, but keep a close eye on the seedlings so they don't dry out. You will notice that the stems and leaves become firmer during the hardening-off period. After 7 to 14 days of this treatment, your plants will be ready for the rigors of the garden.

Protect Plants with a Cold Frame

If you're lucky enough to have a cold frame, you'll find it makes an excellent shelter for seedlings during the hardening-off process. Open the top in the daytime whenever temperatures are warm enough. For extra convenience, you can get an automatic opener to ventilate the cold frame and prevent overheating.

As the seedlings become more hardened, and as temperatures warm, gradually leave the cold frame open longer. For more tips on using a cold frame, see "Plant in Cold Frames" on page 76.

PLANTING THE GARDEN

Decide When to Plant

After a long, cold winter, it's tempting to get out into the garden on the first warm day and start planting. But remember that even though the weather feels warm to you, it may not be warm enough for your crops. Both *soil* and *air* temperatures have to be right for seedlings and transplants to get off to a good start.

Knowing what conditions your crops need will help you pick the best time to begin planting. Seed packets and seedling labels usually give general guidelines on the best planting times. You'll also find planting guidelines in the individual crop entries, starting on page 82.

Some cold-tolerant crops, such as peas and lettuce, are ready for planting as soon as the ground can be worked in the spring. Depending on your climate, this can be as early as late February or as late as early May. When your soil has thawed and dried out enough to be worked, start sowing or setting out transplants of these early crops.

Other crops need warmer soil for germination and good growth. Some, like bean seeds and squash transplants, are planted around the last frost date. This is the average date of the last spring frost in your area. To find out the last frost date, ask local gardeners or contact your local extension service office.

Corn, tomatoes, and melons are a few of the crops that you'll plant about two weeks after the last frost date for your area. But still keep an eye on the weather reports, and protect tender plants if a late frost is predicted.

These general planting suggestions work fine for gardens in most areas. One exception is the West Coast, where spring frosts end early but the soil can be slow to warm up enough for summer crops. And in mountain areas, spring frosts may continue long after the soil temperature is adequate for planting.

Use a soil thermometer to accurately gauge soil temperature. Plant when the soil conditions are ideal. Then be prepared to protect your plantings if weather forecasters predict a cold spell.

NO-SHOW SEEDS

If your seeds fail to germinate after a few weeks, it's time to figure out what went wrong. Below are some of the most common reasons seeds fail to sprout and steps you can take to prevent the problem when you replant.

Seed was too old. See "Starting Seeds Indoors" on page 46 for information on how to test if seeds are still alive.

Seed was planted too deep. Follow depth recommendations on seed packet or in individual crop entries, beginning on page 82.

Seed dried out. Firm the seedbed carefully after planting to eliminate air pockets. Water regularly.

Seed rotted. Improve soil drainage. Wait until soil is warmer and drier to plant.

Seed was attacked by pests. Seed-corn maggots and birds may devour seed; rabbits, cutworms, snails, and slugs may eat young seedlings. See "Preventing Problems" on page 68 for tips on stopping these pests.

Soil was too cold. Check soil temperature before planting.

Soil was too wet. Improve soil drainage. Avoid overwatering.

SOWING SEED IN ROWS

Step 1. *Use the corner of a rake or hoe to open a shallow furrow.*

Step 2. *Drop seeds by hand into the prepared furrow at the proper spacing.*

Step 3. *Sift soil through your fingers to screen out stones, sticks, and soil clumps.*

Pick Plant Spacings

Each plant in your garden will need a certain amount of sun and root space to develop properly. Giving them the space they need will help ensure the best harvest possible.

If you're planting in rows, allow adequate spacing between the rows and between plants within each row. Hill plantings need to have ample space between the hills. You'll find this information on the seed packet or seedling label, or in the individual crop entries, beginning on page 82.

Planting in beds rather than in rows allows you to grow more plants in the same amount of space, because you don't have to allow for paths between rows. Space seeds or transplants evenly over the bed. The distance between each plant is the distance that you would allow between plants in an ordinary row.

Where two different crops meet in rows, hills, or beds, you need to decide how close to plant them. Calculate this spacing by adding the correct distance between two plants of each crop and dividing it by two. For example, if lettuce should be 6 to 8 inches apart and broccoli 18 to 24 inches apart, then lettuce and broccoli should be 12 to 16 inches apart.

Sowing Seed Outdoors

You can sow seeds individually in rows, as shown above, or plant them in beds or hills.

Sow in beds. To broadcast small seeds, mark the area you want to cover. Scatter the seed evenly over prepared soil. Rake the seed in or cover it with soil to get the correct planting depth. Once

Planting grid. *Chicken wire mounted on a wooden frame makes a handy guide for evenly spacing seeds and transplants.*

the seedlings emerge, thin them as needed so each plant has enough room to develop without crowding.

Large seeds, like peas, beans, and squash, are easy to plant individually at the correct spacing.

Sow in hills. Hill planting consists of small groups of seeds with wide spaces between the groups. It doesn't necessarily imply an actual mound, although planting on low mounds *can* improve drainage and reduce the chance of seed decay. Vining crops, like melons, squash, and pumpkins, are common choices for hill planting.

Use rocks or stakes to lay out the spacing of your hills. Plant two or three seeds in each spot at the correct depth; cover as needed.

Label and water. Once seeds are covered, pat the planted area with your fingers or the back of a rake to get good contact between the seed and the soil. Label the area, and water gently to moisten the soil. Keep the soil moist until you see stems and leaves popping above the ground.

Planting Transplants

Transplants adapt well to rows, beds, or hill planting. Once you've prepared the soil, use stakes and string to mark off rows or beds, or use

HANDLING TRANSPLANTS

5"   1" of soil

Soil/compost mix

1. Dig a hole at least as wide and as deep as the pot the transplant is growing in. To give transplants an extra boost, make the hole a few inches deeper and mix a handful of compost into the bottom of the hole. Cover this mixture with an inch of soil.

2. Remove the transplant from its container by placing one hand over the soil, with the plant's stem between two fingers. Carefully turn the plant over until the soil is resting on your hand. Use your other hand to pull off the pot. (If the pot won't come off, tap it a few times on a hard surface to loosen the roots.)

3. Set the transplant in the center of the hole. Steady the root ball with one hand, and use your other hand to fill in soil around it. Pat the soil down firmly around the base of the plant.

A ridge of soil holds water near transplant.

4. Use your fingers to shape a low circular ridge a few inches out from the plant stem. With a gentle hose stream or a watering can, water in the transplant; about a quart of water per plant is a good amount.

pebbles to mark hills. Then set out the plants, as shown on the opposite page.

Keep transplants well watered until you see new growth; then you can start to gradually cut back. If you plan to set in stakes or a trellis, do it soon after planting to avoid injuring growing roots.

Harsh weather right after transplanting can damage even well hardened-off seedlings. If you can, transplant late in the day or on overcast days to minimize transplant shock. If this isn't possible, or if unexpected weather conditions occur, you may need to protect transplants from sun, winds, or cold temperatures.

Sun shields. To protect new transplants from strong sunshine, set up sun shields. Place them on one side (use a shingle or board stuck into the soil), or cover plants altogether (with newspaper or a paper bag). If you can shade the plant on only one side, place the shield to the southwest, angled over the plant. Leave it in place for a few days. Remove whole-plant covers after a day or two or plants will become spindly.

Wind blocks. Besides knocking down young plants, strong winds can draw water out of leaves faster than the limited roots replace it. Set up wind blocks on the side from which the wind is most likely to come. Cut milk jugs or milk cartons in half to make simple

temporary shelters; remove them after a few days.

If your site is always very windy, make a permanent windbreak. Stake medium-height and tall crops at transplanting time to keep the wind from knocking them over.

Cold covers. If you're setting your seedlings out a little early, or if late frosts are predicted, you'll need to protect the transplants from cold temperatures. Make your own covers by cutting the bottoms off of plastic milk jugs or 2-liter soda bottles. (Insert a stick through the top of the jug or bottle into the ground to anchor it.) You can also buy commercial products, like Wallo Water and floating row cover, to keep cold air from tender transplants.

Plastic or glass covers can heat up quickly on sunny days; remove them on warm days and replace them at night. For more tips on protecting plants from cold temperatures, see "Extending the Season" on page 74.

Plastic milk jug shelter

Newspaper tent

Milk jug wind shelter

Commercial hotcap

Paper bag shelter

Milk carton wind shelter

Plastic row cover

Board shelter

Transplant protectors. *Use simple homemade or commercial structures to protect new transplants from sun, wind, or cold.*

WATERING THE GARDEN

When to Water

Pay close attention to water needs in a newly planted garden. Check seedbeds every day—or even twice a day when the weather is hot—and water lightly whenever the surface is dry. Keep the soil around transplants on the wet side for the first week or two as well. Once the seedlings are several inches tall and the transplants begin to grow, you can gradually shift to a pattern of less frequent but more thorough watering.

Look at the Plants

Judging water needs by the way your plants look is popular but not always dependable. Plants that are too dry have dull, rather than glossy, leaves. The leaves may also feel limp. Don't wait till plants wilt to water; by then, the plants are seriously stressed. If your plants do wilt, get out there and water right away; otherwise, they may be permanently damaged.

Test Soil Moisture

Checking the soil gives you a more accurate idea of when you need to water. To do this, dig into the soil with your hand or a trowel. If the surface is dry, dig until you find moist soil. Check the moisture by feel or by noticing a color change: Moist soil is usually darker than dry soil. If you have to dig deeper than 2 or 3 inches to find moisture, it's time to water.

A more sophisticated, although still inexpensive, testing method is a moisture meter. Simply insert the probe into the soil and read the moisture level on the dial.

Time of Day

Early morning is an ideal time to water. Water soaks in before heat causes it to evaporate, and the day's warmth dries the leaves before nightfall, reducing the spread of disease.

Evening watering is also a good option, if you can avoid getting water on the leaves.

If your plants need water desperately, irrigate them as soon as you can—even midday watering is fine in a pinch. Water on the leaves can damage plants in very hot weather, but this is generally not a problem unless temperatures are above 95°F.

How Much to Water

A general rule of thumb for watering is to let the surface dry 1 to 2 inches deep, then add a 1-inch layer of water. Your garden will probably do nicely if you use this method, but your plants may not give optimum yields.

Vegetable crops grow best in soil that is constantly moist. Letting the top inch or two of soil dry out does put some stress on your plants. Your plants will be happiest if you replace the water lost from the soil *before* it gets dry.

The amount of water lost from day to day depends on factors such as soil type, humidity, and temperature. For a method to calculate how much water your soil is losing (and therefore how much you should be adding), refer to "When and How Much to Water" on page 204.

GREEN THUMB TIP

Wilting is a common symptom of water-stressed plants, but it's not the best indicator to go by. Wilting can also mean that the soil is too wet or that the plants are diseased or infested with borers. Plants may also wilt when a day is very hot, even though the soil is moist. Always check the soil before you assume wilting is due to a lack of water.

How Long to Water

Whether you've decided to go with the 1-inch rule of thumb or to calculate water loss from soil, you need to know how long to run your sprinkler, handheld hose, or irrigation system to deliver the right amount of water.

Sprinklers. To test the delivery rate of your sprinkler, gather several empty cans of the same size, and set them in different spots in the area covered by the spray pattern. Check the time when you turn on the sprinkler. Leave it on until at least one can holds 1 inch of water. Next time you water, you'll know just how long to leave the sprinkler running. (If the spray pattern is uneven, move the sprinkler around to distribute the water equally over the area.)

Handheld hoses. To test the water-delivery rate of a handheld hose and nozzle, turn the tap on midway and time how long it takes to fill a 1-gallon container. When the hose fills the container in 30 seconds, it is releasing enough water to add a 1-inch layer of water to 100 square feet of garden in 30 minutes. If the jug fills in less time, close the tap a bit; if it takes longer, open the tap more.

Marking the tap at the right position can help you remember just how far to open it. Water pressure can vary depending on the time of day, so the same setting may not always provide the same water flow. If you want to be precise, test the rate each time before you water.

Irrigation systems. It's good to determine roughly how long it takes for your irrigation system to thoroughly wet the soil. On a day when the top few inches of soil are dry, turn on your irrigation system or soaker hose. Clock how long it takes to moisten the soil to a depth of 1 inch, and make note of that time. You can use it as a base unit, multiplying by the number of inches of soil you want to soak at a particular time. To calculate the output of a drip irrigation system more precisely, see "When and How Much to Water" on page 204.

Watering methods. *Sprinklers are fine for keeping seedbeds moist. But for established plants, ground-level watering from a handheld hose, soaker hose, or a drip system is more efficient.*

FEEDING VEGETABLE CROPS

Rich soil is the best food source for your vegetable crops. If you've been improving your soil over the years, chances are you'll reap great harvests without adding fertilizer. The organic matter you apply once or twice a year feeds the soil microorganisms, which release nutrients that plants use to grow.

Fertilizer can give crops a boost but won't replace basic soil care. Feeding your crops is a plus when:

• You're starting a garden in soil that hasn't been adequately prepared. This can happen when you move to a new home or when you expand your garden.

• You grow crops that benefit from extra fertilizer. Heavy feeders like broccoli and tomatoes love a feeding at planting or a booster feeding later in the season.

• Your crops' condition makes you suspect the soil is in worse shape than you thought. If your crops grow slowly or look pale, booster feedings may help them get through the season.

Feed As You Plant

Fertilizing at planting simply calls for adding an extra step in your routine. You can broadcast and dig in fertilizers just before you plant. Or, place fertilizers directly under a seed row or a transplant—a technique known as *banding.*

Both compost and blended dry organic fertilizers are easy to broadcast or apply in bands. Before you broadcast dry fertilizers, read the label and compute the proper amount to apply. Compost is usually a precious commodity during the growing season. Your plants will get the most benefit from compost if you apply it in bands.

To band fertilizer or compost in a seed row, open a furrow 2 inches deeper than the required planting depth. Spread the fertilizer or compost in the furrow, cover it with 2 inches of soil, and then plant the seeds. For transplants, dig a hole of the appropriate size for the plant. Then shovel out 2 more inches of soil, lay in the fertilizer or compost, replace the extra soil, and plant the transplant.

Give Booster Feedings

Dry fertilizers. Popular dry fertilizers include blood meal, bonemeal, composted manure, cottonseed meal, and rock phosphate. Apply these dry materials by sidedressing—working them into the top inch of soil next to, but not touching, the plants. It takes about two weeks for nutrients from side-dressed fertilizers to become available to plant roots.

Most organic fertilizers are

TRY COMPOST TEA

You can make a nutrient-rich beverage for your plants by adding compost to water and allowing it to steep for three days or more. A good proportion is about 2 cups of solid matter to a gallon of water. Filter the mixture through burlap or cheesecloth, and return the trapped solids to the compost pile or garden. Place the strained liquid in a small sprayer or watering can.

You can also make manure tea from chicken or steer manure. However, manure tea can be more nitrogen-rich and can burn plants. After straining manure tea, be sure to dilute it with more water to a weak tea color before using.

slow-acting and won't burn plant roots. However, some, such as blood meal, contain high enough concentrations of nitrogen that caution is in order. A rule of thumb: Don't apply more than ¼ ounce of actual nitrogen per square yard. Blood meal is 13 percent nitrogen. One pound (16 ounces) contains about 2 ounces of nitrogen. Therefore, you should not apply more than 2 ounces of blood meal per square yard.

Liquid fertilizers. Liquid fertilizers are an especially good choice for booster feedings. The nutrients in them are quickly available to plants. You can water them into the soil or spray them directly on the leaves. Use diluted liquid fertilizers, such as seaweed extract or fish emulsion. You can also make liquid fertilizer, as described in "Try Compost Tea" on the opposite page.

Spray liquid fertilizers directly on leaves for a quick-acting boost. Just remember that fish emulsion can attract cats! Also, the odors of fish emulsion and manure tea may linger on harvested parts of crops that were sprayed too close to harvesttime.

Some gardeners spray their vegetable crops every two or three weeks with dilute seaweed extract, which contains micronutrients and growth hormones in addition to basic plant nutrients.

Compost

Liquid fertilizer on the spot. *Sink a clay pot into the ground near a plant at planting time. Add a handful of compost or manure to it. Fill the pot with water each time you water the plant. The water in the pot will absorb nutrients and seep into the soil through the hole in the pot bottom.*

Foliar feeding is also one of the best ways to supply nutrients to fruit trees and bushes. The tips and instructions on foliar feeding in "Feeding Fruit Crops" on page 203 should also help you in planning foliar feeds for your vegetables.

Custom-feeding. Want to get ultimate performance from your garden? Then you may want to take the time and effort to custom-feed individual crops. Look for feeding recommendations for specific crops in the vegetable crop entries that begin on page 82.

Correct Deficiencies

If your crops are suffering from a nutrient deficiency, it's rarely possible for you to recognize and reverse the problem in the already-growing crops. Vegetables grow so fast that it will be too late by the time you see symptoms. (If you suspect that symptoms you see are due to a nutrient deficiency, refer to "Solving Nutrient Deficiency Problems" on page 341 for more information about symptoms and their causes.)

If your crops have deficiency problems, fight back by working harder to improve overall soil fertility. Include a soil test (with a pH test) in your plans for next year. Test results will help you plan a program of amendments and cover cropping to revitalize your soil. You'll find information on soil testing, adding soil amendments, composting, and planting cover crops in Part 1 of this book.

FENCING OUT ANIMAL PESTS

Animal pests eager to share in the harvest may plague rural, suburban, or even urban gardens. Before you build a fence, figure out what kind of pest is attacking your crops. Then you can choose the most effective fencing system.

Rabbits

To keep out rabbits, skunks, and armadillos, put up a fence of chicken-wire mesh that has 1-inch openings. Make the fence 3 feet high, with an underground "skirt." If this is to be your only fence, support the wire by attaching it to 5-foot metal T-posts driven 2 feet into the ground. You can also add this barrier to the base of an existing fence.

Install the fence, as shown on this page. You can use one 4-foot width of mesh for the entire fence, but you may find it easier to construct the barrier with two smaller widths. Use a 1-foot-wide strip for the underground part, and a 3- to 4-foot-wide one for the aboveground part. The two strips should overlap a few inches.

To make an animal-resistant gate, run the underground chicken-wire skirt across the gate opening, extending it 4 inches above the ground. Set a 2 × 4 across the gate opening at ground level and fasten it to the gateposts. Wrap the 4-inch extension of the underground skirt over the 2 × 4, and fasten it there with staples.

Hang the gate, allowing no more than a 1-inch gap between the bottom of the gate and the ground. Cover the gate, or at least the lower 3 feet of it, with chicken wire. Allow an inch of wire to hang from the bottom of the gate and drag on the ground.

Keep out digging critters. *Extend your fence 6 inches below ground level, then bend the bottom 6 inches outward from the garden.*

Woodchucks

Woodchucks, also known as groundhogs, are good at both digging and climbing. To keep them out, you will need a fence at least 6 feet tall, with an underground chicken-wire extension like the one described on this page. The chicken wire should overlap the bottom of the aboveground fence and should extend 2 feet below the soil surface, curving outward at the bottom. To make the fence harder to climb, attach a 1-foot-wide band of sheet metal near the top.

Raccoons

Gardeners generally find it difficult to exclude raccoons with a fence. Running a low-voltage electric wire along the top of a fence may help, but be sure you install it properly.

Some gardeners have had success by topping an existing fence with a 2-foot section of chicken wire. Attach the bottom foot of the chicken wire to the top of the fence, but leave the top foot loose. When a raccoon tries to climb up, the top of the chicken wire will fold back over him. (This type of fence may also be effective against woodchucks.)

Gophers

Where gophers are common, gardeners often resort to lining their garden beds with aviary wire, as shown below.

If gophers travel above ground to reach your plants, lay another piece of aviary wire across the top of the bed. Fold the 2-inch extensions over it at the edges. Plant before you lay the surface wire, or lay it in spring before perennials and bulbs emerge. Cut openings as needed for transplants.

Deer

Deer are excellent high jumpers. To exclude them you will usually need a 7- to 8-foot barrier. Use strong wire fencing, and stretch it snug to the ground—deer sometimes try to go under or through a fence.

If the deer can't see what's on the other side of the fence, they will be less likely to jump it. Solid wood fences make good barriers, but they can be expensive and create shade in the garden. A cheaper approach is to take advantage of the deer's poor long-jumping ability. Try a double fence (two 4-foot fences with 3 feet between them) or a single 4-foot fence with a slanting wood-and-wire barrier outside of it.

Electric fences are another option for keeping deer out of your crops. Be sure you understand and follow all of the manufacturer's safety instructions before installing the fence, or have a professional install it for you.

Other Exclusion Options

Sometimes animal pests will only attack certain crops, like your sweet corn or bush beans. In this case, you may decide to fence only the sections where you grow susceptible crops, rather than the whole garden.

If your garden is very small and animal pests are a real problem, a different option is to surround the entire garden with fencing. Make a walk-in chicken-wire enclosure, fencing the top as well as the sides. Add underground protection as well, if necessary.

4 × 4 post

Hardware cloth

12"

2 × 4

A deer-deterrent fence. *To the outside of a 4-foot fence, attach 8-foot-long 2 × 4's slanting down to the ground. String wire along the 2 × 4's at 12-inch intervals.*

Aviary wire lines the bed and sticks up 2" above soil surface.

18"

Aviary wire is similar to chicken wire but has smaller holes.

Gopher barrier. *Dig out a planting bed to a depth of 18 inches and line it with aviary wire to prevent gophers from eating your plants.*

CONTROLLING WEEDS

Know Your Weeds

The first step to keeping weeds under control is knowing what kinds of weeds you're dealing with. Once you learn their growth habits and life cycles, you'll know how and when to take action.

Weeds can be annual, biennial, or perennial. Annuals sprout, flower, and die in one year; biennials flower and die the second year. Perennials grow and flower for many years. Get to know the weeds in your garden using a wild plant or weed identification guide. (You'll find titles in "Recommended Reading" on page 362.)

Annual Weeds

Groundsel, lamb's-quarters, pigweed, purslane, and ragweed are some of the most common annual weeds in vegetable gardens. The trick to controlling annual weeds is removing them when they're small, before they flower and set seed.

Pull out the plants or cut them off the soil surface. Leave the roots to decompose in the soil; they won't resprout.

Even if you pull all of your annual weeds for a year, you will still have some the next year. Weed seeds can lay dormant in the soil for many years. To keep them under control, you'll need to weed carefully for a few years. Gradually, you'll notice fewer and fewer annual weeds.

Biennial Weeds

Common burdock, common mullein, and Queen Anne's lace are three common biennial weeds. Simply cut off the flowerstalk to keep biennials from spreading by seed. Or, dig out the entire plant.

SUPER SMOTHER MULCH

Leaf mulch

Newspaper

If you're willing to wait for a year or two before planting, you can simply mulch weeds away. Even the toughest of weeds will eventually succumb to a thick smothering mulch.

Pull or cut existing weeds, water the area well, and apply a thick but porous blocking layer like cardboard or multiple sheets of newspaper. For small annual weeds, a layer of newspaper about 12 sheets thick should do the job. For tough perennials, you might need a pile of papers several inches thick.

Spread the papers or cardboard sheets with overlapping edges. Cover the area with wood chips, chopped leaves, or another attractive organic mulch.

Leave the smother mulch in place for an entire season, then remove or dig in what is left. If the weed roots aren't dead, leave it on for a second season as well. You can plant large crops, such as pumpkins, winter squash, or tomatoes, in holes you make through the mulch; just make sure you pull out any weed shoots that poke through.

Perennial Weeds

Perennial weeds are the biggest headache for vegetable gardeners. Bindweed, Canada thistle, dock, poison ivy, quack grass, and wild garlic are a few of the most notorious perennial weeds.

Perennial weeds reproduce by seed, but they're especially troublesome because they can also spread by thickened roots, bulbs, runners, or other underground plant parts.

As you prepare the soil for planting, hand-dig as many weed roots and bulbs as you can. (Don't till—tillers chop perennial roots into tiny pieces that will sprout all over your garden.) Then let the area sit for a week or two. Any roots that remain will send up new shoots; dig them out and then plant crops.

An easier but slower control method is to cover the soil with black plastic or a thick layer of mulch to smother the shoots. Leave the mulch in place for a year, then remove it; dig out any remaining roots, and plant as usual. See "Super Smother Mulch" on the opposite page for more on this technique.

Plan a Control Strategy

Controlling weeds in your vegetable garden is something you can do practically year-round. Try any or all of the tactics below in each season to keep weeds from getting out of control.

Spring:
- Presprout your weeds
- Plant through black plastic
- Space plants properly

Summer:
- Weed by hand
- Mulch and mulch more
- Solarize the soil

Fall and Winter:
- Weed by hand
- Mulch and mulch more

Weed by Hand

Even if you could prevent all of the weed seeds in your soil from sprouting, you'd still have weeds to deal with. New weeds are entering your garden all the time, blown by the wind, dropped by birds, or brought in on new plants.

Removing weeds with your hands or with cultivating tools is a centuries-old organic technique for weed control. Garden centers and garden supply catalogs carry hundreds of different weeding tools. The trick is to find a tool that feels comfortable for you, and then use it effectively. Here are some tips for getting the most out of your weeding time.

- Control weeds when they're small. A hoe works best on weed seedlings; hand-pull larger weeds.
- Cultivate shallowly to avoid bringing more weed seeds to the surface.
- Always pull weeds before they set seed.
- Weed when the soil is moist, if possible; the weeds will be easier to pull.
- Leave weed tops (unless they've gone to flower or seed) on the soil surface or toss them on the compost pile. Dispose of seedy weed tops and perennial weed roots, or bury them at least 1 foot deep in an area where you won't be likely to dig deeply again.
- Don't give up on weeding in winter. A few short weeding sessions on mild winter days will keep cool-season weeds like chickweed under control.

ORGANIC HERBICIDES

Organic, soap-based herbicides are available, but you're best off saving them to control weeds in paths and paving. Soap-based herbicides are not labeled for use in food gardens. These materials are nonselective contact herbicides, which means that they will damage any plant they touch—crops and weeds alike. If you have used soap-based herbicides around an area where you plan to grow vegetables, wait several days before planting.

Presprout Your Weeds

Presprouting is an easy and effective technique for getting weeds under control before you plant. See "Presprouting a Seedbed" on this page.

If you plan to grow crops with delicate seedlings, such as carrots, onions, or spinach, presprout the area twice. Water the bed again, and give the remaining weed seeds a chance to sprout. One more session with the hoe, and you're ready to plant.

As you weed, cultivate, and plant after presprouting, disturb the soil as little as possible to avoid bringing up more weed seeds.

Plant through Black Plastic

Covering the soil with black plastic blocks the light that many weed seeds need to germinate. Prepare the soil for planting; water if necessary so the soil is moist. Lay the sheet of plastic over the bed, burying the edges in the soil. Sow seeds or set transplants through slits or holes you've cut in the plastic.

Space Plants Properly

Let your crop plants shade the soil to prevent weeds from sprouting. This technique works best with bushy plants, like bush beans and lettuce.

At planting time, set seeds or transplants so the tips of the mature leaves will just touch. Hand-pull weeds or cultivate between plants until they are large enough to shade out the weeds.

Mulch and Mulch More

Organic mulches—straw, compost, chopped leaves, and the like—are a cornerstone of any successful vegetable garden. They provide good conditions for root growth and add organic matter to the soil, and also help to keep weeds under control.

Once your plants are several inches tall, weed thoroughly. Apply a 2- to 3-inch layer of fine-textured mulches

---

PRESPROUTING A SEEDBED

1. As you prepare the soil, dig out as many weed roots, runners, and bulbs as you can.

2. Add any needed amendments to the soil, rake the area smooth, then water it well. Keep the soil moist for seven to ten days, until it is covered with weed seedlings an inch or two high.

3. Carefully pull out the shoots and roots of any perennial weeds. Then use a scuffle or a hula hoe to cut the remaining weed seedlings just below the soil surface.

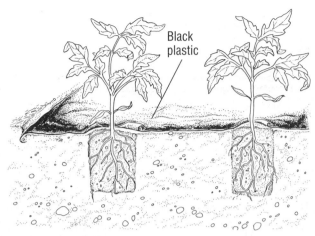

Black plastic

Plastic mulch. *Covering the soil with black plastic mulch keeps weed seeds from sprouting; it also helps warm the soil. If you lift and store the plastic at the end of the season, it should last for several years.*

like grass clippings or chopped leaves; use a 6- to 8-inch layer for loose mulches like straw or spoiled hay. Leave a few inches of bare soil around the base of each plant. Top off the mulch as needed during the growing season to keep it at the right thickness.

Solarize the Soil

Leave part of your garden unplanted in summer, and let the sun control weeds for you. Covering moist, bare soil with clear plastic for several weeks in clear, hot weather will raise soil temperatures enough to kill many weed seeds (as well as many pests and pathogens). You'll find complete details on soil solarization in "Managing Pests Organically" on page 334.

Avoid Importing Weeds

Once you've got your garden weeds under control, do everything possible to avoid bringing in new ones.

First, investigate the quality of any organic matter before you apply it as mulch. Materials like hay and uncomposted horse manure often contain weed seeds. Many seeds can also survive the composting process. A few overripe tomatoes tossed on the pile can yield hundreds of unwanted seedlings when you spread the compost in your garden.

If you're not sure that a given batch of organic matter is weed-free, test it. Mix it half-and-half with sterile potting mix in a flowerpot and water it. In a few weeks you will see what, if any, weeds are sprouting in it.

If many seeds are present, don't use the material as a surface mulch. Look for a different source of organic matter. If you *must* use a weedy batch, let it sit out for a month or two first. Turn the pile once a week to destroy any seedlings and expose new seeds to light. The more seeds that germinate on the pile, the fewer weed problems you'll have once it's in your garden.

Also, be wary of gift plants. If you suspect that the soil they were grown in contains weed seeds or perennial weed roots, grow the plants in a pot or an out-of-the-way spot in your garden for a season. If weeds do pop up, you can nab them before they spread.

6"

Straw mulch. *A deep layer of straw will prevent weed growth and keep the soil moist and at an even temperature—ideal conditions for good root growth.*

PREVENTING PROBLEMS

Can you list the five worst pest problems in your garden? If those problems are the same year after year, it's a signal that you should make a change in your gardening style. You don't have to put up with the same caterpillar invasions, rots, or blights every year. With some ingenuity and planning, you can reduce or prevent nearly all insect, disease, and cultural problems. And, you can do it with safe, organic methods.

Use Good Cultural Practices

Your plants will have the best chance against pests if they have fertile soil with the proper pH, adequate sunlight, and regular deep watering. These common-sense measures also help boost yields and produce good-looking, good-tasting vegetables.

If you have more than occasional pest problems, it could be a sign that your garden needs better basic care. You may need to have your soil tested and add amendments. Perhaps you need to change the way you water your garden so that your plants don't suffer stress between waterings. A simple change like this can prevent your tomatoes from getting blossom-end rot, which is caused by calcium deficiency and is often linked to water stress.

Choose Resistance

You can stack the deck in your favor *before* you start the garden season by choosing crop cultivars that are resistant to pests that are common in your area. Read catalog descriptions carefully to find resistant cultivars. (See "Reading Seed Catalogs" on page 32 for more information.)

Rotate Crops

Rotating crops—changing their position in the garden from year to year—is another cultural practice that can reduce some disease problems. This technique works best if you have a large garden. In a small garden, you may not be able to move a crop far enough from its last planting site to avoid the disease organism or insect that caused the problem. If you've had serious problems with diseases like club root on cabbage-family crops and want to try rotating crops, see "Planning a Practical Garden" on page 44.

TIMED PLANTING

Avoid persistent pests by planting your crop before the pest becomes active in the spring or after the main wave of the pest has come and gone. This tactic can help you avoid problems with cabbage root maggots, carrot rust flies, and onion maggots.

Insects become active after winter dormancy in response to biological cues like soil and air temperatures. So, the date they emerge will vary with the weather from year to year. You may be able to relate the appearance of a certain pest to the development of other plants and animals in your area. For example, you might find that a certain pest always appears two weeks after the apple trees bloom.

You'll need to learn about the life cycle of the pest you're fighting to determine if timed planting will work. Consult a good insect identification guide; you'll find some suggested in "Recommended Reading" on page 362. To find out when various pests become active in your region, contact your local extension office.

Size Up Potential Problems

If you know which pests are most likely to attack your crops, you can choose the right preventive measures to stop those particular pests. Look back at your gardening records for mentions of previous years' pest problems. If you're new to gardening or have moved to a new area, ask nearby gardeners or your local extension office for a list of the most common pests of local vegetable gardens.

Make frequent inspections for signs of insect damage and symptoms of diseases in your garden. If your garden is large, pick out sample plants of each crop rather than trying to look at every plant. Examine fronts and backs of leaves, growing points, blossoms, and the base of the plant at the soil line.

After you examine plants up close, step back. Look at groups of plants. Plants that are a different color than the rest, such as a yellowed or mottled plant, could have a disease.

Protect Your Allies

Your garden probably hosts far more beneficial organisms than pests. Among the beneficial insects flying about your garden are lacewings, lady beetles, syr-

Parasitic wasps feed on nectar from fennel and other small-flowered herbs.

Syrphid flies must eat pollen before laying eggs. Garland chrysanthemum (*Chrysanthemum coronarium*) is one good source.

Lady beetles feed on pollen and nectar from flowers like yarrow (*Achillea* spp.).

Predatory assassin bugs also feed on pollen from weedy plants like wormseed.

Food for beneficials. *Insect predators and parasites need plant food sources as well as their host prey. Be sure your garden includes some of the species shown here to help beneficials thrive.*

phid flies, tachinid flies, and parasitic miniwasps.

Plant food sources. Encourage beneficial insects to stay in your garden by growing small, shallow-necked flowers from which they can sip nectar. Daisies, dill, fennel, mint, mustard, and onion are just a few of the common plants that beneficial insects favor. You'll find more suggestions for plants for beneficials in "Herbs to Lure Beneficials" on page 316.

Make a "bug bath." Provide a water source for beneficials. Fill a shallow dish with small stones, and add enough water to create shallow pools among the stones. Many beneficial insects are tiny and can drown easily, so be sure your "insect bath" has dry landing sites and only shallow water.

Encourage soil-dwelling beneficials. Healthy soil contains fungi and bacteria that fight soilborne organisms that can cause plant diseases. Adding compost to your soil encourages the full range of helpful soil creatures. At the soil surface, ground and rove beetles, spiders and daddy longlegs, and salamanders and lizards offer their assistance. Make them feel welcome by leaving some stones, wood scraps, or undisturbed mulch around your garden for them to hide under.

Don't use pesticides. The single step that will most increase your garden's population of helpers is limiting or eliminating use of pesticides. Even some organically acceptable pesticides, such as pyrethrins or rotenone, are quite poisonous to beneficial insects. If you do use pesticides, use them only on the pest-infested plants, only as often as necessary, and choose ones that break down fastest in the environment.

Barricade Your Plants

Floating row cover. Commercial floating row cover is one of the best pest prevention materials around for home gardens. Made of superlight spunbonded polyproplyene, floating row cover lets light and water through but serves as an impenetrable barrier for insect pests. Some home gardeners cover entire beds with floating row cover from planting to harvest.

Push collar into the soil so half the width is below the surface.

Cutworm collars. Make these simple barriers from a small soup can or half of a toilet paper tube. Push the collar into the soil around the transplant right after planting.

Make a bubble of the material over seed rows or transplants, gathering it to leave room for some growth, then tuck the edges into the soil firmly all around. To protect plants as they grow, make easy-to-remove covered frames like the one shown to the left.

Homemade barriers. You can also keep pests away from seedlings with two simple homemade barriers. Collars made from a tin can or toilet paper tube and slipped around the stem of newly planted transplants will keep them safe from cutworms. These soil-dwelling larvae will chew on the stems of a wide variety of vegetables and can wipe out your crop overnight.

Barriers for animal pests. If birds love to peck at your newly planted seeds,

Staple row cover to inside of frame.

Finish ends like a gift-wrapped package.

Framed row cover. Build a frame of 1 × 2's, using nonrusting galvanized roofing nails to hold it together. Drape the row cover over the frame and cut it to fit.

Screen protector. *To protect seeds from birds, plant seeds in indented rows and lay a chicken-wire strip over each row. Weight the wire with soil or small rocks. Remove the chicken wire once the plants have emerged.*

protect them with chicken wire, as shown on this page. If birds like to peck at the plants as well, drape plastic bird net lightly over your beds to deter them.

Your best preventive solution to deter animals such as rabbits or woodchucks is to fence your garden. For more information on garden fences, see "Fencing Out Animal Pests" on page 62.

Use Repellents

Mix up some potent brews that repel pests from common garden herbs. Many gardeners report keeping their plants pest-free by spraying these mixtures on their crops.

Catnip, chives, marigolds, nasturtiums, rosemary, sage, and thyme are some of the herbs reputed to have insect-repellent properties.

To make a repellent spray, mash or blend 1 to 2 cups of fresh leaves in 2 to 4 cups of water. Let the mix soak overnight. Strain the mix through cheesecloth, and dilute the strained liquid with 2 to 4 cups of water to make a spray. Add a few drops of liquid soap to help the spray stick to the leaves.

Spicy seasonings such as black pepper, chili pepper, ginger, paprika, and red pepper also have repellent qualities. Sprinkle hot dusts around young plants to prevent onion maggot flies and cabbage maggot flies from laying their eggs at the base of the plants. These hot dusts may also deter rabbits and other animals from nibbling on tender young plants.

Deciding on Controls

Sometimes pests get out of balance despite all attempts at prevention. When this happens, don't rush too quickly to wipe out the enemy. Even "natural" fungicides and insecticides can have harmful side effects on your garden. Some botanical poisons kill beneficial insects as well as pests. And sulfur and copper fungicides may damage your plants if you spray them during hot weather or on certain types of plants. So don't take one step forward to control a pest and end up taking several steps back in your quest to have a healthy, naturally balanced garden.

Organic pest controls for vegetable gardens include BT (*Bacillus thuringiensis*), a bacterium that can sicken and kill many kinds of plant-chewing caterpillars. There are also botanical poisons, such as pyrethrins, rotenone, and sabadilla, which have varying degrees of toxicity to humans and other animals.

In a small vegetable garden, it's often not worthwhile to spray fungicides on already diseased plants. For some diseases, such as viruses, there are no sprays (synthetic or otherwise) that will kill or stop the spread of the disease organisms. And most fungicides, including organically acceptable sulfur- and copper-based fungicides, do not cure diseased plants; they mainly help prevent the spread of the disease. Generally, it's best to salvage what harvest you can from diseased crops and then dig and destroy the crop residues. If you do plan to spray sulfur or copper, you can learn more about their use by reading "Sprays and Dusts" on page 210.

To learn more about control methods for fighting problems that get out of hand, read "Managing Pests Organically" on page 334.

VEGETABLES IN CONTAINERS

Choose Your Crops

A surprising variety of vegetable crops will thrive in well-prepared containers. Bush beans, cucumbers, eggplants, lettuce, onions, peppers, potatoes, tomatoes—even corn and melons—are able to adapt to container life.

In general, small, fast-growing crops are the best container performers. When possible, choose dwarf or compact cultivars of normally large plants like cabbage, cucumbers, and melons.

Pick a Container Mix

A good growing mix is the key to successful container gardening. Like good garden soil, a container growing mix should hold some water but allow the excess to drain away freely. But the good soil that produces bumper crops in the garden is not ideal for filling containers. In a pot, straight garden soil tends to become compacted and drain poorly.

Luckily, it's easy to blend or buy a container growing mix that will meet all of your plants' needs. A simple formula for home-blended container mix is equal parts of compost or sphagnum peat, shredded fir or pine bark, and vermiculite or perlite. For each cubic foot of the homemade mix, add the following:

- 4 ounces of dolomitic limestone
- 1 pound of rock or colloidal phosphate
- 4 ounces of greensand
- 1 pound of granite meal
- 2 ounces of blood meal

Care for Container Gardens

Watering

Because plants growing in containers dry out more quickly, you'll need to water them much more frequently than plants in the open ground. If it's warm out, check them daily.

For seeds and new transplants, keep the surface moist. For mature plants, water when the top inch of mix is dry, and keep watering until some seeps out the bottom of the container.

Fertilizing

Since the frequent watering will leach nutrients from the container mix, your plants need supplemental fertilizer. After the first month of growth, water container crops with diluted fish emulsion, seaweed extract, manure tea, or compost tea every two weeks. Watch the response of the plants, and fertilize more or less often accordingly.

FOR BEST RESULTS

- Elevate containers on bricks, small wooden legs, or platforms with wheels to prevent damage to wooden decks and stairs.
- Have a structural engineer examine your roof before you put a container garden on it. It must be built to handle the weight of the pots and the wear of being walked on.
- For gardens on exposed sites like roofs and high decks, stretch burlap or commercially available wind cloth between posts on the side toward the prevailing wind to protect plants from drying and being knocked over.

SIZING UP CROP CONTAINERS

You can grow vegetables in clay, plastic, wood, metal, or even concrete containers. Be sure the containers have drainage holes and will hold enough growing mix for the crops you want to grow. Plants in clay containers need frequent watering, and the containers may be damaged by freezing and thawing. Wood containers protect roots from rapid temperature swings. Metal containers heat up rapidly, which can damage roots, so use a clay or plastic pot as a liner. Below you'll find some ideas for matching crops to containers.

A 6-inch pot holds 2½ quarts of growing mix—enough for 6 radishes, 1 escarole plant, or 1 dwarf tomato plant.

An 8-inch pot holds 1 gallon of growing mix. That's enough root room for 1 lettuce, bush bean, kale, or spinach plant.

A 10-inch pot holds about 2 gallons of growing mix. It can support 1 bush cucumber or pepper plant, 8 bulb onions or beet plants, or 12 carrots or green onions.

A 12-inch pot holds 3½ gallons of growing mix. That's enough for 1 standard-size tomato plant, 1 head of cabbage, 15 long-rooted carrots, or 9 bush pea plants.

A box 1 foot square and 8 inches deep holds 5 gallons of growing mix. It can grow 25 beet plants, 4 to 9 lettuce plants, or 9 to 12 bush bean plants.

A box 1 foot square and 1 foot deep, filled with 7 gallons of growing mix, can hold 1 broccoli, cauliflower, eggplant, melon, or summer squash plant.

A box 2 feet square and 8 inches deep holds 10 gallons of growing mix. That's enough for 12 corn plants or 40 bush bean plants. Or try a mixed salad garden with 10 lettuce plants, 20 green onions, and 10 radishes.

EXTENDING THE SEASON

Spring isn't the only season for planting. Many vegetable crops will grow well in the cool temperatures of fall, if you can get them to start growing at the right time in mid- or late summer. Some, like cabbage and lettuce, will grow well past the first fall frost if they have extra protection from cold nights.

You can also start your garden extra early in spring if you start your seedlings indoors and shelter them from frost until the warm weather arrives.

It's easy to try some simple season-extension tricks to spread your harvest. For a summary of techniques for different times of the year, see "Season-Extension Options" on this page.

Prolong Cool-Season Crops

Shade Your Plants

Once summer's heat starts, many gardeners call an end to cool-season crops like lettuce, peas, and spinach. But if you give them some shade, these succulent spring treats can keep producing well into summer. Shade can also provide welcome relief for eggplants, peppers, and tomatoes in the intense heat of the South and Southwest.

Protect existing plantings with temporary sun shields made from shade cloth, lath, or even snow fence. If you can plan ahead, site late-spring plantings on the east side of a house or garden wall to block hot afternoon sun. Trellises or tall crops, like corn and sunflowers, to the south or west of the crop can also shield plants from the sun.

Choose Heat-Tolerant Cultivars

When you buy seeds or transplants, look for cultivars described as heat-tolerant or "slow to bolt." These generally keep producing into midsummer, especially with some shade.

Extend Fall Harvests

Plan Fall Plantings

Get twice your harvest of cool-season crops with a second planting that will mature in the crisp weather of fall. To decide when to plant, you need to know the average date of the first fall frost in your area. You can get this information from other gardeners in your area or from your local Cooperative Extension office.

SEASON-EXTENSION OPTIONS

Try some or all of these season-extension techniques to get more from your garden space all season long.

To keep cool-season crops producing into summer:
• Shade plants from summer sun.
• Choose heat-tolerant cultivars.

To extend your harvests in fall:
• Plant crops in summer to mature in fall.
• Cover plants to protect them from frost.

To get extra-early spring harvests:
• Start seeds indoors.
• Grow early crops in a cold frame or hotbed.
• Warm the soil with plastic mulch.

You also need to know how long it will take for your crop to mature. Check seed packets or transplant labels for this information. Carrots, for instance, are generally ready to pick about 65 days from sowing; early cauliflower may be ready as soon as 50 days after transplanting. Add 14 days to the stated maturity time, since the plants will mature more slowly in cool fall weather.

Now, take a calendar, record the first frost date, and count backward the number of days it takes your crop to mature. For instance, if your first frost date is October 20, you could sow carrots for fall harvest from mid-July until early August.

Make a minigreenhouse. *Protect peppers, tomatoes, and other tender plants with wire cages wrapped in clear plastic. Cut small vents into the sides for ventilation. Cover the top with plastic, cardboard, or a blanket on frosty nights.*

FROST FACTS

If you're trying to extend the growing season in spring or fall, you'll need to deal with frost sooner or later. Frost is most likely when:

• The night is clear, with bright stars.
• The air is dry (with no condensation on car windows).
• The temperature is 45°F or colder by 10 P.M.

Cold air sinks to the lowest point it can, but it can't travel through a solid surface. So, plants under the overhang of a building or under any kind of surface (such as cloth, plastic, and cardboard) are less likely to be damaged by a light frost.

If you forget to cover your plants, you may be able to revive the hardier crops, such as chard, collards, and mustard. Sprinkle them with water from the hose for awhile before the sun shines on them. (This won't work on frost-tender crops like tomatoes.)

After a frost, don't assume damaged plants are dead. Leave vegetables alone for at least a week, then only remove tissue that is clearly dead. Leave perennials alone until their normal period of growth begins, then prune out dead parts.

Sometimes it can be difficult to get cool-season-crop seed to sprout when the soil is warm. Sowing in the shade of taller plants may help. Or, try sprinkling the seedbed frequently with cool water until the seeds sprout. Start leafy crops like lettuce and spinach indoors under lights in a cool basement or air-conditioned room. When they're large enough for the garden, gradually expose them to more and more sunlight and warmth.

Protect Plants from Frost

To some gardeners, the first fall frost signals the end of the harvest season. But in many areas that first frost is followed by a spell of warmer weather. Getting your plants past that one cold snap can mean the difference between a super harvest and a so-so one.

Frost protectors run the gamut from high tech to homemade. For temporary protection, drape blankets, towels, old sheets, and the like over low-growing or trellised plants. To keep crops growing even longer, you can use more elaborate structures such as cold frames. See "Plant in Cold Frames" on page 76 for more details.

Commercial or homemade growing tunnels are good

Row-cover tunnel. *A tunnel of row cover or plastic supported on metal hoops makes a cheap and easy frost protector.*

protection for low-growing row crops like lettuce. Metal or PVC hoops spaced over the row will keep the cover from crushing the plants below. The tunnel cover, made of clear plastic or commercial row cover, needs to be anchored firmly to the ground at each side and at the ends: use rocks, boards, or commercial fasteners.

If the temperatures are mostly above freezing, cut slits in plastic covers for ventilation. Where days are cool and nights often drop below freezing, unvented plastic is better, although you must lift it on warm, sunny days to keep your crops from getting "cooked" by the heat. When you lift a cover, be sure to put it back on an hour or so before sunset, to trap a bit of the day's warmth.

Get an Early Start

Start Seeds Indoors

If you really want to plant early (and begin picking early!), starting your seedlings indoors is the way to go. Setting out transplants can give you a head start of a month or more over direct-sown seeds. (Don't try this with most root crops, though; they don't transplant

well.) You'll find all the details in "Starting Seeds Indoors" on page 46.

You can gain even more time by setting seedlings out extra early, if you're prepared to protect them from the spring chill. When unseasonably late frosts threaten, protect plants with newspaper tents weighted at the edges with rocks or with blankets or commercial floating row cover propped up on supports. For more plant protection tips, see "Planting Transplants" on page 56.

Plant in Cold Frames

A small commercial or homemade cold frame provides an extra measure of protection against chilly temperatures. At its simplest, a cold frame is a bottomless box with a transparent cover that is tilted toward the south or southeast to catch the sun. More elaborate (and

Fruit-crate cold frame. *You can make a serviceable cold frame from an old fruit crate, two nails, and an unframed pane of Plexiglas.*

Heat-activated
venting arm

Easy-care cold frame. *A cold frame can heat up quickly. Forget to open it one sunny day, and your crop will be cooked. A heat-activated venting arm can save you time and save your crop.*

more effective) models are made of sturdier lumber or even concrete.

For mild-winter areas, the most useful cold frames are small, portable ones. You can easily move these around to protect small plantings of cool-season crops.

In colder climates, a sturdier, nonportable structure will allow you to extend the growing season by a month or more in spring and fall. For added insulation, line the frame with plastic, seal the edges with foam strips, and cover it with glass window sashes. You can also sink the frame partially into the ground or mound earth up around the sides. Another option is to set the frame against a basement window to catch some of the warmth from the house.

On sunny days, heat can build up surprisingly fast inside a closed frame. If the forecast calls for clear weather, prop the frame open a few inches in mid-morning, and close it again about an hour before sunset. If you don't have the time to check the frame so frequently, invest in an automatic opener that will ventilate the cold frame for you. On cold nights, cover the frame with old carpets or with a canvas "comforter" filled with leaves or straw to hold in the day's warmth.

Build a Hotbed

Add a heat source to a cold frame and you have a hotbed. Ideally, your heat source will warm the soil (rather than the air), providing good conditions for root growth. The most common way to do this is with a commercial electric soil cable.

To install the cable, dig out an area 1 foot deep under the cold frame. Add a 1- to 2-inch layer of gravel, then 1 inch of sand or vermiculite. Spread the cable on top, making sure that it doesn't overlap anywhere. Cover it with 2 to 3 inches of sand, then a fine-mesh wire screen to prevent garden tools from cutting into the cable. Fill the bed with good topsoil to bring it up to ground level, and you're ready to plant in the frame.

Warm the Soil

Give summer crops like melons and tomatoes an early start by warming up the soil. Lay black or clear plastic over prepared garden soil a couple of weeks before you plant or transplant the crop. Soil organisms will become active in the warmer soil, releasing nutrients from your organic fertilizers. The warmth and the ready supply of nutrients will encourage good root growth.

Clear plastic warms the soil quickly, but it also provides ideal conditions for weed seeds to sprout. Black plastic warms the soil slightly less than clear, but it prevents weed growth. Remove either type of plastic before planting, or cut slits and plant through it. If you leave clear plastic on the soil, cover it with another mulch during summer to prevent the soil from overheating.

ENDING THE SEASON

As your harvests dwindle after the first fall frost, it can be tempting to forget the garden until next spring. But it's worth your time now to clean up the debris and protect the plants and soil. Next spring, you'll be ready to plant sooner, your soil will be healthier, and pest and disease problems will be at a minimum.

Clean Up the Garden

Save time at year's end by making cleanup a regular part of your gardening time during the season. Pull or cut weeds before they can form seed. Also pull out crops as soon as they are finished bearing.

Collect stakes, temporary trellises, and any row covers you will not be using until next spring. Scrape off clinging soil. To remove insect eggs or disease pathogens, rinse the materials in a 10 percent bleach solution (1 part chlorine bleach to 9 parts water). Spread them out to dry before storing them.

Prepare for the Cold

Pick any remaining crops and prepare them for storage. (You'll find specific storage tips in the individual crop entries that start on page 82.) Prepare hardy perennial crops for winter by trimming off dead or dying leaves.

Hardy root crops like carrots and parsnips can store well in the ground. In cold-winter areas, cover them with a thick mulch of leaves or straw to keep the soil from freezing. Pull aside the mulch and dig the roots as needed. In mild-winter areas, apply a light mulch to bare areas between plants only; don't pile it over the roots. In the coldest zones, don't leave root

Cleaning up spent plants. *After harvest, pull plants from the garden. Check plant roots for signs of disease and insects. All diseased and infested plants should be buried deeply or disposed of in household trash.*

crops in the ground over the winter. Dig and store them before the ground freezes.

Get the Soil in Shape

You have four options for dealing with your garden soil at the end of the season:

1. Leave it alone.
2. Cultivate it.
3. Mulch it.
4. Plant a cover crop.

The option that's best for you depends on the time of year and the amount of time and materials you have.

Leave it alone. If you're really strapped for time, you may choose to do nothing to protect the soil. On the positive side, leaving the soil

New use for old cornstalks. *Pull up cornstalks after harvest, tie several together, and use them as a compost pile aerator.*

undisturbed can help reduce the number of weed seeds that will sprout next spring. Unfortunately, though, bare soil is quite prone to wind and water erosion, as well as compaction. Whenever possible, try to choose another option that will be better for the soil.

Cultivate it. Fall digging or tilling has several advantages. It can kill pests that overwinter in the soil or expose them to birds or other predators. It can also bury plant debris that may harbor overwintering insects. Left rough and unraked, tilled soil will better resist erosion than bare, uncultivated soil. The cycles of freezing and thawing will help break down clods in tough, clayey soil. And, in the spring, tilled soil

Cutworm pupae

Fall cultivation. *Digging or tilling the soil in fall will expose overwintering pests to predators.*

warms faster, so you can plant sooner.

On the downside, fall tilling can increase weed seed germination in the spring. And the soil is still exposed to the elements, so it can be eroded by high winds or hard rain. If you can, follow fall cultivation with a cover crop or a mulch for winter-season soil protection.

Mulch it. In cold winters, applying mulch after the ground is frozen protects the roots and crowns of perennial plants from sudden temperature changes. It also helps to moderate soil temperatures for helpful soil organisms. This protection is most important in cold areas with little snow cover.

In areas with mild, wet winters, mulch prevents heavy rains from eroding bare soil or leaching nutrients out of it. Keep mulches to a minimum around perennial plantings, though, or you'll provide ideal condi-

tions for slugs, snails, and crown and root rots.

Heavy mulches can slow soil warming in spring, so rake them off in late winter to let the sun reach the soil.

Plant a cover crop. Growing cover crops over winter will protect your soil from erosion and enrich it at the same time. Dig or till the soil in late summer and early fall; then sow grains, like oats or wheat, or legumes, such as fava beans or red clover. Work the tender growth into the soil before spring planting to release organic matter and nutrients for your new crop. For more details on planning, planting, and managing cover crops, see "Planting Cover Crops" on page 28.

Cover crops. *Plant clover or other legumes in late summer or early fall to protect and enrich the soil.*

GREEN THUMB TIP

Researchers at the University of Wisconsin have successfully tested a mulching sequence that kills pests that spend winter in the soil. They mulched in the fall, pulled back the mulch and snow for three days during very cold weather, then replaced the mulch until spring. They found that this routine killed more overwintering Colorado potato beetles than when they left the soil unmulched.

SAVING SEEDS

Seed-Saving Basics

A little know-how and patience are all you need to have success saving vegetable seeds. The first thing you need to know is that seeds do not always produce plants that look (or taste) like the one they came from. They contain a mix of genetic material from the mother plant *and* the plant that pollinated the mother plant.

Coping with cross-pollinators. In some cases, the mother plant can be pollinated by a plant that is closely related but nonetheless looks very different. The offspring of the cross may have characteristics of both parents. For

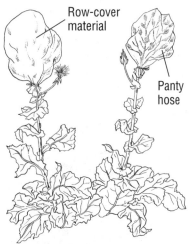

Homemade seed catchers.
Cover seed heads of lettuce and cabbage-family plants with row-cover material or panty hose to foil birds and catch loose seed.

example, broccoli, cabbage, and cauliflower can pollinate each other. Pumpkins and zucchini can also cross-pollinate, producing some strange-looking fruits!

Crossing can also occur between different cultivars of the same crop. Planting two types of summer squash close together may lead to seeds that produce plants unlike either parent. Beets, carrots, corn, cucumbers, onions, peppers, radishes, and spinach are other cross-pollinated crops.

To prevent unwanted cross-pollination, you can enclose the mother plant in a cage or just protect individual flowers with tape or cloth bags. (For crops like squash, you'll need to hand-pollinate the flowers to get fruit.)

Another option is to grow crops or cultivars that bloom at different times. For references with specific guidelines on saving vegetable seed, see "Recommended Reading" on page 362.

Handling hybrids. Hybrids are produced by crossing carefully selected plants to get a specific combination of genes. But when hybrid plants reproduce, the resulting seedlings show a broad range of genetic traits. Some of them will perform like the parents, but

most of them will be inferior.

How do you know if your parent plant is a hybrid? Look for the word "hybrid" or the symbol "F_1" in the seed catalog, on the seed packet, or on the transplant label. Don't try to save seed from hybrid plants.

Sure bets for seed savers. There are many crops that produce useful seed without a lot of fuss. Self-pollinating crops such as beans, endive, lettuce, lima beans, peas, and nonhybrid tomatoes are good crops for the beginning seed saver.

Select Superior Parents

No matter what crops you're saving seed from, always choose high-quality parent plants. They should be disease-free and free of insects, such as pea weevils, that can infest stored seed. Select the plants with the best flavor, the biggest fruit, or the highest yield—whatever you like best about the crop.

Once you've decided which plant you're going to save seed from, mark it with a stake or a piece of yarn. When you go back to harvest the seeds, you'll be sure to get the right plant.

SAVING TOMATO SEED

1. Scrape the pulp and seeds from several fruits, or blend the fruits briefly in a blender. Put in a jar with a cup of water for each cup of fruit pulp and stir.

2. Keep the jar at room temperature for several days, stirring twice a day. Look for bubbles at the surface or for a dense layer of foul-smelling mold. At this point, add some water and stir vigorously until most of the seed has dropped to the bottom.

3. Skim off any floating seeds and mold, and pour off some of the water. Add clean water; stir and skim again. When the seeds are clean, pour off all the water.

4. Spread the clean seeds on a window screen or ceramic plate to dry.

Save the Seed

Seeds like corn, beans, and peas that are held firmly in dry fruit are easy to save. Pick them when the husks or pods are fully dry. Keep them in a warm, dry place out of direct sunlight for two weeks, then shell them.

Cucumbers, peppers, squash, and tomatoes bear seeds inside fleshy fruits. To save seed, pick these fruits when they're fully ripe but before they decay or shrivel up on the plant.

You can remove seed by hand from peppers or squash, but wet fruits, such as cucumber, eggplant, or tomato, are usually fermented and then dried, as shown on this page.

Store the Seed

Sometimes dry seed is mixed with bits of pods and chaff. Separating the seeds from the other material is called *winnowing.*

Winnow seed by pouring it through the stream of air from a small fan or a hair dryer. The seed will fall straight down into a waiting container; the chaff will blow away in the air. Or use sieves or screens to remove the chaff.

Most thoroughly dry seeds store well in airtight containers in a cool place (like a refrigerator). Large seeds like beans and peas shouldn't be stored in airtight containers.

ASPARAGUS *Asparagus officinalis* • Liliaceae

Choosing Plants

For an early-season treat from the vegetable garden, try planting asparagus. This hardy perennial crop is easy to grow but requires a one- to two-year wait after planting before the first harvest.

Asparagus grows in Zones 2 through 9 but is less productive in the Deep South. Warm winters keep the crowns (perennial roots) from storing the reserves needed for strong spring growth.

Choose cultivars resistant to rust and Fusarium wilt. Also, look for new hybrids such as 'Jersey Knight' that produce mostly male plants. Male plants yield more than female plants because females put energy into making berries instead of spears. West Coast and southern gardeners should look for heat-tolerant cultivars.

Crowns

It's easiest to establish asparagus by planting one-year-old crowns. They should produce harvestable spears the year after planting. Select large crowns with thick roots and well-formed buds.

Crowns may be available at your local garden center. For a wider range of cultivar choices, order from a mail-order company.

Seeds

Starting asparagus from seed is cheaper than buying crowns. It requires more care and a two-year wait until harvest. However, stands produced from seed often yield better than stands started from crowns. Check specialty vegetable catalogs to find asparagus seed.

Site and Soil

A well-prepared asparagus bed can produce for 20 or more years. Separate your asparagus patch from your annual vegetables so you won't accidentally till or dig it up.

Choose a site with:
• At least half a day of sun.
• Moderately rich sandy or loam soil.
• pH between 6.5 and 7.5.
Avoid:
• Areas where water puddles on the soil surface.
• Sites exposed to strong winds.
• Sites where asparagus grew previously.

Preparing to Plant

Remove all stones and perennial weeds from the site. Till or dig the soil 1 foot deep. Work in 10 to 20 pounds of compost per 100 square feet. Apply 5 pounds of rock phosphate or calcium phosphate per 100 square feet to supply phosphorus.

Roots will rot in soggy beds. If you have clay soil, prepare raised planting beds to ensure good drainage.

Planting

When to plant. In mild-winter areas, plant crowns in the fall. In colder regions, plant in the spring when soil temperatures reach 50°F and

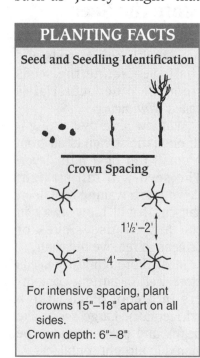

PLANTING FACTS

Seed and Seedling Identification

Crown Spacing

1½'–2'

4'

For intensive spacing, plant crowns 15"–18" apart on all sides.
Crown depth: 6"–8"

Presprout seeds between damp paper towels.

Set pot 3" below soil surface.

Starting asparagus seed indoors. Sow sprouted seeds individually in peat pots in late February or early March. Place pots in a sunny window with bottom heat at 77°F. When sprouts appear, reduce the temperature to 60° to 70°F. When seedlings are from 1 to several inches tall and frost danger is past, plant them 4 to 5 inches apart in a nursery bed outdoors.

night temperatures are above 35°F.

How much to plant. Plant 20 to 40 plants per person, depending on your appetite for asparagus.

Starting plants indoors. In short-season areas, start seeds indoors, as shown in the illustration on this page.

Planting crowns outdoors. Dig 1-foot-wide trenches 6 to 8 inches deep and 4 feet apart in the prepared planting area. Make small mounds of compost 1½ to 2 feet apart in the bottom of the trenches. Drape the long roots of each crown over each mound. Cover the crowns with about 2 inches of soil and gently tamp it down. Continue adding 2 inches of soil every two weeks until the trenches are filled and the soil is slightly mounded over the top.

Sprinkle 1 to 2 pounds of alfalfa meal per 100 square feet over the finished beds. Mulch with 6 to 12 inches of shredded leaves or other organic mulch.

Plan to water the young stand weekly for the first two years of growth whenever the weather is dry.

Planting seeds outdoors. In mild climates, plant seeds outdoors as soon as frost danger is past. Sow two seeds per inch in a nursery bed—a specially prepared temporary bed with good quality, fine soil. Sow seeds ½ inch deep in rows 18 inches apart. Germination takes about 30 days. Add radish seeds to the rows as you plant; they emerge quickly and serve as a row marker.

Thin the seedlings to 4 inches apart when the plants are 3 inches tall.

Transplant nursery-bed plants to a permanent site in late summer or the following spring.

Seasonal Care

Spring

Protect from frost. Late frosts can turn spears brown and soft. Cover emerging spears with leaf mulch or a tarp when frost is predicted.

Cover with floating row cover. If you've had past infestations of asparagus beetles or beet armyworms, cover beds with row cover for the harvest period.

Blanch spears. If you want white asparagus spears, mound organic mulch over the beds as the spears develop.

Allow first spears to grow. If crown rot has weakened your patch in the past, don't cut the first spear that emerges from each crown. It will grow to full size and provide food to the roots during the harvest period, helping to keep the plant strong.

Harvest daily in hot weather. Temperatures above 90°F can cause leaves on spears to sprout prematurely. Harvest daily to avoid this.

Apply mulch. After the harvest is over, spread a 6- to 12-inch layer of leaf mulch.

FOR BEST RESULTS

Plant crowns immediately after you buy them or receive them in the mail. If you can't plant right away, wrap the roots in damp sphagnum moss.

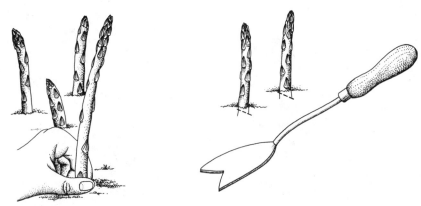

Harvesting asparagus spears. *Snap asparagus spears off at ground level using your thumb and index finger. Or use an asparagus knife to carefully slice through spears just below the soil surface.*

Summer

Clear weeds. Pull weeds that emerge through the mulch until the plants are large enough to smother them.

Water as needed. Keep the soil evenly moist. To test soil moistness, squeeze some soil in your hand. It should form a loose ball without sticking to your fingers; if it doesn't, you need to water.

Fall

Cut down fronds. After the fronds die, cut or mow them off at ground level.

Destroy or dispose of old foliage.

Apply compost. Spread 10 to 15 pounds of compost per 100 square feet.

Mulch. In northern areas, renew leaf mulch to protect the roots during winter.

Harvesting

Harvest asparagus spears in early spring when they are 6 to 10 inches high and the tips are firm, with tight bracts. Don't harvest spindly spears.

In the first year of harvest, pick only for 2 weeks. Extend the harvest each year, until you are harvesting for about 8 weeks (12 weeks in California).

Once a bed is in full production, pick about every three days. When the weather warms and the crop grows fast, you may need to harvest twice a day to keep up with production.

It's best to eat or preserve asparagus right after picking. To store spears up to one week, place them upright in a shallow tray of water in the refrigerator.

Propagation

If you're growing a standard cultivar, you can collect berries from female plants before the first fall frost. Crush the berries in a bag, then soak them in water to wash away the pulp. Collect seeds that sink while soaking; air dry them for a week before storing.

Extending the harvest. *Plant asparagus at a range of depths to spread the harvest. Spears will emerge early from shallowly planted crowns, late from deeply planted crowns.*

Solving Asparagus Problems

Use this table to identify problems in your asparagus patch. Scan the list of symptoms to find the description that most closely matches what you see in your garden. Then refer across the page to learn the cause and the recommended solutions. For some pest problems, by the time you see damage, there is little you can do to fix things in the current season.

In the future, take preventive steps such as clearing away old fronds in fall so pests can't overwinter there. See "Seasonal Care" on page 83 for a schedule of preventive measures. You'll also find illustrations, descriptions, and additional controls for many of the insects and diseases listed below in Part 5 of this book.

SYMPTOMS	CAUSES	SOLUTIONS
Slender, weak, or small spears	Young plants Poor soil Excessive harvesting	It is normal for first-year spears to be slender; do not harvest the first year after planting. If older stands produce weak plants, fertilize them well. Next season, shorten the harvest period to allow plants to recover.
Brown scars or tunnels just beneath the skin of spears	Asparagus miners	Destroy any spears with miners. Plan to pull up old stalks in fall and burn. Miner infestations often increase infection by Fusarium.
Spindly spears with dark sunken areas at or below soil level	Fusarium wilt	Remove and destroy affected plants. Try a single application of rock salt (2 lb. per 100 sq. ft.). If damage is severe, replant in a site not used for asparagus for at least 8 years, using Fusarium-tolerant cultivars.
Spindly spears turn brown at soil line and rot	Crown rot	Remove and destroy affected plants. Replant disease-free stock, preferably in raised beds. Test soil pH and adjust if needed to keep pH above 6.0.
Dark stains on spears; spears chewed by small, orange or blue-black beetles	Asparagus beetles	Damaged spears are edible. Handpick and destroy beetles, larvae, and eggs (laid on stems), or wash them off with a strong spray of water. If beetles are numerous, spray with pyrethrins or rotenone. Remove and destroy old stalks in fall.
Small, reddish spots on spears, stalks, and leaves	Asparagus rust	Spray sulfur at first sign of disease to reduce severity. Strengthen plants with good growing conditions. Cut and destroy stalks in fall. Where infections are severe, replant with resistant cultivars.
Silvery or grayish spears and stalks	Onion thrips	Damaged spears are edible. These tiny sucking insects are barely visible to the naked eye. If infestation is severe, spray neem, pyrethrins, or insecticidal soap.
Leaves chewed; fronds stripped of leaves	Beet armyworms	These green caterpillars are also called the asparagus fern caterpillar. Handpick caterpillars. If a large stand is infested, spray BTK or neem.
Short, stunted plants; tiny, powdery green insects on ferns	Asparagus aphids	Wash aphids off plants with a strong spray of water. For severe infestations, spray neem or pyrethrins. In fall, remove and destroy ferns, or till them into the soil.

BEAN   Phaseolus vulgaris and other species • Leguminosae

Choosing Beans

From snap and kidney beans to lima and scarlet runner beans, there are beans to suit any gardener's taste and growing conditions.

Snap beans (*Phaseolus vulgaris*) are the best-known beans, and there are both bush and pole types. If your summers are short, try bush beans, which usually take less time to mature than pole beans. Pole beans, a good choice for small gardens because they grow vertically up poles or trellises, also produce a higher overall yield than bush types.

If your summers are hot and dry, grow heat- and drought-resistant cultivars. Early-maturing beans are best in cooler regions.

Select cultivars that resist anthracnose, bean mosaic, powdery mildew, rust, and other diseases that commonly affect beans.

If you'd like to be more adventurous in your bean picks, see "A Garden Full of Beans" on the opposite page for more ideas.

Site and Soil

Beans will grow successfully in most gardens as long as they get at least half a day of sun. However, they do best in a light, sandy, well-drained soil with a pH of 5.5 to 6.8. If your garden has heavy soil or drainage problems, build raised beds.

Work compost into the top 6 inches of soil before planting, at a rate of 5 to 10 pounds of compost per 100 square feet.

PLANTING FACTS

Seed and Seedling Identification

Seed Spacing for Bush Beans

2"–4"

18"–36"

Seed Spacing for Pole Beans

4"–6"

3'–4'

For intensive spacing, plant seeds 4"–6" apart on all sides. (Intensive planting not recommended for pole beans.)
Seed depth: 1"

GREEN THUMB TIP

If you're thinking about soaking your bean seeds before planting them, think again. Putting dry seeds in water will make them more brittle and may cause them to crack.

For best bean germination, plant in warm soil. To get a head start, warm the soil by covering it with black plastic. Choose an early cultivar such as 'Venture', and plant through holes poked in the plastic.

Planting

When to Plant

Begin planting your bean crop about two weeks after the last predicted frost. The soil temperature should be at least 60°F. If the soil is too cold and moist, the seeds will rot.

If you live in an area with moderate summers, make several small sowings of bush beans at two-week intervals to spread the harvest through the summer. If your summers tend to be very hot, making repeated sowings is not the best strategy. Beans often drop their blossoms at high temperatures, so you won't get good midsummer crops.

A GARDEN FULL OF BEANS

Try some of the popular home garden beans shown below. Snap beans (*Phaseolus vulgaris*) are a standard; you can choose from green beans, yellow wax beans, purple beans, thin French beans, and broad Italian beans. Kidney beans (*P. vulgaris*) are dark red dried beans used in chili, soups, and salads. Tender lima beans (*P. limensis* or *P. lunatus*) don't tolerate cold temperatures, so wait until three weeks after the last frost before planting them. Scarlet runner beans (*P. coccineus*), native to South America, grow on tender perennial vines that produce bright red blossoms and black- and red-speckled seeds that are eaten fresh or dried. Broad beans, also called fava, horse, or cattle beans (*Vicia faba*), are unusual because they thrive under cool, damp conditions. Black-eyed peas (*Vigna unguiculata* subsp. *unguiculata*) are a Southern favorite that do best in areas with long, hot summers. If you discover that you like growing and eating different cultivars and types, branch out to more unusual beans, like tepary beans—a Southwestern native with white, yellow, blue, or black edible seeds.

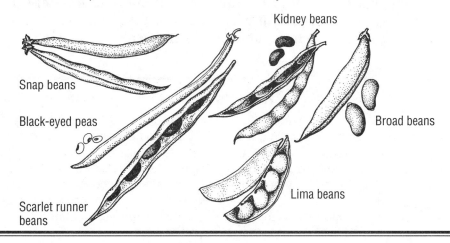

Snap beans

Black-eyed peas

Scarlet runner beans

Kidney beans

Broad beans

Lima beans

Sow beans for a fall harvest 7 to 12 weeks before the first predicted frost. Be sure the crop will mature before frost, because frost will damage bean plants.

How Much to Plant

For fresh eating, grow 10 to 15 bush bean plants per person; for pole beans, plant three to five hills per person.

For canning or freezing, figure that ½ pound of seed will cover a 100-foot row and produce approximately 50 quarts of beans.

Planting Outdoors

Beans are legumes, plants that can supply some of their own nitrogen with the help of certain soil-dwelling bacteria. Your beans may get a growth boost if you treat the seeds with a commercial inoculant containing these bacteria. You can buy inoculant from most mail-order companies that sell bean seeds. See "Pea" on page 148 for instructions on treating seeds with inoculant.

For general instructions on planting seeds, see "Sowing Seed Outdoors" on page 55. For seed depth and spacing information, see "Planting Facts" on the opposite page.

Thinning

Thin your bean seedlings after the first true leaves appear. Thin plants to these distances:

- Bush beans: 4 to 6 inches apart
- Pole beans in rows: 6 to 9 inches apart
- Pole beans in hills: 3 to 4 plants per hill

Seasonal Care

If you keep up with watering, feeding, mulching, and other tasks as your bean plants grow, you will get a more bountiful harvest. For tips on what to do and when to do it for your best bean crop ever, see "Season-by-Season Care: Bean" on page 91. If your plants have problems, see "Solving Bean Problems" on page 92 for a rundown of common symptoms, causes, and solutions.

Harvesting

Bush beans ripen over a shorter period than pole beans. But frequent harvesting of both types keeps them producing longer. To avoid uprooting bush bean plants when you harvest, hold the stem as you remove the pods with your thumbnail and fingers. Use scissors to cut the pods off pole bean plants.

Store green and lima beans in plastic bags in the refrigerator. They will keep for one to two weeks. Surplus beans can and freeze well.

For dry beans, wait to harvest the pods until they have turned brown. (When you shake them, you should hear the seeds rattling inside.) If rain is predicted and the beans need more time to dry, harvest the entire plants and hang them upside down indoors. When the seeds are completely dry and hard, remove them from the pods, as shown on page 90. Store

---

TRAINING BEANS

Pole beans require some kind of support for the twining vines. With staking or trellising, it's possible to grow these vigorous plants in a small space. Supports also ensure that pole beans get enough light and air to stay healthy and produce high yields.

Pole beans cling to a support by wrapping their stems in a spiral around it, so it's important to provide plenty of straight vertical supports. Try simple trellises constructed from stakes and strings, like the ones shown on this page, or a tepee-shaped trellis, as shown on page 90.

Use straight wooden poles 6 to 10 feet long for trellises. Push the poles several inches into the soil when you construct the trellises to anchor them.

Crisscross trellis. *Cross pairs of wooden poles 6 to 9 inches apart to form the framework of this trellis. Then rest a final pole horizontally in the valley formed by the crisscrossed pairs. Tie it to each pair to secure the trellis in place.*

Horizontal pole stabilizes trellis.

6"   Wire

Twine

Vertical trellis. *Sturdy wooden end stakes support two wires strung near the soil level and near the top. Beans climb up twine tied between the wires. Sink the poles 1 foot deep.*

Harvesting green beans. *Green beans are ready to pick when they are about the width of a pencil. The pods should snap when you break them in half.*

Harvesting with care. *Use your thumb and fingernails to pinch beans off plants when you harvest. Yanking or tugging at the pods will damage stems and plant roots.*

Harvesting shell beans. *Harvest fresh shell beans when they are still tender and you can see bumps on the pods made by the enlarged seeds inside.*

them in airtight containers in a cool, dry spot. Dry beans will keep for up to one year.

Extending the Season

Preheat the soil. To get a head start on the season, warm the soil where you plan to plant beans by covering it with black plastic. Cover beds as soon as you can work the soil in spring; then monitor soil temperatures and plant when the soil reaches 60°F. Air temperatures may be too cool for best bean growth if you plant early. Warm the plants as well by covering them with a clear plastic tunnel or with floating row cover.

Start seeds indoors. If your growing season is very short, you can try starting seeds in individual peat pots indoors. Bean transplants are temperamental, so handle them with care.

Sow seeds four weeks before the last predicted frost. Provide plenty of light. The air temperature should be about 55°F. Seeds germinate in 7 to 14 days.

Protect fall beans from frost. If you plant crops that will mature after the first expected frost, be sure to cover them with plastic or floating row cover.

Growing in Containers

Any bush or pole bean you plant in your garden is suitable for growing in containers. Choose a good potting soil rich in nitrogen. Beans grow best in full sun but will tolerate partial shade. Ideally, temperatures should be between 65° and 85°F; do not subject plants to frost. Keep the soil moist, but not soggy. Avoid watering the leaves and flowers directly. For pole beans, put

a stake in the pot at planting time, or move the container next to a wall or trellis for support.

Propagation

It's easy to save bean seed from your own garden for future crops. Mark sections of your bean rows for seed saving at planting. Treat these plants well during the season, and pull and discard weak plants. Be sure the cultivars you choose are not hybrids, because hybrid cultivars don't come true from seed.

Leave at least 150 feet between plantings of different cultivars for seed saving to prevent cross-pollination. Collect bean seeds for propagation as you would dry beans for eating. Wait until the pods have turned brown and you can hear the seeds rattling inside. For small amounts, pick the pods and

BUILDING A BEAN TEPEE

6"–9"

Step 1. *Lash two wooden 8- to 10-foot poles together with strong nylon cord. Then bind on more poles one at a time, using a figure-eight pattern. Use six to eight poles in total.*

Step 2. *Stand the poles up and spread them to form a tepee. Push the poles several inches into the soil. Poke planting holes with a dibble. Plant six to eight pole bean seeds in a hill around each pole.*

Step 3. *After seedlings begin to form true leaves, thin them to three plants per hill. The bean vines will climb the poles and cover the tepee, creating an attractive garden feature.*

spread them out to dry indoors. When the seeds are completely dry (in one or two weeks), remove them from the pods and store in a cool, dry place.

If you are collecting a large number of seeds to preserve, pull up the entire plants and allow them to dry indoors for a week or two. You can then hand-shell the beans, or thresh them in quantity, as shown below.

After threshing, you'll want to winnow your beans—separate the seeds from the bits of dried pods, leaves, and stems (chaff). On a windy day, lay a tarp or a heavy piece of cloth on the ground, then slowly pour the beans from your container onto the cloth. Repeat this process several times, until the wind blows all the chaff away.

Hand-shelling dry beans. *Apply pressure on the seam of the pod with your thumbs to make the pod crack open.*

Threshing in a can. *For fast shelling, pull up whole dried bean plants and bang them against the inside of a clean trash can.*

Threshing in a bag. *Shell large quantities of beans by filling a burlap bag with dried bean plants and beating it with a stick.*

SEASON-BY-SEASON CARE: BEAN

This care guide tells you what to do and when to do it for your best bean harvest ever. Because timing of certain tasks is critical, review all the instructions in this guide in late winter. Locate or buy the products you'll need in advance. To identify specific problems, refer to "Solving Bean Problems" on page 92.

Spring

Choose disease-resistant cultivars. If you've had disease problems with your beans in the past, plan to plant disease-resistant cultivars this year. This is your best option if you've had problems with anthracnose, bean mosaic, downy mildew, powdery mildew, or rust.

Warm the soil before planting. Cover the area where you plan to plant beans with black plastic as soon as the soil can be worked. Beans germinate faster and are less prone to rot in warm soil.

Apply parasitic nematodes to the soil. If you've had past problems with seed-corn maggots or cutworms, drench the soil with parasitic nematodes before planting.

Plant after frost danger is past. Beans grow best in warm conditions. Begin planting about two weeks after the last predicted frost. For best results, the soil temperature should be at least 60°F.

Put up supports for pole beans. Construct trellises or tepees for pole beans at planting time or when the first two leaves appear on the seedlings.

Cover plants with floating row cover. If you've had past problems with bean leaf beetles, flea beetles, Mexican bean beetles, or other pests, cover beds at seeding and keep them covered until plants are large enough to withstand damage.

Mulch. After seedlings appear, mulch with a 3- to 6-inch layer of grass clippings.

Cultivate. Cultivate shallowly around young plants to kill weeds that might compete with the crop.

Thin plants. Thin beans when plants have two true leaves. Unthinned stands will be more prone to disease problems due to poor air circulation.

Summer

Water. Watering is especially important when the pods start to develop. Keep the soil constantly moist but not soggy. Don't overwater; it can cause plants to drop their pods.

Fertilize. To give your crop an extra boost, spray plants with kelp.

Stay away from wet plants. Don't work around your plants when they are wet. Disease organisms spread easily in the film of water covering wet leaves.

Harvest frequently. When beans are ready to harvest, pick every day or so to keep plants productive.

Plant for fall harvest. Sow seeds 7 to 12 weeks before the first predicted frost. Keep seeds and seedlings well watered during hot or dry conditions.

Late Summer/Fall

Harvest dry beans. Pick dry beans when you can hear seeds rattling inside the pods when you shake them.

Protect late crops with floating row cover. Temperatures below 45°F can injure plants and pods. Protect plants by covering them with row cover if low temperatures are predicted.

Clean up. After the crop has winter-killed, pull up the plants and compost them, or mow the bed and mulch. Be sure to pull and destroy any diseased or pest-infested plants.

Solving Bean Problems

Use this table to identify problems on your beans. Scan the list of symptoms to find the description that most closely matches what you see in your garden. Then refer across the page to learn the cause and the recommended solutions. For some disease problems, by the time you see the damage, there is little you can do to save your crop. In the future, your best choice is to plant disease-resistant cultivars whenever possible. For other suggestions for preventing pest problems, see "Season-by-Season Care: Bean" on page 91. You'll also find illustrations, descriptions, and additional controls for many of the insects and diseases listed below in Part 5 of this book.

FLOWER AND POD PROBLEMS

SYMPTOMS	CAUSES	SOLUTIONS
Flowers appear but no pods form	High temperatures Physical injury Drought	Temperatures over 85°F can sterilize blossoms. Heavy rains can knock off blossoms. Pods won't form when plants are water-stressed, so be sure to water adequately. When weather conditions change, or plants recover from water stress, new blossoms should form pods.
Water-soaked brown blotches on pods	Bacterial blight	Pull and destroy infected plants. If crop is nearly ready to pick, try keeping disease in check by spraying copper.
Pitted and brown pods; no sign of bacterial ooze	Cold injury	Temperatures below 45°F usually damage plants and pods. If cold temperatures are predicted, cover late-season crops with floating row cover.
Black or reddish, sunken areas on pods; pods may ooze	Anthracnose	Spray plants thoroughly with copper or bordeaux mix. Handle plants only when leaves are dry. Pull and destroy all crop residues in fall.
Powdery white patches on pods, which may be stunted	Powdery mildew	Mildew usually occurs on late-season plants. Thin plants to promote air circulation. Handle plants only when foliage is dry. Where problem is persistent and in wet weather, spray or dust sulfur every 10–14 days.
Thick cottony white growth on pods; tissue underneath is soft	White mold (Sclerotinia)	Affected plants usually die, so pull and destroy plants at first sign of disease. Thin remaining plants to promote air circulation. Remove and destroy crop residues in fall.
Downy white growth on lima bean pods	Downy mildew	Spray copper at first sign of disease. In fall, remove and destroy crop residues.
Water-soaked tissue on pods, with fuzzy gray mold	Gray mold (Botrytis)	This disease is worse in wet conditions. Pick and destroy affected pods and other plant tissue. Thin plants to promote air circulation.
Mottled, stunted, or deformed pods	Bean mosaic	Pull and destroy infected plants. Control aphids, which spread the virus, and do not handle healthy plants after pulling diseased plants.

LEAF PROBLEMS

SYMPTOMS	CAUSES	SOLUTIONS
Yellow, withered leaves; tiny black or green insects on shoot tips	Aphids	Wash aphids from leaves with a strong spray of water. For severe infestations, spray insecticidal soap, neem, or pyrethrins.
Mottled, puckered leaves with yellow patches	Bean mosaic	Pull and destroy infected plants. Control aphids, which spread the virus, and do not handle healthy plants after pulling diseased plants.
Water-soaked dead spots on leaves	Bacterial blight	Pull and destroy infected plants. If pods are nearly ready to harvest, try to keep disease in check by spraying copper.
Discolored spots on leaves, turning grayish white and powdery	Powdery mildew	Mildew usually occurs on late-season plants. Thin plants to promote air circulation. Handle plants only when foliage is dry. Where problem is persistent and in wet weather, spray or dust sulfur every 10–14 days.
Veins on underside of leaves turn black; black spots on stems, pods	Anthracnose	Spray plants thoroughly with copper or bordeaux mix. Handle plants only when leaves are dry. In fall, pull and destroy all crop residues.
Many small reddish spots on leaves, mostly on leaf undersides	Rust	Spray sulfur at first sign of disease, and repeat every 10–14 days as needed. In fall, remove and destroy crop residues.
Leaves skeletonized; yellowish brown beetles with black spots on plants	Mexican bean beetles	Handpick beetles, larvae (yellow, spiny grubs), and egg masses (bright yellow ovals in clusters). In severe infestations, spray pyrethrins or rotenone. In fall, pull and destroy crop residues.
Large holes chewed in leaves	Bean leaf beetles Caterpillars	Handpicking these pests usually is sufficient. For serious leaf beetle infestations, spray pyrethrins or rotenone. If caterpillars are a serious problem, spray BTK.

WHOLE PLANT PROBLEMS

SYMPTOMS	CAUSES	SOLUTIONS
Seeds fail to sprout or die after coming up	Root rot Damping-off Seed-corn maggots	For rot or damping-off, replant in a new site, waiting until soil is well warmed. If seed-corn maggots are present in seeds, treat soil at a new site with parasitic nematodes. Wait 1 week, and then plant seeds at this new site.
Stunted plants with light green to yellow leaves; roots appear healthy	Nitrogen deficiency	Beans usually produce nitrogen with the aid of natural bacteria in the roots. Waterlogged soil hinders nitrogen production. Feed plants with foliar and root applications of fish emulsion.

BEET   *Beta vulgaris*, Crassa group • Chenopodiaceae

Choosing Plants

Basic beets are round and red; for variety, you can try carrot-shaped beets, candy-striped beets, yellow beets, or white beets. Most main-crop cultivars reach 4 to 6 inches in diameter and can be stored for a few months without losing their taste and texture. 'Lutz Greenleaf' is a main-crop cultivar grown especially for its tasty foliage.

You can select cultivars that tolerate extreme temperatures, or small-rooted cultivars for canning. Select leaf spot–resistant cultivars if you've had problems with Cercospora leaf spot.

PLANTING FACTS

Seed and Seedling Identification

Seed Spacing

1"–2"

12"–18"

For intensive spacing, plant seeds 8" apart on all sides.
Seed depth: 1/4"–1/2"

Site and Soil

Beets prefer full sun but will tolerate light shade. They need well-drained sandy loam with a pH of 6.0 to 6.8. Roots growing in heavy clay soil tend to become deformed. If you have heavy or poorly drained soil, build raised planting beds for your beets.

Dig the planting site to a depth of 1 foot and remove all stones and clods of soil. Beets are heavy feeders, so work in 15 to 20 pounds of rich compost per 100 square feet.

Planting

When to plant. Beets develop the best color, taste, and texture when grown quickly during cool weather (60° to 65°F). Plant in early spring as soon as the soil can be worked and soil temperatures exceed 45°F.

In cool climates, make successive plantings of beets every two weeks for an all-summer harvest, and then plant main-crop cultivars in late summer for a fall harvest. In cool climates, sow beets grown for storage 90 days before the first fall frost. In hot climates, plant beets only in the early spring and fall, or grow them as a late-winter crop.

How much to plant. For fresh eating, plant 5 to 10 feet of garden row per person. For canning, sow 10 to 20 feet per person. One ounce of beet seeds will plant a 75-foot row. Depending on the cultivar, this should produce 200 to 300 beet roots.

Planting outdoors. Beet seeds of most cultivars are actually small fruits that contain four to eight seeds each. Don't seed too thickly because each seed you plant will produce several seedlings.

For general instructions on planting seeds, see "Sowing Seed Outdoors" on page 55. For seed depth and spacing information, see "Planting Facts" on this page .

Thinning. One of the most common mistakes gardeners make with beets is under-thinning. Beets that aren't thinned enough never develop roots worth harvesting. Thin for the first time, when seedlings are 1 to 2 inches high, to 1/2 inch apart. After that, thinning distance depends on the cultivar. See the illustration on the opposite page for details. Eat the tender, young thinnings either raw or cooked. If you want to harvest beet tops for greens, delay thinning until the plants are 6 to 8 inches tall.

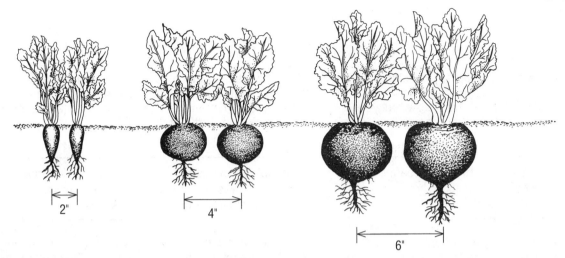

Thinning beets. *To make sure beet roots develop properly, thin them after sprouting. Thin carrot-shaped beets to a final distance of 2 inches apart, standard round roots to 4 inches, and large storage cultivars to 6 inches.*

Seasonal Care

Because beets can be planted in spring, summer, or fall, timing for their care is related more to their size than to the time of year. Follow the guidelines below for success with beets. If you have problems with your beets, refer to "Solving Beet Problems" on page 96.

Water. Keep young beets well watered. The soil surface should be moist, but not wet, at all times. Lack of moisture causes plants to bolt (go to seed) and roots to become cracked, stringy, and tough.

Apply mulch. Lay down a thick mulch of grass clippings or composted leaves between rows of seedlings to keep down weeds and keep soil cool and moist.

Cover plants with floating row cover. If you've had past problems with leafminers or curly top virus (which is spread by leafhoppers), cover plants with row cover from seeding until harvest.

Fertilize. When the first true leaves are fully expanded, drench the plants with kelp or compost tea. Repeat weekly until the plants are 2 to 3 inches tall.

Hill up soil around roots. If the enlarging roots poke up above the soil surface, hill up the soil to keep these "shoulders" from becoming green and tough.

Harvesting

Harvest early cultivars when they reach 2 inches in diameter. Store fall crops in the ground, covered with a 6-inch layer of mulch, or pull the beets and cut off the tops to store in the refrigerator for several weeks. You can also store beets in boxes, layered with sand or peat, at 35° to 45°F for two to five months.

Extending the Season

Get a head start on spring beets by planting them in the fall. Sow seeds when air temperatures are 50° to 65°F. Cover the row with a 1-foot layer of straw for the winter. In spring, when temperatures reach 50° to 60°F, remove several inches of straw every few days until plants are exposed.

Propagation

Beets are biennials, producing seed in the second year. Overwinter plants for seed production under mulch. Beet cultivars will cross-pollinate, and the pollen is wind-borne. If you plan to grow beets for seed, be sure only one cultivar will be in flower at a time. Wait until the seeds at the base of the stalk ripen before collecting them.

Solving Beet Problems

Use this table to identify problems on your beets. Scan the list of symptoms to find the description that most closely matches what you see in your garden. Then refer across the page to learn the cause and the recommended solutions. You'll also find illustrations, descriptions, and additional controls for many of the insects and diseases listed below in Part 5 of this book.

SYMPTOMS	CAUSES	SOLUTIONS
Clear or brownish tunnels between upper and lower leaf surfaces	Leafminers	Handpick and destroy damaged leaves. Undamaged parts of leaves can still be eaten, and roots are unaffected. Spray neem to control larvae in leaves.
Brown or gray spots with distinct reddish margins on leaves	Cercospora leaf spot	This disease is most severe east of the Rocky Mountains. Roots are not affected and are edible. Pick and destroy all affected leaves. Spray copper if problem is severe. Remove and destroy crop residues in fall to eliminate overwintering disease. For future plantings, rotate crops and select Cercospora-tolerant cultivars.
Dwarfed, excessively crinkled leaves; leaf margins roll upward	Curly top virus	Infected plants produce woody, inedible roots. Pull and destroy affected plants. This disease is spread by leafhoppers; if they are numerous, spray with insecticidal soap or pyrethrins.
Large holes chewed in leaves	Beet armyworms Garden webworms	Damage has little effect on yield unless more than half of leaf area is consumed. Handpick caterpillars in rolled sections of leaf edges. If many small caterpillars are present, spray BTK or neem.
Premature seedstalks form; white rings may show in cross section of roots	Heat stress	Sudden exposure to high temperatures, especially in early-spring and late-fall crops, causes plants to bolt (go to seed). Where this is a recurring problem, select heat-tolerant and bolt-resistant cultivars.
Black, dead roots or roots with black dry rot in center	Root rot	Destroy affected roots, and do not replant beets at same site next year. To avoid future damage, plant in well-drained soil when soil has warmed.
Dark, corky scabs on surface of roots	Scab	Scab is only a problem in acidic soils. Affected roots are edible, though skins are blemished. For next season, have your soil tested and apply lime as required to raise soil pH above 6.0 to prevent growth of scab organisms.
Woody roots with many side roots	Curly top virus	Pull and destroy affected plants. This disease is spread by leafhoppers; protect future crops by covering them with floating row cover.

BROCCOLI *Brassica oleracea*, Botrytis group • Cruciferae

Vitamin-rich broccoli is so tasty and versatile that it's become one of the nation's most popular vegetables. Broccoli is a member of the cabbage family, which is also called the crucifers. It requires soil preparation and care similar to cabbage and is vulnerable to many of the same problems. Refer to "Cabbage" on page 100 for basic care information, a schedule of seasonal care, and solutions to pest problems.

Below you'll find specialized information to help you select cultivars and types of broccoli to grow, planting information, and tips to help you get repeated harvests from your crop.

Choosing Plants

For tender, good-tasting broccoli, your plants need extended cool temperatures as they produce flower heads. Work with your climate by selecting a cultivar that will mature before hot weather sets in. Use a fast-maturing type, such as 'Spartan Early' or 'Green Comet Hybrid', in areas with early warm spells. 'Green Duke' is a good choice for even-warmer southern gardens.

Gardeners with cool summers can plant a range of cultivars maturing anywhere from 40 to 85 days from planting.

To extend your harvest, choose an Italian sprouting type like 'De Cicco' that produces many small sideshoots after the main head is cut.

Broccoli raab doesn't head at all but has tender, delicious branches and edible leaves. Romanesco broccoli, with a flavor between that of broccoli and cauliflower, produces a chartreuse, conchshell-shaped head.

If you've had past problems with black rot, downy mildew, or hollow stem, select cultivars that tolerate these diseases.

Planting

When to plant. Sow your spring crop two months before the last expected frost. Seeds should germinate in less than a week. Protect young plants from frost with cloches or floating row cover.

For a fall crop, plant broccoli two to four months before the first frost, depending upon the cultivar. Provide shade during hot spells.

In areas with mild winters, like those found in the Southwest, plant in the fall for a spring harvest. In the Deep South, start plants indoors in mid-December and set them out the middle of February.

Gardeners in cool-summer areas of the Pacific Northwest can grow broccoli nearly year-round.

How much to plant. For fresh eating, plan on growing five to ten plants per person. One plant can produce 2 pounds of main heads and sideshoots.

For direct-seeding, figure that after thinning, a 25-foot row will produce about 15 mature plants.

PLANTING FACTS

Seed and Seedling Identification

Transplant Spacing

18"–24"

2'–3'

For intensive spacing, plant transplants 18" apart on all sides.

Set transplants 2"–3" deeper than they grew in pots or flats.

Starting plants indoors. Start broccoli seeds indoors the way you would cabbage plants, or try this variation. Seven to nine weeks before the last expected frost, plant each seed ¼ inch deep in good potting mix in a 4-inch-deep pot. After the seeds germinate, put the pots in a sunny place where temperatures are between 60° and 65°F. Keep the soil moist, but not wet. When seedlings are 6 inches tall with two to four leaves, they are ready for hardening off and planting outdoors.

Planting outdoors. For fall crops, direct-seeding broccoli can work well. For general instructions on planting seeds, see "Sowing Seed Outdoors" on page 55. Space seeds 1 inch apart and ½ to 1 inch deep in rows 2 to 3 feet apart.

For spacing information for transplants, see "Planting Facts" on page 97. If transplants have floppy or crooked stems, set the plants deeply so that their first true leaves are at soil level. Firm the soil and water well.

Thinning. Crowded plants will produce small heads, so thin to 18 to 24 inches apart once seedlings have two true leaves. Be sure to remove any weak or sick-looking seedlings as you thin.

Harvesting

Harvest broccoli florets early in the morning for the best flavor. Holding out for large broccoli heads isn't the best idea. Heads that look gorgeous one day can begin to overmature the next. The technique for harvesting broccoli is shown in the illustration below left.

FOR BEST RESULTS

Start your spring broccoli crop indoors from seed. That way the seedlings are safe from the effects of temperature dips and dives. If young broccoli plants are exposed to a spell of ten days or more when the temperature stays below 50°F, they may form tiny premature flower heads known as "buttons."

Soak your harvested broccoli in salt water (1 to 2 tablespoons of salt per gallon) for 30 minutes before cooking or storing. This will drive out any cabbageworms hidden in the heads. You can store broccoli wrapped in plastic for about one week in the refrigerator. Blanch and freeze surplus broccoli.

Harvesting broccoli. *Cut main broccoli heads when they reach 3 to 4 inches across and before the flowers open. Cut the stem at an angle with a sharp knife so that water will run off the cut stem. Water collecting on the cut area can lead to stem rot.*

Bonus broccoli. *Continue to water and feed your broccoli plants after cutting the central head. You'll be rewarded with as many as six more cuttings of small but tasty heads that sprout and grow along the stem.*

BRUSSELS SPROUTS
Brassica oleracea, Gemmifera group • Cruciferae

Brussels sprouts belong to the crucifers—the botanical family that also includes cabbage and broccoli. They require similar care to cabbage. Refer to "Cabbage" on page 100 for basic information, seasonal care, and solutions to pest problems.

Here you'll find information on brussels sprout cultivars and timing of planting as well as harvesting tips.

Choosing Plants

Early-maturing dwarf cultivars are exceptionally hardy, but their sprouts cling

Picking sprouts. *Twist or cut sprouts carefully from the stalk. A second crop of smaller sprouts may follow in their place.*

tightly to the stalks, making them more difficult to harvest. Later-maturing cultivars are less hardy. Their sprouts grow away from the main stalk on small stems, making them easier to pick. Hybrids combine the qualities of these two basic types.

Planting

When to plant. Sprouts take 80 to 100 days to mature. Frost improves the taste. Start fall crops indoors in March, April, or May, and set transplants out in May, June, or July, timing plantings to mature as the first frost hits. In long-season areas, sow seeds outdoors in July. In mild climates, plant in the fall for a spring crop.

How much to plant. For fresh eating, grow 5 to 10

plants per person. A direct-seeded row 25 feet long will produce 12 to 15 mature plants.

Planting outdoors. Outdoors, sow seeds ½ inch deep and 2 inches apart. Thin to 18 inches apart. See "Planting Facts" on this page for transplant spacing guidelines.

Harvesting

Brussels sprouts mature from the base of the stem up. You can pick small quantities of sprouts as the plants grow or harvest the whole plant top and store it with the sprouts attached, as shown in the illustrations on this page. Brussels sprouts will keep for up to three weeks in a plastic bag in the refrigerator.

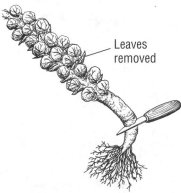

Leaves removed

Sprout "log." *To make a brussels sprout "log," pull up the plant, and cut off all leaves and roots. Store the "log" at 35° to 45°F in a root cellar.*

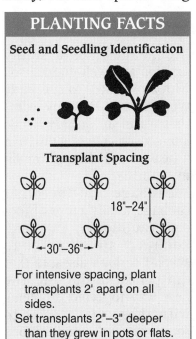

PLANTING FACTS

Seed and Seedling Identification

Transplant Spacing

18"–24"

←30"–36"→

For intensive spacing, plant transplants 2' apart on all sides.
Set transplants 2"–3" deeper than they grew in pots or flats.

CABBAGE
Brassica oleracea, Capitata group • Cruciferae

Cabbage, a reliable storage crop and the raw material for coleslaw and sauerkraut, is a garden classic. It's one of a group of related crops that are commonly called the crucifers, all of which belong to the genus *Brassica.* The information in this entry will help you grow successful cabbage crops. It will also guide you in growing other crucifers, including broccoli, brussels sprouts, cauliflower, collard, kale, kohlrabi, and turnip. (You'll also find specialized information on these crops in their individual entries.)

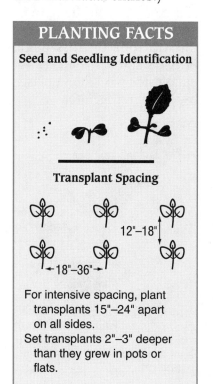

PLANTING FACTS

Seed and Seedling Identification

Transplant Spacing

12"–18"

←18"–36"→

For intensive spacing, plant transplants 15"–24" apart on all sides.
Set transplants 2"–3" deeper than they grew in pots or flats.

Choosing Plants

The cabbage harvest can begin early in the season and stretch into late fall. There are cultivars available that mature from 60 to 180 days from planting.

Early cabbage. If your garden season is short, pick an early-maturing type such as 'Early Jersey Wakefield'. 'Ruby Ball' is an early red cabbage known for its firm, sweet heads.

Late-season cabbage. Grow late-season types, such as 'Penn State Ballhead' and 'Wisconsin Hollander', for a fall harvest or, in mild climates, for a winter harvest.

Storage types. If you plan to store cabbage heads over winter, choose a tight-headed cultivar such as 'Danish Ballhead'. For a winter cabbage that is tasty raw or cooked, pick a white, tight-headed type such as 'Hitstar'.

Problem resistance. To avoid disease problems, select disease-tolerant cultivars such as 'Survivor', 'Greencup', or 'Regalia'.

In areas with hot spells, heat-resistant, high-yielding 'Savoy Queen' is a good choice.

Chinese cabbage. For a variation on the theme of cabbage, try growing Chinese

cabbage and other Oriental cabbage-family plants. For more information on these crops, see "Chinese Cabbage" on page 105.

Site and Soil

Cabbage likes a sunny location and well-drained soil with a pH of 6.0 to 6.8. Early types do best in sandy loams that warm up quickly, while late-season cultivars thrive in a heavier soil that will retain moisture.

Cabbage and the other cabbage-family crops (broccoli, cauliflower, kale, and kohlrabi) are all prone to several serious diseases that can persist in the soil. The best way to avoid problems with these diseases is to rotate cabbage-family crops in your garden. For some diseases, a two-year rotation is sufficient; others require a longer rotation. For more information on rotating cabbage-family crops, see "Rotate Crops for Better Production" on page 45.

Cabbage-family crops will grow best on a site enriched by cover cropping. Dig in the cover crop at least two weeks before setting out transplants.

If you haven't planned ahead and planted a cover crop the previous fall, enrich the soil with compost instead. Spread and work in at least 30 pounds of compost per 100 square feet two weeks before setting out transplants.

To ensure a supply of phosphorus, a major factor in avoiding tipburn, work in an application of calcium phosphate (also called colloidal phosphate) or ground rock phosphate at a rate of 5 pounds per 100 square feet.

Planting

When to Plant

Cabbage is a cool-season crop that can tolerate some frost. You can begin planting cabbage outdoors about four weeks before your last expected spring frost.

Start early cultivars indoors four to six weeks before transplanting the seedlings outside—usually in March in the North and

Standard ball cabbage. *These cabbages vary from reddish purple to light green to white. Stems can range from nonexistent to 20 inches long.*

Pointed-head cabbage. *This storage-type cabbage takes up less space in the garden than other types. 'Early Jersey Wakefield' is one popular cultivar.*

Crinkled-leaved savoy. *Richer in iron than other cabbage, savoy should be eaten fresh because it doesn't store well.*

Chinese cabbage. *Chinese cabbage looks like a cross between lettuce and cabbage. It's become a favorite for salads and stir-fries.*

January or February in the South.

Start mid-season or late types in outdoor flats. Sow mid-season cultivars after the last expected frost. Start late types from the first to the middle of July; transplant them to the garden the first of August in the North and from the middle to late August in warmer regions. Seed fall crops of late types directly in the garden by midsummer.

How Much to Plant

Grow five to ten plants per person for fresh eating.

If you want to grow cabbage for processing, a 100-foot row of 70 early-cabbage plants will produce about 100 pounds; 60 late-maturing types in the same space will produce about 175 pounds.

Starting Plants Indoors

Start early crops of cabbage indoors. For instructions on preparing soil mix and seed flats, see "Starting Seeds Indoors" on page 46.

Sow cabbage seeds ¼ inch deep and 2 inches apart in good potting soil in flats. They will take six to nine days to come up with a germination rate of around 75 percent. Place the flats in a sunny window, a greenhouse, or under plant growth lights. Optimum soil temperature for growing seedlings is

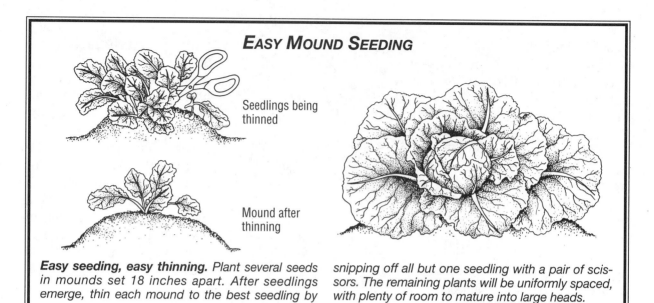

EASY MOUND SEEDING

Seedlings being thinned

Mound after thinning

Easy seeding, easy thinning. Plant several seeds in mounds set 18 inches apart. After seedlings emerge, thin each mound to the best seedling by snipping off all but one seedling with a pair of scissors. The remaining plants will be uniformly spaced, with plenty of room to mature into large heads.

65° to 75°F; keep air temperature around 60°F during the day and 50°F at night.

Planting Outdoors

Seeds. Sow seeds for mid-season and storage crops directly in garden beds. You can sow seeds thinly, ½ inch deep, in traditional rows 2 to 3 feet apart. Or to save seed and make thinning easier, try mound seeding, as shown on this page.

Transplants. If you're buying cabbage transplants, look for sturdy, stocky plants. Check to be sure that there are no flea beetles or small cabbageworms hiding among the leaves.

See "Planting Facts" on page 100 for guidelines for spacing cabbage transplants. Wider spacing results in larger heads, but smaller heads are usually more tender. If you want the best of both worlds, space the plants 6 to 8 inches apart and harvest every other one before maturity.

Thinning

Thin seedlings of early cultivars to 15 to 18 inches apart; thin late cultivars to stand 2 feet apart. Don't pull the extra seedlings—snip them off with scissors to avoid damaging the roots of the remaining plants.

Seasonal Care

Keep close watch on your cabbage-family plants as they grow. Good care will result in a more bountiful harvest. For a seasonal schedule of planting and maintenance, see "Season-by-Season Care: Cabbage" on the opposite page. If your plants have problems, see "Solving Cabbage Problems" on page 106 for a rundown of symptoms, causes, and solutions.

Harvesting

Cabbage is ready to harvest as soon as firm, glossy heads form, even if they are no larger than baseballs. If you leave mature heads on the plants too long, the heads will probably split.

Test for firmness by pressing the back of your hand on the head. Don't pinch heads with your fingers; it may bruise them.

If several of your cabbages are mature at the same time, you can try this trick to hold some of the mature heads in the ground without splitting. Gently grip the head and give it a quarter turn. This will break some of the roots, reducing

SEASON-BY-SEASON CARE: CABBAGE

This care guide tells you what to do and when to do it for your best cabbage-family crops ever. Because timing of certain tasks is critical, review all the instructions in this guide in late winter. Locate or buy the products you'll need in advance. To identify specific problems, refer to "Solving Cabbage Problems" on page 106.

Spring

Start early-cabbage seedlings. Start seeds indoors six weeks before you plan to plant them outside. In cool-season areas, you can make several small sowings for planting every two to three weeks for a staggered harvest.

Choose disease-tolerant cultivars. If you've had disease problems (especially black rot or Fusarium yellows) in the past, plan to plant disease-tolerant cultivars this year.

Check soil pH. If you've had past problems with club root, check the pH in the bed where you plan to plant cabbage-family crops. Add lime to raise the pH above 7.0 if needed.

Cover with floating row cover. If you've had past problems with cabbage loopers, flea beetles, imported cabbageworms, slugs, or other pests, cover plants with row cover immediately after planting and keep them covered until plants are large enough to withstand damage.

Water and mulch. Keep the soil evenly moist and cool by mulching with a 6- to 8-inch layer of straw or grass clippings.

Feed young plants. During the first three weeks after transplanting, feed your plants as you water them. Apply 1 cup per plant of kelp and fish emulsion mixture (1 tablespoon of kelp extract and 1 tablespoon of fish emulsion per gallon of water).

Apply cutworm collars and/or seedling disks. If you've had past problems with cut- worms or root maggots, protect transplants immediately after planting. For cutworms, slide collars made from half a toilet paper tube over transplants and push them about halfway into the soil. For root maggots, apply seedling disks like the one shown on page 104.

Summer

Harvest crops before they overmature. Broccoli and cauliflower may develop loose, ricey heads in hot weather. Early cabbage heads may split if not harvested promptly.

Start crops for fall harvest. Plant late cabbage during the first half of July or 10 to 12 weeks before the first autumn frost. Be sure to space these late and larger cultivars 18 to 24 inches apart so they'll have room to reach their full potential size.

Fall

Plant living mulch. Sow low-growing clover, oats, or rye around fall cabbage crops after they are established. The living mulch will grow on after the harvest, and enrich the soil for the following year.

Cut back on water as late cabbages mature. Provide enough water to keep the soil moist, but cut back on both water and fer- tilizer as the plants mature to keep the heads from splitting. Overhead watering during peri- ods of high humidity or cool weather can cause diseases if the leaves have no chance to dry out.

Plant a winter-cabbage crop. In warm cli- mates, plant a winter-cabbage crop after the weather cools. It will be ready to harvest in late winter or early spring.

Clean up. Remove and destroy or compost all residues of cabbage-family crops to destroy overwintering sites for pests.

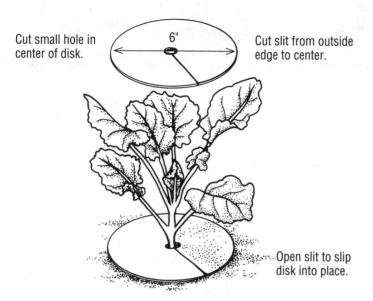

Cut small hole in center of disk.

6"

Cut slit from outside edge to center.

Open slit to slip disk into place.

Prevent root maggot problems. *Cabbage root flies lay eggs by the base of cabbage-family plants—the maggots then tunnel into the roots. Create a fly-proof barricade from a circular piece of thin cardboard.*

water flow to the head. This can hold off splitting for about one week. Heads that split are still edible but don't try to store them, as they will decay easily.

Use a sharp knife to cut the heads off just above the loose outer leaves, keeping just enough of these leaves to protect the head.

For the best flavor, harvest late cabbage after a few frosts but before a hard freeze.

Eat early cabbage, either raw or cooked, as soon as possible after harvest. You can store fresh cabbage heads up to two weeks in the refrigerator.

Storage-type cabbages will keep for several weeks in a covered pit like the one shown on the opposite page.

They will also keep two to three months in a cool, humid root cellar. The optimum temperature is just above 32°F with 90 percent humidity. Cut off all rotted or damaged outer leaves. Space heads so their leaves do not touch.

Extending the Season

The most obvious way to extend the cabbage harvest, if your climate allows, is to plant early, mid-season, and late crops. You can also stagger the plantings of a fresh-use, quick-growing cultivar at two- to three-week intervals, harvesting promptly at maturity.

Propagation

Cabbages don't flower and set seed until their second year. In most areas, you can overwinter cabbage plants for seed production in place in the garden. Mound soil around the stems or cover the plants with loose mulch to protect them.

In areas with severe winters, dig up the plants, put them in containers, and store them in a cool, humid place

Two harvests in one. *When you cut cabbage heads, try leaving at least 2 inches of stalk behind. Little side heads may form a tender and tasty second harvest. Eat them when small like brussels sprouts, or allow them to develop into small cabbages.*

The cabbage pit. *Late cabbage will store well in an outdoor pit for several weeks. Uproot plants and stack them upside down in a pit lined with straw or hay. Top with more straw or hay, then add a thin covering of soil.*

for the winter. Replant them outdoors in early spring.

Make a crisscross slash in the top of the head to help the flowerstalk emerge.

Collect seeds from the browning seed head. Properly stored seeds should last four years.

Cabbage will readily cross-pollinate with other cabbage cultivars and other cabbage-family crops. Separate your seed plants from other pollinators by at least 300 feet.

CHINESE CABBAGE

Want to try Chinese cabbage? Chances are, there are several types of Oriental cabbage-family plants that will grow well in your garden and add new tastes for your cooking. These Oriental cabbages require the same care as standard ball cabbage.

Sweet Chinese cabbage (*Brassica rapa* var. *chinensis*) is a barrel-shaped or cylindrical heading cabbage. It has large, crisp leaves that are good in salads and sautéed dishes, and also when cooked like greens.

Bok choy (*B. rapa,* Chinensis group), or pak choi, has loose, Swiss-chard-like, dark green leaves that cluster but don't form a head. Its leaves are edible, but it is grown primarily for its stalks. The stalks are a great addition to stir-fry dishes and an ingredient in chow mein. You can also eat raw bok choy stalks. Another plus for bok choy is its fast growth—it takes only about 45 to 50 days to mature.

Flat cabbage (*B. rapa* var. *rosularis*), or tatsoi, forms a rosette of dark green, spoon-shaped leaves, and is noted for its cold-hardiness.

In cool-summer areas, plant Oriental cabbages outdoors in early spring at the same time you plant lettuce. These crops are best grown direct from seed. Where summers are hot, Chinese cabbage is extremely likely to bolt (go to seed), so it is best to sow seeds in August into September as a fall crop. In the Deep South, grow it as a winter crop.

Harvest bok choy stalks and flat cabbage leaves as needed. As soon as there is a light frost, harvest the entire crop.

Solving Cabbage Problems

Use this table to identify problems on your cabbage-family crops. Scan the list of symptoms to find the description that most closely matches what you see in your garden. Then refer across the page to learn the cause and the recommended solutions. For many disease problems of cabbage-family crops, you'll need to plan a crop rotation with nonsusceptible crops. To learn more about crop rotation, see "Rotate Crops for Better Production" on page 45. For a schedule of other pest prevention measures for cabbage-family crops, see "Season-by-Season Care: Cabbage" on page 103. You'll also find illustrations, descriptions, and additional controls for many of the insects and diseases listed below in Part 5 of this book.

LEAF PROBLEMS

SYMPTOMS	CAUSES	SOLUTIONS
Large ragged holes in leaves; green caterpillars present	Imported cabbageworms Cabbage loopers	Handpick caterpillars. If many caterpillars are present, spray with BTK or neem. In the future, cover small plants with floating row cover from seedling stage onward.
Holes in leaves, with slime trails present	Slugs	Set out slug traps; check daily and destroy captured slugs. Spread a wide band of wood ash or natural grade diatomaceous earth around plants; renew the dust after each rain. Protect small plants with floating row cover, well secured at the edges.
Small round holes in leaves; small, jumping black insects may be seen	Flea beetles	Although seedlings may be seriously damaged, flea beetle injury has little effect on older plants. If damage is serious, spray rotenone or pyrethrins, and drench soil with parasitic nematodes to control beetle larvae. Next season, plan to cover seedlings with floating row cover.
Distorted leaves with light patches; tiny, powdery gray insects on leaf undersides	Cabbage aphids	Spray a strong stream of water to knock aphids off of plants; repeat weekly as needed. As a last resort, spray insecticidal soap, neem, or pyrethrins.
Silvery brown streaks and spots on leaves	Thrips	These insects are almost too small to see. If damage is severe, spray with neem or insecticidal soap, especially on leaf undersides. Dust natural grade diatomaceous earth at base of plant and on undersides of leaves. In the future, plan to sow thrips-tolerant cultivars.
Large, water-soaked patches coated with white mold on leaves	White rot (Sclerotinia)	Dig and destroy infected plants, including entire root. Remove and destroy all crop debris after harvest. The disease persists in the soil, so practice a 2-year rotation with nonsusceptible crops (beet, corn, onion, spinach).
Leaves with sunken gray areas dotted with black specks	Black leg	Affected plants eventually wilt and die. Pull and destroy all affected plants, disinfecting tools and hands before handling healthy plants. Replant in well-drained soil. In the future, practice a 4-year crop rotation.

SYMPTOMS	CAUSES	SOLUTIONS
Yellow spots on leaves, which turn brown; white mold under leaves	Downy mildew	Spray copper at first sign of disease. Pull and destroy severely infected plants. At end of the season, remove and destroy or till in crop debris.
Distinct gray spots with darker, concentric rings on lower leaves	Alternaria	This disease progresses from lower leaves to rest of head. Spray copper at first sign of infection. Remove and destroy all affected plants and all crop debris to eliminate disease overwintering sites.
Small, hard, light brown warts on leaf surface	Edema	Damage is cosmetic, and heads are edible. The condition usually occurs when nights are cool and days are warm and humid, which causes leaves to take up more water than usual, damaging leaf surface cells.
Yellow wedges on leaf margins; veins turning black	Black rot	Pull and destroy affected plants. In fall, remove crop debris to eliminate overwintering sites. In the future, use a 2-year crop rotation and plant black rot–tolerant cultivars.
Brown tips on leaves	High temperatures Calcium deficiency	Cabbages with tipburn are edible, but will not store well. If outer leaves are affected, high temperatures are likely the cause. In warm regions, plant cultivars adapted to high light and heat. If inner leaves are affected, poor calcium uptake may be the cause. Mulch around plants and keep plants well watered. For next season, ensure soil is fertile with adequate calcium levels.

WHOLE PLANT PROBLEMS

SYMPTOMS	CAUSES	SOLUTIONS
Stems of seedlings collapsed and dark at soil level; plants are stunted	Wirestem	Affected plants may survive but will be stunted. Heads will probably be small but are edible. Pull and destroy severely affected plants. Rotate future crops and plant in well-drained soil, enriched with compost.
Seedlings disappear	Slugs	Replant and set out slug traps. Check traps daily and destroy captured slugs. Spread wood ash or natural grade diatomaceous earth around seedlings; renew the dust after each rain. Protect seedlings with floating row cover, well secured at the edges. If slug problems are severe, start seedlings indoors to produce transplants large enough to withstand some damage when set out.
Stunted plants wilt in midday; roots gnarled with thickened galls	Club root	Pull and destroy severely affected plants. To salvage some harvest from surviving plants, side-dress with compost and keep plants well watered. Plan to rotate crops, with at least 2 years (preferably 7 years) between cabbage-family crops. Add lime to raise soil pH above 7.0. Disinfect tools after using them in infected soil.

(continued)

Solving Cabbage Problems—Continued

WHOLE PLANT PROBLEMS—CONTINUED

SYMPTOMS	CAUSES	SOLUTIONS
Stunted plants wilt in midday; roots are tunneled and rotting; tiny white maggots may be seen in roots	Cabbage root maggots	Pull and destroy seriously affected plants. Drench soil around roots with pyrethrins or parasitic nematodes to save less-damaged plants, which may produce small heads. In the future, put a cardboard disk around bases of transplants or wrap stems with paper for 1"–2" above and below soil line.
Stunted plants wilt in midday; hard, pea-size galls on roots	Root knot nematodes	Pull and destroy severely stunted plants. Pamper remaining plants to salvage some harvest. Rotate future crops with nonsusceptible plants. Solarizing soil will suppress nematodes. In some soils, digging in green manure crops may suppress nematodes.
Yellow leaves with purple edges; lower leaves drop; plants are stunted	Fusarium yellows	There is no cure for this disease; pull and destroy affected plants. The disease persists in soil for many years. Plan to rotate crops and plant Fusarium-tolerant cultivars. Solarizing the soil may help reduce the severity of the problem for future crops.
Cracked, rough, curling leaves; center of head hollow or rotting	Boron deficiency	Spray plants with liquid seaweed extract or boron foliar feed. Plan to have soil tested, and correct a boron deficiency by digging in kelp meal or watering with a borax solution (1 tbsp. borax to 1 gal. water per 100 sq. ft.) before planting next crop.
Broccoli and cauliflower plants form tiny, premature flower heads	Early exposure to cold	If spring-planted transplants are exposed to 10 or more days with temperatures below 50°F, they will produce tiny, "button" heads. Later plantings should not have this problem.
Broccoli and cauliflower with loose or irregular heads	Excessive heat	Heat stress can causing "ricing," or opening of flowers before heads are ready to harvest. Crops grown in cooler parts of the growing season will not have this problem.
Cabbage heads split	Excessive water uptake	Split heads are edible, but must be harvested immediately to avoid rotting. Harvest early cultivars as soon as heads are mature to avoid splitting. To prevent late-crop cabbage from splitting in fall rains, dig around plants or give each head a twist to break some roots. Where problem recurs, plant cultivars resistant to splitting.

CARROT *Daucus carota* var. *sativus* • Umbelliferae

Choosing Plants

The classic carrot types are Chantenay, Nantes, Danvers, and Imperator. New cultivars include round, bite-size, or finger-length carrots for handy snacking. You can select from early types (55 days to maturity) and late types (80 days). For fun and variety, try white, yellow, crimson, or purplish carrots.

Site and Soil

Carrots grow best in a deep, sandy loam. If you have heavier soil, plant short cultivars. Or plant in a raised

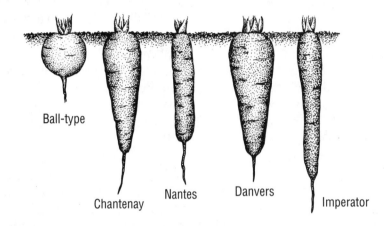

Carrot choices. Ball-type carrots are well suited for containers. Chantenay and heavy Danvers can form good roots even in heavy soils. Nantes are known for fine flavor. Long, slim Imperators need loose, deep, stone-free soil.

PLANTING FACTS

Seed and Seedling Identification

Seed Spacing

3–6 seeds per inch

←12"–14"→

For intensive spacing, plant seeds 3" apart on all sides.
Seed depth: $1/4$"–$1/2$"

bed or raised ridge like the one shown on page 110.

Carrots grow best with half a day of sun and will tolerate growing in light shade.

Work in 10 pounds of compost per 100 square feet to provide a balance of nutrients. Too much nitrogen produces soft, fork-rooted, poor-tasting carrots with rough skins. Rake the bed thoroughly and remove all stones and lumps to ensure that you create a fine seedbed.

Carrots are susceptible to soilborne problems, including carrot weevils, fungal leaf blight, root knot nematodes, and white mold. To reduce severity of these problems, don't replant carrots in the same spot every year; rotate their position in the garden.

Planting

When to plant. Plant an early crop as soon as the soil temperature reaches 45°F and the soil is dry enough to work. Then sow a fall crop, for both fresh eating and storage, in summer; harvest it just before the first frost.

Gardeners in mild-summer areas can have a constant carrot supply by sowing seed every three weeks until $2 1/2$ months before the first frost. In areas with hot summers, stick with spring and fall crops: carrots harvested in midsummer heat are likely to be bitter and resinous.

If carrot rust flies are a problem in your area, delay planting until summer. (You can plant in spring if you cover your carrot bed with floating row cover immediately after planting and leave the cover in place until harvest.)

How much to plant. At each seeding, plant 20 to 40 carrots per person for fresh eating. One-half ounce of carrot seeds, which averages 10,000 seeds, will plant about 300 feet of row.

Planting outdoors. Tiny carrot seeds need moisture to germinate but are easily washed away. Plant right after a heavy rain or after a good watering so the seeds can remain safely in place in already-moist soil.

See "Planting Facts" on page 109 for seeding and spacing information. Plant seeds deeper in warm soil or dry climates.

Carrot seed takes 7 to 20 days to germinate with a germination rate of 50 to 70 percent. Because carrots are so slow to come up, mix in radish or quick-maturing lettuce seeds to mark the rows. Thinning and harvesting the radishes and lettuce also will help keep the soil loose.

Thinning. When the carrot seedlings are 2 inches tall, thin them to 1 inch apart. Thin two weeks later, to 3 to 4 inches apart. An easy way to do your first thinning is to use a rake, as shown on the opposite page.

Seasonal Care

Spring

Apply parasitic nematodes to soil. If you had past problems with carrot rust flies or carrot weevils, drench the soil with parasitic nematodes before planting.

Cover seedbeds with floating row cover. If you've had past problems with aster yellows (spread by leafhoppers) or carrot rust flies, cover your crop with row cover from seeding until harvest.

Keep soil moist. Seedlings dry out and die easily. They also cannot poke through a soil crust. Water gently whenever the soil surface is dry.

Apply mulch. After seedlings emerge, mulch around them with 5 to 8 inches of grass clippings or hay. Gently hand-pull or clip

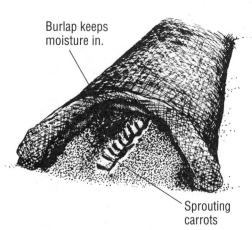

Burlap keeps moisture in.

Sprouting carrots

Raised ridges for carrots. If you don't have raised beds, try planting your carrots in raised ridges. Cover the ridges with wet burlap to help keep in the moisture carrots need for good germination.

> ### GREEN THUMB TIP
>
> Carrot seed can be slow to germinate. To speed germination, spread a layer of seed between two layers of damp paper towels and put it in the refrigerator. Check the seed daily. When white root tips appear, mix the seed with a little dry sand and sow it outdoors.

off weeds that come up near the seedlings.

Thin seedlings. Thin seedlings when they are 2 inches tall, and again two weeks later, to ensure good air circulation around plants and to allow room for roots to enlarge.

Summer

Hill up soil around base of plants. Exposure to light will make carrots bitter and cause the tops of the roots to turn green. Push up 2 inches of soil or mulch around plants to keep roots covered.

Water carefully. Once carrots have been thinned, cut back on water; too much can cause the roots to crack. If the soil dries out completely, gradually remoisten it over a period of several days. A sudden drenching can cause the roots to split.

Plant fall crops. Seed fall crops 85 to 100 days before the first expected fall frost.

Thin with a rake. *A quick way to make your first thinning of carrots is to draw a steel garden rake through the rows.*

Fall

Mulch late carrots. Freezing soil can crack and ruin roots. Apply 8 to 12 inches of mulch to keep soil from freezing.

Cultivate soil. If you've had past problems with wireworms, cultivate next year's carrot patch weekly four to six times in the fall to unearth and destroy wireworms.

Clean up. Remove all crop residues after harvest; destroy pest-ridden or diseased residues.

Harvesting

Begin harvesting carrots as soon as they are big enough to eat; their flavor develops more fully as they mature. With spring crops, pull the roots only as needed. However, don't leave your crop in the ground too long. Carrots left unharvested more than three weeks after they mature tend to be woody.

Leave fall crops in the ground until they are mature. Harvest them all at once, on a day when the ground is moist and the air is dry. (Water the bed to moisten the soil if it's dry.) Hand-pull the crop. If the roots don't pull out easily, carefully loosen the earth around them with a trowel before hand-pulling.

Store carrots for fresh eating in plastic bags in the refrigerator; they will last from three weeks up to three months. To store fall-crop carrots, twist off the tops and place the roots, so that they don't touch, in boxes between layers of moist sand or peat moss. Top them with a thick layer of straw. Carrots stored this way in a humid, cool place will last up to four months.

Extending the Season

Extend your carrot harvest by mulching late plantings with 8 to 12 inches of grass clippings or hay before the ground freezes. Stick in a tall stake as a marker so you can find the crop when it is covered by snow.

Growing in Containers

Small finger-size carrots and ball-shaped types grow well in containers. Some to consider are 'Lady Finger'; tender, 3½-inch 'Little Finger'; 'Tiny Sweet', just 3 inches long; and ball-shaped 'Planet' or 'Thumbelina'.

Plant carrot seeds in lightweight soil mix in an 8- to 12-inch-deep container. Place it in a sunny area. Thin the seedlings at least 2 inches apart.

Propagation

Saving seed from carrots isn't easy to do. Carrots are biennials, producing seed in the second year. You must overwinter plants for seed under mulch, or dig up and store the roots for replanting the second spring. To further complicate things, carrots cross-pollinate freely with other carrot cultivars and with the common weed called Queen Anne's lace. Commercial carrot seed producers separate their cultivars by at least one mile to prevent cross-pollination.

Solving Carrot Problems

To identify problems on your carrots, scan the list of symptoms to find the description that most closely matches what you see in your garden. Then look across the page for the cause and recommended solutions. If roots are damaged, there may be little you can do except search out undamaged portions to harvest. In the future, take preventive steps, like covering your plants with floating row cover to keep pests away. For a schedule of preventive measures, refer to "Seasonal Care" on page 110. You'll also find illustrations, descriptions, and additional controls for many of the problems listed below in Part 5 of this book.

SYMPTOMS	CAUSES	SOLUTIONS
Seedlings fail to appear	Crusted soil Seedling diseases High temperatures	Carrot seedlings can't break through a surface soil crust. Replant seeds ¼" deep, and keep soil moist. In heavy soils, plant radishes in carrot rows to break up crust. Cold, wet soils favor disease development. Reseed in well-drained soil when temperatures are warmer. Shade seedbeds for midsummer crops with burlap (remove at first sign of germination) or floating row cover (this can remain in place all season).
Tan or dark spots on leaves; spots may be ringed with yellow	Fungal leaf blight	Leaves only are infected; roots are edible. If infection is severe, spray copper. Destroy crop debris at end of season. Plan to rotate crops, leaving at least 3 years between carrot-family plants. In the future, plant leaf blight–tolerant cultivars.
Stunted, light yellow leaves; woody roots with tufts of white side roots	Aster yellows	Slightly affected plants may be edible. Leafhoppers spread this disease. There is no cure; therefore pull and destroy affected plants. Control leafhopper problems by spraying neem, insecticidal soap, or pyrethrins in evening.
Winding tunnels in upper part of roots, crown, and lower stems	Carrot weevils	Roots are usually ruined. If you can find any undamaged parts, they are edible. Drenching soil with parasitic nematodes may give some control.
Distorted roots with many forks, galls, and tufts of side roots	Root knot nematodes	Roots are edible though blemished, but will not keep in storage. In the future, practice at least a 2-year rotation with nonsusceptible plants (lettuce, onion, radish). In warm regions, solarizing the soil may reduce nematodes enough to allow good carrot crops.
Tunnels filled with brown, crumbly material in roots; white maggots in roots	Carrot rust flies	Undamaged parts of roots are edible, but they cannot be stored because maggots continue to feed in storage. Drenching soil with parasitic nematodes may give some control. Cover subsequent crops with floating row cover from seeding through harvest.
Roots twisted around each other	Overcrowding	Roots, though deformed, are edible and will store well. For the next crop, plan to thin seedlings as soon as plants are established, leaving 1"–3" between plants in the row.
Roots watery, dark brown, and rotted, with cottony white mold	White mold (Sclerotinia)	Dig and destroy infected roots. Destroy all crop debris after harvest. In the future, practice a 2-year rotation with nonsusceptible crops (beet, corn, onion, spinach). Plant in raised beds to ensure good drainage.

CAULIFLOWER *Brassica oleracea,* Botrytis group • Cruciferae

Crunchy cauliflower belongs to the same botanical family as cabbage. It requires similar care and is vulnerable to many of the same problems. Refer to "Cabbage" on page 100 for care information and solutions to pest problems.

Here you'll find information on choosing cultivars of cauliflower, as well as timing plantings, blanching heads, and harvesting.

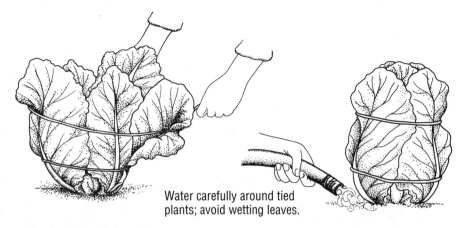

Water carefully around tied plants; avoid wetting leaves.

Blanching cauliflower. Unless you grow a self-blanching cultivar, you'll need to shield cauliflower heads from the sun to keep them white. When the heads are egg-size, fasten the leaves around the head with soft twine, rubber bands, or plastic tape. The leaves and heads must be dry when you wrap them. Unwrap the heads to check growth, or after a heavy rain to let them dry out.

Choosing Plants

Choose cultivars carefully to match your climate and season of planting. Fast-maturing cauliflower cultivars are a good choice for spring or late-summer planting if your area has hot summers. Choose cultivars that mature more slowly for summer growing in areas with cool summers or for winter growing in mild-winter areas.

Planting

When to plant. Start transplants indoors six weeks before you plan to plant them out. Direct-sow your fall crop two to three months before the first fall frost. In mild climates, plant in late autumn for early-spring harvests.

How much to plant. Grow five plants per person; twice that for winter preservation. A 100-foot row will produce 50 to 70 heads.

Planting outdoors. Set transplants out only after daytime temperatures are above 50°F. Extended exposure to cold causes tiny, premature heads, or "buttoning."

Harvesting

Harvest cauliflower heads when they're solid, before the curds begin to roughen and separate. Size depends on weather and cultivar and isn't a good way to judge maturity. Store heads wrapped in plastic in the refrigerator up to one week.

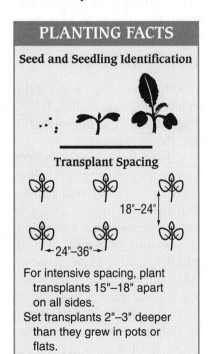

PLANTING FACTS

Seed and Seedling Identification

Transplant Spacing

18"–24"

24"–36"

For intensive spacing, plant transplants 15"–18" apart on all sides.
Set transplants 2"–3" deeper than they grew in pots or flats.

CELERY *Apium graveolens* var. *dulce* • Umbelliferae

Choosing Plants

Garden celery—which was developed from a wild marsh plant—will grow in most any garden if you make sure the soil is kept moist. Choose a heat-resistant cultivar if your springs warm up fast. Bolt-resistant cultivars are always a good choice. Choose an early-maturing cultivar if your spring and fall seasons are short.

Site and Soil

Celery needs rich, water-retentive soil and protection from dry heat. It will thrive in

PLANTING FACTS

Seed and Seedling Identification

Transplant Spacing

6"–8"
24"–36"

For intensive spacing, plant transplants 6"–12" apart on all sides.
Set transplants at the same depth as they grew in pots.

part shade as long as it gets at least half a day of sun. In hot areas it prefers partial shade; try planting it under taller plants.

Celery is a greedy feeder and needs rich soil. Prepare the site by spreading 10 to 20 pounds of compost per 100 square feet. Dig or till about 4 inches deep.

If your soil is clayey, build raised beds adding as much sand, compost, or leaf mold as you can get.

Planting

When to plant. Celery takes 80 to 120 days from seed to harvest. Plant in spring or late summer for fall harvest. Celery is a winter crop in the Deep South.

For a spring crop, start seedlings indoors eight to ten weeks before the last expected spring frost.

Start fall transplants indoors or in a cool, shady area of your garden about two months before you plan to move them to your garden.

How much to plant. Grow 6 plants per person. A 100-foot row will produce 65 plants.

Starting plants indoors. Soak seeds overnight in compost tea to encourage germination. Sow them $1/8$ inch

deep in individual pots or flats. Keep the temperature at 70°F in the daytime and 60°F at night. Keep the soil constantly moist. Once plants emerge, keep the daytime temperature between 65° and 75°F and the nighttime temperature between 60° and 65°F. When flat-grown plants are 4 inches tall, prick them out into pots.

Planting outdoors. Plant transplants out once the nights are consistently 40°F or more. Follow the spacing guidelines in "Planting Facts" on this page. Drench transplants and soil with compost tea. Spread 4 to 8 inches of organic mulch around them.

Seasonal Care

Whether you're growing celery in spring or fall, follow these basic care guidelines to get the best harvest.

Cover with floating row cover. Cover early plantings with row cover to prevent bolting (going to seed). If insect pests were a problem in previous seasons, cover all plantings and leave covered until harvest unless temperatures go above 75°F.

Fertilize. Mix 1 tablespoon of fish emulsion and 2 tablespoons of kelp extract per gallon of water and give each

BLANCHING CELERY

Soil or mulch. *Pile loose soil or mulch up around a single celery plant or a row of plants as they grow.*

Cans. *Blanch individual celery plants by slipping a large metal can with the ends cut out over each plant.*

Boards. *Push a board firmly up against a row of celery and secure it with stakes. Secure a second board on the other side.*

plant ½ cup once a week until they are 8 inches tall.

Water well. Celery insists on evenly moist, but not soggy, soil all season.

Blanch stalks. Even golden "self-blanching" cultivars are sweeter and more tender when blanched. Try one of the blanching methods illustrated on this page.

Harvesting

Cut outside stalks with a sharp knife as needed during the season, being careful not to uproot the plant. To harvest a whole plant, use a spade to cut the plant off just below the soil's surface.

Harvest all your celery before hard frost. Dig plants up, roots and all, and plant them in deep boxes of moist sand. Store the boxes in a cool place and your celery will keep for several months.

Extending the Season

To get a head start in the spring, prewarm the soil by covering it with black plastic for a few weeks. Once the soil temperature is 40°F, set out transplants and cover them with floating row cover until nighttime temperatures remain above 40°F.

Celery will tolerate cold down to about 25°F. Blanching structures give some frost protection. Cover fall crops with row cover and they will remain sound for at least a few extra weeks depending on your weather.

Harvesting celery. *Use a knife to harvest single stalks from the outside of the plant; cut whole plants free with a spade.*

Solving Celery Problems

Use this table to identify problems on your celery plants. Scan the list of symptoms to find the description that most closely matches what you see in your garden. Then refer across the page to learn the cause and the recommended solutions. For some problems, by the time you see the damage, there is little you can do to fix things on the current crop. In the future, take preventive steps such as planting bolt-resistant cultivars and rotating the position of your celery plants. You'll also find illustrations, descriptions, and additional controls for many of the insects and diseases listed below in Part 5 of this book.

SYMPTOMS	CAUSES	SOLUTIONS
Leaves distorted, sticky; small, green insects on plants	Aphids	Spray weekly with a strong stream of water into crowns to remove aphids. Spray severe infestations with insecticidal soap, neem, or pyrethrins.
Stunted, yellow plants; curled leaves; discolored crowns	Fusarium yellows	Pull and destroy affected plants. Solarize soil to reduce amount of disease in the soil. In the future, plant celery in another part of your garden and choose yellows-tolerant cultivars.
Plants stunted; leaf edges brown	Heat	Temperatures above 75°F can stunt celery. Shade plants and keep soil constantly moist. In the future, choose heat-resistant cultivars for summer crops.
Water-soaked, browned tips on youngest leaves; inner leaves and stalks turn black	Black heart (calcium deficiency)	Discard blackened sections of plants; the rest is edible. Mild cases can be salvaged by keeping soil evenly moist, but not soggy, for rest of the season.
Large holes chewed in leaves	Caterpillars	Handpick caterpillars. If damage is severe, spray BTK.
Small plants chewed off; holes in stalks	Slugs	Set out slug traps; check daily and destroy accumulated slugs. Spread wood ash or natural grade diatomaceous earth around plants, renewing the dust after each rain.
Seedstalks develop	Low temperatures	Celery bolts (goes to seed) if plants are exposed to temperatures below 40°F for 10 days or more. Harvest plants as soon as you notice seedstalks forming. In the future, choose bolt-resistant cultivars and delay planting out until weather is warm.
New growth distorted, yellow	Aster yellows	Harvest mildly affected plants immediately. Pull and destroy severely affected plants. If leafhoppers are numerous, spray plants with insecticidal soap or neem to slow spread of the disease.
Crowns and stems with slimy black or brown rot	Various diseases	Harvest undamaged parts of plant immediately. Destroy infected plant material and all crop debris after harvest. In the future, plant celery in another part of your garden.

COLLARD *Brassica oleracea, Acephala group • Cruciferae*

Hardy, nutritious collards belong to the same botanical family as cabbage. They require similar care and are vulnerable to many of the same problems. Refer to "Cabbage" on page 100 for care information and solutions to pest problems.

Here you'll find information on timing plantings, harvesting, and extending your season.

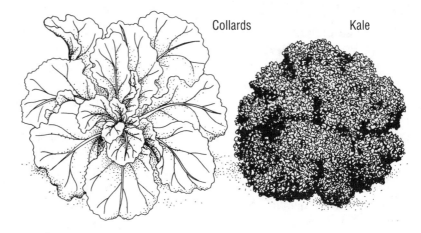

Collards   Kale

Collards and kale. *Both collards and curly kale are nonheading cabbages that make delicious cooked greens. Collards grow well in hot or cool weather, while kale prefers cool weather. You can even harvest kale from under a cover of snow.*

Planting

When to plant. Sow seed outdoors in spring when your soil temperature reaches 50°F. Plant fall crops three

PLANTING FACTS

Seed and Seedling Identification

Seed Spacing

1"

18"–36"

For intensive spacing, plant seeds 6"–12" apart on all sides.
Seed depth: ¼"–½"

months before your first expected frost. In the Deep South, plant in fall for winter harvest.

How much to plant. Grow 3 to 5 plants per person. A 100-foot row will produce 80 to 100 plants.

Planting outdoors. Sow seed ¼ to ½ inch deep in rows 18 to 36 inches apart. Thin plants to 1 to 2 feet apart; you can eat the tender thinnings. The wider the spacing between plants, the larger they will grow.

Harvesting

Start harvesting individual leaves from the base of the plants when the leaves are 8 to 12 inches long.

Extending the Season

For early-spring harvest, start transplants the same way you would cabbage transplants. Before you plant, prewarm the soil by covering it with black plastic for a few weeks. Then once the soil temperature reaches 50°F, set out transplants. Cover them with floating row cover until the chance of frost is past.

Collard plants will last well into the fall without any protection. In fact, light frost actually makes them sweeter. Covering the plants with row cover can extend your harvest even longer, perhaps through the winter.

CORN *Zea mays* • Gramineae

Choosing Plants

Home gardeners love sweet corn (*Zea mays* var. *rugosa*) for its ears of juicy, tender kernels. Dry corns are just as easy as sweet corn to grow. Popcorn (*Z. mays* var. *praecox*) makes a delicious low-calorie grow-your-own snack. Indian or flint corn (*Z. mays* var. *indurata*) is used for decorations and homemade cornmeal. Field or dent corn (*Z. mays* var. *indentata*) is also ground into cornmeal.

Choose yellow, white, or bicolor sweet corn cultivars that are suitable for your area. If your springs tend to be cold and damp, choose an early-maturing cultivar and plant once your soil warms up. Flavor and sweetness vary with cultivar. Standard sweet corn cultivars have the most intense "corny" flavor. Sugar-enhanced cultivars are sweeter and more tender than the standard sweet corn cultivars; super-sweet cultivars are sweeter still. Both stay sweet—without turning starchy—longer after harvesting.

If corn diseases are a problem in your area, consider choosing disease-resistant cultivars. Cultivars are available that resist bacterial wilt, corn leaf blight, corn smut, maize dwarf mosaic, and rust.

Site and Soil

Corn thrives in full sun and a rich loam soil with a pH of 5.5 to 6.8. Corn is a heavy feeder, so work in 20 to 30 pounds of compost per 100 square feet before planting. Prepare soil about 8 inches deep. Build raised beds or hills if the site is poorly drained.

Planting

When to Plant

Wait until your soil is at least 50°F (55°F for super-sweet cultivars) to plant corn in the spring. For continuous harvest, plant an early-season cultivar every two weeks until about ten weeks before the first predicted frost. Or try planting early-, mid-, and late-maturing cultivars at the same time in spring.

How Much to Plant

Grow at least 10 plants per person for fresh corn, 30 to 40 plants per person for frozen or canned corn. One corn plant normally produces two ears (dwarf cultivars may produce up to four ears). One 2-ounce packet of seed will cover 50 to 100 feet of row.

Planting Outdoors

Make a shallow furrow with your hoe blade and sow three seeds together every 8 to 12 inches, then cover with 1 to 2 inches of soil. Space rows 24 to 36 inches apart (24 inches for dwarf cultivars).

Plant a block of several short rows rather than one long row so the plants can pollinate each other.

All corn will pollinate each other if given the chance. This may result in color and texture changes in the kernels. If you're growing more than one cultivar or type of corn, stagger the planting dates or maturity dates so the corn won't be tasseling during the same two-week period. Or, if you have the

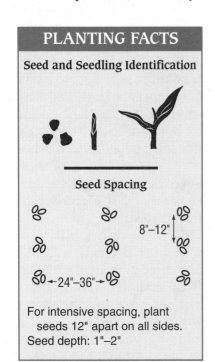

PLANTING FACTS

Seed and Seedling Identification

Seed Spacing

8"–12"

24"–36"

For intensive spacing, plant seeds 12" apart on all sides.
Seed depth: 1"–2"

CORN CARE TECHNIQUES

Hand-pollinating. *Wait until the tassels look loose and open and the pollen is just starting to shed. On a still morning, gently shake pollen from tassels into a paper bag. Mix the collected pollen; sprinkle a little on the silks of each developing ear.*

Controlling ear-worms with oil. *When silks start to turn brown, squirt several drops of mineral oil onto the tips of the ears.*

Controlling borers with granular BTK. *Sprinkle a few granules of BTK in the whorl of leaves to control European corn borers.*

Removing a corn earworm. *Pull the husk back to reveal the ear tip and dig the pest out with a knife. Gather the husk back around the ear and tape it shut.*

Hilling corn. *Use a hoe to push soil around the stalks when seedlings are about 6 inches high. Be careful not to damage the plants' shallow roots as you work.*

space, you can plant them at least 250 feet away from each other to prevent cross-pollination. This is especially important for super-sweet corn, which will be tough and starchy if it is pollinated by standard corn cultivars.

Try interplanting squash, pole beans, or other vining crops with your corn to save garden space.

Thinning

Thin standard-size cultivars in rows to 15 inches apart (8 inches between dwarf types). Snip extra seedlings off at ground level to avoid damaging nearby plants.

Seasonal Care

Once your corn takes off, you'll need to make sure it gets enough water to produce healthy ears of plump kernels. You'll also need to keep the patch free of weeds and fertilize periodically. For complete instructions, see "Season-by-Season Care: Corn" on the opposite page. If you have problems with your corn, refer to "Solving Corn Problems" on page 122 to identify the cause and find solutions.

Harvesting

Check sweet corn ears for ripeness when the silks have turned brown but are still damp to the touch. Pull back

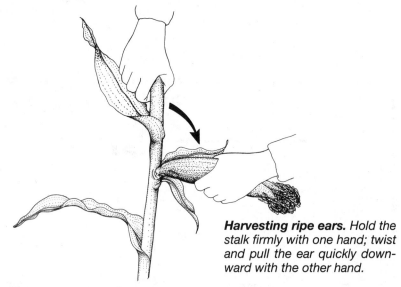

Harvesting ripe ears. Hold the stalk firmly with one hand; twist and pull the ear quickly downward with the other hand.

the husk of an ear part way and poke a kernel with your thumbnail. If the liquid that spurts out is clear, the corn isn't ready to pick yet. If the juice is milky, pick and eat it right away! If no liquid comes out, the corn is past its prime.

Pick sweet corn in the late afternoon and eat it immediately, before the sugar turns to starch. You can refrigerate standard cultivars for two or three days. Sugar-enhanced and super-sweet cultivars will keep in the refrigerator for up to a week or so. Can or freeze excess corn immediately after harvesting.

Leave dry corn ears on the stalk until the husks are dry and brown or until the first hard frost, then bring indoors to finish drying.

Extending the Season

To speed up the warming process in spring, cover the soil with black plastic a few weeks before planting, then protect young plants with floating row cover. If your growing season is very short, start seed indoors in peat pots about four weeks before setting out. Corn does not transplant easily, so handle the seedlings with care and keep them well watered during the adjustment to the garden.

Propagation

If you want to collect seed to sow for future crops, plant open-pollinated cultivars. Tie water-resistant bags (but not plastic) over the ears before the silks appear. When the tassels begin to shed pollen, remove the bags and hand-pollinate each ear. Replace the bags and leave them until the silks turn brown.

Choose well-formed ears to save, and mark them with string or yarn. Harvest when the husks are dry and brown or after the first hard frost. Pull the husks back and hang the ears indoors. Remove the kernels when they are completely dry.

SEASON-BY-SEASON CARE: CORN

This care guide tells you what to do and when to do it for your best corn crop ever. Because timing of certain tasks is critical, review all the instructions in this guide in late winter. Locate or buy the products you'll need in advance. To identify specific problems, refer to "Solving Corn Problems" on page 122. "Preventing Disease Problems" on page 210 explains how to mix and apply sprays. If you apply fungicides or insecticides, only spray affected plants.

Spring

Warm soil with black plastic. Cover soil with plastic a few weeks before planting time to get an early start on the season. Once soil temperature is 50°F, remove plastic and plant.

Apply parasitic nematodes. If corn rootworms, cutworms, or wireworms were a problem previously, drench the soil with parasitic nematodes a few weeks before planting.

Cover seedbed with floating row cover. If daytime temperatures are cool or if corn earworms, European corn borers, maize dwarf mosaic, slugs, Stewart's wilt, or stunt were a problem in the past, cover seedbeds with row cover. If the cover is large enough, you can leave it in place until tassels shed pollen.

Fertilize. When the first leaves emerge, water with compost tea. Repeat weekly for three to four weeks. Spray plants with kelp just before the silks peek out of the young ears.

Hang pheromone traps. If you've had serious problems with worms in ears of corn, hang corn earworm, European corn borer, or fall armyworm traps when plants are 1 foot high or when you remove floating row cover. Spray plants with rotenone-pyrethrins or ryania weekly as long as new moths are caught.

Hill up. Hill soil up around the stalks when the plants are 6 inches high and again when they are 1 foot high, as shown on page 119.

Mulch. After hilling, spread 6 to 8 inches of organic mulch. Or broadcast clover seed under the corn to form a living mulch.

Summer

Scout for insect damage. Check the top leaves for small round holes at least twice a week. If you find holes, spray plants with BTK weekly as long as new holes appear. Or, for European corn borers, sprinkle granular BTK in the whorl of leaves at the growing tip.

Hand-pollinate. If you have a very small corn patch, hand-pollinate twice, two days apart, as shown on page 119.

Pest-proof ears. If you've had past problems with worms in corn ears, squirt a few drops of mineral oil or parasitic nematodes into the tip of each ear after the silk turns brown.

If birds have been a problem, cover each ear with a paper bag after the silk turns brown, or wrap the tip end of the husk with fiberglass-reinforced strapping tape. If raccoons have been a problem, wrap the tip end of the ear with the tape, then loop the tape around the stalk and back to the ear.

Harvest. Check daily for mature ears once the silks begin to turn brown.

Clean up. After harvest is finished, chop up and compost the stalks. Remove and destroy diseased or insect-infested plants.

Fall

Harvest. If you're growing popcorn or other dry corn, pick the ears when the husks are dry and brown or after the first hard frost.

Clean up. After the stalks of late plantings have winter-killed, cut them up and add them to the compost pile or till them under. Remove and destroy diseased or insect-infested plants.

Solving Corn Problems

Use this table to identify problems on your corn. Scan the list of symptoms to find the description that most closely matches what you see in your garden. Then refer across the page to learn the cause and the recommended solutions. For some problems, by the time you see the damage, there is little you can do to save your crop. In the future, your best choices are to plant problem-resistant cultivars whenever possible, encourage native beneficial insects, and rotate your corn patch to a new location each year. For a schedule of other pest prevention measures for corn, see "Season-by-Season Care: Corn" on page 121. You'll also find illustrations, descriptions, and additional controls for many of the insects and diseases listed below in Part 5 of this book.

LEAF AND STALK PROBLEMS

SYMPTOMS	CAUSES	SOLUTIONS
Seedlings do not appear	Cold soil Soil-dwelling insects	Replant when soil is at least 50°F. If soil is warm, culprit may be wireworms or seed-corn maggots. Drench soil with parasitic nematodes and replant, or replant in a new site.
Seedlings chewed off or girdled at soil level	Cutworms	Search for and destroy cutworms hiding in the soil around base of damaged plants. If damage is severe, replant and sprinkle bran mixed with BTK between hills.
Holes in leaves of seedlings; seedlings may disappear	Slugs	Set out slug traps; check daily and destroy trapped slugs. Replant and spread a wide band of wood ash or natural grade diatomaceous earth around plants, renewing the dust after each rain.
Seedlings or older plants stunted and wilted; white larvae feeding on roots	Corn rootworms	Mildly damaged plants may survive. Drench soil around plants with parasitic nematodes to suppress rootworms. Salvage what you can from the planting, and destroy all crop debris after harvest. Replant in a new area or after drenching soil with parasitic nematodes.
Top leaves of untasseled plants with small, round holes	European corn borers	Leaf damage is rarely damaging, but later generations will bore into stalks and ears. Spray plants (tops and undersides) weekly with BTK as long as new damage appears on leaves.
Leaves of plants streaked; plants stunted and bushy	Maize dwarf mosaic	Pull and destroy infected plants. In the future, plant resistant cultivars and control aphids to prevent them from spreading the disease.
Yellow and red streaks on leaves; plants stunted and bushy	Corn stunt	Pull and destroy infected plants. This disease is spread by leafhoppers. In the future, control leafhoppers by spraying insecticidal soap, neem, or pyrethrins.
Leaves with wavy edges and yellow stripes	Bacterial wilt (Stewart's wilt)	Pull and destroy affected plants. In the future, control flea beetles to prevent them from introducing the disease.

SYMPTOMS	CAUSES	SOLUTIONS
Leaves with gray-green or tan spots	Corn leaf blight Fungal leaf spot	Spray plants with sulfur. Respray every 2 weeks as long as new spots appear.
Leaves with small brown dots on top and underside	Rust	Spray plants with sulfur. Respray every 2 weeks as long as new dots appear.
Leaves skeletonized by shiny bronze beetles	Japanese beetles	In early morning, knock beetles from plants into a bucket of soapy water or onto a tarp and destroy them. For severe infestations, spray with pyrethrins or rotenone.
Stalks break off; entry holes in stalks; caterpillars inside stalks	Stalk borers Corn borers	Pull up and shred infested plants. Plant future crops in a new area; plant borer-tolerant cultivars if available.

EAR AND KERNEL PROBLEMS

SYMPTOMS	CAUSES	SOLUTIONS
Silks chewed off; brown insects with pincers present	Earwigs	These insects are normally beneficial, but occasionally they chew corn silk. If damage is severe, lay rolled-up newspapers among plants; earwigs will hide in the newspapers. Once a day, shake earwigs out of the newspaper traps and destroy them.
Silks and kernels eaten; caterpillars usually present	Corn earworms European corn borers	Undamaged portion of ear is edible. Open tip of husks on developing ears and dig out any caterpillars before they cause further damage.
Some or all kernels fail to develop	Poor pollination Nutrient deficiencies Drought Insects	Partially filled ears are still good to eat once developed kernels are ripe. Plant future crops in blocks to ensure good pollination. Also be sure to fertilize adequately, maintain soil moisture, and control insect pests that feed on silks.
Kernels replaced by large, fleshy galls filled with black powder	Corn smut	Remove and destroy deformed ears or galls anywhere on plant as soon as you see them. Remove and destroy garden debris after harvest. Avoid planting corn in this site for 5–7 years.
Husks torn open; kernels pecked	Birds	To prevent further damage of developing ears, cover each with a paper bag or wrap tip end of husks with fiberglass-reinforced strapping tape to keep them closed.
Husks torn open; entire ears missing	Raccoons	Wrap tip end of remaining ears twice around with fiberglass-reinforced strapping tape, then loop tape around stalk and back to ear to frustrate raccoons.

CUCUMBER *Cucumis sativus* • Cucurbitaceae

Cool cucumbers belong to the same botanical family as squash. They require the same site and soil conditions and are vulnerable to many of the same problems. Refer to "Squash" on page 170 for site and soil requirements and solutions to specific problems. Here you'll find general care instructions.

Hill planting. *Plant seeds in a central hill and thin to three plants per hill. The vines will spread in all directions.*

Choosing Plants

The most familiar cucumbers are the dark green slicers, but there are also light green (Armenian), yellow (lemon), and white cultivars. The "burpless" cultivars

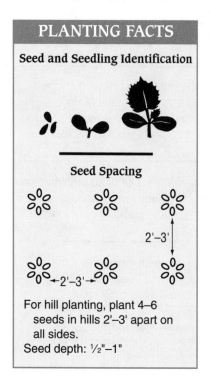

PLANTING FACTS

Seed and Seedling Identification

Seed Spacing

2'–3'

←—2'–3'—→

For hill planting, plant 4–6 seeds in hills 2'–3' apart on all sides.
Seed depth: ½"–1"

may be easier for some people to digest.

Nonbitter cultivars are less prone to becoming bitter when drought strikes and are less attractive to cucumber beetles. Choose disease-resistant cultivars if cucumber mosaic virus or mildew has been a problem.

Gynoecious cultivars, which bear only female flowers, have higher yields than standard cucumbers. They tend to bear all their fruit at once. A few seeds of a standard cultivar will be included in the seed packet to pollinate all those female flowers.

You can grow seedless greenhouse-type cultivars outdoors, but they will develop seeds unless you prevent pollination (by insects). Cover the plants with floating row cover before they flower and leave it on through harvest.

You can make pickles with young slicing cucumbers, but

if you want to make a lot of pickles, choose a pickling cultivar. Tiny pickled cucumbers are called gherkins, but true gherkins (*Cucumis anguria*) are actually a different, closely related plant. Grow them like cucumbers and pickle the small, prickly fruits.

Planting

When to plant. Direct-sow cucumbers when all danger of frost has past. Both the soil and the average air temperature should be at least 60°F.

For a continuous supply of cucumbers, make a second planting five weeks after the first and a third planting three weeks later (if you still have eight frost-free weeks left).

How much to plant. Grow 1 or 2 cucumber plants per person. Fifteen to 20 plants of picklers will yield about 24 pints.

Planting outdoors. Plant outdoors three to four weeks after the last frost date. See "Planting Facts" on the opposite page for spacing recommendations.

Thinning. To avoid disturbing roots, use scissors to snip off extra seedlings. For row plantings, thin to one plant per foot. In hills, thin to three plants per hill.

Seasonal Care

Follow these care guidelines for early, mid-season, and late plantings to get maximum yields.

Cover with floating row cover. Protect early-season plantings from cool temperatures with row cover or cloches. Cover all plantings if you have had problems with cucumber beetles. Remove covers when flowers appear.

Fertilize. Give each plant a cup of compost tea or fish fertilizer every week until the first flowers form. Spray plants with kelp when the first blossoms appear.

Water. Keep the soil moist at all times or your cucumbers will produce poorly formed, unappetizing fruit.

Mulch. Apply an 8- to 10-inch layer of clean straw when the seedlings are about 1 foot long.

Harvest regularly. Once plants start to bear, check them daily for harvestable fruit. Fruit left on the vine too long may become bitter and will depress production of more fruit.

Clean up. Once production drops off, pull up plants and add them to the compost pile or till them under.

Harvesting

Cucumbers are ready to harvest in 50 to 70 days. Begin picking as soon as the fruits are large enough and before the seeds start to harden. To avoid injuring the vines, clip off the fruit. Harvest frequently—daily for pickling types—to keep the vines productive. Remove any overripe fruit immediately. You can refrigerate cucumbers for one to two weeks.

Extending the Season

To get a head start on the season, cover the soil with black plastic several weeks before planting. Cut holes in the plastic when you are ready to plant seeds or transplants.

For the biggest jump, start with transplants. Sow seeds indoors three weeks before your last expected frost. Sow seeds $1/2$ inch deep, two to a pot. The air temperature should be 70° to 85°F; don't let it drop below 60°F at night. Thin to one seedling when the first leaves appear.

Set out transplants one week after the last frost, and cover with cloches.

TRELLISING CUCUMBERS

Twine

5'

4'–5'

Fence-post-and-wire trellis

A-frame trellis made from scrap lumber or bamboo poles

Simple trellises. For healthy fruit and efficient use of garden space, plant cucumbers next to a fence or train them up a trellis.

EGGPLANT *Solanum melongena* var. *esculentum* • Solanaceae

Glossy eggplants are in the same family as tomatoes, peppers, and potatoes. They are even more sensitive to cold than tomatoes but need the same site and soil preparation and are prone to many of the same problems. Refer to "Tomato" on page 180 for site and soil requirements and solutions to specific problems.

Choosing Plants

Eggplants range in color from deep purple or black to lavender to white. There are also yellow, red, and even green eggplants. Fruits may be round, oval, or elongated; bite-size to huge.

Choose early-bearing types if you have a short growing season. If you've had past problems with tobacco mosaic virus on any tomato-family plants in your garden, look for eggplant cultivars that resist the virus.

Planting

When to plant. Heat-loving eggplants require a long, warm growing season. Start seedlings indoors six to eight weeks before your last expected frost.

How much to plant. Grow two or three plants for each person in your family. One 0.25-gram packet (50 to 60 seeds) will produce enough plants to cover at least 100 feet of row.

Starting plants indoors. Soak seeds in compost tea for 15 minutes or overnight to speed germination and reduce disease problems. Plant seeds ¼ inch deep in a soilless medium such as vermiculite. The soil temperature must be at least 70°F; 85°F is ideal. Seeds germinate in 5 to 12 days.

Seedlings thrive in full sun and air temperatures above 70°F. When the first true leaves appear, move

Preheat the soil. *Spread black plastic a few weeks before you plant to warm the soil. Cut slits in the plastic and insert transplants.*

flat-sown seedlings to individual pots.

Planting outdoors. Transplant seedlings when the soil is at least 60°F and the air temperature is consistently above 70°F. Put 1 cup each of kelp meal and bonemeal in each planting hole. See "Planting Facts" on this page for suggested spacing. Water plants in with compost tea.

Seasonal Care

Follow these care guidelines to produce vigorous plants and good-size fruits.

Cover soil with black plastic. Several weeks before transplanting, use black plastic to speed soil warming.

Cover plants with floating row cover. Protect transplants

PLANTING FACTS

Seed and Seedling Identification

Transplant Spacing

18"–24"

24"–36"

For intensive spacing, plant transplants 18" apart on all sides.

Set transplants with first true leaves at soil level.

from cool weather or Colorado potato beetles, flea beetles, and other pests by covering the plants with row cover. Remove cover once night temperatures are consistently warm or plants are too large to fit under cover.

Fertilize. Give each plant 1 cup of compost tea or fish fertilizer every week until the first blossoms appear.

Water. Keep the soil moist, but not soggy, at all times.

Mulch. If you didn't plant through black plastic, apply 8 to 10 inches of straw when the soil is thoroughly warm.

Stake. If your plants get top-heavy, insert stakes to keep them upright.

Plant in Wallo Water. *Eggplants sulk at the slightest draft. Wallo Water releases stored heat at night and blocks chilly winds.*

Clean up. Once frost kills the plants, till them under or pull them up and add them to the compost pile.

Harvesting

Eggplant is ready to pick 55 to 70 days after transplanting. Begin harvesting when the fruit is large enough to use but before the seeds start to harden. The skin should be glossy; fruit that looks dull is usually past prime. Hold the fruit with one hand while cutting the stem with a sharp knife or pruning shears. Pick often to keep the plants productive.

For best taste, cook immediately after harvesting. You can refrigerate eggplant for up to two weeks.

Extending the Season

Eggplants thrive in heat and sulk in cool weather. Prewarm soil with black plastic. Cover plants with floating row cover and use Wallo Water to give transplants extra heat. Or make a minigreenhouse over your eggplants with hoops and slitted clear plastic row cover. Use it in early summer and early fall or whenever daytime temperatures are less than 80°F. If your summers aren't hot, you may leave it on all season.

Harvesting eggplant. *Support the fruit with one hand and cut the stem with a knife.*

Bury edge of plastic in soil.   Metal, fiberglass, or plastic hoop

Make a mini hoop house. *If your daytime temperatures are less than 80°F, keep your plants under a mini hoop house to increase yields. Buy slitted row cover or use clear plastic and cut two rows of closely spaced slits near the peak.*

KALE *Brassica oleracea,* Acephala group • Cruciferae

Hardy, nutritious kale belongs to the same botanical family as cabbage. Kale can survive heat, but hot weather makes it tough and bitter. It likes semishade in hot, sunny climates and thrives in cloudy climates. Refer to "Cabbage" on page 100 for care information and solutions to pest problems.

Here you'll find information on choosing cultivars, timing plantings, harvesting, and extending your season.

Preparing kale. *Kale's stems and midribs can be tough, so cut them out before eating. Chop the leaves and add them to salads, cook them like spinach, or use them in stir-fries or soup.*

Choosing Plants

Hardy, nutritious kale survives winters as far north as Zone 5. Select cultivars with thick, crinkled leaves.

Ornamental kale cultivars come in attractive shades of cream, pink, and purple. They are mild tasting and make attractive garnishes as well as colorful additions to your fall and winter garden.

Planting

When to plant. Where summers are cool, plant in early spring as soon as the soil is at least 50°F. For a fall and winter crop, sow seed six weeks before the first frost. Frost improves kale's taste, and fall crops are less likely to be bothered by pests than spring-grown kale.

How much to plant. Grow two to five plants per person. One-eighth of an ounce of seed will plant a 50-foot row.

Planting outdoors. Sow seed according to the guidelines in "Planting Facts" on this page. Thin seedlings to 8 to 12 inches apart.

Harvesting

Once leaves reach 8 inches in length, harvest individual outer leaves as needed. Harvest lower leaves first. Kale will keep up to two weeks in the refrigerator.

Extending the Season

Kale will withstand freezing temperatures and light snow. If severe cold threatens, cover plants with straw or floating row cover to protect them and stretch your harvest season even longer.

PLANTING FACTS

Seed and Seedling Identification

Seed Spacing

1"

←—— 18"–36" ——→

For intensive spacing, plant seeds 15"–18" apart on all sides.
Seed depth: ¼"–½"

KOHLRABI *Brassica oleracea*, Gongylodes group • Cruciferae

Kohlrabi's mild, sweet taste is a mix of turnip and cabbage. Kohlrabi belongs to the same botanical family as cabbage and is more tolerant of heat than most other cabbage-family plants. Refer to "Cabbage" on page 100 for care information and solutions to pest problems.

Here you'll find information on choosing cultivars, timing plantings, harvesting, and extending your season.

Choosing Plants

Look for crack-resistant, nonfibrous cultivars. Purple kohlrabi, with its colorful skin and pale green flesh, makes a nice addition to raw vegetable trays.

Planting

When to plant. Plant seed as soon as the soil reaches 50°F in spring. In areas with long, cool growing seasons, replant every 2 weeks until the end of May. Sow seed again 10 to 12 weeks before the average date of the first fall frost. In mild-winter regions, grow as a fall, winter, and spring crop.

How much to plant. Grow 10 to 20 plants per person. One packet of seed will plant a 100-foot row.

Planting outdoors. Plant seed according to the guidelines in "Planting Facts" on this page. When seedlings are 4 inches tall, thin to 3 to 6 inches apart.

Harvesting

Harvest kohlrabi "bulbs" before they get large and possibly woody and bitter. Use clippers or a sharp knife to cut the stem just below the "bulb" and trim the top off. You can also eat the leaves raw or cooked.

Kohlrabi will stay fresh in the refrigerator for one week. It will keep for several months packed in moist sand or sawdust in a cool, moist basement or root cellar.

Harvesting kohlrabi. *For crisp, tender kohlrabi "bulbs," harvest the stems when they are 1½ to 2 inches in diameter, or about the size of a silver dollar.*

Extending the Season

For early-spring harvest, start transplants as you would cabbage. Prewarm the soil by covering it with black plastic for a few weeks. Once the soil temperature reaches 50°F, set transplants outdoors. Cover them with floating row cover until chance of frost is past.

Protect fall crops with row cover to extend your fall harvest.

PLANTING FACTS

Seed and Seedling Identification

Seed Spacing

1"–1½"

12"–18"

For intensive spacing, plant seeds 4"–8" apart on all sides.
Seed depth: ¼"–½"

LEEK *Allium ampeloprasum,* Porrum group • Liliaceae

Elegant leeks, the sweetest and the most delicately flavored members of the onion family, are quite cold-hardy. Their care is similar to onions, but they are usually blanched to keep their fleshy stems white. Refer to "Onion" on page 142 for site and soil recommendations, seasonal care suggestions, and solutions to specific problems.

Choosing Plants

Choose early-maturing cultivars if your growing season is short. Choose storage types for winter use.

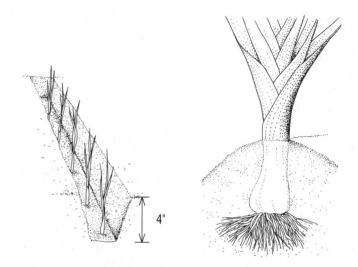

Blanching leeks. *Make blanching easier by planting your leeks in the bottom of a narrow trench. Once they are growing vigorously, gently fill in the trench with soil. Every few weeks, hoe another inch of soil up around the leeks until the hill is 6 to 8 inches above the soil surface.*

PLANTING FACTS

Seed and Seedling Identification

Transplant Spacing

6"

←1'–2'→

For intensive spacing, plant transplants 6" apart on all sides.

Set transplants in 2"-deep holes in the bottom of a 4"-deep planting trench.

Planting

When to plant. Start transplants 12 weeks before the last expected frost. Direct-plant seeds as soon as the soil is at least 40°F. Direct-plant winter crops in late summer.

How much to plant. Ten leeks per person is usually adequate. One packet will plant a 25-foot row.

Starting plants indoors. Sow seed thinly in flats. Keep the temperature at 65° to 70°F during the day and 55° to 60°F at night. Thin seedlings to 2 inches apart.

Planting outdoors. Dig 4-inch-deep trenches spaced 1 to 2 feet apart. Set seedlings in 2-inch-deep holes spaced 6 inches apart in the bottom of the trenches. Or you can plant seeds ¼ inch deep in the bottom of the trenches. Thin seedlings to 6 inches apart.

Harvesting

Pull or dig individual leeks as needed. Refrigerate for a few weeks or store in moist sand for two months.

Extending the Season

Leeks can stay in the ground all winter if temperatures stay above 10°F.

LETTUCE *Lactuca sativa* • Compositae

Choosing Plants

Red or green, crunchy or melting, frilly or flat—lush lettuce is anything but boring. You can choose conventional "iceberg" lettuce or a mix of gourmet leaf lettuces—or try some of both.

Batavian. Also known as summer crisp or French crisp lettuce, this distinctive group is crisp like romaine or crisphead types. Batavians are sweet and juicy—never bitter. They are heat-tolerant and resist bolting (going to seed); you can grow the same cultivars spring, summer, and fall.

Butterhead. For great taste and melting texture, try butterhead, also known as bibb or Boston, lettuce. It is almost as easy to grow as leaf lettuce and far easier than crisphead types. For best results, choose different cool-season and summer cultivars.

Crisphead. Also known as "iceberg" lettuce, crisphead lettuce is the most challenging type to grow and contains fewer vitamins than other types do. It requires a long growing season and rich soil.

Leaf. Loose-leaf lettuce is the fastest-maturing type of lettuce. For best results, choose different cultivars for cool- and warm-season crops.

Romaine. Easy-to-grow romaine or cos lettuce has crunchy, spoon-shaped, nutritious leaves. Some cultivars will grow in spring, summer, and fall—others do best in either cool or summer conditions. Select cultivars to match your needs.

Site and Soil

Lettuce will grow in full sun to part shade. It isn't fussy about soil as long as it is well drained and the pH is between 6.0 and 6.8.

Till or dig 4 inches deep and work in 40 pounds of compost

Butterhead lettuce. *Butterheads form soft green or red heads with white to yellowish hearts.*

Crisphead lettuce. *This familiar lettuce type comes in a range of colors from scarlet to pale green.*

Loose-leaf lettuce. *Colors and textures vary from ruby to greenish yellow and smooth to frilly.*

Romaine lettuce. *Romaine heads have a distinctive vase shape.*

PLANTING FACTS

Seed and Seedling Identification

Seed Spacing

1"

12"–18"

For intensive spacing, plant seeds 9"–12" apart on all sides.
Seed depth: $1/8$"–$1/4$"

per 100 square feet. Prepare raised beds if your soil is not well drained because lettuce is much more prone to disease problems when grown in poorly drained soil.

Planting

When to Plant

Start extra-early crops indoors eight weeks before the last expected frost and transplant them outside under cloches or floating row cover four weeks before the last expected frost.

Lettuce seed will germinate (slowly) when soil temperatures are as low as 35°F. Direct-seed outdoors as early as six weeks before the last expected frost under row cover or two to four weeks before the last expected frost without cover.

Make small plantings every two weeks all spring and summer for continuous harvest through fall or beyond.

How Much to Plant

Plant about 2 feet of row or eight plants per person every two weeks if you want lettuce daily for salads. One-fourth ounce of seed will plant a 100-foot row and produce around 100 heads.

Starting Plants Indoors

Start plants indoors for earlier harvests or to outwit slugs and to save thinning time on later crops. Sow seeds thinly in flats. Keep the temperature between 50° and 60°F. If the temperature is too warm, seedlings will become weak and spindly, won't form heads, and will become bitter. Thin plants to 2 inches apart each way. Harden off seedlings when they reach 3 to 4 inches tall.

Planting Outdoors

Seeds. Broadcast seed and rake the bed gently to cover it, or plant in rows, as shown in "Planting Facts" on page 131.

Transplants. Spacing depends on the harvest size of your cultivar. Follow packet recommendations or in general: Set romaine and crisphead transplants 12 to 16 inches apart, butterhead and batavian transplants 8 to 10 inches apart, and loose-leaf transplants 12 to 15 inches apart. Water transplants immediately with compost tea or fish fertilizer.

Thinning

Thin broadcast beds by pulling a metal rake over the surface when the plants have one true leaf, as shown in the illustration on page 111. Hand-thin seedlings when they have four true leaves to

Lettuce 'Green Ice' April 1

Lettuce 'Green Ice' April 15

Spreading the harvest. *Don't make the common mistake of planting a whole packet of lettuce seed at once in early spring. Make small successive plantings of a few feet of*

the same spacings as recommended for transplants.

Seasonal Care

Follow the guidelines below to harvest your best lettuce crop ever. Good care, especially vigilant watering, will result in a more bountiful harvest. If your plants have problems, see "Solving Lettuce Problems" on page 135 for a rundown of symptoms, causes, and solutions.

Spring and Summer

Start transplants indoors. For the earliest crops, start plants indoors. Select cold-tolerant cultivars for early-spring planting, and cover them with floating row cover to prevent frost damage.

Plant for late-spring and summer harvest. Plant cool-season cultivars in early spring. Choose heat-tolerant, bolt-resistant cultivars for late-spring and summer plantings.

Cover with floating row cover. If insects, insect-spread diseases, slugs, or rabbits have been a problem in the past, cover seedbeds or transplanted seedlings with row cover. You can leave the cover on right through harvest.

Fertilize. Water plants with compost tea or fish emulsion once a week until they are 4 inches tall. Also spray plants once with kelp if they are not growing in nutrient-rich soil.

Water. Keep soil moist, but not soggy, at all times. Avoid wetting leaves, or water in the morning so leaves will dry before nightfall.

Weed. Pull weeds carefully to avoid damaging the crop's shallow roots.

Thin. Thin plants so they don't touch one another to increase air circulation and prevent disease.

Mulch. When plants are 4 to 6 inches tall, apply a thick layer of organic mulch to keep the soil moist, discourage weeds, and keep the leaves free of dirt.

Shade summer lettuce. Hot weather (especially 80°F and over) can make lettuce bolt and become bitter. Grow between or under larger plants or shade your plantings with shade cloth stretched over hoops, as shown on page 134.

To encourage lettuce seed to germinate in hot weather, lay a piece of lumber directly on the ground over the seedbed. As soon as the seeds start to sprout, protect the new seedlings by suspending the board on cinder blocks over the bed for a few weeks, as shown on this page.

Lettuce 'Green Ice' April 29

Lettuce 'Green Ice' May 13

row every two weeks instead. Shade late plantings with a board supported on cinder blocks to keep tender, young seedlings from getting baked by the sun.

Shading summer lettuce.
Midsummer crops may need shading throughout their growth. Use commercial hoops or a homemade wooden frame to support shade cloth.

Plant for fall harvest. As summer starts to cool down, choose cool-season cultivars again.

Fall

Plant for winter harvest. Plant cold-hardy cultivars in your cold frame four weeks before your first expected frost to extend your lettuce harvest into winter.

Cover with floating row cover. When the first freeze threatens, cover plants with row cover.

Clean up. Remove and compost all crop debris.

Harvesting

To preserve crispness, pick lettuce in the early morning. Lettuce quality deteriorates quickly, so don't delay in harvesting mature plants.

Once lettuce starts to bolt, it gets bitter; pull and compost bolting plants.

Shear rows or patches of young leaf lettuce with scissors. The plants will resprout for additional harvests. Harvest the outer leaves from larger plants and let the inner ones grow, or cut entire plants as needed.

You can pick individual outer leaves of batavian, butterhead, and romaine lettuces or harvest entire plants with a sharp knife. Harvest crisphead types when their centers feel firm when you press down gently on them with the back of your hand.

Leaf lettuce wilts quickly and is best eaten fresh picked. To refrigerate leaf lettuce, first rinse it in cool water. Shake off the excess water, and seal lettuce in a plastic bag with a moist paper towel. Head-type lettuces will keep from one to two weeks in the refrigerator, wrapped in a towel inside a plastic bag.

Extending the Season

Make small plantings every two weeks from early spring through late summer for a continuous supply of tender, sweet lettuce.

Speed early crops by starting transplants indoors and planting them out under floating row cover.

Extend your harvest by covering plants or making a late planting in a cold frame.

Growing in Containers

Lettuce is a great container plant if you are dedicated to keeping the soil moist. Use a large container and plant one-quarter of it every two weeks, or use four smaller containers to provide lettuce all season. In hot weather, provide partial shade to help keep the containers cool.

Propagation

Choose open-pollinated or nonhybrid cultivars. Save seed from the *last* plants of each cultivar to bolt. Saving seed from the first plants to bolt may yield quick-bolting offspring.

Lettuce is generally self-pollinated but cultivars occasionally cross with each other. Make sure only one cultivar is in bloom at a time or separate cultivars with a row of a tall crop. Cut a cross in the top of headed types to help the seedstalk emerge.

Lettuce seeds ripen over a month or so. Check the plants for ripe seedpods every few days, starting 12 days after the first flowers open. Shake the seed head over an open paper bag to collect ripe seeds.

Solving Lettuce Problems

Use this table to identify problems on your lettuce. Scan the list of symptoms to find the description that most closely matches what you see in your garden. Then refer across the page to learn the cause and the recommended solutions. For some problems, by the time you see the damage, there is little you can do to save your crop. In the future, your best choices are to plant resistant cultivars whenever possible and cover plants with floating row cover. For a schedule of other pest prevention measures for lettuce, see "Seasonal Care" on page 133. You'll also find illustrations, descriptions, and additional controls for many of the insects and diseases listed below in Part 5 of this book.

SYMPTOMS	CAUSES	SOLUTIONS
Seedlings nipped off and lying on the ground	Cutworms	Search for and destroy cutworms hiding in the soil around the base of damaged plants. Protect future crops by drenching soil with parasitic nematodes or sprinkling bran mixed with BTK over beds for a week before planting.
Seedlings disappear; older plants cut off above soil and missing	Rabbits	Cover plants with floating row cover or fence the garden to prevent further damage.
Seedlings disappear; ragged holes in leaves; slugs or slime trails seen	Slugs	Set out slug traps; check daily and destroy trapped slugs. Spread a wide band of wood ash or diatomaceous earth, or erect copper barriers, around plants; renew dust after each rain. Protect future crops with floating row cover.
Leaves with large, ragged or round holes; caterpillars seen	Caterpillars	Many kinds of caterpillars eat lettuce. Handpick caterpillars or, if they are numerous, spray BTK or neem. Where caterpillars are a common problem, plan to cover plants with floating row cover from seeding until harvest.
Leaves with distorted patches; tiny green or black insects present	Aphids	Aphids feed on lettuce and can spread virus diseases. If aphids are visible, knock them off with a strong stream of water. Cover future crops with floating row cover to prevent problems.
Leaves with silvery, beige streaks	Thrips	Streaked lettuce is edible. Thrips are insects that are almost too small to see. If damage is severe, spray with insecticidal soap or neem, or dust with diatomaceous earth around the base of the plant and on the undersides of leaves.
Lower leaves with rusty, sunken areas on midribs	Bottom rot	Harvest mildly infected plants promptly; undamaged areas are edible. Pull and discard badly infected plants. In the future, plant resistant cultivars or upright cultivars to reduce soil contact. Rotate lettuce with other crops.
Leaves with brown spots on edges (tipburn)	Uneven watering Extreme heat	Pick tipburned heads promptly or they will rot. Uneven watering causes poor calcium uptake and leads to tipburn. Keep soil consistently moist. In the future, choose tipburn-tolerant cultivars.

(continued)

Solving Lettuce Problems—Continued

SYMPTOMS	CAUSES	SOLUTIONS
Outside leaves wilt; entire head rots; white cottony mold present	Lettuce drop (Sclerotinia drop)	Remove and destroy all affected plants, including roots. Do not plant lettuce on the site for 2 years. Plant future crops in raised beds.
Leaves with water-soaked, rotting areas or fuzzy gray mold	Gray mold (Botrytis)	Moist conditions encourage gray mold. Thin vigilantly to increase air circulation. Promptly remove and compost damaged plants and crop debris.
Light yellow patches on leaves; powdery white mold on leaf undersides	Downy mildew	Undamaged leaves are edible; harvest promptly to minimize loss. Increase spacing between plants to promote air circulation. Destroy crop residues at end of season. In the future, plant resistant cultivars, especially for late-season crops.
Leaves water-soaked	Frost damage	Undamaged portions of plants are edible. Early and late plantings may be damaged by frost. Cover plants when frost threatens. In the future, choose cold-tolerant cultivars for early and late plantings.
Leaves upright with wide, colorless central leaf veins	Big vein	Affected plants are edible and symptoms may disappear when conditions become warmer. Next season, plant in raised beds and wait until soil is warm before seeding.
Leaves bitter; seedstalk develops	Hot weather Plants too mature	Plants just beginning to bolt (going to seed) may be edible; taste first to check bitterness. Discard bitter plants. In the future, match cultivars to the seasons, make small plantings every few weeks, and provide shade in warm weather.
Leaves yellow; lower leaves nearly white	Nitrogen deficiency	Soggy soil can cause nitrogen deficiency. Keep soil consistently moist, but not soggy. Fertilize plants with compost tea or liquid fish fertilizer to provide an immediate nitrogen supply. Amend soil before planting next crop.
Plants stunted; hard, pea-size galls on roots	Nematodes	Pull and destroy severely stunted plants. Feed and water remaining plants generously. After harvest, solarize soil then plant nonsusceptible plants (corn, onion, small grains) to reduce nematode population.
Plants stunted; inner leaves are pale and twisted	Aster yellows (lettuce yellows)	Mildly affected plants are edible. Pull and destroy badly affected plants. Protect future crops with floating row cover to keep leafhoppers from introducing the disease.

MELON *Cucumis melo* and *Citrullus lanatus* • Cucurbitaceae

Choosing Plants

Homegrown melons are a luscious, juicy treat that puts store-bought melons to shame. While melons can be tricky to grow, the harvest is worth the effort. Compact, disease-resistant cultivars are the best choice for most home gardens. Northern gardeners should also look for cultivars that mature early.

Cantaloupes. Our American "cantaloupe" (*Cucumis melo* var. *reticulatas*) is more accurately called a muskmelon. True cantaloupes (*Cucumis melo* var. *cantalupensis*) are not widely grown

Trellised melons. *If you're short of space, train your melons up trellises. Support each fruit with a sling made of panty hose.*

in the U.S. You may find these smooth-skinned melons offered as "Charentais" or French melons.

Winter melons. Winter melons (*Cucumis melo* var. *inodorus*) are large and require a long growing season. They include casabas, crenshaws, and honeydews.

Watermelons. Watermelons (*Citrullus lanatus*) can have red or yellow flesh. "Seedless" cultivars contain a few soft seeds and are a little fussier to grow than seeded cultivars.

PLANTING FACTS

Seed and Seedling Identification

Seed Spacing

For hill planting, plant 4–6 seeds in hills 4' or more apart on all sides.
Seed depth: ½"–1"

Site and Soil

Melons need full sun to ripen properly. They do best in fertile, well-drained soil with a pH of 6.0 to 6.8.

Till or dig the soil at least 8 inches deep. Spread 40 pounds of compost and 3 pounds of alfalfa meal per 100 square feet and work it into the top few inches of soil. Another option is to prepare individual hills of compost. Build raised beds or hills if soil drainage is poor.

You can grow melons in a small garden if you plant them against a trellis and support the fruits, as shown on this page.

Planting

When to plant. Direct-sow seeds or set out transplants when the soil temperature is at least 70°F.

How much to plant. You can expect to harvest one or two melons from each compact plant in a short-season garden. Vining plants in long-season areas yield more.

Starting plants indoors. Start plants indoors about the time of your last expected frost, or two to four weeks before you plan to set them out. Plant two or three seeds ½ inch deep in 3- or 4-inch

PLANTING MELON TRANSPLANTS

Step 1. Clip extra seedlings off with scissors to avoid disturbing delicate roots.

True leaves

Step 2. Transplant outdoors in hills when the plants have two or three true leaves.

Hotcap

Step 3. Cover the young transplants with hotcaps to protect them from cold.

pots. For best results, keep soil at 80° to 95°F until seeds germinate. Then keep daytime temperatures between 70° and 75°F; nighttime temperatures between 60° and 65°F. Thin to one seedling per pot when the first true leaves appear.

Planting outdoors. Soak seeds overnight in compost tea, then presprout them indoors at 95°F until the root tips appear. Plant four to six seeds per hill. Sow seeds ½ to 1 inch deep and 2 inches apart. Space hills 4 to 6 feet apart for compact or bush-type melons. For vining melons, allow 6 to 12 feet between hills so the vines will have enough room to spread. Use scissors to clip off the weakest seedlings to leave two or three plants per hill when the first true leaves appear.

Seasonal Care

Melons are in the same botanical family as squash. They require care similar to squash and are vulnerable to many of the same problems. See "Season-by-Season Care: Squash" on page 173 for a schedule of care. If your plants develop problems, refer to "Solving Squash Problems" on page 175 to identify the causes and find solutions.

Melon fruits are more prone to early rotting in the field than squash. To keep your melons intact while they ripen, raise them up on overturned cans or plastic containers, as shown on this page.

Harvesting

Figuring out when a melon is ripe can be the most challenging part of growing them. In general, except for water-

melons, a ripe melon smells sweet and separates easily from the vine. Skin color also changes as melons ripen. Watermelons are ready to pick when the underside of the fruit turns creamy yellow and the tendril at the stem-end turns brown.

Most melons will keep in the refrigerator for one to two weeks. Winter melons keep for a month or so.

Rot-proof your melons. *Prevent rot problems by placing each melon on an overturned tin can.*

OKRA *Abelmoschus esculentus* • Malvaceae

Choosing Plants

Okra is a traditional Southern favorite, but you don't have to live in the South to grow it. If your summers are long and warm enough for raising sweet corn, then you can grow okra too. Look for early-maturing cultivars if your summers are short.

Cultivars of this tropical hibiscus-relative range in height from 2 to 6 feet. If your skin is sensitive to okra's spiny pods, look for the new spineless cultivars. If your garden soil has root knot nematodes, select root knot–tolerant cultivars.

Site and Soil

Okra needs full sun and fertile, well-drained soil with a pH of 6.5 to 6.8.

Till or dig the soil to at least 8 inches deep. Spread 30 pounds of compost per 100 square feet and work it into the top few inches of soil. Try planting okra after an early nitrogen-fixing crop, such as peas, for an extra boost. If your soil is not well drained, prepare raised beds.

Planting

When to plant. In short-season areas, start plants indoors three to four weeks after the last frost date. Plant seed outdoors when the soil has warmed to 68°F. Don't rush it, or your seed will languish and rot. In the Deep South, plant a second crop in June.

How much to plant. Okra plants produce pods over a long period of time, so three or four plants per person are usually adequate. One ounce of seed will plant a 100-foot row.

Starting plants indoors. Sow seeds in 2-inch pots, ¼ inch deep, three seeds per pot. Keep the pots at 80° to 90°F until the seedlings emerge. Grow the seedlings

Ornamental okra. *Okra has creamy yellow, hollyhock-type flowers with reddish centers, making it a lovely plant for ornamental borders. Red cultivars with their red stems, leaf ribs, and pods are especially attractive.*

at 75° to 80°F. Clip off the extra seedlings to leave just one per pot when the first true leaves appear.

Planting outdoors. Soak fresh seeds overnight in compost tea or nick each seed coat with a file to encourage germination. Sow seeds ½ inch deep in light soil; 1 inch deep in heavy soil. Plant seeds 2 to 3 inches apart in rows 2 to 3 feet apart. Another option is to plant groups of three seeds, 12 to 18 inches apart for dwarf cultivars and 24 inches apart for standard cultivars.

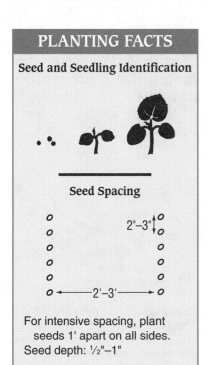

PLANTING FACTS

Seed and Seedling Identification

Seed Spacing

2"–3"

2'–3'

For intensive spacing, plant seeds 1' apart on all sides.
Seed depth: ½"–1"

Set transplants 1 foot apart in rows, being careful not to disturb the roots. Water in with compost tea.

Thinning. When the seedlings are 4 inches tall, clip off weaker seedlings with scissors to leave one per group.

Seasonal Care

Once your okra is up and growing, you'll need to make sure it gets enough water. Use a hoe to keep the patch free of weeds. Follow the guidelines below for a bumper harvest. If you have problems with your okra, refer to "Solving Okra Problems" on the opposite page to identify the causes and find solutions.

Spring
Start plants indoors. Unless you live in a very hot climate, you'll harvest more okra if you get a jump on the season by starting indoors.

Cover soil with black plastic. Prewarm soil by covering it with plastic several weeks before you plan to plant or transplant. Cut slits in the plastic on planting day and plant right through the slits.

Cover beds and transplants. Keep plants covered with floating row cover or slitted plastic spread over hoops until temperatures stay in the 80s. Remove or open the ends of cover when plants start to flower so insects can pollinate them.

Thin. Thin plants to 12 inches apart (or one per group if you seeded in groups) when they are 4 inches tall.

Fertilize. Give each plant a cup of compost tea every three weeks to boost growth.

Summer
Mulch. If you're not using black plastic, spread a 6- to 8-inch layer of organic mulch around plants when the soil is thoroughly warm.

Water. Keep soil consistently moist to keep pods coming.

Harvest. Cut all the harvestable pods every other day.

Cut back plants. In long-summer areas, your plants may get taller than you are. Cut some of your plants off at 2 feet tall in midsummer—when you still have 90 days of warm weather left. Side-dress each plant with compost and water it well. Shortened plants will sprout branches and yield well.

Short-summer gardeners can try pinching out the growing tips of plants when they reach 2 feet tall to keep them short and bushy and easy to cover in the fall.

Fall
Protect plants from cool weather. Cover plants when cold nights threaten.

Clean up. Compost or till in all plant debris after plants are killed by frost. If your plants suffered from disease, don't compost them; destroy them instead.

Harvesting

Use a sharp knife to harvest pods when they are 1 to 6 inches long and still young, soft, and tender. Once plants start producing, harvest at least every other day to keep plants producing until frost.

Be sure to pick large pods even if they are past good eating quality or else the plants will stop flowering and producing new pods. (Just toss the tough pods on the compost heap.)

Okra does not store well. Consume, freeze, or pickle okra pods the day you harvest them. To keep okra fresh for 24 hours, moisten pods and spread them out in a cool place with good air circulation.

Protection for picking. *It's a good idea to wear gloves when you harvest spiny okra cultivars. Some gardeners get an annoying rash from touching the spines.*

Solving Okra Problems

Use this table to identify problems on your okra. Scan the list of symptoms to find the description that most closely matches what you see in your garden. Then refer across the page to learn the cause and the recommended solutions. For a schedule of other pest prevention measures for okra, see "Seasonal Care" on the opposite page. You'll also find illustrations, descriptions, and additional controls for some of the insects and diseases listed below in Part 5 of this book.

SYMPTOMS	CAUSES	SOLUTIONS
Seeds fail to germinate	Old seed Cool soil	Save or buy fresh seed each year. Wait until soil is at least 68°F before planting, and presoak seeds to help soften seed coats.
Seedlings fall over and die	Damping-off Cutworms	Wait until soil is at least 68°F before planting, and keep soil moist but not soggy to avoid damping-off. Control cutworms with a BTK-bran bait or protect transplants with cardboard collars.
Brown, water-soaked pits on pods	Cold injury	Undamaged portions of pods are edible. Protect plants with floating row cover when cool weather threatens.
Holes chewed in pods and/or leaves	Corn earworms Other caterpillars	Undamaged portions of pods are edible. Handpick eggs and caterpillars. If small caterpillars are present, spray BTK or neem.
Pods distorted and puffy	Low soil pH	Adjust soil pH to 6.5 with lime.
Leaves distorted; tiny insects present	Aphids	Knock aphids off with a strong spray of water. If infestation is severe, spray with insecticidal soap, neem, or pyrethrins.
Branches wilt gradually; leaves turn yellow and drop	Verticillium wilt	Pull and destroy all infected plants and all crop debris in fall. In the future, solarize soil to help kill disease organism. Plan a 4- to 6-year rotation with nonsusceptible crops.
Leaves suddenly turn yellow, wilt, and drop	Southern blight (stem rot)	Look for stem rotting at soil level, with white or pinkish mold present on soil around stem to confirm. Dig out and destroy infected plants, including all roots and a thick layer of soil within 6 inches of the stem. Then solarize area to kill disease organism. In the future, plant nonsusceptible crops (corn, small grains) for 4 years before replanting okra or other susceptible crops.
Plants stunted, wilted; hard galls on roots	Root knot nematodes	Pull and destroy severely stunted plants. Give remaining plants the best of care to obtain some harvest. In the future, plant nematode-tolerant cultivars, solarize soil, or plant nonsusceptible crops (corn, onion, small grains) for 4 years to decrease or eliminate root knot nematodes in the soil.

ONION *Allium cepa* and other species • Liliaceae

Choosing Plants

Onions, sweet and hot, add zest to many familiar dishes. Plant a range of colors and types for a plentiful supply of fresh bulbs and greens.

Bulb Onions

Bulb onions can be flat, globular, or spindle shaped, and come in a variety of colors. For storage, choose yellow cultivars recommended for their long storage life. Select a large, mild cultivar that is suited to your region for salads and fresh eating. If you want pearl onions, choose a cultivar that doesn't develop papery outer skins.

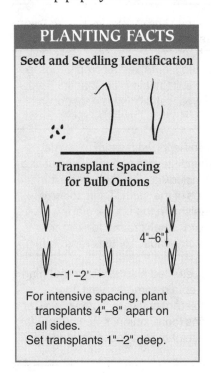

PLANTING FACTS

Seed and Seedling Identification

**Transplant Spacing
for Bulb Onions**

4"–6"

1'–2'

For intensive spacing, plant transplants 4"–8" apart on all sides.
Set transplants 1"–2" deep.

Sets. Sets (immature bulbs grown the previous season) are easy to plant, quick to mature, and the least likely to develop disease problems. Look for bulbs about ½ inch in diameter. See "Green Thumb Tip" on the opposite page for instructions on growing your own sets.

Transplants. Transplants (seedlings started the same season) are sold in bunches, or you can start your own from seed indoors in late winter. They are as easy to grow as sets but may not be available locally.

Seeds. You'll get the widest choice of cultivars if you grow onions from seeds. Seed-grown plants need a long season to mature. Most gardeners should start seeds indoors in late winter for all but the quickest-maturing cultivars.

Green Onions

You can plant bulb onion cultivars close together for harvest early as green onions (scallions). Most gardeners prefer white cultivars.

Perennial bunching onions (*Allium fistulosum*) make great green onions. They grow easily from seed and never form bulbs, and one planting will produce for many years.

FOR BEST RESULTS

Match your bulb onion cultivars to your daylength. Long-day cultivars thrive north of an imaginary line that runs roughly from North Carolina to San Francisco. Short-day cultivars are better suited to areas south of that. If you plant long-day cultivars in the South, you will get enormous green onion plants that never form a bulb. Plant short-day cultivars in the North and they will quickly form tiny bulbs.

Multiplier Onions

These perennial onions divide and form their own sets. Try some for reliable harvests year after year.

Shallots. For mild, onion-garlic flavor, try shallots (*A. cepa,* Aggregatum group). Start most cultivars from sets (divisions). Divide bulbs into individual bulbets for planting. A few cultivars can also be grown from seed. Harvest the tender greens or allow the bulbs to mature. Lift and divide clusters in fall, saving out sets for next spring's planting. Store the remainder for winter eating.

Potato onions. Potato or pregnant onions (*A. cepa,*

Aggregatum group) produce bulbs that taste much like the more familiar bulbing onions. Start them from sets (divisions). Harvest them for green onions or let the clumps mature. Lift and divide clusters in fall, saving out sets for next spring's planting. Store the remainder for winter eating.

Top-setting onions. For the unusual, try Egyptian or top-setting onions (*A. cepa,* Aggregatum group). The underground bulbs are almost too pungent to eat, but the clusters of bulbets that form on top of the stem are delightfully tasty. Plant sets (bulbets) to get started.

Site and Soil

Plant in a well-drained location that gets at least half a day of full sun. Soil pH

Cut tops back to 3"–4".

Trim transplants. *To keep onion transplants from becoming too tall and floppy, clip the tops back every week until they're ready for planting outdoors.*

should be between 6.0 and 6.8 for best results.

Till or dig the soil at least 8 inches deep. Spread 20 pounds of compost per 100 square feet and work it into the top few inches of soil. A sprinkling of wood ashes and bonemeal will help encourage early maturation. Prepare raised beds if your soil is not well drained.

Planting

When to Plant

Plant sets and transplants outdoors as soon as soil temperatures reach 35°F. Direct-plant seeds when soil temperatures reach 40°F. Plant fall green onions four to six weeks before your first expected frost. You can plant perennial onions in fall and mulch them well to protect them over winter.

How Much to Plant

Each set or transplant will make one onion, except for multiplier onions, which yield up to 12 bulbs for each one planted. Two pounds of sets, 400 transplants, or 1 ounce of seed will plant a 100-foot row and yield 1½ bushels of onions.

Starting Plants Indoors

Sow seed thinly ¼ inch deep in flats. Thin the seedlings to 1½ inches apart each way. Or plant small pinches of

seed in individual pots and thin to five or six seedlings. Keep the temperature between 60° and 70°F during the day and 50°F at night.

Planting Outdoors

Plant bulb onion sets or transplants 4 to 6 inches apart in rows 1 to 2 feet apart. Or set plants more closely and use the thinnings for green onions. Set transplants 1 to 2 inches deep. Plant sets pointed end up and covered with 1 inch of soil. Plant pots of seedlings 4 inches apart in the row.

Plant seed ¼ to ½ inch deep and 1 inch apart. You can also plant small pinches of seed every 4 inches in

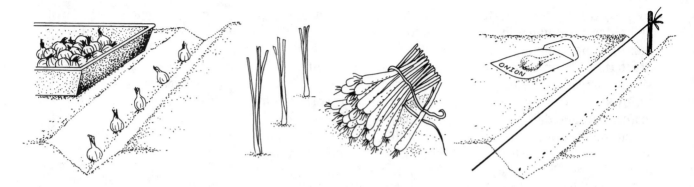

Planting onion sets. *Position sets pointed end up in the bottom of the furrow.*

Planting onion transplants. *Plant transplants in a trench or individual holes.*

Planting onion seeds. *Plant onion seed early, placing seeds 1 inch apart in a shallow furrow.*

rows. Space rows 1 to 2 feet apart. Try mixing in a few radish seeds to serve as a marker crop. The young radish roots may also lure root maggots away from the onions.

For green onions, plant sets or individual transplants 1 inch apart. Plant one to three seeds per inch in rows ¼ to ½ inch deep.

Plant multiplier onion sets 6 to 8 inches apart each way.

Thinning

Thin seedlings to 1 inch apart when they are 4 inches tall. Thin bulb onions to 4 inches apart when they are green onion size. If you planted in clumps, leave the clumps unthinned and harvest the entire clump at one time.

Seasonal Care

Water onions regularly to keep the soil uniformly moist. When you weed, use a hoe to slice weeds just below the surface so you don't disturb the onions' shallow roots. Follow the guidelines below for a bumper harvest. If you have problems with your onions, refer to "Solving Onion Problems" on page 146 to identify the causes and find solutions.

Late Winter

Start transplants. Start seeds indoors 10 to 12 weeks before you plan to plant transplants outdoors.

Spring

Prepare raised beds. If your drainage is iffy or if you have had problems with bulb rots in the past, build beds 4 to 6 inches high.

Prewarm the soil. If smut, purple blotch, or other cool-soil diseases have been a problem in the past, cover the soil with clear plastic for several weeks before planting.

Apply parasitic nematodes. If you've had problems with cutworms or onion maggots in the past, drench the soil with parasitic nematodes at least a week before planting.

Pretreat sets and transplants. Soak sets and transplants in compost tea for 15 minutes before planting. Then dust with bonemeal.

Plant late. If onion maggots have been a problem, delay planting for a month or so to miss the first generation of the pest.

Cover with floating row cover. If onion maggots have been a major problem in the past, cover beds with row cover after planting. Leave the cover on until the soil is thoroughly warm.

Fertilize. Spread ¼ to ½ pound of alfalfa meal over each 10 feet of row when the leaves emerge or a week after transplanting.

Thin. Thin seedlings and plants to reduce disease problems.

Mulch. Mulch around and between the plants with 4 to 6 inches of organic mulch.

Summer

Water. Onion bulbs split in dry conditions, so keep the soil consistently moist. When the tops start to turn yellow, cut back on watering.

Pull bolting plants. If any of your onions bolt (send up a seedstalk), harvest and use them immediately.

Fall

Harvest. When tops start to yellow, the bulbs are maturing. Lift and cure for winter use. Sort out some multiplier onion sets for next spring's planting and store the rest for eating.

Clean up. After harvest, collect plant debris and compost or till it in.

Harvesting

Harvest green onions and bulb onions for immediate use whenever you need them. Allow bulb onions for storage to mature. When the onion tops turn yellow and begin to fall over, it's time to harvest and cure them. Here's how:

1. Using a rake, push over the tops of the onion plants to speed bulb maturation. Keep an eye on the plants for the next week or so, watching for the tops to wilt and turn brown.

STEP 1

2. When a spell of sunny, dry weather is predicted, pull up the onions. Overlap the tops and bulbs to help prevent sunscald. Let the pulled plants dry for two or three days. If rain threatens while the onions are drying in the field, bring them inside an airy shed or garage instead. Spread them on wire mesh or wooden-slat racks to dry.

STEP 2

3. Once the onion skins are dry, cut off the tops within 1 inch of the crown (unless you plan to braid them). Brush gently to remove dirt and loose skins. Spread the bulbs on newspapers in a shady, warm, dry area for a week or two to finish curing.

STEP 3

4. Put the cured onions in mesh bags or an open crate and keep them in a cool, dry place. Or braid the tops together and hang the braid in the kitchen.

STEP 4

Solving Onion Problems

Use this table to identify problems on your onions. Scan the list of symptoms to find the description that most closely matches what you see in your garden. Then refer across the page to learn the cause and the recommended solutions. For some problems, by the time you see the damage, there is little you can do to save your crop. In the future, your best choices are to plant resistant cultivars whenever possible and rotate your onion patch to a new location each year. For a schedule of other pest prevention measures for onion, see "Seasonal Care" on page 144. You'll also find illustrations, descriptions, and additional controls for many of the insects and diseases listed below in Part 5 of this book.

LEAF PROBLEMS

SYMPTOMS	CAUSES	SOLUTIONS
Leaves with dusty gray streaks; seedlings may die	Smut	Surviving plants are edible. In the future, plant smut-free sets or transplants. Also, warm the soil by covering it with clear plastic for 2 weeks before planting.
Leaves with silvery streaks; may have browned tips	Onion thrips	These tiny insects are almost too small to see. Mildly affected plants will mature normally. If damage is severe or weather is wet, spray with insecticidal soap, neem, or pyrethrins. Dust natural grade diatomaceous earth around the base of each plant.
Leaves with purplish or white moldy stripes; oldest leaves dry up	Downy mildew	Pull and destroy affected plants. Thin remaining plants and remove weeds. Keep leaves dry when watering. Remove and destroy all crop debris in fall. Don't replant onions in infected soil; select a new site.
Leaves with white specks; entire top dies rapidly	Botrytis leaf blight (blast)	Pull and compost affected plants. This fungus infects plants through wounds such as those caused by blowing sand and by thrips feeding. In the future, mulch the soil to reduce blowing sand and grit; control thrips by spraying insecticidal soap.
Leaves with water-soaked, purplish, yellow-edged spots	Purple blotch	Spray sulfur to reduce spread of this disease. Surviving plants may produce edible bulbs. Remove and destroy all crop residues in fall. In the future, warm soil by covering it with clear plastic for 2 weeks before planting.
Yellow leaves; stunted plants	Pink root Waterlogged soil Nitrogen deficiency	If roots and bulbs are pinkish, the plants probably have pink root. Pull and destroy plants. If roots appear healthy, but soil is wet, replant in raised beds or in an area with better drainage. If soil is not wet, the problem may be low fertility. Spray plants and drench roots with fish emulsion to supply nitrogen.
Leaves wilted and yellow; soft, brown rot in neck or bulb	Fusarium basal rot	Pull and destroy affected plants. In the future, plant in raised beds, avoid damaging roots when you cultivate, plant Fusarium-tolerant cultivars, and rotate onion crops.

SYMPTOMS	CAUSES	SOLUTIONS
Leaves turn yellow and die, starting at tips; roots rotted with fluffy white mold on them	White rot (Sclerotinia)	Remove and destroy infected plants and all crop debris. Solarize area to help reduce populations of this fungus in the soil. Do not replant in infected soil.
Seedstalks form (bolting)	Cold Uneven soil moisture	Pull and use bolting plants as soon as possible; only the tough seedstalk is inedible. In the future, wait until soil is warm enough in spring before planting, and keep soil evenly moist all season.

ROOT PROBLEMS

SYMPTOMS	CAUSES	SOLUTIONS
No bulbs form	Late planting Inappropriate cultivar Low soil fertility	Onions planted too late in the season (mid-June or later) may not form bulbs. Long-day cultivars won't form bulbs in the South. Bulbs also may not form if plants can't get enough nutrients. In the future, plant suitable cultivars at the correct time; amend soil if fertility is low.
Bulbs with tunnels or cavities	Onion maggots	Bulbs are edible unless internal rot has developed. Drench soil with parasitic nematodes for some control. In the future, rotate onions to another site, plant late to avoid first generation of the pest, try red cultivars, and cover beds with floating row cover.
Bulbs with soft, light-colored patches	Sunscald	Damaged onions are edible if used immediately. In the future, protect bulbs from direct sun. If sunscald is a persistent problem, plant cultivars with hard, dark skins that cover the bulb well.
Bulbs small with pink, shriveled roots	Pink root	Bulbs are edible. In the future, plant pink root–tolerant cultivars and rotate onions to a new site.
Bulbs with large dark smudges at harvest or in storage	Onion smudge	This disease is most serious in wet soil and warm conditions. Destroy infected bulbs and check stored bulbs frequently for signs of infection. In the future, plant smudge-tolerant cultivars in raised beds.
Bulbs rot or shrivel up in storage	Botrytis neck rot Bacterial soft rot Fusarium basal rot	Check stored bulbs frequently and remove damaged bulbs, especially if growing season was wet and cool. In the future, plant cultivars with small necks, choose Fusarium-tolerant cultivars, rotate your onions to another site, cut back on irrigation as bulbs are maturing, and make sure bulbs are well cured before storage.

PEA   *Pisum sativum* • Leguminosae

Choosing Plants

Garden peas. Old-fashioned garden peas (*Pisum sativum* var. *sativum*) bear plump, succulent peas in tough, inedible pods. Choose wrinkled-seeded cultivars, which are sweeter than smooth-seeded types, for your main crop. For early and late harvests, the hardier smooth-seeded cultivars are a better choice. Tiny "petit pois" cultivars are a gourmet treat, but it requires lots of patience to shell them.

Edible-podded peas. Enjoy the crisp, sweet pods and tender peas of edible-podded peas (*P. sativum* var. *macrocarpon*). Choose "stringless" cultivars for easy preparation. *Snow or sugar peas* are best before the peas start to fill out. *Snap peas* can be enjoyed anytime from flat-pod stage until the pods are packed full of fat pea seeds.

Dry peas. Any kind of peas can be grown as dry peas. Cultivars selected for dry-pea production are also available.

Choose bush cultivars for small gardens or if you hate fussing with trellises. Choose tall cultivars for high yields and no-stoop picking. Southern gardeners should look for heat-resistant cultivars.

Site and Soil

Choose a wind-protected site with at least half a day of full sun. Peas do best in a loose, well-drained soil with a pH of 6.0 to 7.5. Peas will grow in heavier soils but will take a few days longer to bear.

In fall or early spring, till or dig the soil at least 8 inches deep. Spread 5 to 10 pounds of compost per 100 square feet and work it into the top few inches of soil. If you're planting an early crop or if your soil is heavy, prepare raised beds. Cover fall-prepared beds with a thick layer of straw; they will be ready for very early planting in the spring.

Planting

When to Plant

Peas grow best when the air temperature is 60° to 65°F. Temperatures above 70°F slow or stop pod development.

In temperate climates, sow seed in late winter or early spring, as soon as the ground can be worked and the soil temperature reaches 40°F. Make small plantings every two weeks as long as temperatures will stay below 80°F for the next month and a half.

For a fall harvest, plant peas in mid- to late summer, when temperatures are less than 80°F and up to six to eight weeks before the first expected frost.

In areas with mild winters, you can plant in the fall for an early-spring harvest.

How Much to Plant

Grow 20 to 40 plants per person per planting. One pound of seeds will plant about 150 feet of row.

Planting Outdoors

Peas are legumes, which means their roots work with

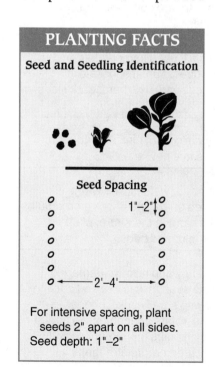

PLANTING FACTS

Seed and Seedling Identification

Seed Spacing

1"–2"

2'–4'

For intensive spacing, plant seeds 2" apart on all sides.
Seed depth: 1"–2"

INOCULATING PEA SEEDS FOR HIGHER YIELDS

Step 1. *Pour a small amount of pea-seed inoculant into a bowl.*

Step 2. *Spread seeds on a plate and spray with kelp solution.*

Step 3. *Dump the wet seeds into the bowl holding the inoculant.*

Step 4. *Pour seeds back and forth between the bowl and container.*

soil bacteria to transform soil nitrogen into forms that plants can use. Coating pea seeds with an inoculant containing these bacteria (available from mail-order seed companies) helps fixation and can boost growth and yield. Before planting, mix seeds with inoculant, as shown on this page.

Sow seeds 1 to 2 inches deep and 1 to 2 inches apart. Plant dwarf cultivars in a single row or a 3-inch-wide band. Allow 18 inches between rows. Or broadcast dwarf cultivars in 18-inch-wide beds so they will support themselves. Plant tall climbing cultivars in single rows or 3-inch bands next to a trellis. Or sow them in an 8-inch band centered under the trellis, and train the plants up both sides. Space trellised rows 2 to 4 feet apart.

Thinning

Thin peas to 2 to 3 inches apart when the plants are 2 to 3 inches tall.

Seasonal Care

Follow the guidelines below to keep your plants healthy and productive. If you have problems with your peas, refer to "Solving Pea Problems" on page 152 to identify the causes and find solutions.

Fall

Prepare bed. To get a jump on early-spring planting, prepare a bed for your first spring peas the fall before.

Late Winter to Spring

Cover soil with black plastic. Lay plastic over your fall-prepared bed several weeks before planting to warm the soil. Remove the plastic on planting day.

Cover seedbed with floating row cover. Cover early plantings to keep the soil warm and protect plants from extreme cold. Remove cover once daytime temperatures are in the 60s and nights stay above freezing. Pea seedlings can withstand light freezes; replace cover temporarily if frost threatens after blossoms appear.

Provide support. Put up a trellis or other support before planting, at planting time, or when the seedlings are a few inches tall. For trellis ideas, see "Peas Love Warm Companions" on page 150 and the illustrations on page 151.

Mulch. When seedlings are 3 inches tall, apply a 2- to 6-inch layer of grass clippings

PEAS LOVE WARM COMPANIONS

Why not grow two crops in the space of one and provide extra benefits for both? Plant peas and a warm-season crop together and reap extra harvests. Peas and tomatoes work especially well together.

Plant peas in a ring around the outside of tomato cages in early spring. The peas will climb up the wire. Transplant tomatoes into the cages as the weather allows. The peas will protect the tomatoes from cool winds before they fade away and leave behind an extra boost of nitrogen for the hungry tomatoes.

You can also train peas up a wooden A-frame covered with a twine grid. Interplant a few cucumbers between the peas when the weather warms. As the peas fade away, the cucumbers will be filling in the space, grateful for the extra nitrogen left behind by the peas.

Reverse the pairing for fall crops, letting the warm-season crop provide cooling shade for the seedling peas. A row of trellised tomatoes can provide cooling midsummer shade for a row of heat-shy pea seedlings. Peas and tomatoes are a mutually beneficial combination, but any tall crop can provide shade.

to control weeds and keep the soil cool and moist.

Summer

Water. Peas thrive in cool, moist soil. Keep it consistently moist but not soggy.

Clean up. When you have finished harvesting, mow the bed or cut the plants off and compost them.

Late Summer to Fall

Plant. Plant for fall and winter harvests as your climate allows. Mulch new plantings and provide partial shade if the weather is still warm at planting time.

Protect late crops from frost. Cover plants with floating row cover when frost threatens.

Clean up. When the plants are no longer productive or frost kills them, mow the bed or cut the plants off and compost them.

Harvesting

Follow the guidelines below to decide when your peas are ready for picking. For all types, handle plants tenderly as you harvest. To avoid uprooting the plants, use scissors to cut the pods off, or hold the plant with one hand while you gently pull the pods off with the other. Harvest daily to keep plants productive. Pick overripe pods if you find any and

Trellising peas. _Tall cultivars need a 5- to 8-foot-high trellis. Pound tall stakes firmly into the soil at the ends of the row or every 10 to 15 feet. Stretch a strip of 4- to 6-inch mesh netting from end to end._

compost them. You can refrigerate fresh peas for up to one week.

Garden peas. Begin checking garden peas about two weeks after the blossoms appear. If they're plump and the peas are just touching, pick them. Don't wait too long, hoping for bigger peas, because they'll get starchy.

Snap peas. Both the tender pods and juicy seeds are edible. For best flavor and highest yield, harvest the pods when they are bulging with seeds. This is usually about two weeks after the flowers appear. Eat snap peas whole or snap them into pieces. They are great raw, or cook them as you would snap beans.

Snow peas. Harvest snow pea pods when they're 3 to 4 inches long but still flat, before the seeds start to swell. Check larger pods for strings and pull them off. Eat snow peas raw or cook them whole.

Dry peas. Harvest dry peas when the pods are brown and dry, and the seeds rattle. Remove the seeds, allow them to dry for about three weeks, and then store in airtight containers.

Extending the Season

For early crops, warm the soil with black plastic and cover with floating row cover. For an extended harvest, sow seeds every two weeks until mid-spring, or plant cultivars with different maturing rates all at once. Plant again in late summer for fall harvest.

Growing in Containers

Peas make fine container plants. Choose dwarf types, such as 'Little Marvel', and provide support. Sow seeds in containers that are 12 inches deep and care for them like garden-grown peas.

Propagation

Pea flowers are mostly self-fertilizing, but it's best to have just one cultivar blooming at a time if you plan to save seed from the plants. Or separate blooming cultivars by planting a row of another tall vegetable between them.

Don't just save seed from the pods you happen to miss during harvest. Plan ahead, and mark a section of row early in the season specifically for seed production. Pull up and discard any poor-looking or sickly plants during the season. Harvest your seed as you would dry peas for eating.

Pea bush supports. _Bush cultivars benefit from a row of 2-foot-tall twiggy branches to grow through. Push the cut ends of the branches firmly into the soil at planting time._

Solving Pea Problems

Use this table to identify problems on your peas. Scan the list of symptoms to find the description that most closely matches what you see in your garden. Then refer across the page to learn the cause and the recommended solutions. For some problems, by the time you see the damage, there is little you can do to save your crop. In the future, your best choices are to plant resistant cultivars whenever possible, rotate your pea patch to a new location each year, and cover your plants with floating row cover. For a schedule of other pest prevention measures for peas, see "Seasonal Care" on page 149. You'll also find illustrations, descriptions, and additional controls for many of the insects and diseases listed below in Part 5 of this book.

FLOWER AND POD PROBLEMS

SYMPTOMS	CAUSES	SOLUTIONS
No flowers; plants large and healthy	Too much nitrogen	Plants may outgrow problem. In the future, avoid high-nitrogen fertilizers, and plant peas where heavy feeders, such as melons or tomatoes, grew last season.
Flowers appear, but no pods form	Weather conditions Nutrient imbalance	Hot weather can cause blossom-drop; heavy rains can knock flowers off. Wait for more flowers to form. If weather is not at fault, spray plants with kelp to provide nutrients.
Water-soaked spots on pods; spots may become slimy or dry up	Bacterial blight	Pull and destroy infected plants and all crop debris. Do not save seed for replanting. In the future, plant disease-free seed and practice a 3-year crop rotation.
Pods puckered and scarred	Thrips	Damage is superficial; peas and pods are edible. For severe thrips problems, wash plants with a strong stream of water or spray with insecticidal soap or neem. In the future, maintain vigorous, well-watered plants.
Pods with bumps or ridges; plants stunted	Viral diseases	Pull and discard diseased plants. In the future, plant cultivars resistant to pea enation and mosaic. Aphids can spread viral diseases. Plant very early in spring before aphids are active or cover with floating row cover.
Peas with ragged holes; silk webbing in pods	Pea moths	Uninfested peas are edible. Open snap pea pods to check for infestation. Pick and destroy yellowing pods. Collect and destroy crop debris and cultivate soil.
Peas hollowed out; cream-colored larvae may be present	Pea weevils	Discard damaged peas. Remove and destroy all crop debris after harvest. Do not save potentially infested seed for replanting. In the future, cover plants with floating row cover through blossom period to exclude weevils.

LEAF AND PLANT PROBLEMS

SYMPTOMS	CAUSES	SOLUTIONS
Seeds fail to emerge; young seedlings die	Cold soil Soil insects	Cold soil encourages rots and damping-off diseases. Replant when soil is warmer; plant in raised beds if your garden has heavy, wet soil. If seeds have been chewed, or if plants are snipped off at the soil line, drench soil with parasitic nematodes and wait a week before replanting.

SYMPTOMS	CAUSES	SOLUTIONS
Young plants disappear	Animal pests and/or birds	Birds, rabbits, woodchucks, and other animals love to nibble tender pea seedlings. Replant and cover with floating row cover until plants are at least 1' tall, or fence the entire garden.
Leaves with small notches cut out; seedlings chewed	Pea leaf weevils	Weevils rarely cause serious damage unless plants are small. In the future, cover plants with floating row cover until they are at least 1' tall.
Young leaves and shoots curled and sticky	Pea aphids	Aphids can spread viral diseases. Wash aphids off plants with a strong spray of water or spray with insecticidal soap or neem.
Leaves with tiny yellow flecks; fine webbing under leaves	Spider mites	Spider mites are generally more problematic when weather is hot and dry. Spray infested plants with water or insecticidal soap.
Powdery white coating on leaves or stems	Powdery mildew	Spray or dust plants with sulfur every 10–20 days to reduce spreading. Do not save seed for replanting. In the future, buy disease-free seed of tolerant cultivars.
Yellow patches on leaves; powdery coating on leaf undersides	Downy mildew	Pull and destroy all affected plants and remove crop debris. Thin out remaining plants and avoid wetting leaves when watering. In the future, plant tolerant cultivars.
Leaves with yellow patches or patterns; plants stunted	Viral diseases	Pull and discard infected plants. Choose resistant cultivars. Aphids can spread viral diseases. Plant very early before aphids are active, and cover plants with floating row cover.
Water-soaked spots on leaves; spots become slimy or dry up	Bacterial blight	Pull and destroy infected plants. Collect and destroy all crop debris after harvest. Replant in a new location using disease-free seed. Practice a 3-year crop rotation.
Leaves with large holes; caterpillars may be present	Loopers Other caterpillars	Caterpillars usually don't cause severe damage. Handpick caterpillars or spray plants with BTK or neem.
Plants stunted and wilted; stem tissue discolored	Fusarium wilt Other wilt diseases	Pull and destroy affected plants and remove crop debris. In the future, plant in raised beds, choose tolerant cultivars, and plant in other sites for 3–5 years.
Plants pale and stunted; roots rotted	Various root rots	Remove and destroy infected plants. In the future, plant in raised beds and fertilize to maintain vigor.

PEPPER Capsicum annuum var. annuum • Solanaceae

Choosing Plants

Once just Christmasy red and green, peppers now come in a wide range of colors. Cultivars may also mature to orange, yellow, white, purple, or brown. Northern gardeners should choose cold-tolerant or early-maturing cultivars. Southerners need cultivars with heat tolerance. Select disease-resistant cultivars when available.

If you buy pepper plants, choose sturdy seedlings with dark green leaves and no fruit. Flower buds are okay if you fertilize and water the plants well at planting.

Grow a pepper fiesta. *You can harvest an exciting mixture of tastes, shapes, and colors from backyard pepper plants. Choose from some of the popular peppers shown here.*

PLANTING FACTS

Seed and Seedling Identification

Transplant Spacing

18"–24"

2'–3'

For intensive spacing, plant transplants 18" apart on all sides.

Set transplants with first true leaves at soil level.

Sweet Peppers

Bell peppers. Often called green peppers, these sweet-tasting, blocky peppers have thick walls. Fruits start out pale yellow, light to dark green, or purple, and ripen to yellow, orange, red, or dark brown.

Frying or salad peppers. These peppers tend to be longer than they are wide and have thinner walls than bell peppers do. While they resemble hot peppers, frying peppers have a mellow flavor. Caribbean, Italian, and other ethnic sweet peppers are in this group. Fruits start yellow and ripen to red.

Pimiento peppers. Thick-walled, heart-shaped, and very sweet when ripe, pimiento peppers are also known as squash peppers or cheese peppers. Most cultivars ripen red or orange, a few ripen yellow.

Other sweet peppers. Various small or oddly shaped sweet peppers are available, including the commonly grown sweet cherry peppers.

Hot Peppers

Hot peppers are becoming a national passion. No matter how tough or tender your taste buds, there are hot peppers to suit your palate. In general, hot cultivars will be less hot if your summer weather is cool or cloudy.

Chili peppers. Chili peppers have long or triangular fruits only an inch or two wide. The typical canned "green chilis" are Anaheim-type peppers. Ripened red chili peppers are used fresh, dried, or even smoked as the basis of many flavorful dishes. Choose from mild to medium-hot cultivars.

Small hot peppers. Often, the smaller the pepper, the hotter its fire. Long, skinny cayenne peppers are hot. Thumb-size jalapeños are hotter and widely used. (Look for milder jalapeño cultivars if you want the flavor without the burn.) Tiny peppers, such as 'Habañero', 'Thai Hot', and 'De Arbol', are hotter still. Even handling the seeds and then touching your eyes can be a painful experience. Use surgical gloves when cutting and preparing hot peppers, and don't touch anything else until after you've discarded the gloves and washed your hands well with soap.

Site and Soil

Peppers need full sun, protection from the wind, and well-drained soil with a pH of 5.5 to 6.9.

Dig or till the soil at least 12 inches deep. Spread 20 to 30 pounds of compost per 100 square feet and work it into the top few inches of soil. Prepare raised beds if your soil drains poorly.

Planting

When to plant. Set transplants out two to three weeks after the last average frost, when the soil temperature has reached at least 65°F.

How much to plant. Grow two or three plants per person. A packet of seed will produce at least 20 transplants.

Starting plants indoors. Start seeds indoors 6 to 8 weeks before the last frost, or 8 to 11 weeks before transplanting. Soak seeds for 15 minutes, or as long as overnight, in compost tea. Plant seeds ¼ inch deep in individual pots, two to a pot. For best results, the soil should be at least 85°F.

Grow seedlings at 65° to 75°F during the day, 60° to 65°F at night. Snip off extra plants to leave one per pot when the seedlings get their first true leaves.

Planting outdoors. Put ½ cup each of bonemeal and kelp meal into each planting hole. Set sweet peppers 1½ to 2 feet apart; allow 2 to 3 feet between rows. Space hot peppers 12 to 18 inches apart.

High temperatures and exposure to the sun can cause sunscalded fruit. Try one of the planting schemes illustrated on this page to prevent sunscald on your peppers.

Shade peppers with corn or trellised crops, such as beans.

Plant peppers 1–1½ feet apart in a block.

Preventing sunscald. *In hot climates, shade peppers by planting them in the shadow of taller crops or by planting them in a dense block to help protect the fruit from bright afternoon sun.*

Seasonal Care

Warm temperatures and evenly moist soil are critical ingredients for producing healthy, good-tasting peppers. For a complete listing of things you can do to help your pepper plants thrive, see "Season-by-Season Care: Pepper" on the opposite page.

Peppers are in the same botanical family as tomatoes. However, they are more sensitive to cold than tomatoes are. If your pepper plants seem healthy and have blossoms, but never form fruit, the problem could be temperature sensitivity. Pepper flowers may drop off if temperatures fall below 60°F. To avoid this problem, cover plants if cool nights are predicted. When temperatures rise, new flowers should set fruit.

Peppers are prone to most of the same insect and disease problems as tomato. Refer to "Solving Tomato Problems" on page 186 for solutions to many common problems. Two insect pests unique to peppers are pepper maggots and pepper weevils. When these insects feed on flowers and small fruits, the flowers and fruits turn yellow and drop. Larger fruits are misshapen. If your peppers have these problems, collect and destroy all dropped and damaged flower buds and fruit. If damage is severe, spray the plants with pyrethrins or rotenone.

Chili ristras. *String hot peppers together with a needle and strong thread (through the stem, not the fruit). Hang the ristra in a sunny window to dry, then move it out of the sun to avoid fading. Use the dry peppers in cooking.*

Harvesting

Cut fruit off the plant leaving some of the stem attached to the pepper. Harvest "green" or immature peppers whenever they are large enough for your purposes. For maximum sweetness or flavor, harvest ripe peppers after they have completely changed to their mature color.

Peppers will usually keep in the refrigerator for up to two weeks. Freeze or dry any excess fruit.

Harvest all usable fruit before the first frost, or cut the entire plants and hang them indoors to allow the fruit to continue ripening.

Extending the Season

Cover the bed with black plastic four to six weeks before your last expected frost to warm the soil. Set out transplants in Wallo Water when the soil is 65°F and cover them with slitted plastic spread over hoops. Remove plastic once nights remain above 60°F and daytime temperatures are in the 80s.

Replace plastic when nights dip below 60°F or days are consistently less than 70°F.

Propagation

Choose open-pollinated (nonhybrid) cultivars if you want to save seed. Peppers are mostly self-pollinated, but separate different cultivars with a row of another tall crop to avoid occasional cross-pollination. Mark your best-looking healthy plants and leave one of the best fruits on each to ripen to the point of shriveling. If necessary, pull up the plants and hang them indoors to finish ripening. Once the peppers are fully ripe, cut them in half, scoop out the seeds, and spread them out to dry.

SEASON-BY-SEASON CARE: PEPPER

This care guide tells you what to do and when to do it for your best pepper harvest ever. Because timing of certain tasks is critical, review all the instructions in this guide in late winter. Locate or buy the products you'll need in advance. Peppers suffer from many of the same problems as tomatoes. If you have problems with your peppers, refer to "Solving Tomato Problems" on page 186 to identify the causes and find solutions.

Spring

Cover the soil with black plastic. Several weeks before planting time, spread black plastic over the soil to prewarm it. When the soil is at least 65°F, cut slits in the plastic and plant transplants through the slits.

Cover transplants. Use cloches, floating row cover, or slitted plastic spread over hoops to keep plants warm and protect them from disease-spreading insects. Remove the cover when the daytime temperatures are in the 80s. If temperatures don't exceed 80°F before bloom time, be sure to open the ends of the covers when blossoms appear.

Fertilize. Give each plant 1 cup of compost tea or fish emulsion once a week until the plants are growing well.

Summer

Fertilize. Spray plants with Epsom salts and kelp (1 teaspoon Epsom salts per gallon of kelp solution) when the first flowers open.

Water. Keep the soil constantly moist, but not wet. Keep water off foliage and fruit by watering plants at the base.

Mulch. If you're not using black plastic, spread 6 to 8 inches of organic mulch around the plants when the soil is warm.

Spray plants with BTK. Spray plants with BTK if small caterpillars are present.

Spray plants with copper. If light or dark spots develop on the leaves, or small wartlike spots appear on the fruit, spray affected plants with copper. If spot-producing diseases have been a severe problem in the past, spray plants with copper when the fruit sets.

Spray plants with pyrethrins-rotenone. If pepper maggots or pepper weevils have been a severe problem in the past, spray plants with pyrethrins-rotenone when the fruit begins to set.

Pull and destroy permanently wilted plants. Permanent wilting may be due to root knot nematodes and various wilt diseases. If roots of pulled plants have numerous small swellings (a sign of nematodes), treat the soil with a chitin-containing product.

Harvest. Begin picking peppers when they are large enough to eat. Use pruners so you don't damage or uproot the plants. If you find fruits with dark, sunken spots with concentric rings, destroy the fruits and spray affected plants with copper. If you find fruits with tips that are sunken and dark (blossom-end rot), or if skin has light-colored patches (sunscald or cold injury), pick and use them as soon as possible.

Fall

Protect plants from cool temperatures. Cover plants with slitted plastic spread over hoops when nights dip below 50°F or days are consistently less than 70°F.

Harvest all fruits before hard frost. Even fruits on covered plants will be damaged if the temperature drops more than a few degrees below freezing. Pick all usable fruits or pull up the plants and hang them indoors.

Clean up. When plants stop bearing or are killed by frost, pull up and compost them or till them under.

POTATO *Solanum tuberosum* • Solanaceae

Choosing Plants

Variety is the reason to grow potatoes in your backyard garden. While potatoes are cheap and plentiful in grocery stores, the selection is far from exciting. Grow your own, and you can have yellow, purple, or blue potatoes in a range of sizes and textures.

If you plan to grow a large crop and store potatoes into the winter, select cultivars with good keeping quality.

You can buy true seed for certain potato cultivars. For best results, however, buy certified disease-free "seed" potatoes.

Disease resistance. Potatoes can suffer from serious fungal and bacterial diseases. Eggplant, pepper, tomato, and potato are related and can suffer from many of the same diseases. One way to lessen disease problems in large gardens is to plan a rotation of all tomato-family crops. But if you have a small garden, this may be hard to achieve. A better option is to select disease-resistant and disease-tolerant cultivars. Cultivars are available that resist or tolerate early blight, late blight, scab, Verticillium wilt, and viruses.

Site and Soil

Potatoes do best in a light, fertile sandy or loamy soil with a pH of 5.0 to 6.8. Potatoes need potassium and phosphorus to produce healthy tubers. Loosen the soil deeply, because potato roots will penetrate up to 2 feet deep. Another option is to build raised planting beds.

Spread 20 to 30 pounds of compost per 100 square feet and work it into the top several inches of soil before planting.

Planting

When to Plant

In northern regions, begin planting early cultivars as soon as the ground can be

PLANTING FACTS

Seed Potato Spacing

8"–12"

30"–36"

For intensive spacing, plant seed potatoes 9"–12" apart on all sides.
Planting depth varies with planting method.

GREEN THUMB TIP

Potatoes take less time to mature and are less likely to rot if you presprout them before planting. Cut and cure seed potato pieces, then place them in wooden flats or shallow boxes. Leave them outside under shelter or in a cool room indoors for one to two weeks. Tubers need plenty of light and cool temperatures to sprout; don't subject them to direct sunlight or frost, however. Plant potato pieces when the sprouts are still short—less than 1 inch long.

worked—about two to four weeks before the last frost date. If you plant mid-season and late potatoes, keep in mind that they must be ready to harvest by the first frost in autumn. In areas with mild winters, start potatoes in early spring for a summer harvest. Or plant in fall or winter and harvest in spring.

How Much to Plant

A single potato plant yields 2 to 5 pounds of potatoes. Plant 10 to 15 plants per person. Five to 8 pounds of seed potatoes will plant 100 feet of row.

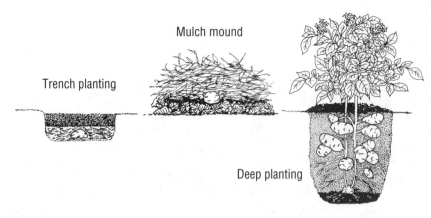

Planting potatoes. Trench planting is the most common potato-planting method. Mulch mounds make harvesting easy and keep the tubers clean. Deep planting potatoes can lead to high yields, but requires more labor and is not recommended for regions with cool, damp weather.

Planting Outdoors

Seed potatoes that are egg-size or smaller can be planted whole. Cut larger tubers into pieces. There should be two or three eyes (buds) on each piece. Spread the pieces out in a well-ventilated place with plenty of light. Let them dry for a day or until the cut sides have hardened. If the weather is damp, sprinkle the pieces with sulfur dust to prevent rotting.

There are three common methods for planting potatoes. Whichever method you choose, always plant seed pieces with the eyes facing upward.

Trench planting. To plant in trenches, prepare 4- to 6-inch-deep rows spaced 3 feet apart. Place potato pieces 10 to 15 inches apart at the bottom of the trench. Cover with 1 to 2 inches of compost, then add soil to fill the trench. Hill up plants as needed.

Mulch mounds. To plant in mulch mounds, start in the fall by mounding up leaves. The following spring, place the potato pieces on top of the partially decomposed leaves. Mulch with a 1- to 1½-foot layer of straw or hay. Add mulch as needed to keep the tubers covered.

Deep planting. To deep-plant, prepare 12-inch-deep holes. (This task is easier if you use a post-hole digger.) Add 2 inches of compost, place a potato piece in each hole, then add about 2 inches of soil. Gradually add soil as the plants grow, until the holes are completely filled. Mulch with a thin layer of compost and straw.

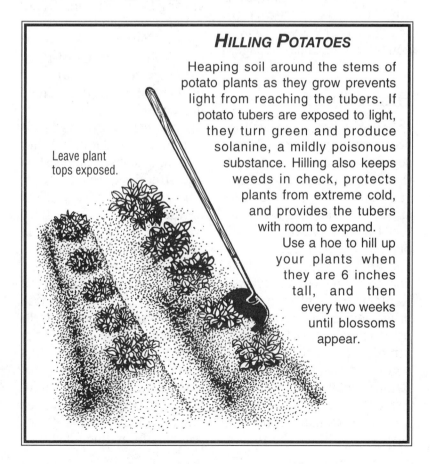

HILLING POTATOES

Heaping soil around the stems of potato plants as they grow prevents light from reaching the tubers. If potato tubers are exposed to light, they turn green and produce solanine, a mildly poisonous substance. Hilling also keeps weeds in check, protects plants from extreme cold, and provides the tubers with room to expand.

Use a hoe to hill up your plants when they are 6 inches tall, and then every two weeks until blossoms appear.

Leave plant tops exposed.

Potatoes are ready to dig when foliage withers.

Cure potatoes and clean them before storing.

HARVESTING POTATOES

Seasonal Care

As your potatoes grow, it's important to keep moisture in and weeds out. If you've planted in trenches, you'll also need to hill up plants. For details on watering and mulching your potato crop, see "Season-by-Season Care: Potato" on the opposite page.

Harvesting

You can begin harvesting potatoes shortly after blossoms appear on the plants. At this stage, the young tubers (called "new" potatoes) are small, thin skinned, and perfect for boiling. To harvest, push your hand through the soil at the base of the plant and gently remove the tubers. Replace the soil to protect other developing potatoes. If potatoes were mulch-planted, simply reach through the straw and remove the tubers. Eat new potatoes immediately.

Most potatoes take 90 to 120 days to mature from a seed potato. Once the tubers are full-size, the foliage will start to turn brown. Dig up the tubers as needed; you can store them in the ground for several weeks as long as the weather stays cool and dry. Be sure to finish harvesting before the first frost.

Use a spading fork to carefully dig up tubers. Shake off excess dirt, then move them indoors to dry. Eat any bruised or pierced potatoes immediately.

Curing is a process that toughens the delicate tuber skin and helps prolong storage life. To cure potatoes, spread the tubers out on newspapers in a dark place where the temperature is about 60°F. Leave for one to two weeks.

After curing, brush dirt off the tubers, then place them in bushel baskets or other well-ventilated wooden containers. Store in a cool, dark place that stays about 40°F. Do not expose the potatoes to light. Stored properly, they will keep for four to six months. Check regularly for rotting tubers.

Extending the Season

If your climate is suitable, plant early, mid-season, and late potatoes. Protect early potatoes with straw mulch or cloches.

To get a head start on the season, try presprouting your potatoes, as described in "Green Thumb Tip" on page 158.

Growing in Containers

You can grow potatoes in barrels, trash cans, or compost bins by planting in mulch mounds. Put a layer of soil in the bottom, then add a layer of straw, then another of compost or well-rotted manure. Place the potato pieces in the compost. As the vines grow, gradually add more compost or manure. To harvest, simply empty out the container.

Propagation

You can save tubers from your plants to be next year's seed potatoes. Choose the best-looking tubers from the healthiest plants for your seed. (Don't save seed potatoes if you've had disease problems in your garden.) Store the seed tubers over winter as you would other potatoes.

SEASON-BY-SEASON CARE: POTATO

This care guide tells you what to do and when to do it for your best potato harvest ever. Because timing of certain tasks is critical, review all the instructions in this guide in late winter. Locate or buy the products you'll need in advance. If you have problems with your potatoes, refer to "Solving Potato Problems" on page 162 to identify the causes and find solutions.

Spring

Set out wireworm traps. If you've had past problems with wireworms, put out pieces of store-bought potatoes in the bed two weeks before you plan to plant your crop. Every few days, remove the potato traps (they should be full of wireworms), destroy them, and set out more. If wireworms have been a severe problem, delay planting until late spring.

Plant seed potatoes. Start potatoes as soon as the soil can be worked—about two to four weeks before the last predicted frost. Be sure to use certified, clean seed potatoes.

Cover plants with floating row cover. If you've had past problems with caterpillars, Colorado potato beetles, flea beetles, or leafhoppers, protect this year's crop by covering beds with row cover before plants appear.

Water. Keep soil evenly moist. Water thoroughly during droughts. Don't overwater; soggy conditions will cause potatoes to rot.

Fertilize. Drench plants with 1 cup of compost tea per plant when the first sprouts emerge. Repeat in ten days. Spray plants two or three times before bloom with a mix of 2 tablespoons of liquid seaweed in 1 gallon of compost tea.

Hill up plants. Push soil up around the base of the plants periodically until the plants flower. For details, see "Hilling Potatoes" on page 159.

Mulch. A thick mulch of hay or straw helps keep soil moisture even and prevents weed problems. If you can get hay or straw, begin applying it a few weeks after planting, continuing until you've put down a 6- to 8-inch-deep layer. Broadcast 1 pound of soybean meal or alfalfa meal per 100 square feet into the mulch so that it won't rob nutrients from the potato crop as it breaks down.

Spray pyrethrins or rotenone. If you've had past problems with flea beetle larvae damage to tubers, prepare to spray adult flea beetles as soon as they appear.

Summer

Harvest. Begin harvesting "new" potatoes soon after the plants blossom.

Plant fall crop. Be sure to plant early enough so that tubers can mature before the first frost.

Fall

Harvest. Dig up mature potatoes before the first frost. Cure tubers thoroughly, then clean dirt off the tubers and store them.

Clean up. Remove all crop residues and damaged potatoes. Compost them, or if you've had any disease or insect problems, destroy them or put them in sealed containers with household trash.

Cultivate. Work the top few inches of soil to unearth and kill Colorado potato beetles that would overwinter in the soil. If you've had problems with wireworms, cultivate several times over a four- to six-week period.

Plant for early-spring harvest. In areas with mild winters, plant potatoes in fall or winter, whenever the ground is workable.

Solving Potato Problems

Use this table to identify problems on your potatoes. Scan the list of symptoms to find the description that most closely matches what you see in your garden. Then refer across the page to learn the cause and the recommended solutions. For some pest problems, by the time you see the damage, there is little you can do to fix things in the current season. But pest-damaged potatoes usually are good to eat if you peel the scarred skin off or cut out damaged areas. Damaged potatoes generally don't store well. In the future, take preventive steps, such as planting certified disease-free seed. For a schedule of preventive measures for potatoes, see "Season-by-Season Care: Potato" on page 161. You'll also find illustrations, descriptions, and additional controls for many of the insects and diseases listed below in Part 5 of this book.

LEAF AND PLANT PROBLEMS

SYMPTOMS	CAUSES	SOLUTIONS
Planted seed fails to sprout or rots before emergence	Sprout inhibitor treatment Fungal or bacterial rot	Potatoes from the grocery store are usually treated to prevent sprouting, so you should not use them for seed. Various rot disease organisms can attack potatoes, especially in cold, wet soil. Replant with certified disease-free seed in a well-drained site when soil is above 45°F.
Light green stipples and brown spots on leaflets; wedge-shaped insects on leaf undersides	Leafhoppers	Several species of leafhoppers attack potatoes; potato leafhoppers occur in eastern half of North America. Severely attacked plants may die from leafhopper damage or from viruses spread by leafhoppers. Inspect plants; if you find more than 1 leafhopper per 10 leaves, spray insecticidal soap, neem, pyrethrins, or rotenone.
Large holes in leaves; black and orange striped beetles on plants	Colorado potato beetles	Knock beetles off plants into cans of soapy water or onto a tarp and destroy them. Inspect leaves and shoots; handpick beetles, larvae (orange, humpbacked grubs), and bright yellow egg clusters. Moderate leaf damage won't lower yields. For severe problems, spray BTSD, neem, or pyrethrins.
Puckered, curled leaves; small, pink or green insects on leaf undersides	Potato aphids	Native parasites and predators usually keep aphids in check. If aphids are numerous or if you live in an area where potato viruses spread by aphids are a problem, wash aphids from plants with a strong spray of water or spray insecticidal soap, neem, or pyrethrins.
Small, round holes in leaves; small, jumping black insects may be seen on plants	Flea beetles	Leaf injury by flea beetles has little effect on yield, but flea beetle larvae feeding on tubers can cause serious damage. Spray rotenone or pyrethrins to control adults. Drench soil with parasitic nematodes to control larvae.
Large, ragged holes in leaves; caterpillars may be seen on plants	Caterpillars	Several species of caterpillars may attack potatoes. Plants can withstand some damage without lowering yield. Handpick caterpillars, or spray BTK or neem.

SYMPTOMS	CAUSES	SOLUTIONS
Gray, water-soaked patches on leaves; plants may collapse suddenly	Late blight	Late blight is most severe in northern and eastern North America, especially in cool, wet weather. Spray copper or bordeaux mixture at first sign of disease; repeat every 7–10 days. To prevent blight from spreading to tubers, cut vines just below the soil line and remove all foliage 2 weeks before harvest.
Rolled, tough, light green leaves with yellowish or reddish edges	Leafroll virus Other viruses	Tubers from infected plants have brown areas but are edible when damaged areas are cut out. Pull and destroy infected plants. For future crops, control aphids immediately as their feeding spreads the virus.
Leaves turn yellow between veins, edges curl up; ooze exudes from cut stems	Bacterial ring rot	Pull and destroy all infected plants. Disinfect your hands and tools before handling healthy plants. Collect and destroy all crop debris. Do not save seed from infected plants.
Leaves with gray-brown spots with concentric rings	Early blight	Plants stressed by drought, nutrient deficiency, or insect damage are most likely to be infected. Spray copper or bordeaux mixture at first sign of disease; repeat every 7–10 days. Hill soil over roots to prevent infection of tubers and wait to harvest until plant foliage has died. Plan to practice a 2- to 3-year crop rotation with all tomato-family crops.
Tunnels in leaves and stems; shoots wilt and die	Potato tuberworms	This is a pest in California and the South; it infests potatoes in the field and in storage. Pull and destroy infested plants and tubers. Next season, plant potato sets deeply. Keep soil hilled 2" deep over developing tubers, and mulch plants to keep adults from laying eggs. Plan to practice a rotation with all tomato-family crops.
Branches or whole plant gradually wilts, leaves drop; stem interior turns brown	Verticillium wilt	Pull and destroy all infected plants. In warm regions, try solarizing the soil before planting. Plan to practice a 4- to 6-year crop rotation with all tomato-family crops.

TUBER AND ROOT PROBLEMS

SYMPTOMS	CAUSES	SOLUTIONS
Holes in eyes of tubers, with pinkish webbing and crumbly residues around holes	Potato tuberworms	This is a pest in California and the South; it infests potatoes in the field and in storage. Pull and destroy infested plants and tubers; carefully check all tubers for evidence of larvae before storing. Next season, plant potato sets deeply. Keep soil hilled 2" deep over developing tubers, and mulch plants to keep adults from laying eggs. Plan to practice a rotation with all tomato-family crops.

(continued)

Solving Potato Problems—Continued

TUBER AND ROOT PROBLEMS—CONTINUED

SYMPTOMS	CAUSES	SOLUTIONS
Small, round holes in potato sets or tubers; slender, brown larvae may be present	Wireworms	Undamaged parts of tubers are edible, but damaged tubers cannot be stored. Wireworms are worse in soil recently turned from sod and for a few years thereafter. Drenching soil with parasitic nematodes may give some control.
Networks of fine tunnels, cracks, and scabby areas on surface of tubers	Tuber flea beetles	Damaged tubers are edible, once surface damage is removed, but they cannot be stored. Drench soil with parasitic nematodes to control larvae.
Brown or black, crusty scabs on skin of tubers	Scab	Damage is only cosmetic; tubers are edible and can be stored. Scab fungus grows in neutral or alkaline soils; add sulfur to acidify neutral soils if necessary. Avoid use of fresh manure and alkaline soil amendments (bonemeal, lime, wood ashes) where potatoes will be grown.
Tubers are misshapen, with knobs and cavities, but otherwise healthy	Alternating wet and dry conditions	Misshapen potatoes are edible; they will store well if handled carefully to avoid breaking knobs, which would allow rot organisms to enter. Avoid future problems by correcting the irrigation system if necessary to ensure more even watering. Mulch plants to conserve moisture.
Small bumps on tubers; galls on other roots; brown flecks in tuber flesh	Nematodes	Undamaged portions of tubers are edible, but they cannot be stored. Pull and destroy all infested plants, including all roots and undersize tubers. In warm regions, try solarizing the soil before planting. Plan to practice a 3- to 5-year rotation with nonsusceptible crops (corn, onion, small grains).
Ring of black rot at stem end of tubers; light brown layer in tuber flesh	Bacterial ring rot	Pull and destroy all infected plants. Disinfect your hands and tools before handling healthy plants. Collect and destroy all crop debris. Do not save seed from infected plants.
Center of tuber is hollow; tubers are unusually large, but otherwise healthy	Waterlogged soil Excessive rate of growth	Internal cavities develop when tubers grow too quickly. Tubers are edible, but may not store well. Don't overfertilize and keep soil evenly moist, especially when plants are young. Avoid overwatering while tubers are expanding.
Green skin on tubers; green color may extend into flesh	Exposure to light	Tubers are edible if all green-tinged skin and flesh are removed (do not eat green areas). In the future, make sure growing tubers are well covered with soil or mulch. Store potatoes in a completely dark place.

PUMPKIN   *Cucurbita* spp. • Cucurbitaceae

Care of pumpkins is similar to that of winter squash. See "Squash" on page 170 for seasonal care information and solutions to problems. Here you'll find special information on choosing cultivars, growing giant pumpkins, and harvesting pumpkins.

Tending the pumpkin patch. Place boards under developing pumpkins; it will help prevent them from rotting. To keep your pumpkins round and evenly colored, lift and turn them regularly.

One-quarter turn each week until harvest

Choosing Plants

Pumpkin cultivars vary according to size (from 1 to 800 pounds), color (deep orange to yellow or even white), shape (uniformly round to long necked), and rate of maturity (90 to 120 days). The skin may be smooth or ribbed.

Some pumpkin types have sweeter, smoother flesh and are better suited for cooking than others. If you have limited garden space, choose bush or compact cultivars. There are also early-maturing pumpkins.

Planting

Plant pumpkins according to the guidelines in "Planting Facts" on this page.

To grow huge pumpkins for show, choose 'Atlantic Giant' or another cultivar developed for that purpose. Start seeds indoors, then set transplants out where they will receive full sun at least eight hours a day. Dig in plenty of composted cow manure or compost before planting. Allow 25 feet between hills; thin to one plant per hill. Protect plants from wind, and correct pest problems immediately. By midsummer, channel each plant's energy to one pumpkin by removing all other fruits. Fertilize plants regularly with compost tea.

Harvesting

Wait to harvest until the vines have died back and the shells are tough—90 to 120 days, depending on the cultivar. To test for ripeness, poke the shell with your thumbnail; if the skin doesn't break or dent easily, the pumpkin is ready to pick. Store pumpkins as you would winter squash.

PLANTING FACTS

Seed and Seedling Identification

Seed Spacing

4'–8'

4'–8'

For hill planting, plant 6 seeds in hills 4'–8' apart on all sides.
Seed depth: ¾"–2"

RADISH *Raphanus sativus* • Cruciferae

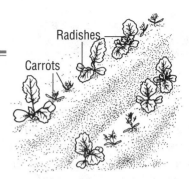

Interplant radishes. Sow radish seed with other vegetables. The radishes will be ready to harvest just when slower crops take off.

Choosing Plants

Easy-to-grow radishes come in early, mid-season, and late cultivars. Color choices include white, scarlet, red, and yellow. Early, or spring, types, which mature in 20 to 30 days, need cool temperatures to produce good-quality roots. If the weather or the soil is too warm, they are small and unpleasantly pungent. Mid-season radishes, bred to withstand summer heat, require 30 to 40 days to develop. The much-larger late, or winter, radishes need decreasing temperatures and daylengths during the 60 to 70 days they take to mature.

Site and Soil

Radishes like a rich, loose, well-drained, sandy loam. Add aged manure for quick growth to prevent tough and woody-tasting roots. In clay soil, add lots of compost and sand before planting to avoid a crop of misshapen roots. Till the planting area to a depth of 6 inches for quick-growing radishes and up to 2 feet for the big winter types.

Planting

When to plant. Make small succession plantings of spring radishes every ten days in April and May and again in August and September. Plant mid-season types from June to mid-August. Plant late radishes in midsummer in the North for a fall harvest, and in late summer in the South for an early-winter harvest.

How much to plant. Only winter radishes can be stored. So, for spring and summer types, make small successive plantings for a constant, moderate supply for fresh eating. One ounce of radish seed will plant a 100-foot row.

Planting outdoors. Sow seed ¼ to ½ inch deep and ½ to 1 inch apart. Thin seedlings to 2 inches apart; 3 to 4 inches for winter radishes.

Seasonal Care

Radish care is simple because the crop grows so fast. Be sure to weed and water regularly; dry soil causes cracked, woody roots.

Radishes are in the cabbage family. If problems develop, see "Solving Cabbage Problems" on page 106 for solutions.

Harvesting

Pull radishes as soon as the roots are mature; they quickly become cracked and tough if left in the soil.

Radishes as houseplants. Grow radishes on a sunny windowsill for winter harvests.

PLANTING FACTS

Seed and Seedling Identification

Seed Spacing

1–2 seeds per inch

←10"–12"→

For intensive spacing, plant seeds 2"–4" apart on all sides.
Seed depth: ¼"–½"

RHUBARB *Rheum rhabarbarum* • Polygonaceae

Choosing Plants

This long-lived perennial thrives in Zones 2 through 8. Grow most cultivars from root divisions (sold as crowns). Rhubarb is generally trouble-free as long as it is planted in well-drained soil.

Site and Soil

Separate rhubarb from annual vegetables so you won't till it up accidentally.

Choose a site with:
• At least half a day of sun. (Partial shade is good in warmer regions.)
• Light, moderately rich soil.
• pH between 6.5 and 7.5.
Avoid:
• Areas where water puddles.

PLANTING FACTS

Crown Spacing

30"–36"

←–30"–36"–→

For intensive spacing, plant crowns 2' apart on all sides. Crown depth: 2"–3"

Dig or till a 3-foot-wide bed 1½ feet deep. Mix in a 6-inch layer of compost.

Planting

When to plant. Plant crowns in early spring.

How much to plant. Three plants are adequate for most families.

Planting outdoors. Dig holes large enough in which to spread out the roots. Sprinkle 1 cup of bonemeal in each hole. Place crowns with buds facing up and spread out roots. Cover and water well.

Seasonal Care

Fertilize. Rake back loose mulch and spread 2 inches of compost in very early spring.

Thin plants. If stalks were thin and crowded last year, dig up and divide the roots in early spring. Replant sections with two or three buds.

Mulch. When plants sprout, add 4 inches of organic mulch.

Remove flowerstalks. Cut off stalks as they appear.

Inspect crowns. Wet soil conditions can cause the plants to wilt and the roots to rot. Destroy rotted plants, and replant in a well-drained site or in raised beds. The rhubarb curculio occasionally

Blanching rhubarb. *Set an open-ended box over a sprouting plant. Blanched stalks will be longer and a week earlier than usual.*

bores into the stem or crown to lay its eggs. Handpick adults or spray severe infestations with rotenone.

Winterize. Remove and compost the foliage when it dies down in the fall. Apply a thick layer of organic mulch.

Harvesting

Don't harvest rhubarb the first year after planting. The second year, harvest for one or two weeks. The third year, harvest for one to two months. From then on, harvest as long as you please.

Pick thick stalks with fully developed leaves. Twist and pull them off the crown or cut them with a sharp knife. Trim off and compost the leaves. Don't eat rhubarb leaves; they are poisonous.

SPINACH *Spinacia oleracea* • Chenopodiaceae

Choosing Plants

The thick, savoyed (puckered) leaves of spinach are a nutritious treat in salads. You can also grow smooth-leaved cultivars, which are easier to wash clean of sand and grit. If you live in an area where spring warms up quickly, look for cultivars that resist heat and bolting (going to seed).

Site and Soil

Spinach will grow in sun or light shade. (It prefers shade in warm weather.) Soil should be light and well drained with a pH of 6.0 to 7.0. Till or dig 4 inches deep.

PLANTING FACTS

Seed and Seedling Identification

Seed Spacing

1"–2"

12"–18"

For intensive spacing, plant seeds 6" apart on all sides.
Seed depth: ¼"–½"

Spread 10 to 15 pounds of compost per 100 square feet and work it into the top few inches. If your soil drains slowly, prepare raised beds.

Planting

When to plant. Plant in early spring as soon as the soil is at least 35°F. Make small successive plantings every two to three weeks until daytime temperatures are consistently over 70°F. Resume planting when temperatures stay below 75°F; continue until a few weeks before the first expected frost. Plant spinach in cold frames in the fall for winter and early-spring harvest.

In the South, start planting in early fall for late-fall through spring harvests.

How much to plant. Plant ten plants per person per planting. A packet of seed will plant about 25 feet.

Planting outdoors. Soak seed in compost tea for 15 minutes to overnight. Sow seed as directed in "Planting Facts" on this page. Thin to 2 to 4 inches apart.

Seasonal Care

Follow these guidelines for a bumper spinach harvest.

Quick spinach harvests. Use a push hoe to quickly sever the plants just below ground level. This technique also works for clearing out plants that are overgrown or have gone to seed.

Cover with floating row cover. Protect early plantings from cold and all plantings from insect damage. Leave on until harvest in cool weather.

Fertilize. Water weekly with 1 cup of kelp meal plus fish emulsion per foot of row until plants are 3 inches tall.

Mulch. Spread 3 to 6 inches of mulch after thinning.

Provide shade. Cover warm-season plantings with shade cloth over hoops.

Harvesting

Pick individual outside leaves once they are at least 3 inches long or cut entire plants just below the ground. Spinach will keep in the refrigerator up to one week.

Solving Spinach Problems

Use this table to identify problems on your spinach. Scan the list of symptoms to find the description that most closely matches what you see in your garden. Then refer across the page to learn the cause and the recommended solutions. Avoid problems by covering your spinach with floating row cover and giving the plants proper care. For details, see "Seasonal Care" on the opposite page. You'll also find illustrations, descriptions, and additional controls for many of the insects and diseases listed below in Part 5 of this book.

SYMPTOMS	CAUSES	SOLUTIONS
Leaves with clear or brownish blotches or squiggles	Leafminers	Undamaged parts of leaves are edible. Handpick and destroy damaged leaves. Spray severely infested plants with neem. In the future, protect plants with floating row cover from seeding until harvest.
Leaves with pale yellow spots; spots have grayish mold on undersides	Downy mildew (blue mold)	Remove and destroy affected plants. To reduce problems, thin plants and avoid wetting leaves when watering. In the future, plant resistant cultivars, avoid planting spinach in the site for 3 years, and plant in well-fertilized raised beds.
Yellow, deformed leaves	Curly top virus Mosaic virus	Destroy infected plants. Control aphids, which spread viruses as they feed. Plant mosaic-tolerant cultivars.
Leaves distorted; tiny black, green, or pink insects on leaf undersides	Aphids	Wash aphids off plants with a strong stream of water. Spray severely infested plants with insecticidal soap, neem, or pyrethrins. (Spinach may be sensitive to these sprays, so test-spray a small area first.) In the future, grow smooth-leaved cultivars (which offer fewer places for aphids to hide), or protect plants with floating row cover from seeding until harvest.
Leaves with numerous small, round holes	Flea beetles	Leaves with holes are edible. If damage is serious, pick off damaged leaves and spray plants with pyrethrins-rotenone. Drench soil with parasitic nematodes to control beetle larvae. In the future, cover plants with floating row cover until they are well established or through harvest.
Leaves with large, ragged holes	Loopers Beet armyworms	Handpick caterpillars. If small caterpillars are present, spray plants with BTK or neem. In the future, cover plants with floating row cover from seeding to harvest.
Seedstalks appear prematurely	Cold or heat	Harvest leaves of bolting (going to seed) plants as soon as possible; then pull up and compost the plants. In the future, plant bolt-resistant cultivars. Cover early plantings with floating row cover. Plant early in warm regions to avoid summer heat, mulch plants to cool the soil, and plant in partial shade.

SQUASH *Cucurbita* spp. • Cucurbitaceae

Choosing Plants

Gardeners separate squash into two main groups, summer and winter. Summer squash are harvested immature and used fresh; winter squash are allowed to mature on the vine and can be stored for many months. All squash need the same conditions and care.

You can select bush cultivars of many types of squash, a good option if your space is limited. Early-maturing types are suitable for regions with short growing seasons.

Summer squash. Summer squash cultivars (mostly

PLANTING FACTS

Seed and Seedling Identification

Seed Spacing

3'–8'

3'–8'

For hill planting, plant 6 seeds in hills 3'–8' apart on all sides.
Seed depth: ¾"–1"

Cucurbita pepo) take 48 to 75 days from seeding to harvest. Dark green zucchini is the most familiar type, but there are also light green, yellow, and white cultivars. Plant one or two plants of several cultivars.

Dual-purpose squash. A few squash cultivars are harvested both as summer squash and mature winter squash. 'Eat-It-All' and 'Jersey Golden Acorn' are two examples. Pick young fruits until midsummer—then let the rest of the fruits mature for winter use.

Winter squash. Winter squash cultivars (*C. maxima, C. mixta, C. moschata,* and *C. pepo*) are ready to harvest in 75 to 120 days. There is an enormous variety from which to choose, including

acorn, buttercup, butternut, delicata, hubbard, and spaghetti squash. Most cultivars are long vined, but some bush cultivars are available.

Site and Soil

Squash will grow in full sun or part shade (such as under tall vegetables like corn). Choose a well-drained site with fertile soil with a pH of 5.5 to 6.8. Dig or till the soil 8 inches deep. Spread 10 to 20 pounds of compost per 100 square feet and work it into the top few inches, or prepare individual hills of compost. If drainage is poor, build raised beds or plant your squash seeds or transplants in hills 2 to 3 feet wide and 8 to 10 inches high.

GREEN THUMB TIP

If you have a small garden, but lots of lawn that gets full sun, try this innovative way of growing vining squash.

1. Dump two wheelbarrowfuls of soil mixed with compost or well-rotted manure in a pile on the lawn.

2. Spread the pile out over the lawn with a rake or hoe to make an 8- to 12-inch-deep circular bed.

3. Plant 6 to 14 seeds in a circle on top of the bed.

4. When the seeds germinate and grow, don't thin. Simply allow the most vigorous plants to take over.

To water, put a hose in the middle of the circle and let the water run for a while. Mow the grass around the bed until the vines start to run. Don't mow over the vines; just do less mowing as the vines spread!

Planting

When to Plant

Plant seeds or plants outdoors when the soil temperature has reached 60°F—at least one week after the last frost. Young plants cannot tolerate cold and will be damaged by temperatures below 35°F. Make additional plantings of summer squash: one six weeks later and another four weeks after that to have a continuous harvest right up until frost.

How Much to Plant

One summer squash plant per person per planting is plenty. For a supply of winter squash that will last all winter, grow four to six plants per person.

Starting Plants Indoors

Start seeds indoors in individual 3-inch pots two to three weeks before your last expected frost. Plant two seeds per pot and cut off the extra seedlings when they get their first true leaves.

Planting Outdoors

Soak seeds in compost tea for 15 minutes to overnight. Sow seeds ¾ to 1 inch deep. Handle transplants carefully to avoid injuring the roots.

To plant in hills, for bush cultivars allow 3 to 6 feet between hills; 6 to 8 feet for vining types. Plant two transplants or six seeds in a circle on top of each hill.

Trellising vining squash. *Vertical growing keeps vines and fruits off the ground, away from soilborne disease problems and crushing feet. This wood-and-wire-mesh lean-to works well—just be sure young fruits don't get caught halfway through a hole in the wire.*

To grow squash in rows, for bush cultivars plant one transplant or two seeds every 2 to 3 feet in rows spaced 4 to 6 feet apart. For vining types, plant every 3 to 4 feet and space rows 8 to 12 feet apart. You can plant vining squash closer together if you support them on trellises.

Thinning

Thin to leave two plants per hill or one plant per pair of seeds when plants have two true leaves.

Seasonal Care

To produce a good crop, squash plants need plenty of water as well as protection from pests. For complete details on taking care of your squash plants, see "Season-by-Season Care: Squash" on page 173. For information on how to deal with troublesome pests, see "Solving Squash Problems" on page 175.

Harvesting

Squash flowers are delicious fried, stuffed, or cooked

SQUASH AND CORN

Squash and corn are famous companion plants. Squash leaves shade the soil and reduce weed growth, and their prickly stems may make raccoons think twice about entering the patch. The corn provides shade for the squash in the heat of the summer and doesn't mind if the vines wander up it.

If you really want to make your garden space work, plant pole beans next to your corn as well. The beans will climb happily skyward while feeding the corn extra nitrogen.

Preventing borer problems. *To keep out squash vine borers, wrap panty hose around the stems at the base of young plants.*

in soups or stews. Just remember that if you pick female flowers, you'll be reducing the number of squash fruits that will form. Also, don't harvest the male flowers so heavily that there's no pollen to fertilize the female flowers.

Summer squash. Harvest summer squash fruits with a sharp knife when they are still

small—about 3 or 4 inches across or 4 to 6 inches long. Larger squash are edible but the skin and seeds get tough as they get larger. Pick off and compost any large fruits that sneak by you; leaving them on the vine will decrease the plant's productivity.

You can store summer squash in the refrigerator for about one week. Freeze, can, dry, or pickle surplus fruits.

Winter squash. Let winter squash fruits ripen fully on the vine before picking. You shouldn't be able to pierce the skin with your fingernail. Harvest before the first hard frost. Fruit exposed to light frost is often more flavorful but doesn't keep as well. Pick fruits with hand pruners or a sharp knife, leaving a few inches of the stem attached.

Always hold the squash itself—don't lift it by the stem; a snapped-off stem can

Squash bug traps. *Lay scrap boards on the ground around the plants. The bugs will hide under them. Lift the boards carefully in the early morning and squash the pesky bugs.*

cause the fruit to rot. Use a soft cloth to brush off any soil, and sort out any bruised or stemless fruit to use immediately. Cure the healthy fruits in the sun or in a well-ventilated place at room temperature for ten days.

Winter squash will keep for up to five months if cured properly and stored in a dry place at 50° to 55°F. Place squash so the air can circulate around them as much as possible.

Extending the Season

To get a head start on the season, warm the soil with black plastic a few weeks before planting. Start seed indoors about four weeks before transplanting. Protect seedlings from the cold with cloches or floating row cover;

Harvesting winter squash. *Cut butternut and other winter squash from the vine using hand pruners or a sharp knife. Leave a few inches of the stem attached to the fruit.*

SEASON-BY-SEASON CARE: SQUASH

This care guide tells you what to do and when to do it for your best squash harvest ever. Because timing of certain tasks is critical, review all the instructions in this guide in late winter. Locate or buy the products you'll need in advance. If you have problems with your squash, refer to "Solving Squash Problems" on page 175 to identify the causes and find solutions.

Spring

Cover soil with black plastic. Prewarm the soil to get your plants off to a faster start. On planting day, cut slits in the plastic and insert seeds or transplants through the slits into the soil beneath.

Start seeds indoors. If your growing season is short, start seeds indoors two to three weeks before your last expected frost.

Direct-sow seeds. Plant outdoors whenever the soil is at least 60°F.

Interplant radishes. Try planting radish seeds on your squash hills. Many gardeners report that radishes repel squash pests. Let the radishes remain in place all season.

Cover seeds and plants with floating row cover. Protect squash plants from cool weather and insects (and the diseases they spread) by covering them with row cover from planting until the first female flowers open.

Fertilize. Spray plants with compost tea plus kelp (2 tablespoons kelp meal per gallon of tea) at transplanting or two weeks after seedlings come up. Spray again in three weeks or when the first flowers appear.

Provide support. If your space is limited, put up a trellis or other vertical support for vining squash cultivars. The wooden lean-to trellis, shown on page 171, works well for squash. Or interplant your squash crop with your corn.

Water. Keep soil evenly moist. Water deeply, especially during dry spells. To prevent problems with diseases, always water from below. Drip irrigation works well for squash. Squash plants may wilt slightly on hot days even when the soil is moist. This is normal and won't harm the plants.

Mulch. If you're not using black plastic, spread 8 to 10 inches of loose organic mulch around the plants when the soil is thoroughly warm.

Summer

Hand-pollinate flowers. If you have just a few plants or the weather is cool, pollinate each female flower when it opens.

Fertilize. When the first fruits set, water each plant well with compost tea or dump a shovelful of compost over the base of the stem.

Raise fruits off the ground. Winter squash fruits resting on the ground or on moist mulch are prone to rot. Place scraps of board, tin cans, or other objects under the developing fruits to keep them off the ground.

Harvest. Pick summer squash at least every other day. Harvest while still small and tender.

Prune. For vining cultivars, pinch off shoot tips, flowers, and small fruits in late summer to encourage the larger fruits to mature.

Fall

Harvest. Pick winter squash when they are fully mature and before the first hard frost.

Clean up. Pull and compost vines as soon as production drops off or when frost kills them. Till site after pulling vines to expose insects hiding in the soil, and plant a cover crop suited to the season.

Storing winter squash. *You can store winter squash through the winter in a cool (50° to 55°F) cellar or garage. Hubbards are the best keepers; acorn squash keep only a few months.*

remove when the weather turns warm and the plants are established.

Make a second planting of summer squash one to six weeks after the first planting. Follow up with a third planting four weeks later, and you'll have a continuous harvest that lasts until frost.

To extend your harvest, cover plants in fall when light frost threatens.

Growing in Containers

Choose bush cultivars. Sow seeds directly in outdoor pots (2 feet by 2 feet by 2 feet) filled with very fertile, well-drained soil. Place the pots in full sun. Water regularly; never let the soil dry out. Hand-pollinate, as shown at right, to ensure complete pollination. Fertilize weekly with compost tea.

Propagation

Choose open-pollinated (nonhybrid) cultivars for seed saving. If you grow more than one type of squash (or your neighbor does), ensure the seeds' purity by bagging the flowers before they open and hand-pollinating them.

Don't bag the flowers until the buds are on the verge of opening (when the green buds have begun to turn orange). Cover the same number of female and male buds with small paper bags (don't use plastic); tie them closely to the stem. The next day, cut off and unbag the male flowers and remove their petals. Unbag each female flower, open it, and rub the stamen of the male flower against the sticky stigma at the tip of the pistil. (For an illustration of the parts, see below.) Cover the female flower again with the bag to keep insects out. With string or ribbon, mark the stems of the female flowers you have pollinated. Wait four or five days, then remove the bags.

Harvest the seed from both summer and winter squash when the fruits are fully mature. Cut them open, scoop out the pulp, and put it in a container of water. Work the pulp with your fingers until the seeds separate from it. Wash the seeds; spread them out to dry for about a week. Store in an airtight container.

Hand-pollinating a squash flower. *Transfer pollen from the male stamen to the female pistil using a small brush. Or remove a male blossom, pluck off the petals, and rub the stamen against the pistil of the female flower.*

Solving Squash Problems

Use this table to identify problems on your squash and squash-family plants. Scan the list of symptoms to find the description that most closely matches what you see in your garden. Then refer across the page to learn the cause and the recommended solutions. For some problems, by the time you see the damage, there is little you can do to save your crop. In the future, your best choices are to plant resistant cultivars whenever possible, rotate your squash patch to a new location each year, and protect young plants with floating row cover. For a schedule of other preventive measures, see "Season-by-Season Care: Squash" on page 173. You'll also find illustrations, descriptions, and additional controls for many of the insects and diseases listed below in Part 5 of this book. *Caution:* Cucumber, melon, and squash leaves are easily burned by insecticidal soap and copper-containing sprays. Use the most diluted sprays recommended on the label, and use them sparingly in the cool of the morning or evening. Do not spray drought-stressed plants or plants in direct sun. Also avoid spraying when the temperature is above 80°F.

FLOWER AND FRUIT PROBLEMS

SYMPTOMS	CAUSES	SOLUTIONS
Flowers appear, but no fruit	Lack of female flowers Lack of pollination	The first flowers are usually male and do not form fruit. Female flowers have a swelling at the base of the flower; male flowers don't. If you see both male and female flowers, but no fruit forms, the problem may be lack of pollination due to low bee populations or cool weather. You can hand-pollinate flowers; see bottom illustration on the opposite page for instructions.
Flowers chewed; tunnels in fruit	Pickleworms	Pale green caterpillars may be found inside fruit. Pick and destroy damaged fruit. Spray plants with BTK when damaged flowers are found. Crush rolled sections of leaves, which have pupae inside. Support fruit off the ground on tin cans or other supports to prevent worms from entering them. In the future, plant tolerant cultivars or early-maturing cultivars as early as possible to miss late-emerging pests. Plant summer squash as a trap crop to lure pickleworms away from melon and cucumber.
Fruit knobby, blotched, bitter, and off-flavored	Mosaic viruses	Pull and destroy infected plants. Control aphids, cucumber beetles, and other insects, and disinfect hands and tools after working with diseased plants to prevent disease from spreading. In the future, plant mosaic-tolerant cultivars and protect young plants from disease-carrying insects with floating row cover until female flowers open.
Fruit misshapen	Diseases Poor pollination	If leaves also show symptoms of disease, that is probably also the cause of the misshapen fruit. If no leaf symptoms are present, misshapen fruit may be due to poor pollination during hot or cool weather. Wait for weather to moderate, or hand-pollinate flowers if bee activity is low. See bottom illustration on the opposite page for instructions.

(continued)

Solving Squash Problems—Continued

FLOWER AND FRUIT PROBLEMS—CONTINUED

SYMPTOMS	CAUSES	SOLUTIONS
Fruit rots	Diseases Poor pollination Contact with soil	If leaves also show symptoms of disease, that is probably also the cause of the fruit rot. If young fruit on healthy plants rot from the blossom end, they may not have been well pollinated due to hot or cool weather. Wait for weather to moderate, or hand-pollinate flowers if bee activity is low. See bottom illustration on page 174 for instructions. If rot starts on underside where fruit rests on the ground, raise young fruit off the ground on tin cans or other supports, or spread clean mulch on the soil where fruit will rest.

LEAF AND WHOLE PLANT PROBLEMS

SYMPTOMS	CAUSES	SOLUTIONS
Leaves with holes; leaves may wilt	Cucumber beetles	These greenish yellow, black striped or greenish yellow, black spotted insects can spread bacterial wilt and viral diseases as they feed. Spray plants with pyrethrins-rotenone as soon as you see beetles. Drench soil with parasitic nematodes weekly to control larvae. Remove and destroy all crop residues when plants stop yielding. In the future, plant beetle- and disease-tolerant cultivars and protect plants with floating row cover until female flowers open.
Leaves with pale flecks; fine webbing under leaves	Spider mites	Spray leaves top and bottom with water once a week to control this pest, which thrives in dry conditions.
Leaves with whitish, powdery spots; turning brown and dry	Powdery mildew	Pick and destroy badly affected leaves. Rinse leaves thoroughly top and bottom with water once a week to slow spread of the disease. Severely infected plants yield poorly if at all, so pull them up and destroy. In the future, plant powdery mildew–resistant cultivars.
Leaves with small yellow to brown spots; purplish mold on leaf undersides	Downy mildew	Spray copper or bordeaux mixture every 5–7 days to reduce spread of the disease. In the future, plant tolerant cultivars.
Leaves with yellow, brown, or tan spots or blotches	Leaf spots Other diseases	Spray copper every 7–10 days to slow spread of the diseases. Thin plants to promote air circulation and avoid wetting foliage. Clean up and destroy crop debris. In the future, plant cultivars with multiple-disease resistance and plan at least a 2-year crop rotation with all squash-family crops.

SYMPTOMS	CAUSES	SOLUTIONS
Leaves turn yellow; leaves sticky and coated with black mold	Whiteflies	A few whiteflies do little damage—simply wash black mold off with water. Spray severe infestations with insecticidal soap. Pick and destroy heavily infested lower leaves, where immature whiteflies develop. In northern areas, plant seed or grow your own transplants to avoid importing whiteflies from greenhouse-grown plants.
Leaves with pale to brown blotches; shoots blacken and die back	Squash bugs	Handpick adults, which are oval and dark brown to black, and nymphs, which are powdery green, reddish, or gray. Lay boards around plants; check under them daily and destroy hiding squash bugs. Spray severe infestations with rotenone to control nymphs, with sabadilla to control adults. In the future, plant tolerant cultivars and cover plants with floating row cover until female flowers open.
Leaves and shoots distorted and curled	Melon aphids	Wash aphids off leaves with a strong spray of water. Spray severe infestations with insecticidal soap or neem. In the future, cover plants with floating row cover until female flowers open.
Leaves small, distorted, and mottled yellow; plants stunted	Mosaic viruses	Pull and destroy affected plants. Control aphids, cucumber beetles, and other insects, and disinfect hands and tools after working with diseased plants to prevent disease from spreading. In the future, plant mosaic-tolerant cultivars and protect young plants from disease-carrying insects with floating row cover until female flowers open.
Leaves wilt at midday, but recover at night	Bacterial wilt	Confirm diagnosis by cutting stem of one plant; a string of sticky bacterial ooze inside indicates bacterial wilt. Pull and destroy severely affected plants. Spray plants with copper to reduce spread of the disease. Spray pyrethrins-rotenone to control cucumber beetles, which spread the disease. In the future, cover plants with floating row cover until female flowers open to prevent insects from infecting plants.
Vines suddenly wilt; stem rotted or chewed at soil line	Squash vine borers	Once a plant wilts, it is hard to save it. In the future, choose borer-tolerant cultivars. Cover plants with floating row cover until female flowers open, then spray just the bottom 6" of the stem with BTK or pyrethrins-rotenone once a week, or wind a strip of cloth around base of the stem to cover it, as shown top left on page 172.

SWEET POTATO *Ipomoea batatas* • Convolvulaceae

Choosing Plants

Sweet potatoes come in white, yellow, and dark orange with brown or reddish brown skin. Dark orange sweet potatoes are called "yams," but true yams belong to the genus *Dioscorea* and are seldom grown north of Zone 10.

Sweet potatoes are grown from tuber sprouts called slips. Buy certified disease- and pest-free slips from a reputable nursery or start your own. Gardeners in the North should choose early-maturing cultivars. Southern gardeners should choose disease-resistant cultivars.

Site and Soil

Sweet potatoes prefer full sun, and loose, slightly acidic soil—pH 5.5 is ideal. Spread 10 to 20 pounds of compost

Starting sweet potato slips. Six weeks before the planting-out date, place tubers in a box of moist sand, sawdust, or chopped leaves. Keep the box at 70° to 80°F. When sprouts are 6 inches long and have little roots, snap them off the tuber. Cut off the bottom inch of the slip to help reduce tuber-borne disease problems.

per 100 square feet and work it into the top few inches. Avoid fresh manure and other nitrogen-rich fertilizers. If your soil is heavy or poorly drained, build 10-inch-high raised beds.

Planting

When to plant. Plant slips once the soil is at least 70°F.

How much to plant. Two to five plants per person is usually enough. Each plant produces 2 to 3 pounds.

Starting plants indoors. You can start your own sweet potato slips from tubers saved from your last year's crop (choose the last tubers to sprout and be sure they are healthy) or from purchased, untreated ones.

Follow the instructions with the above illustration for growing slips.

Planting outdoors. Dig holes 6 inches deep and 12 inches apart in rows 3 to 4 feet apart. In raised beds, plant a single row of slips down the center of the bed. Bury slips up to their top leaves, firm the soil, and water well.

Seasonal Care

Keep your soil moist all summer long to grow plump tubers. If your plants develop problems, refer to "Solving Sweet Potato Problems" on the opposite page to identify the causes and find solutions. Follow the guidelines below to harvest a bumper crop.

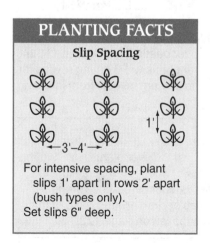

PLANTING FACTS

Slip Spacing

←— 3'–4' —→   1'

For intensive spacing, plant slips 1' apart in rows 2' apart (bush types only).
Set slips 6" deep.

Cover soil with black plastic. Prewarm the soil by covering it a few weeks prior to planting. On planting day, cut slits in the plastic and plant slips through the slits.

Mulch. If you're not using black plastic, mulch the vines with 6 inches of organic mulch two weeks after planting.

Water. Keep soil consistently moist but not soggy. Stop watering two weeks before harvesting.

Harvesting

Start checking tuber size 70 days after planting and harvest them when they reach the size you like. Dig tubers carefully by inserting a digging fork about a foot away from the main stem and lifting the soil. Harvest all tubers when frost nips the vines or when the vines yellow and die down.

Leave tubers in the sun for several hours. Then cure in a hot, well-ventilated area for 10 to 15 days. Store cured tubers at room temperature.

Solving Sweet Potato Problems

Use this table to identify problems on your sweet potatoes. Scan the list of symptoms to find the description that most closely matches what you see in your garden. Then refer across the page to learn the cause and the recommended solutions. For a schedule of other preventive measures, see "Seasonal Care" on the opposite page. You'll also find illustrations, descriptions, and additional controls for many of the insects and diseases listed below in Part 5 of this book.

SYMPTOMS	CAUSES	SOLUTIONS
Leaves with veins chewed; leaves wilted	Sweet potato flea beetles	Spray rotenone or pyrethrins to control adults. Remove bindweed and dichondra plants which is where larvae feed. In the future, cover plants with floating row cover until June; in the South, delay planting until June.
Stems turn black at soil line; leaves yellow; plants stunted	Black rot	Remove and destroy all diseased plants, roots, and crop debris. In the future, buy disease-free stock and plan a 3- to 4-year crop rotation.
Tubers tunneled; white grubs in tunnels	Sweet potato weevils	Unchewed parts of tubers may be edible (check for bitterness). Don't store roots that may contain larvae. Remove and destroy all crop debris, volunteer sweet potatoes, and morning glories in the area. In the future, buy weevil-free stock and cover plants with floating row cover until harvest.
Tubers with lengthwise cracks in surface	Growth cracks	Damaged tubers are edible. In the future, plant crack-resistant cultivars and keep the soil evenly moist.
Tubers with dark patches which may crack; tubers shrivel	Scurf	Diseased roots are edible but don't keep well. In the future, plant resistant cultivars, purchase disease-free stock, and plan a 2- to 3-year crop rotation.
Tubers with round, sunken black spots or patches	Black rot	Remove and destroy all diseased plants, roots, and crop debris. In the future, plant resistant cultivars, purchase disease-free stock, and plan a 3- to 4-year crop rotation.

TOMATO *Lycopersicon esculentum* • Solanaceae

Choosing Plants

Whether your personal favorite is a solid 1-pound beefsteak or a dish of dainty cherry tomatoes, you can't beat the quality and flavor of a garden-grown tomato. The most popular types for back-yard gardens are red, orange, and yellow, but there are also pink and white cultivars.

Large beefsteak tomatoes are especially well suited for slicing. Pear-shaped Italian or paste types, with thick skins and few seeds, are good for canning, juicing, or cooking. Fresh cherry tomatoes are popular in salads and make

Choosing tomato transplants. *If you buy tomato transplants, pick compact, sturdy plants and avoid weak, overgrown seedlings.*

Labels on figure: Healthy transplant — No blossoms on plant — Large, closely spaced leaves — Unhealthy transplant — Long stem — Flowers on plant — Yellowing lower leaves — Roots protruding from pot

tasty little snacks. Cultivars with high sugar content ("low acid") are also available.

Growth Habit

One important choice to make is whether to grow *determinate* or *indeterminate* tomatoes. Determinate types are bushy and compact; the plants set all their fruit within about a two-week period, and then decline. These types are perfect for producing a crop for processing.

Indeterminate cultivars are normally pruned and staked. The vines, which can reach 20 feet, produce fruit until the first frost or until they succumb to disease.

Days to Maturity

When selecting cultivars, consider your growing sea-son. Early types mature rapidly—55 to 70 days from transplanting—and are ideal for short-season regions; mid-season tomatoes are ready to harvest in 70 to 80 days; late-maturing types can take up to 90 days to mature.

Problem Resistance

The initials V, F, N, and T appearing after a cultivar name indicate a cultivar's resistance to Verticillium wilt(V), Fusarium wilt(F), nematodes(N), and tobacco mosaic virus(T). Southern gardeners should consider growing heat-resistant types.

Site and Soil

Tomatoes need at least six to eight hours of direct sun each day. (In areas with very

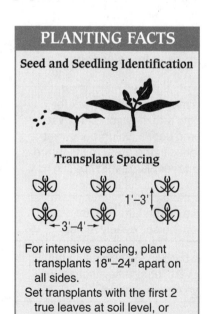

PLANTING FACTS

Seed and Seedling Identification

Transplant Spacing

1'–3'
3'–4'

For intensive spacing, plant transplants 18"–24" apart on all sides.

Set transplants with the first 2 true leaves at soil level, or strip lower leaves and lay plants horizontally in a trench.

PLANTING TOMATOES IN TRENCHES

Remove lower leaves.

New top growth

New roots

Preparing plants. *Strip off all but the top set of leaves from the stems.*

Planting. *Set plants horizontally in a 2- to 3-inch-deep trench and firm the soil.*

New growth. *The plant top will turn upward and the buried stem will produce roots.*

hot summers, provide partial shade.) Tomatoes do best in a loose, rich, well-drained soil with a pH between 5.5 and 6.8.

If you've had disease problems with past tomato crops, it's best to select a site where tomato, potato, eggplant, and pepper have not been planted for the past two or three years.

Add generous amounts of compost or well-rotted manure, and prepare rows. If your soil is heavy or your growing season is short, plant your tomatoes in raised beds.

Planting

When to Plant

Move transplants outdoors about one week after the last expected spring frost. Nighttime air temperatures should be consistently above 50°F and daytime temperatures should be at least 65°F. Or, if your growing season is long enough, sow seeds directly in the ground when the soil temperature is at least 60°F. Tomato plants cannot tolerate frost. They will thrive when air temperatures are between 70° and 75°F.

How Much to Plant

Grow two to four plants of slicing types per person. If you plan to can or freeze tomatoes and/or sauce, plant at least six plants of a paste or processing tomato.

Starting Plants Indoors

Sow seeds indoors six to eight weeks before you plan to set plants outdoors in the garden. Plant them ¼ inch deep in flats filled with a sterile potting mix; space seeds 1 inch apart. Gently spray the planted seed flats with water, then place the flats inside plastic bags. Provide good drainage and maintain soil temperature between 75° and 85°F. Seeds will germinate in seven to ten days.

Remove the plastic bags when the seedlings emerge. Place the flats in a sunny window or under fluorescent light. The air temperature should be 70°F or below. Keep the soil constantly moist, and fertilize weekly with manure tea or fish emulsion.

Move the strongest seedlings to 4-inch peat pots when the first true leaves appear. Plant deeper than before to keep the stems sturdy. Decrease the amount of water and increase the amount of light the seedlings receive. Select the healthiest seedlings, then gradually harden them off several days before transplanting outdoors.

Planting Outdoors

Move plants outdoors when all danger of frost has past. Choose an overcast day for transplanting. Dig large holes for the seedlings. Put 1 cup of kelp meal and 1 cup of bonemeal in the bottom of each hole to provide potassium and phosphorus. Set the transplants lower than they grew in the pot. If your transplants have long, leggy stems, plant them in trenches, as shown in the illustrations on page 181.

If you're sowing seeds directly in the garden, plant them 1/2 inch deep every 2 inches. Whether transplanting or direct-sowing, allow 1 to 3 feet between staked plants in rows spaced 3 feet apart. For tomatoes that will not be staked, space 3 feet apart in rows set 4 feet apart. Water well after planting, and cover with cloches.

Removing suckers. *Snap small suckers off at the base with your fingers. Cut off large, fleshy suckers with a sharp knife or pruning shears.*

Seasonal Care

Tomatoes need even moisture and regular feeding to produce the best yields. You may also want to support your plants in cages or train them on a trellis. Staked plants have lower overall yields than plants that are left to sprawl, but they produce more tomatoes per square foot. The fruit of staked plants is also less susceptible to disease and tends to have a higher vitamin C content.

Methods for supporting tomatoes fall under three general categories: cages, stakes, and trellises. (If you use stakes or trellises, you'll need to tie the plants loosely to the support with string or twine.) Choose the method that works best for you, and don't be afraid to experiment. See "Make-Your-Own Tomato Cages" on the opposite page and the illustrations on page 184 for ideas.

All tomato plants tend to produce suckers—shoots that appear between the main stem of the plant and the petioles (stems of the leaves). You may want to prune off suckers to keep plants within bounds and to channel their energy into producing fruit rather than leaves.

For a schedule of care for tomato plants, see "Season-by-Season Care: Tomato" on page 185. If your tomatoes develop problems, refer to "Solving Tomato Problems" on page 186 to identify the causes and find solutions.

Harvesting

Tomatoes are ready to harvest 55 to 90 days from transplanting. Fruits are ready to pick when they have

---

GREEN THUMB TIP

Southern gardeners can take advantage of their long, warm summers by planting a second, late-season tomato crop cloned from their first planting. In early summer, when your tomato plants are established, cut off several healthy 8-inch-long suckers, then plant them in containers. Provide partial shade and plenty of water. After two weeks, strip all but the top set of leaves from the new plants. Transplant, burying the stem up to the leaves. Within a few weeks, you'll have fresh tomatoes when other gardeners have long since harvested theirs.

MAKE-YOUR-OWN TOMATO CAGES

Commercial tomato cages are convenient, but if you grow indeterminate tomatoes, the cages often aren't large enough or strong enough to give the plants good support.

You can make heavy-duty, long-lasting cages inexpensively using concrete reinforcing wire. To make two cages that will support even your largest plants, gather the following:

- 16-foot length of heavy wire mesh (5 feet wide)
- Cinder blocks
- Heavy-duty bolt cutters
- Pliers
- Four wooden stakes

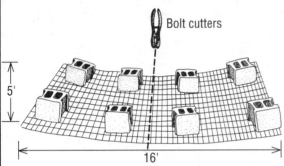

Bolt cutters

5'

16'

1. Start by spreading the roll of wire mesh out flat on the ground. Put cinder blocks around the perimeter of the mesh to hold it down, then use bolt cutters to cut through the center of the mesh. Wear gloves and heavy clothing to protect yourself from being scratched by the ends of the wire that are exposed as you make cuts.

Cut on both sides
of vertical wire.

2. Now use the bolt cutters to sever the bottom horizontal wire along one end of the mesh. This leaves tines that you can stick in the ground to help anchor the cage.

3. Carefully remove the cinder blocks from the wire (the wire may spring up forcefully as you remove the blocks), and stand the wire upright. Bend the edges toward each other to form a cylinder. Use pliers to twist the clipped edges together, or secure the edges together with medium-gauge wire.

4. Put the cage in place over a tomato plant. Pound in a wooden stake on either side of the cage to help anchor it more securely.

developed their full mature color. Fruits can pass their prime quickly, so be sure to check your plants daily. You can also harvest tomatoes when they begin to show stripes of mature color. Let them ripen at room temperature out of direct sunlight.

To avoid injuring the vine, cut the fruit off with pruning shears or twist it off gently while holding the vine. If a light frost is predicted, cover the plants at night with plastic, blankets, or sheets to protect the fruits.

Don't refrigerate tomatoes because cold causes loss of flavor and texture. Instead, can or freeze extra tomatoes.

Harvest all fruit before the first hard frost. Wrap harvested fruits that are still green in newspaper and put them in a dark place where the temperature is between 55° and 60°F. They will ripen over a period of weeks. Check wrapped fruit frequently and toss out any that are rotting.

Extending the Season

If your growing season is long enough, you can extend your harvest by planting early, mid-season, and late cultivars. For a head start on the season, warm the soil with black plastic, then set out transplants two weeks earlier than you would ordinarily. Plant in raised beds, and protect seedlings with cloches. To ensure against frost damage in the fall, cover plants with plastic, blankets, or sheets.

Growing in Containers

Tomatoes are well suited for growing in containers. Sow seeds indoors six to eight weeks before transplanting, then move outdoors when all danger of frost has past. Plant standard cultivars in large containers (1 foot wide by 2 feet deep) and provide vertical support. Dwarf types such as 'Pixie' or 'Tiny Tim' fit nicely in pots measuring 6 inches wide by 6 inches deep.

Use a loose, fertile potting soil with good drainage. Provide full sun at least six to eight hours every day, and water regularly. Side-dress with compost until the plants are established, then water with manure tea or fish emulsion weekly.

Propagation

If you're saving seed, select nonhybrid cultivars. To avoid cross-pollination, don't grow different types near each other. Choose the best fruits from the healthiest and fastest-maturing plants, and harvest when they are completely ripe. Refer to "Saving Tomato Seed" on page 81 for step-by-step instructions for separating the seeds from the tomato pulp.

Corral staking tomatoes. *Position stakes 10 feet apart along a row of plants and weave twine or cloth strips in figure-eight fashion around the plants and stakes.*

Trellising tomatoes. *Use concrete reinforcing wire and fasten it to heavy wooden end posts with metal staples. Tie the stems of the plants loosely to the trellis with string or twine.*

SEASON-BY-SEASON CARE: TOMATO

This care guide tells you what to do and when to do it for your best tomato harvest ever. Because timing of certain tasks is critical, review all the instructions in this guide in late winter. Locate or buy the products you'll need in advance. If you have problems with your tomatoes, refer to "Solving Tomato Problems" on page 186 to identify the causes and find solutions.

Early Spring

Cover soil with black plastic. Prewarm the soil to get a head start on the season and get your plants off to a faster start. On planting day, cut slits in the plastic and insert seeds or transplants through the slits into the soil beneath.

Start seeds indoors. Sow seeds indoors six to eight weeks before transplanting.

Spring

Direct-sow seeds. Plant outdoors whenever the soil is at least 60°F.

Set out transplants with cutworm collars. Put collars made of paper or cardboard around the stems of newly planted transplants to prevent cutworm feeding.

Cover transplants with cloches. This step will lessen transplant shock. Remove the covers when the weather warms up.

Cover plants with floating row cover. If you've had past problems with serpentine leafminers or flea beetles, cover plants securely with row cover rather than cloches. Keep the cover on until plants blossom.

Provide support. Insert stakes or trellises when you transplant; set out cages when plants are still young.

Water. Tomatoes need evenly moist soil. Water well at planting time. Continue watering deeply, especially during dry spells. To avoid problems with disease, water from the bottom and early in the day.

Mulch. Hand-pull weeds until the plants are established and the ground has warmed up, then apply a thick mulch of straw, grass clippings, or composted leaves.

Fertilize. If your plants are growing in poor soil, water each plant with 1 cup of fish emulsion solution (1 tablespoon per gallon of water) weekly from planting time until the first blossoms form.

Summer

Cover plants with floating row cover. If you've had past problems with tomato pinworms, covering the plants may help keep worms from attacking the fruits. Shake covered plants daily to ensure good pollination (plants are wind pollinated).

Spray copper. Where bacterial spot infections have been severe in the past, begin spraying copper as soon as fruit forms.

Provide partial shade. In areas with very hot summers, sunscald or blossom-drop may occur if plants or fruits aren't protected.

Harvest. Pick fruit when it is fully ripe.

Fall

Cover plants. For an extended harvest, protect plants with plastic, blankets, or sheets when a light frost is predicted.

Harvest. Continue picking fruit of indeterminate types until the first hard frost.

Clean up. After harvest ends, clear away all fallen fruit and plant debris and compost it. If your plants suffered from insect or disease problems, do not compost crop residues; destroy them or put them in sealed containers with your household trash.

Solving Tomato Problems

Use this table to identify problems on your tomato plants. Scan the list of symptoms to find the description that most closely matches what you see in your garden. Then refer across the page to learn the cause and the recommended solutions. For some disease problems, by the time you see the damage, there is little you can do to fix things in the current season. In the future, plant resistant cultivars. If you can, plan a 3- to 4-year rotation of tomato-family crops. For a schedule of pest-preventive measures for tomatoes, see "Season-by-Season Care: Tomato" on page 185. You'll also find illustrations, descriptions, and additional controls for many of the insects and diseases listed below in Part 5 of this book.

FLOWER AND FRUIT PROBLEMS

SYMPTOMS	CAUSES	SOLUTIONS
Blossoms appear, but few or no fruit develop	Cold nights or excessive heat Excess nitrogen	Early-season flowers may drop if nights are colder than 55°F. In summer, flowers may drop if temperatures exceed 90°F. When the weather changes, new blossoms should develop normal fruit. Nitrogen can stimulate leaf and stem growth and not fruit. Do not fertilize, and see if fruit development improves.
Fruit distorted at blossom end (cat-faced), otherwise healthy	Cold injury to flower buds	Cat-faced fruit is edible. Fruit that develops later in the season should be normal. In the future, wait to plant until weather is settled and warm.
Sunken, brownish black area starting at blossom end of fruit	Blossom-end rot	The condition is caused by poor calcium uptake, which is related to an uneven supply of water. Mulch plants and be sure they are deeply and evenly watered. For next season, ensure soil is fertile, with adequate calcium levels, and plant blossom-end rot–resistant cultivars.
Deep holes chewed in fruit; caterpillars may be present	Tomato fruitworms Hornworms	Undamaged portions of fruit are edible. Handpick fruitworms; spray BTK weekly for fruitworms if infestations are severe. Handpick hornworms daily. If many young hornworms are present, spray BTK every few days.
Fruit with small, water-soaked spots that later become scabby	Bacterial spot (bacterial blight)	Fruit is edible, but use it promptly because it may rot quickly. Collect and destroy all crop debris. In the future, plant disease-free seed.
Mottled, rough, or deformed fruit	Tobacco mosaic virus Other viruses	Fruit is usually still edible though of lower quality. Once plants are infected, there is no cure. Pull and destroy all affected plants. Wash hands, preferably in milk, and disinfect tools before handling healthy plants. In the future, plant cultivars with multiple-virus tolerance.
Concentric cracks in fruit around stem	Growth cracks	Cracked fruit is edible. Harvest cracked fruit immediately because it may rot quickly. Pick all fruit as soon as it ripens to prevent cracking. Keep soil evenly moist and mulch plants to help prevent fruit cracking.

SYMPTOMS	CAUSES	SOLUTIONS
Tan, leathery patches on side of fruit exposed to sun	Sunscald	Undamaged parts of fruit are edible; use ripe fruit immediately because it will rot quickly. Feed and water plants to stimulate vigorous leaf growth so that fruit won't be exposed.
Dark tunnels in fruit; tiny, mottled worms in fruit	Tomato pinworms	This pest occurs mostly in California. Undamaged parts of fruit are edible. Plan to remove or till under all crop debris and eliminate all tomatoes in the area for at least 3 months before growing another crop.

LEAF AND WHOLE PLANT PROBLEMS

SYMPTOMS	CAUSES	SOLUTIONS
Seedlings chewed off or girdled at soil level	Cutworms	Search for and destroy cutworms hiding in the soil around the base of damaged plants. Use a flashlight at night to catch feeding cutworms. Where infestations are severe, drench soil with parasitic nematodes, spray neem on plants, or use a bran bait mixed with BTK sprinkled between rows.
Sticky coating on leaves; tiny, white insects fly around leaves	Whiteflies	A light infestation does little damage. Black mold may grow on leaves and fruit; wash mold from leaves with water, wipe it off picked fruit. To control heavy infestations, spray insecticidal soap, neem, or pyrethrins frequently. Pick and destroy heavily infested lower leaves, where immature whitefly scales develop. In northern areas, plan to grow plants from seed to avoid bringing in whiteflies on purchased transplants.
Gray-brown spots with concentric rings on leaves	Early blight	Plants stressed by drought, deficiency, or insect damage are most affected. Spray copper or bordeaux mixture at first sign of disease; repeat every 7–10 days.
Leaves curl down; small, pink, green, or black insects on leaf undersides	Aphids	Native parasites and predators usually keep aphids in check. For a severe infestation, wash aphids from plants with a strong stream of water, or spray insecticidal soap, neem, or pyrethrins.
Leaves eaten, leaving only stems; large caterpillars on plants	Hornworms	Light feeding won't lower yield. Handpick hornworms daily. If many young caterpillars are present, spray BTK every few days.
Leaves with gray, water-soaked patches; white mold grows on lower side of spots in moist weather	Late blight	This disease is most severe in the North and East, especially in cool, wet weather. Spray copper or bordeaux mixture at first sign of disease; repeat every 7–10 days. Collect and destroy all crop debris and tomato-family weeds.

(continued)

Solving Tomato Problems—Continued

LEAF AND WHOLE PLANT PROBLEMS—CONTINUED

SYMPTOMS	CAUSES	SOLUTIONS
Dark brown spots on leaves	Bacterial spot	To reduce spread of the disease, spray with copper as soon as you see symptoms; repeat every 1–2 weeks (may not be effective in wet weather). Collect and destroy all crop debris. In the future, plant disease-free seed.
Lower leaves and stem turn bronze with a greasy sheen; leaves dry up	Tomato russet mites	Russet mites are microscopic; it's easy to mistake their feeding damage for a disease. Spray or dust sulfur to control mites but don't apply it too often or plants may suffer damage.
Mottled, puckered areas on leaves; growth may be stunted	Tobacco mosaic virus Various viruses	Once plants are infected by a virus, there is no cure. Pull and destroy all affected plants. Wash hands, preferably in milk, and disinfect tools before handling healthy plants. In the future, plant cultivars with multiple-virus tolerance.
Light-colored, water-soaked spots with dark margins on leaves	Bacterial spot Cercospora leaf spot	To reduce spread of the disease, spray with copper as soon as you see symptoms; repeat every 1–2 weeks (may not be effective in wet weather). Collect and destroy all crop debris. In the future, plant disease-free seed.
Small round holes in leaves	Flea beetles	Leaf injury by these small, black, jumping insects causes little damage unless plants are small. If damage is severe, spray rotenone or pyrethrins to control adults; drench soil with parasitic nematodes to control larvae.
Leaves speckled with pale yellow dots; fine webbing on leaves	Spider mites	Spider mites thrive in hot, dry weather. Native predators usually keep mites in check. Wash mites from leaves with a strong stream of water weekly. Spray insecticidal soap if infestations are severe.
Plants grow poorly; lower leaves turn yellow; roots with swollen galls	Root knot nematodes	Pull and destroy severely infected plants and give remaining plants extra care to salvage some harvest. In warm regions, solarizing the soil will suppress nematodes. In the future, plant nematode-resistant cultivars and practice a 3- to 5-year rotation with nonsusceptible crops (corn, onion, small grains).
Plant gradually wilts, leaves turn yellow; inside of lower stems brown or yellow	Verticillium wilt Fusarium wilt	Nematode injury increases susceptibility to wilts. Pull and destroy infected plants and remove crop debris in fall. Solarizing the soil will help control these disease organisms in warm regions. In the future, plant verticillium/fusarium/nematode-resistant (VFN) cultivars.

TURNIP *Brassica rapa*, Rapifera group • Cruciferae

Choosing Plants

Turnips and their close kin, rutabagas (*Brassica napus*), are grown for their sweet roots. Turnip greens also are rather sweet when cooked.

Turnips take 30 to 60 days to produce harvestable roots, which may be round or oblong. Choose from all white or yellow roots, or white roots with green, pink, or violet upper halves. Grow root cultivars for greens or choose a cultivar selected for abundant greens production.

Rutabagas, also called Swedish turnips, take 75 to 120 days to yield their large roots. Most cultivars are yellow with purple upper halves.

PLANTING FACTS

Seed and Seedling Identification

Seed Spacing

1–2 seeds per inch

←8"–12"→

For intensive spacing, plant seeds 4" apart on all sides.
Seed depth: ¼"–½"

Site and Soil

Turnips and rutabagas like full sun and loose soil with a pH of 5.5 to 6.8.

Dig or till soil at least 8 inches deep to loosen it for good root growth. Spread 30 pounds of compost per 100 square feet and work it into the top few inches of soil.

Planting

When to plant. Turnips and rutabagas need cool weather to thrive and produce tender roots.

Sow small plantings of turnips every two weeks in early spring and late summer in the North. Southern gardeners can plant them in the fall. Fall crops are usually more productive and better tasting than spring-grown turnips unless you have long, cool springs.

Plant spring turnips outdoors about three weeks before the last average frost or once the soil is at least 40°F. Sow fall crops in late summer about two months before the first fall frost, when daytime temperatures average about 75°F. In southern regions, sow seed in early to late fall for fall and winter harvests.

Plant rutabagas about

Hilling turnips. *Push soil up over the crown of turnips to prevent frost damage.*

three months before your first expected fall frost.

How much to plant. For turnips, plant a few feet of row per person per planting. If you plan to store your rutabagas, plant up to 10 feet of row per person. One-half ounce of seed will plant a 100-foot row.

Planting outdoors. For spring crops, sow seed ¼ inch deep. For fall crops, sow seed ½ inch deep. Broadcast seeds in the planting area or bed or sow them ½ to 1 inch apart in rows spaced 8 to 12 inches apart.

Thinning. When seedlings are a few inches tall, thin turnip seedlings to 4 inches apart and rutabaga seedlings to 7 inches apart.

Seasonal Care

Turnips and rutabagas belong to the cabbage family and may suffer from many of the same problems as cabbage. Minor leaf damage won't lower yields. However, if you want to harvest turnip greens for eating, or if your crop has a severe problem, you may need to take action. See "Solving Cabbage Problems" on page 106 to identify the cause of the problem and find solutions.

Close attention to watering, weeding, and thinning will help guarantee the success of your turnip or rutabaga crop. Follow the guidelines below to ensure a bountiful harvest.

Cover soil with black plastic. Cover soil a few weeks before planting to get early-spring plantings in sooner.

Cover seedbed with floating row cover. Cover your earliest plantings with row cover to keep them warm.

Water. Keep the soil evenly moist to encourage fast growth and good flavor.

Thin. When plants are a few inches tall, thin to their final spacings.

Mulch. When plants are 5 inches tall, add a 2- to 4-inch layer of organic mulch. This is especially important for rutabagas.

Hill up late crops. Pull soil up over the roots to protect them from early frosts. See the illustration on page 189.

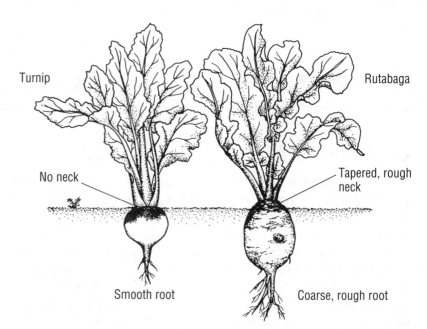

Turnip · No neck · Smooth root · Rutabaga · Tapered, rough neck · Coarse, rough root

Turnips and rutabagas. *Harvest fast-growing turnips when the roots are 1 to 3 inches in diameter. Larger roots may be pithy and bitter. Rutabagas grow slowly and can be harvested when they are 4 to 6 inches in diameter without losing quality.*

Harvesting

One good source of turnip greens is the tops of thinned seedlings. These young greens are sure to be tender and sweet. Pick other greens anytime once they are large enough to use. Be sure to leave enough tops behind to keep the roots alive.

For the tenderest roots, harvest when they are from 1 to 3 inches in diameter. If you wait too long, the roots will become pithy, woody, stringy, and bitter tasting. If your soil is hard, carefully loosen the earth at the base of the leaves with a digging fork before you pull them.

Heirloom 'Gilfeather' turnips can still be harvested when they get larger than most turnips—up to 6 inches across. (It's thought that they

may be a turnip-rutabaga hybrid.)

Harvest rutabaga roots in late fall when they are 4 to 6 inches across. A few light frosts will improve their flavor. Dig the large roots with a digging fork.

Choose sound, undamaged turnips and rutabagas for storage. Brush off large clods of soil, but don't wash them before storing. Trim tops off an inch above the roots with a sharp knife.

Turnips will keep for several months in a cool, damp place, such as a basement or root cellar.

Rutabagas will keep for up to six months in a cool, damp storage area.

In mild areas, you can overwinter roots in the ground by covering them with a thick mulch.

UNUSUAL VEGETABLES

Planting a crop you've never tried before adds more fun to your gardening. It's exciting to see how an untried plant grows and to reap new flavors in your harvest. If you discover that you have a flair for the unusual, there are almost unlimited possibilities in specialty vegetable catalogs. (You'll find the names of several in "Sources" on page 358.) Here's an introduction to 25 interesting crops that you may want to sample in your home garden. For specific instructions on how to plant seeds and transplants, see "Planting the Garden" on page 54.

NAME / PLANT TYPE / TIME UNTIL HARVEST	DESCRIPTION AND USES	GROWING GUIDELINES
Artichoke, globe *Cynara scolymus* Perennial in Zones 8 through 10 (annual north of Zone 8). First harvest 3–12 months after planting.	Whole artichokes are usually steamed. Hearts are used in salads and pasta dishes.	Plant seeds or plants (root divisions) in spring. Space plants 2'-3' apart. Harvest flower buds when they are large and firm, before they start to open.
Artichoke, Jerusalem *Helianthus tuberosus* Perennial in Zones 2 through 9. First harvest 7–12 months after planting.	Use peeled tubers raw in salads. Steamed or broiled tubers go well in soups and casseroles. May also be pickled.	Plant tubers in fall or spring. Dig after foliage has died down in fall. Dig as needed over winter. Mulch where ground freezes. In very cold regions, dig tubers in fall and store in moist sand.
Arugula; Rocket *Eruca vesicaria* subsp. *sativa* Cool season. 40–60 days.	Leaves and flowers add a spicy flavor to green salads, soups, and sauces.	Sow small plantings in place every 3 weeks for a continuous supply. Plant seeds ¼" deep. Thin plants to 6"–10" apart. Harvest by the leaf as needed, or cut whole small plants. Once plants bolt (send up a flowerstalk), leaf flavor will be sharper.
Basella; Malabar spinach *Basella alba* Warm season. 70 days.	Leaves and shoot tips are good steamed or fresh in salads.	Plant seeds or transplants after danger of frost is past. Space plants 3' apart and train them up a 6' fence or trellis. Harvest leaves and shoot tips as needed.
Celeriac *Apium graveolens* var. *rapaceum* Cool season. 190 days.	Roots have a mild celery flavor. Serve them peeled and julienned in salad, steamed and mashed with potatoes, or chopped in soup.	Direct-sow seeds in long-season regions. Where summers are short, start seeds indoors 10–12 weeks before last spring frost; plant out after danger of frost is past. Keep plants well watered. Harvest when root crowns are 2"–5" in diameter.

(continued)

Unusual Vegetables—Continued

NAME / PLANT TYPE / TIME UNTIL HARVEST	DESCRIPTION AND USES	GROWING GUIDELINES
Chard; Swiss chard; Perpetual spinach *Beta vulgaris,* Cicla group Cool and warm seasons. 50–60 days.	Use young red or green leaves in salads; serve mature leaves and leafstalks as a cooked green.	Plant seeds from early spring until late summer for harvest until frost. In mild-winter regions, harvest right through winter. Plant seeds thinly ½" deep. Thin plants to 6" apart. Snap off individual outer leaves or cut off entire plant 1" above the ground.
Chicory; Radicchio *Chichorium intybus* Cool season. 40–70 days.	Young red or green leaves as well as blanched leaves inside mature heads make a mildly bitter addition to salads. Heads are also grilled or sautéed and served with pasta. Radicchio cultivars add color to your cooking.	Make small plantings of leaf cultivars every few weeks starting in early spring. Choose radicchio cultivars to match your planting season. Some may need to be cut back to form heads.
Chicory, whitloof; Belgian endive *Chichorium intybus* Cool season. 110–130 days.	Roots are dug in fall and forced to grow indoors to produce a pale, tender head called a "chicon" in the winter. Chicons are used fresh in salads or served lightly cooked.	Sow seeds outdoors in late spring. Dig roots in fall and cut off tops 2" above the crown. Trim roots to 8" long and bury them upright in a container of moist sand or peat. Keep them medium moist and place container in a dark place with temperatures between 50°–60°F. Harvest pale sprouts when they're 4"–6" tall. Under good conditions a second crop may sprout.
Corn salad; Lamb's lettuce; Mâche *Valerianella locusta* Cool season. 40–50 days.	The spoon-shaped leaves make a mild, slightly minty addition to spring or winter salads.	Plant seeds in early spring or late fall. Thin plants to 2" apart. Harvest entire rosettes when they are 2½" tall.
Cress, garden; Peppergrass *Lepidium sativum* Cool season. 10–15 days.	The flat or curly, pungent leaves brighten salads and sandwiches any time of year.	Plant seeds shallowly in pots anytime or in garden beds from early spring through fall. Plant every 10 days for continuous harvest. Harvest plants when they are 2" tall.
Cress, upland; Winter cress *Barbarea verna* Warm season. 50 days.	The pungent leaves make a sprightly addition to salads.	Plant seeds shallowly from mid-spring to late summer. Thin plants to 4"–6" apart. Harvest individual leaves as needed.

NAME / PLANT TYPE / TIME UNTIL HARVEST	DESCRIPTION AND USES	GROWING GUIDELINES
Endive; Escarole *Chichorium endiva* Cool season. 60–90 days.	Frilly-leaved cultivars are called endive; broad, lettuce-leaved cultivars are called escarole. Leaves of either add a mild bittersweet flavor to salads or can be sautéed or braised and served with pasta.	Grow much like lettuce. Direct-sow seeds from early spring on. Thin to 8" apart. In warm weather, harvest plants very young. When cooler, grow to maturity. You can blanch mature plants to produce a milder flavor by resting a 6"-diameter plastic bowl upside down over plant top for 2–3 weeks.
Fennel, Florence; Finocchio *Foeniculum vulgare* var. *azoricum* Cool season. 65–120 days.	Use thickened leaf bases raw in salads for a celery-anise flavor. Braise or bake for a milder anise flavor.	Make small plantings every few weeks, starting in early spring. Where seasons are short, start plants indoors in individual pots. Space plants 6"–12" apart. Harvest when "bulb" or leaf base is 2½"–4" across at the widest part.
Husk cherry; Strawberry tomato *Physalis* spp. Warm season. 75 days.	The sweet orange or yellow fruit can be eaten fresh or made into pies and preserves.	Grow like a tomato. Harvest small fruits when the husks are brown; the fruits turn color and become slightly soft. Remove husk before use.
Mustard greens *Brassica juncea, B. rapa,* and hybrids Cool season. 25–60 days.	Use young leaves in salads; cook older leaves.	Starting in early spring, make small plantings every 2 weeks for a continuous supply. Space plants 3"-6" apart for young greens, 12" apart for mature plants. Harvest individual outside leaves or whole plants.
New Zealand spinach *Tetragonia expansa* Warm season. 55–70 days.	Leaves and shoot tips taste rather like spinach. Use the crop as a substitute for spinach.	Plant seeds around time of the last expected spring frost. Soak seeds overnight in water in the refrigerator before planting to speed germination. Harvest leaves or 4"-6" shoot tips as needed. Pinch out growing tips to keep plants from bolting (going to seed) in extremely hot weather.

(continued)

Unusual Vegetables—Continued

NAME / PLANT TYPE / TIME UNTIL HARVEST	DESCRIPTION AND USES	GROWING GUIDELINES
Orach; Mountain spinach *Atriplex hortensis* Cool season. 40–60 days.	Withstands light frost, thrives in shade, and tolerates warm weather. Red-leaved type keeps its color when cooked. Add young red or green leaves to salads. Later, harvest tops of plants and ends of branches to use as a cooked green.	Plant seeds ¼" deep in early spring and make repeat sowings every 3–4 weeks. Thin plants to 15"–18" apart in rows 2' apart. Pinch out flowers to encourage branching and new leaf formation.
Parsnip *Pastinaca sativa* Cool season. 80–120 days.	Use sweet, white roots baked, steamed and mashed with potatoes, or chopped in soups and casseroles.	Plant seeds in early spring. Soak seeds overnight to speed germination. Sow ½" deep. Thin plants to 4"–6" apart. Harvest when large enough to use or after the first frost. Harvest mulched plantings all winter but before growth begins again in spring.
Peanut *Arachis hypogea* Warm season. 100–150 days.	Enjoy mature seeds raw or roasted as a snack. Also use them in cooking or grind them to make peanut butter. Boil immature pods in salted water and eat.	Peanuts need very warm days and warm nights and well-drained soil. In the South, sow after soil has warmed; in the North, sow right after last spring frost. Remove seeds from shells, but leave skins intact. Thin plants to 1' apart. Hill up soil around plants when they are 1' tall. Pull up plants and harvest mature peanuts when shells are hard and skins are pink or red.
Salsify; Oyster plant *Tragopogon porrifolius* Cool season. 120–150 days.	White-skinned roots look like slender parsnips but taste something like oysters. Peel roots and boil them with a little lemon juice to keep them from browning, or sauté or bake them.	Sow seeds ½" deep in early spring in deeply worked soil. Thin plants to 4"–6" apart. Dig roots in fall or winter.
Salsify, black; Scorzonera *Scorzonera hispanica* Cool season. 120–150 days.	Leave flavorful black skin intact when boiling roots. You can also sauté or bake roots.	Sow seeds ½" deep in early spring in deeply worked soil. Thin plants to 4"–6" apart. Dig roots in fall or winter.

NAME / PLANT TYPE / TIME UNTIL HARVEST	DESCRIPTION AND USES	GROWING GUIDELINES
Sorrel *Rumex* spp. Perennials in all hardiness zones. 60 days.	The lemony leaves are good in sauces and soups or used sparingly in salads.	Plant seeds or seedlings once the chance of frost is past. Thin to 8" apart. Plant in part shade and remove seedstalks as they appear. Harvest large leaves as needed.
Sunflower *Helianthus annuum* Warm season. 90–110 days.	Roast seeds at 275°F for 45 minutes and salt if desired. Pick seedlings before true leaves form and add them to salads.	Plant seeds ½" deep when the chance of frost is past. Thin plants to 1'–3' apart, depending on mature size. As flowers fade, cover seed heads with cheesecloth or panty hose to keep birds from eating the seeds. Let seeds dry hard outdoors or cut the head with several inches of stem and hang it to dry indoors in a warm, airy spot. Rub the head on wire mesh set over a bucket to remove the seeds.
Tomatillo; Husk tomato *Physalis ixocarpa* Warm season. 65–90 days.	Use the sweet-tart fruit in green salsa and other Mexican sauces.	Grow like a tomato. Harvest immature green fruits when they fill the papery husk; harvest ripe fruits when husk loosens and fruit turns pale yellow. Remove husk before using.
Watercress *Nasturtium officinale* Perennial in Zone 3 and warmer. 60 days.	The piquant leaves and shoots add zip to salads and sandwiches.	Plant seeds ¼" deep in early spring. Watercress likes to grow in a few inches of cold, running water, but it will grow in the garden if you keep the soil moist. Or plant in large pots and rest pots in a deep saucer of water. Harvest 4"–6" shoots in spring.

GROWING FRUITS

PART 3

DECIDING WHAT TO GROW

Fruit growing is a perennial love affair, not an annual fling. Plan ahead and plant fruits that suit your site and your lifestyle.

Select a Site

To grow fruit successfully, you need a site that gets full or almost full sun. Fruits don't sweeten up if they get less than half a day of full sun; they're also more prone to problems. For ways to evaluate how much sun your yard gets, see "Selecting a Site" on page 6. If you're short on sunny space, try planting fruit behind flower beds or in foundation plantings that receive full sun.

Once you've determined which sites get the most sun, measure and record the location and size of prospective fruit-growing areas. Now you're ready to decide what to grow.

Fruit for containers. *If your heart is set on growing fruit that's not hardy in your area, consider container growing. Many fruits, such as this fig, or lemons or limes, will thrive in large tubs or pots.*

List Fruits to Grow

The best rule to follow is grow what you like. Make a list of the fruits your family enjoys that you'd like to try growing. Cross off any that won't thrive in your hardiness zone. You can grow nonhardy fruit in containers. See "Fruit in Containers" on page 224 for guidelines.

Plan for a Long Harvest

To get the most from your fruit, select crops that will be ready for harvest at different times throughout the season. Use the chart on the opposite page to evaluate your list of fruits to grow. You can plan for a steady stream of fruit through the summer or choose ones that ripen before or after an annual summer vacation.

To spread the harvest out as much as possible, choose early-, mid-, and late-ripening cultivars of each crop.

For example, here's a planting that would provide a full season of fruit from two short rows of plants and four trees.

Late-spring harvest:
An early- and a late-season Junebearing strawberry, ten plants each
Early-summer harvest:
An early red raspberry
Summer harvest:
An early-season plum and mid-season peach
Late-season harvest:
A late-summer and a fall apple; select cultivars that will pollinate each other

Note Vital Statistics

Next, jot down some vital statistics on the fruits remaining on your list. The plant entries, starting on page 228, are a good place to start. Note the following for each:

• Plant sizes available and how much space each will take
• If you need more than one plant for proper pollination
• How many years it will take from planting to harvest
• Expected yield

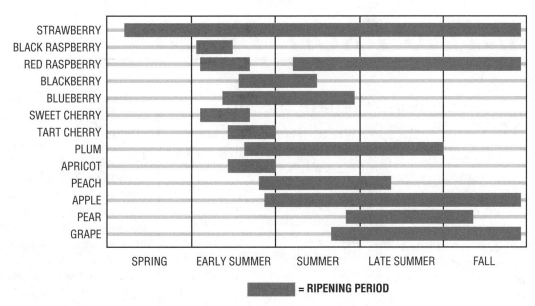

Season of ripening. *Individual cultivars usually ripen over a few days to a few weeks, but by carefully choosing a range of fruit types and cultivars, you can have luscious ripe fruit from spring through late fall.*

Narrow Your Options

Your prospective fruit-growing area may automatically limit the number or kinds of fruit you can plant. But even if you have loads of space, limit your choices until you know how much time and effort each plant will require.

Use the questions below to evaluate the fruit on your list. Then make a final list of fruits you'd like to grow.

How much fruit can I use? You can give away fruit, but growing ten times what your family could ever eat is lots of work. Figure out how much you can really use and plant accordingly.

How much time do I have? Don't choose many high-care fruits. Apples, blueberries, citrus, grapes, and pears are good choices for weekend gardeners, since ripe fruits will last on the plant a few days until you can pick.

How long am I willing to wait for my plants to bear? If you want fruit next year, include some raspberries and strawberries in your plan. Keep in mind that most dwarf tree fruits will bear sooner than standard-size ones.

What can't I buy easily? If you can't buy good raspberries or apricots locally, consider growing them instead of fruit you can find in local stores. Also consider growing outstanding cultivars of common fruits that aren't readily available at the store.

Draw Your Plan

Once you have a final list of fruit you'd like to grow, use the measurements you made of your yard and potential fruit-growing sites to map your planting on graph paper. Choose a scale that lets you fit each area onto the paper with room to write fruit names and show details. For example, if you decide a 1/4-inch square equals 2 feet, a 4-foot shrub will take up 1/2 inch and a 15-foot tree a little less than 2 inches. For a large yard, tape sheets of paper together.

Sketch your choices onto a copy of your map. Use the spacing recommended and don't crowd plants or overlap tree outlines. Crowded plants are unhealthy and unproductive. You may need to eliminate plants on your list. When it all fits and the arrangement pleases you, you're ready to prepare the site(s) and order plants to plant next year.

PLANTING FRUIT TREES

Take the time to plant your fruit trees properly and you will be rewarded with years of bounteous harvests.

To pick the best location for your trees, read "Selecting a Site" on page 6. Check the individual plant entries, starting on page 228, for information on site preparation, spacing, and other requirements.

Prepare the Site

While it's best to start preparing your planting area at least a full year before you plan to plant, it's hard to be that patient sometimes. Here's what to do if you have trees to plant now.

Deeply till an area at least 6 feet in diameter for each tree. Be careful to dig out every perennial weed. Shape the soil into a 6-inch-high raised bed if desired. Test the soil pH and add lime or sulfur to adjust pH if necessary.

Sprinkle 1 gallon of compost, 1 cup of blood meal or seed meal, and 1 cup of kelp meal over the soil for each tree. Rake the additions into the top few inches of soil.

FOR BEST RESULTS

Plant bareroot trees immediately. If you must hold them for more than two days, dig a trench with one vertical and one slanted side in a sheltered spot. Lay the roots against the slanted side and cover them with moist soil. Plant trees permanently as soon as possible.

Prepare the Tree

Bareroot trees. Shorten lanky roots to 18 inches, and trim injured roots back to healthy tissue. Soak the roots in compost tea for a few hours. Dust the roots with a mixture of 2 cups of kelp meal and 1 cup of bonemeal just before planting.

Other trees. Drench the root balls with compost tea. Remove pots and loosen circling roots. Leave balled-and-burlapped (B&B) trees wrapped.

Plant the Tree

Bareroot trees. Follow the step-by-step planting instructions on the opposite page. If tunneling rodents are a problem in your area, see "Preventing Animal Damage"

Bareroot tree

Balled-and-burlapped (B&B) tree

Container-grown tree

Fruit tree choices. *Choose dormant bareroot trees with plump buds, flexible twigs, and moist, healthy roots. Choose freshly dug balled-and-burlapped trees with large, solid root balls. Choose container-grown plants with moist soil and no gaps between soil and trunk or pot.*

on page 214 for instructions on installing a gravel collar below the soil line as you fill in the hole.

Other trees. Dig a hole in the center of your prepared area about 8 inches wider and ½ inch deeper than the dimensions of the root ball. Roughen the sides and bot-tom of the hole with a spade.

Set the root ball in the hole. The top of a root ball should be ½ inch lower than the sur-rounding soil so the soil will cover the edges. Carefully slide out wrapping after positioning a B&B tree. Then follow the rest of the planting procedure as for a bareroot tree.

Aftercare

Paint the trunk with diluted white interior latex paint, and install wire animal guards.

Keep the soil around newly planted trees consistently moist for the first growing season. Regularly remove weeds growing under the tree.

PLANTING A BAREROOT TREE

Step 1. *Dig a hole in the cen-ter of your prepared area large enough so the roots can be spread out without touching the sides or bottom. Roughen the sides and bottom of the hole with a spade to help the roots grow into the sur-rounding soil.*

Soak tree roots in compost tea before planting.

Position graft union 2" above soil level.

Step 2. *Mound soil in the hole and spread the roots over it. The tree should be slightly higher than it grew in the nursery to allow for settling.*

Make a small ridge to hold water.

Step 3. *Fill the bottom few inches with soil, then slosh in water or compost tea. Continue adding layers of soil and soak-ing them until the hole is full.*

Step 4. *Pound in a stake a few inches away from the trunk. Tie the tree loosely to the stake half to three-quarters of the way up the trunk.*

Mulch

4" ring of bare soil

Step 5. *Spread 8 to 10 inches of loose, organic mulch in a 6-foot-diameter circle around the tree. Leave the area near the base of the trunk bare.*

PLANTING VINES AND BUSHES

Berries bear better if you plant them properly. So spend extra time getting your blueberries, grapes, and other fruits off to a good start.

To decide where to plant your vine or bush, read "Selecting a Site" on page 6. Check the individual plant entries, starting on page 228, for information on site preparation, and spacing, pH, and other requirements.

Prepare the Site

It's best to start preparing your planting area at least a full year before you plan to plant. But if you haven't

Surface of root ball is ¼" lower than surrounding soil.

Planting a container-grown bush. A potted bush doesn't require immediate planting. Keep it well watered, and take time to prepare the planting area. When you do plant, set the top of the root ball slightly below soil level.

made advance preparations, here's what to do now.

Dig out all perennial weeds in the bed or planting area. Deeply till the bed or a circle at least 4 feet in diameter for each plant. Test the soil pH and adjust it if necessary. See "Soil Testing" and "Improving Your Soil" on pages 10 and 12, respectively, for instructions.

Spread 10 pounds of compost, 5 pounds of alfalfa or seed meal, and a ¼ pound of kelp meal over the prepared soil for each plant. Work the amendments into the top few inches of soil.

Install permanent trellises for grapes or kiwis before you plant. See "Staking and Trellising" on page 207 for more information.

Planting

If you're planting bareroot plants, dig holes large enough to spread the roots out. For container-grown plants, dig holes about 4 inches wider than the root ball. Roughen the sides and bottoms, as shown in the "Step 1" illustration on page 201.

Bareroot plants. Shorten lanky roots and trim injured roots back to healthy tissue. Then soak them in compost

tea for a few hours. (See "Try Compost Tea" on page 60 for a recipe.) Just before planting, dust the roots with a mixture of 2 cups of kelp meal and 1 cup of bonemeal.

Mound soil in the bottom of the hole to spread the roots over, adjusting the height so the plant will be at the same level it grew in the nursery. Spread the roots out evenly.

Container-grown plants. Drench the potting mix with compost tea. Take the plants out of the pots and loosen circling roots. Set them in the hole, as shown on this page.

Backfilling

Fill the bottom few inches around the roots or root ball with the soil removed from the hole. Slosh in compost tea or diluted fish emulsion to thoroughly soak and settle the soil. Continue adding and soaking layers of soil until the hole is full.

Aftercare

If you plan to install drip irrigation, do so now. See "Watering Fruit Crops" on page 204 for instructions.

Mulch the planting bed with a layer of organic mulch, leaving about 4 inches of bare soil around each plant.

FEEDING FRUIT CROPS

Fruit crops need an annual feeding to produce a bountiful harvest year after year. Compost makes a good main meal, and other fertilizers such as bonemeal, alfalfa meal, and seed meals (cottonseed meal or soybean meal) provide an extra boost for certain fast-growing fruits.

Measuring new growth. Raised rings and a change in twig diameter mark the end of one season's growth and the start of the next. Check the individual crop entries for how much growth is desirable for each type of fruit you grow; adjust the amount of fertilizer you use accordingly.

Feed the Roots

For grapes, raspberries, and strawberries, spread fertilizer evenly over the entire bed.

For bushes, spread fertilizer over the entire bed or in a circular band under each bush, starting a few inches from the trunk and extending a foot or so outside the drip line.

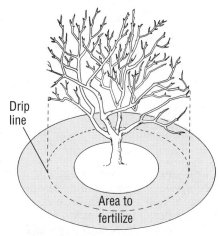

Feeding a fruit tree. Spread fertilizer in a band extending from a foot inside the drip line to a few feet outside the drip line.

Under trees, spread fertilizer in a circular band starting a foot or so inside the drip line and extending a few feet outside the drip line, as illustrated below left.

You'll find recommendations for each fruit in the "Season-by-Season Care" calendars in the individual crop entries, starting on page 228.

Feed the Leaves

Foliar feeding by spraying liquid fertilizer on a plant's leaves is a quick way to correct temporary or specific nutrient deficiencies. Prepare the sprays listed below according to the label instructions. Add ¼ teaspoon of vegetable oil or liquid soap per gallon of spray to help the material stick to the leaves.

Strain your spray with cheesecloth or panty hose as you pour it into your sprayer. Adjust the sprayer to a fine mist. Spray in the early evening, covering both the upper and lower surfaces of the leaves until liquid drips off the leaf edges. If it rains within a day, respray.

Kelp. Seaweeds, such as kelp, absorb and concentrate many of the ocean's trace elements or micronutrients. Kelp sprays can correct trace-element deficiencies rapidly.

Chelated nutrient sprays. Chelated trace elements are readily absorbed by plants. Compost tea (see "Try Compost Tea" on page 60) contains natural chelates. Chelated calcium sprays are good for treating calcium uptake problems.

WATERING FRUIT CROPS

Plants grow best when the top foot or two of the soil is moist, but not wet, at all times. Frequent, short waterings are the best way to maintain ideal soil moisture.

You can water fruits and berries with a hose, but they'll be better off with a drip irrigation system. Drip systems moisten the soil slowly without flooding it, make it easy to apply the right amount of water, and distribute it evenly. Plus, you don't have to haul and hold hoses each time you water.

When and How Much to Water

Here's an easy and accurate method for maintaining your soil's moisture. To use it, you'll need to calculate the gallons-per-hour (gph) rating of your system. For porous pipes, multiply the gph rating per foot listed on the package by the total length. For in-line emitters, multiply the total length by the number of emitters per foot and the emitter rating.

1. Decide how often you are willing to water. Daily is best, especially in arid areas, but two or three times a week will work. The number of days between waterings is your *watering interval.*

2. Measure rainfall. Place a rain gauge in an open area of your garden. Read and empty it every potential watering day.

3. Calculate how much water your garden lost. To determine water lost, look up your current weather conditions in the table "Making Up for Lost Water" on the opposite page. Multiply the number of inches of water lost per day for your conditions by your watering interval to get the total inches of water lost.

4. Compare rainfall to water loss.
• If rainfall about equaled the amount of water your garden lost, skip this watering.
• If you got more than twice as much water as your garden lost, skip this watering *and* any waterings scheduled for the next three or four days.
• If you got less rain than your garden lost, you'll need to water. To determine how many inches of water to add, subtract the inches of rain received from the inches of water lost.

5. Calculate how much water you need to add. Multiply the inches of water you need to add by the number of square feet you will be watering. Divide the result by the conversion factor for your current weather conditions from the table to determine how many gallons you need to add. (Drip irrigation systems are less efficient at high temperatures; the conversion factor takes account of this difference in

Low-tech drip watering. *For a temporary drip system, punch one or two pencil-lead-size holes in the bottoms of 1-gallon plastic jugs. Nestle them into the mulch around a newly planted tree, or set them on the soil surface for a potted tree. Fill them with a hose as needed.*

efficiency.) Note that if you had no rain, there's an alternate way to figure how much water to add. Simply look at the table to find the number of gallons of water lost per day per 100 square feet. Multiply that number by your watering interval. Then multiply by the number of square feet you will be watering.

6. Calculate the number of hours to run your drip system. Find this number by dividing the total gallons by your system's gph rating.

Drip Irrigation Systems

Here are two drip systems that work well for fruit crops. Keep in mind that some systems work best on level ground and that the spacing and design of your system will depend on your soil type.

Porous pipes. Porous pipes "leak" water all along their length. They will work for runs up to 200 feet if your yard is reasonably level. Space multiple lines 6 to 12 inches apart in sandy soil, 18 to 24 inches in clay soil.

Making Up for Lost Water

Your garden loses water two ways: through the plants' leaves and directly from the soil surface. To keep your crops growing well, you need to replace the water that is lost and not replaced by rain. This table gives you estimated daily water loss based on humidity and temperature. Using the water loss figures and the calculations described under "When and How Much to Water" on the opposite page, you can determine precisely how much water your garden needs.

MOISTURE LEVEL OF AIR AND AVERAGE HIGH TEMPERATURE (°F)	INCHES OF WATER LOST PER DAY	GALLONS OF WATER LOST PER DAY PER 100 SQUARE FEET	DRIP EFFICIENCY CONVERSION FACTOR (INCHES OF WATER TO GALLONS OF WATER)
Humid and under 70°	0.10	5.15	1.94
Dry and under 70°	0.15	7.73	1.94
Humid and 70°–80°	0.20	10.87	1.84
Dry and 70°–80°	0.25	13.59	1.84
Humid and 80°–100°	0.30	16.31	1.84
Dry and 80°–100°	0.35	19.03	1.84
Humid and 100°+	0.40	23.03	1.74
Dry and 100°+	0.45	25.90	1.74

In-line emitter tubing. In-line emitter tubing has discrete openings every few inches to every few feet. Choose a type of emitter tubing, such as T-tape, that resists clogging and controls how much water comes out of each emitter. T-tape is suitable for runs up to 700 feet and works fine even on hilly terrain.

Choose tubing with 2-gallons-per-hour (gph) emitters spaced 6 to 12 inches apart for sandy soil, 0.5-gph emitters 18 to 24 inches apart for clay soil. Space multiple lines 6 to 12 inches apart in sandy soil, 18 to 24 inches in clay soil.

Drip System Design

You can use any combination of drip systems to suit your plantings. Join different sections of the system with supply lines made of solid tubing. Include a water filter, pressure regulator, back flow preventer, and/or timer as required by local laws or system requirements. Garden centers and catalogs sell starter kits and components, and many will help design a custom system.

You can design a circular drip irrigation layout for fruit trees, or use parallel lines of emitter tubing. If you choose a circular layout, start with two concentric circles of tubing, as shown in the illustration below left. For large trees, you may need to add an additional ring in order to keep directing water at the actively growing roots.

If you decide on a parallel layout, be sure the emitters cover the entire area of the tree's root zone, as shown in the illustration below right.

A single length of in-line emitter tubing may supply enough water for a row of berry plants, if you have clay soil. For berries growing in sandy soil or wide raised beds, use two parallel lengths of tubing.

Circular drip layouts. *The best way to water a tree is by laying concentric rings of in-line emitter tubing around it. This puts the water where it counts, right over the tree's most active roots.*

Drip line / Add tubing as tree grows.

Parallel drip layouts. *You can also water the area under a tree with parallel lengths of in-line emitter tubing. Keep the tubing at least 1 foot away from the trunk.*

Drip line / Add tubing as tree grows.

STAKING AND TRELLISING

Staking, trellising, and propping help plants stand strong even when they are wet, windblown, and loaded with fruit. The type of support and materials used depends on whether a plant needs a permanent trellis or just temporary support to get it established or protect its heavy branches close to harvest.

Materials

Here are some common materials used to stake and trellis plants.

Wood. Wood is strong, light, and easy to cut. Buy naturally rot-resistant wood posts made of cypress, redwood, or cedar. Pressure-treated (also called CCA-treated) posts are also used for trellising fruit crops. However, these posts contain toxic synthetic chemicals which organic gardeners would not find acceptable for their standards.

Steel. Steel is reasonably strong, light, and inexpensive. Choose heavyweight (12 gauge) U- or T-posts. If you need to make holes in steel posts to insert bolts, use a power drill with a carbide-tip drill bit.

Fiberglass. Fiberglass is lightweight, strong, and rot proof. Choose "ultraviolet coated" O-posts.

Plastic. Recycled plastic "wood" is as easy as wood to cut and lift. It won't rot and should last a long time. Different brands vary in strength and stiffness, so ask your supplier if the brand they carry will work for what you have in mind.

Stakes and Props

Temporary stakes. Trees planted in windy sites need to be staked for a year or two so they will develop a strong trunk while they are getting established. Grapevines also need staking for the first year or two, until they can be supported fully on a trellis. Choose untreated wood or bamboo for temporary stakes. See the "Step 4" illustration on page 201 to see how to set stakes for fruit trees; the top right illustration on page 260 shows how to stake a grape vine.

Permanent stakes. Fruit trees on very dwarfing rootstocks and black raspberries need permanent stakes. Choose a 6-foot steel post for a very dwarf tree or a black raspberry; an 8-foot post for a semidwarf tree.

Props. Props temporarily protect branches of fruit trees that are heavily laden with fruit from breaking. To make a prop, cut a V-shaped notch in one end of each of two lengths of untreated lumber. Place the notches together under the branch and brace the bottom ends against the soil surface.

Setting Stakes and Posts

Pound in steel and pointed wooden posts and stakes with a sledge unless your soil is very hard or rocky. Rent a tubular post driver to speed up the job.

Fiberglass, plastic "wood," and large wooden posts need predug holes. Rent a high-quality post-hole digger—either a manual or machine-powered one. If your soil is rocky, you'll also need a digging bar to dislodge rocks. Dig a straight-sided hole about twice the diameter of your post and one-third as deep as the post is long.

Rest the larger end of your post on the bottom of the hole and have someone hold it upright. Shovel in a few inches of soil around the post and pack the soil down firmly

T-trellis. *This trellis uses T-shaped supports set at intervals up to 30 feet apart. It's a good design for fallbearing raspberries. The trellis wires hold up the raspberry canes, making the fruit easy to pick. The ground area remains clear, so it's convenient to cut back the canes to soil level after the fall harvest.*

with a tamping tool or a length of 2 × 4. Keep adding soil and packing it down until the hole is full.

Trellises

Construct permanent trellises out of sturdy materials that will last as long as the plants they support. Steel fence posts are very durable and work well for all styles of trellises.

T-Trellis

A light-duty T-trellis is perfect for fallbearing raspberries. Build T-trellis supports with 6-foot steel posts and 2½-foot 1 × 2's. Use rust-resistant ¼-inch carriage bolts ½ inch longer than the joints are thick. Drill ¼-inch holes in the posts with a carbide-tip drill bit, then insert and tighten the

bolts. Use flat washers inside both the head and nut next to wood or plastic. Pound a nail into the ends of each crosspiece.

Trellis support. *Use three bolts to fasten each crosspiece on a support like this.*

Pound the T-trellis supports into the midline of the row every 30 feet so the crosspiece is 36 inches off the ground and at right angles to the row. String the trellis with synthetic baling twine, looping it once around each nail. Tie the twine to firmly anchored stakes at the ends of each row.

During the summer, tuck leaning canes inside the twine to keep them from straying. If the canes fall sideways within the trellis, you may need to add cross-ties, as shown above.

This trellis system works well for fallbearing raspberries because it's easy to remove the trellis wires to prune off or mow down the canes each fall. You can even remove the supports if needed to make mowing more convenient, and then reconstruct the trellis.

V-Trellis

Summerbearing raspberries and erect blackberries thrive on a sturdy V-trellis. Set pairs of 6-foot-long posts (angled so they are 1 foot apart at the soil line, 3 feet apart at the top) straddling the row every 30 feet.

String the trellis with synthetic baling twine or wire. Tie it to firmly anchored stakes at the ends of each row, as shown on the right.

Allow the vegetative canes to grow upright in the center of the V all summer. After winter pruning, tie the canes to the trellis wires with twist ties or twine. After harvest, snip the ties and prune out the fruited canes.

Fence Trellis

Grapes, thornless blackberries, and espaliered fruit trees need a strong, long-lasting trellis. Set 8-foot posts every 30 feet along the midline of the row.

The weight of your plants will pull the two end posts inward unless you anchor them securely. To anchor them, drive a 4-foot steel post $3^1/2$ feet into the ground at a 45-degree angle away from the end post and in line with the row. The top of the anchor post should be about 6 feet beyond the end post. For maximum support, connect the top of the end post to the top of the anchor post with steel cable or heavy wire.

String the trellis with monofilament plastic wire or high-tensile, rust-resistant, 12-gauge metal fence wire. Plastic is much easier to work with than metal. Use $1^1/2$-inch-long U-shaped metal staples to attach wires to

Tie half the canes to each side.

|← 1' →|

V-trellis. *Raspberry stands trained as shown here have an open center, which gives new canes light and room to grow.*

wooden posts. Insert them until they just touch the wire, so it can slide easily. Use specially designed wire clips for other types of post.

See "Grape" on page 258 for instructions on pruning and training grapes onto a fence trellis. Creating espaliered fruit trees on a trellis is a special technique that allows you to grow fruits like apples and peaches in a small space. If you'd like detailed instructions for fruit tree espalier, refer to "Sources" on page 358 for titles of books on fruit production that provide complete information on this technique.

Use just the top wire for grapes.

Use 3 equally spaced wires for blackberries and fruit trees.

Fence trellis. *Grapes, thornless blackberries, and espaliered fruit trees grow best when trained against a fence or fence trellis like this one.*

PREVENTING DISEASE PROBLEMS

Prevention is the best medicine when it comes to controlling diseases. Lay the groundwork for your prevention program by:

• Planting fruits that suit your climate and site.
• Not planting large patches of one fruit type or cultivar.
• Selecting disease-resistant cultivars whenever possible.
• Giving your soil and plants the best possible care.

Most disease organisms need moisture to grow and reproduce. Deprive them of moisture and they won't be so quick to make your life miserable.

Your goal is to create conditions where dew and raindrops on plants evaporate as quickly as possible. Take advantage of "Nature's fungicides"—air and sunshine—to keep diseases from becoming big problems. Avoid shaded or boxed-in areas where the air never stirs. Also be sure to keep fruit crops properly pruned to prevent branch crowding. Follow the spacing and pruning recommendations in the individual plant entries, starting on page 228.

Sprays and Dusts

You won't always be able to prevent disease problems with cultural methods alone. Sometimes you'll need to fall back on organically acceptable fungicides, such as those listed below.

It is important to apply fungicides *before* you see disease symptoms. Most organically acceptable controls only protect plants from becoming infected; they can't cure them. The control must be on the plant before a spore or other disease-causing particle lands there to do any good. A few controls, such as lime-sulfur, can stop an infection even if the disease has started to invade the plant.

Antitranspirants. These commercial products are designed to block water loss from leaves. You can also use them to seal out diseases. Apply them *before* you see disease symptoms, diluted as per the label instructions.

Compost tea. Compost tea contains beneficial organisms, nutrients, and many other compounds. Research shows that spraying plants with compost tea can prevent or reduce certain disease problems. Spray *before* you see symptoms for best results. See "Try Compost Tea" on page 60 for instructions for making compost tea.

Streptomycin. This antibiotic is produced by a common soil bacterium, *Streptomyces avermitilis.* Streptomycin is the most effective product for controlling fire blight bacteria. Apply according to label instructions.

Sulfur. This naturally occurring element is an effective preventive fungicide.

Spray preventively. *When a fungal spore first lands on a leaf, as shown here, it's vulnerable to organic controls. A protective layer of a fungicide, such as sulfur, creates a barrier that prevents the spore from germinating. Once a spore germinates and grows into a leaf, it is difficult or impossible to stop it with organic controls.*

Fungal spores that land on sulfur-coated leaves are literally burned. Mix according to label instructions and spray *before* you see disease symptoms. Reapply after rain or every 10 to 14 days.

Caution: In hot weather (above 80°F), sulfur is highly phytotoxic and will damage plants. Sulfur plus oil also damages growing plants. Do not use sulfur within one month of an oil spray. High concentrations of sulfur damage soil microbes, so don't spray it directly on the soil.

Lime-sulfur. Lime-sulfur, also called calcium polysulfide, is more effective—and caustic—than either lime or sulfur alone. It can actually penetrate leaves and kill recently germinated disease spores. Unfortunately it is also more likely to damage growing plants. Use it only when more benign methods haven't worked. It is often used on dormant plants just before or just as the buds open and tends to be quite safe for plants at that stage. Apply according to the label directions. The cautionary measures for sulfur sprays also apply to lime-sulfur sprays. Repeat in 10 to 14 days if necessary.

Bordeaux mix. Bordeaux mix is copper sulfate plus hydrated lime. It is less toxic to plants and nontarget organisms than copper alone. It controls many of the same dis-

eases as lime-sulfur and is used the same way. See "Lime-sulfur" above for details.

Copper. This naturally occurring element is a powerful, nonspecific fungicide and herbicide.

Caution: Copper is toxic to animals and beneficial insects. It is also toxic to plants; repeated applications can stunt them. It damages beneficial soil organisms and accumulates in the soil. Use copper only as a last resort, when nothing else works. Avoid spraying it directly on the soil. Always apply copper according to label directions.

Safe Spraying

Just because a fungicide or insecticide is considered organic doesn't mean it's harmless. To use organically acceptable sprays and dusts safely, adhere to the following guidelines.

- Wear protective clothing, as shown on the right, when mixing, applying, and cleaning up sprays and dusts.
- Mix and apply exactly according to directions. Measure carefully with measuring cups and spoons. Use these cups and spoons only for garden chemicals.
- Wash your measuring cups and spoons, sprayer, clothing, and skin thoroughly when you finish.
- Store fungicides in their original containers. Keep them closed and away from food and children.
- Check product labels for "reentry time." This will tell you how long you should stay out of an area after spraying to avoid exposure to substances that could be harmful to your health. For example, you should wait 24 hours before walking through an area sprayed with sulfur or handling plants sprayed with sulfur.

Cover hair.

Goggles

Dust mask

Rubber apron

Tuck sleeves into gloves.

Rubber gloves

Tuck pants into boots.

Rubber boots

PREVENTING PEST PROBLEMS

Prevention is the best way to keep insect pests at reasonable levels. Keep your fruits and berries healthy by providing optimum care, and you'll help them withstand attacks by pest insects. Enlist recruits in your fight against pests by attracting beneficial insects and animals. See "Protect Your Allies" on page 69 for details on attracting beneficials.

There is also an arsenal of commercial and homemade barriers and traps that will keep insects from attacking your fruit crops. And if preventive measures fail, you may need to resort to using naturally derived insecticidal sprays and dusts.

GREEN THUMB TIP

Instead of buying sticky coating to trap pests, try using axle grease, which is less expensive. Or mix equal parts of petroleum jelly or mineral oil and liquid dish soap. For easy cleaning and reuse, cover traps with plastic sandwich bags or plastic kitchen wrap before spreading on the coating. When the trap fills up with insects or loses its stickiness, remove and discard the plastic covering. Rewrap with fresh plastic and recoat.

Keep Pests Off

Garden cleanup. Destroy dropped fruits where pests such as apple maggots and codling moths may hide. Also clean up fallen leaves and fruits at season's end.

Floating row cover. Use floating row cover to keep pests like tarnished plant bugs or plum curculios away from your crops. Spread row cover over plants *before* insects arrive. For small plants like strawberries, spread it loosely over the bed and seal the edges with soil. Cover bushes and trees with a large sheet; gather and tie it tightly around the base or trunk. Uncover plants during flowering so pollinators can pollinate.

Shaking. To capture Japanese beetles and plum curculios, spread a tarp or an old sheet under the plant, then shake the plant until the pests drop off. Dump pests into soapy water.

Water. A strong spray of water can knock aphids and spider mites right off plants. Repeat sprays as needed.

Stick Pests Down

Traps lure insects by sight and/or smell, and catch them on a sticky surface. You can buy traps or make your own,

as shown on the opposite page. Some commercial traps come coated with sticky stuff, or you may need to buy sticky coating such as Tangle-Trap to apply to uncoated traps.

Sticky band traps. Sticky band traps work for crawling pests like gypsy moths. To sticky-band a tree, wrap plastic kitchen wrap around the trunk and spread a band of sticky coating on the plastic.

Pheromone traps. Insect sex scents, or pheromones, will lure male insects. You can use pheromone traps to monitor pest populations. When males begin landing in the traps, it's time to take action with other control methods.

Stop Pests with BTK

BTK (*Bacillus thuringiensis* var. *kurstaki*) controls caterpillars such as fruitworms and leafrollers. Mix and apply according to label instructions. Add 1 tablespoon of molasses per gallon to encourage insects to feed on sprayed foliage.

Soaps and Oils

Soaps. Soaps kill pests such as aphids by washing off their protective coatings. Mix and apply commercial insecticidal soap according to label instructions.

You can also use 1 to 3 teaspoons of household soap—not detergent—per gallon of water. The effectiveness of dish soap will vary from brand to brand.

Oils. Oils smother insect eggs and immature insects. *Dormant oils* are heavy oils only used on dormant plants to control overwintering pests such as scale or peach twig borers. *Summer* or *superior*

oils are lighter and can also be used on leafed-out plants to control pests such as woolly apple aphids. Mix and apply according to label instructions.

As a substitute for summer oil, you can use 1 tablespoon of plain vegetable oil and ¼ teaspoon of liquid soap per quart of water. Shake vigorously and spray.

Caution: Oil plus sulfur can damage plants. Don't use them within 30 days of each other.

Botanical Poisons

If insect pest problems threaten to destroy your harvest or even kill your plants, you may choose to use an organically acceptable insecticide like pyrethrins or rotenone. These substances are toxic to a range of pests and often also to beneficial insects. To learn how and when to use these substances, see "Insecticides and Fungicides" on page 339.

MAKING STICKY TRAPS

RECTANGLE TRAP

Step 1. *To make a sticky rectangle trap, cut a rectangle from the side of an empty bleach bottle.*

Step 2. *Paint the rectangle bright yellow for aphids or white for tarnished plant bugs. When it is dry, slip it into a sandwich bag.*

Step 3. *Poke a hole through the bag and plastic to insert a wire hook. Coat both sides with sticky coating.*

BALL TRAP

Screw eye to attach hanger

Step 1. *To make sticky ball traps, paint apple-size balls red for apple maggots or apple-green to attract plum curculios.*

Secure plastic wrap with twist tie.

Step 2. *After the paint dries completely, insert a screw eye into each ball, and wrap it in plastic kitchen wrap.*

Step 3. *Coat the plastic wrap with a sticky coating, and hang the balls in your fruit trees or bushes.*

PREVENTING ANIMAL DAMAGE

Chances are your wild neighbors will take an interest in whatever fruit you grow. Here are some ways to protect your plants and keep your harvests for yourself.

Trunk Protection

A few ill-placed nibbles of bark can girdle and kill your tree. You can protect young trees and shrubs from bark-gnawing rodents with wire collars like the one shown above right.

If you live in an area where tunneling critters such as pine voles chew on tree

Twist ties fasten cylinder.

Set collar 1"–3" below soil line.

Wire collars. *Cut an 18-inch square of ¼-inch hardware cloth for each tree. (Use 18-inch by 3-foot pieces for taller collars if you live in a deep-snowfall area.) Bend the wire and slip it around the tree trunk.*

roots, protect your young trees with underground gravel collars. This is easiest to do at planting, but you can carefully remove the soil around established trees and replace it with gravel.

To install a gravel collar when planting, backfill with soil as usual up to the top of the side roots. Then water generously to settle the soil. Next, build a cone of ¼- to ½-inch gravel around the main taproot and trunk up to a few inches above the eventual soil surface level. Backfill carefully around the gravel with soil. The top few inches of gravel above the soil line will settle leaving a layer of gravel between the tree and the soil.

Repellents

You may be able to shoo animals away from your fruits by offending or scaring them.

6'

6'

8'

Hardware cloth

Be sure there are no gaps at soil level.

Walk-in fruit cage. *If birds or animal pests harvest more berries than you do, build a cage like this one out of 2 × 4's and hardware cloth. Secure the door with a padlock if raccoons are a problem. A 6- by 8-foot, 6-foot-tall cage will accommodate two blueberry plants.*

If you make a plant taste or smell like something yucky, moochers will munch elsewhere. Smells that say *Danger! Predator alert!* will make animals skedaddle. Try commercial repellents or see "Make-Your-Own Repellents" on this page for some bad-tasting and foul-smelling things to try in your garden.

You can buy shiny balloons and streamers or fake snakes, hawks, and owls, or make your own scare devices, to frighten birds and make them think their worst enemy is about to gobble them up. Put scare devices out just before you expect problems, and move them from place to place at least every two days. Birds and animals quickly learn to ignore things that stay in the same place.

Barriers

Fences. If repellents don't keep large animals such as raccoons and deer at bay, you need a good fence. A low electric fence works well for raccoons. Try a temporary 6-foot-high chicken-wire fence around individual trees to stop deer. Or fence the entire area. See "Fencing Out Animal Pests" on page 62 for more fence ideas. See "Staking and Trellising" on page 207 for information on selecting and installing fence posts.

If your pests have wings or

MAKE-YOUR-OWN REPELLENTS

Tastes and Smells

Soap—the cheapest and smelliest deodorant soap you can buy—is a good animal repellent. Cut bars of soap in half (wrapper and all) and drill a hole in each half. Then hang the soap pieces at about chest height every 5 to 10 feet in trees or around your berry beds.

Human hair (get it from a barber), dog and cat droppings, or used cat litter can be put in small cheesecloth or muslin bags and hung around your garden, too. Walk your dog and encourage him to mark his territory. Or use a squirt bottle full of human urine to mark it yourself.

Make your own antideer spray by mixing 1 egg or 2 egg yolks per quart of water. Spray plants liberally. You'll need to reapply the spray after rain.

Sights and Sounds

Aluminum pie pans and shiny pinwheels help repel birds. Hang them from stakes so they flash in the breeze.

Discourage nocturnal visitors by leaving a radio or some blinking lights on at night in the garden. Better still, use a motion detector to switch them on when anything approaches.

Strawberry-pecking birds may get disgusted and go elsewhere if you paint some strawberry-sized rocks red and sprinkle them around your patch just before the real berries get ripe.

---

are world-class climbers or jumpers, you'll need more than a fence.

Netting. Drape netting directly over your plants, and secure every inch of the edge to the ground or gather it around the trunk. Netting can be hard to handle and may knock fruit off as you uncover it; "robbers" may reach through and grab fruit where the netting touches it. But it's quick and works well for fruits, such as cherries, that you harvest all at once.

Cages. Netting- or wire-covered frames are more convenient for fruits, such as blueberries, that you harvest over a long period. See the bottom illustration on the opposite page for one cage idea.

PRUNING AND TRAINING BASICS

Pruning and training strengthen fruit trees and berry bushes, slow their growth, and keep them open to sunlight and air movement. Here you'll find general guidelines for shaping fruit trees. For specific instructions on pruning fruit trees and information on pruning vine and bush fruits such as blueberries, grapes, and raspberries, see the individual plant entries starting on page 228.

Pruning

Early pruning pays; a few cuts when a plant is young are more effective and less disruptive to the tree than ones made later. Remember these pruning basics.

• Use clean, sharp tools. Bypass pruners make cleaner cuts than anvil pruners. A small, folding handsaw is good for slightly larger cuts.
• Prune on a dry day to help minimize diseases.
• Always prune to just above a distinct point: an outward-facing bud, branch, or the trunk. Don't leave stubs.

To prune effectively, you need to know the difference between the two basic types of cuts. When you cut back to a bud in the middle of a twig or branch, you are making a *heading cut.* Heading cuts stimulate buds farther back on the branch to grow. If you remove a whole twig or branch flush with another branch, you are making a *thinning cut.* Thinning cuts encourage branches that remain to continue growing without triggering excessive growth. Use them to encourage branches you select to grow. See the illustration on this page for more on heading and thinning cuts.

When you cut a branch back to a larger branch or the trunk, you're using a thinning cut. See the illustration on the opposite page for the correct way to handle larger branches.

Heading cuts

Thinning cuts

Regrowth after heading

Regrowth after thinning

Heading and thinning cuts. *Save yourself time and years of pruning headaches by knowing the difference between these types of cuts. Heading cuts cause lots of new branches that you'll just have to remove later. Use thinning cuts to encourage well-spaced or positioned branches to grow. They won't trigger excessive new growth.*

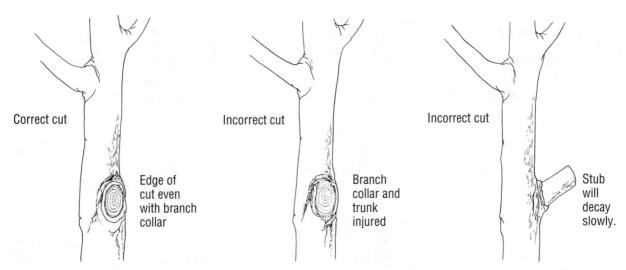

Removing a branch. *Cut as close to the branch collar—the raised ridge of bark at the base of the branch— as possible without cutting into it. Cutting into the collar damages the tree, leaving it open to disease.*

Training

Strong, productive trees have branches that arise from the trunk at a 45- to 60-degree angle. Such branches grow slowly, bear sooner than more vertical ones, and make lots of fruit buds.

Train branches that are too vertical by spreading them when they are young. To see if a branch is too vertical, put your forefinger in the crotch. If you can see light below your finger, the angle is too narrow and the shoot needs spreading.

Round toothpicks make good spreaders for young shoots. Insert one end of the toothpick into the trunk 2 inches above the base of the shoot. Spread the shoot slightly beyond 45 to 60 degrees. Then insert the other end into the shoot. You can also clip a clothespin to the trunk just above a shoot to spread it down and out.

Larger branches need larger spreaders. You can hang weights on branches to spread them—anything from clothespins to large rocks will work. You can make weights by filling tin cans with concrete. Insert a hook of coat-hanger wire while the concrete is soft. See "Make-Your-Own Spreaders" on this page for another kind you can make.

MAKE-YOUR-OWN SPREADERS

Spread branches with these simple spreaders made from 1 × 1's and 2-inch finishing nails. Cut lengths of lumber from 6 to 36 inches, depending on the branch you need to spread. Pound finishing nails into either end. Then clip off the heads of the nails. Gently spread the branches and use the nails to hold the spreaders in place.

Rest nailed end on spool while pounding second nail in.

Clip nail head at angle with wire cutters.

REVIVING NEGLECTED PLANTINGS

Neglected fruits and berries can become healthy and fruitful again with the proper care. To decide if yours are worth renovating, clear away growth around them and prune off any stems that arise from below the graft union. Then wait for a crop. If it's tasty, your plants may have potential. Replant fruits and berries that are badly diseased, especially if disease-resistant cultivars are available. As you begin your renovation, help your plants regain vigor by following the instructions on pruning, mulching, fertilizing, and other care in the individual crop entries, beginning on page 228.

Apples and Pears

Although it takes patience and effort, you can bring even badly neglected apples and pears back into bearing. See "Taming an Abandoned Apple Tree" on the opposite page for directions on reclaiming a young, moderately overgrown apple tree. The procedure is much the same for pears and very old apples.

Blueberries

Blueberry plants live for many years, and even very neglected ones are worth saving. Reclaim overgrown bushes by cutting some of the oldest canes off at ground level each winter over three to five years.

Brambles

Overgrown blackberries or raspberries may be worth saving if they bear high-quality fruit. If the fruit is small and crumbly, dig the plants out and destroy them.

Begin your renovation in winter by cutting all the canes off at ground level. In early spring, mark 1-foot-wide rows in which you'll allow new canes to grow. Leave at least 7 feet between rows. As new growth emerges, keep the space between your rows mowed. Weed, fertilize, and mulch the canes in the new rows.

Grapes

Grapevines can bear for hundreds of years, so renovated vines probably have many productive years ahead of them. Start by repairing or replacing the trellis or support if necessary. Then select one of the two pruning methods described in "Grape" on page 258.

To reclaim a spur-pruned vine, cut all the canes that sprout from the main side branches back to two-bud spurs in late winter. Thin out the spurs, saving the youngest ones.

To reclaim a cane-pruned vine, or a grossly overgrown vine, cut off all the canes and branches a few buds or 10 inches away from where the top of the trunk will be. New canes will grow near the top of the trunk the following season; select two strong ones in early summer and rub off all the others.

Stone Fruits

Most stone fruits, including apricots, cherries, peaches, and plums, are not very long-lived. If your trees are more than 10 to 15 years old, they have little chance of becoming productive again. Sweet cherries live and bear longer than other stone fruits, but you won't be able to reach cherries on large trees. Consider replanting with new dwarf ones.

If you have older stone fruits that are still bearing, plant new ones in a new location. Care for the older trees until the new ones begin to bear, then remove the old trees.

TAMING AN ABANDONED APPLE TREE

Bringing an overgrown apple tree such as this one back into full production is a three-year project, since drastic pruning will cause massive regrowth and sunscald. Start any renovation by removing all dead and damaged branches.

Your goals are to shorten the tree so you can reach the fruit and to thin out the crowded branches so the sun and the air can reach every part of the tree. For large overgrown trees, you may need an arborist to help you.

Year one. In early spring, just before the buds show green, cut one-third of the tallest main branches back to an outward growing limb or bud no more than 10 to 14 feet above the ground. Cut large branches off in sections, rather than in one long piece. In summer, rub or prune off water sprouts (new vertical branches).

YEAR 1

Before pruning · After pruning

Year two. Cut another third of the tallest main branches back as you did in the first year of renovation. Also, continue to let air and light into the tree center; remove water sprouts or bend them over and weight them down to grow new fruit-bearing or fruitful branches.

YEAR 2

Before pruning · After pruning

Year three. Remove the last third of the tall main branches and continue summer care as in the previous years. If your tree has a sound trunk, it should continue to bear fruit for many more years.

YEAR 3

Before pruning · After pruning

PROPAGATING BERRY PLANTS

Transplanting Runners

Most strawberry plants spread by producing dozens of runners—tiny plantlets on the end of long, slender stems.

A simple trick makes it fast and easy to transplant runners, as shown on the right. Select a runner with a tip that's almost touching the ground. Dig a small hole in the soil under the tip. Put a small soil-filled pot into the hole. After the runner roots, snip the stem, lift the pot, and transplant the new plant into the garden.

Alpine strawberries and day-neutral cultivars produce few if any runners. It's best to propagate these plants by dividing them in early spring. See "Dividing Herbs" on page 313 for details.

TRANSPLANTING
STRAWBERRY RUNNERS

Use a wire hairpin to secure the runner tip.

Lift pot after runner roots, and transplant.

Transplanting Suckers

Red raspberries and some thorny blackberries spread naturally by sending up new shoots from their roots. To transplant these shoots, called suckers, first cut off all but 4 to 6 inches of the shoot. Then insert a shovel vertically between the sucker and the main plant, a few inches from the sucker and 6 inches deep, to sever the sucker from the mother plant. Lift the sucker with the shovel and snip any remaining roots that hold the sucker in place. Transplant

Shorten sucker to 4"–6" before transplanting.

TRANSPLANTING RED
RASPBERRY SUCKERS

the sucker to its new location and water generously.

Tip Layering

Black raspberries and trailing blackberries spread by tip layering—growing roots where the tip of a cane touches the ground.

In early summer, when your plants are about 3 feet tall, cut them back to 30 inches. This will encourage formation of sideshoots that will droop toward the ground. When the tips of the shoots start to look stretched in midsummer, dig a small hole under the tip of each shoot. Then put the tip of the shoot on the bottom of the hole and firm the soil over it. In late fall, cut the rooted tip layer from the mother plant and transplant it.

*TIP LAYERING
BLACK RASPBERRIES*

Mound Layering

Propagate currants and gooseberries by covering the base of the plant with soil. This encourages the lowest branches to form roots. You can also propagate dwarfing apple rootstocks by mound layering.

If your plant has four or five side branches close to the ground, simply cover the base of the plant with 8 to 12 inches of soil or sawdust in early spring.

If your plant has few branches close to the ground, cut it back to 1 or 2 inches in early spring. As sideshoots develop, make a small pile of soil or sawdust over the bases of the shoots. Continue to add soil or sawdust every few weeks until the mound is 8 to 12 inches tall.

The following spring, carefully scoop the soil or sawdust away from the plant as soon as the soil is dry enough to work. Cut off all but one of the rooted plants and transplant them. The shoot you leave attached will grow and bear fruit.

Hardwood Cuttings

Expand your vineyard by cutting short sections of dormant wood from your best grapevines and making them take root. Currant, fig, gooseberry, peach, quince, and some plum hardwood cuttings also root reliably.

Prune off sections of the previous season's growth in midwinter for hardwood cuttings. Discard the skinny shoot tips and cut the rest into 8- to 12-inch sections. You'll need to know which end is up on each cutting, so use this simple trick: Make an angled cut just above the top bud on each cutting and a flat cut just below the bottom bud. (Discard the short budless sections between cuttings.) Dip the flat end of each cutting in rooting (hormone) powder. Tag each set of cuttings with their cultivar name. Wrap the cuttings in moist sphagnum moss and put them in a plastic bag in the coldest part of the refrigerator.

In early spring, retrieve your cuttings from cold storage. Plant them outdoors in full or part sun as soon as you can work the soil. Space the cuttings 4 to 6 inches apart in a row, flat end down, with only the top bud exposed.

After one year of growth, the cuttings should be ready for grafting or transplanting to permanent locations.

MOUND LAYERING

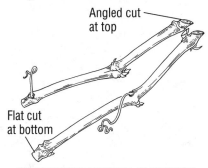

GRAPE HARDWOOD CUTTINGS

BUD GRAFTING FRUIT TREES

To create a bud-grafted tree, you'll join wood from two different cultivars or species. The roots grow from the *rootstock* cultivar; the trunk and branches grow from a bud cut from the *scion* cultivar. Bud grafting is the technique of inserting the scion bud into a slit in the bark of the rootstock.

If you or a friend have a tree of the cultivar you want to propagate, you can collect scion wood from that. If not, order scion wood from a mail-order company. Order scion wood in the spring for delivery in late summer. When it arrives, store it in

Scion grows
from single
bud.

Rootstock is
cut back to
graft union. — Graft union

A BUD-GRAFTED TREE

GROW-YOUR-OWN ROOTSTOCKS

You can create your own rootstocks from seeds or cuttings or by mound layering. Seedling rootstocks will produce full-size trees; to produce dwarfing rootstocks, you must start with cuttings from dwarf cultivars or practice mound layering.

To start rootstocks from seed, harvest seeds from ripe fruits. For apple and pear, pick out seeds from the core. For peaches and apricots, crack the pits and remove the seeds.

Plant the seeds immediately in your garden. Space seed 4 inches apart in a row; cover them with ½ to 1 inch of soil. Cover the row with chicken wire (as shown in the illustration on page 71) to protect the seeds from animals.

The seeds will sprout the following spring. Seedlings will be ready to graft a year later. Select vigorous seedlings at least as big around as a pencil for grafting and discard the others.

For directions for mound layering and taking cuttings, see "Mound Layering" and "Hardwood Cuttings" on page 221.

---

the refrigerator until the day you plan to bud.

Your choice of rootstock may significantly affect your tree's final size and performance. It will not affect the size or kind of fruit your tree bears. In general, choose the same type of rootstock as scion: apple for apple, peach for peach. Closely related plants may work too; quince rootstocks work well for pears. Check with your supplier to learn more about rootstock characteristics.

Buy a suitable rootstock and plant it in early spring of the season you plan to bud. If you are more adventurous, see "Grow-Your-Own Rootstocks" on this page.

When to Bud Graft

Budding isn't hard to do; judging *when* to do it is trickier. And picking the right time is critical for success.

The favorable time period for budding lasts for a few weeks to a few months in late summer and early fall, depending on your climate. You can bud anytime after the rootstock's growth has slowed. However, you can't wait too long, because the inserted bud needs three weeks of nights with temperatures above 50°F to begin forming a living connection to the rootstock.

Checking the rootstock. As summer winds down,

check your rootstock weekly. It's ready to bud when the new growth slows down and starts to harden. If it's still soft and producing new leaves, wait a week and check it again.

Once your rootstock is ready, water it well. If you ordered scion wood, you can now remove it from the refrigerator and proceed with making bud grafts.

Taking scion cuttings. If you will cut your own scion wood, now is the time to begin checking your scion wood tree. The buds in the crook of each leaf on this year's new growth need to be firm and plump. If they are still soft, wait a week and check them again.

SCION CUTTINGS

Once the buds on the scion wood are firm, you can take cuttings. Do this early in the morning. Take the center third of this year's growth. Snip off the leaves, leaving ½-inch leaf-stem "handles." Put the lower ends of the cut-

tings in water and store the cuttings in a cooler until you're ready to bud.

Budding Technique

You're now ready to make bud grafts. Here's how:

1. Strip the leaves off the bottom 10 inches of your rootstock. Make a T-shaped cut through the bark 4 to 6 inches above the ground. Do not cut into the wood.

STEP 1

2. Cut a bud off the scion wood, starting ¾ inch below the bud. Cut deep enough to get a sliver of wood behind the bud. Hold the bud by its leaf-stem handle only.

STEP 2

3. Lift the flaps of the T-shaped cut with the knife tip and slide the bud in, making sure it is right side up.

STEP 3

4. Wrap masking tape around the rootstock above and below the bud. Then tape a 4-inch strip of plastic wrap over the budded area to keep it moist. Label your new tree and give it a good drink.

STEP 4

Four weeks later, remove the plastic wrap. If the bud's plump and green, you did it!

When the tree starts to leaf out next spring, cut off the top of the rootstock ⅝ inch above the inserted bud. Angle the cut away from the bud. During the summer, remove any shoots that sprout below the bud. Transplant the tree the following spring.

FRUIT IN CONTAINERS

The best choices for container fruits are trees that are genetic dwarfs or are growing on dwarfing rootstocks, along with slow-growing or nonvigorous cultivars of bushes or vines. Check your choice's pollination requirements; some fruits won't bear without a pollinator.

Picking Containers

Containers come in a wide range of sizes and styles. Be sure all the containers you choose have drainage holes.

Large containers are best. A dwarf tree needs one at least 2 feet wide and 3 feet deep; bushes or vines need 2 feet by 2 feet. Strawberries need pots at least 8 inches deep.

Plastic and fiberglass containers are lightweight, fairly inexpensive, and come in many styles. Avoid thin, stiff pots, which get brittle with cold and age.

Wooden containers are natural looking and protect roots from rapid temperature swings. Choose containers made of naturally rot-resistant wood. Avoid ones constructed of pressure-treated lumber.

Planting

Before you fill a pot or plant a plant, arrange your containers where you'll want them to stay. Even lightweight containers are astonishingly heavy when full of potting mix. Buy or build dollies for large containers you'd like to be able to move.

Potting mixes. Potted fruits and berries grow best in a lightweight potting mix that holds plenty of moisture but drains well. Look for a coarse commercial mix that doesn't contain synthetic fertilizer. Or mix your own by combining equal parts of compost or peat moss, pulverized pine or fir bark, and perlite or vermiculite. Add 1 cup of greensand, 1 cup of rock or colloidal phosphate, 1 cup of bonemeal, and ¼ cup of blood meal, cottonseed meal, or soybean meal to each cubic yard of commercial or homemade mix.

Potting. The day before you plant, thoroughly wet the potting mix in a large bucket or garden cart.

On planting day, cover the drainage hole(s) with a layer of paper towels or newspaper to prevent the mix from washing out. A layer of pot shards or gravel is unnecessary and may block the drainage hole.

Soak bareroot plants in compost tea before planting. Trim damaged, overly long, or circling roots.

Build a mound of mix to spread a bareroot plant's roots over. Place container-grown plants on a layer of mix. Adjust the height of the mix so the soil line on the plant or the top of the root ball is 1 inch below the container's rim; fill to within 1 inch of the rim. Firm the mix

Plate-type swivel casters

Easy-move plant dolly. *All you need is a circle of ³/₄-inch exterior-grade plywood and five large swivel casters to build this handy back saver. Use ³/₄-inch round-headed wood screws to attach the casters.*

PLANTING A STRAWBERRY BASKET

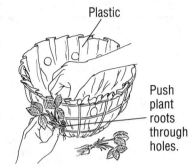

Plastic

Push plant roots through holes.

Step 1. *Line a 12-inch wire basket with plastic, and cut eight holes in it. Insert a plant through each hole as you add mix.*

4" unglazed clay pot serves as water reservoir.

Step 2. *Plug the hole in a clay pot with a cork, and sink it in the center of the basket. Plant four plants around it.*

Step 3. *The plants will grow and cascade over the basket. The sunken pot is a hidden reservoir for easy watering.*

gently as you fill, and settle by watering thoroughly.

Seasonal Care

Frequent watering is the key to successful container growing. Always water before plants dry out, as dry mix is very hard to re-wet. Every other watering, feed by watering with compost tea or extra-dilute kelp or fish fertilizer. Check the pH of the potting mix once a month. Add a pinch of lime if it falls below 6.0; a pinch of sulfur or a spoonful of diluted vinegar if the pH climbs above 7.0.

Besides watering and feeding, container plants need the same care plants in the ground do. See the individual plant entries, starting on page 228, for general care and pest problems.

Winter care. Plants in containers are more cold-tender than those in the ground. See "Protecting Frost-Tender Plants" on page 227 for outdoor care suggestions. See "Indoor Citrus" on page 252 for instructions on bringing trees indoors.

You'll need to repot and root-prune your plants every few years in the early spring just before the plants start to grow. Water well then carefully tip the container onto its side and slide the root ball out. Loosen circling roots and prune them back to an inch or so from the outside of the root ball. Then repot with fresh potting mix and water well again.

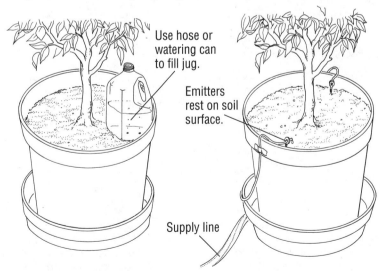

Use hose or watering can to fill jug.

Emitters rest on soil surface.

Supply line

Container drip systems. *Drip-watering is perfect for containers. Choose jugs with one or two pencil-lead-size holes punched in the bottoms or a drip irrigation system with individual emitters.*

PREPARING FRUIT FOR WINTER

While it's tempting to put off garden cleanup until spring, it's best to do it before winter arrives. You'll have fewer insect and disease problems come spring if you do. Here's a checklist of garden-keeping chores to remember as fall fades into winter.

Deal with plant debris. Put fallen leaves and dropped fruits from healthy plants right in the compost pile, or cover them with a thick layer of mulch. Burn the debris from plants that were diseased or pest-ridden, or dispose of it in sealed containers with your household trash. Scour trees, bushes, and vines for mummified fruit, and pick any you find off into a trash bag.

Dig out weeds. Remove any pesky perennial weeds that sneaked by you during the growing season now while they are easy to see.

Clean and store traps. Strip the insect-clogged plastic off reusable traps and store them. If the sticky coating is right on the trap, clean it off with a citrus-oil household cleaning product. Discard disposable traps.

Do therapeutic pruning. Once plants go dormant, check them for any disease symptoms, and prune off diseased twigs and branches. Burn or dispose of prunings. To keep from spreading the problems, dip your pruners in a 10 percent bleach solution between cuts. Put the rest of the pruning off until the proper time. See the individual plant entries, starting on page 228, for specific pruning instructions.

Protect trunks. Protect young fruit trees from sunscald by wrapping the trunk

PREVENTING WINTER RODENT DAMAGE

Step 1. In early autumn, before leaves fall, rake loose mulch back to the tree line to prevent rodents from nesting in mulch under your fruit trees.

Step 2. In late fall, after all the leaves have fallen, and small rodents have found winter homes elsewhere, rake loose mulch back over the fallen leaves and fruit.

Step 3. Spread new mulch on top of the old mulch to make a layer 8 to 10 inches thick. Don't let mulch touch the trunk of the tree.

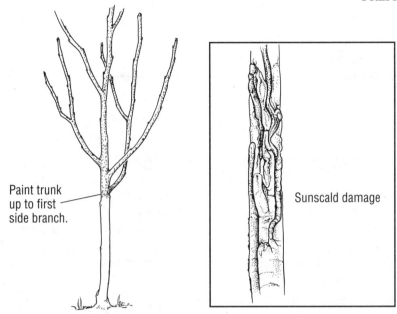

Paint trunk up to first side branch.

Sunscald damage

Protect trees with paint. Protecting trees with a coating of diluted white interior latex paint prevents sunscald, which causes bark cracks that leave the tree open to invasion by disease and insect pests.

coating, and lures now so you'll have them when you need them next spring.

Protect container fruits. Plants growing in containers are less hardy than they would be growing in the ground. If your potted tree wouldn't survive winter in the ground a zone *colder* than the one you live in, you'll need to protect it. Move pots to an unheated basement after the plants go dormant or pile bags of dry leaves around and over the pot to insulate it. Potted frost-tender plants will need to come in before your first frost in the fall.

with a white plastic tree guard or by painting it with white interior latex paint diluted 1:1 with water. Paint from 1 inch below ground up to the first scaffold branch. For protection from disease and borers as well, dilute the paint 1:1 with lime-sulfur solution. Renew paint each fall.

Check trunks for borers. Remove wire collars, and dig about 1 inch of soil away from the trunks of apricot, cherry, peach, and plum trees. If you find borer holes or gummy ooze, dig the borers out with a sharp, flexible wire or squirt parasitic nematodes into the holes. Renew protective paint on trunks, and then replace the soil and wire collars.

Renew defenses. Hungry deer and rabbits nibble tender twigs in winter. Hang fresh bars of soap or spray trees with another repellent before they start foraging. Small rodents also nibble bark in winter. Make sure your wire collars are in good shape. See "Preventing Animal Damage" on page 214 for more on keeping four-footed pests at bay.

Complete garden records. The best time to fill in blanks in your records left during those oh-so-busy weeks in summer is now, while your memory is fresh. By next spring, you'll be too busy to have time for reconstructing old records.

Check supplies. Also take time to check your supplies of chemicals and insect traps. Order dormant oil, lime-sulfur, kelp extract, replacement traps, sticky

PROTECTING FROST-TENDER PLANTS

With a little extra work, you can grow blackberries, grapes, and figs outdoors north of their hardiness zone limits. Here's how.

Train blackberries and grapes on a low trellis. In fall, cut the trellis ties and bend the canes right to the ground. Cover them with wire mesh and then a thick layer of straw to prevent cold damage. In spring, uncover them and tie them to the trellis again.

Protect fig trees by tying the branches together and either wrapping them in layers of old carpet or building a cage around them and filling the cage with dry leaves or straw.

APPLE Malus pumila and other species • Rosaceae

Choosing Trees

Apples are a great fruit for gardeners from chilly Zone 3 to mild Zone 9. Most cultivars will thrive over a wide range of climates. Apples have a chilling requirement, so gardeners in Zones 8 and 9 should select cultivars that will bloom and set fruit despite mild winters. Gardeners in Zones 3 and 4 should avoid late-ripening cultivars.

One of the most common mistakes gardeners make when shopping for apple trees is buying whatever the local discount garden center

Apple tree sizes. Five factors influence apple tree height: cultivar vigor, pruning, soil type, climate, and the dwarfing effect of the rootstock. A vigorous cultivar grafted on a dwarf rootstock and a nonvigorous cultivar grafted on a semidwarf rootstock may eventually reach the same height.

has for sale at planting time. These trees are probably common commercial cultivars selected because the fruit ships well, not because the trees are suited to local conditions. They are also almost guaranteed to be susceptible to many apple diseases.

For success with apples, study mail-order catalogs that offer a selection of disease-resistant and less-common apple cultivars. Visit farmers' markets to find and taste-test unusual cultivars before you order, so you'll know whether you like the flavors of the cultivars you're considering.

Rootstocks

Any apple tree you buy is grafted onto a rootstock. The rootstock type influences how tall the tree will eventually grow. Most gardeners choose trees grafted on semidwarf or dwarf rootstocks because they will remain relatively small and easy to maintain. Semidwarf and dwarf trees also bear fruit sooner than full-size trees do. Zone 3 gardeners should plant full-size trees because they are the most hardy.

Ask what kind of rootstock a tree has before you buy. Knowing the rootstock cultivar will give you a better idea

of how big your tree will eventually grow. Your supplier can also tell you if the cultivar you choose is especially vigorous or not.

Pollination

Most apple cultivars can't pollinate themselves very well, so plant at least two cultivars for cross-pollination. A few cultivars produce no viable pollen (catalogs may refer to these trees as triploids). Be sure to check the catalog or ask your supplier to find out if any of the cultivars you choose are triploids. If they are, you'll need to plant at least two pollen-producing cultivars in addition to the triploid cultivar.

Yield

You can expect to harvest at least a bushel of apples each year from a large dwarf or semidwarf tree at maturity (five years from planting). Smaller harvests begin two to three years after planting.

An ideal apple tree. *This tree's Christmas-tree shape prevents shading of branch tips. Branches have wide attachment angles. The distinct layers of branches allow good air movement through the tree.*

Site and Soil

You can grow apples from Zone 3 through Zone 9 if you match cultivars to your climate.

Choose a site with:
- Full sun.
- Moderately rich soil.
- pH between 6.5 and 6.8.

Avoid:
- Low spots where frost tends to settle.
- Areas where water puddles in spring or after a rain.
- Sites where an apple tree grew previously.

Preparing to Plant

Start preparing the soil a full year before you plan to plant apple trees. Have the soil tested and adjust the pH if necessary. Dig out *every* perennial weed. Plant a cover crop such as sweet clover or buckwheat over the planting area. If you're only planting a few trees, you can prepare and plant cover crops on 10-foot-diameter planting circles at the precise locations where you plan to plant. During the preparation year, mow the cover crop whenever it reaches 8 to 10 inches in height. See "Planting Cover Crops" on page 28 for more details on choosing and managing cover crops.

Planting

Plant apple trees in either early spring or fall. Avoid fall planting in Zone 5 and colder. See "Planting Fruit Trees" on page 200 for complete instructions.

Spacing

Plant full-size trees 20 to 30 feet apart each way. Plant semidwarf trees 10 to 15 feet apart each way; dwarf trees 6 to 8 feet apart each way.

Seasonal Care

Between planting and harvesting, be sure to keep up with feeding and caring for your trees. For a complete guide on what to do when for a successful crop, see "Season-by-Season Care: Apple" on page 232. To identify and treat specific problems, see "Solving Apple Problems" on page 234.

Training Young Trees

Apple trees grow best when trained in a central leader form, which means that the tree has one main trunk with many side branches. Use the technique described below to help your tree develop strong, well-positioned branches during its first few years of growth. (If pruning is new for you, read "Pruning and Training Basics" on page 216 before you train your trees.)

Training at Planting

At planting, cut the main trunk back to 2 to 2½ feet. Cut off about one-third of each side branch.

Some trees are prepruned. If you buy apple trees at a nursery, ask whether they need

2'–2½'   Graft union

TRAINING AT PLANTING

Cut off root-
stock sucker.

Branch
spreader

FIRST SUMMER TRAINING

Shorten side
branches.

FIRST WINTER TRAINING

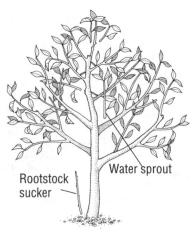

Rootstock
sucker

Water sprout

SECOND SUMMER TRAINING

pruning at planting. If you receive trees via the mail, look for pruning instructions in the packaging with your trees.

First Summer Training

When the new side branches are 12 to 18 inches long, it's time to select three or four main branches and prune off the others. Choose branches that point in four different directions. Each branch should be 4 to 8 inches above or below the nearest branch. Cut off all other branches at the main trunk (the central leader). Do not prune the central leader itself.

Spread each branch so that the angle between trunk and branch is between 45 and 60 degrees. See "Training" on page 217 for how-to spreading instructions.

First Winter Training

In late winter or early spring, shorten each branch, cutting off one-third to one-half of the length. This will encourage side branches to grow. Remove any new shoots

that are growing at a narrow angle and competing with the central leader. If the central leader has grown very tall, cut it back to about 2 feet above the crotch of the uppermost side branch.

Second Summer Training

When the new side branches are 12 to 18 inches long, select another "layer" of three or four main branches about 1½ feet above the previous season's main branches. Cut off other new branches, including any water sprouts (vertical branches) or suckers (sprouts near the soil line). Spread the chosen branches as needed.

Second Winter Training

In late winter or early spring, shorten side branches to encourage branching. Remove one-third to one-half of the previous season's new growth. Remove any new shoots that are growing at a narrow angle and competing with the central leader. If necessary, cut back the central

leader to about 2 feet above the crotch of the uppermost side branch.

Training until Bearing

Depending on the vigor and size of your tree, it may not start bearing for three or more years. Continue to prune and spread branches as you did in the second growing season and winter. Once your tree starts bearing large crops, your pruning method will change.

Pruning Bearing Trees

Once your tree starts to bear fruit, its growth will slow and it will need less pruning. Your task now is to help your tree bear generous crops of juicy, ripe apples. Note: If you have a bearing tree that has been neglected, see "Reviving Neglected Plantings" on page 218 for pruning instructions.

Growing-Season Pruning

When growth slows and stops in mid- to late summer,

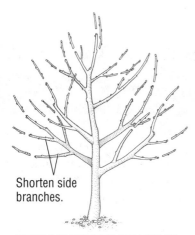

Shorten side branches.

SECOND WINTER TRAINING

cut off any vigorous vertical shoots leaving a $\frac{1}{8}$- to $\frac{1}{4}$-inch stub. Each such stub will tend to form a fruiting spur next season. Use thinning cuts as needed to remove branches to open up the tree to light and air. Cut back branches that are pointing straight down to a more horizontal branch.

Your trees may send up suckers from near the soil line. You can cut or rub these off at any time of year.

Winter Pruning

Over time, your trees may develop a "hole" or empty

Prune vertical shoots, leaving short stubs.

GROWING-SEASON PRUNING

space in the outside shell of branch tips. If this happens, late winter is the best time to encourage new branches to grow and fill in the empty area. Head back branches on the inside of the hole, making cuts just above buds that face toward the hole.

Harvesting

Apples are ready to pick when they taste ripe, not "green" or starchy, but before they get mealy and bland. Once the apples start to change color, pick an apple every few days for a taste test.

Harvest early-ripening or summer apple cultivars when they taste ripe. Eat or process them within a few weeks.

Later fall-ripening apple cultivars will keep in storage for a longer time, some as long as six months. Harvest apples for storage just slightly underripe—they will ripen in storage. Let a few ripen on the tree for eating right away.

How to Pick Apples

• Gently lift and twist each apple to pick it. Keep the stem attached to the fruit. Leave the spur attached to the tree.
• Handle apples carefully to avoid bruising them.
• Set aside bruised and pest-damaged apples to use first.

Storing

Root cellars are ideal for long-term apple storage. Apples keep best at 80 to 90 percent relative humidity and 32° to 40°F (colder than usual refrigerator temperature). If you don't have a root cellar, set up an old refrigerator in the basement or garage for apple storage. Check your apples weekly and remove spoiling fruits.

It's best to store fruits and roots in separate areas. Fruits release ethylene gas as they ripen. The gas makes root crops, like carrots, taste bitter and reduces their storage life.

BE GENTLE WITH SPURS

Apple trees bear fruit mainly on stubby branches called spurs. These spurs live and bear fruit for many years. Don't pull spurs off or damage them when you pick apples—broken spurs mean fewer fruit in the future.

Correct pruning helps increase yields by encouraging the formation of new spurs and by keeping the tree open so light reaches every spur.

Fruit spurs

SEASON-BY-SEASON CARE: APPLE

This care guide tells you what to do and when to do it for your best apple harvest ever. Because timing of certain tasks is critical, review all the instructions in this guide in late winter. Locate or buy the products you'll need in advance. To identify specific problems, refer to "Solving Apple Problems" on page 234. "Preventing Disease Problems" on page 210 explains how to mix and apply sprays.

Dormant buds

Late Winter

Fertilize. Spread 5 to 10 pounds of compost in a band under and just beyond the drip line before buds start to swell.

Scrape tree bark. If codling moths were a problem last year, scrape off loose bark to remove cocoons.

Spray oil. If aphids, codling moths, mites, scales, or fire blight was a problem last year, spray with dormant oil before buds start to swell. Be sure to do this at least 30 days before you plan to spray lime-sulfur or sulfur.

Buds starting to swell

Early Spring

Hang codling moth traps. If codling moths were a problem last year, hang one or two pheromone traps per tree two weeks before bud break. Check traps twice a week. If more than five moths are caught, wait until most of the petals have fallen, then spray ryania four times at one- to two-week intervals.

Spray lime-sulfur. If apple scab or powdery mildew was a problem last year, spray once with lime-sulfur after buds start to swell but before green leaf tips emerge from the buds.

Spray kelp. Kelp sprays help improve bud hardiness and can increase fruit set. Apply three times: when you first see green tips, when leaves are ½ inch long, and when buds are fat and pink.

Spray bordeaux mix. If fire blight was a problem last year, spray tree with bordeaux mix when you first see green tips. If you spray bordeaux mix, you don't need to spray lime-sulfur or sulfur at the same time—bordeaux mix alone will provide adequate disease protection.

Spray streptomycin. If fire blight was a problem last year, spray tree with streptomycin sulfate when buds show pink. Repeat after four or five days if weather is warm and humid.

Hang white sticky traps. If tarnished plant bugs were a problem last year, hang one to four traps per tree when buds start to swell to help provide control. If you catch more than one bug per trap, spray trees with sabadilla when buds show pink.

Petals falling

Spring

Spray calcium. If your fruit had corky spots under the skin or got soft around the core in storage last year, spray tree with calcium chloride when petals fall.

Spray BTK. If fruitworms or leafrollers were a problem last year, spray tree with BTK when petals fall.

Hang green sticky ball traps. If plum curculios were a problem last year, hang one to four traps per tree when petals fall. Start control measures as soon as you trap a curculio or see curculios or damage symptoms on young fruits. To control, hit branches with a padded stick twice daily to knock curculios off onto tarps spread on the ground, and then destroy the pests. Or, immediately after knocking trees free of curculios, enclose each tree in floating row cover closed at the trunk; remove the cover six weeks after bloom. Or spray trees with rotenone-pyrethrins or ryania every few days as long as new curculios are active.

Spray sulfur. If apple scab or powdery mildew was a problem last year, spray tree with sulfur when weather is wet or humid and temperature is above 59°F. Repeat after each rain or at seven- to ten-day intervals until mid-summer.

Small fruit

Early Summer

Hang red sticky ball traps. If apple maggots were a problem last year, hang one to eight traps per tree about four weeks after the first blooms open. Hang the traps halfway up the tree and 2 feet in from the branch tips. The traps should not touch any leaves if possible.

Thin fruit. When fruits are the size of a jelly bean, it's time to thin. Leave one fruit per cluster and allow about 6 inches between fruits.

Replace codling moth lures. Rebait codling moth traps six to eight weeks after you put them out. Check traps weekly. If moths are caught, spray ryania immediately. Repeat at one- to two-week intervals as long as new moths are caught.

Developing fruit

Summer

Pick up dropped fruit. Gather and destroy dropped fruits at least weekly. Drops often contain insect pests that crawl into the soil to overwinter.

Put up apple tree bands. If codling moths are a problem, put bands of corrugated cardboard or burlap around trunks to trap larvae as they leave the tree to pupate. Check under bands daily and destroy larvae.

Prune. Prune bearing trees after growth has slowed in late summer. See "Pruning Bearing Trees" on page 230 for details.

Leaves falling

Fall

Renew mulch. When the leaves start to fall, rake the loose mulch away from tree trunks to leave a bare area under the branches. Once all leaves have fallen, push the raked mulch back on top of the fallen leaves. Add new mulch to make a 6- to 8-inch layer.

Clean up. After leaves fall, pick off remaining fruits and cut out swollen or deformed twigs and branches. Destroy collected fruits and prunings. Clean and store insect traps.

Winterize trunks. Check wire sleeves and white paint on young trees and replace or renew as needed. See page 226 for more information on trunk protection.

Solving Apple Problems

Use this table to identify problems on your apple trees. Scan the list of symptoms to find the description that most closely matches what you see in your garden. Then refer across the page to learn the cause and the recommended solutions. For some pest problems, by the time you see the damage, there is little you can do to fix things in the current season. But pest-damaged apples usually are good to eat if you peel the scarred skin off or cut out damaged areas. Pest-damaged fruit generally doesn't store well. In the future, take preventive steps such as spraying sulfur to prevent certain diseases. For a schedule of preventive measures for apples, see "Season-by-Season Care: Apple" on page 232. You'll also find illustrations, descriptions, and additional controls for many of the insects and diseases listed below in Part 5 of this book.

FLOWER AND FRUIT PROBLEMS

SYMPTOMS	CAUSES	SOLUTIONS
Deformed flowers that don't open; whitish velvetlike patches on flower stems	Powdery mildew	Spray tree with sulfur when weather is wet or humid and temperature is above 59°F. Repeat after each rain or every 7–10 days until midsummer. In late fall, prune out and destroy twigs with a powdery-white coating.
Flowers wilting rapidly and turning dark brown	Fire blight	Prune off infected shoots 6"–12" below areas that show symptoms. Disinfect pruners between cuts. Destroy infected shoots. Spray copper after petals drop and during summer if weather is wet.
Few or no young fruit on apparently healthy tree	Tree too young Spring-frost damage Alternate-year bearing	For young trees, wait one or more seasons—full-size trees may take up to 8 years to bear. On older trees, flowers damaged by late-spring frosts often open but no fruit forms. Certain cultivars alternate between a heavy crop one year and a very light crop the next year. For more even harvests overall, thin fruit in heavy-bearing years.
Crescent-shaped scars or small, loose flaps of skin on young fruit	Plum curculios	This pest is found only in eastern North America. Scarred fruit don't contain insects and are edible. To control, strike branches with a padded stick twice daily to knock curculios off onto a tarp; destroy collected curculios. Or spray with rotenone-pyrethrins or ryania every few days. Continue as long as new curculios are active.
Brown or olive green spots on fruit, or knobby fruit with corky, cracked areas	Apple scab	Scabby fruits are edible. Spray tree with sulfur when weather is wet or humid and temperature is above 59°F. Repeat after each rain or weekly until midsummer.
Deep corky scars or indentations on fruit	Fruitworms Leafrollers Tarnished plant bugs	Ripe deformed fruit do not contain insects and are edible. If you see lots of caterpillars feeding on leaves, spray tree with BTK or neem. Remove and destroy rolled up leaves. If you don't see any caterpillars, damage may be due to tarnished plant bugs. Refer to "Season-by-Season Care: Apple" on page 232 for suggestions for preventing tarnished plant bug problems in the future.

SYMPTOMS	CAUSES	SOLUTIONS
Rough, brown patches or netlike patterns on fruit skin	Powdery mildew	Ripe scarred fruits are edible. Spray tree with sulfur when weather is wet or humid and temperature is above 59°F. Repeat after each rain or every 7–10 days until midsummer. In late fall, prune out and destroy twigs with a powdery-white coating.
Small, red, white-centered spots on fruit	San Jose scale	Ripe spotted fruit are edible, but peel skin first. To prevent problems next year, spray tree with dormant oil before buds start to swell.
Small yellow-orange spots or bumps on fruit	Cedar apple rust	This disease is found only in eastern North America. Ripe spotted fruit are edible. Remove and destroy all infected leaves and excess fruit.
Raised, half-moon-shaped brown patches on older fruit	Plum curculios	This pest is found only in eastern North America. Scarred fruit don't contain insects and are edible. To control, strike branches with a padded stick twice daily to knock curculios off onto a tarp; destroy collected curculios. Or spray with rotenone-pyrethrins or ryania every few days. Continue as long as new curculios are active.
Dimpled, knobby fruit	Apple maggots	Fruit will contain small white maggots, brown tunnels, and discolored areas, but undamaged portions are edible. Plan to hang red sticky ball traps in trees next spring to catch adult flies.
Holes in fruits; holes surrounded by dark brown sawdust	Codling moths	Pinkish white larvae may be present near the core. Undamaged areas of ripe fruit are edible. Collect and destroy all dropped fruit. Ring the trunk with sticky band traps or corrugated cardboard bands to trap larvae leaving the tree to pupate. Check inside bands daily and destroy larvae.
Uninjured fruit rotting before or as they ripen	Bacterial or fungal fruit rots	Remove and destroy rotting fruit. Prune out and destroy any cankered twigs or branches. Plan on applying sulfur or lime-sulfur next season to prevent future problems.
Small black spots on fruit that won't rub off	Black rot	Remove and destroy rotting fruit. Prune out and destroy any cankered twigs or branches. Plan on applying sulfur or lime-sulfur next season to prevent future problems.
Small black spots on fruit that rub off	Harmless fungi	Ripe spotted fruit are edible. Wipe fruit with a damp cloth to remove spots.
Small corky pockets under skin of ripe fruit	Nutrient deficiency	Unaffected parts of fruit are edible. Plan on spraying kelp and calcium next year to prevent future problems.

(continued)

Solving Apple Problems—Continued

LEAF AND SHOOT PROBLEMS

SYMPTOMS	CAUSES	SOLUTIONS
Flat or raised, brown or olive green spots on leaves	Apple scab	Spray tree with sulfur when weather is wet or humid and temperature is above 59°F. Repeat after each rain or weekly until midsummer.
Small yellow-orange spots on leaves	Cedar apple rust	This disease occurs only in eastern North America. Remove and destroy all infected leaves and fruit. Fungicidal sprays are of little use.
Twisted, sticky, sooty young leaves	Aphids	Native predators and parasites usually keep aphids in check. Control large outbreaks with a strong spray of water or spray tree with insecticidal soap or neem.
Whitish, powdery or velvetlike patches on leaves and shoot tips	Powdery mildew	Spray tree with sulfur when weather is wet or humid and temperature is above 59°F. Repeat after each rain or every 7–10 days until midsummer. In late fall, prune out and destroy twigs with a powdery-white coating.
Shoots rapidly turn brown; shoot tip often forms a crook	Fire blight	Prune off infected shoots 6"–12" below areas that show symptoms. Disinfect pruners between cuts. Destroy infected shoots.

BRANCH, TRUNK, AND WHOLE TREE PROBLEMS

SYMPTOMS	CAUSES	SOLUTIONS
Rough, cracked, or gummy areas on twigs or branches	Bacterial and fungal diseases	Prune out and destroy cankers as soon as possible. Allow wounds to dry, then paint large wounds with a 1:1 mix of white interior latex paint and lime-sulfur.
Cottony white masses on twigs or branches	Woolly apple aphids	Spray tree with summer oil or neem during growing season or dormant oil in late winter. Ring trunk and major branches with sticky band traps in spring and fall.
Small gray bumps on bark; leaves turn yellow	San Jose scale	Spray tree with dormant oil in late winter to control.
Weak growth, but no apparent sign of insects or disease	Boring insects Root or collar rot	Inspect base of the trunk. If you find holes and sawdust due to borers, poke a straightened paper clip into the holes to kill borers, or inject parasitic nematodes. Trim away damaged wood. Paint trunk with white interior latex paint to prevent sunscald, which creates entry sites for borers. If you don't find holes, use a knife to peel back bark at trunk base. If wood is dark and discolored, tree will not recover. Remove and destroy the tree. Replant in a new site.

APRICOT *Prunus armeniaca* • Rosaceae

Apricots look like miniature peaches, but they have a rich, aromatic flavor all their own. They are related to peaches, and care of both kinds of trees is similar. Refer to "Peach" on page 268 for information on seasonal care, solving pest problems, and harvesting.

Here you'll find specialized facts about apricots, including the best cultivars and rootstocks for your area, as well as pollination, yield, and pruning information.

Choosing Trees

You can grow apricots successfully in Zones 4 through 9. Most cultivars grow well in Zones 6 through 8.

Apricots are prone to frost damage. Some cultivars to try in cold areas are 'Scout' (Zone 4) and 'Jerseycot' or 'Hargrand' (Zone 5).

If your area has humid summers, select disease-resistant cultivars such as 'Jerseycot', 'Alfred', or those whose names start with 'Har-'. Only gardeners in the arid Southwest should plant commercial cultivars such as 'Royal' or 'Perfection'.

Rootstocks. Buy trees that are grafted on apricot seedling rootstocks rather than peach rootstocks if you

have a choice. 'Myrobalan' plum rootstock is the best choice for clayey soils.

Pollination. Most apricot cultivars are self-fruitful, but you'll often get more fruit per tree if you plant two different cultivars.

Yield. Expect 50 to 100 pounds of apricots per tree each year beginning two years after planting. Yields will be lower if late frosts cause blossom damage.

Site and Soil

Apricots need the same conditions and soil as peaches but will tolerate a wide range of pH: from 5.5 to 8.0.

Planting

Plant trees in early spring or fall. Avoid fall planting in Zones 4 through 6. See "Planting Fruit Trees" on page 200 for complete instructions.

Spacing. Plant trees 15 to 20 feet apart each way.

Training and Pruning

Train your apricot trees to a central leader shape as you would an apple tree. See "Training Young Trees" on

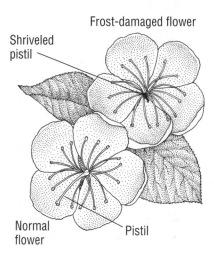

Frost-damaged flower
Shriveled pistil
Normal flower
Pistil

Frost damage. *Apricots bloom early, but temperatures of 26°F or below will damage swelling buds. Examine exposed flowers a few days after a cold snap. Pistils of damaged flowers will be dark and shriveled; they will not bear fruit.*

page 229 for directions. Wait until just after the trees leaf out or bloom to do your spring pruning.

Once your trees are bearing, you'll prune them more as you would peaches. See "Pruning Bearing Trees" on page 270 for instructions. Unlike peaches, apricots bear on one-, two-, three-, and four-year-old spurs. Because of this, you don't need to thin out the old wood as heavily as you would for peaches. Each year, remove a few of the oldest branches.

If you have a year with very heavy fruit set on your apricot tree, thin the fruits to about 2 inches apart.

BLACKBERRY *Rubus* spp. • Rosaceae

Raising blackberries is similar to growing their cousins, the raspberries. Refer to "Raspberry" on page 284 for information on site preparation, seasonal care, solving pest problems, and harvesting. Below you'll find suggestions for the best blackberry cultivars for your area, spacing requirements, and training and trellising instructions.

Are your blackberries ripe? *To be sure, wait until the berries lose their shine and separate easily from their stems. Blackberries are less delicate than raspberries—they can stand up to being piled into quart baskets.*

Choosing Plants

You can grow blackberries from Zones 4 through 9. Erect, thorny cultivars such as 'Illini Hardy' are hardy to warmer parts of Zone 4. Other erect cultivars such as 'Rosborough' are well suited to hot, dry climates.

Semi-erect, thornless blackberries such as 'Navaho' and 'Arapaho' are hardy in Zones 5 through 9. Trailing blackberries, sometimes called dewberries, are hardy only to Zone 7.

Blackberries have a wide range of ripening times, beginning in early summer and continuing through fall.

Pollination. Blackberries are self-fertile; you can plant one cultivar and harvest a full crop.

Yield. Each blackberry plant in your patch should produce 10 to 15 pounds of berries yearly once the plants are mature (two or three years).

Planting

Plant blackberry plants as you would raspberries.

Spacing. Plant erect cultivars 4 feet apart in rows. They will spread and fill in the row, forming a continuous stand. Plant semi-erect and trailing cultivars 6 to 8 feet apart in rows. These types will not spread nor form a stand. Leave at least 8 feet between rows of plants, more for thorny cultivars.

Training Plants

Erect cultivars. Erect blackberries hold themselves up but it's best to keep them caged in a V-trellis, as shown at the top on page 209.

Each summer pinch off the tips of the new canes when they are 3 feet tall. Cut off the canes that have fruited flush with the soil as soon as harvest is complete. In late winter, remove canes outside the 18-inch-wide row and thin the remaining canes to leave four to six sturdy canes per foot of row. Shorten all side branches to 12 to 18 inches.

Semi-erect and trailing cultivars. These vigorous types need support. The fence-type trellis shown at the bottom on page 209 is an excellent choice.

Each summer pinch off the tips of new, skyward-reaching canes when they reach the top of their trellis. Cut off the canes that have fruited flush with the soil as soon as harvest is complete. In late winter, thin the canes to leave eight to ten sturdy canes per plant. Tie them securely to the trellis. Shorten all side branches to 12 to 18 inches.

BLUEBERRY   *Vaccinium* spp. • Ericaceae

Choosing Plants

Unlike many of the fruits we grow, blueberries are a native American crop. Gardeners in Zones 2 through 9 can enjoy growing blueberries. Try extending your harvest season by planting cultivars with different ripening seasons. Select two- or three-year-old virus-indexed plants.

Highbush blueberries. Gardeners in Zones 4 through 7 should grow highbush blueberries (*Vaccinium corymbosum*), which are native to the mid-Atlantic region. They grow to about 6 feet tall.

Lowbush blueberries. The cold-hardy lowbush blueberry (*V. angustifolium*) thrives in Zones 2 through 6. This spreading, 1- to 2-foot-tall groundcover bears small, high-quality berries. A few superior cultivars are available from specialty mail-order sources. (See "Sources" on page 358 for addresses of specialty fruit suppliers.)

Midhigh blueberries. Hybrid midhigh cultivars combine the berry size of highbush blueberries and the hardiness of lowbush blueberries in a 2- to 4-foot-tall bush. They require the same care as highbush blueberries.

Rabbiteye blueberries. Rabbiteye or southern high-bush blueberries (*V. ashei*) are native to the Southeast. The plants are heat- and drought-tolerant, thrive in Zones 7 through 9, and can grow as tall as 15 feet.

Pollination

Some types and cultivars of blueberries require cross-pollination; others are partially self-fertile. Plant two or more cultivars for good fruit set.

Yield

Highbush plants will bear up to 6 pounds of berries every year once they reach eight years old. Smaller harvests will start two years after planting. Midhigh plants yield about 3 pounds of berries per year at maturity. Rabbiteye plants yield slightly more than 6 pounds yearly and come into full production in just five years. Expect a few cups of berries per plant per year for lowbush blueberries.

Site and Soil

Blueberries need acid soil to thrive. If acid-loving wild plants such as mountain laurel grow in your area, you can probably grow blueberries easily. If your soil isn't acid enough, you'll need to add sulfur to lower the pH.

Choose a site with:
• Full sun. (Blueberries tolerate partial shade, but produce less fruit than bushes growing in full sun.)
• High levels of organic matter.
• pH between 4.0 and 5.0.
Avoid:
• Low spots where frost tends to settle.
• Areas where water puddles in spring or after a rain.
• Sites near wild blueberries, which can harbor viral diseases.

BEATING THE ALKALINE BLUES

If your soil's pH is 7.0 or above, it will be hard to make it acid enough for blueberries to grow well. Try growing a few plants in a raised bed instead. Use equal parts sand and peat moss mixed with a bucketful of compost to create a mix that's fairly acid and provides enough nutrients for good growth. Or, for a productive patio pair, plant two midhigh cultivars in half barrels filled with the same mixture. See "Fruit in Containers" on page 224 for care instructions for fruits in containers.

LOWERING SOIL pH

Blueberries require a much lower pH than most garden plants. Unless you have naturally acidic soil, you'll probably need to add material to your planting site to lower the soil pH. For existing stands of blueberries, you can try applying an acidic organic mulch such as oak leaves or pine needles.

A more precise way to correct soil pH for blueberries is to test the pH level and then add sulfur as needed. The table below shows the pounds of sulfur needed per 100 square feet to drop soil pH to 4.5, based on initial soil pH. Soil pH changes more easily in sandy soil than in clay soil; the table recommends different quantities for sandy, loamy, and clay soils. Work half the recommended amount of sulfur into the top 4 to 6 inches of soil in early spring and the balance in early fall.

INITIAL SOIL pH	POUNDS OF SULFUR PER 100 SQUARE FEET		
	SAND	LOAM	CLAY
5.0	0.4	1.2	1.8
5.5	0.8	2.4	3.6
6.0	1.2	3.5	5.3
6.5	1.5	4.6	6.7
7.0	1.9	5.8	8.7

Preparing to Plant

Start preparing the soil a full year before you plan to plant blueberries. Have the soil tested and adjust the pH if necessary. Ask your soil-testing lab to recommend how much sulfur you need to add to lower the pH to 4.5. Or you can test the soil pH yourself, and try following the guidelines in "Lowering Soil pH" on this page.

The season before you plant, also dig out *every* perennial weed. Plant a buck-wheat cover crop over the entire planting area. In fall, plant a winter cover crop such as hairy vetch or winter rye. See "Planting Cover Crops" on page 28 for more details on choosing and managing cover crops.

Mow or till your cover crop a few weeks before planting time. Then shape the soil into a 6-inch-high, 4-foot-wide raised bed. This is especially important if water puddles on the site in the spring or after a rain.

Planting

Plant bareroot blueberries in spring as soon as the chance of heavy frost is past. You can plant container-grown blueberries anytime from spring through late summer. See "Planting Vines and Bushes" on page 202 for planting instructions.

Surround plants with a 4-foot-wide, 6- to 12-inch-deep strip of organic mulch after planting. Leave the mulch about 4 inches deep where it touches the stems.

Spacing

Plant highbush blueberries 5 feet apart in a row; rabbit-eye blueberries 8 feet apart. Set lowbush blueberries 2 feet apart each way; plants will fill in the area within six years.

Seasonal Care

You will harvest more berries and have fewer problems if you feed and care for your plants regularly. See "Season-by-Season Care: Blueberry" on page 242 for directions for caring for your blueberries throughout the year. To identify and treat specific problems, see "Solving Blueberry Problems" on page 244.

Training Bushes

Blueberries are generally self-shaping and only need some thinning each winter to stay healthy and productive.

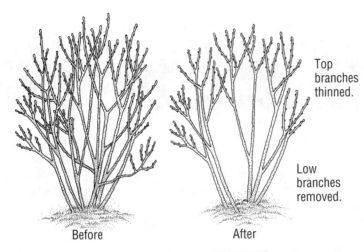

Top branches thinned.

Low branches removed.

Before   After

PRUNING HIGHBUSH BLUEBERRIES

Follow the instructions below to ensure years of generous harvests.

Pruning
Highbush Blueberries

Young bushes. Remove all flower clusters the first two years to let the bush concentrate on growing. Don't prune, except to remove dead or diseased wood or canes that are growing close to the ground.

Three- to eight-year-old bushes. Prune in late winter or early spring just before growth begins each year. Remove prostrate canes and canes that are less than 2 feet tall, cutting them off flush with the base of the bush. If more than two or three new upright canes grew the previous summer, remove the extras. Choose canes from the center for removal (this opens the bush to air and sunlight), and cut them off flush with the base of the bush. On the remaining canes, cut off side branches that are within 18 inches of the ground. Thin out side branches near the top of the bush if the bush is very dense.

Mature bushes. Prune like three- to eight-year-old bushes with one additional step: Cut two or three of the oldest canes off flush with the base of the plant each year. This will keep the bush productive.

Pruning
Rabbiteye Blueberries

Prune rabbiteye blueberries like highbush types but leave three or four new canes each year rather than two or three. Plants will reach full size in five years. At that time, start removing three or four of the oldest canes each year.

Pruning
Lowbush Blueberries

The best tool for pruning lowbush blueberries is a lawn mower. Pruned plants will not bear the season following pruning, so if you want berries every year, divide your patch in half and mow the halves in alternate years. Mow stems to the ground in late winter.

If your patch is too small to mow easily, you can hand-prune it instead. If you'd like some berries each year, just cut off the older stems at ground level and leave the younger stems to bear.

Harvesting

Taste-test blueberries before harvesting. A blueberry that has just turned blue is not at its best for eating. Wait a few days for full sweetness and aroma. Tickle clusters of blue fruits, and the ripe ones will drop into your hand. Don't pick underripe berries because they won't ripen further after picking. If you need to pull at a fruit, it isn't ripe yet. Berries hang on the bush after they are ripe, so picking twice a week is adequate. To prevent picked berries from being crushed, pile them no more than 5 inches deep in your picking containers.

Storing

Blueberries will keep in your refrigerator for about a week. If you need to store them longer, they will keep two weeks in a spare refrigerator set at 31° to 32°F (colder than usual refrigerator temperature). Freeze excess berries.

SEASON-BY-SEASON CARE: BLUEBERRY

This care guide tells you what to do and when to do it for your best blueberry harvest ever. Because timing of certain tasks is critical, review all the instructions in this guide in late winter. Locate or buy the products you'll need in advance. To identify specific problems, refer to "Solving Blueberry Problems" on page 244. "Preventing Disease Problems" on page 210 explains how to mix and apply sprays.

Dormant buds

Late Winter

Prune. Prune yearly to keep bushes productive. See "Training Bushes" on page 240 for details.

Spray oil. If aphids or scales were a problem last season, spray with dormant oil before buds start to swell. Be sure to do this at least 30 days before you plan to spray lime-sulfur or sulfur.

Test and adjust pH. Scrape back mulch under a bush, take a soil sample from the top 6 inches of soil, and replace mulch. Determine the soil pH and adjust as needed. See "Lowering Soil pH" on page 240 for more information.

Buds starting to swell

Early Spring

Spray lime-sulfur. If phomopsis twig blight was a problem last season, make an application of lime-sulfur when the buds start to swell.

Spray copper. If bacterial blight was a problem last season, spray bushes with copper as soon as the buds start to swell. Repeat every two weeks if the weather is cool and wet.

Stir mulch surface. Use your hands or a rake to gently stir the top ½ inch of the mulch around your plants when buds are fat and swollen. This helps prevent a disease called mummy berry that can ruin the crop.

Spray kelp. Kelp sprays help improve bud hardiness and can increase fruit set. Apply three times: when you first see green tips, when leaves are ½ inch long, and three weeks later.

Full bloom

Spring

Fertilize. Each spring, sprinkle blood meal or alfalfa meal around plants on top of the mulch at a rate of ½ pound of fertilizer per plant.

Remove flowers from newly planted bushes. Remove all blossoms the first two years so that plants can put their energy into shoot and root growth.

Spray sulfur. If fruit rots were a problem last year, and if humidity is high or weather is wet, spray plants when they are in full bloom. Reapply every seven to ten days and after rains through harvest.

Spray compost tea. If weather is dry, spray compost tea instead of sulfur. Reapply every seven to ten days and after rains through harvest.

Spray pyrethrins or rotenone after bloom. If cherry fruitworms are a severe problem in your area, spray pyrethrins or rotenone after the bloom period is over to kill fruitworms before they bore into fruits.

Hang sticky traps. If blueberry maggots were a problem last year, hang red sticky spheres or yellow rectangular sticky traps baited with fruit fly (*Rhagoletes*) attractant 4 inches above your bushes when the berries appear. Use one trap per highbush plant or one trap every 5 feet for lowbush plants. Leave the traps in place until you finish harvesting the fruits.

Remove wilted shoot tips. Blueberry tip borers burrow into new growth, causing it to wilt. If you find wilted twigs, snip them off a few inches below damage and destroy them.

Cover bushes with screening. If blueberry maggots are a severe problem in your area, enclose bushes with floating row cover or a cage covered with nylon window screening after the fruit has set. This will prevent females from reaching the berries and laying eggs on them.

Developing berries

Early Summer

Cover bushes with netting. Birds can strip berries from plants before they ripen. Cover bushes with netting just before the berries start to change color. If there are lots of hungry birds in your yard, consider protecting your bushes with a walk-in blueberry cage, like the one shown at the bottom on page 214.

Remove flowers from young plants. For highbush and rabbiteye blueberries, pick off flower clusters during the first two years of growth to encourage the plants to develop strong vegetative and root growth.

Ripe berries

Summer

Clean up rotting or infested berries. Remove and destroy rotting or infested fruits on or under your plants as soon as you see them.

Drench soil with parasitic nematodes. If your bushes were damaged by black vine weevils this year, drench the soil around your bushes with parasitic nematodes. The nematodes will control the weevil larvae, which feed on plant roots.

Leaves falling

Fall

Renew mulch. When the leaves start to fall, rake the loose surface mulch away from the bush to leave a bare circle under the branches. Once all leaves have fallen, spread loose mulch back over them and add new mulch to make a 6- to 8-inch layer.

Clean up. After leaves fall, pick off any remaining fruits and cut out any swollen or deformed twigs and branches. Destroy the collected fruits and prunings. Clean insect traps and store them in a dry place until next season.

Control animal pests. Rabbits and deer like to munch on blueberry stems in winter. Keep them away with repellents or by building a walk-in blueberry cage. See "Preventing Animal Damage" on page 214 for details.

Solving Blueberry Problems

Use this table to identify problems on your blueberries. Scan the list of symptoms to find the description that most closely matches what you see in your garden. Then refer across the page to learn the cause and the recommended solutions. For some pest problems, by the time you see the damage, there is little you can do to fix things in the current season. In the future, take preventive steps such as spraying sulfur to prevent certain diseases. For a schedule of preventive measures for blueberries, see "Season-by-Season Care: Blueberry" on page 242. You'll also find illustrations, descriptions, and additional controls for many of the insects and diseases listed below in Part 5 of this book.

FLOWER AND FRUIT PROBLEMS

SYMPTOMS	CAUSES	SOLUTIONS
Water-soaked brown spots and/or fuzzy gray mold on blossoms and berries	Botrytis blight	Pick and destroy all affected blossoms and fruit. Prune foliage to increase air circulation.
Shriveled, soft berries that drop early; whitish maggots inside berries	Blueberry maggots	Collect and destroy soft or dropped berries. Infested berries drop early, so delay harvest until berries are thoroughly ripe to avoid infested berries.
Deformed or shriveled berries that drop early; small white grubs feeding inside	Plum curculios	This is a pest only in eastern North America. Twice a day strike bushes with a padded stick to knock curculios onto a tarp spread under bushes; destroy collected curculios. Spray with rotenone, ryania, and/or pyrethrins weekly as soon as first scars are seen on developing fruit.
Tan to salmon-colored berries, which later become gray and hard	Mummy berry	Collect and destroy all dropped and mummified berries, or rake mummies into rows and cultivate them into the soil. Prune foliage to increase air circulation. If plants are severely infected, destroy them and replant with resistant cultivars.
Berries webbed together; white or greenish caterpillars feeding inside	Cherry fruitworms Cranberry fruit- worms	Pick and destroy damaged fruit. Harvest berries daily to minimize damage.
Fruit disappears	Birds	Birds can strip fruit from bushes very quickly before berries are fully ripe. To avoid losing next year's crop to birds, plan to cover bushes with bird netting before berries start to turn blue.

LEAF AND SHOOT PROBLEMS

SYMPTOMS	CAUSES	SOLUTIONS
Young leaves yellow with veins remaining green	Iron deficiency	Iron deficiency occurs when soil pH is too high. Apply foliar sprays of chelated iron when plants are well leafed out. In the future, reduce soil pH with acidic mulches (oak leaves, pine needles). Lightly top-dress alkaline soils with sulfur once a year.

SYMPTOMS	CAUSES	SOLUTIONS
Leaves webbed together; caterpillar inside some webs	Blueberry leafrollers Other leafrollers	Native parasites usually keep leafrollers in check. In light infestations, pick off leaves with webbing and destroy. Spray neem if defoliation is serious. When berries start to ripen, shake plants to knock mature larvae onto a tarp. Collect and destroy larvae.
Leaves skeletonized; bronze beetles on leaves	Japanese beetles	In early morning, knock beetles from plants into a bucket of soapy water or onto a tarp and destroy. If infestation is severe, spray with pyrethrins or rotenone frequently. For complete protection, cover plants with floating row cover or nylon window screening after fruit has set.
Small, half-circle notches in margins of mature leaves	Black vine weevils	At night, shake plants over a tarp to knock adult weevils from leaves (late April through summer). Collect and destroy weevils. Where leaves are severely notched, spray pyrethrins or rotenone in early June, repeating only if fresh notches appear on leaves. Drench soil with parasitic nematodes in late summer and early fall to control larvae, which feed on roots and can girdle stems.
Blackened areas on buds and leaves; wilted shoots	Mummy berry	Prune and destroy infected foliage. Prune foliage to increase air circulation. If plants are severely infected, destroy them and replant with resistant cultivars.
Fuzzy gray mold covering leaves and shoots	Botrytis blight	Prune and destroy all affected leaves and shoots. Prune foliage to increase air circulation.
Water-soaked areas on 1-year-old shoots	Bacterial blight	Prune and destroy all affected wood. Spray copper as soon as symptoms appear and again when half of leaves have fallen. If damage is severe, replant with blight-tolerant cultivars.
Reddish, gray, or black tapering swellings on stems	Blueberry cane canker	This disease is most common in the South. Prune out wood with cankers, disinfecting tools between cuts, or dig and destroy severely infected plants. If cane canker problems persist, replant with rabbiteye blueberries or resistant cultivars of highbush blueberries.
Circular, reddish spots on stems; dead leaves show up bright red from a distance	Fusicoccum canker (Godronia canker) Phomopsis twig blight	Symptoms of these two diseases are similar. Bull's-eye patterns in spots indicate Fusicoccum. Phomopsis infection sometimes causes leaf spots as well as stem symptoms. Prune and destroy infected stems well below infection point, disinfecting tools between cuts. For Fusicoccum, spraying copper at 2-week intervals may help. In the future, replant with resistant or tolerant cultivars.

CHERRY *Prunus* spp. • Rosaceae

Choosing Trees

Cheerful cherries deserve a place in your garden. Thanks to new self-pollinating cultivars and dwarfing rootstocks, luscious sweet cherries are now fairly easy for home gardeners to grow. Tart cherries tolerate cold winters, hot and wet summers, and imperfect soil drainage better than sweet cherries.

Sweet cherries. Sweet cherries (*Prunus avium*) thrive in Zones 5 through 9. Choose soft-fleshed, non-cracking cultivars such as 'Lapins' and 'Sam' where spring and early summer are humid or rainy. 'Windsor' resists brown rot. Yellow cultivars may be less attractive to birds.

Tart cherries. Tart cherries (*P. cerasus*) are small, spreading trees and thrive in Zones 4 through 9. 'Northstar' resists brown rot.

Rootstocks

Any cherry tree you buy will be grafted on a rootstock. Rootstock type influences tree performance in various soil types. Some rootstocks also provide size control—especially important for normally large sweet cherry trees.

Sweet cherries. 'Mazzard' is a good rootstock for heavier, wetter soil. 'Mahaleb' is better for light soil and droughty conditions. For dwarf trees, select naturally dwarf (or genetic dwarf) cultivars such as 'Garden Bing'. Full-size cultivars are also available grafted onto a dwarfing rootstock such as 'Damil' (also called 'GM 61/1') or 'Gisela'.

Tart cherries. 'Mazzard' and 'Mahaleb' are the most common rootstocks. Full-size tart cherry trees grow to about 15 feet; for a smaller tree, buy one grafted on 'Damil'.

Pollination

Sweet cherries. Most sweet cherry cultivars need cross-pollination. Also, certain cultivars can't pollinate other cultivars; ask your supplier to recommend good pollinator combinations. A few cultivars, such as 'Garden Bing' and 'Stella', are self-fertile; you can plant just one and harvest a full crop.

Tart cherries. All tart cherry cultivars are self-fertile. You can expect a good harvest from a single tree.

Yield

A mature full-size sweet cherry tree will produce 50 to 100 pounds of fruit yearly (smaller harvests begin five to six years after planting).

Mature tart cherry trees yield 30 to 50 pounds of fruit per year (smaller harvests begin four to five years after planting).

Site and Soil

You can grow cherries in Zones 4 through 9 if you match types and cultivars to your climate.

Choose a site with:
• Full sun.
• Moderately fertile soil.
• pH between 6.0 and 6.8.
Avoid:
• Low spots where frost tends to settle.

BUSH CHERRIES

Bush cherries grow on shrubs that laugh at drought, poor soil, and winter cold (they are hardy to Zone 3). Try one of three types: Western sand cherry (*Prunus besseyi*), Nanking cherry (*P. tomentosa*), or fall-fruiting hybrid bush cherries 'Jan' and 'Joy'. Nanking cherries and fall-fruiting bush cherries are sweet enough for fresh eating; Western sand cherries are better cooked.

• Areas where water puddles in spring or after a rain (especially important for sweet cherries).
• Sites where a cherry, peach, or plum tree grew previously.
• Sites near wild chokecherries, which can harbor viral diseases that also infect cherry trees.

Prepare planting sites for cherries the same way you would for peach trees. See "Preparing to Plant" on page 269 for details.

Planting

Plant cherry trees in either early spring or fall. Avoid fall planting in Zones 4 through 6. If your planting site has any drainage problems, build the soil up into a raised bed. See "Planting Fruit Trees" on page 200 for complete planting instructions.

Spacing

Plant full-size sweet cherry trees 20 to 30 feet apart each way; dwarf trees 8 to 12 feet apart. Plant tart cherry trees 15 to 20 feet apart.

Seasonal Care

To produce its best crop, your tree will need feeding and other attention during the season. "Season-by-Season Care: Cherry" on page

248 makes your job simple with directions for caring for your trees throughout the year. For solutions to specific problems with your trees, see "Solving Cherry Problems" on page 251.

Training and Pruning

It's best to train sweet cherry trees to a central leader shape, as you would apples. However, tart cherry trees respond better to open center training, which is also used for peach trees.

Sweet Cherries

Sweet cherry trees are trained almost the same way apple trees are trained. Before you make any pruning cuts, read "Training Young Trees" on page 229. Then review the following exceptions to those instructions.

Planting time. Do not shorten the main stem or side branches of a cherry at planting time. Thin out branches if they are crowded.

First growing season. Select main branches that are 12 to 15 inches apart along the main stem (compared to 4 to 8 inches for apples).

Be extra careful not to choose a branch that's directly in line above another branch. One branch will take over and choke out the other.

First winter. Shorten side

FOR BEST RESULTS

Sweet cherries. Buy 4- to 5-foot-tall one-year-old trees with ½- to ¾-inch-diameter trunks. One to three branches 2½ to 3 feet up the trunk are a plus.

Tart cherries. Choose 4- to 5-foot-tall two-year-old trees with ½- to ¾-inch-diameter trunks.

branches by no more than one-third. An exception: If one branch has outgrown the other branches and the main stem, cut it back as much as needed so it's the same length as the other branches.

Pruning until bearing. Follow the guidelines above in succeeding years. Keep in mind that sweet cherries grow more slowly and branch less than apples. Your cherry tree will need less pruning than an apple and take a few more years to reach bearing size.

Once the tree is about 8 feet tall, cut the central leader back to a weak side branch each spring.

Pruning bearing trees. Prune bearing sweet cherry trees just after harvest. Next year's fruit buds are forming at this time, and it's important to allow light into the tree to help their growth. Use thinning cuts to keep the center of the tree open to increase air movement and decrease brown rot problems.

SEASON-BY-SEASON CARE: CHERRY

This care guide tells you what to do and when to do it for your best cherry harvest ever. Because timing of certain tasks is critical, review all the instructions in this guide in late winter. Locate or buy the products you'll need in advance. To identify specific problems, refer to "Solving Cherry Problems" on page 251. "Preventing Disease Problems" on page 210 explains how to mix and apply sprays. *Caution:* Don't substitute lime-sulfur for sulfur on cherry trees while fruit is present; lime-sulfur can damage the fruit.

Dormant buds

Late Winter

Fertilize. Spread 5 to 10 pounds of compost in a band under and just beyond the drip line before buds start to swell.

Avoid pruning. Hold off pruning your cherry trees until spring to decrease the risk of pruning-induced cold injury and canker development.

Spray oil. If aphids or scales were a problem last season, spray with dormant oil before buds start to swell. Be sure to do this at least 30 days before you plan to spray lime-sulfur or sulfur.

Spray lime-sulfur. If black knot was a problem last season, spray lime-sulfur once in late winter and again when the buds start to swell.

Buds swelling

Very Early Spring

Spray lime-sulfur. If cherry leaf spot or brown rot was a problem last season, spray lime-sulfur when the buds start to swell.

Spray kelp. Kelp sprays help improve bud hardiness and can increase fruit set. Apply three times: when leaves are ½ inch long, when flowers are open, and when green fruits are visible.

Full bloom

Spring

Prune. Prune young sweet cherry trees and tart cherry trees just before, during, or just after bloom. See "Training and Pruning" on page 247 for instructions.

Spray sulfur. If the weather is wet or humid and at least 70°F when flowers are open, spray trees with sulfur to help control brown rot.

Hang green sticky ball traps. Plum curculio can be a major problem east of the Rocky Mountains. Hang one to four traps per tree when petals fall. Start control measures as soon as you trap a curculio or spot damage on young fruits. To control, hit branches with a padded stick twice daily to knock curculios off onto tarps spread on the ground, and then destroy the pests. Or, immediately after knocking trees free of curculios, enclose each tree in a large piece of floating row cover, tying it securely around the trunk; remove the cover six weeks after bloom. Or spray trees with rotenone-pyrethrins or ryania every few days as long as new curculios are active.

Hang traps for cherry fruit flies. If cherry fruit fly larvae were a problem last year or the year before, hang traps two weeks after petals fall. Hang rectangular yellow sticky traps in trees. Attaching a small vial of ammonium carbonate to each trap increases its effectiveness. Or hang one to eight red sticky ball traps per tree. Position the traps halfway up the tree and 2 feet in from the branch tips. The traps should not touch any leaves if possible. In areas where fruit fly numbers are high, spray pyrethrins or rotenone weekly as soon as the first flies appear in traps.

Spray BTK. If you've had past problems with green fruitworms in your cherries, watch for webbing and/or pale green caterpillars on leaves. Spray affected trees with BTK as soon as you notice the damage.

Spray calcium. If your sweet cherries tend to crack, spray calcium three times. Start when fruits are pea size; repeat every two weeks.

Spray sulfur. If cherry leaf spot was a problem last year, spray sulfur every two to three weeks, beginning when you first see spots on leaves. Repeat sprays whenever the weather is wet or humid and the spots are spreading, until all leaves have fallen in fall.

Pick up dropped fruit. Gather and destroy dropped fruit at least weekly. If you have problems with cherry fruit flies, gather and destroy dropped fruit daily to reduce future infestations.

Developing fruit

Early Summer

Spray sulfur. If brown rot was a problem on your fruit last year, spray trees with sulfur when the fruits begin to color. Remove rotting fruits as soon as you spot them.

Net trees. When the fruits start to color, drape netting over the tree and fasten the edges securely so no birds can sneak in.

Ripe fruit

Summer

Prune. Prune bearing sweet cherry trees now. See "Training and Pruning" on page 247 for instructions.

Leaves falling

Fall

Renew mulch. When leaves start to fall, rake loose mulch away from the trunk to leave a bare circle under the branches. Once all leaves have fallen, push the loose mulch back into place. Apply new mulch to make a 6- to 8-inch layer.

Winterize trunks. Peachtree borer larvae bore into the bark near the soil line and up about 1 foot. If your trees have wire sleeves around them, remove them and dig about 1 inch of soil away from the base of the trunk. If you find borer holes or gummy ooze, dig the borers out with a sharp flexible wire or squirt parasitic nematodes into the holes. Renew paint and replace soil and wire sleeve. See page 226 for more information on trunk protection.

Clean up. After leaves fall, pick off any remaining fruits and cut out any swollen or deformed twigs and branches. Destroy collected fruits and prunings. Clean and store insect traps for next season.

WHERE CHERRIES BEAR FRUIT

Tart cherries bear fruit on fruit spurs and on the bottom 7 inches of one-year-old shoots. The following year, this portion of the shoot becomes a bare area, not new spurs. Prune and fertilize your trees so they produce new shoots at least 10 inches long to keep them productive. Sweet cherries develop differently. They produce only one flower bud on each one-year-old shoot. All the other buds will form fruiting spurs in the following year.

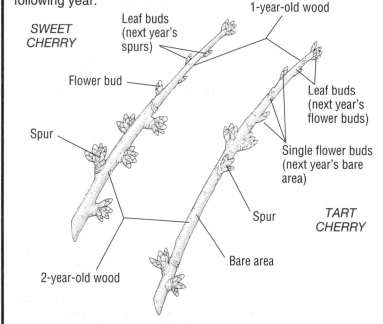

SWEET CHERRY

Leaf buds (next year's spurs)

1-year-old wood

Flower bud

Leaf buds (next year's flower buds)

Spur

Single flower buds (next year's bare area)

Spur

TART CHERRY

Bare area

2-year-old wood

Tart Cherries

Train your tart cherries as you would a young peach tree. See "Training Young Trees" on page 270 for step-by-step directions. There are a few differences, so review the following exceptions before you pick up your pruners.

Planting time. Don't shorten the main stem or side branches. Thin out extra branches if needed.

First growing season. In the summer, select up to five main branches. Be especially careful not to choose a branch that is directly in line above another branch. One branch will take over and choke out the other.

Second growing season. If one branch outgrows the other branches or the main stem, head it back severely.

Pruning bearing trees. Keep the center of a bearing tree open to increase air movement and decrease brown rot. Thin out old wood

less heavily than suggested for peaches. A few of the oldest branches a year is fine.

Harvesting

Sweet cherries. Sweet cherries do not ripen off the tree, so picking underripe fruit is a waste. However, ripe sweet cherries rot quickly if left on the tree. Once your cherries are fully colored, taste a few. If they're not rich and sweet, wait and sample again every day or two to catch your cherries at their best. Pick nearly ripe cherries quickly if rain falls; otherwise they will probably split and spoil on the tree.

Tart cherries. Pick cherries for cooking when they are fully colored but still firm. For fresh eating, let them ripen and soften on the tree.

How to Pick Cherries

Pick cherries with the stems attached. Carefully lift the stems away from the spur to avoid damaging the spur.

Storing

Cherries will keep in your refrigerator for three to seven days. For longer storage, keep them in a spare refrigerator set at 31° to 32°F (colder than usual refrigerator temperature). Firm-fleshed sweet cherries will keep for up to three weeks; firm-ripe tart cherries up to one week.

Solving Cherry Problems

Use the table below to identify problems on your cherry trees. Scan the list of symptoms to find the description that most closely matches what you see in your garden. Then refer across the page to learn the cause and the recommended solutions. Cherry trees suffer from many of the same problems as peaches; if you don't find symptoms below that match your problem, also refer to "Solving Peach Problems" on page 274. For some pest problems, by the time you see damage, there is little you can do to fix things in the current season. However, in the future you can take preventive measures, such as spraying sulfur to prevent certain diseases. For a suggested schedule of preventive measures for cherries, see "Season-by-Season Care: Cherry" on page 248. You'll also find illustrations, descriptions, and additional controls for many of the insects and diseases listed below in Part 5 of this book.

SYMPTOMS	CAUSES	SOLUTIONS
Shriveled, soft fruit drops early; small, white maggots feeding inside	Cherry fruit flies	Pick up dropped fruit daily and destroy. Plan to hang sticky traps next spring to monitor pests.
Fruits crack, split open near harvesttime; no pests present	Rain and warm weather	Cherries may split open if they take up too much water too fast. Some cultivars are more susceptible than others. Harvest and refrigerate ripe fruit immediately after rain.
Tiny purplish spots on leaves; leaves turn yellow and drop	Cherry leaf spot	This disease occurs mainly in the East and Midwest. Tart cherries are most susceptible. Spray copper to reduce severity. Prune to increase air circulation. Replace severely infected trees with resistant cultivars.
Curled leaves with a sticky coating; small, shiny black insects on leaf undersides	Black cherry aphids	No treatment may be necessary as cherry aphids leave trees by midsummer. If infestation is severe, remove aphids with strong spray of water or spray insecticidal soap or neem.
Leaves chewed and webbed together; pale green caterpillars present	Green fruitworms	Leaf damage is usually not significant, but caterpillars later bite into fruit and may completely consume it. Spray BTK or neem as soon as leaf damage is noticed.
Leaves wilting and dying; gummy, sunken areas on branches	Bacterial canker	Young trees are most affected. Prune out infected branches well below canker, disinfecting tools between cuts. Destroy prunings. Replace severely affected trees with resistant cultivars.
Leaves on one or more branches turn yellow and wilt in late summer	Verticillium wilt	Prune out and destroy affected branches. Trees may recover if they are prevented from growing too vigorously; avoid high-nitrogen fertilizers and prune as little as possible.
Coal black, knotty swellings on twigs and branches	Black knot	Fruit produced is edible, though yields decrease as tree weakens. In late winter, prune infected branches and twigs 4"–6" below knots, disinfecting tools between cuts.

CITRUS *Citrus* spp. and others • Rutaceae

Choosing Trees

For fragrant flowers, handsome evergreen foliage, and delicious fruit on a low-maintenance tree, think citrus! Gardeners in Zones 9 and 10 can grow citrus outdoors year-round. Zone 8 gardeners can grow cold-tolerant types outdoors year-round. In Zone 7 and north, grow potted citrus trees outdoors in the summer and indoors in the winter. See "Indoor Citrus" on this page for specific instructions. The illustration on the opposite page shows the range of cold tolerance for different types of citrus trees.

Choose more than one type of fruit or several cultivars of one type with different ripening times to spread out your harvest. Look for cultivars that hold well on the tree. If you can, visit a farmers' market or group of citrus enthusiasts and sample a range of cultivars to help decide which to buy.

Buy certified virus-free trees because viral diseases can cause major problems for citrus trees. Select young trees without fruits on them. Also look for a straight trunk with a strong, well-healed graft and unblemished, deep green leaves.

Oranges and Grapefruits

Most types of oranges are small to medium-size trees. They thrive in containers, especially if they are grafted on a dwarfing rootstock. Grapefruits are large trees; most are not suitable for containers.

There are three types of sweet orange (*Citrus sinensis*): common, navel, and blood. 'Marrs', 'Washington' (a navel orange), and 'Moro' (a blood orange) are good for containers.

Most mandarin oranges (*C. reticulata*), also called tangerines, are hardy to 20°F. 'Changsha' satsuma (one type of mandarin) is hardy to about 10°F.

Calamondins are hardy to at least 20°F, thrive in small containers, and bear small, tart fruits. Pummelo fruits (*C. grandis*) are larger and less juicy than grapefruits. Tangelos have thin-skinned, aromatic fruits.

Lemons and Limes

Most lemons (*C. limon*), limes (*C. aurantifolia*), and

INDOOR CITRUS

Most citrus trees make good container plants. A 5-gallon pot is sufficient for a dwarf tree such as a kumquat. For a larger tree, choose at least a 20-gallon planter. Water potted plants regularly and use a liquid fertilizer such as kelp extract at least once a month during the growing season.

Protect your tree from cold temperatures by moving it indoors. If your area has only a few weeks of too-cold weather, you can put your tree in an unheated, glassed-in porch or in a garage (close the door at night). Put the tree back outside when the danger of damaging temperatures is past.

If your winters are long and cold, move the tree indoors in the fall when nighttime temperatures drop near freezing. Citrus needs an indoor spot with at least half a day of full sun to thrive. Mist the leaves frequently to keep the humidity up, and maintain warm days (70° to 75°F) and cool nights (45° to 55°F). Hand-pollinate flowers with a cotton swab or artist's brush daily.

When nighttime temperatures stay above 45°F in the spring, move the tree outdoors to a sheltered, partially shaded spot for the summer. Put the tree outside for a few hours the first day and increase the time outside a few hours every day.

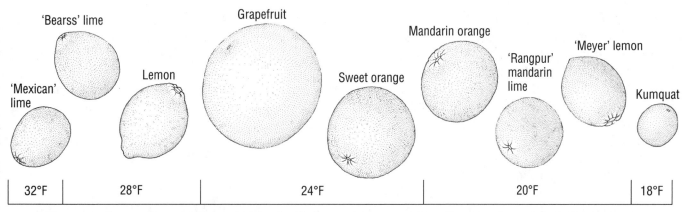

Citrus hardiness. *Exposed fruits of all types of citrus may suffer damage at 26° to 28°F. However, foliage and branches of mature citrus trees vary in hardiness.* *The range of hardiness is represented in the illustration above. Young growth is less cold-hardy than older growth on the same tree.*

their hybrids are small trees and grow well in containers.

True limes only grow well in hot, frost-free areas. Hybrid limequats have small limelike fruits and are hardy to 20°F.

Cold-Hardy Citrus

Kumquats (*Fortunella* spp.) tolerate temperatures as low as 18°F. They bear small fruits that you eat rind and all. Meiwa kumquat is the sweetest.

Trifoliate orange (*Poncirus trifoliata*) will produce flowers and fruits as far north as Zone 6. Juice from the hard, bitter fruit makes a passable drink. It is usually grown for its ornamental value.

A trifoliate–sweet orange hybrid, 'Morton' citrange is hardy to 12°F and produces large, juicy, acid fruits for juice. For juicy, sweetish fruits for fresh eating, try 'Thomasville' citrangequat, a small fruit that is hardy to 10°F.

Rootstocks

Trifoliate orange or sour orange seedlings are commonly used for rootstocks. Check with your supplier for disease-resistant rootstocks recommended for your area. 'Flying Dragon' is a dwarf rootstock for containers.

Pollination

Most citrus are self-fertile so you can plant one tree and harvest a full crop.

Yield

Citrus trees start bearing significant crops in three or four years. Annual yields range from a few dozen fruits on a very dwarf tree to bushels on a mature, full-size tree.

Site and Soil

Citrus trees need full sun and protection from wind. In extremely hot places, trees benefit from partial shade.

Choose a site with:
• Full sun.
• Deep, fertile soil.
• pH between 6.0 and 6.5.
Avoid:
• Low spots where frost tends to settle.
• Areas where water puddles in spring or after a rain.
• Soil with high salt concentration.

Preparing to Plant

Start preparing the soil a full year before you plan to plant. Have the soil tested and adjust the pH if necessary. Dig out *every* perennial weed. Plant a cover crop over the entire planting area. If you're only planting one tree, prepare and plant a 6- to 10-foot-diameter circle. During the preparation year, mow the cover crop whenever it reaches 8 to 10 inches in height. See "Planting Cover Crops" on page 28 for more details on choosing and managing cover crops.

If the site you've chosen has less than excellent drainage, build the soil up into a large 6-inch-high raised bed. If your soil has high concentrations of salt, don't use it to make the raised bed. Buy topsoil and mix it with compost instead.

Planting

Plant bareroot trees when frost danger is past but when weather is still cool. Plant container trees at the same time for best results. See "Planting Fruit Trees" on page 200 for planting instructions.

Keep the graft union 6 to 8 inches above the soil level. Paint the trunk or wrap it with tape, as explained in "Preparing Fruit for Winter" on page 226.

Install drip irrigation or shape the surface of the soil into a doughnut-shaped watering basin a few inches deep. The inner edge of the basin should be a few inches away from the trunk and the outer edge should be beyond the tips of the branches. Water your new tree deeply after planting. Keep the soil consistently moist for the first growing season.

Spread 3 to 4 inches of coarse organic mulch such as wood chips under the tree from the outside edge of the watering basin to within a few inches of the trunk.

Spacing

Space trees as far apart as their mature height.

Seasonal Care

You will harvest more fruit and have fewer problems if you feed and care for your tree regularly. See "Season-by-Season Care: Citrus" on the opposite page for directions for caring for your tree throughout the year. For solutions to specific pest problems, refer to "Solving Citrus Problems" on page 256.

Training Trees

Citrus trees are self-shaping and need very little pruning. Remove crossing branches and rootstock suckers when you notice them. Head back upright growth anytime to limit size of young trees. Remove dead wood once a year from mature trees.

If frost strikes your trees, spray them with kelp extract. Then wait—perhaps as long as six months—until you're sure which parts of the tree have died to prune off the dead wood. If you remove large branches, some remaining branches may be suddenly exposed to full sun. Paint any newly exposed branches white to prevent sunscald, as described on page 226.

Harvesting

Citrus fruits ripen at specific times. Record the harvest season of each tree you plant when you buy it. Watch trees for fruit that shows mature color, but keep in mind that color is not a reliable indicator of ripeness—green skin may contain orange flesh. When you think fruit is ready to harvest, pick a sample and taste it. Continue weekly tastings until the fruit is ripe. Harvest fruits with pruners.

Storing

You don't have to pick all the ripe fruit on your tree at once; many types of fruit can remain on the tree for up to three months without damage. Your supplier can tell you how long your choices will last on the tree. Or you can test by sampling fruit from your trees weekly to find out how long they hang before starting to get puffy and dry. If you must harvest a large amount of fruit at once, store it in the refrigerator. It should keep for up to several months.

SEASON-BY-SEASON CARE: CITRUS

This care guide tells you what to do and when to do it for your best citrus harvest ever. Because timing of certain tasks is critical, review all the instructions in this guide in late winter. Locate or buy the products you'll need in advance. To identify specific problems, refer to "Solving Citrus Problems" on page 256. "Preventing Disease Problems" on page 210 explains how to mix and apply sprays.

Late Winter/Early Spring

Prune. Remove any dead or damaged wood. If scab was a serious problem in the last year, thin out some branches to improve air movement through the tree. If brown rot was a serious problem last year, prune off the low parts of branches that droop within 2 feet of the ground.

Clean up. After harvest, gather and remove fallen fruits.

Fertilize. Choose one of these three options each year. *Compost:* 50 pounds per inch of trunk diameter, applied in February. *Fish, seed, or alfalfa meal:* 10 pounds per inch of trunk diameter, applied in thirds in February, April, and June. *Blood meal:* 5 pounds per inch of trunk diameter, applied in thirds in February, April, and June. Spread fertilizer evenly over the entire watering-basin area. If your tree made more than 12 to 18 inches of new growth last year, apply only half the recommended amounts.

Spray kelp. Kelp provides micronutrients and may increase fruit set. Spray trees when new growth is $\frac{1}{2}$ inch long. Repeat after three weeks.

Spring and Summer

Water. Water trees slowly and deeply once or twice a week.

Watch for pests. Inspect your trees once a week for pest problems. Check both the top surface and the undersides of leaves, as well as twigs, flowers, and fruits. Act quickly to combat any insect or disease problems before they become serious.

Fall and Winter

Spray oil. If scales, bud mites, or red mites have been a severe problem in the past, spray trees with summer oil on a day in early fall when the temperature will stay below 80°F.

Spray bordeaux mix. If brown rot was a serious problem in the last year, spray the ground and lower branches with bordeaux mix before the fall rains start. Repeat in late winter.

Enlarge watering basin. For young, rapidly growing trees, enlarge the watering basin each fall. It should span the area from 1 foot inside the drip line out to 2 feet beyond the drip line. If you use a drip irrigation system, move and add to the system to cover the same area.

Renew mulch. Add new mulch on top of the old to make a 3- to 4-inch layer. The mulch should cover an area slightly larger than the watering basin, but the ground near the base of the trunk should be left unmulched.

Renew trunk paint. Repaint exposed trunk with diluted white interior latex paint if old paint is wearing off.

Protect from frost. When frost threatens, protect your trees. Cover trees with old blankets and quilts or large cardboard boxes. Or build wooden frames and cover them with plastic. Don't drape plastic directly over trees; contact with cold plastic can damage trees. Remove or vent shelters in mid-morning the following day to keep trees from overheating.

Solving Citrus Problems

Use this table to identify problems on your citrus trees. Scan the list of symptoms to find the description that most closely matches what you see in your garden. Then refer across the page to learn the cause and the recommended solutions. In some cases, diseases or insects damage the rind of citrus fruit, but the pulp and juice inside are unharmed. Also, native predators and parasites will keep many pests in balance as long as the trees are growing vigorously. Refer to "Season-by-Season Care: Citrus" on page 255 for a care schedule that will help ensure that your trees stay pest-free. You'll also find illustrations, descriptions, and additional controls for many of the insects and diseases listed below in Part 5 of this book.

FLOWER AND FRUIT PROBLEMS

SYMPTOMS	CAUSES	SOLUTIONS
Distorted flowers and fruit	Citrus bud mites	This mite is mostly a pest of lemons in west coastal areas. Damage is cosmetic; pulp and juice from affected fruit are edible. If damage is severe, spray summer oil once, either in May/June or in fall (not in hot, dry weather, which will damage leaves).
Maturing, healthy fruit suddenly drops; no pests present	Sudden temperature change Drought Nutrient stress	Keep trees evenly watered, especially while fruit is maturing. Be sure to maintain soil fertility.
Small, round, reddish bumps on fruit	California red scale	Affected fruit is unharmed as scales are only on the rind. If leaves turn yellow and drop, spray summer oil once in late summer or early fall (not in hot, dry weather, which will damage leaves). For severe infestations, release parasitic wasps, *Aphytis melinus.*
Brown, corky scars on fruit rind	Citrus scab	This disease only damages rind; fruit is still edible. Plan to prune foliage to increase air circulation, especially during spring growth period.
Scarred tissue on fruit rind encircling stem end	Citrus thrips	Fruit is unharmed as scars are only cosmetic. No control is necessary.
Mature fruit soft, light brown, with a pungent odor; rind may develop white mold	Phytophthora brown rot	Pick and destroy fruit at first sign of damage. Check stored fruit frequently for signs of rot. Prune out low-hanging branches and cover soil around trees with mulch.

LEAF AND SHOOT PROBLEMS

SYMPTOMS	CAUSES	SOLUTIONS
Holes chewed in leaves (and fruit); slimy trails left behind	Snails	Install copper bands around trunks to form a permanent snail barrier. Prune low branches so they do not touch the ground.

SYMPTOMS	CAUSES	SOLUTIONS
Curled leaves covered with sticky coating; tiny pear-shaped insects on leaf undersides	Aphids	Wash leaves with water to remove sticky coating; if fruits have black mold on rind, simply wipe it off. If young trees are severely attacked, wash aphids from trees with a strong spray of water or spray insecticidal soap or neem.
Leaves covered with sticky coating; tiny white insects fly around leaves	Citrus whiteflies	Wash leaves with water to remove sticky coating; if fruits have black mold on rind, simply wipe it off. If attack is severe, spray insecticidal soap or neem, ensuring good coverage on undersides of leaves. Control ants, which remove whitefly predators, by using sticky bands around tree trunks.
Leaves and shoots covered with sticky coating; oval, powdery white crawling insects on trees	Citrus mealybugs	Wash leaves with water to remove sticky coating; if fruits have black mold on rind, simply wipe it off. Control ants, which remove mealybug predators, by using sticky bands around tree trunks. For severe infestations, spray neem or release Australian lady beetles, *Cryptolaemus montrouzieri.*
Pale yellow flecks on leaves; minute red mites present on young leaves	Citrus red mites	If infestation is severe, spray summer oil once in early fall (not in hot, dry weather, which will damage leaves).
Leaves turn light green, then yellow, starting with oldest leaves; no mites or insects present	Nitrogen deficiency	If symptoms appear in spring, it may be due to cool soil conditions that temporarily prevent uptake of nutrients. Check soil fertility and incorporate blood meal, fish meal, or other nitrogen source if necessary.
Youngest leaves turn yellow with dark green veins	Iron deficiency	Trees may not be able to take up iron from the soil if soil pH is high or soil is waterlogged. Correct poor soil conditions and ensure good drainage. If tree is severely affected, treat soil with iron chelates and/or apply foliar sprays of chelated iron.

WHOLE TREE PROBLEM

SYMPTOMS	CAUSES	SOLUTIONS
Trunk with gummy sap coming from cracks; sunken cankers develop; leaves turn yellow and drop	Brown rot gummosis (Phytophthora root rot)	Cut out cankered bark well into healthy tissue and allow wound to dry; paint wound with copper fungicide. Change irrigation system, if necessary, to ensure that water does not contact tree trunk and that soil never becomes waterlogged. If tree is severely affected, remove and replant with a tree grafted onto Phytophthora-tolerant rootstock.

GRAPE Vitis spp. • Vitaceae

Choosing Vines

Classic European wine grapes (*Vitis vinifera*), also called vinifera grapes, demand sunny, dry summers. They are hardy to Zone 6 and will grow well as far south as Zone 9. European grapes are generally mild and sweet, and suited to fresh eating or drying, and they make excellent wine.

If your area has humid summers, you shouldn't plant vinifera grapes. You can successfully grow American grapes, hybrids, or muscadines.

American grapes (*V. labrusca,* others, and hybrids) tolerate cold winters (Zones 4 through 7), summer humidity, and certain pests.

'Concord', with its strong "foxy" flavor, is the classic American grape cultivar. Most seeded and seedless table grapes are American grapes with some vinifera in their parentage (this crossbreeding has muted the sharpness of their flavor). American grapes are best for fresh eating, jelly, and juice.

Certain crosses of vinifera and American grapes are called French or French-American hybrids. They combine the hardiness and problem resistance of American types with the flavor and wine-making quality of European cultivars.

Muscadines (*V. rotundifolia*) are adapted to the warm, humid climate of the Southeast (Zones 7 through 10). These vines are robust plants that produce small clusters of large berries. Muscadines are enjoyed fresh or made into jelly or wine.

Check with your supplier for cultivars that will do well in your area. Choose disease-resistant cultivars such as those listed in "Problem-Resistant Table Grapes" on this page whenever possible.

Pollination

Grapes are self-fertile, except for some muscadine

PROBLEM-RESISTANT TABLE GRAPES

Grapes can be difficult to grow organically, especially in areas with humid summers. Stack the cards in your favor by planting American table grape cultivars with disease resistance, such as the ones listed below. New resistant cultivars are released every year, so also ask your supplier about new releases. In the listings below, A = anthracnose, BL = black rot, BU = bunch rot, DM = downy mildew, and PM = powdery mildew.

CULTIVAR (RESISTANCE)	DESCRIPTION
'Alwood' (A, BL, DM, PM)	Blue black, seeded
'Campbell's Early' (BL)	Purple black, seeded
'Canadice' (DM, PM)	Red, seedless
'Catawba' (BU)	Red purple, seeded
'Concord' (A, BU, DM)	Black, seeded
'Delaware' (A, BL, BU)	Light red, seeded
'Einset' (BU)	Red, seedless
'Fredonia' (BL, BU)	Black, seeded
'Himrod' (DM)	Green yellow, seedless
'Ives' (BL, BU, PM)	Black, seeded
'Mars' (A, BL, DM, PM)	Blue, seedless
'Moore Early' (A)	Purple black, seeded
'Niagara' (A, BU)	Yellow green, seeded
'Steuben' (BL, DM, PM)	Blue black, seeded
'Stover' (DM)	Light green, seeded
'Worden' (BL)	Purple black, seeded

cultivars, so you can plant one cultivar and harvest a full crop. Muscadine growers: Ask your supplier whether the cultivar you choose needs a pollinator and which cultivars are good pollinators.

Yield

Expect a yearly harvest of 10 to 20 pounds of grapes from each vine after four or five years growth (smaller harvests start as soon as two years after planting).

Site and Soil

You can grow grapes successfully almost anywhere in North America if you select cultivars to match your climate.

Choose a site with:
- Full sun.
- Well-drained soil.
- pH between 5.0 and 6.0.

Avoid:
- Low spots where frost tends to settle.
- Areas where water puddles in spring or after a rain.
- Sites near wild grapes, which can be a source of disease or insect pests.

Preparing to Plant

Start preparing the soil a full year before you plan to plant grapevines. Have the soil tested and adjust the pH if necessary. Dig out *every*

---

perennial weed. Plant a cover crop such as sweet clover or buckwheat over the entire planting area. During the preparation year, mow the cover crop whenever it reaches 8 to 10 inches in height. See "Planting Cover Crops" on page 28 for details on choosing and managing cover crops.

It's best to decide how you plan to train your vines and to build an appropriate trellis before you plant. See "Training Young Vines" on page 260 for suggestions.

Planting

Plant grapes in either early spring or mid-fall. See "Planting Vines and Bushes" on page 202 for complete instructions for planting grapevines.

Right after planting, insert a long, lightweight wooden or bamboo stake next to the vine and tie it to the top wire of the trellis.

Spacing

Plant European, American, and hybrid grapes 8 feet apart in a row. Space muscadines 15 to 20 feet apart in rows. If you're planting more than one row, leave at least 8 feet between rows; 10 feet between rows for muscadines.

Seasonal Care

You will harvest more grapes and have fewer problems if you feed and care for your vines regularly. See "Season-by-Season Care: Grape" on page 262 for directions for caring for your vines throughout the year. If you have problems, see "Solving Grape Problems" on page 265 to identify the problems and find solutions.

Training Young Vines

Here's a simple training method for backyard gardeners. Vines grow along the top wire of a tall trellis; gravity pulls the new growth neatly down on either side.

The bottom trellis shown on page 209 will support one vine or a row of vines. You can also train grapevines up a wall or arbor, but it's harder to reach them to pick and prune.

Pruning at Planting

Cut your vine back to two buds. Be sure to leave two

Cut vine back
to 2 buds.

PRUNING AT PLANTING

buds *above* the graft union if it's a grafted vine.

First Summer Training

Let your vine grow freely the first growing season. Tie it loosely to the stake every foot or so (leave enough slack in the ties so that you could slip your little finger in) to keep it off the ground. Remove any flower clusters that form. Rub off shoots that sprout below the graft union if it's a grafted vine.

First Winter Pruning

Prune your vine in late winter after the coldest weather is past. Use the guidelines below to determine how to prune the vine.

Nonvigorous growth. If your vine didn't grow as high as the top wire of the trellis, cut it back to two buds, just as you did when you planted it. Treat it like a newly planted vine for another growing season. Next winter it will be ready for pruning like a vigorous one-year-old vine, as described below.

Vigorous growth. If your vine did reach the top wire of the trellis, it is time to select a trunk. Choose the straightest, sturdiest cane that is at least as tall as the top trellis wire. Cut off all other canes flush to that chosen cane. Tie the cane loosely to the stake and the trellis. Then cut it off just above the top trellis wire.

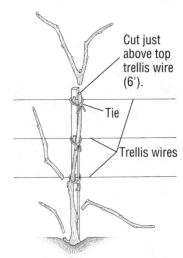

Cut just
above top
trellis wire
(6').

Tie

Trellis wires

FIRST WINTER PRUNING

Second Summer Training

Let the topmost five buds develop into sideshoots and grow sideways along the trellis or arbor. Carefully break off any lower sideshoots, but not the leaves, that form on the trunk. Remove any flower clusters that form.

Second Winter Pruning

In late winter, select two sturdy, pencil-size canes, one headed each way along the trellis. Tie them loosely to the trellis wire or arbor every foot or so. Rub off extra buds along these canes, leaving one bud every 4 to 5 inches.

Leave 1 bud
every 4"–5".

Select 2 canes.

SECOND WINTER PRUNING

Then cut back the canes so that each cane has just ten buds. Cut all other canes off flush with the trunk.

Third Summer Training

Each of the buds on the canes you left at winter-pruning time will produce a fruiting shoot this summer. Remove most of the flower clusters, leaving just five on each cane. Also, rub off any shoots that sprout below the top few inches of the trunk. On grafted vines, be sure to rub off all shoots that sprout below the graft union.

Pruning Bearing Vines

There are two basic methods of pruning bearing vines: cane pruning and spur pruning. Up to this point, training for both methods has been the same.

Beginning in the third winter after planting, pruning differs for the two methods. For cane-pruned vines, you will select new main branches every year. On spur-pruned vines, you will maintain the same main branches year after year.

Most grape cultivars can be pruned either way with good results. A few cultivars will be more productive with one method compared to the other, depending on where they tend to bear fruit. Check with your supplier for guidance. And don't worry—if one method doesn't work well for a specific cultivar, you can change to the other method the next winter.

Third Winter Pruning

Cane-pruned vines. In late winter, cut the ties that held last year's main branches to the trellis or arbor. Examine the canes that have grown along these main branches. On each main branch, select one pencil-size cane near the trunk to become the new main branch. You can also choose canes that have

Cut canes back to 2-bud spurs.

Main branch   Main branch

SPUR-PRUNED VINE: THIRD WINTER

sprouted directly from the top of the trunk.

You may also want to select and save two two-bud stubs near the top of the trunk or the base of the new main branches. These are your insurance in case one of the main branches is lost to disease or winter cold.

After you have decided which canes and two-bud stubs to save, cut off all the other canes, including last year's main branches. Make cuts flush with the trunk or the new main branches except where you have chosen to leave two-bud stubs. Pull the cut canes off the trellis.

Tie the new main branches loosely to the trellis wire every foot or so. Rub off buds on these branches, leaving one every 4 to 5 inches. Cut back the branches so each has just ten buds.

Spur-pruned vines. In late winter, renew the ties that hold the main branches to the trellis or arbor. Cut each of the canes that has sprouted from these branches back to two

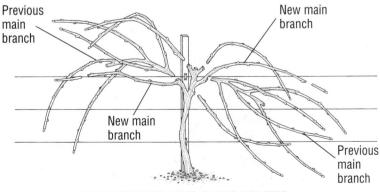

Previous main branch

New main branch

New main branch

Previous main branch

CANE-PRUNED VINE: THIRD WINTER

(continued on page 264)

SEASON-BY-SEASON CARE: GRAPE

This care guide tells you what to do and when to do it for your best grape harvest ever. Because timing of certain tasks is critical, review all the instructions below in late winter. Locate or buy the products you'll need in advance. To identify specific problems, refer to "Solving Grape Problems" on page 265. "Preventing Disease Problems" on page 210 explains how to mix and apply sprays.

Late Winter

Dormant buds

Prune. Prune your vine each winter when the plant is dormant. If your winters are very cold, wait to prune until after the coldest weather has past. Pruning close to bud break may cause sap to drip; this doesn't harm the plant.

Fertilize. Spread 10 to 15 pounds of compost per 10 feet of row each year under the vines in late winter. For muscadines, spread 20 to 40 pounds of compost per 10 row feet.

Spray dormant oil. If scales or grape mealybugs were a problem on your vines last year, spray dormant oil now.

Early Spring

Buds starting to swell

Spray lime-sulfur. If anthracnose, black rot, downy mildew, or powdery mildew was a problem last year, spray when buds start to swell, but before any green shows.

Spray kelp. When leaf buds start to open, spray plants with kelp to increase bud hardiness and fruit set. Repeat every two to four weeks until small green fruits are visible.

Spray copper or sulfur. If black rot, downy mildew, or powdery mildew was a problem last year, spray copper or sulfur when buds show green if the weather is wet or humid and the temperature is above 59°F. Use copper for black rot and downy mildew, and sulfur for powdery mildew. Do not spray copper while flowers are open; spray sulfur instead. Respray after each rain or every one to two weeks. Stop in midsummer if the weather stays warm and dry and there is little disease present.

Full bloom

Spring

Hang grape berry moth traps. If grape berry moths were a problem last year, hang one grape berry moth trap per 100 feet of row when the flower buds appear. Check traps every few days. Spray vines with BTK one week after the first moth appears in a trap. Repeat every few days until no new moths are caught.

Fertilize. Muscadines need an extra feeding now. Spread 8 to 10 pounds of alfalfa meal per vine when small green grapes are visible.

Developing clusters

Early Summer

Thin fruit. When your vine sets an especially heavy crop, thin out excess clusters while the fruits are still small and hard. Cut off some fruit clusters completely. Leave just one cluster per spur or cane on young vines, two clusters on mature vines. On the clusters that remain, cut off some of the little branchlets to make the clusters more open. This is especially important on cultivars with very tight or large clusters.

Bag clusters. Use small paper bags to protect fruit from insects, diseases, and birds. Cut a tiny hole in the bottom corner of a paper bag to allow water to escape. Slip the bag over the cluster. Fold the top of the bag tightly around the stem. Be sure that there's enough space in the bag for the fruit to enlarge, and staple the bag closed without crushing the stem.

Watch for cane dieback. Various diseases cause stunting or death of entire branches. If you find elongated, sunken spots on canes, prune the canes 6 inches below the spots. Destroy the prunings.

Scrape bark. If you've had past problems with grape mealybugs, scrape all loose bark off your vines to expose the mealybugs to bright summer sun and heat. Exposure to high temperatures will kill the mealybugs.

Ripe clusters

Summer

Remove leaves around fruit. Pull or cut off a handful of leaves around every cluster in late summer so air can circulate around developing fruits, minimizing diseases such as bunch rot. Be sure to leave one leaf over each cluster to prevent sunscald. Or clip

pieces of floating row cover onto the vines so that they cover the clusters and protect the berries from intense sunlight.

Tip long canes. Cut back canes to 6 feet if they are getting in your way on the ground.

Cover vines with netting. Birds ruin fruits by pecking holes in them. The damaged fruits also attract bees and wasps. If you haven't protected your fruits by enclosing them in paper bags, drape netting over the vines now.

Spray sulfur. If rot was a problem on your fruit last year, spray vines with sulfur. Once the fruits begin to color, apply sulfur when the weather is wet or humid and the temperature is below 85°F. Repeat every ten days or after rain. Don't wait until you see rot to spray!

Remove and destroy rotting berries. Remove rotting fruit as soon as you see it.

Leaves falling

Fall

Renew mulch. When the leaves start to fall, rake the loose mulch away from the trunk to leave a bare strip under the trellis. Once all leaves have fallen, push the mulch back into place and add new mulch to make a 6- to 8-inch layer. See "Preventing Winter Rodent Damage" on page 226 for more information on mulching.

Clean up. After leaves fall, pick off any remaining fruits and cut out any swollen or deformed canes. Destroy collected fruits and prunings. Clean and store insect traps for next season.

buds. When you're done, there will be a two-bud spur every 4 to 5 inches along the main branches. Cut any extra spurs off flush with the main branches.

Fourth Summer Training

Each of the buds left after the winter pruning will produce a new shoot. Rub off any shoots that sprout below the graft union on grafted vines.

Once the new shoots grow, cane-pruned vines will look just like they did the previous summer. Spur-pruned vines will have thicker main branches and two shoots coming out of each spur.

Fourth Winter Pruning

In the fourth and subsequent years, adjust the severity of pruning depending on how vigorously your vines are growing. Look for these clues to determine how much pruning your vine needs.

- If the previous summer's canes are less than 4 feet long and smaller around than a pencil, leave four fewer buds or spurs than you did last winter.
- If the previous summer's canes are more than 8 feet long and larger around than a pencil, leave four more buds or spurs than you did last winter.
- If the previous summer's canes are about as big around as a pencil and 5 to

SPUR-PRUNED VINE: FOURTH WINTER

6 feet long, keep the same number of buds as you did last winter.

Cane-pruned vines. Prune your bearing vine in late winter as described for pruning in the third winter. Rub off more buds or fewer buds along the main branches if needed. You will continue to select new main branches each year and cut off the ones from the previous season.

Spur-pruned vines. In late winter, renew the ties that hold the main branches to the trellis or arbor. These branches are part of the permanent structure of the vine and will get larger and heavier each year.

Select one pencil-size shoot near the base of each two-bud spur and cut it back to two buds. Cut the other shoot that emerges from the spur off flush with the spur.

If you need more spurs, you can select shoots that have sprouted directly from the main branches and cut them back to two buds. You may want to replace old, overgrown spurs with new ones the same way.

Otherwise, cut any shoots growing from the trunk or main branches off flush at their source.

Harvesting

Pick grapes when they are fully ripe; they will not ripen further after harvest. With American, European, and hybrid grapes, cut bunches off whole when the berries are fully colored, sweet, and full flavored.

Spot-pick muscadine grapes every two days because they ripen unevenly and tend to drop when very ripe.

Storing

Grapes keep well in your refrigerator. If you have a lot, store them in a spare refrigerator set at 31° to 32°F (colder than usual refrigerator temperature). Some European cultivars such as 'Emperor' and 'Ribier' will keep as long as six months. Other grapes will last two months at most. Muscadine grapes are the most perishable and will keep no more than three weeks.

Solving Grape Problems

Use this table to identify problems on your grapes. Scan the list of symptoms to find the description that most closely matches what you see in your garden. Then refer across the page to learn the cause and the recommended solutions. For some pest problems, by the time you see the damage, there is little you can do to fix things in the current season. In the future, take preventive steps such as spraying sulfur to prevent certain diseases. For a schedule of preventive measures for grapes, see "Season-by-Season Care: Grape" on page 262. You'll also find illustrations, descriptions, and additional controls for many of the insects and diseases listed below in Part 5 of this book.

FRUIT PROBLEMS

SYMPTOMS	CAUSES	SOLUTIONS
White powdery patches on early fruit; skins split on ripening grapes	Powdery mildew	Pick and destroy infected fruit. Prune excess foliage and clear away weeds to improve air circulation. At first sign of disease, spray or dust with sulfur; repeat weekly. Replace severely infected vines with resistant cultivars.
Round, tan spots on fruit; fruit shrivels and darkens	Black rot	This is a common problem east of the Rockies. Pick and destroy mummified fruit. Prune excess foliage and clear away weeds to improve air circulation. Spray with sulfur or copper; repeat weekly through harvest. Replace severely infected vines with more resistant cultivars.
Small, sunken, dark-ringed spots on fruit	Anthracnose (bird's-eye rot)	Remove and destroy infected fruit. Prune excess foliage and clear away weeds to improve air circulation. Spray copper every 10–14 days if weather is wet to prevent spread of the disease. Replace severely infected vines with resistant cultivars.
Fruit water-soaked and soft, with fuzzy gray or tan mold	Botrytis bunch rot	Infections appear in late summer when fruit is ripening. Remove and destroy all infected bunches and prune foliage to increase air circulation. Thin berries in the bunch and remove leaves and shoots that are shading or touching bunches.
Grapes webbed together, with holes eaten in berries	Grape berry moths	Pick and destroy infested berries and leaves with cocoons, which are inside rolled sections of leaf. In fall, collect and destroy all fallen leaves to control overwintering pupae. The following spring, begin spraying BTK shortly after fruit has set.
Sticky coating on fruit; tiny white insects fly around leaves	Grape whiteflies	Black mold may grow on fruit; wash or wipe it off before eating. Wash sticky coating from leaves with water. Spray insecticidal soap or neem, ensuring there is good coverage on undersides of lower leaves.

(continued)

Solving Grape Problems—Continued

FRUIT PROBLEMS—CONTINUED

SYMPTOMS	CAUSES	SOLUTIONS
Sticky coating on fruit; white, powdery, wingless insects on canes and leaf stems	Grape mealybugs	These pests occur in the West. Black mold may grow on fruit; wash or wipe it off before eating. Native parasites and predators usually keep mealybugs in check. If not, use sticky tree bands to prevent ants from protecting mealybugs from predators. Scrape off all loose bark to expose mealybugs to high summer temperatures, which kill them. For large infestations, spray neem or release Australian lady beetles, *Cryptolaemus montrouzieri.*
Holes in fruit	Birds	Pick and compost damaged fruit. To prevent further damage, drape a net over vines, or enclose each cluster in a paper bag. Cut a small hole in bottom corner of bag so water can escape, and staple top so it fits tightly around stem.

LEAF PROBLEMS

SYMPTOMS	CAUSES	SOLUTIONS
Leaves skeletonized; bronze beetles on plants	Japanese beetles	In early morning, knock beetles from vines into a bucket of soapy water or onto a tarp and destroy. Mild to moderate damage will not harm vines or affect yield. If infestation is severe, spray with pyrethrins or rotenone frequently.
Pale green stipples along leaf veins; leaves lose color and dry up	Leafhoppers	Native parasites and predators usually keep leafhoppers in check. Spray insecticidal soap or neem if infestation is severe enough to cause leaves to turn yellow and drop.
White or mottled patches on young leaves; grayish patches on older leaves	Powdery mildew	Prune excess foliage and remove weeds and surrounding vegetation to improve air circulation. At first sign of disease, spray or dust with sulfur; repeat weekly. Replace severely infected vines with resistant cultivars.
White cottony growth on leaf undersides; small yellow spots on leaves	Downy mildew	Prune excess foliage and remove weeds and surrounding vegetation to improve air circulation. At first sign of disease, spray copper; repeat weekly. Remove and destroy all diseased leaves and shoots in fall. Replace severely infected vines with resistant cultivars.
Sunken, dark-ringed spots on leaves	Anthracnose	Remove and destroy infected leaves and other tissue. Prune excess foliage and clear away weeds to improve air circulation. Spray copper every 10–14 days if weather is wet. Replace severely infected vines with resistant cultivars.

SYMPTOMS	CAUSES	SOLUTIONS
Red spots on young leaves; spots enlarge, turn brown or grayish tan	Black rot	This is a common problem east of the Rockies. Prune excess foliage and clear away weeds to improve air circulation. For susceptible cultivars, plan to spray bordeaux mixture or copper before and after bloom, 10 days later, and again in early June. Replace severely infected vines with more resistant cultivars.
Green galls on leaf undersides; minute yellowish eggs and insects inside gall	Grape phylloxera	Prune out and destroy leaves with galls. Leaf gall phylloxera cause little direct damage unless extremely numerous; however, they are an indicator that the much more damaging root-attacking form of phylloxera may be present. Only European cultivars are susceptible to root phylloxera; American types are resistant. There is no treatment for root phylloxera. Provide good irrigation and fertile soil to slow decline of infested vines. When vines become unproductive, replant with grapes grafted onto phylloxera-resistant rootstock.

WHOLE PLANT PROBLEMS

SYMPTOMS	CAUSES	SOLUTIONS
Vines stunted; root tips have small, brown galls with tiny insects inside	Grape phylloxera	Damage from root-attacking form of phylloxera is limited to European cultivars not grafted onto resistant rootstock. There is no treatment. Provide good irrigation and fertile soil to slow decline of infested vines. When vines become unproductive, replant with grapes grafted onto phylloxera-resistant rootstock.
Vines decline; hard galls grow on trunks, usually at soil level	Crown gall	No treatment is available for this disease on grape. Pull and destroy vines when they become unproductive. Replant disease-free stock in a site where crown gall has not been present. Dip the new plants in Galltrol before planting. To minimize opportunities for infection, avoid injury to bark and plan to prune shoots while they are still small to speed healing.
Vines slowly decline; light gray bumps (scale insects) on or under bark	Grape scale	Scrape off loose bark to expose immature scales. Plan to spray dormant oil in late winter and radically prune back old growth to remove scale and renew vines.
Vines stunted; leaves appear scorched, with red and brown edges	Pierce's disease	This bacterial disease is common in the South. There is no control, and vines eventually die. Replant with muscadine cultivars or resistant American cultivars.

PEACH *Prunus persica* • Rosaceae

Choosing Trees

Peaches and their fuzz-less nectarine sisters are popular home fruit trees in Zones 5 through 9. Most gardeners are familiar with yellow-fleshed, freestone peaches, but there are other types that grow well in backyards too. White-fleshed peaches are deliciously sweet. Firm-fleshed, golden clingstones are renown for their aromatic flesh and canning quality. And for the really adventurous, there are flat peaches that look like a doughnut with a pit instead of a hole. 'Stark Saturn' is one.

Every peach cultivar needs a specific period of cold weather before it will resume growth and flower in spring. Once that requirement is met, the tree will open its flowers on the first warm day. Therefore, it's important to match peach and nectarine cultivars carefully to the length and severity of winter in your area.

In Zone 5 and the colder regions of Zone 6, choose a "high-chill" cultivar, such as 'Reliance', that will not be ready to open its buds until spring arrives in earnest. In Zones 8 and 9, choose a "low-chill" cultivar, such as 'Desert Gold'.

You can keep a full-size peach tree pruned to 10 to 12 feet high, and they are the best choice for most gardeners. If space is very limited, you may want to consider planting a genetic dwarf cultivar.

PROBLEM-RESISTANT PEACHES

Peaches aren't normally known for their problem resistance, but there are some resistant cultivars available. Resistance isn't immunity, but every little bit helps. When you're choosing peach trees, look for the resistant cultivars listed here or check with your supplier for new releases. In the list below, B = peachtree borer, BR = brown rot, BS = bacterial leaf spot, C = canker, and LC = peach leaf curl.

CULTIVAR (RESISTANCE)	FLESH COLOR/PIT TYPE
'Belle of Georgia' (BR)	White, freestone
'Biscoe' (BS)	Yellow, freestone
'Canadian Harmony' (BS)	Yellow, freestone
'Candor' (BS)	Yellow, freestone
'Dixired' (B, LC)	Yellow, clingstone
'Earlired' (BS)	Yellow, freestone
'Elberta' (B, BR, C)	Yellow, freestone
'Encore' (BS)	Yellow, freestone
'Floridagrande' (BS)	Yellow, freestone
'Frost' (LC)	Yellow, freestone
'Harbelle' (BS)	Yellow, freestone
'Harbrite' (BS, C)	Yellow, freestone
'Harcrest' (BR, BS, C)	Yellow, freestone
'Harken' (BS, LC)	Yellow, freestone
'June Gold' (BS, LC)	Yellow, freestone
'La Premier' (BR, C)	Yellow, freestone
'Loring' (BS, C, LC)	Yellow, freestone
'Norman' (BS)	Yellow, freestone
'Ranger' (BS)	Yellow, freestone
'Raritan Rose' (C)	White, freestone
'Red Haven' (LC)	Yellow, freestone
'Redskin' (C)	Yellow, freestone
'Reliance' (C)	Yellow, freestone
'Topaz' (BS)	Yellow, freestone

Call your local extension office to see what cultivars are best suited to your conditions. While you have them on the line, also inquire about problems peaches suffer in your area. Ask them to recommend resistant cultivars.

Rootstocks

Any peach tree you buy will be grafted onto a rootstock. Most are grafted onto peach seedlings.

If nematodes are a problem in your area, select trees grafted onto 'Nemaguard' or 'Okinawa' rootstocks.

If your winters get cold and stay cold, 'Siberian C' rootstock will make your trees more cold-hardy. However, if your winter weather fluctuates between warm and cold, stick with seedling rootstocks.

Peach cultivars grafted onto currently available dwarfing rootstocks tend to die young. If you want a dwarf tree, ask your supplier to recommend a genetic (naturally) dwarf cultivar.

Pollination

Most peaches and nectarines are self-fertile; you only need one tree to get a crop. A few heirloom cultivars, such as 'J. H. Hale' and 'Chinese Cling', are not self-fertile; you'll need a second cultivar to produce a crop.

Yield

On the average, you can expect to harvest 2 to 2½ bushels of fruit per year from a mature full-size tree. Smaller harvests start three to fours years after planting.

Site and Soil

You can succeed with peaches in Zones 5 through 9 if you select cultivars to match your climate.

Choose a site with:
• Full sun.
• Fertile soil.
• pH between 6.0 and 7.0.
Avoid:
• Low spots where frost tends to settle.
• Areas where water puddles in spring or after a rain.
• Sites where a peach tree grew previously.
• Sites near wild chokecherries, which can harbor viral diseases.

Preparing to Plant

Start preparing the soil a full year before you plan to plant peach trees. Have the soil tested and adjust the pH if necessary. Dig out *every* perennial weed. Plant a cover crop, such as sweet clover or buckwheat, over the entire planting area. If you're only planting one tree, prepare and plant a cover crop on a 10-foot-diameter circle of ground.

FOR BEST RESULTS

Buy one-year-old trees with a trunk diameter of ½ inch. One to three branches 2½ to 3 feet up the trunk are a plus.

During the preparation year, mow the cover crop whenever it reaches 8 to 10 inches in height. See "Planting Cover Crops" on page 28 for more details on choosing and managing cover crops.

Planting

Plant peach trees in either early spring or fall. Avoid fall planting in Zones 5 and 6. If you have any doubts about how well the site drains, build the soil up into a raised bed. See "Planting Fruit Trees" on page 200 for complete planting instructions.

Spacing

Plant full-size peach trees 15 to 20 feet apart each way. Plant trees with dwarfing rootstocks 8 to 12 feet apart and genetic dwarfs as close as 3 feet apart.

Seasonal Care

Peach trees are notoriously susceptible to insect and disease problems. Your trees will have the best chance of resisting problems if they are growing vigorously. See

"Season-by-Season Care: Peach" on page 272 for a schedule of care and preventive pest control measures. If your trees develop problems, refer to "Solving Peach Problems" on page 274 to identify the causes and find solutions.

Training Young Trees

Peaches are trained to a vase or open center form. To help your tree develop strong, well-positioned branches during its first few years of growth, follow the technique described below.

Training at Planting

At planting, cut the main trunk back to 2 to 2½ feet.

Cut side branch back by a third.

TRAINING AT PLANTING

Remove all spindly or damaged side branches flush with the trunk. Cut off about one-third of each remaining side branch.

Some trees come prepruned. If you buy a tree at a nursery, ask whether it has been pruned. If you order a tree from a mail-order supplier, look for pruning instructions in the tree's packaging.

First Summer Training

Once the new growth on your tree is 12 to 18 inches long, it's time to select four main branches and prune off the others. Select four branches that emerge in different directions from the trunk. Be sure that each main branch will be 4 to 8 inches above or below the branches closest to it.

Cut off all unwanted branches at the main trunk. Cut the main trunk off at an angle just above the top main branch. Spread each main branch so that the angle between the trunk and the branch is between 45 and 60 degrees. See "Training" on page 217 for how-to spreading instructions.

Second Year Training

In the spring, when the new leaves are just beginning to show, cut off about one-third of the previous season's growth on each

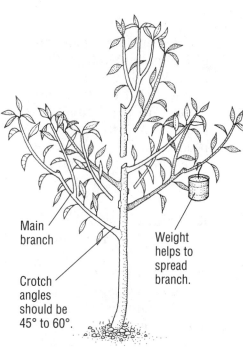

Main branch

Crotch angles should be 45° to 60°.

Weight helps to spread branch.

FIRST SUMMER TRAINING

branch. This will encourage side branching along the main branches.

In late summer, remove any new shoots coming from the trunk. Also remove or weight any strongly vertical shoots.

Pruning Bearing Trees

Follow the guidelines below to help your tree bear generous, problem-free harvests for many years. Peaches bear fruit only on one-year-old wood. You need to stimulate the tree to keep producing new growth or you won't have any fruit-bearing wood in the next year. Careful pruning will achieve this while not letting the tree get so tall you can't reach its fruit.

Third and Fourth Year Pruning

At bloom time, cut off about one-third of the previous season's growth from every shoot tip.

In late summer, use thinning cuts to remove crowded shoots. Also remove or weight any strongly vertical shoots. It is important to keep the tree open to sunlight and air movement to reduce problems with disease and encourage good fruit development.

Pruning Mature Trees

At bloom time, remove any dead wood. Cut back branches that hang down to a horizontal branch.

Use thinning cuts to remove the longest side branches, making the cuts back into old wood. You want to remove about a third of the branches every year. This will encourage new fruit-bearing wood to grow and help keep the tree compact.

In late summer, use thinning cuts to remove crowded or weak shoots. Also remove or weight any strongly vertical shoots.

Harvesting

Peaches don't sweeten up after you pick them, so wait until the fruits are perfectly ripe to harvest. Ripe fruit shows no green and is slightly soft. It parts easily from the stem, and most important, it tastes delectable.

Weight pulls vertical shoot down.

Late-summer pruning. Thin out crowded shoots in late summer. Putting a small weight, such as a tin can filled with concrete, on the end of a new upright shoot will pull it to horizontal, encouraging it to become a new fruitful branch.

How to Pick Peaches

• Cradle a ripe fruit in your hand and lift with a slight twisting motion.
• Handle peaches gently to avoid bruising them.

Storing

Ripe peaches are highly perishable and last just a few days at room temperature. You can store ripe fruits for a few days in your refrigerator, but it is too warm for longer storage and may make your fruit pithy or water-soaked. For longer storage, put slightly underripe fruits in a spare refrigerator set at 31° to 32°F (colder than usual refrigerator temperature); they will last two to four weeks.

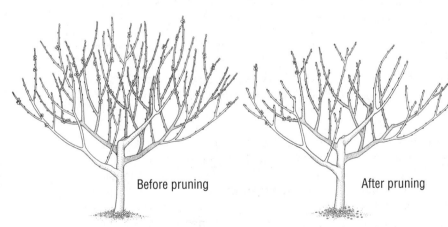

Before pruning   After pruning

Pruning peach trees. Three- and four-year-old peach trees will bear some fruit but need continued training to reach their best mature form. Notice the contrast between a blooming three-year-old peach tree before and after pruning. Shortening all of the previous year's shoots by one-third opens the tree to light and air and will stimulate new growth during the season.

SEASON-BY-SEASON CARE: PEACH

This care guide tells you what to do and when to do it for your best peach harvest ever. Because timing of certain tasks is critical, review all the instructions in this guide in late winter. Locate or buy the products you'll need in advance. To identify specific problems, refer to "Solving Peach Problems" on page 274. "Preventing Disease Problems" on page 210 explains how to mix and apply sprays. *Caution:* Copper and copper-containing compounds can defoliate peach trees. Don't substitute them for lime-sulfur or sulfur.

Late Winter

Dormant buds

Fertilize. Spread 5 to 10 pounds of compost in a band under and just beyond the drip line before buds start to swell.

Spray oil. If aphids, scales, European red mites, or peach twig borers were a problem last season, spray with dormant oil before buds start to swell. Be sure to do this at least 30 days before you plan to spray lime-sulfur or sulfur.

Early Spring

Buds starting to swell

Spray lime-sulfur. If bacterial leaf spot, brown rot, or peach scab was a problem last season, spray tree with lime-sulfur when the buds start to swell.

Hang pheromone traps. If peachtree borers, peach twig borers, or oriental fruit moths damaged your trees last year, hang one or two pheromone-baited traps per tree when the buds start to swell. Check traps every few days. If you catch borer moths, wait 10 to 14 days and then spray trees with BTK or neem every 10 to 14 days for several weeks. If you catch oriental fruit moths, follow the same procedure, but spray BTK only.

Hang white sticky traps. If tarnished plant bugs were a problem last year, hang one to four traps per tree when buds start to swell to help provide control. If you catch more than one bug per trap, spray trees with sabadilla when buds show pink.

Spray kelp. Kelp sprays help improve bud hardiness and can increase fruit set. Apply kelp: when you first see green tips, when leaves are 1/2 inch long, when buds are fat and pink, and then every three to four weeks all summer.

Spring

Full bloom

Prune. Prune your trees during or just after bloom to help decrease pruning-induced cold injury and canker disease development.

Spray sulfur. If the weather is wet or humid and at least 70°F when your peaches have open flowers, spray trees with sulfur to help control brown rot. Repeat when petals start to fall.

Spray BTK. If you've caught peach twig borers in your pheromone traps, spray BTK now.

Fertilize. After petal-fall, spread 2 cups of bonemeal and 1 cup of alfalfa meal in a band under and just beyond the drip line. (If flower buds were killed by frost, skip this feeding.)

Hang green sticky ball traps. If plum curculios were a problem last year, hang two traps per tree when petals fall. Start control measures as soon as you trap a curculio or see curculios or damage symptoms on young fruits. To control, hit branches with a padded stick twice daily to knock curculios off onto tarps spread on the ground, and then destroy the pests. Or, immediately after knocking trees free of curculios, enclose each tree in floating row cover and tie it closed at the trunk; remove the cover six weeks after bloom. Or spray trees with rotenone-pyrethrins or ryania every few days as long as new curculios are active.

Developing fruit

Early Summer

Thin fruit. When fruits are the size of a jelly bean, it's time to thin. Leave one fruit about every 6 to 8 inches.

Replace lures in pheromone traps. Rebait traps six to eight weeks after you put them out. Check oriental fruit moth traps weekly. If moths are caught, spray BTK immediately. Repeat weekly as long as new moths are caught.

Ripe fruit

Summer

Pick up dropped fruit. Gather and destroy dropped fruit weekly. Drops may contain insect pests that crawl into the soil to overwinter.

Spray sulfur. If peach scab and bacterial leaf spot were a major problem on your fruit last season, spray trees with sulfur or lime-sulfur every 10 to 21 days until harvest if weather is wet or humid and spots are spreading. If brown rot was a problem on your fruit last year, you'll need to spray sulfur if the weather is wet or humid to prevent recurrence of rotting fruit. Once the fruits begin to color, spray every ten days or after any rain. Don't spray if temperatures are above 85°F.

Remove and destroy rotting fruit. Remove rotting fruits as soon as you see them.

Leaves falling

Fall

Renew mulch. When the leaves start to fall, rake the loose mulch away from the trunk. After all leaves have fallen, replace the mulch and add new mulch to make a 6- to 8-inch layer.

Winterize trunk. Peachtree borer larvae bore into the bark from near the soil line to about 1 foot up the trunk. If trees have wire sleeves around the trunks, remove them and pull the soil away from the trunk an inch or so down. If you find borer holes or gummy ooze, dig the borers out with a sharp, flexible wire, or squirt parasitic nematodes into the holes. Renew paint and replace soil and wire sleeve. See page 226 for more information on protecting tree trunks from insect and rodent damage.

Spray bordeaux mix. If your trees suffered from shothole disease or peach leaf curl during the growing season, spray them with bordeaux mix after leaves fall to reduce problems next year.

Clean up. After leaves fall, pick off any remaining fruits and cut out any swollen or deformed twigs. Destroy collected fruits and prunings. Clean and store insect traps.

Solving Peach Problems

Use this table to identify problems on your peach trees. Scan the list of symptoms to find the description that most closely matches what you see in your garden. Then refer across the page to learn the cause and the recommended solutions. For some pest problems, by the time you see the damage, there is little you can do to fix things in the current season. You may be able to salvage some edible sections of damaged fruit. In the future, take preventive steps, such as spraying sulfur to prevent certain diseases. For a schedule of preventive measures, see "Season-by-Season Care: Peach" on page 272. You'll also find illustrations, descriptions, and additional controls for many of the insects and diseases listed below in Part 5 of this book.

FLOWER AND FRUIT PROBLEMS

SYMPTOMS	CAUSES	SOLUTIONS
Flowers appear, but no fruit	Frost injury Lack of pollination	This is a common problem in northern areas, when late frosts may ruin flowers. Cool, wet spring weather may also prevent pollination by bees.
Tree appears healthy, but produces few flowers and fruit	Excessive pruning Tree too old Winter injury to buds	Overpruning can reduce fruit production because peaches only bear fruit on 1-year-old wood. Trees will not bear much fruit if most of the 1-year-old wood is pruned off. Peach trees produce well for about 10 years, then production declines. If your trees are old, replant at a new site, and remove the old trees. A late cold spell can kill flower buds. Trees will not produce any fruit in that season but should resume normal production next year.
Small brown dots and/or fuzzy gray mold on fruit; entire fruit rots	Brown rot	Harvest any unaffected ripe fruit immediately. Remove and destroy infected fruit and twigs. Collect and destroy all mummified fruit remaining on tree. Spray sulfur or copper 1–3 weeks before harvest if weather is wet to protect ripening fruit. Prune trees to increase air circulation.
Olive green spots on immature fruit; fruit becomes distorted	Peach scab	Lightly damaged fruit is edible. Collect and destroy infected fruit, dropped fruit, and fallen leaves. Prune to increase air circulation.
Sunken, corky scars on fruit	Tarnished plant bugs	Though blemished, fruit is edible. Remove all crop debris from around trees in fall.
Crescent-shaped scars on young fruit; fruit may drop prematurely	Plum curculios	This pest is found only in eastern North America. Scarred fruit don't contain insects and are edible. To control, strike branches with a padded stick twice daily to knock curculios off onto tarps; destroy collected curculios. Or spray with rotenone-pyrethrins or ryania every few days. Continue as long as new curculios are active.
Gummy residues on immature fruit; pinkish caterpillars inside fruit	Oriental fruit moths	Undamaged areas of ripe fruit are edible. Immature fruit with residue or signs of entry around stem end should be picked and destroyed to kill larvae inside.

SYMPTOMS	CAUSES	SOLUTIONS
Holes in fruit, with gummy residues by holes; brown caterpillars inside fruit	Peach twig borers	Undamaged areas of mature fruit are edible. Unripe, damaged fruit should be picked and destroyed to kill larvae inside. Spray dormant oil during winter to control overwintering larvae under bark. Next spring, plan to spray BTK at bloom time to control the borers before fruit forms.

LEAF AND SHOOT PROBLEMS

SYMPTOMS	CAUSES	SOLUTIONS
Curled leaves, with a sticky coating; tiny green insects on leaf undersides	Green peach aphids	Native parasites and predators usually keep aphids in check. If aphid numbers are high, wash them from trees with a strong spray of water or spray trees with insecticidal soap or neem.
Small, light green to black spots on leaf undersides	Peach scab	Collect and destroy affected leaves and rake up fallen leaves. Prune to increase air circulation. For trees with persistent infections, spray lime-sulfur or sulfur every 1–3 weeks during humid weather, starting at bud break.
Small, round purple spots on leaves, with centers dropped out	Shothole disease (peach blight)	This disease cannot be controlled during growing season. To reduce its spread, avoid wetting foliage while watering. While trees are dormant, prune out infected shoots and buds, which have a glazed appearance.
Fine, yellow stipples on leaves; minute reddish mites on leaf undersides	European red mites	Native predatory mites usually keep mites in check. For minor infestations, spray water or insecticidal soap. For severe infestations, spray summer oil when leaf buds are developing or release purchased predatory mites (e.g., *Metaseiulus occidentalis* or other species adapted to the local climate).
Dark spots on leaves; spots fall out, leaving holes	Bacterial leaf spot	This disease is common east of the Rockies. Fruit produced is edible but may be of poor quality. To reduce spread of the disease, spray copper every 10–14 days. Replace severely affected trees with resistant cultivars.
White or gray powdery patches or coating on leaves and shoots	Powdery mildew	At first sign of disease, spray or dust sulfur, and repeat every 10–14 days, or more frequently in humid weather. Prune out and destroy affected shoots and leaves. Prune to increase air circulation.
Thickened, crisp, distorted, reddish leaves; growing shoots may die back	Peach leaf curl	This disease is worse in wet weather. Pick and destroy affected leaves as soon as symptoms are visible. Spraying trees with kelp once a month during growing season may reduce future damage.

(continued)

Solving Peach Problems—Continued

LEAF AND SHOOT PROBLEMS—CONTINUED

SYMPTOMS	CAUSES	SOLUTIONS
Shoot tips die back; pinkish caterpillar inside shoot stem	Oriental fruit moths	Prune out and destroy affected tips to prevent a new generation from damaging ripening fruit. Spray summer oil to kill eggs and larvae.
Shoot tips die back; brown caterpillars inside shoot stem	Peach twig borers	Prune out affected tips and destroy. Spray dormant oil during winter to control overwintering larvae under bark. Next spring, plan to spray BTK at bloom time to control the first generation of peach twig borers before they bore into shoots.
Young shoots wilt and die; stems girdled by sunken, brown cankers	Brown rot	Prune and destroy infected twigs. Spray sulfur or copper 1–3 weeks before harvest if weather is wet to protect ripening fruit. Prune trees to increase air circulation. Collect and destroy all mummified fruit.
Abnormally shortened shoots, bearing hundreds of deformed, discolored leaves	Peach rosette virus	This disease is found only in eastern North America. There is no cure. Remove infected trees and replant with certified virus-free stock. In areas where this virus is common, control leafhoppers, which spread the disease, by spraying with insecticidal soap.

WHOLE TREE PROBLEMS

SYMPTOMS	CAUSES	SOLUTIONS
Small, hard or soft bumps on leaves or branches; leaves turn yellow	Scales	Spray tree with dormant oil in late winter to control. Also control ants, which encourage scale insects, by applying sticky bands to tree trunks.
Branches do not leaf out in spring or they wilt and die during growing season	Bacterial canker	Young or stressed trees are often most affected. Prune out infected branches well below wilted zone, disinfecting tools between cuts. Help trees avoid stress by keeping them well-watered and maintaining soil fertility.
Tree loses vigor; caked sawdust and gummy residue may be seen at base of trunk	Peachtree borers	Weak trees or trees that have bark injuries are most susceptible to invasion by borers. Remove soil several inches deep around base of trunk and look for borer holes containing cream-colored larvae. Dig out larvae with a sharp knife or kill them by working a flexible wire into the holes. If soil around tree is not mulched, cultivate around the trunk in June and July to kill pupae. Maintain vigorous trees by watering adequately and maintaining soil fertility.

PEAR *Pyrus communis* and hybrids • Rosaceae

Whether you have a partridge or not, a fruiting pear tree is a worthwhile addition to your garden. Hardy in Zones 4 through 9, pears suffer from fewer pest and disease problems than most other tree fruits.

Pears are closely related to apples. Many aspects of raising backyard pears and apples are the same. Refer to "Apple" on page 228 for information on site preparation, seasonal care, and solving pest problems.

Below you'll find specific information on choosing pear trees, training, and harvesting. You'll also find special information on and solutions for two pear problems: pear psylla and fire blight.

Choosing Trees

The pears that are most familiar to us are European pears (*Pyrus communis*). Their cousins the Asian pears (hybrids of *P. pyrifolia, P. ussuriensis,* and *P. bretschneideris*) are gaining popularity and are equally easy to grow. The fruits are often round and have crisp, sweet, juicy flesh.

Fire blight, a bacterial disease that causes branches to wilt suddenly and die, can be a major problem for pear trees. If your springs are warm and wet, or if your summers are hot and humid, you should be sure to select cultivars with resistance to fire blight. 'Kieffer', 'Magness', and 'Moonglow' are three good choices.

Rootstocks

Any pear tree you buy will be grafted onto a rootstock. The rootstock has a major influence on how tall your tree will grow and how disease-resistant it will be. Most gardeners choose trees grafted on one of the dwarfing, fire-blight–resistant 'OH × F' rootstocks.

Pollination

You must plant at least two cultivars to get a good crop of pears. However, not all cultivars can pollinate each other. Be sure to ask your supplier whether the cultivars you select are a good match as pollinators.

Yield

Expect a yearly harvest of 3 or more bushels of pears from a mature full-size tree. You will harvest 1 bushel annually from a mature dwarf tree. Smaller harvests

start eight to ten years after planting a full-size tree; three to five years after planting a dwarf tree.

Site and Soil

Pears need the same site and soil conditions as apple, except that they prefer soil with a pH between 6.0 and 6.5. They will tolerate poorly drained soil slightly better than apples will.

Planting

Plant trees in early spring or fall. Avoid fall planting in Zones 4 through 6. See "Planting Fruit Trees" on page 200 for complete instructions.

Spacing

Plant full-size trees 15 to 20 feet apart each way and dwarf trees 8 to 12 feet apart each way.

MULTIPLE-TRUNK TRAINING

Fire blight is a bacterial disease that can spread through a plant's vascular system. The bacteria move downward from the point of infection. If the bacteria reach the main trunk and roots, the entire tree may die.

In areas where fire blight is a major problem, try training your pears to have multiple trunks. If one or more of the trunks become infected with fire blight, you can prune off the infected wood. Your tree will survive and bear fruit on its other trunks.

To create a multiple-trunk tree, allow four or five well-spaced branches to grow vertically during the first summer after planting. (Don't use branch spreaders.) These branches will all serve as trunks.

In the second year, choose and spread side branches that point outward from each of the trunks. Remove all side branches that point into the tree's interior. Thereafter, just imagine that the trunks are one large trunk and prune according to the directions on page 230 for a central leader tree.

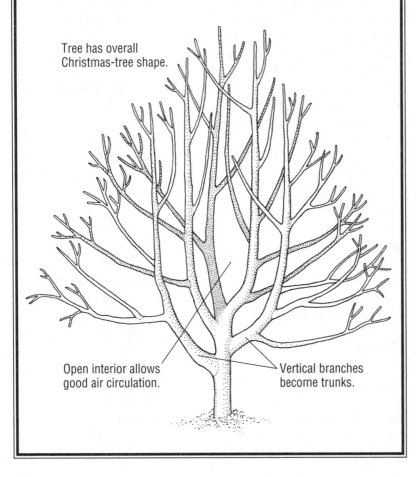

Tree has overall Christmas-tree shape.

Open interior allows good air circulation.

Vertical branches become trunks.

Pear Problems

Pears have one unique problem insect: pear psylla. Also, they are generally more susceptible to fire blight than apples and other fruits are.

Pear psyllids are tiny red or green insects that suck plant juices. As they feed, they release a sticky honeydew that supports the growth of black sooty mold. The black mold is usually the first symptom noticed.

The sooty mold that grows on psylla honeydew looks a bit like the blackening caused by fire blight. To diagnose the cause of a black coating on pear leaves, rub an affected leaf with a wet finger: Sooty mold black washes off, but fire blight black doesn't.

Both problems are encouraged by soft, succulent growth, so limit fertilizer applications to your pear trees. Pruning can also stimulate unwanted succulent growth. Use branch spreaders rather than pruning cuts to keep your pear tree's growth open to light and air. When you do prune, use only thinning cuts.

If you have a mature pear tree that puts out too much new growth every year, try slowing it down by replacing the mulch under it with turfgrass. The grass should soak up nutrients and water, and thus reduce the growth of the tree. Mow the grass and remove the clippings regularly.

If you find pear psyllids on your trees during the growing season, spray insecticidal soap or summer oil to control them. Follow up to prevent problems next year by spraying trees with dormant oil in early spring, just as buds are swelling.

Training Pear Trees

Train your pear trees to a central leader shape as you would an apple tree. See "Training Young Trees" on page 229 for directions. Be sure to spread branches whenever possible and make as few pruning cuts as possible. If fire blight is a severe problem in your area, you may want to try multiple-trunk training, as described on the opposite page.

Harvesting

European pears. For best eating quality, pick European pears before they soften on the tree. Harvest when their green color lightens and the stem separates easily from the spur. ('Seckel' pears are an exception; they can be left to ripen on the tree if you don't want to store them.) Use a gentle lift-and-twist

---

QUINCE

Quince (*Cydonia oblonga*) is used as a dwarfing rootstock for pears, but it is a worthwhile fruit in its own right. The hard, aromatic fruits make delicious preserves, and the trees are less vulnerable to pest problems than either apples or pears.

Quince is hardy in Zones 5 through 9. Plant one of the small, low-care trees (they are self-fertile) and it will reward you with up to a bushel of fuzzy yellow fruit starting three years after planting.

Care for your quince the same way as you would a pear. Prune it as an open center tree like you would a peach tree. It needs little pruning after its initial shaping—light thinning each year will do.

Harvest quinces when they are fully colored and fragrant. Frost does not damage them. You can refrigerate them for up to two months. The fruits are hard and astringent even when ripe but are delicious when cooked into jelly or added to applesauce.

---

motion when you pick pears to avoid damaging the spurs.

Early-ripening pear cultivars come to ripeness over a period of about one week; make three passes to harvest them all at the proper ripeness. In general, you can pick later-maturing cultivars all at once.

Asian pears. Asian pears ripen well on the tree. Pick them when their skins change color and they taste good. Ripe Asian pear stems part readily from the spur when you lift the fruit with a slight twist.

Storing

You can store mature, hard European pears or ripe Asian pears in your refrigerator for a few weeks. For longer storage, put them in a spare refrigerator set at 31° to 32°F (colder than usual refrigerator temperature). The length of storage varies with cultivar. If the fruits start to shrivel, the humidity is too low. Try covering them with a sheet of paper towel and misting it with water to keep the humidity level high.

At room temperature, European pears will soften and ripen in three to seven days. If you have European pears stored in the refrigerator, remember to take them out about a week before you plan to eat them. They are ready to enjoy when the flesh next to the stem gives a little when you press on it. Don't wait for them to get soft all over or you may find the core is overripe when you take that first bite.

PLUM   *Prunus* spp. • Rosaceae

There are two major types of plums—European plums (*Prunus domestica*) and Japanese plums (*P. salicina*)—and a few less well known ones. Plums may be purple, blue, red, yellow, or green.

Plums are related to cherries and peaches, and some aspects of their care are the same. Refer to "Peach" on page 268 for information on site preparation. If you have problems with your plums, refer to "Solving Cherry Problems" on page 251 and "Solving Peach Problems" on page 274 to identify the causes and find solutions.

Choosing Trees

European plums. European plums have firm-fleshed fruits the size of golf balls. Extra-firm-fleshed European plums with blue skins are known as prunes. Astringent damson plums (*P. institia*) are smaller and are used in cooking. Most European plums are hardy in Zones 5 through 9. A few are hardier; check with your supplier for names of hardy cultivars.

Japanese plums. Somewhat larger than European plums, Japanese plums are soft, juicy fruits. Their sweet flesh can be tart at the center.

Japanese plums are hardy in Zones 6 through 10.

American plums and hybrids. Wild plums native to North America lack the fruit size or quality of the European or Japanese cultivars but make up for it with their extreme cold- and drought-hardiness. Hybrid plums combine hardiness (some as far north as Zone 4) with somewhat larger fruits.

Plums are generally easy to grow except in areas with hot, humid summers. But Southeasterners can beat rots, spots, and knots by planting one of the disease-resistant cultivars developed by the Alabama Agricultural Experiment Station. Look for 'AU-Rosa', 'AU-Roadside', and other cultivars starting with 'AU-'.

Rootstocks

Choose 'Mariana', 'Damas', or 'Myrobalan' plum root-

FOR BEST RESULTS

Buy one-year-old Japanese plum trees with $1/2$-inch-diameter trunks. Choose two-year-old European plum trees the same size. One to three branches $2^1/2$ to 3 feet up the trunk are a plus.

---

stocks for heavy or poorly drained soils. Peach rootstocks may be a better choice in sandy soil. 'Mariana' is the most winter-hardy rootstock for plums. If you want a very small tree, buy one grafted on 'Pixie' rootstock.

Pollination

Plan to plant two different cultivars. Most European plums will set some fruit without cross-pollination, but nearly all will yield better when cross-pollinated by another European cultivar.

Japanese plums must be cross-pollinated by either a Japanese or American type. American plums also need cross-pollination for best yields. Check with your supplier for specific matchmaking recommendations.

Yield

You can expect to harvest about 50 pounds of fruit from each mature full-size plum tree every year. Smaller harvests start three to five years after planting.

Site and Soil

You can grow plums in Zones 4 through 10 if you choose cultivars to match your climate.

Choose a site with:
- Full sun.
- Moderately fertile soil. (Japanese cultivars need richer soil.)
- pH between 6.0 and 6.8.

Avoid:
- Low spots where frost tends to settle (especially for Japanese cultivars).
- Areas where water puddles in spring or after a rain. (European cultivars will tolerate clayey soil.)
- Sites where a cherry, peach, or plum tree grew previously.

Planting

Plant plum trees in either early spring or fall. Avoid fall planting in Zones 4 through 6. If your soil isn't well drained, build it up into a raised bed. See "Planting Fruit Trees" on page 200 for complete planting instructions.

Spacing

Plant plum trees 15 to 20 feet apart each way. Plant dwarf trees and less vigorous cultivars, such as some of the bushy American hybrids, 8 to 12 feet apart.

Seasonal Care

You will harvest more plums and have fewer problems if you feed and care for your trees regularly. See "Season-by-Season Care:

Where plums bear fruit. Plum trees form short, stubby spurs that bear fruit season after season. Japanese plums tend to overbear, so remove some spurred branches as you prune to help thin the crop. For European plums, preserve as many of the spurred branches as possible.

Plum" on page 282 for directions for caring for your trees throughout the year.

Training Plum Trees

European plums. Most European plum cultivars have upright growth. Train them to a central leader form as you would apples. See "Training Young Trees" on page 229 for directions. Prune the trees just after they leaf out or bloom.

Once your trees are bearing, prune them more as you would peaches. See "Pruning Bearing Trees" on page 270 for instructions. Since plums bear on spurs as well as on one-year-old wood, you don't need to thin out the old wood as much as instructed for peaches. A few of the oldest branches a year is fine.

Japanese plums. Most Japanese plum cultivars tend to grow in a graceful spreading shape. Select four or five main branches and train them to an open center form as you would peaches. See

"Training Young Trees" on page 270 for details.

Harvesting

Plums develop their mature color a few weeks before they ripen. Gently squeeze fruits every few days to test ripeness. When they are slightly soft, taste one. If the flavor is rich and sweet, they are ripe; pick the soft ones right away. The fruits on a tree will ripen over a week to ten days. Harvest ripe fruits every day or two during the ripening period.

Storing

Ripe plums will keep a few days in your refrigerator. For longer storage, put them in a spare refrigerator set at 31° to 32°F (colder than usual refrigerator temperature). Soft Japanese types will keep for one to two weeks. European types will keep two to four weeks. Prune-type plums, with their firm flesh and high sugar content, keep even longer.

SEASON-BY-SEASON CARE: PLUM

This care guide tells you what to do and when to do it for your best plum harvest ever. Because timing of certain tasks is critical, review all the instructions in this guide in late winter. Locate or buy the products you'll need in advance. Plums are closely related to cherries and peaches, and share many of the same problems. If you have problems with your plum trees, refer to "Solving Cherry Problems" on page 251 and "Solving Peach Problems" on page 274. "Preventing Disease Problems" on page 210 explains how to mix and apply sprays.

Late Winter

Dormant buds

Fertilize. Spread 5 to 10 pounds of compost in a band under and just beyond the drip line before buds start to swell.

Spray oil. If aphids, peachtree or peach twig borers, or scales were a problem last season, spray with dormant oil before buds start to swell. Be sure to do this at least 30 days before you plan to spray lime-sulfur or sulfur.

Early Spring

Buds starting to swell

Spray lime-sulfur. If bacterial leaf spot, brown rot, or black knot was a problem last season, spray the tree with lime-sulfur when the buds start to swell. For black knot only, spray again one week later.

Spray kelp. Kelp sprays help improve bud hardiness and can increase fruit set. Apply three to six times: when the leaves are ½ inch long, when the flowers are open, when small green fruits are visible, and every three to four weeks all summer.

Hang oriental fruit moth traps. If oriental fruit moth damage was a problem last year, hang one or two pheromone-baited traps per tree when the buds start to swell to monitor the pest. Check traps every few days. When you catch the first oriental fruit moth, wait 10 to 14 days and then spray trees with BTK.

Spring

Full bloom

Prune. Prune your trees during or just after bloom to help decrease pruning-induced cold injury and canker disease development.

Spray sulfur. If the weather is wet or humid and at least 70°F when your plums have open flowers, spray trees with sulfur to help control brown rot. Repeat when petals start to fall.

Fertilize. After petal-fall, spread 2 cups of bonemeal and 1 cup of alfalfa meal in a band under and just beyond the drip line. (If flower buds were killed by frost, skip this feeding.)

Hang green sticky ball traps. If plum curculios were a problem last year, hang two traps per tree when petals fall. Start control measures as soon as you trap a curculio or see curculios or damage symptoms on young fruits. To control, hit branches with a padded stick twice daily to knock curculios off onto tarps spread on the ground, and then destroy the pests. Or, immediately after knocking trees free of curculios, enclose each tree in floating row cover and tie it closed at the trunk; remove the cover six weeks after bloom. Alternatively, you can spray trees with rotenone-pyrethrins or ryania every few days as long as new curculios are active.

Developing fruit

Early Summer

Thin fruit. When fruits are the size of a jelly bean, it's time to thin. Leave one fruit every 1 to 3 inches for small-fruited cultivars and every 4 to 5 inches for large-fruited cultivars.

Replace oriental fruit moth trap lures. Rebait traps six to eight weeks after you put them out. Check traps weekly. If moths are caught, spray BTK immediately. Repeat weekly as long as new moths are caught.

Spray lime-sulfur. If bacterial leaf spot was a problem last year, spray the tree with lime-sulfur every two to three weeks, beginning when you first see spots on leaves. Repeat sprays whenever the weather is wet or humid and the spots are spreading, until all leaves have fallen in autumn.

Ripe fruit

Summer

Remove wilted shoot tips. If you've had past problems with peach twig borers or oriental fruit moths, be on the lookout for wilting shoot tips. If you find any, use pruners to snip them off a few inches below the damaged area. Destroy the infested prunings.

Pick up dropped fruit. Gather and destroy dropped fruit at least weekly.

Spray sulfur. If brown rot was a problem on your fruit last year, spray trees with sulfur every ten days or after any rain once the fruits begin to color and the weather is wet or humid and the temperature is below 85°F.

Remove and destroy rotting fruit. Remove rotting fruits as soon as you see them.

Leaves falling

Fall

Renew mulch. When the leaves start to fall, rake the loose mulch away from the trunk. After all leaves have fallen, replace the mulch and add new mulch to make a 6- to 8-inch layer.

Winterize trunk. Peachtree borer larvae bore into the bark from near the soil line to about 1 foot up. To check for borer invasion, remove wire sleeve and pull the soil away from the trunk an inch or so down. If you find borer holes or gummy ooze, dig the borers out with a sharp, flexible wire, or squirt parasitic nematodes into the holes to kill the borers. Renew paint and replace soil and wire sleeve. See page 226 for more information on trunk protection.

Spray bordeaux mix. If your trees suffered from shothole disease or peach leaf curl during the growing season, spray them with bordeaux mix after leaves fall to reduce problems next year.

Clean up. After leaves fall, pick off any remaining fruits and cut out any swollen or deformed twigs. Destroy collected fruits and prunings. Clean and store insect traps.

RASPBERRY *Rubus* spp. • Rosaceae

Choosing Plants

Raspberries come in a mouthwatering medley of red, yellow, purple, and black fruits. Fallbearing red and yellow raspberries are the most winter-hardy (Zones 3 through 8). Black raspberries are less winter-hardy (Zones 4 or 5 through 9) but produce better than reds in regions with hot summers.

'Bababerry', a fallbearing red raspberry, is an exception and does well even in Zone 9.

Depending on what types you grow, you can harvest raspberries from early summer through fall. Ask your supplier to recommend cultivars that bear over a long season or at the time of year when you want berries.

Also ask your local nursery or extension office about diseases and pests that cause serious problems in your region. See "For Best Results" on the opposite page for information on virus-free raspberries. "Problem-Resistant Raspberries" on this page lists cultivars resistant to some of the most common raspberry problems.

Pollination

Raspberries are self-fertile, so you can plant just one cultivar and harvest a full crop.

Yield

You'll pick your first crop 8 months (fallbearers) to 20 months (fall-planted summerbearers) after planting. You can expect to harvest 4 to 6 pounds of raspberries each year from each plant once the plants are mature (two or three years after planting).

PROBLEM-RESISTANT RASPBERRIES

Plan for problem-free berries by choosing cultivars that resist problems that are common in your area. These cultivars should have a better chance to grow and produce well. In general, birds are less attracted to yellow raspberries than to other colors. For other problems, select the cultivars listed below or ask your supplier for new resistant releases. In the list below, A = aphids, AN = anthracnose, CG = crown gall, GM = gray mold, PM = powdery mildew, RR = root rot, and SB = spur blight.

CULTIVAR (RESISTANCE)	COLOR/BEARING TIME
'Algonquin' (RR, SB)	Red, summer
'Allen' (PM)	Black, summer
'Amity' (RR, SB)	Red, fall
'Autumn Bliss' (RR)	Red, fall
'Black Hawk' (AN)	Black, summer
'Boyne' (RR)	Red, summer
'Bristol' (PM)	Black, summer
'Canby' (A)	Red, summer
'Festival' (AN, PM, RR, SB)	Red, summer
'Haida' (A, RR, SB)	Red, summer
'Haut' (AN)	Black, summer
'Heritage' (PM)	Red, fall
'Latham' (RR)	Red, summer
'Lowden' (AN)	Black, summer
'Matsqui' (GM)	Red, summer
'Meeker' (GM)	Red, summer
'Newburgh' (AN, RR)	Red, summer
'Royalty' (A, RR)	Purple, summer
'Skeena' (A)	Red, summer
'Success' (SB)	Purple, summer
'Summit' (RR)	Red, fall
'Willamette' (AN, CG, PM)	Red, summer

Site and Soil

You can grow raspberries successfully in Zones 3 through 9 if you select cultivars to match your climate.

Choose a site with:
- Full sun.
- Fertile soil with lots of organic matter.
- pH between 5.5 and 6.5.

Avoid:
- Low spots where frost tends to settle.
- Areas where water puddles in spring or after a rain.
- Sites where berry plants, grapes, or tomato-family plants grew previously.
- Sites near wild raspberries or old cultivated plantings, which can harbor viral diseases. Remove wild plants within 600 feet of your planting.

Preparing to Plant

Start preparing the soil a full year before you plan to plant raspberries. Have the soil tested and adjust the pH if necessary. Spread greensand (1 pound per 100 square feet) if the potassium level is low. Dig out *every* perennial weed. Plant a cover crop, such as sweet clover or buckwheat, over the entire planting area. During the preparation year, mow the cover crop whenever it reaches 8 to 10 inches in height. See "Planting Cover Crops" on page 28 for more details on cover crops.

Shape the soil into a 3-foot-wide raised bed before planting if your soil tends to stay soggy after rain. Spread 100 pounds of compost, 50 pounds of alfalfa meal, and 3 pounds of kelp meal per 100 square feet and work it into the top few inches of soil.

Planting

Green tissue-culture plants. Plant actively growing tissue-culture plants anytime after the last spring frost through late summer. Spray the leaves with an antitranspirant as you unpack the plants.

Planting raspberries. *Set up your trellis before you plant. That way you won't crush young plants underfoot while you set the posts and string the wire. When you plant, center the plants between the trellis wires.*

Summer

Cut canes flush with ground.

Winter

Remove canes growing outside row.

Pruning summerbearing raspberries. *In the summer, cut all fruit-bearing canes to the ground after harvest. In late winter, thin the canes, leaving three to five canes per foot of row.*

After planting, water them in with compost tea. They will need frequent watering until they are established.

Dormant tissue-culture plants. Plant dormant plants in early spring or mid-fall. Water them in with compost tea. Mulch fall plantings immediately to prevent frost from heaving the tiny plants out of the soil.

Nursery-matured tissue-culture plants and bareroot canes. Plant dormant plants in early spring or fall. Soak roots in compost tea for 20 minutes just before planting. Then dust roots with a mixture of 2 parts kelp meal to 1 part bonemeal and plant. Cut the canes to the ground after planting to reduce cane-borne diseases.

For all types of plants, it's best to install drip irrigation lines immediately after planting. Lay the drip line a few inches away from the plants. Then spread a strip of straw mulch 3 feet wide and 6 to 8 inches deep (the plants should be centered in this mulch strip). Leave small bare areas around the plants. For more details on drip irrigation, see "Watering Fruit Crops" on page 204.

Spacing

Plant red raspberries 3 feet apart in the row; yellow and purple raspberries, 2 feet apart. These types will spread and fill in the row. Space black raspberries 3 feet apart in the row; they will not spread. If you are planting more than one row of raspberries, leave at least 7 feet between rows. That will give you a 4-foot-wide aisle to work from between your 3-foot-wide mulched rows.

Seasonal Care

To reap the best harvests and avoid problems, feed and care for your raspberries regularly. See "Season-by-Season Care: Raspberry" on page 288 for directions for caring for your raspberries throughout the year.

Adequate watering is especially important from the time when flowers form through the harvest. Water-stressed raspberries will form little or no fruit. See "Watering Fruit Crops" on page 204 for ways to gauge when and how much to water.

Training Plants

Trellising

A basic bramble trellis is a single wire stretched between a single row of posts set firmly in the ground. Tie the canes to the wire each winter after pruning. You can also tie black raspberry plants to individual fence posts.

The V-trellis, shown at top on page 209, works well for summerbearing raspberries.

For fallbearing raspberries, a removable trellis, like the one shown at top on page 208, makes winter pruning easier.

Pruning

Fallbearing raspberries. After harvesting the fall crop, most gardeners cut all the canes to the ground during the winter. Use a heavy-duty lawn mower; you can also use pruning shears.

You can let the fall-fruiting canes overwinter and bear a second, but much smaller, crop of berries the next summer. If you choose this second option, prune them like summerbearing raspberries.

Summerbearing raspberries. Prune summerbearers twice each year. In midsummer, cut fruit-bearing canes off at ground level as soon as they finish bearing.

In late winter, remove any canes outside the 1-foot-wide row. Cut these canes off flush with the ground. Then remove canes within the row so that only three to five sturdy, evenly spaced canes remain per foot. Remove slender or bent canes. Don't cut back the cane tips, except for winter-killed portions, because that is where next summer's fruit is waiting.

Black raspberries. Black raspberries need pruning three times a year. When the new canes are 3 feet tall, pinch back the tips to 28 inches. This encourages side branching, which results in more berries next season.

In midsummer, cut fruit-bearing canes off at ground level as soon as they finish bearing. In late winter, remove slender and short canes so that only four to six thick, sturdy canes remain per plant. Then trim back all side branches to 10 to 12 inches. Remove slender or bent canes first.

Harvesting

Pick raspberries when they are thoroughly ripe; unripe fruits will not ripen off the plant. A ripe fruit is soft and comes free from the plant with little force.

Harvest berries in the morning after the dew is gone but before the sun heats the berries. Go over your patch at least every other day to prevent fruits from becoming overripe.

Pick any overripe or rotting fruit you find to prevent the spread of pests. Carry a spare basket so that you can keep damaged and overripe fruits separate from the good ones. Dispose of the reject fruit in the center of a hot compost pile or with your household trash.

Raspberries are delicate fruits. Pick ripe berries with a light touch and place them gently into shallow containers (three to four berries deep) to prevent crushing. Do not dump berries from one container into another; it will damage the fruit. Place harvested raspberries in the shade and refrigerate them as soon as possible.

Storing

Raspberries are extremely perishable. They will keep in your refrigerator for only a day. For longer storage, put them in a spare refrigerator set at 31° to 32°F (colder than usual refrigerator temperature) for up to three days.

Summer

28"

Winter

Cut canes flush with ground.

Pruning black raspberries. *In summer, cut new canes back to 28 inches tall; remove fruit-bearing canes after harvest. In late winter, remove short canes, leaving four to six sturdy canes per plant; shorten side branches.*

SEASON-BY-SEASON CARE: RASPBERRY

This care guide tells you what to do and when to do it for your best raspberry harvest ever. Because timing of certain tasks is critical, review all the instructions in this guide in late winter. Locate or buy the products you'll need in advance. Also, timing of certain tasks, such as pruning, differs for summerbearing raspberries and fallbearing raspberries. Be sure to note whether the task you plan to do is for all raspberries or only for one type. To identify specific problems, refer to "Solving Raspberry Problems" on page 290. "Preventing Disease Problems" on page 210 explains how to mix and apply sprays.

Late Winter

Dormant buds

Prune summerbearers. Thin out extra canes and prune side branches (on black raspberries only). Be sure to remove any canes damaged by cold. If canes snap off at ground level while you are handling them, the plants may have a crown borer problem. If several canes break off from one crown, dig up and destroy that plant.

Fertilize. Spread 10 to 15 pounds of compost for each 10 feet of row, broadcasting it over the straw mulch. Spread 5 pounds of compost under each black raspberry plant.

Early Spring

Buds starting to swell

Spray lime-sulfur. If powdery mildew, leaf spot, cane diseases, or spider mites were a problem last year on summerbearing raspberries, spray just as the buds first show green. For cane diseases only, also spray sulfur when the new canes reach 2 feet in height.

Hang white sticky traps. If tarnished plant bugs were a problem last year, hang one trap every 10 feet in summerbearing raspberries when buds start to swell. If you catch more than one bug per trap, spray plants with sabadilla when the flower buds appear.

Spray kelp. Kelp sprays help improve bud hardiness and can increase fruit set. For summerbearing raspberries, apply kelp when you first see green tips, when leaves are ½ inch long, and when the flower buds appear.

Summerbearing raspberries in bloom

Spring

Spray rotenone. If raspberry fruitworms were a problem last year, spray summerbearing raspberries with rotenone and/or pyrethrins when the flower buds appear. Repeat just before flowers open. If cane borers were a severe problem last year, spray once just before flowers open.

Spray compost tea. Just before flowers open, spray summerbearing raspberries with compost tea to help prevent gray mold. Spray in the early morning of a clear day so foliage will dry fast. Respray a few days later if weather is wet or humid.

Spray kelp. Kelp sprays help improve bud hardiness and can increase fruit set. For fallbearing raspberries, spray kelp when the shoots are 1 foot tall, 2 feet tall, and when the flower buds appear.

Weed. Begin weeding your stand of raspberries now, and continue all season long. Also mow the aisles between rows if vegetation grows to help air circulate around your plants. This will reduce disease problems.

Ripe summerbearing raspberries

Early Summer/Summer

Prune. Cut suckers that are growing outside a 1-foot-wide strip off flush with the ground. If the new canes in the row are very dense, thin them out also. Top new black (but not red) raspberry canes to encourage branching.

Spray compost tea. Compost tea sprays can help prevent gray mold. Spray summerbearing raspberries as fruit first forms. Spray in early morning of a clear day so foliage will dry fast. If your summerbearing raspberries have had gray mold problems in the past, repeat the spray every few days through harvest whenever the weather is humid or wet.

Remove damaged and dropped fruits. Clean up dropped berries, and pick moldy, damaged, or overripe berries from summerbearing raspberries. Destroy the collected berries.

Watch for virus symptoms. Yellow patterns on leaves or small, crumbly berries could be symptoms of viral diseases. Orange blisters on black and purple raspberries is rust disease. Dig up and destroy all such plants immediately.

Watch for wilted canes. Cane dieback may be caused by borers or cane diseases. Look for small entry holes near base of wilted area. Prune off and destroy infested canes or cane tips. If you can't find an insect entry hole on discolored canes, the problem is probably disease. Cut these canes off at the base and destroy them.

Cut out spent canes. Once you harvest the last berries from summerbearing raspberries, cut the canes that bore fruit off flush with the ground.

Late Summer/Fall

Leaves falling

Hang white sticky traps. If tarnished plant bugs were a problem last year, hang one trap every 10 feet in fallbearing raspberries when flower bud clusters appear. If you catch more than one bud per trap, spray plants with sabadilla when the flower buds appear.

Spray compost tea. As fallbearing raspberries form fruit, spray compost tea to help prevent gray mold. Spray in early morning of a clear day so foliage will dry fast. If your plants have had gray mold problems in the past, repeat the spray every few days through harvest whenever the weather is humid or wet.

Remove damaged and dropped fruits. Clean up dropped berries, and pick moldy, damaged, or overripe berries from fallbearing raspberries. Destroy the collected berries.

Watch for virus symptoms. If the berries from your fallbearing raspberries are small, crumbly, and fall apart when you pick them, they may have a viral disease called crumbly berry. Dig up and destroy infected plants.

Prune. For fallbearing raspberries, cut all canes off at ground level once all the leaves have fallen.

Renew mulch. For summerbearing raspberries, renew the mulch after all the leaves have fallen. For fallbearing raspberries, renew mulch after pruning. Add new mulch on top of the old to make a 6- to 8-inch layer.

Solving Raspberry Problems

Use this table to identify problems on your raspberries. Scan the list of symptoms to find the description that most closely matches what you see in your garden. Then refer across the page to learn the cause and the recommended solutions. For some pest problems, by the time you see the damage, there is little you can do to fix things in the current season. In the future, take preventive steps, such as spraying lime-sulfur to prevent or reduce severity of certain diseases. For a schedule of preventive measures for raspberries, see "Season-by-Season Care: Raspberry" on page 288. You'll also find illustrations, descriptions, and additional controls for many of the insects and diseases listed below in Part 5 of this book.

FRUIT PROBLEMS

SYMPTOMS	CAUSES	SOLUTIONS
Soft, watery berries, with fuzzy gray mold	Gray mold (Botrytis)	Pick and destroy all infected fruit. Pick ripe fruit daily. Thin canes and prune foliage to increase air circulation.
White or grayish powdery patches or coating on berries	Powdery mildew	At first sign of disease, apply sulfur; reapply every 10–14 days. Remove and destroy all infected fruit, shoots, and leaves. Thin canes and prune foliage to increase air circulation.
Small, dry, and flavorless berries	Drought Verticillium wilt	If conditions have been dry, water deeply and mulch any unmulched plants. If new fruit does not improve, the cause may be Verticillium wilt. There is no cure; dig and destroy infected plants. Replant in another site, using resistant cultivars where available.
Small, crumbly berries	Crumbly berry virus	This disease occurs only on red raspberries. There is no cure; dig and destroy infected plants. Replant in a new site with certified virus-free stock.
Small, white larvae feeding inside berries	Raspberry fruit-worms	Collect and destroy infested fruit and fruit that drops early. Plan to spray pyrethrins or rotenone before bloom next year to prevent problems.

LEAF, SHOOT, AND CANE PROBLEMS

SYMPTOMS	CAUSES	SOLUTIONS
Dark spots on leaves; leaves drop early	Raspberry leaf spot	Thin canes and prune foliage to promote air circulation.
Yellow flecks on leaves; leaf edges curl; fine webbing on leaf undersides	Spider mites	Native predators usually keep mites in check. For minor infestations, spray water or insecticidal soap. For severe infestations, release purchased predatory mites, *Metaseiulus occidentalis.*
Bright orange dots or powdery coating on leaf undersides	Orange rust	This disease spreads from wild bramble plants. Red raspberries are not susceptible. There is no cure; dig and destroy infected plants. Replant in a new site at least 600' away from wild brambles.

SYMPTOMS	CAUSES	SOLUTIONS
Leaves skeletonized; green larvae on undersides of leaves	Raspberry sawflies	Sawflies rarely cause significant damage to vigorous canes. If damage is severe, spray pyrethrins or neem.
Leaves skeletonized; bronze beetles on plants	Japanese beetles	In early morning, knock beetles from canes into a bucket of soapy water and destroy. For a heavy infestation, spray frequently with pyrethrins or rotenone.
Gray spots with purplish margins on leaves and shoots	Anthracnose	Remove infected canes at ground level. Thin canes and prune foliage to promote air circulation. Dig and destroy severely infected plants; replant with resistant cultivars.
White or grayish powdery patches on leaves and shoots	Powdery mildew	At first sign of disease, apply sulfur; reapply every 10–14 days (do not apply when temperatures exceed 80°F). Remove and destroy all infected fruit, shoots, and leaves. Thin canes and prune foliage to increase air circulation.
Leaves wilt and turn yellow, starting at base of cane; canes die back	Verticillium wilt	This fungal disease is incurable; dig and destroy affected plants. Replant at a new site, using resistant cultivars where available.
Discolored areas at leaf bases; blotches on new canes; shoots may die back	Spur blight	Remove infected canes at ground level. Thin canes and prune foliage to promote air circulation. Dig and destroy severely infected stand; replant using resistant cultivars.
Large purplish or brown cankers on canes; side-shoots wilt	Cane blight	Black raspberries are most affected. Remove infected canes at ground level. Thin canes and prune foliage to promote air circulation.
Tips of new shoots die back; white grubs inside base of canes	Cane borers	Prune out and destroy infected canes at first sign of injury.
Canes are weak and break off easily; some canes stunted or dying	Raspberry crown borers	Larvae girdle and tunnel into the base of canes and main roots, especially on stressed plants. In late fall, dig and destroy severely infested crowns.

WHOLE PLANT PROBLEM

SYMPTOMS	CAUSES	SOLUTIONS
Tumors or galls on canes, crown, and roots	Crown gall	Prune out and destroy infected canes, disinfecting tools between cuts. Dig and destroy severely infected plants. Replant at a new site using resistant cultivars; dip crowns in Galltrol before planting.

STRAWBERRY *Fragaria × ananassa* • Rosaceae

Choosing Plants

Strawberries bear their first crop in as little as three months after planting. They will grow anywhere from Zones 3 through 10. There are two types of garden strawberries to choose from.

Junebearing strawberries. Junebearing strawberries ripen a single crop over a week to ten days in late spring. Junebearers are a great choice for preserving because you get lots of fruit all at once. Plant early-, mid-, and late-season cultivars to spread out your harvest. These plants take their cue to flower from daylength, so be sure to choose cultivars suited to your region's latitude.

Everbearing strawberries. Everbearing strawberries bear two crops each season, one in spring and a second, smaller one in fall. 'Quinalt' is one of the better standard cultivars.

Day-neutral cultivars, such as 'Tribute' and 'Tristar', are a big improvement over standard everbearing cultivars. They bear great-tasting, full-size fruit throughout the growing season. They have one disadvantage: they will bear themselves to death if you ignore their needs. If you can pick and de-runner them every few days and apply water consistently, day-neutrals are a strawberry lover's dream-come-true.

Whatever type of strawberry you grow, look for one-year-old plants with lots of light-colored roots and single crowns. When selecting cultivars, remember to consider disease resistance. (See "Problem-Resistant Strawberries" on this page for some choices.) Strawberries also are subject to viral diseases, so purchase certified disease-free plants from a nursery rather than accepting plants from friends.

Pollination

Almost all strawberry cultivars are self-fruitful, so

PROBLEM-RESISTANT STRAWBERRIES

Plan for problem-free berries by choosing cultivars that resist problems that are common in your area. Choose from the list below or check with your supplier for new resistant releases. All the cultivars listed are Junebearers unless otherwise indicated. In the list below, GM = gray mold, LS = leaf spot and leaf scorch, PM = powdery mildew, RS = red stele, TPB = tarnished plant bug, and V = Verticillium wilt.

CULTIVAR (RESISTANCE)	BEARING TIME
'Catskill' (V)	Mid-season
'Darrow' (RS, V)	Early-season
'Delite' (RS, V)	Late-season
'Earliglow' (GM, LS, RS, V)	Early-season
'Empire' (V)	Early-season
'Fletcher' (LS, V)	Late-season
'Guardian' (LS, RS, V)	Mid-season
'Honeoye' (TPB)	Mid-season
'Lateglow' (RS, V)	Late-season
'Midway' (RS)	Mid-season
'Redchief' (LS, PM, RS)	Mid-season
'Robinson' (V)	Mid-season
'Sparkle' (RS, TPB)	Mid-season
'Sunrise' (RS, V)	Early-season
'Surecrop' (LS, PM, RS, V)	Mid-season
'Tribute' (LS, PM, RS, V)	Day-neutral (everbearing)
'Tristar' (LS, PM, RS, V)	Day-neutral (everbearing)

ALPINE STRAWBERRIES

Alpine strawberries are a type of wild wood strawberry (*Fragaria vesca*). The runnerless plants bear tiny but highly flavored fruit from spring through fall. They are easy to grow from seed. Set plants just 1 foot apart in sun or even partial shade and care for them like their larger garden cousins. Be sure to try the pale yellow pineapple-flavored variant, 'Pineapple Crush'.

you can plant one cultivar and harvest a full crop. Your supplier will tell you if a cultivar you've chosen needs a pollinator.

Yield

You can expect to harvest about 1 quart of berries per plant per year starting in midsummer (everbearers) or the spring after planting (Junebearers).

Site and Soil

You can succeed with strawberries in Zones 3 through 10 if you select cultivars to match your climate.

Choose a site with:
• Full sun.
• Fertile soil with lots of organic matter.
• pH between 5.5 and 6.5.

Avoid:
• Low spots where frost tends to settle.
• Areas where water puddles in spring or after a rain.
• Sites where lawn, strawberries, raspberries, potatoes, or tomatoes grew previously.

Preparing to Plant

Start preparing the soil a full year before you plan to plant strawberries. Have the soil tested and adjust the pH if necessary. Dig out *every* perennial weed. Plant a buckwheat cover crop over the entire planting area. If you live in an area with sunny, hot summers, solarize the soil during midsummer to help prevent potential weed and disease problems. Replant buckwheat after solarizing. In fall, plant a winter cover crop, such as hairy vetch or winter rye. See "Planting Cover Crops" on page 28 for more details on choosing and managing cover crops and "Solarizing Soil" on page 338 for solarization instructions.

Mow or till your cover crop a few weeks before planting time. Then shape the soil into 6-inch-high, 3-foot-wide raised beds. This is especially important if water puddles on the site in the spring or after a rain, because strawberries are more prone to disease problems when grown in poorly drained soil.

Planting

In Zones 3 through 6, plant strawberries in early spring, as soon as you can work the soil. In Zones 7 through 10, plant strawberries in either late winter or mid-fall.

Growing Systems

You will harvest more good-size berries and have fewer disease problems if you manage your strawberries' growth. Left unmanaged, they can grow so thickly that they'll choke themselves out. Here are two systems that will keep your strawberries productive.

Hill system. In this system, you'll plant crowns fairly close together in double rows down a raised bed. This system is good for strawberries that don't produce large numbers of runners (day-neutrals and standard everbearers), because you must remove all runners that form.

You can use straw mulch or black plastic mulch when planting strawberries in hills. If you use black plastic, spread it tightly over the bed two to four weeks before planting. At planting time, cut 6-inch crosses through the plastic at each spot where you want to set a plant.

Set everbearers 1 foot apart in a double row (1 foot between rows) centered in the raised bed. Plant day-neutrals

Planting the hill system. *Set plants relatively close together in a double row, staggering the plants in the row.*

closer: 8 inches apart in a double row 8 inches apart. Stagger the plants in the rows to give each plant more room.

Matted row system. In this system, you'll plant crowns far apart in single rows and allow runners to fill in the space between crowns. This system is good for strawberries that produce lots of runners (Junebearers and vigorous standard everbearers); it also requires less work than the hill system.

Set plants 18 inches apart in a single row running down the center of a raised bed. If you're planting in a conventional plot, leave 4 feet between rows. Straw or other organic mulch is the best choice for this system.

Setting Plants

Strawberries are usually sold as bundles of bareroot plants. If you cannot plant immediately, moisten the roots, put the plants in a plastic bag, and refrigerate them.

Follow these steps when you are ready to plant.

1. Use scissors to cut all the roots back to 4 inches from the base of the crown.
2. Soak the roots in compost tea for 15 to 20 minutes, then dust roots with a mixture of 2 cups of kelp meal plus 1 cup of bonemeal.
3. Dig a 6-inch-deep, 6-inch-diameter hole for each plant. Build a 5-inch-high cone of soil and compost in the center of the hole.
4. Drape the plant's roots over the cone and fill the hole in with soil. Take special care to set each plant so that its crown is just half covered with soil.
5. Tuck 2 to 4 inches of straw or pine needles around each plant (unless you've put down black plastic already). Then give each plant a pint of compost tea to settle the soil and get growth off to a good start.

Seasonal Care

You will harvest more berries and have fewer problems if you feed and care for your plants regularly. See "Season-by-Season Care: Strawberry" on page 296 for directions for caring for your strawberry plants throughout the year. If you have problems with your berries, refer to "Solving Strawberry Problems" on page 297 to

Planting a matted row. *Set plants relatively far apart in single rows. Runners will take root and fill in the row.*

identify the causes and find solutions.

Training Plants

Follow the instructions below to ensure years of generous harvests.

Newly planted strawberries. Remove all flowers once a week for three months after planting so the plants can grow sturdy roots.

Hill system. Remove all runners every few weeks during the growing season.

Matted row system. Allow the plants to produce runners in the space between crowns and to spread within an 18-inch-wide band along the length of the row. Remove runners outside the 18-inch-wide area every few weeks during the growing season.

Harvesting

Pick strawberries when the fruits are red and taste good; they won't ripen further off the plant. Leave the green caps attached to the berries unless you plan to use them immediately.

Storing

Strawberries will last a few days in your refrigerator. You can store strawberries for up to a week in a spare refrigerator set at 31° to 32°F (colder than usual refrigerator temperature).

RENOVATING BEDS

Renovating strawberry beds after harvest will lengthen their productive life. When you renovate, you remove old leaves that harbor pests and disease organisms, clear out perennial weeds that compete for water and nutrients, and fertilize the bed.

1. After the last berries are picked, use hand clippers or your lawn mower set to 1½ to 2 inches and mow off the leaves and stems. (Be sure the blade is high enough so you are not cutting into the crowns.) Use the bagger of your mower to collect the leaves or rake them up and remove them.

Strawberry crowns

Weeds

2. After mowing, dig up any strawberry plants outside the designated row. Remove every single weed; be sure to dig out roots of perennial weeds. In matted rows, thin out some of the smaller plants so that the remaining plants are at least 6 inches apart each way.

3. When all the weeds and extra strawberry plants have been removed, spread a 1-inch layer of compost over the entire bed. (Use part soil or all soil if you're short on compost.) Then water the bed with diluted fish fertilizer and apply straw mulch.

Compost

SEASON-BY-SEASON CARE: STRAWBERRY

This care guide tells you what to do and when to do it for your best strawberry harvest ever. Because timing of certain tasks is critical, review the instructions in this guide in late winter. Locate or buy the products you'll need in advance. To identify specific problems, refer to "Solving Strawberry Problems" on the opposite page. "Preventing Disease Problems" on page 210 explains how to mix and apply sprays.

Late Winter

Remove mulch. When pale new leaves begin to grow, pull the mulch back off the crowns to give them light. Tuck the mulch around the plants to keep the soil moist and the berries clean during the growing season.

Early Spring

Spray kelp. Spray plants with a mixture of compost tea and kelp (2 teaspoons of kelp per gallon of tea) when you first see the flower buds; repeat every week until the flowers open.

Cover plants with floating row cover. If tarnished plant bugs were a problem last year, cover beds when new growth starts. Leave the cover on until the first flower buds show white. Tarnished plant bugs overwinter in garden refuse, so clean out all dead plant debris in your beds before you apply the cover.

Spray sabadilla. If you've had severe problems with tarnished plant bugs in the past, you can spray sabadilla during bloom to control the bugs. However, sabadilla also kills honeybees and other pollinators, so be sure to spray in late evening after honeybees have returned to their hives.

Remove flowers from newly planted plants. Pinch off flower stems every week for three months after planting.

Late Spring

Remove runners from hills. Pinch off runners every few weeks all season if you are using the hill system.

Spray sulfur. If you've had problems with gray mold in the past, and if humidity is high or weather is wet, spray when buds show white. Reapply every week or so and after rains.

Spray compost tea. If weather is dry, or if your plants haven't suffered previous problems with gray mold, spray compost tea instead of spraying sulfur.

Cover beds with netting. Cover bed completely with netting before berries start to ripen to keep out birds. Support netting away from fruit with metal hoops or other frame for best results.

Control slugs. Handpick slugs at night and trap them in shallow saucers of beer, or install copper flashing around your strawberry bed.

Pick off rotting berries. Don't leave rotting berries in the garden; put them into a separate container for disposal.

Summer

Renovate Junebearers. Renovate the bed after harvest to maintain productivity. See "Renovating Beds" on page 295 for instructions.

Fall

Renovate day-neutrals and everbearers. Once these plants stop producing new berries, renovate the bed to maintain its long-term productivity. See "Renovating Beds" on page 295 for complete instructions.

Apply mulch. In late fall, after you have had a few freezes, cover your plants with 4 to 6 inches of straw or other weed-free organic mulch. In areas with mild, wet winters, use floating row cover instead of organic mulch.

Solving Strawberry Problems

Use this table to identify problems on your strawberry plants. Scan the list of symptoms to find the description that most closely matches what you see in your garden. Then refer across the page to learn the cause and the recommended solutions. For some pest problems, by the time you see the damage, there is little you can do to fix things in the current season. In the future, take preventive steps, such as spraying sulfur to prevent certain diseases. For a schedule of preventive measures for strawberries, see "Season-by-Season Care: Strawberry" on the opposite page. You'll also find illustrations, descriptions, and additional controls for many of the insects and diseases listed below in Part 5 of this book.

FLOWER AND FRUIT PROBLEMS

SYMPTOMS	CAUSES	SOLUTIONS
Rotting blossoms; berries with soft watery spots or fuzzy gray mold	Gray mold (Botrytis)	Infections are worse in wet weather. Pick ripe fruit daily. Thin plants to improve air circulation. If gray mold keeps ruining crops each year, replant with more resistant cultivars on a sunny site with good air circulation.
Misshapen or distorted (cat-faced) berries	Poor pollination Tarnished plant bugs	Frost or cool, wet weather during bloom can interfere with pollination, resulting in distorted berries. Though odd-looking, berries will taste fine. If late-spring frosts threaten, cover beds with a tarp or blanket. Tarnished plant bugs rarely cause serious damage in home gardens, and damaged berries are still edible. To avoid problems with these insects, keep beds weeded and renovate beds after harvest ends.

LEAF PROBLEMS

SYMPTOMS	CAUSES	SOLUTIONS
Leaves have purple spots with tan centers or tan margins	Leaf spot Leaf blight	Several similar leaf spot and blight diseases occur in strawberries. Berries may also develop spots. Keep problems in check by thinning plants and by renovating beds after harvest ends. For severe infections, spray copper every 10–14 days if weather is wet.
White, powdery patches on leaves; undersides of leaves reddish	Powdery mildew	At first sign of disease, spray lime-sulfur or sulfur every 1–2 weeks (but not if temperatures are over 80°F). Keep beds weeded and plants thinned to promote air circulation. Renovate beds after harvest ends.
Youngest leaves crinkled or puckered; leaves later appear bronzed	Cyclamen mites	Remove and destroy affected plants as soon as damage is noticed. Replant every year with clean plants. For serious, repeated infestations, experiment with releases of purchased predatory mites, *Amblyseius cucumeris.*
Sticky coating on leaves; pale green or yellowish insects on leaf undersides	Strawberry aphids	Aphids cause little direct damage; however, they can spread viral diseases in some areas. Wash aphids from plants with a strong spray of water. In areas where viruses are a concern, spray pyrethrins or neem.

(continued)

Solving Strawberry Problems—Continued

LEAF PROBLEMS—CONTINUED

SYMPTOMS	CAUSES	SOLUTIONS
Silken webbing around leaves; small caterpillars in webbing	Leafrollers	Handpick rolled leaves containing caterpillars and destroy. Leafrollers rarely cause much damage. If you have a severe leafroller problem, spray neem. Renovate beds after harvest ends.
Masses of white foam on leaves and stems	Spittlebugs	In spring, these larvae of leafhoppers feed inside a protective mass of bubbles. Wash them off plants with water. Spittlebugs rarely cause significant damage.
Yellow stippling and brown edges on leaves; fine webbing on leaf undersides	Spider mites	For light infestations, rinse plants with water. For heavy infestations, spray insecticidal soap or release purchased predatory mites, *Metaseiulus occidentalis*.
Small half-circles clipped from edges of leaves	Root weevils	Spray pyrethrins or rotenone when you see fresh notches to control adult weevils (do not spray during bloom period). Drench soil with parasitic nematodes in spring and late summer to control larvae feeding in the roots.

WHOLE PLANT PROBLEMS

SYMPTOMS	CAUSES	SOLUTIONS
Stunted, wilted plants; roots black and water-soaked	Black root rot	There is no cure for this fungal disease. Dig and destroy plants. Replant in another site, with well-drained, fertile soil and good sun exposure.
Stunted, wilted plants, with a reddish color in spring; roots with few sideshoots	Red stele disease	Roots will appear red inside in early spring. This disease persists in the soil. Dig and destroy plants. Replant in another site, with well-drained soil in full sun, using certified disease-free plants and resistant cultivars.
Stunted, wilted plants; no obvious root damage	Verticillium wilt	There is no cure for this fungal disease; dig and destroy plants. Replant in another site with resistant cultivars, but not in soil used to grow other Verticillium-susceptible plants (peppers, potatoes, tomatoes).
Plants wilt and collapse; fat white grubs in hollowed-out crown	Strawberry crown moths Crown borers	Dig infested plants and destroy. Replanting in a new site at least 300' away will help if crown borers are the problem, because adults are weevils that do not fly. Maintain vigorous plants.
Plants stunted and wilted; white grubs with brown heads in crown and roots	Root weevils	Drench soil with parasitic nematodes in spring and in August to control larvae in the root zone, where they cause the most damage. Spray pyrethrins or rotenone if you see fresh notches in leaves to control adult weevils (do not spray during bloom period).

UNUSUAL FRUITS

If you'd like to try something exotic in your garden, unusual fruits are a great conversation piece—and they taste terrific too! You'll be surprised at the range of lesser-known berries and tree fruits that will grow in temperate regions. If your curiosity about unusual fruits increases, there are dozens offered in specialty fruit catalogs. (You'll find the names of several in "Sources" on page 358.) Here are 15 interesting fruits that you may want to try in your home garden.

NAME / PLANT TYPE / HARDINESS	PLANTING AND CARE	HARVESTING
Cranberry, bog; Thanksgiving cranberry *Vaccinium macrocarpon* Creeping evergreen plant. Zones 2 through 7.	Bog cranberries need wet feet, acid soil, and full sun. Set plants 3'–4' apart. Plant at least 2 for pollination. They require no pruning.	Expect your first harvest after a year or two. Tart, red fruits are ready to harvest in early fall when they are dark red.
Cranberry, highbush *Viburnum trilobum* Shrub, to 10'. Zones 2 through 9.	Plant in full sun or part shade in well-drained or slightly moist soil. Space plants 3'–5' apart in a hedge, further apart for individual plants. Each winter, prune wood that is more than 3 years old.	Bushes often fruit the year after planting. Clusters of tart, red fruit will hang decoratively from late summer almost through winter. Pick as you need them. Each fruit has a seed that must be strained out after cooking.
Currant *Ribes* spp. Shrubs, to 4'. Zones 3 through 7.	Plant in full sun or part shade. They will grow in poor soil but pH should be close to 6.5. Space bushes 6' apart or 3' apart in a hedge. Each winter, cut off any shoots older than 3 years and thin to leave 6 shoots.	Expect your first crop of tangy, translucent fruit the second season after planting. Hold thorny branches up with one gloved hand and clip off fully colored clusters with your other hand. Serve fresh with sugar or use for preserves.
Elderberry *Sambucus canadensis* Shrub, to 10'. Zones 2 through 9.	Elderberry tolerates a wide range of soils in full sun or part shade. Plants are partially self-fruitful but yield better crops if another elderberry (a seedling or a different cultivar) is growing nearby. Prune each winter, thinning out spindly suckers and removing all wood older than 3 years.	Expect your first harvest the year after planting. To harvest, cut whole clusters off when fruits are dark blue or purplish black and soft to the touch. Clusters of white flowers are also edible.
Fig *Ficus carica* Tree or large shrub. Zones 6 through 10.	Figs need full sun, good drainage, and soil with a pH of 5.5–8.0. North of Zone 7, select a protected, south-facing site and provide winter protection. Space trees 5'–25' apart, depending on cultivar and region (plants grow larger in the South).	Plants usually produce fruit after the first year. Check trees daily in season and pick fruit that's soft and almost fully colored. Ripen at room temperature for a day or two. Ripe fruit will last 1 week in the refrigerator.

(continued)

Unusual Fruits—Continued

NAME / PLANT TYPE / HARDINESS	PLANTING AND CARE	HARVESTING
Gooseberry *Ribes* spp. Shrubs, to 4'. Zones 3 through 7.	Plant in full sun or part shade. They will grow in poor soil but pH must be close to 6.5. Space bushes 6' apart. Each winter, cut off any shoots that are more than 3 years old and thin to leave 6 shoots per plant.	Expect your first crop of tangy fruit the second season after planting. Hold thorny branches up with one hand (be sure to wear a glove) and pluck soft, fully colored berries with your other hand. Gooseberries make great jam.
Jostaberry *Ribes nidigrolaria* Shrub, to 6'. Zones 3 through 7.	Plant in full sun or part shade. They will grow in poor soil but pH must be close to 6.5. Space bushes 8' apart. Each winter, cut off any shoots that are more than 3 years old and thin to leave 6 shoots per plant.	Expect your first crop of these black currant–gooseberry hybrids the second season after planting. Hold thorny branches up with one gloved hand and pluck soft, fully colored berries with your other hand. Jostaberries taste like mellow black currants.
Jujube *Ziziphus jujuba* Tree, to 30'. Zones 5 through 10.	Jujubes need full sun but aren't picky about soil. Plant 2 trees to increase fruit set. Prune lightly in winter.	Expect your first crop after 2–3 years. Shiny, cherry- to plum-size fruits have mahogany skin and crisp, white flesh similar to apple flesh.
Juneberry; Serviceberry *Amelanchier* spp. Shrubs or small trees. Zones 3 through 8.	Juneberries grow in most soils and full sun to part shade. Prune lightly to shape or thin bushes each winter.	Expect your first harvest 2–3 years from planting. Clusters of pink to purple fruits look and taste somewhat like blueberries, with almond overtones.
Kiwi *Actinidia* spp. Deciduous vines. Fuzzy kiwi (*A. chinensis*) grows in Zones 7 through 9. Hardy kiwi (*A. arguta* and *A. kolomikta*) grows in Zones 3 through 9.	Kiwis need full sun and well-drained soil with a pH of 5.0–6.5. Plant a male and a female, unless the cultivar you choose is self-fertile. Provide 200 sq. ft. of trellis per vine. Pinch back the vine when it reaches the trellis and encourage 2 to 4 side branches to grow. Pinch tips off when they get to the trellis edges. Throughout summer, when sideshoots reach 8" in length, pinch them back to 4". In winter, remove any side branches older than 3 years.	Expect your first fruit after 2–6 years. Fuzzy kiwis have fuzzy, egg-size, green-fleshed fruits. Hardy kiwis produce smooth, grape-size, green- or red-fleshed fruits. Pick fruits slightly firm (but after seeds turn black); they will keep in the refrigerator for months. You can also let fruits ripen fully on the vine for fresh eating. Ripen stored fruits at room temperature for a few days before eating. Peel fuzzy kiwis before eating; eat hardy kiwis with the skin on.

NAME / PLANT TYPE / HARDINESS	PLANTING AND CARE	HARVESTING
Lingonberry *Vaccinium vitis-idaea* and *V. vitis-idaea* var. *minus* Small evergreen shrubs. Zones 2 through 7.	Lingonberries need part shade (full sun in northern areas) and well-drained soil with a pH below 5.8. Space plants 2' apart.	Expect your first harvest after 2 years. Use tangy red berries as you would cranberries.
Mulberry *Morus* spp. Trees. Zones 5 through 9.	Plant in full sun, spacing 20'-30' apart. Avoid planting over walks or patios because the fruits drop and stain. Check with your supplier about winter hardiness and possible pollination needs.	Expect your first harvest after 2-4 years. Soft fruits are blackberry-like and may be black, purple, red, or white. Harvest fruits in quantity by shaking them off branches onto a clean cloth spread on the ground. Harvest fully ripe for fresh eating; harvest slightly underripe for jams and pies.
Pawpaw; Michigan banana *Asimina triloba* Tree. Zones 5 through 8.	Plant trees 15' apart in full sun to part shade and well-drained soil with a pH of 5.0-7.0. Mulch thickly with leaves or straw to keep roots cool and moist and to cushion falling fruit. Prune lightly to keep tree in bounds and to stimulate fruiting on old trees.	Seedlings bear in about 6 years; grafted plants in 2-3 years. Pick banana-pineapple-mango-flavored fruits fully ripe or just as they begin to soften to finish ripening indoors. Either way, fruit is ready to eat when greenish yellow skin turns brown or black. Tree-ripened fruits have a stronger flavor than those ripened off the tree.
Persimmon *Diospyros* spp. Trees. Asian persimmon (*D. kaki*) is hardy to Zone 7; American persimmon (*D. virginiana*) is hardy to Zone 5.	Plant grafted trees 15'-30' apart in full sun and well-drained soil. Most cultivars of Asian persimmons and a few cultivars of American persimmons bear fruit without pollination. Prune Asian persimmons as you would apple or peach trees; American persimmons need little pruning.	Grafted trees often bear some fruit the year after planting. Harvest Asian persimmons by clipping fruit from the tree. Pick astringent cultivars when they are very soft and their skins are almost translucent. Pick fruits of nonastringent cultivars while they are fully colored yet firm. Pick American persimmons when fruit is very soft or falls to the ground.
Pomegranate *Punica granatum* Semi-deciduous shrub or tree. Zones 8 through 10.	Plant trees in a hot, sunny site with well-drained soil. Space plants 15' apart or 6' apart in a hedge or with dwarf cultivars. Prune lightly to remove dead wood and shape the plant.	Expect your first harvest in 3-4 years. Cut round, jewel-like fruits off plant as soon as they turn fully red. Slightly underripe fruits will store for many months if kept cool and dry.

GROWING HERBS

DECIDING WHAT TO GROW

Beautiful, versatile herbs fit well into any kind of garden. Most are easy to grow, and they come in a surprising variety of colors, shapes, sizes, and flavors. The hardest part of herb gardening can be deciding which herbs you absolutely must grow. One good place to start is to select herbs for their uses.

Herbs for Cooking

If you're just starting with herbs, or if your garden space is limited, you'll probably want to stick with basic culinary herbs. Homegrown herbs straight from the garden offer the freshest of flavors—something you just can't get from store-bought herbs. It's also easy to dry herbs at home; their savory flavors will remain to add a taste of summer to midwinter meals.

Some of the most dependable culinary herbs include basil, garlic, oregano, parsley, sage, and thyme. Other popular choices include chives, dill, mint, rosemary, and tarragon. You'll learn more about growing these and other culinary herbs in "Favorite Herbs," beginning on page 322.

Herbs for Home Remedies

Herbs are also a traditional ingredient in many home remedies. Grow herbs like chamomile and mint to brew teas that help relieve stress. Add slices of fresh gingerroot, or fresh fennel seeds, to the tea to calm an upset stomach. Or substitute horehound or hyssop leaves, and add a little honey, to soothe sore throats.

If you decide to grow and use herbs for medicinal purposes, keep these important safety tips in mind.

- Make sure each plant is correctly identified before you use it for medicine.

Herbs for the kitchen. *Culinary herbs, such as sage, rosemary, and thyme, add fabulous flavor to home-prepared meals. Use them fresh or tie bunches to air dry.*

- Limit daily use to 3 tablespoons of dried or 9 tablespoons of fresh herbs.
- Don't mix herbal remedies with medical prescriptions.

See "Recommended Reading" on page 362 for books that offer more information on preparing and using herbal medicines safely.

HINTS FOR HERBAL COOKING

Fresh and dried homegrown herbs are interchangeable in most recipes. When substituting fresh herbs for dried, use two to three times more fresh. To release the flavor of dried herbs, crush the foliage between your hands before adding it to recipes.

Most herbs don't require cooking; you can add them just before serving. Or, for the freshest flavor, simply add a pinch of herbs to each plate at serving time.

Herbs for Crafts

Making craft projects with herbs is a creative and delightful way to bring your garden indoors. You can work with fresh and dried herbs to make wreaths, potpourris, and fragrant oils. The uses are really only limited by your imagination!

Many common herbs are great for craft projects. Instead of a ribbon bow, for instance, add small bunches of dried leafy herbs like thyme or sage to wreaths or gift wrapping. Braid fresh garlic heads together with bunches of herbs, then hang them to dry in the kitchen; later, use scissors to cut away the bulbs or dried herbs as needed.

Create a personalized potpourri by mixing together your favorite dried herbs, flowers, and spices. Mint,

Dual-purpose herbs. *Versatile herbs like mint and sage are tasty in tea and pretty in potpourri.*

rosemary, sage, and thyme are just a few of the herbs that hold their fragrance well when dried.

Selecting Herbs

Once you know what you want your herbs for, it's time to choose specific kinds.

First, look for species that are adapted to the conditions your garden has to offer. Most thrive in average, well-drained garden soil with full sun. Mint is one exception—it grows best in moist soil and can tolerate a few hours of shade each day. Parsley can also take some shade.

Experiment with different cultivars of herbs to find out which ones grow best in your climate. For example, regular rosemary usually only survives winter in Zone 8 and warmer, but the cultivar 'Arp' may overwinter in areas as cold as Zone 6. Common garden sage is hardy in most northern gardens, but 'Tricolor' sage needs winter protection in cold climates.

Cultivars can also vary in leaf and flower type, flavor, fragrance, and growth habit. Common garden sage, for instance, normally has gray leaves. But there is also 'Purpurascens', a purple-leaved cultivar; 'Icterina', a green-and-yellow-leaved cultivar; and 'Tricolor', a particularly showy cultivar with

Herbs for arrangements. *Oregano and yarrow are two of the many herbs that blend well into fresh or dried arrangements.*

cream-, red-, and green-striped foliage.

Some herbs even have cultivars that lend themselves best to specific uses. For example, you can choose dill cultivars that produce abundant foliage (such as 'Dukat' or 'Fernleaf') for tossing with salads or cultivars like 'Bouquet' that produce lots of seeds to add to pickle recipes.

If you're new to herb growing, you'll probably find all the choices you're prepared to cope with at your local garden center. Read the seed packet or the plant label to find out the traits of each herb you're considering. As you gain experience and want a wider variety of cultivars, start investigating specialty seed and plant catalogs; a few are listed in "Sources" on page 358.

PLANNING A PRACTICAL GARDEN

Once you've decided *what* herbs you want to grow, you need to figure out *where* you're going to put them. If you just want to grow a few herbs, you may decide to tuck them into a flower bed or the vegetable garden. If you really want to get into growing and using herbs, a separate herb garden can be a fun and useful part of your yard. Either way, here are a few points to keep in mind.

Match Plants to Place

For healthy, vigorous herbs, give your plants the best possible conditions. It's true that many herbs can adapt to poor, dry soil, but that doesn't mean they thrive in it; fertile, well-prepared garden soil will encourage much better growth.

Also be sure to match each herb to the right garden conditions. For example, place mint where it will get plenty of moisture. Plant heat-loving herbs, such as basil, in full sun; they'll be weak and spindly in shade. For more on choosing the best spot to grow your herbs, see "Selecting a Site" on page 6.

Leave Room to Grow

Just like vegetables, herbs need room to spread without crowding their neighbors. For the right spacing between plants, follow the guidelines in "Favorite Herbs," beginning on page 322, or on the seed packet or transplant label. Crowding in lots of herbs won't give you better harvests; the plants won't grow as well, and you'll be left with lots of thinning and dividing to keep plants healthy.

If you're growing perennial herbs that will spread—such as mint and horseradish—plan some kind of containment system, or soon you'll have nothing but the spreaders! See the illustration on page 310 for one way to handle these exuberant herbs. Or set aside a separate area of the garden where they can spread without endangering more delicate plants.

Pick a Practical Site

While it's important to give your herbs the conditions they like, you'll also want to consider *your* needs. You'll be most likely to use your herbs if they're close to the house. If you frequently snip a few herbs for cooking, a small herb garden (or container planting) near the kitchen door will save you lots of time. A garden of herbs for crafts can double as a colorful flower bed to liven up a boring spot in your backyard.

Also plan your garden for

HERBS FOR TOUGH SPOTS

Most herbs grow best in sun and average, well-drained soil, but not all gardens can offer these ideal conditions. Here are some suggestions of herbs that can adapt to less-than-perfect sites.

Shade-tolerant herbs. Bay, bee balm, chamomile, chervil, comfrey, ginger, lemon balm, mint, and sweet woodruff are good candidates for lightly shaded gardens.

Herbs for moist spots. Angelica, borage, comfrey, ginger, horseradish, lovage, mint, sweet cicely, and violets can take plenty of moisture (although not standing water!).

Herbs for dry spots. Save these herbs for garden dry spots: aloe, anise, catnip, tarragon, and thyme.

Diagramming your herb garden. *Plan your garden layout on paper before you plant. Refer to your plan when figuring how many herbs to buy or sow. A simple garden like this one can provide fresh herbs all season long.*

easy care. Choose a site near a water supply for moisture-loving herbs like mint. And allow for paths so you can comfortably reach into all parts of the garden without stepping on the soil. Make at least one path wide enough so you can get into the center of a large garden with tools and a wheelbarrow or garden cart. Planting in raised beds helps to ensure good drainage and makes harvesting easier.

Grow a Specialty Garden

One fun thing you can do with herbs is to mix them with other plants to create special theme gardens. Here are some ideas to get you started.

Marinara garden. A planting of tomatoes, onions, basil, garlic, marjoram, oregano, Italian parsley, rosemary, and thyme will provide all the fixings for your favorite pasta sauce.

Pesto garden. Fill one garden with basil, garlic, and parsley so you'll be sure to have plenty of pesto supplies.

Fresh salad garden. Start your salad garden with cucumbers, tomatoes, chives, garlic, parsley, and thyme. Every two to three weeks throughout the season make successive sowings of arugula, lettuce, mustard greens, radicchio, basil, cilantro, dill, and fennel so you'll have a steady supply of zesty salad fixings.

Meadow herb garden. Plant tough herbs like bee balm, horseradish, mint, tansy, and yarrows in a low-maintenance area to create a meadowlike effect. These herbs won't need much care, and they'll provide plenty of material for cooking or crafts. A mixed planting like this is also a great way to attract pest-controlling beneficial insects to your yard.

Mix Herbs and Ornamentals

With their charming flowers and lovely leaves, many herbs do double duty as ornamentals. Plan on mixing some of them into foundation plantings, flower beds, and container gardens.

Count on these herbs to provide lots of attractive blossoms: bee balm, borage, chamomile, chives, dill, feverfew, anise hyssop, lavender, nasturtium, pot marigold, rue, sage, sweet cicely, and yarrow.

For great-looking foliage, try the purple-leaved cultivars of basil. Use dramatic gray and silver foliage—lamb's ears, lavender, sage, southernwood, and wormwood—as a background for colorful flowers. Look for variegated cultivars of scented geranium, mint, oregano, and thyme. For extra interest, add the feathery foliage of dill, fennel, parsley, and other members of the carrot family.

PLANTING HERBS

Get your herbs off to a good start by planting them properly. Vigorous herbs start with healthy soil, so before you plant, take a close look at your soil and improve it if necessary. See "Evaluating Your Soil" on page 8 and "Improving Your Soil" on page 12 for details.

Starting from Seeds

Growing from seed is economical but takes more time and care than buying plants. As a general rule, growing from seed is best for annuals and biennials. It's also a good choice when you want more than just a plant or two.

Herbs for direct sowing. These herbs can be sown directly in the garden: basil, borage, German chamomile, chervil, cilantro, dill, fennel, mustard, and parsley. See "Planting the Garden" on page 54 for directions on direct sowing.

Herbs for indoor sowing. For an extra-early crop, start basil, sweet marjoram, and parsley indoors. Sow a second crop outdoors when soil temperatures are warmer for a continuous supply of fresh herbs. See "Starting Seeds Indoors" on page 46 for directions on indoor sowing.

Easy perennials from seed. Catnip, chives, feverfew, and lemon balm are easy to grow from seed sown indoors or out.

Starting with Plants

Buying plants is the way to go if you want just a few plants of each herb to start. It's generally a good choice for perennial herbs. For the best success, buy the following herbs as plants: garlic (bulbs), scented geranium, horseradish (roots), lavender, lovage, mint, oregano, rosemary, sage, tarragon, and thyme. Start with one or two plants. For more on selecting herb plants, see "Green Thumb Tip" on this page.

For a selection of companies that offer a wide variety of herb seeds and plants, see "Sources" on page 358.

Planting Technique

Plant annual herbs just as you would vegetables. Since perennial herbs will grow in your garden for several years or more, take extra care to get

Unpotting herbs. *Support the stem of the herb between your fingers as you remove the plant from the pot.*

GREEN THUMB TIP

Knowledgeable herb gardeners sniff before they buy. That's because many specialty herbs—including oregano and French tarragon—don't come true from seed. Seedlings may have no fragrance whatsoever or a coarse facsimile of the best culinary aromas. Don't buy plants hoping they'll develop fragrance and flavor as they grow—they won't. Even small plants should have the full-blown, pungent aromas these herbs are grown for. To test aroma, gently rub a leaf between your fingers and take a good whiff.

Settling new plants. *Use your fingers to shape a shallow trench around the plant.*

them off to a good start. Plant perennial herbs in the spring or fall, when temperatures are cool and soil moisture is plentiful. Overcast days are best for planting, so plants have time to recover from transplant shock. Transplant in the evening so that plants will have a cool, dark period during which to adjust to life in the garden.

Preparing for planting. Give your herbs a good drink before you plant by soaking them in a shallow tub of water, weak compost tea, or liquid seaweed solution. When you're ready to plant, pinch away any dead stems, leaves, and spent blossoms, and pull and discard weed seedlings growing in the pot. Then dig a hole that's deep enough so you can set the plant at the same depth it grew previously.

Removing plants from pots. To remove a plant from its pot, hold one hand over the top of the pot with your fingers slipped around the stem. Turn the pot upside down with the other hand, and tap the bottom. Then gently squeeze out the plant while keeping the ball of soil and roots intact. Loosen roots that are tightly intertwined, and cut away bent or broken ones.

Settling plants in the soil. Center the plant in the hole, making sure it is sitting at the same depth it was in the pot: plants planted too deeply can rot; ones planted too shallowly can dry out. Then replace the soil.

Firm the soil around the stem, forming a shallow trench to hold water and direct it to the plant's roots.

Water gently and thoroughly. Mulch with an organic mulch like cocoa bean hulls to keep plant leaves clean and help retain soil moisture.

Planting in Tough Spots

Perennial herbs are ideal problem solvers in the landscape. Since many will grow well in hot, dry sites, use them as groundcovers on a hard-to-mow slope or as edgings along a fence or tough-to-trim spot. Herbs are also a good choice for filling in rocky sites. They'll serve as a permanent mulch, hold the soil, and outcompete weeds. Chamomile (German and Roman), lavender, oregano, and thyme are good choices for sites with dry soils. Try sweet woodruff in wet spots.

Planting herbs between rocks. *To plant herbs in a rock garden or other rocky site, dig a planting pocket between the rocks with a trowel. Replace some of the soil with good garden loam, settle the plant in place, and water thoroughly.*

MAINTAINING HERBS

It's hard to find plants that are easier to grow than herbs. They resist pests, are troubled by few diseases, and ask only for good light and soil in return. For information on watering and weeding, see "Watering the Garden" and "Controlling Weeds" on pages 58 and 64, respectively.

Control Invasive Herbs

Some perennial herbs, such as horseradish and mint, grow so vigorously they will engulf their better-behaved neighbors. Here are some control tactics to use.

Impermeable mulch. Mulch around invasive herbs with a 1-inch-thick layer of newspaper. Cover the newspaper with an attractive mulch like cocoa bean hulls or bark chips. Renew the mulch each season to prevent the spread of invasive herbs.

Herbal islands. Plant invasive herbs in island beds, surrounded by lawn. Weekly mowing around the bed will keep the spreaders in check.

Sunken containers. Plant invasive herbs in large containers sunk in the soil to keep roots from spreading through the entire bed.

1. Use a hammer and a nail to punch several drainage holes in the bottom of a large bucket. Five-gallon plastic buckets are ideal.
2. Dig a hole in the soil that fits the bucket, so the rim projects 3 to 4 inches above the soil surface.
3. Put the bucket in the hole and fill it with garden soil.
4. Plant the herb in the bucket, water thoroughly, then mulch.

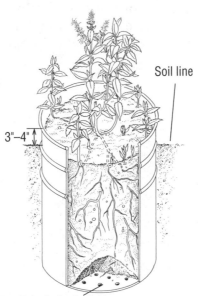

Soil line

3"–4"

Poke holes in bottom.

Plant in a bucket. *Roots can't get through the bucket walls, and the bucket rim stops creeping stems that spread along the soil surface. Trim away stems that sneak over the top.*

Prepare Perennials for Winter

Stop harvesting from perennial herbs in late summer or early fall, about three weeks before the first frost is expected. After frosts begin and plant growth slows, pull away and compost dead leaves and blossoms. Don't feed in fall; give plants a boost with compost or other amendments in spring.

After the soil freezes, mulch hardy perennials with chopped leaves or straw to protect them from heaving out of the soil during periods of freezing and thawing. Remove the mulch in spring.

Tender perennial herbs, such as bay and rosemary, need protection in most parts of the U.S. In zones where they're not hardy, grow them in containers and bring them indoors over the winter. See "Herbs in Containers" on page 318 for more on container culture. In areas where an herb is marginally hardy, try growing it on the south side of a brick or stone wall. In winter, protect marginally hardy plants with barriers, such as overturned buckets or burlap. Antitranspirants like Wilt-Pruf can lessen wind and salt damage.

RESTORING NEGLECTED HERBS

Step 1. Set aside time to clear out weeds and renew the bed. You can do this anytime the soil is workable. The best time for rejuvenating a neglected bed of perennial herbs like this one is just before or after the growing season.

Step 2. Use a garden fork to dig deep-rooted perennial weeds like bindweed, dandelion, and dock. Be sure to remove all the roots.

Step 3. Mow the bed. Set the mowing height at 3 to 5 inches above the soil to avoid damaging the crowns of perennial herbs you would like to save.

Step 4. Rake over the bed. Clear away pieces of weed roots as you find them, as well as dead leaves, stems, and old mulch from around the herbs.

Step 5. After you've cleared away the debris, add any needed soil amendments and rake them into the soil. Also spread a fresh layer of mulch like compost or cocoa bean hulls to help control weeds. Pull and discard any new sprouts of perennial weeds.

PROPAGATING HERBS

Propagating herbs is easy and fun. There's no better way to spread a favorite herb to a new part of your garden or share a beloved plant with neighbors and friends.

There are two types of propagation methods: sexual and asexual. Growing from seed is a sexual method. Seed-sown plants have characteristics from *both* parents, so they're often not identical to the plant from which you collected seed. For information on herbs that can easily be grown from seed, see "Starting from Seeds" on page 308.

Asexual, or vegetative, propagation methods use the roots, bulbs, or stems of a plant to make an exact copy of it. Cuttings, division, and layering are all asexual methods used to propagate herbs. Use an asexual method to propagate plants with special characteristics that don't come true from seed. Oregano is a good example: Seed-sown plants can be tasteless and flavorless, because they can lack the aromatic oils that give this culinary herb its flavor. Seed-sown mints may smell minty, but they cross-pollinate so readily seedlings may not have special flavors or other characteristics you're looking for. See "Propagating Common Herbs" on page 315 for a list of herbs and recommended methods.

Growing Herbs from Cuttings

Basil, scented geranium, lavender, sage, tarragon, and thyme are a few of the herbs that grow well from cuttings.

To take cuttings, use sharp garden shears or a sharp knife to cut 3- to 5-inch pieces of stem with at least two nodes. Keeping them from wilting is essential; take only as many cuttings as you can pot in a half hour. If you can't pot cuttings up immediately, roll them in a damp paper towel to keep them moist.

Fill pots or flats with sterile, moistened medium. A mixture of equal parts perlite, vermiculite, and shredded peat moss is ideal. Remove the leaves on the bottom half of the cutting, leaving only a few leaves at the top. Push the cutting into the medium. About 1 inch of the cutting, and at least one node, should be below the soil. (This is often referred to as "sticking" a cutting.) Label each pot or each row in a flat with the name of the plant and the date. Keep the medium moist and out of direct sunlight for several days.

Allow at least one month for new roots to form. Remove

Taking cuttings. *Take cuttings from annual and perennial herbs when they have new shoots and leaves, but not just before or during bloom.*

Cut between 2 nodes.

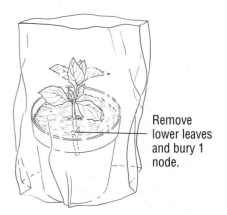

Remove lower leaves and bury 1 node.

Humidity for cuttings. *To maintain high humidity around your cutting, put the pot inside a plastic bag with the top left open for ventilation.*

STEP 1

STEP 2

STEP 3

any leaves that fall. You'll know roots have formed when new growth starts and when the plant responds to light.

You can speed the process of root formation by stimulating new root growth with commercial rooting hormone powders or your own solution made from willow stems. To make it, soak willow stem pieces in water 24 hours. Remove the stem pieces, then soak the new cuttings in the solution for 24 hours before planting.

Dividing Herbs

Use division to separate a mature clump of herbs, such as chives or oregano, into lots of smaller herb plants. It's handy for renovating overgrown plants that have died out in the middle, too.

Divide perennial herbs in either early spring or fall, when soil moisture is high and daytime temperatures remain cool. Before you start, check the soil moisture. If the soil is very wet, wait a few days to divide your plants. If it is quite dry, moisten it before you dig.

1. Use a shovel to dig around a mature clump of herbs. After you've loosened the entire plant, gently lift it from the soil. You may want to set it on a tarp so you don't cover the herbs remaining in the garden with soil.

2. Use your hands or a trowel to gently separate the clump into individual plants. If the clump you're working with is very large and hard to handle, use a shovel to slice new plants away from the parent.

Sometimes a large clump of herbs dies out in the middle or has a ring of healthy plants surrounding overcrowded ones. In these cases, discard and compost the center of the clump and make your divisions from the healthy outer edges.

3. Plant each new division in a pot or replant them in the garden. Water thoroughly after potting them up or planting. Replant a healthy section of renovated clumps after you have discarded the unhealthy center.

Division Made Easy

You don't have to dig up an entire clump to divide it. If you want only one plant from a larger clump, use a trowel or a sharp spade to slice it off one side without digging up the entire plant. This is a good way to give a piece of an herb to a visiting friend or neighbor. You can also use it to cut back a clump that has strayed too far on one side.

Count on Volunteers

One super-easy way to propagate herbs from seed is to let them self-sow. German chamomile, cilantro, dill, and fennel are a few herbs that reseed enthusiastically.

To take advantage of volunteer seedlings, don't disturb the soil in spring until the seeds have germinated. Keep track of what grew where last season, so you'll know where to look for seedlings. You might want to put these self-sowers in their own bed.

If you can't tell which seedlings are weeds and which are herbs, gently touch the seedlings and sniff. Most herb seedlings have their characteristic fragrance. Once the volunteers have germinated, wait until they have at

---

LAYERING HERBS

Layering is a quick, easy way to make lots of new, fairly large plants of herbs, such as marjoram and thyme, outdoors, right in the garden.

Spring and summer are the best seasons for layering, because plants are actively growing then and will readily form new roots.

Slip clothespin over stem.

Step 1. Pinch off leaves along the middle of a low-growing stem. Gently bend the stem to ground level.

Pin stem to soil.

Step 2. Gently poke the middle of the stem into the soil about 1 inch deep. Be sure to bury at least one node. Leave the stem tip exposed.

Cover stem with soil.

Step 3. Mound soil over the stem. Keep the soil moist and leave the plant undisturbed until roots have formed. To check for roots, tug gently at the stem tip.

Separate rooted stem.

Step 4. When the layered plant has rooted, sever its connection to the parent plant. Then dig it and pot it up or move it to a new spot in the garden.

PROPAGATING COMMON HERBS

Basil. Sow seed directly in the garden or move transplants outdoors after all danger of frost is past. Or propagate by cuttings.

Bee balm. Divide plants in spring or grow from cuttings.

Calendula. Sow seed indoors in spring. Move plants outdoors as early as the soil can be worked. In the South, sow outdoors in fall.

Caraway. Sow seed outdoors in spring or fall. Reseeds readily.

Catnip. Sow seed outdoors in spring or propagate by division or cuttings. Reseeds readily.

Chamomile, German. Sow seed outdoors in early spring. Reseeds readily.

Chamomile, Roman. Propagate by division, layering, or cuttings. Reseeds readily.

Chervil. Sow seed outdoors in early spring or fall. Transplants poorly. Reseeds readily.

Chives. Sow seed indoors in late winter; transplant in early spring. Or propagate by division.

Cilantro (Coriander). Sow seed outdoors in spring. Reseeds readily.

Dill. Sow seed outdoors in spring. Transplants poorly. Reseeds readily.

Fennel. Sow seed outdoors in spring or fall. Transplants poorly. Reseeds readily.

Garlic. Plant individual cloves from bulbs in fall for harvest the following summer. Or sow bulbils from flower heads or seed.

Geranium, scented. Propagate by cuttings.

Horseradish. Propagate by division.

Lavender. Propagate by cuttings or layering.

Lemon balm. Propagate by cuttings, layering, or division. Or sow seed outdoors in spring. Reseeds readily.

Lovage. Propagate by division in spring or seed sown outdoors in late summer or fall.

Marjoram, sweet. Sow seed indoors in spring and transplant outdoors after all danger of frost has past. Divide plants in fall or layer them in summer and bring indoors to overwinter.

Mint. Propagate by division, layering, or cuttings.

Oregano. Propagate by division, layering, or cuttings.

Parsley. Sow seed or move transplants to garden when soil temperatures reach 50°F.

Rosemary. Propagate by layering or cuttings.

Sage. Propagate by division, layering, or cuttings. Or sow seed outdoors in late spring or indoors in winter.

Santolina. Propagate by cuttings, layering, or division.

Savory, summer. Sow seed indoors and transplant to garden after all danger of frost is past.

Savory, winter. Propagate by division, layering, or cuttings. Or sow seed outdoors in late spring.

Sorrel. Propagate by division or seed sown outdoors in late spring.

Tansy. Propagate by division or cuttings.

Tarragon. Propagate by division or cuttings.

Thyme. Propagate by division, layering, or cuttings.

---

least two true leaves. Use a trowel to lift seedlings from the soil and transplant them to a new site.

Saving Herb Seeds

Instead of allowing herbs to self-sow, you can harvest the seeds before they mature and fall to the soil. It's easy to save seeds from annuals, like basil and dill. It's more difficult to harvest seeds from perennials.

To collect and save your own seeds, monitor the plants weekly once they bloom. Check seed formation; seeds usually darken as they mature. Harvest seeds by cutting the seed heads into small paper bags. Allow to air dry, then store in a dark, cool spot in sealed, labeled containers.

COMPANION PLANTING

To enjoy your herbs and put them to work defending your garden at the same time, use them as companion plants. Companion planting is a mixture of folklore and scientific fact; experiment to find out what works for you.

Herb Companions

Herbs that repel. Try planting garlic with bush beans to repel aphids, and catnip with eggplant to repel flea beetles. A ring of chives under an apple tree is said to discourage apple scab. Other herbs used to repel pests include anise, borage, calendula, cilantro, dill, scented geranium, mint, rosemary, sage, and tansy.

Herbs that help. Some herbs seem to enhance the growth of other plants. Pair borage with strawberries, chervil with radishes, sage with cabbage-family crops, and summer or winter savory with onions. Also try basil or thyme around tomatoes. Tarragon is said to enhance the growth of most garden vegetables.

Herbs that hinder. Garden lore is filled with examples of herbs that inhibit neighboring plants. Among them: Dill slows the growth of tomatoes, and sage hinders the growth of onions. Garlic harms neighboring beans and peas. Marigold, sunflower, and wormwood also hinder the growth of many plants.

Herbs as trap crops. You can use herbs as traps that lure pests away from your crops. Dill and lovage have been used to lure hornworms from tomatoes, for example.

HERBS TO LURE BENEFICIALS

You can use herbs to keep the beneficial insects in your garden happy and well fed. To lure and support the most beneficials, plant some herbs from each of the following groups. For more on attracting beneficials, see "Protect Your Allies" on page 69.

Daisy-Family Herbs

These will attract assassin bugs, honeybees, hover flies, lacewings, lady beetles, and parasitic wasps. Goldenrod is one of the most effective daisy-family members for attracting beneficials. Other daisy-family herbs include chamomile, coreopsis, marigold, sunflower, tansy, and yarrow.

Mint-Family Herbs

Members of the mint family have aromatic foliage and many small two-lipped flowers. If you're not sure a plant is a mint, check for the characteristic square stem. Mints attract honeybees, hover flies, parasitic wasps, and other beneficials. In addition to mint, try attracting beneficials with bee balm, catnip, hyssop, lavender, sweet marjoram, oregano, sage, and thyme.

Carrot-Family Herbs

Members of the carrot family attract hover flies, lacewings, lady beetles, parasitic wasps, and other beneficials. It's easy to recognize their umbrella-shaped flower clusters. Angelica, anise, caraway, dill, and fennel are carrot-family crops.

Other Herbs

Chives and onions are also popular with beneficial insects, as are cover crops like buckwheat and clovers. Many common weeds, including dandelion, lamb's-quarters, and wild mustard, also attract beneficials.

Chervil with lettuce. *The small white flowers of chervil will attract beneficial insects to your garden.*

Roman chamomile and strawberries. *Chamomile is thought to improve the flavor of many crops. It also attracts beneficials.*

Mint. *Mints attract beneficials and repel pests but will take over your garden. Grow them in containers sunk in the soil.*

How to Use Companions

You can mix and match herbs with most other plants, as long as you're meeting the growth requirements of each individual. Here are some guidelines to follow when choosing companions.

• Choose companion plants that have the same requirements for sunlight, water, season, and temperature.

• Plant perennial herbs with perennial crops. You can pair strawberries and Roman chamomile or lemon thyme in the same bed. Or let asparagus share space with tarragon. You *can* sow seeds of shallow-rooted annual herbs, such as cilantro or dill, around established perennial fruits and vegetables, but don't dig and set in plants—you would disturb the root system of the perennial.

• Avoid using invasive herbs, such as horseradish or mint, as companion plants—they will quickly take over. Instead, grow invasive herbs in pots near the garden. Slow-spreading perennials, such as thyme, make fine companions.

• Avoid planting closely related plants that might attract the same pests. For example, don't sow dill among the carrots.

Plant herbs as scattered clumps among pest-prone plants or plants whose growth you'd like to improve. Or plant a border of herbs around your garden to protect the area inside. Plant pest-attracting herbs away from the vegetable garden, as a decoy. Here's another option: Plant herbs in pots, then move them around in the garden as they're needed to attract or repel insects.

Basil with tomatoes. *When grown as a companion crop, basil is said to improve the flavor of the tomatoes.*

Dill and carrots. *Don't plant members of the same family together. Dill and carrots both belong to the carrot family.*

HERBS IN CONTAINERS

Herbs are great container plants. Potted herbs won't produce the big harvests you'd reap from garden-grown herbs, but with a few pots in a sunny site, you can produce plenty of fresh herbs and some to dry as well. All the better if they're close to the kitchen door, a step away from the soup or sauce pot.

Growing tender herbs, such as rosemary and bay, in containers makes it easy to move them indoors in winter for protection. Potted herbs can grow indoors under lights or on a windowsill in winter.

Care Basics

Give your herbs a happy home by selecting good containers and potting mixes and by providing water and fertilizer regularly. For a make-it-yourself potting soil recipe, see "Pick a Container Mix" on page 72.

Containers. Whether you grow indoors or out, select a container that has drainage holes. Good drainage is critical for most herbs. Clay containers are good choices for herbs, such as rosemary, that like dry soil. Choose concrete, plastic, or wood for herbs, such as mint, that like plenty of moisture. Don't leave clay or concrete containers outdoors in winter, though, because they'll freeze and crack.

Choose containers large enough to allow 1 to 2 inches of space around the root ball. For groups of herbs, consider using half-barrels with holes drilled in the bottom. For example, you can grow a clump of chives, an oregano plant, and a thyme plant for several years in a single barrel. You'll need to prune back the oregano and thyme plants periodically to keep them from taking over. If plants become rootbound, move up to a larger container. When repotting, freshen the potting mix with compost.

Watering. Container-grown herbs will need more frequent watering than ones growing in the garden. In general, it's best to water the soil thoroughly and frequently in hot, dry environments. In cool, wet weather, water less frequently. Don't allow plants to sit in water. To check for soil moisture, press your finger into the top inch of soil.

Feeding. Herbs will benefit from a seasonal spray of liquid kelp or fish emulsion.

Overwintering Herbs

Grow nonhardy herbs in containers. It's often easiest—on both you and the plants—to grow nonhardy herbs, such as rosemary, in containers

---

TIPS FOR HOUSE HERBS

Basil, bay, chives, dill, marjoram, mints, oregano, parsley, rosemary, sage, and winter savory make good houseplants. Use the tips below to keep housebound herbs happy in winter.

• Give your herbs as much light as possible. A sunny, south-facing window is ideal. Or grow them under fluorescent lights.
• Keep humidity up. Set plants in trays filled with stones, then water them. Or mist plants daily with a spray mister.
• When in doubt, choose clay pots.
• Harvest sparingly and regularly to promote growth.
• Start with healthy, disease- and pest-free plants.
• For best results, don't grow herbs indoors permanently. They'll appreciate an annual summer vacation outside. Or start new plants each fall.

year-round. In spring, sink the pots in the garden or leave them above ground on a terrace or patio. In fall, move them to a protected place (still outdoors), such as against a wall with a southern exposure or a cold frame. Allow them to go through a gradual cooling period outdoors until nighttime lows average just less than 40°F. Then bring them indoors to a sunny room that stays between 40° and 60°F. Water just enough to keep them from drying out.

When spring returns, repot and replenish the soil with compost as necessary. Then gradually expose them to outdoor temperatures and light again. Good candidates for this treatment are bay, scented geranium, lemon verbena, myrtle, and rosemary.

Take annual cuttings. Another way to overwinter herbs is to take cuttings or divide plants in late summer, grow the cuttings or divisions in pots over the winter, and replant in spring. Try overwintering basil, scented geranium, lemon verbena, sweet marjoram, rosemary, and pineapple sage in this manner.

Indoor Pest Control

Although herbs are relatively pest-free in the garden, keep your eyes out for pests on ones grown indoors. Aphids, mealybugs, scale, spider mites, and whiteflies will attack potted herbs. Check leaves and stems periodically for signs of these pests, and control infestations with a spray of insecticidal soap. Or try wiping insects away with a cotton ball dipped in rubbing alcohol. Repeat the control measures several times to control generations that hatch later.

MAKE HARDY HERBS THINK IT'S SPRING

To grow an indoor harvest of hardy perennial herbs, you'll have to trick them into thinking spring has arrived. Otherwise, they'll remain dormant until the next season. Here's how.

1. Pot up herb divisions or cuttings in the fall. Trim the top growth to a height of 2 inches. (Remember to dry the trimmings for use in recipes or craft projects.)

2. Place the pot inside a plastic bag. Seal the bag, and place it on a shelf in your refrigerator for two weeks. Move it to the freezer section for two weeks, then back to the refrigerator section for two more weeks.

3. Remove the pot from the refrigerator, prop open the bag, and leave the pot in a sunny location. New growth will begin in the center. Harvest foliage as needed. In the spring, move the plant back to the garden.

HARVESTING HERBS

When and How to Harvest

To get the best harvest from your herbs, let your plants become established before you begin harvesting. Annual herbs, such as basil and dill, should be growing vigorously and have two or three pairs of true leaves. Don't take more than a few leaves from perennial herbs, such as chives or tarragon, the first year. Let them become established before taking major harvests.

Once your herbs are established and growing robustly, you can harvest continuously

all season. Either snip leaves and blossoms as needed, or take larger harvests to preserve for winter.

For most herbs, cut just above a node when you harvest to encourage new bushy growth. Chives and parsley are exceptions. To harvest chives, grab a handful of foliage and cut all the way through the bunch, a few inches above the base. With parsley, harvest the outside stems first. When harvesting herb blossoms, leave several inches of stem attached.

Stop harvesting perennial herbs a month or so before the first fall frost is expected so they can store up the food reserves they need to weather the winter. Harvest annuals right up until frost. Harvest roots, such as horseradish, while the plants are dormant, just before or after the growing season.

Harvesting annual herbs. *Don't pick from annual herbs, such as fennel, unless they are growing actively. Cut the stems just above a node.*

Flavors and foliage color can also change from season to season. Members of the cabbage family, such as the salad herbs arugula and mustard, are mild flavored in spring and autumn but hot in summer. Some herbs, including thyme, take on a reddish hue as winter approaches. Intense heat and sun can act to fade the color of herb foliage, such as basil.

Storing Fresh Herbs

To preserve the best flavor, aroma, and color, keep fresh herbs cool and dry after harvest. Avoid washing foliage and blossoms. If the leaves are gritty, swish bunches of herbs through a pan of icy cold water, then shake and pat dry. Or use a salad spinner—they're not just for salad greens; they're great for drying herbs as well.

Harvesting perennial herbs. *Let perennial herbs become established for a year before taking a large harvest. Cut just above a node to encourage new bushy growth.*

Flavor and Color

Herb flavor can vary from year to year, depending on climate, weather, and cultural practices. Hot and dry weather conditions help to concentrate flavors and stunt growth. At the other extreme, lots of moisture dilutes flavors and promotes lush growth.

Store fresh herbs in the refrigerator between paper towels in resealable plastic bags. They'll last for two weeks or more.

Set herb blossoms in a shallow bowl of water covered with plastic wrap in the refrigerator. Or place cut blossoms between paper towels, and put them in a resealable plastic bag. Kept cold, fresh blossoms will last up to ten days.

Freezing Herbs

Your freezer is one of the best places to preserve the homegrown flavor of herbs. You can freeze herbs individually, or mix them together in special blends. Try basil, oregano, and thyme; chives and dill; lemon verbena and tarragon; or basil and minced garlic.

Chop herb foliage with a sharp knife or scissors. (Use a food processor for large batches.) Then use a canning funnel to pack the chopped herbs into resealable plastic bags. Squeeze the air from the bags, seal them, and label them with the date and kind of herb. To use, just break off a piece and add it to the recipe—no thawing required!

Drying Herbs

Drying herbs is an easy way to preserve your harvest.

Canning funnel — Chopped herbs

FREEZING HERBS

You can dry herbs in any clean, dry, dark, dust-free, well-ventilated environment.

The faster your herbs dry, the better. Spread herbs on screens or hang them to air dry for up to seven days. If foliage remains limp and damp after seven days, move it to a baking sheet in an oven set at 100°F or at the lowest possible setting. Remove the leaves when they are dry and crispy.

Screen drying. Make simple drying screens by stapling hardware cloth or window screening over a wooden frame. Strip leaves from their stems, then place the leaves in a single layer on screens.

Hanging herbs to dry. Gather fresh herbs in small bunches and hang them to dry. Five or six stems per bunch are best; you can make larger bunches, but they won't dry as fast. Secure the bunches with small rubber bands, then hang them from hooks or nails in a well-ventilated spot away from light.

Drying herbs with a dehydrator. For quick drying, a commercial food dehydrator is ideal. Just spread individual leaves or small sprigs of herbs, such as parsley, onto the trays, and turn the dehydrator on. In many cases, they'll dry overnight.

Storing Dried Herbs

Store dried herbs in airtight jars in the dark. For best flavor, store whole leaves or sprigs; crumble them just before use. Continue using dried herbs as long as they have good flavor. Refresh your supply from the garden each growing season.

FOR BEST RESULTS

Harvest herbs grown for foliage *before* the plants flower. Whether you plan on using them fresh, frozen, or dried, this will give you the best flavor from your herbs. Choose healthy, tender foliage from the top of the plant. Unless you've mulched, soil and debris accumulate on the lower leaves.

Harvest foliage and edible flowers in the morning, just after the dew has dried. For the best-quality edible blossoms, such as borage, chives, or nasturtium, pick just before they are fully opened.

FAVORITE HERBS

BASIL, SWEET

Ocimum basilicum • Labiatae

Basil's pungent flavor enhances any summer garden recipe. Plant a sampling of basil cultivars, including lemon-, cinnamon-, and anise-flavored types. You can choose among cultivars that are low-growing, stocky, or tall, with variegated, crinkled, purple, green, or smooth leaves. Basil is an annual that will grow in Zones 4 through 10.

Growing Guidelines

Grow basil in any well-drained soil amended with plenty of organic matter. It needs heat and full sun to grow well.

Plant seeds indoors six weeks before the last expected frost. For the best germination, maintain soil temperature at 70°F. When seedlings sprout, keep air temperature at 65°F. Plant both seeds and plants outdoors after danger of frost, when soil temperature averages 50°F or higher. Continue sowing at two-week intervals. Plant small-leaf types 6 to 8 inches apart. Cultivars with large leaves need 1 to 1½ feet between plants.

Pinch the terminal blossoms as they form to encourage leaf production. Cover plants with plastic or cloth sheets if temperatures drop below 40°F.

Solving Problems

Cover plants with floating row cover when temperatures drop below 40°F to prevent cold injury on leaves. Stake tall plants to prevent stems from breaking during summer storms.

Harvesting

Begin harvesting as soon as plants have several leaf pairs. Frequent harvests encourage

Stripping basil stems. *Try this quick trick for removing basil leaves from the stem. Circle the top of a basil stem with thumb and fingers of one hand. Grasp and pull the stem with your other hand.*

new growth. After harvesting, wrap dry foliage in paper towels and store in resealable plastic bags in the refrigerator at 40°F or more.

Propagation

Make new plants by taking terminal stem cuttings, then rooting them in sterile medium. Or, collect seeds from darkened seedstalks.

CHERVIL

Anthriscus cerefolium • Umbelliferae

Hardy annual chervil starts the growing season early and offers a delicate anise flavor to recipes. Chervil will grow in Zones 3 through 7.

Growing Guidelines

Chervil prefers a rich, humusy, slightly acid soil. Plant chervil in early spring or fall, since it prefers cool temperatures and bolts (goes to seed) at the first sign of heat. Direct-sow seeds shallowly, then thin seedlings to 9 to 12 inches. Chervil transplants poorly. Make successive sowings every two weeks until plants begin to bolt.

Pinch away flowers as they form to prolong foliage harvests. In warm climates, you can grow chervil all winter. In the North, plant chervil in cold frames in fall. Or sow chervil indoors in pots, then keep the plants in a cool room at 40° to 50°F.

Solving Problems

Cover small seedlings with floating row cover to protect them from rabbits, groundhogs, or other animal pests. Also keep mulch away from base of plants or they may suffer damage from earwigs.

Harvesting

Snip the feathery leaves six to eight weeks after sowing. Use chervil fresh, because dried leaves have little flavor. Cooking destroys the flavor of chervil.

Propagation

The easiest way to propagate chervil is to allow some plants to bolt and form seed heads. The seed will self-sow, providing you with a new crop.

CHIVES

Allium schoenoprasum • Liliaceae

Chives have a delicate onion flavor and beautiful, globelike pink and lavender blossoms. This perennial herb will thrive in Zones 3 through 9.

Growing Guidelines

Chives require well-drained soil, low in nitrogen, and full sun. In late winter, sow

Replant divisions at same depth as they grew previously.

Propagating chives. Dig mature plants every three years in spring or fall. Work large clumps apart with your fingers to create small clumps of four to six bulbs each.

seeds indoors. Sow clumps of 10 to 12 seeds in pots, or scatter seeds in flats. When seedlings are 2 inches tall, cut groups of seedlings into clumps. Plant clumps 5 to 10 inches apart as soon as the soil can be worked. You can also sow seeds directly outdoors.

Solving Problems

Keep mulch away from the base of plants to improve air circulation and prevent disease problems. Chives compete poorly with other plants, so weed diligently.

Harvesting

Cut foliage as long as plants are growing actively. Leave a few inches of growth behind. Harvest blossoms at any stage. Stop harvesting two to four weeks before the first fall frost. Chives are best when used fresh.

Use back of rake to tamp seeds in place.

Rake soil surface lightly to cover seeds.

Planting in bands. *Broadcast seeds of cilantro and other herbs in 6-inch-wide bands.*

Foliage regrows after cutting.

Easy harvesting. *Grab a handful of leaves and cut 1 to 2 inches above the soil surface.*

CILANTRO

Coriandrum sativum • Umbelliferae

Cilantro is an annual herb that produces an abundance of glossy green foliage. It also produces seeds, which are called coriander seeds. Both foliage and seeds are just right for Mexican cuisine. Cilantro will grow in Zones 2 through 9.

Growing Guidelines

Grow cilantro in any rich, well-drained soil in full sun to partial shade. Sow seeds directly outdoors ½ inch deep after danger of frost is past. Make repeat sowings every few weeks for continuous harvest. Seed in rows or in bands, as shown at left on this page. Thin seedlings planted in rows to 4 inches apart. Thin plants planted in bands to stand 2 inches apart. Cilantro transplants poorly. This herb likes plenty of water and will tolerate light frost.

Solving Problems

Cilantro is an easy-to-grow, trouble-free herb. Avoid heavy applications of nitrogen for

the best flavor. Seed-producing cultivars may require staking.

Harvesting

Begin pinching foliage as soon as the plants have several leaves. Harvest handfuls regularly as long as the plants are growing vigorously. Foliage regrows after cutting. Cilantro foliage dries and freezes poorly. Harvest and dry the seeds when they are brown, before the seed heads shatter. Store the dried seeds in the dark in airtight containers.

Propagation

Allow mature plants to self-sow in the fall, then avoid disturbing the soil where seedlings will come up.

DILL

Anethum graveolens • Umbelliferae

Use dill foliage—often called dill weed—fresh, dried, or frozen for its characteristic pickle flavor. Dill weed also adds a zesty touch to fresh summer salads. Add the seeds to any pickled vegetable recipe. This annual herb grows in Zones 2 through 9. Choose 'Dukat' or 'Fernleaf' cultivars for plenty of tasty foliage and few seeds.

Growing Guidelines

Dill needs good drainage but moist soil, and full sun. Sow seeds shallowly outdoors in early spring or fall, then keep the soil moist for the best germination. To produce lots of foliage, broadcast the seeds in bands, as shown at left on the opposite page, and thin the seedlings to stand several inches apart. For seed-producing cultivars, thin plants to stand 6 inches apart. Sow every two to three weeks for continuous harvest. Dill transplants poorly. Weed diligently in areas seeded with dill, because small dill seedlings don't compete well against other plants. Dill will withstand light frost.

Solving Problems

Cover plants with floating row cover to keep out rabbits and groundhogs. Handpick any caterpillars that chew on foliage. Tall seed-producing cultivars may require staking to prevent the seedstalks from flopping to the ground.

Harvesting

Begin harvesting eight to ten weeks after sowing outdoors. Pick fresh leaves from the stem, or harvest with scissors if planted in bands. Refrigerate fresh foliage wrapped in a paper or cloth towel inserted in a plastic bag. Dill weed freezes well, whole or chopped. For seed production, allow plants to flower. Harvest seeds anytime, or when they are dry and light brown for the best flavor. You can air dry both seeds and foliage, then store in airtight containers.

Propagation

Save some of your collected seed to plant next year's crop. Dill also self-sows easily.

FENNEL

Foeniculum vulgare • Umbelliferae

Fennel is a semihardy perennial usually grown as an annual. You'll find two kinds of fennel in seed catalogs. *Foeniculum vulgare* produces lots of licorice-flavored, feathery leaves and seeds, used to flavor foods. *F. vulgare* var. *azoricum,* also called Florence fennel, produces a licorice-flavored swollen bulb that is eaten as a vegetable. Fennel will grow in Zones 6 through 9.

Growing Guidelines

Sow both types outdoors as soon as the soil can be worked. Cover shallowly and keep the soil moist. For a continuous harvest, sow at two- to three-week intervals. Fennel transplants poorly. It will tolerate light frost.

Solving Problems

Florence fennel bolts (goes to seed) in hot climates; mulch the soil to keep it cool and moist. Fennel is rarely bothered by pests. Plant fennel away from its close relatives, including carrot, dill, and parsley, to avoid pests.

Harvesting

Begin harvesting foliage eight to ten weeks after sowing outdoors. You can harvest foliage continuously as needed. To produce edible seeds, allow flowers to mature, but cut the seed heads before they shatter. Put the seed heads on paper towels to finish drying and then store. Heat destroys fennel's flavor, so add it to cooked foods just before serving. Pull Florence fennel bulbs as soon as the base begins to thicken. Neither fennel leaves nor bulbs preserve well.

Propagation

Propagate both fennel and Florence fennel by saving your own seed for next year's crop.

GARLIC

Allium spp. • Liliaceae

Garlic's aromatic bulbs are a seasoning and a vegetable in one. Softneck types (*Allium sativum* subsp. *sativum*) have tops that flop over as they dry, so they're best for braiding. Hardneck garlic (*A. sativum* subsp. *ophioscorodon*) has a stiff, upright flower-stalk. Flavor and storage life vary with culti-var. Grow elephant garlic (*A. ampeloprasum,* Ampeloprasum group) for its giant, mild-flavored cloves. All garlic types are perenni-als grown as annuals.

Growing Guidelines

Plant garlic in full sun in well-drained soil. Plant in mid-fall or early spring as soon as the soil is workable. Buy whole bulbs from local garlic growers for the best crop. Separate bulbs into individual cloves, as shown on this page. Set softneck and hardneck cloves 1 to 2 inches deep and 6 to 8 inches apart. Plant elephant garlic 3 inches deep and 8 to 12 inches apart. Fall plantings produce shoots immediately, then become dormant until spring.

In the spring, side-dress with compost or blood meal, or spray with liquid kelp. Keep soil uniformly moist until the tops begin to die, then stop watering to allow bulbs to mature.

Solving Problems

Mildew or rot on garlic can indicate overwa-tering or poor drainage. Garlic can suffer from many of the same problems as onions. See "Solving Onion Problems" on page 146 for other symptoms and solutions to problems.

Harvesting

Harvest garlic when 75 percent of the leaves have turned brown. Pull fall-planted garlic in late June or early July. Pull spring-planted gar-lic at the end of the season. Use a digging fork to lift mature garlic from the soil. Lay the whole plants in an airy, dark, dry spot for

Planting garlic. *Press with your thumbs where you feel indentations in the garlic bulb to break it open. Separate individual cloves. Plant only large, solid cloves. Push each clove into well-loosened soil, root side down.*

several weeks to cure. Then trim away leaves and fibrous roots, and brush away dust. Store garlic at 32° to 35°F and 65 percent relative humidity. You can also dry chopped, peeled cloves to make "instant" garlic.

Propagation

Save your largest, healthiest bulbs to plant next year's crop.

GINGER

Zingiber officinale • Zingiberaceae

Ginger's flavor is a cross between hot, spicy, and citrusy. Ginger is a tender perennial that overwinters in Zones 9 and 10. It adapts well to pots in cool climates.

Growing Guidelines

Ginger prefers fertile, moist, well-drained garden soil. Buy tuberous rhizomes from the grocery store or specialty greenhouses. Hold the rhizomes at 65° to 70°F until sprouts form at each eye, then plant the rhizomes horizontally in beds or pots, loosely covered with soil. Keep the soil moist.

Harvesting

Begin harvests 6 to 12 months after planting. Slide potted ginger from the container, then use a sharp knife to trim away the amount of root needed. Replant the remaining root. Outdoors or in large containers, just dig down in the soil next to the plant and slice away a piece of root. Brush away soil, then store ginger in the refrigerator for several months, wrapped in paper towel and plastic wrap.

Propagation

To propagate, break away new sections of the rhizome as they form.

HORSERADISH

Armoracia rusticana • Cruciferae

Pungent horseradish root adds life to meat dishes. You can also toss the tender, inner leaves with fresh summer salads. Horseradish is a perennial that will grow in Zones 5 through 8.

Growing Guidelines

Buy dormant horseradish roots in spring or fall. Work the soil deeply before planting. Space new roots 1 to 2 feet apart and 1 to 2 feet deep. Horseradish spreads quickly and is difficult to eradicate. Prevent its spread by planting in bottomless 5-gallon containers sunk into the soil.

Harvesting

Harvest horseradish as shown on this page. Store unwashed roots in dry sand in a cool cellar, or in the refrigerator.

Propagation

Horseradish propagates readily by root cuttings in spring or fall.

Harvesting horseradish. *Use a trowel or shovel to dig the root clear. Break or cut off as much root as you need, then replace the soil. Before grating or processing, cut away the crown and peel the root.*

MARJORAM, SWEET

Origanum majorana • Labiatae

Marjoram's floral fragrance livens recipes, potpourris, and other crafts. A tender perennial, marjoram will overwinter in Zones 9 and 10 but is usually grown as an annual.

Growing Guidelines

Marjoram prefers full sun and well-drained soil. Sow seeds shallowly indoors six to eight weeks before the last spring frost. Seeds germinate in one to two weeks at 70°F. Transplant to the garden after all danger of frost is past. Space individual plants 8 inches apart. In the fall, dig plants and transfer them to containers for winter harvests indoors. Replant them again in spring.

Harvesting

Harvest marjoram regularly to promote bushy growth. Begin harvesting five to six weeks after transplanting or when plants are growing vigorously. Harvest continuously as needed. Marjoram holds its flavor when dried.

Propagation

Propagate by seed in spring or by stem cuttings anytime. Divide plants in the fall.

MINT

Mentha spp. • Labiatae

Mint offers flavors and forms to suit every need. Most mints are tough perennials, so they're easy herbs for beginners. Choose from fruity apple, lemon, orange, and pineapple mints, plus standard peppermint and spearmint. Mint will grow in Zones 5 through 9.

Growing Guidelines

Plant mint in full sun or partial shade. Mint prefers rich, moist, but well-drained soil. It's best to start mint from cuttings or divisions, as mint often doesn't come true from seed.

Mint can spread aggressively, choking out plants around it. To prevent its spread, plant mint in 5-gallon containers with holes punched in the bottom for drainage, as shown in the illustration on page 310. Side-dress annually with compost or organic fertilizer for the heaviest production.

Harvesting

Harvest heavily and continuously to encourage new growth, then stop harvesting two to four weeks before fall frosts. Mint foliage freezes and dries well.

Propagation

Divide plants every three to five years. Take stem cuttings whenever plants are growing vigorously.

OREGANO

Origanum spp. • Labiatae

Tomatoes would only be half as popular without the biting flavor of oregano. Flavor varies with cultivar, so try several to find your favorite. Oregano is a perennial and will grow in Zones 5 through 9. Not all types will survive winter in cold climates.

Growing Guidelines

Grow oregano in full sun and well-drained, rich garden soil. This herb likes dry, rocky locations and also grows well in containers. It's best to buy plants, as seedlings are variable in flavor and other qualities. Space plants 1 to 2 feet apart.

Solving Problems

Keep mulch away from the stems to promote air circulation and prevent disease problems. Watch for aphids and spider mites, especially on potted plants. Use a strong spray of water to wash away pests, or spray them with insecticidal soap.

Harvesting

Harvest fresh leaves all season as long as plants are growing vigorously. Stop harvesting two to four weeks before the first frost. Oregano keeps its flavor well when dried.

Propagation

Divide plants every three to five years. Take stem cuttings whenever plants are growing actively. Oregano crosses freely, so seedlings from saved seed often don't look, smell, or taste like the mother plant.

PARSLEY

Petroselinum crispum • Umbelliferae

Parsley has plenty to offer: It's an attractive garnish, rich in vitamins, and an excellent addition to most recipes. Parsley is a biennial grown as an annual; it will grow in Zones 5 through 9.

Growing Guidelines

Parsley grows best in rich, moist, well-drained soil in full sun to partial shade. Sow seeds outdoors when soil temperature averages 50°F. Seeds germinate slowly, often requiring up to six weeks. You can speed germination by soaking the seeds in water overnight before planting. Or freeze seeds in ice cubes, then plant the cubes.

Although you can sow seeds indoors in individual peat pots six to eight weeks before the last frost, you may find that parsley transplants poorly. For best success, transplant when seedlings have only a few true leaves. Space plants 8 to 10 inches apart; thin seedlings to the same spacing. For winter harvests, sow seeds in pots in late summer, then bring the pots indoors.

Solving Problems

Parsley has few pest problems. Handpick occasional chewing caterpillars. Keep mulch away from the crown to promote air circulation and prevent disease problems.

Harvesting

Begin harvesting as soon as plants are growing vigorously. Cut leaves as shown in the illustration on this page. Parsley dries and freezes well.

Propagation

If parsley plants survive the winter in your area, you can collect seed after the plants bloom in the spring.

Picking parsley. *Snip individual outer stems from your plants. They will continue to produce new growth all season long.*

ROSEMARY

Rosmarinus officinalis • Labiatae

Rosemary has a strong floral scent that stands out in cooked dishes and baked goods. This half-hardy perennial is an evergreen in Zones 8 through 10. Choose from upright or prostrate cultivars.

Growing Guidelines

Rosemary needs full sun to light shade and rich soil with excellent drainage. Seedlings grow very slowly, so you'll probably want to buy plants or seek cuttings from an established herb garden. Space plants 1 to 2 feet apart. Grow rosemary outdoors all year where winter temperatures remain above 10°F. If you live in an area with colder winter temperatures, you can try overwintering rosemary in pots. Dig the plants in fall, and plant them in clay pots. Set them in a cool (45°F), sunny location, and water infrequently.

Solving Problems

Rosemary has few pest problems in the garden. Potted plants are frequently bothered by mildew, so provide good air circulation and don't mist the foliage. Watch out for aphids, mites, and scales on potted plants. Control them with a spray of insecticidal soap. Wipe away scales with a cotton ball dipped in rubbing alcohol.

Harvesting

Harvest continuously as long as plants are growing actively. Strip the needles from the stems, then chop them before using. Rosemary dries well. You can preserve rosemary in vinegar, oil, honey, or jelly.

Propagation

Propagate by stem cuttings when plants are growing vigorously. You can also propagate rosemary by layering stems in spring. If you want to grow rosemary from seed, sow seeds several months before you want plants for the garden.

SAGE

Salvia officinalis • Labiatae

Sage is an herb gardener's delight. The perennial, shrubby plants grow quickly without becoming invasive. Sage flowers attract hummingbirds and beneficial insects. In the kitchen, add fresh or dried sage to roasting meats, poultry, fresh tomatoes, and bean dishes. Sage will grow in Zones 4 through 8.

Growing Guidelines

Sage prefers full sun to partial shade and rich, well-drained soil. Buy plants or grow your own from seed. Sow seeds indoors six to eight weeks before the last spring frost. Seeds germinate within three weeks at 60° to 70°F. Transplant outdoors after all danger of frost is past. Space new plants 18 to 24 inches apart.

Harvesting

Harvest leaves when plants are growing actively. Harvest the sweet, edible blossoms of honeydew melon sage and pineapple sage for fresh salads and as a garnish—just pull the petals from their centers. Sage leaves dry and freeze well.

Propagation

Divide plants every three to five years. You can also propagate sage by stem cuttings, root division, and layering. For instructions for layering sage, see the illustrations on page 314.

TARRAGON, FRENCH

Artemisia dracunculus var. *sativa* • Compositae

French tarragon offers a strong, unusual licorice flavor that stands out in cooked dishes. Tarragon is a hardy perennial that will grow in Zones 4 through 8.

Growing Guidelines

French tarragon needs full sun or partial shade and a loose, rich, well-drained garden soil. Don't start plants from seed because French tarragon does not make viable seed, and types other than French don't offer the same flavor. Start by buying French tarragon plants, or get divisions or cuttings from established herb gardens. Space the new plants 1 to 2 feet apart. For the best foliage flavor, remove the flower stems when they form.

Solving Problems

French tarragon has few pest problems. Wash away occasional insect pests with a strong spray of water. Keep mulches away from the crown to avoid disease problems.

Harvesting

Harvest foliage continuously as long as plants are actively growing. Foliage wilts immediately when picked, so don't count on tarragon as a garnish. Tarragon does not dry well. To preserve fresh tarragon, add it to salad vinegars.

Propagation

Divide plants every three to five years. You can also propagate French tarragon by taking stem cuttings or layering stems when plants are growing vigorously.

THYME

Thymus vulgaris • Labiatae

The bittersweet flavor of thyme seems right for almost any dish, from vegetables and meats to soups and casseroles. This perennial comes in upright and prostrate forms. Choose upright cultivars for culinary use, since low-growing types are often gritty with rain-splashed soil. There are also variegated thymes, lemon thyme, and other scented forms. Thyme will grow in Zones 5 through 9.

Growing Guidelines

Thyme likes full sun to partial shade. Choose a well-drained site with sandy soil. Thyme seed is hard to find and rarely true to type, so it's best to start with plants or divisions. Space new plants 1 foot apart.

Once established, thyme is easy to keep looking good and producing well. Prune it lightly as needed to maintain its attractive shape.

Solving Problems

Thyme has few pest problems. On potted plants, control spider mites with a spray of water or insecticidal soap.

Harvesting

Harvest foliage continuously from actively growing plants. Strip leaves from the stems before drying. Thyme dries and freezes well.

Propagation

Divide plants every three to five years. Take cuttings in spring when plants are growing actively, or layer the stems.

CONTROLLING PESTS AND DISEASES

corn earworm, cucumber beetles, cutworms,
European corn borer, flea beetles, hornworms,
imported cabbageworms, Japanese beetle,
leafhoppers, leafminers, leafrollers, Mexican bean
beetle, oriental fruit moth, peachtree borers, plum curculio, scales, slugs, snails, spider mites, squash bug,
squash vine borer, tarnished plant bug, and whiteflies

Solving Disease Problems.................... 354

Symptom descriptions and prevention and control
measures for 14 common fruit and vegetable
diseases: alternaria blight, anthracnose, bacterial leaf
spot, brown rot, Cytospora canker, club root, downy
mildew, fire blight, Fusarium wilt, late blight, mosaic,
powdery mildew, rust, and Verticillium wilt

MANAGING PESTS ORGANICALLY

When you garden organically, you know your fruits and vegetables will be nutritious and taste great. Close inspection of your harvest may reveal brown bumps on the apple skin or an occasional earworm in the tip of an ear of corn. But those flaws are the trade-off for choosing safe, organic pest control methods over synthetic chemical pesticides.

Your organic garden may not be problem-free, but with a little thought and planning, it will be *nearly* problem-free. You'll manage pest problems by building the soil, taking good care of your plants, encouraging native beneficial insects and animals, and using your wits to outwit pests.

When you manage pests organically, you think about your garden as a living system. Your role is to help this natural system work as well as it possibly can.

THE ABCs OF PEST CONTROL

The theory of managing pests organically may seem complicated, but the practice is quite simple. There are lots of special pest control devices like red sticky balls for apple maggots and cardboard seedling disks for cabbage maggots. However, chances are you won't have to use many of them.

For most gardeners, managing pests organically involves five simple things: compost, water, floating row cover, good bugs, and hand power.

Compost. How does compost help control pests? Quite simply, compost is the best all-around soil conditioner and fertilizer you can add to your soil. Healthy, nutrient-rich soil means vigorous plants that are less likely to suffer pest and disease problems.

Compost tea is also a great quick vitalizer for plants that are lagging. When sprayed on foliage, compost tea may even offer some protection against plant diseases. So make compost, and use it liberally in your garden.

Water. A strong spray of water directed on plants can blast away many pests, including aphids and spider mites. Water your crops diligently so your plants don't suffer water stress. Water in the morning so foliage has time to dry (moist conditions favor disease development).

Floating row cover. For fruit and vegetable crops, floating row cover is one of the best pest control devices around. Plants benefit from the protection from wind. And, in most cases, the extra heat trapped by the cover also helps promote growth of young plants. Best of all, a properly applied row cover keeps out virtually all insect pests. This prevents insect-feeding damage and also prevents insect-transmitted disease problems, including bacterial wilt and some viruses.

Good bugs. Native lady beetles, parasitic wasps, predatory wasps, ground beetles, and various bugs and flies consume uncounted pest insects in your garden. While you may rarely see these beneficials, rest assured they will be there if you take some simple steps to provide them with food, water, and shelter.

Hands. Your hands are great pest controllers. Handpick large insects and dump them in a bucket of soapy water. If you're squeamish about touching insects, use tweezers or chopsticks, or wear disposable plastic gloves.

Handpick diseased leaves and destroy them. Prune away and destroy diseased branches on apple, raspberry, and other fruit crops. Pull weeds by hand around disease-prone crops, like grapes, to help promote air circulation.

Keeping the Garden Healthy

Normal gardening tasks, such as soil care, planting, and watering, can have important effects on pest problems. In a well-managed organic garden, plants are healthy because they get plentiful nutrients from a soil that's rich in organic matter. They're naturally pest resistant because they aren't stressed for water or light. So even if they have a few chewed or blighted leaves, vigorous plants will probably produce a fine harvest of fruits or vegetables.

Here's a quick summary of cultural practices that can help prevent pest problems.

- Add organic matter to your garden every year.
- Pick plants suited to local conditions.
- Don't let plants suffer water stress.
- Try foliar feeding to make sure plants get enough nutrients.
- Rotate crops that have had disease problems in the past; change their location in the garden every year.
- Clean up plant debris and fallen fruit throughout the season.
- Keep good garden records.

Many of these practices are a commonsense part of your gardening routine. But it's important to remember how

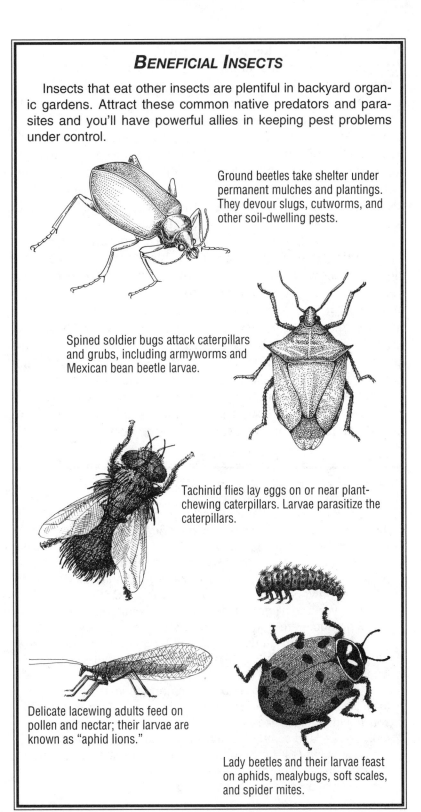

BENEFICIAL INSECTS

Insects that eat other insects are plentiful in backyard organic gardens. Attract these common native predators and parasites and you'll have powerful allies in keeping pest problems under control.

Ground beetles take shelter under permanent mulches and plantings. They devour slugs, cutworms, and other soil-dwelling pests.

Spined soldier bugs attack caterpillars and grubs, including armyworms and Mexican bean beetle larvae.

Tachinid flies lay eggs on or near plant-chewing caterpillars. Larvae parasitize the caterpillars.

Delicate lacewing adults feed on pollen and nectar; their larvae are known as "aphid lions."

Lady beetles and their larvae feast on aphids, mealybugs, soft scales, and spider mites.

helpful they are in keeping your garden free of pest problems. If you have questions about any of these practices, you'll find more information about all of them in this book. Just scan the listings in the contents or refer to the index to find the pages where these topics are covered.

Record Keeping

One thing that might puzzle you is how keeping garden records can help solve pest problems. You need records because memory is fallible but remembering details is important in organic pest management. Even if you have a good memory, chances are you won't remember from year to year exactly what you planted, where you planted it, and what problems it had.

For example, if one tomato cultivar thrived while another moped and developed disease problems, you'll need to know the cultivar names so you can buy the successful cultivar again next year. Also, you can't plan a crop rotation unless you have accurate records of where things were planted for the past three to (for some long-lived disease organisms) five years. And to choose disease-resistant cultivars, you will want a list of the disease problems you've seen in your garden in past seasons in order to make the best choices.

Encouraging Beneficials

Enticing beneficial insects and animals to your garden is a form of biological pest control. It's an effective and fun way to control pests.

You can encourage predators and parasites that prey on insect pests by:

- Putting up birdhouses to attract insect-eating birds.
- Planting pollen- and nectar-producing flowers as a food source for beneficial insects.
- Putting out a shallow water bath for beneficial insects to drink from.
- Leaving some mulched or cover-cropped areas in your garden undisturbed through the season to provide shelter for beneficials.
- Putting an overturned flowerpot with a "doorway" broken in the side in your garden to shelter a toad.

You can learn more about attracting beneficial insects by reading "Protect Your Allies" on page 69.

Buying Beneficials

You can nudge the beneficial balance in your favor by buying certain species of beneficial insects and releasing them in your garden. Buying beneficials is most effective when you have a specific pest problem and release a specific

---

BATTLING PESTS WITH BT

BT is the abbreviation for *Bacillus thuringiensis,* a bacterium that parasitizes insect larvae. Different strains of the bacterium have specific hosts (insects that they attack).

BTK (*B. thuringiensis* var. *kurstaki*) kills common pest caterpillars, including cabbage loopers, codling moth larvae, imported cabbageworms, and tomato hornworms. BTSD (*B. thuringiensis* var. *san diego*) attacks Colorado potato beetles.

BT products are now widely available from mail-order suppliers and even in garden centers. BT comes in liquid, powder, dust, and granules. Be sure to follow label directions when applying.

Because BT is nontoxic to humans and animals, you might think it's okay to spray it less selectively and less carefully than you would a poison like rotenone. But BT can infect and kill butterfly larvae, and some research studies have shown that pests are developing resistance to BT. So spray carefully—only spray infested plants, and only spray after you've tried using other controls, like barriers and handpicking.

predator or parasite to attack it. This ensures that the beneficial you release has a food source to help it get established in its new environment.

Some beneficial insects are a better buy than others. For example, *Trichogramma* wasps are tiny wasps that lay eggs on the eggs of pests such as codling moths and corn earworms. The wasp larvae parasitize the eggs. However, they only provide effective control when released in large numbers over a large crop area. A release in a home garden probably won't have any noticeable effect on pests.

You probably know that lady beetles are among the best insect predators in home gardens. While you can buy and release lady beetles in your garden, you're better off encouraging native lady beetles to take up residence instead. Lady beetles are migratory; chances are the first thing that purchased lady beetles will do when released is fly off to find a new home.

Two pest predators that home gardeners can generally release successfully are aphid midges and lacewings.

Aphid midges. This insect can control more than 60 species of aphids. You buy cocoons to distribute in your garden or fruit trees.

Lacewings. This predator eats aphids, thrips, small caterpillars, mites, and other soft-bodied insects. While

---

NAILING PESTS WITH NEMATODES

Most gardeners are familiar with root knot nematodes, which infect roots of many garden plants, causing stunting and poor growth. So it may be a surprise to learn that there are species of nematodes that are helpful!

Parasitic nematodes attack their hosts and release a bacterium that paralyzes and kills the host within 24 to 48 hours. Use nematodes to control armyworms, Colorado potato beetle larvae, cutworms, Japanese beetle grubs, onion maggots, strawberry root weevils, and other pests.

You'll probably have to order parasitic nematodes from a mail-order supplier. Ask the supplier to recommend the particular species of nematode that is effective for the pest you want to kill. Nematodes are applied as a soil drench; follow label instructions. Control is most successful when nematodes are applied to moist soil in late afternoon or evening.

---

many of the lacewing eggs may die during shipping, those that survive will do a good job of eating pests.

You'll find other specific recommendations for beneficials to buy in the individual crop entries in Parts 2 and 3 of this book.

Barriers and Traps

If pests can't land on or crawl onto your plants, they can't chew on them, tunnel into them, or lay eggs on them. This simple principle has inspired the creation of a battery of barriers and traps for everything from apple maggots to slugs. Familiar examples of these controls are floating row cover and sticky traps. You'll find directions for creating and using many common barriers and traps in

"Preventing Problems" on page 68 and "Preventing Pest Problems" on page 212.

Slug Barriers and Traps

Slugs and snails are the most infamous pests we fight with barriers and traps. These notorious slimers trouble gardens in most areas of North America. Gardeners have devised many ingenious ways to barricade slugs and snails from plants and to trap and kill the slimy creatures. You may want to try some of the following slug barriers and traps.

Copper strips. Slugs and snails avoid contact with copper. Scientists hypothesize that the pests get an electric shock when they touch it. Whatever the reason, copper makes a very effective barrier against slugs and snails. You can buy strips of copper

SOLARIZING SOIL

Heat can be a killer. And we're not talking about the heat of a summer afternoon beating down on us when we work in the garden. The heat of the sun can literally kill microorganisms, nematodes, and weed seeds in the soil. Using the sun's heat to kill soil pests is called *solarization,* and it can be effective in areas where skies are mostly clear and daytime temperatures stay above 85°F for at least four weeks.

To use this method, prepare the soil in an area at least 6 feet by 9 feet as if for planting, and rake it as smooth as possible. Water it well. If possible, snake a soaker hose over the area. Then spread 1- to 2-mil-thick clear plastic tightly over the area. Tuck the edges of the plastic into the soil. The plastic will trap the sun's heat in the covered area, causing the soil temperature to rise as high as 160°F.

If you've put a soaker hose under the plastic, resoak the soil partway through the process, which will increase the effectiveness of the sun's heat. After four weeks, remove the plastic. Let the soil dry to the right consistency for planting. Because you've killed weed seeds in the top few inches of soil, you should have few weed problems as long as you don't turn up new weed seeds from lower levels. When you plant, only make shallow furrows or dig individual holes for setting transplants, disturbing the soil as little as possible.

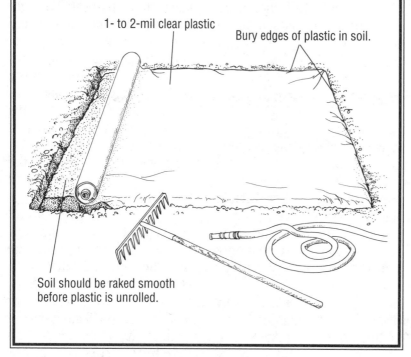

1- to 2-mil clear plastic

Bury edges of plastic in soil.

Soil should be raked smooth before plastic is unrolled.

especially designed for slug barriers. Put strips around tree trunks to keep snails from climbing the trunks. Also bury strips around the edge of a garden bed, leaving 2 to 3 inches of the copper exposed. Bend the top 1/2 inch of the strip outward at a right angle to form a lip.

Board traps. Slugs and snails like to hide in dark, moist places during the day. Put boards, shingles, or even grapefruit rinds around your garden. Check the traps daily and collect and destroy the hiding slugs and snails.

Beer traps. Set a shallow container, such as an aluminum pie plate, in the garden with the rim flush to the soil surface. Fill the container with beer. The slugs are attracted to the beer. They will drown in it or, if they survive, you can pluck them off and put them in a container of soapy water. Use one trap for every 10 square feet of garden area you want to protect.

Dehydrating barriers. The rough surface of natural grade diatomaceous earth, wood ashes, and cinders injures the skin of slugs and snails, causing them to dehydrate and die. Protect individual plants or groups of plants by dusting a 2-inch-wide strip of these materials around them. Renew the materials after rain.

Insecticides and Fungicides

If a pest problem catches you unprepared, you often must choose between letting nature take its course and spraying pesticides. Your decision will depend on the kind of crop attacked—it's more important to intervene to save a fruit tree than a head of lettuce. It will also depend on the severity of the problem and on your personal opinions about the use of pesticides.

Deciding Whether to Spray

Organically acceptable pesticides are botanical poisons (such as rotenone and pyrethrins) derived from plants and mineral fungicides (such as sulfur). What are the reasons for avoiding pesticides? First is potential risk to yourself. Some of these materials are toxic to humans as well as insects. Each time you apply them, you run the risk of making a mistake and inhaling or otherwise exposing yourself to the toxin.

Second is potential risk to the environment. While it's been shown that botanical pesticides break down quickly into less harmful products after application, there are still potential dangers. For example, rotenone kills fish if it is sprayed into water or if spray runoff contaminates water.

The third reason is potential harm to the natural balance in your garden. Many botanical poisons kill a wide range of insects, including beneficial ones. Applying poison sprays can undo all the work you've done to encourage beneficials in your garden.

Whether to use botanical poisons is a personal choice. In many cases, you may want to salvage what harvest you can from a pest-stricken plant. Sometimes, though, your best bet is to pull up and destroy the problem plants. Then replant, and take action early to protect the plants from a repeat performance by the pest.

If you decide to use an insectide or fungicide, always take proper safety precautions, as shown on page 211, and follow label instructions.

Fungicides

Antitranspirants, streptomycin, and sulfur- and copper-based sprays are acceptable fungicides for use in organic gardens. Compost tea also has fungicidal properties. In general, fungicides are used more on fruit crops than on vegetable crops. For more information on these products, see "Sprays and Dusts" on page 210.

Botanical Poisons

Although botanical poisons are organically acceptable, they can be toxic to you and other living creatures, including beneficial insects. Use them only for severe problems and as a last resort. When you do use them, treat them with respect. Use a respirator instead of a dust mask when spraying botanical poisons. Mix and apply according to label instructions. Spray only pest-infested plants.

Neem. Neem is the common name for azadirachtin, a natural insecticide extracted from the seeds of the neem tree. This tropical tree is native to India (it will grow in parts of Florida). Neem is a broad-spectrum insect repellent and poison thought to be mild on beneficials. It controls many pests, including aphids. Scientists are also testing neem's potential as a fungicide. It is almost nontoxic to mammals and is biodegradable. If you have a choice among botanical poisons effective against a particular pest, you should use neem first.

Pyrethrins. Pyrethrins, the active ingredients extracted from pyrethrum daisies, quickly kill many chewing and sucking insects, including codling moths and spider mites. Pyrethroids are a synthetic version of pyrethrins. They are more toxic than pyrethrins. Read product labels carefully to make sure you're using a *pyrethrins* product.

Rotenone. Rotenone is a nonselective, slow-acting poison derived from Peruvian cubé, Malaysian derris, or Brazilian tembo plants. Rotenone kills most beetles and other insects with chewing mouthparts. It is also toxic to birds, fish, and many beneficial insects. Residues remain on plant parts at least one week after application. To be completely safe, you may want to avoid spraying rotenone within two weeks of harvest. Some people are highly allergic to rotenone and suffer violent reactions to food that has been sprayed even after a week-long post-spray period.

Ryania. Ryania is a broad-spectrum insecticide extracted from *Ryania speciosa,* a tropical shrub. It kills chewing and sucking insects, including caterpillars such as codling moths and corn earworms. It is also labeled for use against citrus thrips. Ryania is more toxic to pests than it is to beneficial insects. However, it is also toxic to mammals and water life. It does not break down quickly. Allow several weeks to pass between spraying ryania and harvesting your crops.

Sabadilla. Sabadilla is made from the seeds of *Schoenocaulon officinale,* a lilylike plant native to Venezuela. It is toxic to mammals and can cause severe reactions in people who are allergic to it. It kills hard-to-control pests such as squash bugs and tarnished plant bugs. However, because of its toxicity, make sabadilla your last-choice botanical pesticide. Use it only if others fail and if a crop failure is imminent. Sabadilla is toxic to bees; don't spray while they are active.

Diagnosing Plant Problems

One commonsense rule is to identify the cause of a problem before you try to control it. But while it's easy to notice that a plant has a problem, how can you decide what's causing the problem? Examine the plant carefully. Look at the undersides of leaves as well as the tops.

Remember that insects can take many forms. Adult insects may be flies, beetles, or moths. Immature insects include caterpillars, maggots, and grubs. Scale insects may look like bumps on a leaf or stem. And some insect pests have very distinctive eggs, such as the bright yellow eggs laid by Mexican bean beetles.

Check the base of the stem for discoloration or holes (entry points for borers). Notice whether all the plants or just one in an area is affected.

Keep in mind that insects and diseases aren't the only causes of plant problems. Plants suffering from a nutrient deficiency sometimes show diseaselike symptoms, such as leaf discoloration and stunting. Look for patterns in symptoms to help you decide the cause. If symptoms do not spread from one plant to another, it may indicate that the cause is a deficiency rather than disease. Refer to "Solving Nutrient Deficiency Problems" on the opposite page for a listing of symptoms of nutrient deficiencies.

Once you've noted all the symptoms you can, there are several ways to make an identification. In the individual crop entries, there are "Solving Problems" tables that list symptoms and causes for common problems. Also, you'll find illustrations and descriptions of 30 common insect pests in "Solving Insect Problems," beginning on page 342. Or you may want to consult specialized insect or disease identification guides, such as the ones listed in "Recommended Reading" on page 362.

If you're truly stumped, seek help from your local extension office. Take a fresh sample of the damaged plant, plus any insects or insect eggs, to the office and ask for help in identifying the problem.

Solving Nutrient Deficiency Problems

Nutrient deficiency symptoms usually appear first on one part of a plant. Symptoms are grouped here according to where they first occur. This table also suggests organic soil amendments and fertilizers you can use to help remedy deficiencies. For more information on these amendments and fertilizers, refer to "Improving Your Soil" on page 12.

SYMPTOMS APPEAR FIRST ON OLDER OR LOWER LEAVES

NUTRIENT	SYMPTOMS	SOURCES OF NUTRIENT
Nitrogen	Leaves yellow. Plants light green overall. Growth stunted.	Alfalfa meal, blood meal, fish emulsion, fish meal, guano, soybean meal
Phosphorus	Foliage red, purple, or very dark green. Growth stunted.	Bonemeal, colloidal phosphate, rock phosphate
Potassium	Tips and edges of leaves yellow, then brown. Stems weak.	Granite meal, greensand, Sul-Po-Mag, wood ashes
Magnesium	Leaves yellow, but veins still green. Growth stunted.	Dolomitic lime, Epsom salts
Zinc	Leaves yellow, but veins still green. Leaves thickened. Growth stunted.	Chelated zinc spray, kelp extract, kelp meal

SYMPTOMS APPEAR FIRST ON YOUNGER OR UPPER LEAVES

NUTRIENT	SYMPTOMS	SOURCES OF NUTRIENT
Calcium	Buds and young leaves die back at tips.	Gypsum, lime, oyster shells
Iron	Leaves yellow, but veins still green. Growth stunted.	Chelated iron spray, kelp extract, kelp meal
Sulfur	Young leaves light green overall. Growth stunted.	Flowers of sulfur, gypsum
Boron	Young leaves pale green at base and twisted. Buds die.	Borax, chelated boron spray
Copper	Young leaves pale and wilted with brown tips.	Kelp extract, kelp meal
Manganese	Young leaves yellow, but veins still green. Brown spots scattered through leaves.	Kelp extract, kelp meal
Molybdenum	Leaves yellow, but veins still green. Growth stunted.	Kelp extract, kelp meal

SOLVING INSECT PROBLEMS

Scan the illustrations in this alphabetical guide as a quick route to identifying insect pests or the damage they cause. If you find a picture that resembles what you see in your garden, check the small map next to the picture. This range map shows in green the regions where the pest is found. It will confirm whether that pest is found in your area. Read the description of the pest and damage to help confirm the identity of the pest.

Also use this guide to help plan your strategy for fighting the pests that appear in your garden year after year. The controls listed here include preventive measures that you can put in place *before* the pest infests your crop. Preventive controls, such as covering crops with floating row cover, and environment-friendly controls, like BT and neem, are listed first. Toxic botanical poisons, such as pyrethrins and rotenone, are listed last.

INSECT

DESCRIPTION & CONTROLS

APHIDS

Adults

Description: Tiny (1/32"–1/8") pear-shaped insects that cluster on plants, particularly near growing tips. Aphids suck plant sap, causing leaves, buds, and flowers to be stunted and distorted. Severely infested leaves and flowers will drop off the plant. Sooty mold often grows on sticky honeydew they secrete. Aphids may be green, pink, black, dusty gray, or have a white fluffy coating. Nymphs look like adults; some adults have wings. Their feeding can spread viral diseases.

Plants attacked: Most small fruits, vegetables, and fruit trees.

Controls: Spray plants frequently with a strong stream of water to knock aphids off. Attract native predators. Release purchased aphid midges, lacewings, or parasitic wasps. Apply neem or spray insecticidal soap. For fruit trees, spray dormant oil in late winter to kill eggs. As a last resort, spray pyrethrins or rotenone.

APPLE MAGGOT

Maggot in fruit   Maggot

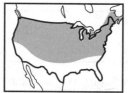

Description: White, 1/4" maggots that tunnel through fruit, causing it to drop prematurely. Maggots hatch from eggs laid on the fruits by adult flies. These small, dark flies have transparent wings patterned with dark bands.

Plants attacked: Apple, blueberry; occasionally cherry and plum.

Controls: Collect and destroy dropped fruit daily until September, twice a month in fall. Hang apple maggot traps in apple trees from mid-June until harvest (1 per dwarf tree, 6 per full-size tree). Plant clover groundcover to attract predatory beetles. Grow late-maturing cultivars to avoid damage because early cultivars tend to be most affected.

INSECT	DESCRIPTION & CONTROLS

ARMYWORMS

Beet armyworm

Description: Pale green caterpillars with stripes down their sides. The most common species found in gardens are beet armyworms and fall armyworms. They feed at night and can destroy whole plants in 1 night. Adults are pale, gray brown moths.

Plants attacked: Many garden crops.

Controls: Cover plants with floating row cover from seeding until flowering or harvest. Handpick larvae, or spray BTK or neem.

CABBAGE LOOPER

Larva

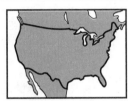

Description: Green caterpillars with 2 white lines down their backs chew large holes in leaves. They move by looping their bodies. Caterpillars hatch from eggs laid on leaf undersides by adult moths, which are gray with a silver spot on each forewing.

Plants attacked: Cabbage-family crops and many other vegetables.

Controls: Handpick several times weekly. Attract native parasitic wasps. Till in crop residues before adults emerge in spring. Spray larvae with BTK or neem. As a last resort, spray larvae with pyrethrins.

CABBAGE MAGGOT

Maggots

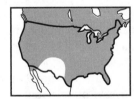

Description: White, tapering, ¼" maggots that bore into roots, stunting or killing plants. First sign of an infestation is plants that wilt in midday. Their feeding allows disease organisms to enter roots. Maggots hatch from eggs laid at stem bases by small, gray, long-legged flies.

Plants attacked: Cabbage-family crops.

Controls: Cover seedlings with floating row cover, burying edges in soil. Put cardboard seedling disks or tar-paper squares around bases of transplants. Wrap stems with paper for 1"–2" above and below the soil line. Burn or destroy seriously affected plants; also, burn or destroy roots when harvesting tops. Drench around roots with pyrethrins or parasitic nematodes. Try repelling egg-laying flies by mounding wood ashes, diatomaceous earth, or hot pepper around base of stems.

INSECT

DESCRIPTION & CONTROLS

CODLING MOTH

Adult

Larva

Entry hole

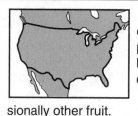

Description: These gray brown moths lay eggs on leaves, fruit, or twigs. Eggs hatch into pink or creamy white caterpillars with brown heads. Caterpillars tunnel through fruits to the center.

Plants attacked: Apple, pear, and occasionally other fruit.

Controls: In early spring, scrape loose bark to remove overwintering cocoons, and spray dormant oil. Grow cover crops to attract native parasites and predators, especially ground beetles that eat pupae. Trap larvae in sticky tree bands or bands of corrugated cardboard. Check cardboard bands daily and destroy larvae. In areas with severe infestations, hang 1 or 2 pheromone traps per tree 2 weeks before bud break. Check traps twice a week. If moths appear in traps, spray ryania every 1–2 weeks, starting when the majority of petals have fallen.

COLORADO POTATO BEETLE

Larva

Eggs

Adult

Description: Yellowish orange beetles with 10 lengthwise black stripes on their wing covers. They lay clusters of yellow, oval eggs on leaves. Eggs hatch into small, dark orange, humpbacked grubs with black spots along their sides. Adults and larvae chew leaves. They can kill small plants and may reduce yields of mature plants.

Plants attacked: Eggplant, potato, and tomato.

Controls: Plant cultivars that tolerate beetle feeding. Cover plants with floating row cover from planting until mid-season. In spring, knock beetles from plants into cans of soapy water or onto a tarp and destroy them. Handpick beetles, larvae, and eggs. Attract native predators and parasites. Mulch plants with a deep layer of straw. In large plantings, release spined soldier bugs or predatory stink bugs. Apply sprays of BTSD when first egg masses start to appear to control young larvae. Drench soil with parasitic nematodes to attack larvae as they prepare to pupate. Cultivate in the fall to destroy overwintering beetles. Spray weekly with neem or pyrethrins.

INSECT	DESCRIPTION & CONTROLS

CORN EARWORM/ TOMATO FRUITWORM

Larva

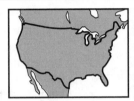

Description: Light yellow, green, pink, or brown caterpillars with yellow heads and white and dark stripes along their sides. They chew holes in leaves, eat buds, and tunnel into ripe fruits. In corn, they feed on fresh silks, then move down the ear eating kernels. Adults are tan moths with a 1½"–2" wingspan.

Plants attacked: Corn and many vegetable and fruit crops.

Controls: Plant corn cultivars with tight husks to prevent larvae from entering. Attract native parasitic wasps and predatory bugs. Spray BTK every 3–4 days on leaves and fruits of plants where fruitworms are feeding. Spray larvae with neem. Apply 20 drops of mineral oil onto silks of each ear 3–7 days after silks appear. After corn silks start to dry, spray BTK or squirt parasitic nematodes into tips of ears. Open cornhusks and dig out larvae in tip before they damage main ear. Paint pyrethrins-and-molasses bait (3 parts spray solution to 1 part molasses) around base of plants to kill emerging adults. In areas with severe corn earworm problems, hang pheromone traps when plants are 1' high. If moths appear in traps, spray rotenone-pyrethrins weekly as long as new moths are caught.

CUCUMBER BEETLES

Spotted   Striped

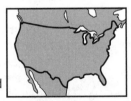

Description: Yellow or greenish yellow beetles with black spots or stripes on their wing covers. They feed on leaves and blossoms. Larvae are white grubs that feed on roots. Their feeding can transmit some viral and bacterial diseases.

Plants attacked: Squash-family crops and other vegetables.

Controls: Plant cultivars that tolerate cucumber beetles, bacterial wilt, and mosaic. Cover seedlings or plants with floating row cover (be sure to hand-pollinate covered squash-family plants). Pile deep straw mulch around plants. Drench soil weekly with parasitic nematodes to control larvae. Remove and destroy crop residues after harvest. If your crops have suffered serious disease problems in the past due to cucumber beetle feeding, spray pyrethrins or rotenone as soon as first beetles are seen.

INSECT

DESCRIPTION & CONTROLS

CUTWORMS

Damage

Larva

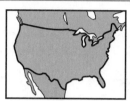

Description: Fat, greasy-looking, gray or dull brown, 1"–2" caterpillars with shiny heads. They feed at night on stems of seedlings and transplants. They may cut completely through stems or eat entire seedlings. During the day they rest below the soil surface near plant stems. Adults are brown or gray moths.

Plants attacked: Most vegetable crops.

Controls: Scatter moist bran mixed with BTK and molasses over surface of beds 1 week before setting out plants. Or, 1 week before planting, drench soil with parasitic nematodes. Put collars made of paper, cardboard, or plastic around transplant stems at planting, pushing collars into soil until about half of the collar is below soil level. (A toilet paper roll cut in half is an easy-to-make collar.) In the morning dig in soil around base of damaged transplants to destroy larvae hiding below the surface. Set out transplants later in the season to avoid damage. Spray undamaged plants with neem to lessen severity of attacks in areas where cutworms are a serious problem.

EUROPEAN CORN BORER

Larva

Description: Beige caterpillars with small brown spots. They feed on corn leaves and tassels and beneath husks; they also tunnel in stems and pods of other crops. Older larvae burrow in cornstalks and ears. Adults are yellowish brown moths.

Plants attacked: Corn, bean, onion, pepper, potato, and tomato.

Controls: Plant tolerant corn cultivars and those with strong stalks. Spray BTK twice, a week apart, on leaf undersides and into tips of ears. Apply granular BTK to corn whorl (part of plant where new leaves emerge) once some feeding is noticed on leaves. Attract native parasitic flies and wasps. Shred or dig in deeply all infested crop residues after harvest. For severe infestations on young plants, spray pyrethrins or ryania when larvae begin feeding.

| INSECT | DESCRIPTION & CONTROLS |

FLEA BEETLES

Adult

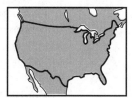

Description: Tiny black, brown, or bronze beetles that jump like fleas when disturbed. They chew many small, round holes in leaves and can severely damage or kill seedlings. Their feeding can also spread viral diseases. Larvae are thin, white grubs with brown heads; they feed on plant roots.

Plants attacked: Most vegetable crops.

Controls: Delay planting to avoid peak populations. Cover seedlings with floating row cover until adults die off. Flea beetles prefer full sun, so interplant crops to provide shade for susceptible plants. Drench soil with parasitic nematodes to control larvae. For severe infestations, spray with neem, pyrethrins, or rotenone.

HORNWORMS

Tobacco hornworm

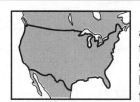

Description: Large green caterpillars with a horn on the tail and diagonal white marks on their sides. The most common hornworms in gardens are tobacco hornworms and tomato hornworms. They feed on leaves, stems, and fruits, and can kill young plants. Adults are large gray moths with a 4"–5" wingspan.

Plants attacked: Tomato-family crops.

Controls: Handpick caterpillars from foliage. Attract native parasitic wasps. Spray BTK while caterpillars are still small. Till after harvest to destroy overwintering pupae.

IMPORTED CABBAGEWORMS

Larva

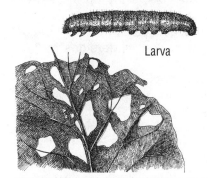

Description: Velvety green caterpillars with a fine yellow stripe down the back. They eat large ragged holes in leaves, soiling plants with dark green droppings. Caterpillars hatch from yellow eggs laid on leaf undersides by white butterflies.

Plants attacked: Cabbage-family crops.

Controls: Cover small plants with floating row cover. Handpick the caterpillars. Use yellow sticky traps to catch female butterflies. Spray with BTK or neem every 1–2 weeks. If this pest has been a severe past problem, try planting red cabbage cultivars, which are less attractive to them.

INSECT

DESCRIPTION & CONTROLS

JAPANESE BEETLE

Adult

Larva

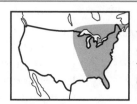

Description: Metallic blue green beetles with bronze wing covers and long legs. They eat flowers and skeletonize leaves. Larvae are fat white grubs with brown heads; they feed on roots of lawn grasses and garden plants.

Plants attacked: Most garden crops.

Controls: In early morning, shake beetles from plants onto tarps, then drown them in soapy water. Cover plants with floating row cover or screening. Drench sod with parasitic nematodes to kill larvae. Allow lawns to dry out between waterings or to go dormant in summer to kill eggs. Aerate lawn with spiked sandals to kill larvae. Spray beetles with pyrethrins or rotenone.

LEAFHOPPERS

Adult

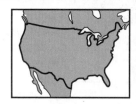

Description: Wedge-shaped, slender, green or brown, $1/10$"–$1/2$" insects. They jump rapidly into flight when disturbed. Nymphs look like pale, wingless adults. Adults and nymphs suck juices from stems and leaf undersides. Their toxic saliva distorts and stunts plants, and causes tipburn and yellowed, curled leaves. Feeding spreads viral diseases.

Plants attacked: Most fruit and vegetable crops.

Controls: Cover plants with floating row cover. Wash nymphs from plants with strong sprays of water. Attract native predators and parasites. Spray with insecticidal soap, neem, pyrethrins, or rotenone.

LEAFMINERS

Leafminer tunnels

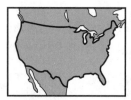

Description: Pale green, stubby maggots that tunnel in leaves. They often destroy seedlings but don't cause serious harm to large plants. Maggots hatch from white eggs laid in clusters on leaf undersides by tiny black flies.

Plants attacked: Many vegetable crops.

Controls: Cover seedlings with floating row cover. Pick and destroy mined leaves and remove egg clusters. Remove nearby dock or lamb's-quarters, which are hosts for beet leafminers. Attract native parasitic wasps. Spray plants with neem to control larvae in leaves.

INSECT	DESCRIPTION & CONTROLS

LEAFROLLERS

Larva

Webbing

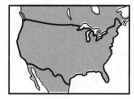

Description: Green caterpillars with brown or black heads. Caterpillars spin webs at branch tips and feed on enclosed buds, leaves, and developing fruit. They hatch from eggs laid on bark or leaves by brown moths.
Plants attacked: Most fruit crops.
Controls: Scrape egg masses from branches in winter. Spray dormant oil in late winter to kill eggs. Handpick caterpillars from young trees weekly. Handpick webs and destroy. Attract native parasitic insects. Apply BTK to larvae before they spin webs. Spray neem or pyrethrins.

MEXICAN BEAN BEETLE

Adult

Larva

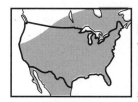

Description: Small, oval, yellowish brown beetles with black spots on wing covers. The yellow eggs laid by beetles on leaf undersides hatch into fat, yellowish orange grubs with long, branching spines. Larvae and adults skeletonize leaves.
Plants attacked: All types of beans.
Controls: Plant tolerant snap and lima bean cultivars. In the South, plant early-season bush beans to avoid damage. Attract native predators and parasites. Cover young plants with floating row cover. Handpick larvae and adults daily. Release spined soldier bugs to control early generation. Release parasitic wasps (*Pediobius* spp.) when weather warms. Remove and destroy crop residues as soon as plants are harvested. Spray weekly with pyrethrins or rotenone.

ORIENTAL FRUIT MOTH

Larva

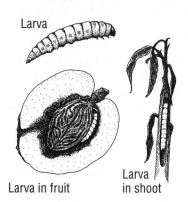

Larva in fruit

Larva in shoot

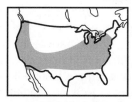

Description: Small, dark gray moths that lay eggs on trees in spring. Eggs hatch into white to pinkish gray caterpillars with brown heads; they bore into green twigs, causing twig wilting and dieback. Later generations of caterpillars bore into developing fruit, sometimes leaving gummy masses on fruit skin.
Plants attacked: Most tree fruits.
Controls: Where possible, plant early-bearing peach and apricot cultivars that ripen before midsummer. Cultivate soil 4" deep around unmulched trees in early spring to destroy overwintering larvae. Attract native parasitic wasps and flies. Pick and destroy immature fruits that show signs of infestation. Spray summer oil to kill eggs and larvae.

INSECT

DESCRIPTION & CONTROLS

PEACHTREE BORERS

Adult

Description: White caterpillars with dark brown heads that bore beneath tree bark at the base of the tree and also into main roots near the surface. Gummy sawdust marks entrance holes of burrows. Borer damage can kill young or weak trees; older trees are less affected. Adults are blue black, wasplike moths with yellow or orange bands across the body.

Plants attacked: Apricot, cherry, nectarine, peach, and plum.

Controls: Since adult borer moths are attracted to injured trees, avoid mechanical injury to trunks. Attract native parasitic wasps and predators. Beginning in late summer, inspect tree trunks and remove soil several inches deep around base of trunk to look for borer holes containing cream-colored larvae. Dig out larvae with a sharp knife or kill them by working a flexible wire into the holes. Cultivate soil around the trunk in summer to kill pupae.

PLUM CURCULIO

Damage

Adult

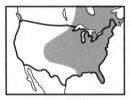

Description: Small, brownish gray beetles with warty, hard wing covers and a long snout. Adults feed on petals, buds, and young fruit. They lay eggs under a crescent-shaped cut in the skin of developing fruits. Eggs hatch into plump, white grubs with brown heads. Larvae feed inside fruit, causing it to drop, rot, or become deformed.

Plants attacked: Apple, apricot, cherry, peach, pear, and plum.

Controls: Knock beetles out of trees onto a tarp by sharply tapping branches with a padded stick; gather and destroy beetles. (This control is only effective if repeated twice a day throughout the growing season.) Or, immediately after knocking trees free of curculios, enclose each tree in floating row cover and tie it closed at the trunk; remove the covers 6 weeks after bloom. Every other day, pick up and destroy all fallen fruit, especially early drops. In areas where severe infestations occur, check developing fruit for egg scars twice a week. Spray with rotenone, ryania, and/or pyrethrins weekly as soon as the first scars are seen on developing fruit. Do not use pesticides before petals drop; it kills beneficial pollinators.

INSECT

SCALES

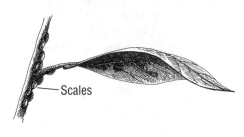

Scales

DESCRIPTION & CONTROLS

Description: Adult females look like small, hard or soft, round or oval bumps on stems, leaves, and fruits. They are legless and wingless. They weaken plants by sucking sap from them; severely infested plants may die. Most scale secrete a sticky substance called honeydew as they feed. Sooty mold, a black fungus, grows on the honeydew. Adult males are minute flying insects with yellow wings. Nymphs are tiny crawling insects.

Plants attacked: Many fruit crops.

Controls: Attract native parasites and predators. Scrub scales gently from twigs with a soft brush and soapy water and rinse well. Apply dormant oil sprays before buds break in early spring. Prune and destroy branches and twigs that are significantly infested. Apply summer oil during summer. As a last resort, spray pyrethrins or rotenone.

SLUGS AND SNAILS

Slug

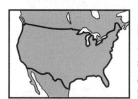

Description: Soft-bodied, gray, tan, green, black, yellow, or spotted wormlike animals. Slugs have no shells; snails have coiled shells. Banana slugs, found in high-rainfall areas along both coasts of North America, can be 4"–6" long. They rasp large holes in foliage, stems, and bulbs, leaving a trail of mucus behind. They are most damaging in wet years or regions.

Plants attacked: Almost any tender plant.

Controls: Wrap copper strips or commercial slug tape around trunks of trees, or use 4"–8" strips of copper flashing as edging for garden beds. Trap under flowerpots or boards; then collect and destroy. Trap in shallow pans of beer buried with the container lip flush to soil surface. Encourage predatory beetles by maintaining permanent paths of clover, sod, or stone mulch. Cover plants with floating row cover, but be sure to remove any slugs in the bed or row before putting on the cover. Protect seedlings temporarily with wide bands of cinders, wood ashes, or natural grade diatomaceous earth spread on the soil.

INSECT

DESCRIPTION & CONTROLS

SPIDER MITES

Spider mite webbing

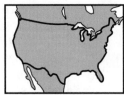

Description: Minute 8-legged creatures; most form fine webbing where they feed. They suck juice from cells on leaf undersides, weakening plants and causing leaves to drop. First signs of damage are yellow speckled areas and webbing on leaves.

Plants attacked: Many vegetables, fruits, and herbs.

Controls: Native predatory mites and beetles usually provide control. For minor infestations, spray water or insecticidal soap. For severe infestations, release purchased predatory mites. For fruit trees or bushes, spray dormant oil and lime-sulfur in late winter.

SQUASH BUG

Nymph

Adult

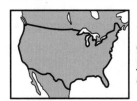

Description: Brownish black, flat-backed, ½" bugs. Nymphs are wingless and whitish green or gray. Adults and nymphs suck plant juices, causing leaves and shoots to blacken and die back.

Plants attacked: Squash-family crops.

Controls: Plant tolerant cultivars. Maintain vigorous plant growth. Handpick eggs, nymphs, and adults from leaf undersides. Support vines off the ground on trellises. Attract native parasitic flies. Cover plants with floating row cover (be sure to hand-pollinate covered plants). Spray rotenone to control nymphs, sabadilla to control adults.

SQUASH VINE BORER

Adult

Larva

Description: Narrow-winged, olive brown moths with clear hind wings and red-ringed abdomens. They lay eggs on stems near the base of plant. Eggs hatch into larvae that bore into vines. Their feeding causes vines to wilt suddenly. Girdled vines rot and die.

Plants attacked: Squash-family crops.

Controls: Plant tolerant cultivars. Plant early or very late to avoid main egg-laying period. Fertilize plants for vigorous growth. Cover vines with floating row cover early in the season (hand-pollinate flowers on covered plants). Spray base of plants with rotenone or pyrethrins repeatedly to kill young larvae before they enter vines. Try saving attacked vines by slitting infested stems and removing borers; heap soil over vines to induce rooting. Or inject infested vines with parasitic nematodes every 4" along lower stem.

INSECT	DESCRIPTION & CONTROLS

TARNISHED PLANT BUG

Nymph

Adult

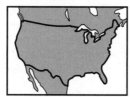

Description: Oval, light green to brown, mottled, ¼" bugs. Nymphs resemble adults but are yellow green and wingless. Adults and nymphs suck plant juices, causing shoot and fruit distortion, bud drop, wilting, stunting, and dieback.

Plants attacked: Most garden crops.

Controls: Cover plants with floating row cover. Tarnished plant bugs overwinter in dead garden refuse, so be sure to clean out all dead plant debris in the bed before putting the row cover over the plants. Attract native predatory bugs. Release purchased minute pirate bugs. Remove all crop debris at end of season. Spray pyrethrins in spring and early summer; if this is not effective, spray sabadilla as a last resort.

WHITEFLIES

Whiteflies

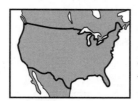

Description: Adults are minute sucking insects with powdery white wings. Whiteflies rest on leaf undersides and fly upward when disturbed. Larvae are flattened, legless, translucent scales on leaf undersides. Nymphs and adults suck plant juices, weakening plants. They also secrete a sticky, sugary substance called honeydew. Sooty mold, a black fungus, grows on the honeydew. Whitefly feeding can also spread viral diseases. Whiteflies can only overwinter in warm southern U.S., but they are commonly introduced in gardens throughout North America on infested greenhouse stock and transplants.

Plants attacked: Citrus and many vegetable crops.

Controls: Vacuum adults from leaves. Attract native parasitic wasps and predatory beetles. Wash the sticky coating from leaves with water. Spray with neem, insecticidal soap, kinoprene (sold as Enstar), or garlic oil. As a last resort, spray with pyrethrins or rotenone.

Solving Disease Problems

There are no instant solutions for most plant disease problems. However, if your crops get enough water and nutrients, and there is good air circulation around the plants, they often bear a good harvest despite some disease symptoms. And, in the long term, there are safe and effective steps you can take so your next crop won't suffer the same fate. Use this table to help confirm a suspected disease problem. Look to the "Controls" section for solutions to protect future crops. This section also points out when spraying organically acceptable fungicides will help prevent the spread of a disease. Only use fungicides preventively when you know from past experience that a crop is likely to suffer from serious disease problems. For information on safe use of fungicides, such as sulfur and copper, refer to "Preventing Disease Problems" on page 210.

DISEASE	SYMPTOMS	CONTROLS
Alternaria blight	Leaves show brown to black spots that enlarge and develop concentric rings (like a target). Heavily blighted leaves dry up and die. Sunken spots appear on fruits and tubers. Affects many vegetables and fruit trees. Known as early blight on nightshade-family crops.	Plant resistant cultivars. Soak seed in a disinfecting solution before planting. Spray copper at first sign of infection. Dispose of infected annual crops, and practice a 3-year rotation.
Anthracnose	Fruits and pods develop small, dark, sunken spots. Bean, cucumber, melon, and tomato are often affected. Also a problem with raspberry and gooseberry. Symptoms on canes and leaves appear as gray spots surrounded by red or purple margins. Sideshoots may wilt, and entire canes may die. On some plants, pinkish spore masses appear in the center of the spots in wet weather.	Plant resistant cultivars. Planting disease-free seed and rotating crops may help prevent anthracnose. For cane plants, apply lime-sulfur spray just as leaf buds break in spring. Prune out and destroy dead wood. For other crops, spray thoroughly with copper or bordeaux mix. Destroy severely infected cane plants and all annual crop residues in fall.
Bacterial leaf spot	Appears as small, dark spots on fruit tree leaves; spots dry up and fall out, leaving shot holes. Small, sunken dark spots or cracks form on fruit. On vegetable crops, small brown or purple spots appear on leaves; leaves eventually turn yellow and die. Affects apricot, peach, plum, also cabbage-family, squash-family, and tomato-family crops.	If you've had past problems with bacterial leaf spot on fruit trees, spray copper on dormant trees. Spray again after bloom every 10–14 days if weather is wet. Check with supplier before spraying because some types of copper fungicide burn leaves. On pepper and tomato, apply streptomycin sulfate every 4–5 days if weather is wet. Limit high-nitrogen fertilizers. Destroy infected vegetable plants. Use a 3-year rotation to reduce problems.

DISEASE	SYMPTOMS	CONTROLS
Brown rot	Flowers and new growth wilt and decay. Developing or mature fruit show soft, brown spots that enlarge rapidly and may grow gray mold. These fruit later shrivel and dry up. Affects apricot, cherry, peach, and plum.	Collect and destroy withered fruit from trees and the ground around them. Cut out infected twigs. If you've had past brown rot problems, and the weather is wet, spray bordeaux mix or copper in spring at bud swell. Spray sulfur at full bloom and when petals fall, and also 1–3 weeks before harvest.
Canker, Cytospora	Infection causes sunken, oozing cankers to form on trunk or twigs. May cause wilting or death of branches or trees. Affects apricot, cherry, peach, and plum.	Avoid mechanical injury because fungus enters through wounds. Cut out cankers, and paint cut area with a 1:1 mix of lime-sulfur and white interior latex paint. Protect trunks from sunscald by painting them with white interior latex paint before January. If problems remain severe, replant with resistant or tolerant cultivars.
Club root	Infected cabbage-family plants wilt during the heat of the day; older leaves turn yellow and drop. Roots are distorted and swollen.	Select resistant cultivars, and buy uninfected plants. Plan to rotate crops, with at least 2 years and preferably 7 years between cabbage-family crops. Add lime to raise soil pH above 7.0 to suppress the disease. Disinfect tools after using them in infected soil. Help infected plants survive by watering well and side-dressing with compost. Pull and destroy severely infected plants.
Downy mildew	White to purple downy growth forms on underside of leaves and along stems. Affects many fruit and vegetable crops.	Plant tolerant cultivars and disease-free plants. Follow a 3-year rotation, and remove and dispose of infected plants. For annual crops, spray copper as soon as symptoms appear. On perennials, such as grapes, remove and destroy badly infected leaves. Try sprays of bordeaux mix or other copper-based fungicides to reduce spread of the disease.
Fire blight	Young, tender shoots die back suddenly. Leaves turn brown or singed looking and remain on the twig. Areas of bark may become water-soaked and ooze. Affects apple, pear, and quince.	Select resistant cultivars. Cut off blighted twigs at least 12" below decay on a dry day. Disinfect pruning tools between cuts. Limit high-nitrogen fertilizers. Spray with streptomycin sulfate (Agrimycin) according to label instructions.

(continued)

Solving Disease Problems—Continued

DISEASE	SYMPTOMS	CONTROLS
Late blight	First symptom is water-soaked spots on lower leaves. Downy white growth appears on leaf undersides. In wet weather, plants will rot and die. Affects nightshade-family crops.	Plant resistant cultivars. Presoak seed in a disinfecting solution. Dispose of all infected plants and tubers. Spraying bordeaux mix can help control outbreaks during wet weather.
Mosaic	Mottled green and yellow foliage or veins. Leaves may be wrinkled or curled; growth may be stunted. This viral disease can appear on bean, tomato, and many other crops.	Plant resistant or tolerant cultivars. Mosaic is spread by insects, especially aphids and leafhoppers. Keep insects away from crops by covering them with floating row cover. Remove and destroy infected plants.
Powdery mildew	Mildew forms a white to grayish powdery growth, usually on upper surfaces of leaves. Leaves of severely infected plants turn brown and shrivel. Fruit ripens prematurely and has poor texture and flavor. Infects apple, cucumber, grape, melon, and many other crops.	Plant resistant cultivars. Prune or stake plants to improve air circulation. Dispose of infected plants. Applying a 0.5% solution of baking soda (1 tsp. baking soda in 1 qt. water) may help to control the disease. If you've had past problems with powdery mildew, apply sulfur every 7–14 days when weather is wet to prevent an outbreak.
Rust	Infected plants develop reddish brown powdery spots on leaves and stems. Leaves turn yellow, and growth is stunted. Different species of rust fungi infect apple, asparagus, bean, brambles, carrot, corn, onion, and other crops.	Provide good air circulation. Remove and destroy seriously infected plants or plant parts. Starting early in the season, dust or spray plants with sulfur to prevent infection or keep mild infections from spreading. For bramble fruits, immediately destroy any infected plants and replant with resistant cultivars.
Wilt, Fusarium and Verticillium	Infected plants wilt and may turn yellow. Leaves may drop prematurely, and severely infected plants may die. Affects a wide range of fruits and vegetables, especially cherry, peach, strawberry, melon, pepper, and tomato.	Select resistant cultivars. Crop rotation does not control these diseases well because so many crops are susceptible. Solarizing the soil before planting may help.

USDA Plant Hardiness Zone Map

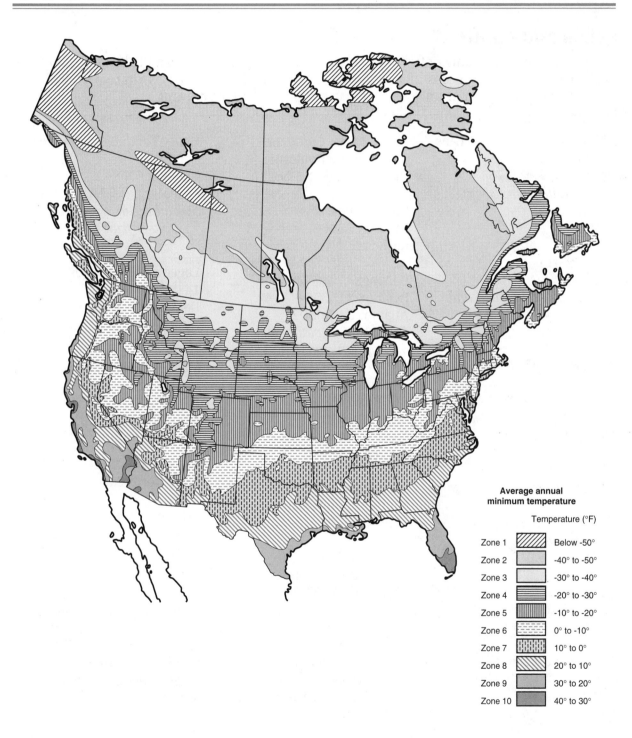

Average annual minimum temperature

Temperature (°F)

Zone 1		Below -50°
Zone 2		-40° to -50°
Zone 3		-30° to -40°
Zone 4		-20° to -30°
Zone 5		-10° to -20°
Zone 6		0° to -10°
Zone 7		10° to 0°
Zone 8		20° to 10°
Zone 9		30° to 20°
Zone 10		40° to 30°

SOURCES

Seeds and Plants

The following companies offer fruit trees and bushes, vegetable seeds and sets, and herbs. Some are large companies that offer a wide range of crops and cultivars, and others are smaller businesses that specialize in a particular type of plant.

Ahrens Nursery & Plant Labs
P.O. Box 145
Huntingburg, IN 47542
Berry plants from tissue culture

Bear Creek Nursery
P.O. Box 411
Northport, WA 99157
Fruit trees; scion wood and bud wood, budded trees, rootstocks

W. Atlee Burpee & Co.
300 Park Avenue
Warminster, PA 18974

Champlain Isle Agro Associates
Isle LaMotte, VT 05463
Tissue culture bramble plants

The Cook's Garden
P.O. Box 535
Londonderry, VT 05148

DeGiorgi Seed Co.
6011 N Street
Omaha, NE 68117

Edible Landscaping
P.O. Box 77
Afton, VA 22920
Specializes in fruit

The Gourmet Gardener
8650 College Boulevard
Overland Park, KS 66210

Harris Seeds
P.O. Box 22960
Rochester, NY 14692

Hastings
P.O. Box 115535
Atlanta, GA 30302
Specializes in plants for southern climates

Ed Hume Seeds, Inc.
P.O. Box 1450
Kent, WA 98035
Specializes in untreated vegetable seed

Johnny's Selected Seeds
2580 Foss Hill Road
Albion, ME 04910

J. W. Jung Seed Co.
335 South High Street
Randolph, WI 53957

Le Jardin du Gourmet
P.O. Box 75
St. Johnsbury Center, VT 05863
Vegetable seed in small and inexpensive packets

Henry Leuthardt Nurseries, Inc.
P.O. Box 666
East Moriches, NY 11940
Specializes in small fruit and espalier fruit trees

Logee's Greenhouses
141 North Street
Danielson, CT 06239
Herbs

Meadowbrook Herb Garden Catalog
P.O. Box 578
Fairfield, CT 06430

Native Seeds/SEARCH
2509 North Campbell Avenue #325
Tucson, AZ 85719
Southwestern native and heirloom vegetable and herb seed

New York State Fruit Testing Cooperative Assoc. Inc.
P.O. Box 462
Geneva, NY 14456-0462
Annual membership fee. New and time-tested fruit cultivars

Nichols Garden Nursery
1190 North Pacific Highway
Albany, OR 97321
Herbs and vegetables

North Star Gardens
19060 Manning Trail North
Marine on St. Croix, MN
55047
Specializes in berries

Owens Nursery
P.O. Box 193
Gay, GA 30218
Specializes in muscadines

Park Seed Co.
P.O. Box 31
Greenwood, SC 29647

Piedmont Plant Co.
P.O. Box 424
Albany, GA 31703
*Field-grown vegetable
transplants*

Pinetree Garden Seeds
Route 100
New Gloucester, ME 04260
*Inexpensive, small seed
packets*

Raintree Nursery
391 Butts Road
Morton, WA 98356
*Specializes in fruits, nuts,
and edible plants*

Redwood City Seed Co.
P.O. Box 361
Redwood City, CA 94064

Ronniger's Seed Potatoes
Star Route
Moyie Springs, ID 83845

St. Lawrence Nurseries
Rural Route 5, Box 324
Potsdam, NY 13676
*Specializes in northern hardy
fruits and nuts*

Sandy Mush Herb Nursery
Route 2, Surrett Cove Road
Leicester, NC 28748
*Specializes in rare and
unusual plants*

Seed Savers Exchange
3076 North Winn Road
Decorah, IA 52101
*Annual membership fee.
Heirloom fruits and
vegetables*

Seeds Blüm
Idaho City Stage
Boise, ID 83706
*Heirloom vegetable and herb
seed*

Seeds Trust High Altitude
Gardens
P.O. Box 4619
Ketchum, ID 83340
*Specializes in seed for high
altitudes and cold climates*

Shepherd's Garden Seeds
6116 Highway 9
Felton, CA 95018

Southmeadow Fruit Gardens
Box SM
Lakeside, MI 49116
Unusual fruit cultivars

Stark Bro's Nurseries &
Orchards Co.
Highway 54
Louisiana, MO 63353
Fruits

Stokes Seeds, Inc.
Box 548
Buffalo, NY 14240

Territorial Seed Co.
P.O. Box 157
Cottage Grove, OR 97424
*Vegetable seed for the
maritime climates of the
Pacific Northwest*

Tomato Growers Supply Co.
P.O. Box 2237
Fort Myers, FL 33902

Well-Sweep Herb Farm
317 Mount Bethel Road
Port Murray, NJ 07865

Specialty Crops

The following companies specialize in the crops of a particular ethnic background, in exotic crops, or in unusual crops.

Exotica Rare Fruit Co.
P.O. Box 160
Vista, CA 92085

Hopkins Citrus and Rare
  Fruit Nursery
5200 SW 160th Avenue
Fort Lauderdale, FL 33331

J. L. Hudson, Seedsman
P.O. Box 1058
Redwood City, CA 94064

Sunrise Enterprises
P.O. Box 330058
West Hartford, CT
  06133-0058
Asian vegetable seed

Whitman Farms
3995 Gibson Road NW
Salem, OR 97304
Currrants and gooseberries

Cultivar and Sources Reference Books

Refer to the books below when you want to find a source for a particular cultivar of a plant, especially if it's an unusual or heirloom cultivar. These books can also give you more comprehensive information on sources of plants and supplies. If your local library doesn't have these books, ask if they can acquire them for you through interlibrary loan.

Barton, Barbara J. *Gardening by Mail: A Source Book.* 4th ed. Boston: Houghton Mifflin, 1994.

Facciola, Stephen. *Cornucopia: A Source Book of Edible Plants.* Vista, Calif.: Kampong Publications, 1990. (Available from Kampong Publications, 1870 Sunrise Drive, Vista, CA 92084)

Whealy, Kent, ed. *Fruit, Berry and Nut Inventory.* Decorah, Iowa: Seed Saver Publications, 1989. (Available from Seed Savers Exchange, 3076 North Winn Road, Decorah, IA 52101)

Whealy, Kent, ed. *Garden Seed Inventory.* 2d ed. Decorah, Iowa: Seed Saver Publications, 1988. (Available from Seed Savers Exchange, 3076 North Winn Road, Decorah, IA 52101)

Gardening Equipment and Supplies

The following companies offer merchandise such as organic fertilizers, composting equipment, animal repellents and traps, beneficial insects and microbes, shredders, sprayers, tillers, row cover and shading materials, irrigation equipment, hand tools, and carts.

Bountiful Gardens
19550 Walker Road
Willits, CA 95490
*Also offers organically grown
herb and vegetable seed*

DripWorks
380 Maple Street
Willits, CA 95490
*Drip irrigation and pond
liners*

Gardener's Supply Co.
128 Intervale Road
Burlington, VT 05401

Gardens Alive!
5100 Schenley Place
Lawrenceburg, IN 47025

Harmony Farm Supply
P.O. Box 460
Graton, CA 95444

A. M. Leonard, Inc.
P.O. Box 816
Piqua, OH 45356

Necessary Trading Co.
P.O. Box 305
422 Salem Avenue
New Castle, VA 24127
*Soil amendments and organic
pest controls; large
quantities only*

Peaceful Valley Farm Supply Co.
P.O. Box 2209
Grass Valley, CA 95945

Pest Management Supply
311 River Drive
Hadley, MA 01035
Traps and pheromone lures

Raindrip, Inc.
21305 Itasca Street
Chatsworth, CA 91311

The Urban Farmer Store
2833 Vicente Street
San Francisco, CA 94116
*Water-conserving irrigation
systems and other supplies*

Soil-Testing Laboratories

The following companies will test soil samples from home gardens. Some companies also make recommendations for adding soil amendments based on test results. Be sure to mention you need an organic recommendation.

A & L Agricultural Labs
7621 White Pine Road
Richmond, VA 23237

Biosystem Consultants
P.O. Box 43
Lorane, OR 97451

Cook's Consulting
Rural Delivery 2, Box 13
Lowville, NY 13367

Timberleaf
5569 State Street
Albany, OH 45710

Wallace Labs
365 Coral Circle
El Segundo, CA 90245

RECOMMENDED READING

The following books and periodicals provide in-depth information on specialized topics related to growing fruits, vegetables, and herbs. Your local Cooperative Extension Service office also has problem identification guides and other gardening publications.

Books

Adams, William D., and Thomas R. Leroy. *Growing Fruits and Nuts in the South*. Dallas, Tex.: Taylor Publishing Company, 1992.

Ashworth, Suzanne. *Seed to Seed*. Decorah, Iowa: Seed Savers Exchange, 1991.

Bartholomew, Mel. *Square Foot Gardening*. Emmaus, Pa.: Rodale Press, 1981.

Bradley, Fern Marshall, and Barbara W. Ellis, eds. *Rodale's All-New Encyclopedia of Organic Gardening*. Emmaus, Pa.: Rodale Press, 1992.

Bubel, Mike, and Nancy Bubel. *Root Cellaring*. 2d ed. Pownal, Vt.: Storey Communications, 1991.

Bubel, Nancy. *The New Seed-Starter's Handbook*. Emmaus, Pa.: Rodale Press, 1988.

Coleman, Eliot. *Four-Season Harvest: How to Harvest Fresh, Organic Vegetables from Your Home Garden All Year Long*. Post Mills, Vt.: Chelsea Green Publishing, 1992.

Ellis, Barbara W., ed. *Rodale's Illustrated Encyclopedia of Gardening and Landscaping Techniques*. Emmaus, Pa.: Rodale Press, 1990.

Ellis, Barbara W., and Fern Marshall Bradley, eds. *The Organic Gardener's Handbook of Natural Insect and Disease Control*. Emmaus, Pa.: Rodale Press, 1992.

Ettlinger, Steve. *The Complete Illustrated Guide to Everything Sold in Garden Centers (Except the Plants)*. New York: Macmillan Publishing Company, 1990.

Gershuny, Grace. *Start with the Soil*. Emmaus, Pa.: Rodale Press, 1993.

Gershuny, Grace, and Deborah L. Martin, eds. *The Rodale Book of Composting*. Emmaus, Pa.: Rodale Press, 1992.

Gessert, Kate Rogers. *The Beautiful Food Garden: Creative Landscaping with Vegetables, Herbs, Fruits, & Flowers*. Pownal, Vt.: Storey Communications, 1987.

Greene, Janet, et al. *Putting Food By*. 4th ed. New York: Viking Penguin, 1991.

Hall, Walter. *Barnacle Parp's Guide to Garden & Yard Power Tools: Selection, Maintenance and Repair*. Emmaus, Pa.: Rodale Press, 1983.

Harrington, Geri. *Grow Your Own Chinese Vegetables*. Pownal, Vt.: Garden Way Publishing, 1978.

Hill, Lewis. *Fruits and Berries for the Home Garden*. Rev. ed. Pownal, Vt.: Garden Way Publishing, 1992.

Hill, Lewis. *Secrets of Plant Propagation*. Pownal, Vt.: Storey Communications, 1985.

Hupping, Carol, et al. *Stocking Up III*. Emmaus, Pa.: Rodale Press, 1986.

Hylton, William H., and Claire Kowalchik, eds. *Rodale's Illustrated Encyclopedia of Herbs*. Emmaus, Pa.: Rodale Press, 1987.

Jeavons, John. *How to Grow More Vegetables Than You Ever Thought Possible on Less Land Than You Can Imagine*. Rev. ed. Berkeley, Calif.: Ten Speed Press, 1991.

Kourik, Robert. *Drip Irrigation for Every Landscape and All Climates.* Santa Rosa, Calif.: Metamorphic Press, 1992.

Larkcom, Joy. *Oriental Vegetables.* New York: Kodansha America, 1991.

McClure, Susan, and Sally Roth. *Rodale's Successful Organic Gardening: Companion Planting.* Emmaus, Pa.: Rodale Press, 1994.

Michalak, Patricia S. *Rodale's Successful Organic Gardening: Herbs.* Emmaus, Pa.: Rodale Press, 1993.

Michalak, Patricia S., and Linda A. Gilkeson. *Rodale's Successful Organic Gardening: Controlling Pests and Diseases.* Emmaus, Pa.: Rodale Press, 1994.

Michalak, Patricia S., and Cass Peterson. *Rodale's Successful Organic Gardening: Vegetables.* Emmaus, Pa.: Rodale Press, 1993.

Mother Earth News Staff. *The Healthy Garden Handbook: An Illustrated Guide to Combating Insects, Garden Pests, and Plant Diseases.* New York: Simon & Schuster, 1989.

Ogden, Shepherd. *Step by Step Organic Vegetable Gardening.* New York: HarperCollins Publishers, 1992.

Peirce, Pam. *Golden Gate Gardening: The Complete Guide to Year-Round Food Gardening in the San Francisco Bay Area and Coastal California.* Davis, Calif.: agAccess, 1993.

Pleasant, Barbara. *Warm-Climate Gardening.* Pownal, Vt.: Garden Way Publishing: Storey Communications, 1993.

Reich, Lee. *Uncommon Fruits Worthy of Attention.* Reading, Mass.: Addison-Wesley Publishing, 1991.

Rogers, Marc. *Saving Seeds.* Pownal, Vt.: Storey Communications, 1990.

Stevens, David, and Kenneth A. Beckett. *The Contained Garden: A Complete Illustrated Guide to Growing Plants, Flowers, Fruits, & Vegetables Outdoors in Pots.* New York: Penguin USA, Studio Books, 1983.

Medic, Kris. *Rodale's Successful Organic Gardening: Pruning.* Emmaus, Pa.: Rodale Press, 1995.

Van Atta, Marian. *Growing & Using Exotic Foods.* Sarasota, Fla.: Pineapple Press, 1991.

Weiss, Gaea, and Shandor Weiss. *Growing & Using the Healing Herbs.* Emmaus, Pa.: Rodale Press, 1985.

Identification Guides

Borror, Donald J., and Richard E. White. *A Field Guide to the Insects of America North of Mexico.* The Peterson Field Guide Series. Boston: Houghton Mifflin, 1970.

Carr, Anna. *Rodale's Color Handbook of Garden Insects.* Emmaus, Pa.: Rodale Press, 1979.

Fisher, Bill. *Growers Weed Identification Handbook.* Oakland, Calif.: ANR Publications, 1985.

Smith, Miranda, and Anna Carr. *Rodale's Garden Insect, Disease & Weed Identification Guide.* Emmaus, Pa.: Rodale Press, 1988.

Periodicals

Common Sense Pest Control Quarterly
Bio-Integral Resource Center (BIRC)
P.O. Box 7414
Berkeley, CA 94707

National Gardening
National Gardening Association
180 Flynn Avenue
Burlington, VT 05401

Organic Gardening
Rodale Press, Inc.
33 East Minor Street
Emmaus, PA 18098

INDEX

Note: Page references in *italic* indicate tables.
  Boldface references indicate illustrations.

A

Abelmoschus esculentus,
  139–41, *141*
Air circulation, site selection
  and, 6
Alfalfa meal, as soil amendment,
  14
Allium ampeloprasum,
  Ampeloprasum group, 326–27
Allium ampeloprasum, Porrum
  group, *49,* 130
Allium cepa. See Onion
Allium cepa, Aggregatum group,
  142–43
Allium sativum subsp. *sativum,*
  326–27
Allium sativum subsp.
  ophioscorodon, 326–27
Allium schoenoprasum, 323
Alternaria blight, *354*
Amendments. *See* Soil amend-
  ments
Anethum graveolens, 324–25
Animal damage, prevention of,
  62–63, 70–71, 214–15, 227
Anthracnose, *354*
Anthriscus cerefolium, 322–23
Antitranspirants, for disease
  prevention, 210
Aphid midges, as beneficials, 337
Aphids, 342, **342**
Apium graveolens var. *dulce,*
  114–16, *116*
Apium graveolens var.
  rapaceum, 191
Apple, 228–36
    choosing trees, 228
    harvesting, 231

pest control for, *234–36*
planting, 229
problem solving for, *234–36*
pruning bearing trees,
  230–31, **231**
renovating, 218, 219, **219**
season-by-season care of,
  232–33
site and soil for, 229
spurs, 231
training young trees,
  229–30, **229–31**
tree size and, **228**
Apple maggot, 342, **342**
Arachis hypogea, 194
Armoracia rusticana, 327
Armyworms, 343, **343**
Artemisia dracunculus var.
  sativa, 331
Artichoke
    globe, *191*
    Jerusalem, *191*
Arugula, *191*
Asimina triloba, 301
Asparagus, 82–85
    pest control for, *85*
    problem solving for, *85*
Asparagus officinalis, 82–85, *85*
Atriplex hortensis, 194
Avena sativa, as cover crop, 29

B

Bacillus thuringiensis (BT), for
  pest control, 71, 336
Bacillus thuringiensis var.
  kurstaki (BTK), for pest con-

trol, **119,** 212, 336
Bacillus thuringiensis var. *san
  diego* (BTSD), for pest control,
  336
Bacterial leaf spot, *354*
Banding fertilizers, 60
Barbarea verna, 192
Bareroot plants, planting,
  200–201, **201,** 202
Barriers
    for pest control, 70–71, **70,
      71,** 212, 337–38
    for preventing animal dam-
      age, 62–63, **62, 63,** 215
Basella, *191*
Basella alba, 191
Basil, sweet, 322
Batavian lettuce, 131
Bean, 86–93
    average seed life of, 47
    choosing plants, 86
    container growing of, 89
    harvesting, 88–89, **89**
    pest control for, *92–93*
    planting, 86–88, **86**
    problem solving for, *92–93*
    propagation of, 89–90, **90**
    season-by-season care of, 91
    season extension for, 89
    site and soil for, 86
    tepee for, **90**
    trellising, 88, **88**
    types of, 87, **87**
Beds
    planning of, 44
    raised (*see* Raised-bed
      garden)
    seed sowing in, 55–56

Notice that $y = \dfrac{k}{x}$ is a rational equation. Its graph for $k > 0$ and $x > 0$ is shown. From the graph, we can see that as x increases, y decreases.

y decreases

$y = \dfrac{k}{x}, k > 0, x > 0$

as x increases

EXAMPLE 3   Suppose that u varies inversely as w. If u is 3 when w is 5, find the constant of variation and the inverse variation equation.

Solution Since u varies inversely as w, we have $u = \dfrac{k}{w}$. We let $u = 3$ and $w = 5$, and we solve for k.

$$u = \dfrac{k}{w}$$

$$3 = \dfrac{k}{5} \quad \text{Let } u = 3 \text{ and } w = 5.$$

$$15 = k \quad \text{Multiply both sides by 5.}$$

The constant of variation k is 15. This gives the inverse variation equation

$$u = \dfrac{15}{w}$$

☐

PRACTICE

3   Suppose that b varies inversely as a. If b is 5 when a is 9, find the constant of variation and the inverse variation equation. ▪

EXAMPLE 4   **Using Inverse Variation and Boyle's Law**

Boyle's law says that if the temperature stays the same, the pressure P of a gas is inversely proportional to the volume V. If a cylinder in a steam engine has a pressure of 960 kilopascals when the volume is 1.4 cubic meters, find the pressure when the volume increases to 2.5 cubic meters.

Solution

1. UNDERSTAND. Read and reread the problem. Notice that we are given that the pressure of a gas is _inversely proportional_ to the volume. We will let P = the pressure and V = the volume. The constant of variation is represented by k.

2. TRANSLATE. Because P is inversely proportional to V, we write

$$P = \dfrac{k}{V}$$

When $P = 960$ kilopascals, the volume $V = 1.4$ cubic meters. We use this information to find k.

$$960 = \dfrac{k}{1.4} \quad \text{Let } P = 960 \text{ and } V = 1.4.$$

$$1344 = k \quad \text{Multiply both sides by 1.4.}$$

Thus, the value of k is 1344. Replacing k with 1344 in the variation equation, we have

$$P = \dfrac{1344}{V}$$

Next we find P when V is 2.5 cubic meters.

(Continued on next page)

3. SOLVE.

$$P = \frac{1344}{2.5} \quad \text{Let } V = 2.5.$$

$$= 537.6$$

4. INTERPRET.

Check: Check the proposed solution in the original problem.

State: When the volume is 2.5 cubic meters, the pressure is 537.6 kilopascals. ☐

PRACTICE

4 Use Boyle's law as stated in Example 4. When $P = 350$ kilopascals and $V = 2.8$ cubic meters, find the pressure when the volume decreases to 1.5 cubic meters. ◼

OBJECTIVE

3 Solving Problems Involving Joint Variation

Sometimes the ratio of a variable to the product of many other variables is constant. For example, the ratio of distance traveled to the product of speed and time traveled is always 1.

$$\frac{d}{rt} = 1 \quad \text{or} \quad d = rt$$

Such a relationship is called **joint variation.**

Joint Variation

If the ratio of a variable y to the product of two or more variables is constant, then y **varies jointly as,** or **is jointly proportional to,** the other variables. If

$$y = kxz$$

then the number k is the **constant of variation** or the **constant of proportionality.**

✔ CONCEPT CHECK

Which type of variation is represented by the equation $xy = 8$? Explain.

a. Direct variation   **b.** Inverse variation   **c.** Joint variation

---

⚠ **EXAMPLE 5** **Expressing Surface Area**

The lateral surface area of a cylinder varies jointly as its radius and height. Express this surface area S in terms of radius r and height h.

Solution Because the surface area varies jointly as the radius r and the height h, we equate S to a constant multiple of r and h.

$$S = krh$$

In the equation, $S = krh$, it can be determined that the constant k is 2π, and we then have the formula $S = 2\pi rh$. (The lateral surface area formula does not include the areas of the two circular bases.) ☐

PRACTICE
5 The area of a regular polygon varies jointly as its apothem and its perimeter. Express the area in terms of the apothem a and the perimeter p. ■

OBJECTIVE

4 Solving Problems Involving Combined Variation

Some examples of variation involve combinations of direct, inverse, and joint variation. We will call these variations **combined variation.**

EXAMPLE 6 Suppose that y varies directly as the square of x. If y is 24 when x is 2, find the constant of variation and the variation equation.

Solution Since y varies directly as the square of x, we have

$$y = kx^2$$

Now let $y = 24$ and $x = 2$ and solve for k.

$$y = kx^2$$
$$24 = k \cdot 2^2$$
$$24 = 4k$$
$$6 = k$$

The constant of variation is 6, so the variation equation is

$$y = 6x^2$$ □

PRACTICE

6 Suppose that y varies inversely as the cube of x. If y is $\dfrac{1}{2}$ when x is 2, find the constant of variation and the variation equation. ■

△ **EXAMPLE 7** Finding Column Weight

The maximum weight that a circular column can support is directly proportional to the fourth power of its diameter and is inversely proportional to the square of its height. A 2-meter-diameter column that is 8 meters in height can support 1 ton. Find the weight that a 1-meter-diameter column that is 4 meters in height can support.

Solution

1. **UNDERSTAND.** Read and reread the problem. Let w = weight, d = diameter, h = height, and k = the constant of variation.

2. **TRANSLATE.** Since w is directly proportional to d^4 and inversely proportional to h^2, we have

$$w = \frac{kd^4}{h^2}$$

(Continued on next page)

3. SOLVE. To find k, we are given that a 2-meter-diameter column that is 8 meters in height can support 1 ton. That is, $w = 1$ when $d = 2$ and $h = 8$, or

$$1 = \frac{k \cdot 2^4}{8^2} \quad \text{Let } w = 1, d = 2, \text{ and } h = 8.$$

$$1 = \frac{k \cdot 16}{64}$$

$$4 = k \quad \text{Solve for } k.$$

Now replace k with 4 in the equation $w = \dfrac{kd^4}{h^2}$ and we have

$$w = \frac{4d^4}{h^2}$$

To find weight w for a 1-meter-diameter column that is 4 meters in height, let $d = 1$ and $h = 4$.

$$w = \frac{4 \cdot 1^4}{4^2}$$

$$w = \frac{4}{16} = \frac{1}{4}$$

4. INTERPRET.

Check: Check the proposed solution in the original problem.

State: The 1-meter-diameter column that is 4 meters in height can support $\frac{1}{4}$ ton of weight. □

PRACTICE
7 Suppose that y varies directly as z and inversely as the cube of x. If y is 15 when $z = 5$ and $x = 3$, find the constant of variation and the variation equation. ▪

✔ Vocabulary, Readiness & Video Check

State whether each equation represents direct, inverse, or joint variation.

1. $y = 5x$ **2.** $y = \dfrac{700}{x}$ **3.** $y = 5xz$ **4.** $y = \dfrac{1}{2}abc$

5. $y = \dfrac{9.1}{x}$ **6.** $y = 2.3x$ **7.** $y = \dfrac{2}{3}x$ **8.** $y = 3.1st$

Martin-Gay Interactive Videos

See Video 6.7 ⬤

Watch the section lecture video and answer the following questions.

OBJECTIVE 1
9. Based on the lecture before ▦ Example 1, what kind of equation is a direct variation equation? What does k, the constant of variation, represent in this equation?

OBJECTIVE 2
10. In ▦ Example 3, why is it not necessary to replace the given values of x and y in the inverse variation equation in order to find k?

OBJECTIVE 3
11. Based on ▦ Example 5 and the lecture before, what is the variation equation for "y varies jointly as the square of a and the fifth power of b"?

OBJECTIVE 4
12. From ▦ Example 6, what kind of variation does a combined variation application involve?

6.7 Exercise Set MyMathLab®

If y varies directly as x, find the constant of variation and the direct variation equation for each situation. See Example 1.

1. $y = 4$ when $x = 20$
2. $y = 5$ when $x = 30$
3. $y = 6$ when $x = 4$
4. $y = 12$ when $x = 8$
5. $y = 7$ when $x = \dfrac{1}{2}$
6. $y = 11$ when $x = \dfrac{1}{3}$
7. $y = 0.2$ when $x = 0.8$
8. $y = 0.4$ when $x = 2.5$

Solve. See Example 2.

9. The weight of a synthetic ball varies directly with the cube of its radius. A ball with a radius of 2 inches weighs 1.20 pounds. Find the weight of a ball of the same material with a 3-inch radius.

10. At sea, the distance to the horizon is directly proportional to the square root of the elevation of the observer. If a person who is 36 feet above the water can see 7.4 miles, find how far a person 64 feet above the water can see. Round to the nearest tenth of a mile.

11. The amount W of water used varies directly with the population N of people. Kansas City has a population of 467,000 people and used 36.5 billion gallons of water in fiscal year 2013. Find out how many billion gallons of water we would expect Springfield to use if we know that its population is 160,000. Round to the nearest tenth of a billion. (*Source: Kansas City Water Board*)

12. Charles's law states that if the pressure P stays the same, the volume V of a gas is directly proportional to its temperature T. If a balloon is filled with 20 cubic meters of a gas at a temperature of 300 K, find the new volume if the temperature rises to 360 K while the pressure stays the same.

If y varies inversely as x, find the constant of variation and the inverse variation equation for each situation. See Example 3.

13. $y = 6$ when $x = 5$
14. $y = 20$ when $x = 9$
15. $y = 100$ when $x = 7$
16. $y = 63$ when $x = 3$
17. $y = \dfrac{1}{8}$ when $x = 16$
18. $y = \dfrac{1}{10}$ when $x = 40$
19. $y = 0.2$ when $x = 0.7$
20. $y = 0.6$ when $x = 0.3$

Solve. See Example 4.

21. Pairs of markings a set distance apart are made on highways so that police can detect drivers exceeding the speed limit. Over a fixed distance, the speed R varies inversely with the time T. In one particular pair of markings, R is 45 mph when T is 6 seconds. Find the speed of a car that travels the given distance in 5 seconds.

22. The weight of an object on or above the surface of Earth varies inversely as the square of the distance between the object and Earth's center. If a person weighs 160 pounds on Earth's surface, find the individual's weight if he moves 200 miles above Earth. Round to the nearest whole pound. (Assume that Earth's radius is 4000 miles.)

23. If the voltage V in an electric circuit is held constant, the current I is inversely proportional to the resistance R. If the current is 40 amperes when the resistance is 270 ohms, find the current when the resistance is 150 ohms.

24. Because it is more efficient to produce larger numbers of items, the cost of producing a certain computer DVD is inversely proportional to the number produced. If 4000 can be produced at a cost of $1.20 each, find the cost per DVD when 6000 are produced.

25. The intensity I of light varies inversely as the square of the distance d from the light source. If the distance from the light source is doubled (see the figure), determine what happens to the intensity of light at the new location.

△ **26.** The maximum weight that a circular column can hold is inversely proportional to the square of its height. If an 8-foot column can hold 2 tons, find how much weight a 10-foot column can hold.

10 feet

2 ton

8 feet

?

MIXED PRACTICE

Write each statement as an equation. Use k as the constant of variation. See Example 5.

27. x varies jointly as y and z.

28. P varies jointly as R and the square of S.

29. r varies jointly as s and the cube of t.

30. a varies jointly as b and c.

For each statement, find the constant of variation and the variation equation. See Examples 5 and 6.

31. y varies directly as the cube of x; $y = 9$ when $x = 3$

32. y varies directly as the cube of x; $y = 32$ when $x = 4$

33. y varies directly as the square root of x; $y = 0.4$ when $x = 4$

34. y varies directly as the square root of x; $y = 2.1$ when $x = 9$

35. y varies inversely as the square of x; $y = 0.052$ when $x = 5$

36. y varies inversely as the square of x; $y = 0.011$ when $x = 10$

▶ **37.** y varies jointly as x and the cube of z; $y = 120$ when $x = 5$ and $z = 2$

38. y varies jointly as x and the square of z; $y = 360$ when $x = 4$ and $z = 3$

Solve. See Example 7.

△▶ **39.** The maximum weight that a rectangular beam can support varies jointly as its width and the square of its height and inversely as its length. If a beam $\frac{1}{2}$ foot wide, $\frac{1}{3}$ foot high, and 10 feet long can support 12 tons, find how much a similar beam can support if the beam is $\frac{2}{3}$ foot wide, $\frac{1}{2}$ foot high, and 16 feet long.

40. The number of cars manufactured on an assembly line at a General Motors plant varies jointly as the number of workers and the time they work. If 200 workers can produce 60 cars in 2 hours, find how many cars 240 workers should be able to make in 3 hours.

△ **41.** The volume of a cone varies jointly as its height and the square of its radius. If the volume of a cone is 32π cubic inches when the radius is 4 inches and the height is 6 inches, find the volume of a cone when the radius is 3 inches and the height is 5 inches.

△ **42.** When a wind blows perpendicularly against a flat surface, its force is jointly proportional to the surface area and the speed of the wind. A sail whose surface area is 12 square feet experiences a 20-pound force when the wind speed is 10 miles per hour. Find the force on an 8-square-foot sail if the wind speed is 12 miles per hour.

43. The intensity of light (in foot-candles) varies inversely as the square of x, the distance in feet from the light source. The intensity of light 2 feet from the source is 80 foot-candles. How far away is the source if the intensity of light is 5 foot-candles?

44. The horsepower that can be safely transmitted to a shaft varies jointly as the shaft's angular speed of rotation (in revolutions per minute) and the cube of its diameter. A 2-inch shaft making 120 revolutions per minute safely transmits 40 horsepower. Find how much horsepower can be safely transmitted by a 3-inch shaft making 80 revolutions per minute.

MIXED PRACTICE

Write an equation to describe each variation. Use k for the constant of proportionality. See Examples 1 through 7.

45. y varies directly as x

46. p varies directly as q

47. a varies inversely as b

48. y varies inversely as x

49. y varies jointly as x and z

50. y varies jointly as q, r, and t

51. y varies inversely as x^3

52. y varies inversely as a^4

53. y varies directly as x and inversely as p^2

54. y varies directly as a^5 and inversely as b

REVIEW AND PREVIEW

Find the exact circumference and area of each circle. See Section 2.3.

△ **55.**   △ **56.**

4 in.   6 cm

△ **57.**

9 cm

△ **58.**

7 m

Find each square root. See Section 1.3.

59. $\sqrt{81}$

60. $\sqrt{36}$

61. $\sqrt{1}$

62. $\sqrt{4}$

63. $\sqrt{\dfrac{1}{4}}$

64. $\sqrt{\dfrac{1}{25}}$

65. $\sqrt{\dfrac{4}{9}}$

66. $\sqrt{\dfrac{25}{121}}$

CONCEPT EXTENSIONS

Solve. See the Concept Check in this section. Choose the type of variation that each equation represents. ***a.*** *Direct variation* ***b.*** *Inverse variation* ***c.*** *Joint variation*

67. $y = \dfrac{2}{3}x$

68. $y = \dfrac{0.6}{x}$

69. $y = 9ab$

70. $xy = \dfrac{2}{11}$

71. The horsepower to drive a boat varies directly as the cube of the speed of the boat. If the speed of the boat is to double, determine the corresponding increase in horsepower required.

72. The volume of a cylinder varies jointly as the height and the square of the radius. If the height is halved and the radius is doubled, determine what happens to the volume.

73. Suppose that y varies directly as x. If x is doubled, what is the effect on y?

74. Suppose that y varies directly as x^2. If x is doubled, what is the effect on y?

Complete the following table for the inverse variation $y = \dfrac{k}{x}$ for each given value of k. Plot the points on a rectangular coordinate system.

x	$\dfrac{1}{4}$	$\dfrac{1}{2}$	1	2	4
$y = \dfrac{k}{x}$					

75. $k = 3$ **76.** $k = 1$ **77.** $k = \dfrac{1}{2}$ **78.** $k = 5$

Chapter 6 Vocabulary Check

Fill in each blank with one of the words or phrases listed below.

rational expression	equation	complex fraction	opposites	synthetic division
least common denominator	expression	long division	jointly	directly	inversely

1. A rational expression whose numerator, denominator, or both contain one or more rational expressions is called a(n) _____.

2. To divide a polynomial by a polynomial other than a monomial, we use _____.

3. In the equation $y = kx$, y varies _____ as x.

4. In the equation $y = \dfrac{k}{x}$, y varies _____ as x.

5. The _____ of a list of rational expressions is a polynomial of least degree whose factors include the denominator factors in the list.

6. When a polynomial is to be divided by a binomial of the form $x - c$, a shortcut process called _____ may be used.

7. In the equation $y = kxz$, y varies _____ as x and z.

8. The expressions $(x - 5)$ and $(5 - x)$ are called _____.

9. A(n) _____ is an expression that can be written as the quotient $\dfrac{P}{Q}$ of two polynomials P and Q as long as Q is not 0.

10. Which is an expression and which is an equation? An example of an _____ is $\dfrac{2}{x} + \dfrac{2}{x^2} = 7$, and an example of an _____ is $\dfrac{2}{x} + \dfrac{5}{x^2}$.

Chapter 6 Highlights

DEFINITIONS AND CONCEPTS	EXAMPLES

Section 6.1 Rational Functions and Multiplying and Dividing Rational Expressions

A rational expression is the quotient $\dfrac{P}{Q}$ of two polynomials P and Q, as long as Q is not 0.

$$\frac{2x-6}{7}, \quad \frac{t^2-3t+5}{t-1}$$

To Simplify a Rational Expression

Step 1. Completely factor the numerator and the denominator.

Step 2. Apply the fundamental principle of rational expressions.

Simplify.

$$\frac{2x^2+9x-5}{x^2-25} = \frac{(2x-1)(x+5)}{(x-5)(x+5)}$$

$$= \frac{2x-1}{x-5}$$

To Multiply Rational Expressions

Step 1. Completely factor numerators and denominators.

Step 2. Multiply the numerators and multiply the denominators.

Step 3. Apply the fundamental principle of rational expressions.

Multiply: $\dfrac{x^3+8}{12x-18} \cdot \dfrac{14x^2-21x}{x^2+2x}$

$$= \frac{(x+2)(x^2-2x+4)}{6(2x-3)} \cdot \frac{7x(2x-3)}{x(x+2)}$$

$$= \frac{7(x^2-2x+4)}{6}$$

To Divide Rational Expressions

Multiply the first rational expression by the reciprocal of the second rational expression.

Divide: $\dfrac{x^2+6x+9}{5xy-5y} \div \dfrac{x+3}{10y}$

$$= \frac{(x+3)(x+3)}{5y(x-1)} \cdot \frac{2 \cdot 5y}{x+3}$$

$$= \frac{2(x+3)}{x-1}$$

A rational function is a function described by a rational expression.

$$f(x) = \frac{2x-6}{7}, \quad h(t) = \frac{t^2-3t+5}{t-1}$$

Section 6.2 Adding and Subtracting Rational Expressions

To Add or Subtract Rational Expressions

Step 1. Find the LCD.

Step 2. Write each rational expression as an equivalent rational expression whose denominator is the LCD.

Step 3. Add or subtract numerators and write the result over the common denominator.

Step 4. Simplify the resulting rational expression.

Subtract: $\dfrac{3}{x+2} - \dfrac{x+1}{x-3}$

$$= \frac{3 \cdot (x-3)}{(x+2) \cdot (x-3)} - \frac{(x+1) \cdot (x+2)}{(x-3) \cdot (x+2)}$$

$$= \frac{3(x-3) - (x+1)(x+2)}{(x+2)(x-3)}$$

$$= \frac{3x-9 - (x^2+3x+2)}{(x+2)(x-3)}$$

$$= \frac{3x-9 - x^2-3x-2}{(x+2)(x-3)}$$

$$= \frac{-x^2-11}{(x+2)(x-3)}$$

DEFINITIONS AND CONCEPTS	EXAMPLES

Section 6.3   Simplifying Complex Fractions

Method 1: Simplify the numerator and the denominator so that each is a single fraction. Then perform the indicated division and simplify if possible.

Simplify: $\dfrac{\dfrac{x+2}{x}}{x-\dfrac{4}{x}}$

Method 1: $\dfrac{\dfrac{x+2}{x}}{\dfrac{x\cdot x}{1\cdot x}-\dfrac{4}{x}}=\dfrac{\dfrac{x+2}{x}}{\dfrac{x^2-4}{x}}$

$=\dfrac{x+2}{x}\cdot\dfrac{x}{(x+2)(x-2)}=\dfrac{1}{x-2}$

Method 2: Multiply the numerator and the denominator of the complex fraction by the LCD of the fractions in both the numerator and the denominator. Then simplify if possible.

Method 2: $\dfrac{\left(\dfrac{x+2}{x}\right)\cdot x}{\left(x-\dfrac{4}{x}\right)\cdot x}=\dfrac{x+2}{x\cdot x-\dfrac{4}{x}\cdot x}$

$=\dfrac{x+2}{x^2-4}=\dfrac{x+2}{(x+2)(x-2)}=\dfrac{1}{x-2}$

Section 6.4   Dividing Polynomials: Long Division and Synthetic Division

To Divide a Polynomial

To divide a polynomial by a monomial, divide each term in the polynomial by the monomial.

Divide: $\dfrac{12a^5b^3-6a^2b^2+ab}{6a^2b^2}$

$=\dfrac{12a^5b^3}{6a^2b^2}-\dfrac{6a^2b^2}{6a^2b^2}+\dfrac{ab}{6a^2b^2}$

$=2a^3b-1+\dfrac{1}{6ab}$

To divide a polynomial by a polynomial other than a monomial, use **long division.**

Divide $2x^3-x^2-8x-1$ by $x-2$.

$$
\begin{array}{r}
2x^2+3x-2 \\
x-2\overline{\smash{)}2x^3-\ x^2-8x-1} \\
\underline{2x^3-4x^2} \\
3x^2-8x \\
\underline{3x^2-6x} \\
-2x-1 \\
\underline{-2x+4} \\
-5
\end{array}
$$

The quotient is $2x^2+3x-2-\dfrac{5}{x-2}$.

A shortcut method called **synthetic division** may be used to divide a polynomial by a binomial of the form $x-c$.

Use synthetic division to divide $2x^3-x^2-8x-1$ by $x-2$.

$$
\begin{array}{r|rrrr}
2\,\rfloor & 2 & -1 & -8 & -1 \\
 & \downarrow & 4 & 6 & -4 \\
\hline
 & 2 & 3 & -2 & -5
\end{array}
$$

The quotient is $2x^2+3x-2-\dfrac{5}{x-2}$.

DEFINITIONS AND CONCEPTS	EXAMPLES

Section 6.5 Solving Equations Containing Rational Expressions

To Solve an Equation Containing Rational Expressions

Multiply both sides of the equation by the LCD of all rational expressions. Then apply the distributive property and simplify. Solve the resulting equation and then check each proposed solution to see whether it makes a denominator 0. If so, it is an **extraneous solution.**

Solve: $x - \dfrac{3}{x} = \dfrac{1}{2}$

$$2x\left(x - \frac{3}{x}\right) = 2x\left(\frac{1}{2}\right) \quad \text{The LCD is } 2x.$$

$$2x \cdot x - 2x\left(\frac{3}{x}\right) = 2x\left(\frac{1}{2}\right) \quad \text{Distribute.}$$

$$2x^2 - 6 = x$$

$$2x^2 - x - 6 = 0 \qquad \text{Subtract } x.$$

$$(2x + 3)(x - 2) = 0 \qquad \text{Factor.}$$

$$x = -\frac{3}{2} \quad \text{or} \quad x = 2 \qquad \text{Solve.}$$

Both $-\dfrac{3}{2}$ and 2 check. The solutions are 2 and $-\dfrac{3}{2}$.

Section 6.6 Rational Equations and Problem Solving

To Solve an Equation for a Specified Variable

Treat the specified variable as the only variable of the equation and solve as usual.

Solve for x.

$$A = \frac{2x + 3y}{5}$$

$$5A = 2x + 3y \quad \text{Multiply both sides by 5.}$$

$$5A - 3y = 2x \quad \text{Subtract } 3y \text{ from both sides.}$$

$$\frac{5A - 3y}{2} = x \quad \text{Divide both sides by 2.}$$

Problem-Solving Steps to Follow

Jeanee and David Dillon volunteer every year to clean a strip of Lake Ponchartrain Beach. Jeanee can clean all the trash in this area of beach in 6 hours; David takes 5 hours. Find how long it will take them to clean the area of beach together.

1. UNDERSTAND.

1. Read and reread the problem.

Let x = time in hours that it takes Jeanee and David to clean the beach together.

	Hours to Complete	**Part Completed in 1 Hour**
Jeanee Alone	6	$\dfrac{1}{6}$
David Alone	5	$\dfrac{1}{5}$
Together	x	$\dfrac{1}{x}$

2. TRANSLATE.

2. In words:

part Jeanee can complete in 1 hour	+	part David can complete in 1 hour	=	part they can complete together in 1 hour
↓		↓		↓

Translate:

$$\frac{1}{6} \quad + \quad \frac{1}{5} \quad = \quad \frac{1}{x}$$

DEFINITIONS AND CONCEPTS	EXAMPLES
Section 6.6 Rational Equations and Problem Solving (continued)	

3. SOLVE.

3. $\dfrac{1}{6} + \dfrac{1}{5} = \dfrac{1}{x}$

$5x + 6x = 30$ Multiply both sides by $30x$.

$11x = 30$

$x = \dfrac{30}{11}$ or $2\dfrac{8}{11}$

4. INTERPRET.

4. *Check* and then *state*. Together, they can clean the beach in $2\dfrac{8}{11}$ hours.

Section 6.7 Variation and Problem Solving	

y **varies directly as** *x*, or *y* **is directly proportional to** *x*, if there is a nonzero constant *k* such that

$$y = kx$$

y **varies inversely as** *x*, or *y* **is inversely proportional to** *x*, if there is a nonzero constant *k* such that

$$y = \dfrac{k}{x}$$

y **varies jointly as** *x* and *z*, or *y* **is jointly proportional to** *x* and *z*, if there is a nonzero constant *k* such that

$$y = kxz$$

The circumference of a circle *C* varies directly as its radius *r*.

$$C = \underset{k}{\underline{2\pi}}\,r$$

At a constant temperature, pressure *P* varies inversely with volume *V*.

$$P = \dfrac{k}{V}$$

The lateral surface area *S* of a cylinder varies jointly as its radius *r* and height *h*.

$$S = \underset{k}{\underline{2\pi}}\,rh$$

Chapter 6 Review

(6.1) Find the domain for each rational function.

1. $f(x) = \dfrac{3 - 5x}{7}$

2. $g(x) = \dfrac{2x + 4}{11}$

3. $F(x) = \dfrac{-3x^2}{x - 5}$

4. $h(x) = \dfrac{4x}{3x - 12}$

5. $f(x) = \dfrac{x^3 + 2}{x^2 + 8x}$

6. $G(x) = \dfrac{20}{3x^2 - 48}$

Write each rational expression in lowest terms.

7. $\dfrac{x - 12}{12 - x}$

8. $\dfrac{5x - 15}{25x - 75}$

9. $\dfrac{2x}{2x^2 - 2x}$

10. $\dfrac{x + 7}{x^2 - 49}$

11. $\dfrac{2x^2 + 4x - 30}{x^2 + x - 20}$

12. The average cost (per bookcase) of manufacturing x bookcases is given by the rational function

$$C(x) = \dfrac{35x + 4200}{x}$$

   a. Find the average cost per bookcase of manufacturing 50 bookcases.

   b. Find the average cost per bookcase of manufacturing 100 bookcases.

   c. As the number of bookcases increases, does the average cost per bookcase increase or decrease? (See parts **a** and **b**.)

Perform each indicated operation. Write your answers in lowest terms.

13. $\dfrac{4 - x}{5} \cdot \dfrac{15}{2x - 8}$

14. $\dfrac{x^2 - 6x + 9}{2x^2 - 18} \cdot \dfrac{4x + 12}{5x - 15}$

15. $\dfrac{a - 4b}{a^2 + ab} \cdot \dfrac{b^2 - a^2}{8b - 2a}$

16. $\dfrac{x^2 - x - 12}{2x^2 - 32} \cdot \dfrac{x^2 + 8x + 16}{3x^2 + 21x + 36}$

17. $\dfrac{4x + 8y}{3} \div \dfrac{5x + 10y}{9}$

18. $\dfrac{x^2 - 25}{3} \div \dfrac{x^2 - 10x + 25}{x^2 - x - 20}$

19. $\dfrac{a - 4b}{a^2 + ab} \div \dfrac{20b - 5a}{b^2 - a^2}$

20. $\dfrac{3x + 3}{x - 1} \div \dfrac{x^2 - 6x - 7}{x^2 - 1}$

21. $\dfrac{2x - x^2}{x^3 - 8} \div \dfrac{x^2}{x^2 + 2x + 4}$

22. $\dfrac{5x - 15}{3 - x} \cdot \dfrac{x + 2}{10x + 20} \cdot \dfrac{x^2 - 9}{x^2 - x - 6}$

(6.2) Find the LCD of the rational expressions in each list.

23. $\dfrac{5}{4x^2y^5}, \dfrac{3}{10x^2y^4}, \dfrac{x}{6y^4}$

24. $\dfrac{5}{2x}, \dfrac{7}{x - 2}$

25. $\dfrac{3}{5x}, \dfrac{2}{x - 5}$

26. $\dfrac{1}{5x^3}, \dfrac{4}{x^2 + 3x - 28}, \dfrac{11}{10x^2 - 30x}$

Perform each indicated operation. Write your answers in lowest terms.

27. $\dfrac{4}{x - 4} + \dfrac{x}{x - 4}$

28. $\dfrac{4}{3x^2} + \dfrac{2}{3x^2}$

29. $\dfrac{1}{x - 2} - \dfrac{1}{4 - 2x}$

30. $\dfrac{1}{10 - x} + \dfrac{x - 1}{x - 10}$

31. $\dfrac{x}{9 - x^2} - \dfrac{2}{5x - 15}$

32. $2x + 1 - \dfrac{1}{x - 3} \left(\text{or } \dfrac{2x + 1}{1} - \dfrac{1}{x - 3} \right)$

33. $\dfrac{2}{a^2 - 2a + 1} + \dfrac{3}{a^2 - 1}$

34. $\dfrac{x}{9x^2 + 12x + 16} - \dfrac{3x + 4}{27x^3 - 64}$

35. $\dfrac{2}{x - 1} - \dfrac{3x}{3x - 3} + \dfrac{1}{2x - 2}$

△ **36.** Find the perimeter of the heptagon (a polygon with seven sides).

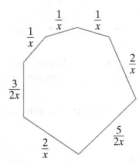

(6.3) Simplify each complex fraction.

37. $\dfrac{1 - \dfrac{3x}{4}}{2 + \dfrac{x}{4}}$

38. $\dfrac{\dfrac{x^2}{15}}{\dfrac{x + 1}{5x}}$

39. $\dfrac{2 - \dfrac{3}{2x}}{x - \dfrac{2}{5x}}$

40. $\dfrac{1 + \dfrac{x}{y}}{\dfrac{x^2}{y^2} - 1}$

41. $\dfrac{\dfrac{5}{x} + \dfrac{1}{xy}}{\dfrac{3}{x^2}}$

42. $\dfrac{\dfrac{x}{3} - \dfrac{3}{x}}{1 + \dfrac{3}{x}}$

43. $\dfrac{\dfrac{1}{x - 1} + 1}{\dfrac{1}{x + 1} - 1}$

44. $\dfrac{\dfrac{x - 3}{x + 3} + \dfrac{x + 3}{x - 3}}{\dfrac{x - 3}{x + 3} - \dfrac{x + 3}{x - 3}}$

If $f(x) = \dfrac{3}{x}$, $x \neq 0$, find each of the following.

45. $f(a + h)$

46. $f(a)$

47. Use Exercises 45 and 46 to find $\dfrac{f(a + h) - f(a)}{h}$.

48. Simplify the results of Exercise 47.

(6.4) Perform the indicated operation.

49. $(4xy + 2x^2 - 9) \div 4xy$

50. Divide $12xb^2 + 16xb^4$ by $4xb^3$.

51. $(3x^4 - 25x^2 - 20) \div (x - 3)$

52. $(-x^2 + 2x^4 + 5x - 12) \div (x + 2)$

53. $(2x^3 + 3x^2 - 2x + 2) \div (2x + 3)$

54. $(3x^4 + 5x^3 + 7x^2 + 3x - 2) \div (x^2 + x + 2)$

Use synthetic division to find each quotient.

55. $(3x^3 + 12x - 4) \div (x - 2)$

56. $(x^5 - 1) \div (x + 1)$

57. $(x^3 - 81) \div (x - 3)$

58. $(3x^4 - 2x^2 + 10) \div (x + 2)$

If $P(x) = 3x^5 - 9x + 7$, use the remainder theorem to find the following.

59. $P(4)$

60. $P(-5)$

61. $P\left(-\dfrac{1}{2}\right)$

△ **62.** If the area of the rectangle is $(x^4 - x^3 - 6x^2 - 6x + 18)$ square miles and its width is $(x - 3)$ miles, find the length.

$$\boxed{\begin{array}{c} x^4 - x^3 - 6x^2 - 6x + 18 \\ \text{square miles} \end{array}} \quad \begin{array}{c} x - 3 \\ \text{miles} \end{array}$$

(6.5) Solve each equation.

63. $\dfrac{3}{x} + \dfrac{1}{3} = \dfrac{5}{x}$

64. $\dfrac{2x + 3}{5x - 9} = \dfrac{3}{2}$

65. $\dfrac{1}{x - 2} - \dfrac{3x}{x^2 - 4} = \dfrac{2}{x + 2}$

66. $\dfrac{7}{x} - \dfrac{x}{7} = 0$

Solve each equation or perform each indicated operation. Simplify.

67. $\dfrac{5}{x^2 - 7x} + \dfrac{4}{2x - 14}$

68. $\dfrac{4}{3 - x} - \dfrac{7}{2x - 6} + \dfrac{5}{x}$

69. $3 - \dfrac{5}{x} - \dfrac{2}{x^2} = 0$ **70.** $2 + \dfrac{15}{x^2} = \dfrac{13}{x}$

(6.6) Solve each equation for the specified variable.

△ **71.** $A = \dfrac{h(a + b)}{2}$ for a

72. $\dfrac{1}{R} = \dfrac{1}{R_1} + \dfrac{1}{R_2}$ for R_2

73. $I = \dfrac{E}{R + r}$ for R

74. $A = P + Prt$ for r

75. $\dfrac{1}{x} = \dfrac{1}{y} - \dfrac{1}{z}$ for x

76. $H = \dfrac{kA(T_1 - T_2)}{L}$ for A

Solve.

77. The sum of a number and twice its reciprocal is 3. Find the number(s).

78. If a number is added to the numerator of $\dfrac{3}{7}$, and twice that number is added to the denominator of $\dfrac{3}{7}$, the result is equivalent to $\dfrac{10}{21}$. Find the number.

79. Three boys can paint a fence in 4 hours, 5 hours, and 6 hours, respectively. Find how long it will take all three boys to paint the fence working together.

80. If Sue Katz can type a certain number of mailing labels in 6 hours and Tom Neilson and Sue working together can type the same number of mailing labels in 4 hours, find how long it takes Tom alone to type the mailing labels.

81. The speed of a Ranger boat in still water is 32 mph. If the boat travels 72 miles upstream in the same time that it takes to travel 120 miles downstream, find the speed of the current.

82. The speed of a jogger is 3 mph faster than the speed of a walker. If the jogger travels 14 miles in the same amount of time that the walker travels 8 miles, find the speed of the walker.

(6.7) Solve each variation problem.

83. A is directly proportional to B. If $A = 6$ when $B = 14$, find A when $B = 21$.

84. According to Boyle's law, the pressure exerted by a gas is inversely proportional to the volume as long as the temperature stays the same. If a gas exerts a pressure of 1250 kilopascals when the volume is 2 cubic meters, find the volume when the pressure is 800 kilopascals.

MIXED REVIEW

For expressions, perform the indicated operation and/or simplify. For equations, solve the equation for the unknown variable.

85. $\dfrac{22x + 8}{11x + 4}$ **86.** $\dfrac{xy - 3x + 2y - 6}{x^2 + 4x + 4}$

87. $\dfrac{2}{5x} \div \dfrac{4 - 18x}{6 - 27x}$

88. $\dfrac{7x + 28}{2x + 4} \div \dfrac{x^2 + 2x - 8}{x^2 - 2x - 8}$

89. $\dfrac{5a^2 - 20}{a^3 + 2a^2 + a + 2} \div \dfrac{7a}{a^3 + a}$

90. $\dfrac{4a + 8}{5a^2 - 20} \cdot \dfrac{3a^2 - 6a}{a + 3} \div \dfrac{2a^2}{5a + 15}$

91. $\dfrac{7}{2x} + \dfrac{5}{6x}$

92. $\dfrac{x - 2}{x + 1} - \dfrac{x - 3}{x - 1}$

93. $\dfrac{2x + 1}{x^2 + x - 6} + \dfrac{2 - x}{x^2 + x - 6}$

94. $\dfrac{2}{x^2 - 16} - \dfrac{3x}{x^2 + 8x + 16} + \dfrac{3}{x + 4}$

95. $\dfrac{\dfrac{1}{x} - \dfrac{2}{3x}}{\dfrac{5}{2x} - \dfrac{1}{3}}$ **96.** $\dfrac{2}{1 - \dfrac{2}{x}}$

97. $\dfrac{\dfrac{x^2 + 5x - 6}{4x + 3}}{\dfrac{(x + 6)^2}{8x + 6}}$ **98.** $\dfrac{\dfrac{3}{x - 1} - \dfrac{2}{1 - x}}{\dfrac{2}{x - 1} - \dfrac{2}{x}}$

99. $4 + \dfrac{8}{x} = 8$

100. $\dfrac{x - 2}{x^2 - 7x + 10} = \dfrac{1}{5x - 10} - \dfrac{1}{x - 5}$

101. The denominator of a fraction is 2 more than the numerator. If the numerator is decreased by 3 and the denominator is increased by 5, the resulting fraction is equivalent to $\dfrac{2}{3}$. Find the fraction.

102. The sum of the reciprocals of two consecutive even integers is $-\dfrac{9}{40}$. Find the two integers.

103. The inlet pipe of a water tank can fill the tank in 2 hours and 30 minutes. The outlet pipe can empty the tank in 2 hours. Find how long it takes to empty a full tank if both pipes are open.

104. Timmy Garnica drove 210 miles in the same amount of time that it took a DC-10 jet to travel 1715 miles. The speed of the jet was 430 mph faster than the speed of the car. Find the speed of the jet.

105. Two Amtrak trains traveling on parallel tracks leave Tucson at the same time. In 6 hours, the faster train is 382 miles from Tucson and the trains are 112 miles apart. Find how fast each train is traveling.

△ **106.** The surface area of a sphere varies directly as the square of its radius. If the surface area is 36π square inches when the radius is 3 inches, find the surface area when the radius is 4 inches.

107. In 2014, 29 out of 50 American adults owned a smart phone. At this rate, how many smart phones would you predict are owned in a community with a 2014 adult population of 43,560? Round to the nearest whole number.

108. Currently, 8 out of 25 U.S. Internet users purchase digital music. At this rate, how many Internet users purchase digital music in a group of 2000 Internet users?

109. Divide $(x^3 - x^2 + 3x^4 - 2)$ by $(x - 4)$.

110. C is inversely proportional to D. If $C = 12$ when $D = 8$, find C when $D = 24$.

Chapter 6 Getting Ready for the Test

1c

MULTIPLE CHOICE *Select the correct choice.*

▶ **1.** Choose the expression that is equivalent to $\dfrac{-x}{4 - x}$.

A. $\dfrac{1}{4}$ **B.** $-\dfrac{1}{4}$ **C.** $\dfrac{x}{4 - x}$ **D.** $\dfrac{x}{x - 4}$

▶ **2.** Choose the expression that is **not** equivalent to $\dfrac{x + 3}{x - 1}$.

A. $\dfrac{-(x + 3)}{-(x - 1)}$ **B.** $\dfrac{-x + 3}{1 - x}$ **C.** $\dfrac{-x - 3}{-x + 1}$ **D.** $\dfrac{-x - 3}{1 - x}$

▶ **3.** For which of these values (if any) is the expression $\dfrac{x + 3}{x^2 + 9}$ undefined?

A. -3 **B.** 3 **C.** -3 and 3 **D.** 0 **E.** none of these

MATCHING *Match each rational expression to its simplified form. Letters may be used more than once.*

▶ **4.** $\dfrac{y - 6}{6 - y}$ **5.** $\dfrac{y + 3}{3 + y}$ **A.** 1

▶ **6.** $\dfrac{x - 2}{-2 + x}$ **7.** $\dfrac{m - 4}{m + 4}$ **B.** -1

C. neither 1 nor -1

MULTIPLE CHOICE *Select the correct choice.*

▶ **8.** $\dfrac{5}{x + 5} \cdot \dfrac{7(x + 1)}{x + 5} =$

A. $\dfrac{35(x + 1)}{x + 5}$ **B.** $\dfrac{35(x + 1)}{(x + 5)^2}$ **C.** $\dfrac{12(x + 1)}{x + 5}$ **D.** $\dfrac{7(x + 1)}{x(x + 5)}$

▶ **9.** $\dfrac{x - 3}{x + 5} - \dfrac{x - 1}{x + 5} =$

A. $\dfrac{-4}{x + 5}$ **B.** $\dfrac{-4}{(x + 5)^2}$ **C.** $\dfrac{-2}{x + 5}$ **D.** $\dfrac{-2}{(x + 5)^2}$

▶ **10.** The LCD of $\dfrac{5}{4x + 8}$ and $\dfrac{9}{8x - 8}$ is

A. $(4x + 8)(8x - 8)$ **B.** $32(x + 2)(x - 1)$ **C.** $4(x + 2)(x - 1)$ **D.** $8(x + 2)(x - 1)$

▶ **11.** Write $\dfrac{2x^{-1}}{y^{-2} + (5x)^{-1}}$ without negative exponents.

A. $\dfrac{\dfrac{2}{x}}{\dfrac{1}{y^2} + \dfrac{1}{5x}}$ **B.** $\dfrac{\dfrac{1}{2x}}{\dfrac{1}{y^2} + \dfrac{1}{5x}}$ **C.** $\dfrac{y^2 + 5x}{2x}$ **D.** $\dfrac{\dfrac{2}{x}}{\dfrac{1}{y^2} + \dfrac{5}{x}}$

▶ **12.** Multiply the given equation through by the LCD of its terms. Choose the correct equivalent equation once this is done.

Given equation: $3 - \dfrac{10x}{4(x + 1)} = \dfrac{5}{6(x + 1)}$

A. $3 - 10x = 5$ **B.** $3 - 3 \cdot 10x = 2 \cdot 5$ **C.** $3 \cdot 12(x + 1) - 3 \cdot 10x = 2 \cdot 5$ **D.** $4(x + 1) - 3 \cdot 10x = 2 \cdot 5$

13. Translate to an equation. Let x be the first even integer.

"The sum of the reciprocals of two consecutive even integers is $\dfrac{9}{40}$."

A. $x + (x + 2) = \dfrac{9}{40}$ **B.** $\dfrac{1}{x} + \dfrac{1}{x+1} = \dfrac{9}{40}$ **C.** $\dfrac{1}{x} - \dfrac{1}{x+2} = \dfrac{9}{40}$ **D.** $\dfrac{1}{x} + \dfrac{1}{x+2} = \dfrac{9}{40}$

MATCHING *Match each statement with its translation. Use each letter once.*

14. y varies inversely as x

15. y varies directly as x

16. y varies jointly as x and z

17. y varies directly as x^2

18. y varies inversely as x^2

A. $y = kx^2$

B. $y = kx$

C. $y = kxz$

D. $y = \dfrac{k}{x}$

E. $y = \dfrac{k}{x^2}$

Chapter 6 Test   MyMathLab® You Tube

Find the domain of each rational function.

1. $f(x) = \dfrac{5x^2}{1 - x}$

2. $g(x) = \dfrac{9x^2 - 9}{x^2 + 4x + 3}$

Write each rational expression in lowest terms.

3. $\dfrac{7x - 21}{24 - 8x}$

4. $\dfrac{x^2 - 4x}{x^2 + 5x - 36}$

5. $\dfrac{x^3 - 8}{x - 2}$

Perform the indicated operation. If possible, simplify your answer.

6. $\dfrac{2x^3 + 16}{6x^2 + 12x} \cdot \dfrac{5}{x^2 - 2x + 4}$

7. $\dfrac{5}{4x^3} + \dfrac{7}{4x^3}$

8. $\dfrac{3x^2 - 12}{x^2 + 2x - 8} \div \dfrac{6x + 18}{x + 4}$

9. $\dfrac{4x - 12}{2x - 9} \div \dfrac{3 - x}{4x^2 - 81} \cdot \dfrac{x + 3}{5x + 15}$

10. $\dfrac{3 + 2x}{10 - x} + \dfrac{13 + x}{x - 10}$

11. $\dfrac{2x^2 + 7}{2x^4 - 18x^2} - \dfrac{6x + 7}{2x^4 - 18x^2}$

12. $\dfrac{3}{x^2 - x - 6} + \dfrac{2}{x^2 - 5x + 6}$

13. $\dfrac{5}{x - 7} - \dfrac{2x}{3x - 21} + \dfrac{x}{2x - 14}$

14. $\dfrac{3x}{5} \cdot \left(\dfrac{5}{x} - \dfrac{5}{2x} \right)$

Simplify each complex fraction.

15. $\dfrac{\dfrac{5}{x} - \dfrac{7}{3x}}{\dfrac{9}{8x} - \dfrac{1}{x}}$

16. $\dfrac{\dfrac{x^2 - 5x + 6}{x + 3}}{\dfrac{x^2 - 4x + 4}{x^2 - 9}}$

Divide.

17. $(4x^2y + 9x + 3xz) \div 3xz$

18. $(4x^3 - 5x) \div (2x + 1)$

19. Use synthetic division to divide $(4x^4 - 3x^3 - x - 1)$ by $(x + 3)$.

20. If $P(x) = 4x^4 + 7x^2 - 2x - 5$, use the remainder theorem to find $P(-2)$.

Solve each equation for x.

21. $\dfrac{5x + 3}{3x - 7} = \dfrac{19}{7}$

22. $\dfrac{x}{x - 4} = 3 - \dfrac{4}{x - 4}$

23. $\dfrac{3}{x + 2} - \dfrac{1}{5x} = \dfrac{2}{5x^2 + 10x}$

24. $\dfrac{x^2 + 8}{x} - 1 = \dfrac{2(x + 4)}{x}$

25. Solve for x: $\dfrac{x + b}{a} = \dfrac{4x - 7a}{b}$

▶ **26.** The product of one more than a number and twice the reciprocal of the number is $\frac{12}{5}$. Find the number.

▶ **27.** If Jan can weed the garden in 2 hours and her husband can weed it in 1 hour and 30 minutes, find how long it takes them to weed the garden together.

▶ **28.** Suppose that W is inversely proportional to V. If $W = 20$ when $V = 12$, find W when $V = 15$.

▶ **29.** Suppose that Q is jointly proportional to R and the square of S. If $Q = 24$ when $R = 3$ and $S = 4$, find Q when $R = 2$ and $S = 3$.

▶ **30.** When an anvil is dropped into a gorge, the speed with which it strikes the ground is directly proportional to the square root of the distance it falls. An anvil that falls 400 feet hits the ground at a speed of 160 feet per second. Find the height of a cliff over the gorge if a dropped anvil hits the ground at a speed of 128 feet per second.

Chapter 6   Cumulative Review

1. Translate each phrase into an algebraic expression. Use the variable x to represent each unknown number.

  a. Eight times a number

  b. Three more than eight times a number

  c. The quotient of a number and -7

  d. One and six-tenths subtracted from twice a number

  e. Six less than a number

  f. Twice the sum of four and a number

2. Translate each phrase into an algebraic expression. Use the variable x to represent each unknown number.

  a. One third subtracted from a number

  b. Six less than five times a number

  c. Three more than eight times a number

  d. The quotient of seven and the difference of two and a number.

3. Solve for y: $\dfrac{y}{3} - \dfrac{y}{4} = \dfrac{1}{6}$

4. Solve for x: $\dfrac{x}{7} + \dfrac{x}{5} = \dfrac{12}{5}$

5. In the United States, the annual consumption of cigarettes is declining. The consumption c in billions of cigarettes per year since the year 2004 can be approximated by the formula
$$c = -11.8t + 390$$
where t is the number of years after 2004. Use this formula to predict the years that the consumption of cigarettes will be less than 200 billion per year.

6. Olivia has scores of 78, 65, 82, and 79 on her algebra tests. Use an inequality to find the minimum score she can make on her final exam to pass the course with a 78 average or higher, given that the final exam counts as two tests.

7. Solve: $\left| \dfrac{3x + 1}{2} \right| = -2$

8. Solve: $\left| \dfrac{2x - 1}{3} \right| + 6 = 3$

9. Solve for x: $\left| \dfrac{2(x + 1)}{3} \right| \le 0$

10. Solve for x: $\left| \dfrac{3(x - 1)}{4} \right| \ge 2$

11. Graph the equation: $y = -2x + 3$

12. Graph the equation: $y = -x + 3$

13. Determine whether the following relations are also functions.

  a. $\{(-2, 5), (2, 7), (-3, 5), (9, 9)\}$

  b.

  c.

Input	Correspondence	Output
People in a certain city	Each person's age	The set of nonnegative integers

14. If $f(x) = -x^2 + 3x - 2$, find

  a. $f(0)$

  b. $f(-3)$

  c. $f\left(\dfrac{1}{3}\right)$

15. Find the intercepts and then graph $3x + 4y = -12$.

16. Find the intercepts and then graph $3x - y = 6$.

17. Find an equation of the line with slope -3 containing the point $(1, -5)$. Write the equation in slope–intercept form $y = mx + b$.

18. Find an equation of the line with slope $\dfrac{1}{2}$ containing the point $(-1, 3)$. Use function notation to write the equation.

19. Graph $x \geq 1$ and $y \geq 2x - 1$.

20. Graph $2x + y \leq 4$ or $y > 2$.

21. Use the elimination method to solve the system.
$$\begin{cases} 3x - 2y = 10 \\ 4x - 3y = 15 \end{cases}$$

22. Use the substitution method to solve the system.
$$\begin{cases} -2x + 3y = 6 \\ 3x - y = 5 \end{cases}$$

23. Solve the system. $\begin{cases} 2x - 4y + 8z = 2 \\ -x - 3y + z = 11 \\ x - 2y + 4z = 0 \end{cases}$

24. Solve the system. $\begin{cases} 2x - 2y + 4z = 6 \\ -4x - y + z = -8 \\ 3x - y + z = 6 \end{cases}$

25. The measure of the largest angle of a triangle is $80°$ more than the measure of the smallest angle, and the measure of the remaining angle is $10°$ more than the measure of the smallest angle. Find the measure of each angle.

26. Kernersville office supply sold three reams of paper and two boxes of manila folders for $21.90. Also, five reams of paper and one box of manila folders cost $24.25. Find the price of a ream of paper and a box of manila folders.

27. Use matrices to solve the system.
$$\begin{cases} x + 2y + z = 2 \\ -2x - y + 2z = 5 \\ x + 3y - 2z = -8 \end{cases}$$

28. Use matrices to solve the system. $\begin{cases} x + y + z = 9 \\ 2x - 2y + 3z = 2 \\ -3x + y - z = 1 \end{cases}$

29. Evaluate the following.
  a. 7^0 **b.** -7^0
  c. $(2x + 5)^0$ **d.** $2x^0$

30. Simplify the following. Write answers with positive exponents.
  a. $2^{-2} + 3^{-1}$ **b.** $-6a^0$ **c.** $\dfrac{x^{-5}}{x^{-2}}$

31. Simplify each expression. Assume that a and b are integers and that x and y are not 0.
  a. $x^{-b}(2x^b)^2$ **b.** $\dfrac{(y^{3a})^2}{y^{a-6}}$

32. Simplify each expression. Assume that a and b are integers and that x and y are not 0.
  a. $3x^{4a}(4x^{-a})^2$ **b.** $\dfrac{(y^{4b})^3}{y^{2b-3}}$

33. Find the degree of each term.
  a. $3x^2$ **b.** -2^3x^5 **c.** y
  d. $12x^2yz^3$ **e.** 5.27

34. Subtract $(2x - 7)$ from $2x^2 + 8x - 3$.

35. Multiply: $[3 + (2a + b)]^2$

36. Multiply: $[4 + (3x - y)]^2$

37. Factor: $ab - 6a + 2b - 12$

38. Factor: $xy + 2x - 5y - 10$

39. Factor: $2n^2 - 38n + 80$

40. Factor: $6x^2 - x - 35$

41. Factor: $x^2 + 4x + 4 - y^2$

42. Factor: $4x^2 - 4x + 1 - 9y^2$

43. Solve: $(x + 2)(x - 6) = 0$

44. Solve: $2x(3x + 1)(x - 3) = 0$

45. Simplify each rational expression.
  a. $\dfrac{2x^2}{10x^3 - 2x^2}$
  b. $\dfrac{9x^2 + 13x + 4}{8x^2 + x - 7}$

46. For the graph of $f(x)$, answer the following:

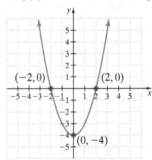

  a. Find the domain and range.
  b. List the x- and y-intercepts.
  c. Find the coordinates of the point with the greatest y-value.
  d. Find the coordinates of the point with the least y-value.
  e. List the x-values whose y-values are equal to 0.
  f. List the x-values whose y-values are less than 0.
  g. Find the solutions of $f(x) = 0$.

47. Subtract: $\dfrac{5k}{k^2 - 4} - \dfrac{2}{k^2 + k - 2}$

48. Subtract: $\dfrac{5a}{a^2 - 4} - \dfrac{3}{2 - a}$

49. Solve: $\dfrac{3}{x} - \dfrac{x + 21}{3x} = \dfrac{5}{3}$

50. Solve: $\dfrac{3x - 4}{2x} = -\dfrac{8}{x}$

Rational Exponents, Radicals, and Complex Numbers

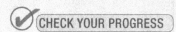

CHECK YOUR PROGRESS

In this chapter, radical notation is reviewed, and then rational exponents are introduced. As the name implies, rational exponents are exponents that are rational numbers. We present an interpretation of rational exponents that is consistent with the meaning and rules already established for integer exponents, and we present two forms of notation for roots: radical and exponent. We conclude this chapter with complex numbers, a natural extension of the real number system.

What Is Zorbing?

New Zealand is the home of some great extreme adventures. For example, bungee jumping, base jumping, and zorbing originated in New Zealand. Invented in 1995, zorbing is climbing inside a large, double-chambered ball and rolling down a hillside track. The creators have also provided zorbs for a show at Sea World, San Diego, created snow zorbing, and produced the zurf, which is zorbing at the beach. Since its inception, zorbing has spread throughout the world, including a site in Amesbury, Massachusetts.

NASA has even investigated using a zorb-like rover to investigate Mars, called the tumbleweed rover.

In Section 7.3, Exercises 125 and 126, we will explore aspects of zorbs and zorbing.

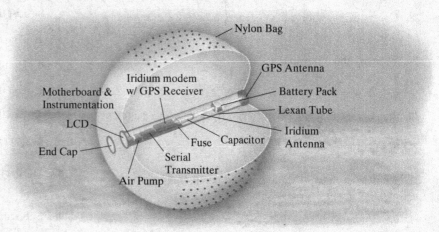

Tumbleweed Rover Architecture

If volume V or surface area A are known, then radius r can be calculated using

$$r = \sqrt[3]{\frac{3V}{4\pi}} \text{ or } r = \sqrt{\frac{A}{4\pi}}$$

7.1 | Radicals and Radical Functions

OBJECTIVES

1 Find Square Roots.
2 Approximate Roots.
3 Find Cube Roots.
4 Find nth Roots.
5 Find $\sqrt[n]{a^n}$ Where a Is a Real Number.
6 Graph Square and Cube Root Functions.

OBJECTIVE

1 Finding Square Roots

Recall from Section 1.3 that to find a **square root** of a number a, we find a number that was squared to get a.

Thus, because

$$5^2 = 25 \quad \text{and} \quad (-5)^2 = 25,$$

both 5 and -5 are square roots of 25.

Recall that we denote the **nonnegative**, or **principal**, **square root** with the **radical sign**.

$$\sqrt{25} = 5$$

We denote the **negative square root** with the **negative radical sign**.

$$-\sqrt{25} = -5$$

An expression containing a radical sign is called a **radical expression**. An expression within, or "under," a radical sign is called a **radicand**.

radical expression: $\overset{\text{radical sign}}{\sqrt{a}}_{\text{radicand}}$

Principal and Negative Square Roots

If a is a nonnegative number, then
$\sqrt{a}$ is the **principal**, or **nonnegative**, **square root** of a
$-\sqrt{a}$ is the **negative square root** of a

EXAMPLE 1 Simplify. Assume that all variables represent nonnegative real numbers.

a. $\sqrt{36}$ **b.** $\sqrt{0}$ **c.** $\sqrt{\dfrac{4}{49}}$ **d.** $\sqrt{0.25}$

e. $\sqrt{x^6}$ **f.** $\sqrt{9x^{12}}$ **g.** $-\sqrt{81}$ **h.** $\sqrt{-81}$

Solution

a. $\sqrt{36} = 6$ because $6^2 = 36$ and 6 is not negative.

b. $\sqrt{0} = 0$ because $0^2 = 0$ and 0 is not negative.

c. $\sqrt{\dfrac{4}{49}} = \dfrac{2}{7}$ because $\left(\dfrac{2}{7}\right)^2 = \dfrac{4}{49}$ and $\dfrac{2}{7}$ is not negative.

d. $\sqrt{0.25} = 0.5$ because $(0.5)^2 = 0.25.$

e. $\sqrt{x^6} = x^3$ because $(x^3)^2 = x^6.$

f. $\sqrt{9x^{12}} = 3x^6$ because $(3x^6)^2 = 9x^{12}.$

g. $-\sqrt{81} = -9.$ The negative in front of the radical indicates the negative square root of 81.

h. $\sqrt{-81}$ is not a real number. □

PRACTICE

1 Simplify. Assume that all variables represent nonnegative real numbers.

a. $\sqrt{49}$ **b.** $\sqrt{\dfrac{0}{1}}$ **c.** $\sqrt{\dfrac{16}{81}}$ **d.** $\sqrt{0.64}$

e. $\sqrt{z^8}$ **f.** $\sqrt{16b^4}$ **g.** $-\sqrt{36}$ **h.** $\sqrt{-36}$ ■

Recall from Section 1.3 our discussion of the square root of a negative number. For example, can we simplify $\sqrt{-4}$? That is, can we find a real number whose square is -4? No, there is no real number whose square is -4, and we say that $\sqrt{-4}$ is not a real number. In general:

The square root of a negative number is not a real number.

> **Helpful Hint**
>
> - Remember: $\sqrt{0} = 0$.
> - Don't forget that the square root of a negative number is not a real number. For example,
>
> $$\sqrt{-9} \text{ is not a real number}$$
>
> because there is no real number that when multiplied by itself would give a product of -9. In Section 7.7, we will see what kind of a number $\sqrt{-9}$ is.

OBJECTIVE

2 Approximating Roots

Recall that numbers such as 1, 4, 9, and 25 are called **perfect squares,** since $1 = 1^2, 4 = 2^2, 9 = 3^2,$ and $25 = 5^2$. Square roots of perfect square radicands simplify to rational numbers. What happens when we try to simplify a root such as $\sqrt{3}$? Since there is no rational number whose square is 3, $\sqrt{3}$ is not a rational number. It is called an **irrational number,** and we can find a decimal **approximation** of it. To find decimal approximations, use a calculator. For example, an approximation for $\sqrt{3}$ is

$$\sqrt{3} \approx 1.732$$
$$\uparrow$$
$$\text{approximation symbol}$$

To see if the approximation is reasonable, notice that since

$$1 < 3 < 4,$$
$$\sqrt{1} < \sqrt{3} < \sqrt{4}, \text{ or}$$
$$1 < \sqrt{3} < 2.$$

1 and 4 are perfect squares closest to but less than and greater than 3, respectively.

We found $\sqrt{3} \approx 1.732$, a number between 1 and 2, so our result is reasonable.

EXAMPLE 2 Use a calculator to approximate $\sqrt{20}$. Round the approximation to 3 decimal places and check to see that your approximation is reasonable.

Solution $$\sqrt{20} \approx 4.472$$

Is this reasonable? Since $16 < 20 < 25$, $\sqrt{16} < \sqrt{20} < \sqrt{25}$, or $4 < \sqrt{20} < 5$. The approximation is between 4 and 5 and thus is reasonable. □

PRACTICE

2 Use a calculator to approximate $\sqrt{45}$. Round the approximation to three decimal places and check to see that your approximation is reasonable. ▪

OBJECTIVE

3 Finding Cube Roots

Finding roots can be extended to other roots such as cube roots. For example, since $2^3 = 8$, we call 2 the **cube root** of 8. In symbols, we write

$$\sqrt[3]{8} = 2$$

> **Cube Root**
>
> The **cube root** of a real number a is written as $\sqrt[3]{a}$, and
>
> $$\sqrt[3]{a} = b \text{ only if } b^3 = a$$

From this definition, we have

$$\sqrt[3]{64} = 4 \text{ since } 4^3 = 64$$
$$\sqrt[3]{-27} = -3 \text{ since } (-3)^3 = -27$$
$$\sqrt[3]{x^3} = x \text{ since } x^3 = x^3$$

Notice that, unlike with square roots, *it is possible to have a negative radicand when finding a cube root.* This is so because the *cube* of a negative number is a negative number. Therefore, the *cube root* of a negative number is a negative number.

EXAMPLE 3   Find the cube roots.

a. $\sqrt[3]{1}$ **b.** $\sqrt[3]{-64}$ **c.** $\sqrt[3]{\dfrac{8}{125}}$ **d.** $\sqrt[3]{x^6}$ **e.** $\sqrt[3]{-27x^{15}}$

Solution

a. $\sqrt[3]{1} = 1$ because $1^3 = 1$.

b. $\sqrt[3]{-64} = -4$ because $(-4)^3 = -64$.

c. $\sqrt[3]{\dfrac{8}{125}} = \dfrac{2}{5}$ because $\left(\dfrac{2}{5}\right)^3 = \dfrac{8}{125}$.

d. $\sqrt[3]{x^6} = x^2$ because $(x^2)^3 = x^6$.

e. $\sqrt[3]{-27x^{15}} = -3x^5$ because $(-3x^5)^3 = -27x^{15}$.

PRACTICE

3   Find the cube roots.

a. $\sqrt[3]{-1}$ **b.** $\sqrt[3]{27}$ **c.** $\sqrt[3]{\dfrac{27}{64}}$ **d.** $\sqrt[3]{x^{12}}$ **e.** $\sqrt[3]{-8x^3}$

OBJECTIVE

4   Finding *n*th Roots

Just as we can raise a real number to powers other than 2 or 3, we can find roots other than square roots and cube roots. In fact, we can find the **nth root** of a number, where *n* is any natural number. In symbols, the *n*th root of *a* is written as $\sqrt[n]{a}$, where *n* is called the **index.** The index 2 is usually omitted for square roots.

> **Helpful Hint**
>
> If the index is even, such as $\sqrt{}$, $\sqrt[4]{}$, $\sqrt[6]{}$, and so on, the radicand must be nonnegative for the root to be a real number. For example,
>
> $$\sqrt[4]{16} = 2, \text{ but } \sqrt[4]{-16} \text{ is not a real number.}$$
> $$\sqrt[6]{64} = 2, \text{ but } \sqrt[6]{-64} \text{ is not a real number.}$$
>
> If the index is odd, such as $\sqrt[3]{}$, $\sqrt[5]{}$, and so on, the radicand may be any real number. For example,
>
> $$\sqrt[3]{64} = 4 \quad \text{and} \quad \sqrt[3]{-64} = -4$$
> $$\sqrt[5]{32} = 2 \quad \text{and} \quad \sqrt[5]{-32} = -2$$

✔ **CONCEPT CHECK**

Which one is not a real number?

a. $\sqrt[3]{-15}$ **b.** $\sqrt[4]{-15}$ **c.** $\sqrt[5]{-15}$ **d.** $\sqrt{(-15)^2}$

EXAMPLE 4   Simplify the following expressions.

a. $\sqrt[4]{81}$ b. $\sqrt[5]{-243}$ c. $-\sqrt{25}$ d. $\sqrt[4]{-81}$ e. $\sqrt[3]{64x^3}$

Solution

a. $\sqrt[4]{81} = 3$ because $3^4 = 81$ and 3 is positive.

b. $\sqrt[5]{-243} = -3$ because $(-3)^5 = -243$.

c. $-\sqrt{25} = -5$ because -5 is the opposite of $\sqrt{25}$.

d. $\sqrt[4]{-81}$ is not a real number. There is no real number that, when raised to the fourth power, is -81.

e. $\sqrt[3]{64x^3} = 4x$ because $(4x)^3 = 64x^3$.   □

PRACTICE
4   Simplify the following expressions.

a. $\sqrt[4]{10,000}$ b. $\sqrt[5]{-1}$ c. $-\sqrt{81}$ d. $\sqrt[4]{-625}$ e. $\sqrt[3]{27x^9}$ ■

OBJECTIVE
5   Finding $\sqrt[n]{a^n}$ Where _a_ Is a Real Number

Recall that the notation $\sqrt{a^2}$ indicates the positive square root of a^2 only. For example,

$$\sqrt{(-7)^2} = \sqrt{49} = 7$$

When variables are present in the radicand and it is _unclear whether the variable represents a positive number or a negative number_, absolute value bars are sometimes needed to ensure that the result is a positive number. For example,

$$\sqrt{x^2} = |x|$$

This ensures that the result is positive. This same situation may occur when the index is any _even_ positive integer. When the index is any _odd_ positive integer, absolute value bars are not necessary.

Finding $\sqrt[n]{a^n}$

If n is an _even_ positive integer, then $\sqrt[n]{a^n} = |a|$.

If n is an _odd_ positive integer, then $\sqrt[n]{a^n} = a$.

EXAMPLE 5   Simplify.

a. $\sqrt{(-3)^2}$ b. $\sqrt{x^2}$ c. $\sqrt[4]{(x-2)^4}$ d. $\sqrt[3]{(-5)^3}$

e. $\sqrt[5]{(2x-7)^5}$ f. $\sqrt{25x^2}$ g. $\sqrt{x^2 + 2x + 1}$

Solution

a. $\sqrt{(-3)^2} = |-3| = 3$ When the index is even, the absolute value bars ensure that our result is not negative.

b. $\sqrt{x^2} = |x|$

c. $\sqrt[4]{(x-2)^4} = |x - 2|$

d. $\sqrt[3]{(-5)^3} = -5$

e. $\sqrt[5]{(2x-7)^5} = 2x - 7$ Absolute value bars are not needed when the index is odd.

f. $\sqrt{25x^2} = 5|x|$

g. $\sqrt{x^2 + 2x + 1} = \sqrt{(x+1)^2} = |x + 1|$ □

PRACTICE
5   Simplify.

a. $\sqrt{(-4)^2}$ b. $\sqrt{x^{14}}$ c. $\sqrt[4]{(x+7)^4}$ d. $\sqrt[3]{(-7)^3}$

e. $\sqrt[5]{(3x-5)^5}$ f. $\sqrt{49x^2}$ g. $\sqrt{x^2+16x+64}$

OBJECTIVE
6   Graphing Square and Cube Root Functions

Recall that an equation in x and y describes a function if each x-value is paired with exactly one y-value. With this in mind, does the equation

$$y = \sqrt{x}$$

describe a function? First, notice that replacement values for x must be nonnegative real numbers, since $\sqrt{x}$ is not a real number if $x < 0$. The notation $\sqrt{x}$ denotes the principal square root of x, so for every nonnegative number x, there is exactly one number, $\sqrt{x}$. Therefore, $y = \sqrt{x}$ describes a function, and we may write it as

$$f(x) = \sqrt{x}$$

In general, radical functions are functions of the form

$$f(x) = \sqrt[n]{x}.$$

Recall that the domain of a function in x is the set of all possible replacement values for x. This means that if n is even, the domain is the set of all nonnegative numbers, or $\{x \mid x \geq 0\}$ or $[0, \infty)$. If n is odd, the domain is the set of all real numbers, or $(-\infty, \infty)$. Keep this in mind as we find function values.

EXAMPLE 6   If $f(x) = \sqrt{x-4}$ and $g(x) = \sqrt[3]{x+2}$, find each function value.

a. $f(8)$ b. $f(6)$ c. $g(-1)$ d. $g(1)$

Solution

a. $f(8) = \sqrt{8-4} = \sqrt{4} = 2$ b. $f(6) = \sqrt{6-4} = \sqrt{2}$

c. $g(-1) = \sqrt[3]{-1+2} = \sqrt[3]{1} = 1$ d. $g(1) = \sqrt[3]{1+2} = \sqrt[3]{3}$

PRACTICE
6   If $f(x) = \sqrt{x+5}$ and $g(x) = \sqrt[3]{x-3}$, find each function value.

a. $f(11)$ b. $f(-1)$ c. $g(11)$ d. $g(-6)$

Helpful Hint

Notice that for the function $f(x) = \sqrt{x-4}$, the domain includes all real numbers that make the radicand ≥ 0. To see what numbers these are, solve $x - 4 \geq 0$ and find that $x \geq 4$. The domain is $\{x \mid x \geq 4\}$, or $[4, \infty)$.

The domain of the cube root function $g(x) = \sqrt[3]{x+2}$ is the set of real numbers, or $(-\infty, \infty)$.

EXAMPLE 7   Graph the square root function: $f(x) = \sqrt{x}$

Solution To graph, we identify the domain, evaluate the function for several values of x, plot the resulting points, and connect the points with a smooth curve. Since $\sqrt{x}$ is not a real number for negative values of x, the domain of this function is the set of all nonnegative numbers, $\{x \mid x \geq 0\}$, or $[0, \infty)$. We have approximated $\sqrt{3}$ in the table on the next page to help us locate the point corresponding to $(3, \sqrt{3})$.

(Continued on next page)

x	$f(x) = \sqrt{x}$
0	0
1	1
3	$\sqrt{3} \approx 1.7$
4	2
9	3

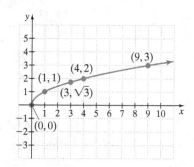

Notice that the graph of this function passes the vertical line test, as expected.

PRACTICE
7 Graph the square root function: $h(x) = \sqrt{x+2}$

The equation $f(x) = \sqrt[3]{x}$ also describes a function. Here, x may be any real number, so the domain of this function is the set of all real numbers, or $(-\infty, \infty)$. A few function values are given next.

$$f(0) = \sqrt[3]{0} = 0$$
$$f(1) = \sqrt[3]{1} = 1$$
$$f(-1) = \sqrt[3]{-1} = -1$$
$$f(6) = \sqrt[3]{6}$$
$$f(-6) = \sqrt[3]{-6}$$
$$f(8) = \sqrt[3]{8} = 2$$
$$f(-8) = \sqrt[3]{-8} = -2$$

Here, there is no rational number whose cube is 6. Thus, the radicals do not simplify to rational numbers.

EXAMPLE 8 Graph the function: $f(x) = \sqrt[3]{x}$

Solution To graph, we identify the domain, plot points, and connect the points with a smooth curve. The domain of this function is the set of all real numbers. The table comes from the function values obtained earlier. We have approximated $\sqrt[3]{6}$ and $\sqrt[3]{-6}$ for graphing purposes.

x	$f(x) = \sqrt[3]{x}$
0	0
1	1
-1	-1
6	$\sqrt[3]{6} \approx 1.8$
-6	$\sqrt[3]{-6} \approx -1.8$
8	2
-8	-2

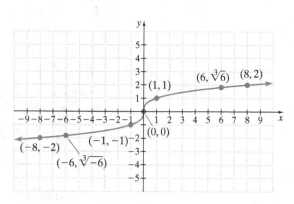

The graph of this function passes the vertical line test, as expected.

PRACTICE
8 Graph the function: $f(x) = \sqrt[3]{x} - 4$

✓ Vocabulary, Readiness & Video Check

Use the choices below to fill in each blank. Not all choices will be used.

is	cubes	$-\sqrt{a}$	radical sign	index
is not	squares	$\sqrt{-a}$	radicand	

1. In the expression $\sqrt[n]{a}$, the n is called the _____, the $\sqrt{}$ is called the _____, and a is called the _____.

2. If $\sqrt{a}$ is the positive square root of $a, a \neq 0$, then _____ is the negative square root of a.

3. The square root of a negative number _____ a real number.

4. Numbers such as 1, 4, 9, and 25 are called perfect _____, whereas numbers such as 1, 8, 27, and 125 are called perfect _____.

Fill in the blank.

5. The domain of the function $f(x) = \sqrt{x}$ is _____.

6. The domain of the function $f(x) = \sqrt[3]{x}$ is _____.

7. If $f(16) = 4$, the corresponding ordered pair is _____.

8. If $g(-8) = -2$, the corresponding ordered pair is _____.

Martin-Gay Interactive Videos

See Video 7.1 🔴

Watch the section lecture video and answer the following questions.

OBJECTIVE 1
9. From ▦ Examples 5 and 6, when simplifying radicals containing variables with exponents, describe a shortcut you can use.

OBJECTIVE 2
10. From ▦ Example 9, how can you determine a reasonable approximation for a non-perfect square root without using a calculator?

OBJECTIVE 3
11. From ▦ Example 11, what is an important difference between the square root and the cube root of a negative number?

OBJECTIVE 4
12. From ▦ Example 12, what conclusion is made about the even root of a negative number?

OBJECTIVE 5
13. From the lecture before ▦ Example 17, why do you think no absolute value bars are used when n is odd?

OBJECTIVE 6
14. In ▦ Example 19, the domain is found by looking at the graph. How can the domain be found by looking at the function?

7.1   Exercise Set   MyMathLab° ▶

Simplify. Assume that variables represent nonnegative real numbers. See Example 1.

1. $\sqrt{100}$

2. $\sqrt{400}$

3. $\sqrt{\dfrac{1}{4}}$

4. $\sqrt{\dfrac{9}{25}}$

5. $\sqrt{0.0001}$

6. $\sqrt{0.04}$

7. $-\sqrt{36}$

8. $-\sqrt{9}$

9. $\sqrt{x^{10}}$

10. $\sqrt{x^{16}}$

11. $\sqrt{16y^6}$

12. $\sqrt{64y^{20}}$

Use a calculator to approximate each square root to 3 decimal places. Check to see that each approximation is reasonable. See Example 2.

13. $\sqrt{7}$

14. $\sqrt{11}$

▶ **15.** $\sqrt{38}$

16. $\sqrt{56}$

17. $\sqrt{200}$

18. $\sqrt{300}$

Find each cube root. See Example 3.

19. $\sqrt[3]{64}$

20. $\sqrt[3]{27}$

▶ **21.** $\sqrt[3]{\dfrac{1}{8}}$

22. $\sqrt[3]{\dfrac{27}{64}}$

23. $\sqrt[3]{-1}$

24. $\sqrt[3]{-125}$

25. $\sqrt[3]{x^{12}}$

26. $\sqrt[3]{x^{15}}$

▶ **27.** $\sqrt[3]{-27x^9}$

28. $\sqrt[3]{-64x^6}$

Find each root. Assume that all variables represent nonnegative real numbers. See Example 4.

29. $-\sqrt[4]{16}$

30. $\sqrt[5]{-243}$

▶ 31. $\sqrt[4]{-16}$

32. $\sqrt{-16}$

▶ 33. $\sqrt[5]{-32}$

34. $\sqrt[5]{-1}$

35. $\sqrt[5]{x^{20}}$

36. $\sqrt[4]{x^{20}}$

▶ 37. $\sqrt[6]{64x^{12}}$

38. $\sqrt[5]{-32x^{15}}$

39. $\sqrt{81x^4}$

40. $\sqrt[4]{81x^4}$

41. $\sqrt[4]{256x^8}$

42. $\sqrt{256x^8}$

Simplify. Assume that the variables represent any real number. See Example 5.

▶ 43. $\sqrt{(-8)^2}$

44. $\sqrt{(-7)^2}$

▶ 45. $\sqrt[3]{(-8)^3}$

46. $\sqrt[5]{(-7)^5}$

47. $\sqrt{4x^2}$

48. $\sqrt[4]{16x^4}$

49. $\sqrt[3]{x^3}$

50. $\sqrt[5]{x^5}$

▶ 51. $\sqrt{(x-5)^2}$

52. $\sqrt{(y-6)^2}$

53. $\sqrt{x^2 + 4x + 4}$
   (*Hint:* Factor the polynomial first.)

54. $\sqrt{x^2 - 8x + 16}$
   (*Hint:* Factor the polynomial first.)

MIXED PRACTICE

Simplify each radical. Assume that all variables represent positive real numbers.

55. $-\sqrt{121}$

56. $-\sqrt[3]{125}$

57. $\sqrt[3]{8x^3}$

58. $\sqrt{16x^8}$

59. $\sqrt{y^{12}}$

60. $\sqrt[3]{y^{12}}$

61. $\sqrt{25a^2b^{20}}$

62. $\sqrt{9x^4y^6}$

63. $\sqrt[3]{-27x^{12}y^9}$

64. $\sqrt[3]{-8a^{21}b^6}$

65. $\sqrt[4]{a^{16}b^4}$

66. $\sqrt[4]{x^8y^{12}}$

▶ 67. $\sqrt[5]{-32x^{10}y^5}$

68. $\sqrt[5]{-243x^5z^{15}}$

69. $\sqrt{\dfrac{25}{49}}$

70. $\sqrt{\dfrac{4}{81}}$

71. $\sqrt{\dfrac{x^{20}}{4y^2}}$

72. $\sqrt{\dfrac{y^{10}}{9x^6}}$

73. $-\sqrt[3]{\dfrac{z^{21}}{27x^3}}$

74. $-\sqrt[3]{\dfrac{64a^3}{b^9}}$

75. $\sqrt[4]{\dfrac{x^4}{16}}$

76. $\sqrt[4]{\dfrac{y^4}{81x^4}}$

If $f(x) = \sqrt{2x + 3}$ and $g(x) = \sqrt[3]{x - 8}$, find the following function values. See Example 6.

77. $f(0)$

78. $g(0)$

79. $g(7)$

80. $f(-1)$

81. $g(-19)$

82. $f(3)$

83. $f(2)$

84. $g(1)$

Identify the domain and then graph each function. See Example 7.

▶ 85. $f(x) = \sqrt{x} + 2$

86. $f(x) = \sqrt{x} - 2$

87. $f(x) = \sqrt{x - 3}$; use the following table.

x	$f(x)$
3	
4	
7	
12	

88. $f(x) = \sqrt{x + 1}$; use the following table.

x	$f(x)$
-1	
0	
3	
8	

Identify the domain and then graph each function. See Example 8.

89. $f(x) = \sqrt[3]{x} + 1$

90. $f(x) = \sqrt[3]{x} - 2$

91. $g(x) = \sqrt[3]{x - 1}$; use the following table.

x	$g(x)$
1	
2	
0	
9	
-7	

92. $g(x) = \sqrt[3]{x + 1}$; use the following table.

x	$g(x)$
-1	
0	
-2	
7	
-9	

REVIEW AND PREVIEW

Simplify each exponential expression. See Sections 5.1 and 5.2.

93. $(-2x^3y^2)^5$

94. $(4y^6z^7)^3$

95. $(-3x^2y^3z^5)(20x^5y^7)$

96. $(-14a^5bc^2)(2abc^4)$

97. $\dfrac{7x^{-1}y}{14(x^5y^2)^{-2}}$

98. $\dfrac{(2a^{-1}b^2)^3}{(8a^2b)^{-2}}$

CONCEPT EXTENSIONS

Determine whether the following are real numbers. See the Concept Check in this section.

99. $\sqrt{-17}$

100. $\sqrt[3]{-17}$

101. $\sqrt[10]{-17}$

102. $\sqrt[15]{-17}$

Choose the correct letter or letters. No pencil is needed, just think your way through these.

103. Which radical is not a real number?

   a. $\sqrt{3}$ **b.** $-\sqrt{11}$ **c.** $\sqrt[3]{-10}$ **d.** $\sqrt{-10}$

104. Which radical(s) simplify to 3?

   a. $\sqrt{9}$ **b.** $\sqrt{-9}$ **c.** $\sqrt[3]{27}$ **d.** $\sqrt[3]{-27}$

105. Which radical(s) simplify to -3?

   a. $\sqrt{9}$ **b.** $\sqrt{-9}$ **c.** $\sqrt[3]{27}$ **d.** $\sqrt[3]{-27}$

106. Which radical does not simplify to a whole number?

   a. $\sqrt{64}$ **b.** $\sqrt[3]{64}$ **c.** $\sqrt{8}$ **d.** $\sqrt[3]{8}$

For Exercises 107 through 110, do not use a calculator.

107. $\sqrt{160}$ is closest to

   a. 10   **b.** 13   **c.** 20   **d.** 40

108. $\sqrt{1000}$ is closest to

   a. 10   **b.** 30   **c.** 100   **d.** 500

△ **109.** The perimeter of the triangle is closest to

   a. 12   **b.** 18

   c. 66   **d.** 132

110. The length of the bent wire is closest to

   a. 5   **b.** $\sqrt{28}$

   c. 7   **d.** 14

111. Explain why $\sqrt{-64}$ is not a real number.

112. Explain why $\sqrt[3]{-64}$ is a real number.

The Mosteller formula for calculating adult body surface area is $B = \sqrt{\dfrac{hw}{3131}}$, where B is an individual's body surface area in square meters, h is the individual's height in inches, and w is the individual's weight in pounds. Use this information to answer Exercises 113 and 114. Round answers to 2 decimal places.

△ **113.** Find the body surface area of an individual who is 66 inches tall and who weighs 135 pounds.

△ **114.** Find the body surface area of an individual who is 74 inches tall and who weighs 225 pounds.

115. Escape velocity is the minimum speed that an object must reach to escape the pull of a planet's gravity. Escape velocity v is given by the equation $v = \sqrt{\dfrac{2Gm}{r}}$, where m is the mass of the planet, r is its radius, and G is the universal gravitational constant, which has a value of $G = 6.67 \times 10^{-11}$ m^3/kg·s^2. The mass of Earth is 5.97×10^{24} kg, and its radius is 6.37×10^6 m. Use this information to find the escape velocity for Earth in meters per second. Round to the nearest whole number. (*Source*: National Space Science Data Center)

116. Use the formula from Exercise 115 to determine the escape velocity for the moon. The mass of the moon is 7.35×10^{22} kg, and its radius is 1.74×10^6 m. Round to the nearest whole number. (*Source*: National Space Science Data Center)

117. Suppose a classmate tells you that $\sqrt{13} \approx 5.7$. Without a calculator, how can you convince your classmate that he or she must have made an error?

118. Suppose a classmate tells you that $\sqrt[3]{10} \approx 3.2$. Without a calculator, how can you convince your friend that he or she must have made an error?

Use a graphing calculator to verify the domain of each function and its graph.

119. Exercise 85   **120.** Exercise 86

121. Exercise 89   **122.** Exercise 90

7.2 Rational Exponents

OBJECTIVE

1 Understanding the Meaning of $a^{1/n}$

So far in this text, we have not defined expressions with rational exponents such as $3^{1/2}$, $x^{2/3}$, and $-9^{-1/4}$. We will define these expressions so that the rules for exponents will apply to these rational exponents as well.

Suppose that $x = 5^{1/3}$. Then

$$x^3 = (5^{1/3})^3 = 5^{1/3 \cdot 3} = 5^1 \text{ or } 5$$

using rules for exponents

Since $x^3 = 5$, x is the number whose cube is 5, or $x = \sqrt[3]{5}$. Notice that we also know that $x = 5^{1/3}$. This means

$$5^{1/3} = \sqrt[3]{5}$$

> **Definition of $a^{1/n}$**
>
> If n is a positive integer greater than 1 and $\sqrt[n]{a}$ is a real number, then
>
> $$a^{1/n} = \sqrt[n]{a}$$

Notice that the denominator of the rational exponent corresponds to the index of the radical.

EXAMPLE 1   Use radical notation to write the following. Simplify if possible.

    a. $4^{1/2}$ **b.** $64^{1/3}$ **c.** $x^{1/4}$ **d.** $0^{1/6}$ **e.** $-9^{1/2}$ **f.** $(81x^8)^{1/4}$ **g.** $5y^{1/3}$

Solution

    a. $4^{1/2} = \sqrt{4} = 2$ **b.** $64^{1/3} = \sqrt[3]{64} = 4$

    c. $x^{1/4} = \sqrt[4]{x}$ **d.** $0^{1/6} = \sqrt[6]{0} = 0$

    e. $-9^{1/2} = -\sqrt{9} = -3$ **f.** $(81x^8)^{1/4} = \sqrt[4]{81x^8} = 3x^2$

    g. $5y^{1/3} = 5\sqrt[3]{y}$

PRACTICE

1   Use radical notation to write the following. Simplify if possible.

    a. $36^{1/2}$ **b.** $1000^{1/3}$ **c.** $x^{1/3}$ **d.** $1^{1/4}$

    e. $-64^{1/2}$ **f.** $(125x^9)^{1/3}$ **g.** $3x^{1/4}$

OBJECTIVE

2 Understanding the Meaning of $a^{m/n}$

As we expand our use of exponents to include $\dfrac{m}{n}$, we define their meaning so that rules for exponents still hold true. For example, by properties of exponents,

$$8^{2/3} = (8^{1/3})^2 = (\sqrt[3]{8})^2 \quad \text{or}$$
$$8^{2/3} = (8^2)^{1/3} = \sqrt[3]{8^2}$$

> **Definition of $a^{m/n}$**
>
> If m and n are positive integers greater than 1 with $\dfrac{m}{n}$ in simplest form, then
>
> $$a^{m/n} = \sqrt[n]{a^m} = (\sqrt[n]{a})^m$$
>
> as long as $\sqrt[n]{a}$ is a real number.

Notice that the denominator n of the rational exponent corresponds to the index of the radical. The numerator m of the rational exponent indicates that the base is to be raised to the mth power. This means

$$8^{2/3} = \sqrt[3]{8^2} = \sqrt[3]{64} = 4 \quad \text{or}$$

$$8^{2/3} = (\sqrt[3]{8})^2 = 2^2 = 4$$

From simplifying $8^{2/3}$, can you see that it doesn't matter whether you raise to a power first and then take the nth root or you take the nth root first and then raise to a power?

> **Helpful Hint**
>
> Most of the time, $(\sqrt[n]{a})^m$ will be easier to calculate than $\sqrt[n]{a^m}$.

EXAMPLE 2   Use radical notation to write the following. Then simplify if possible.

    a. $4^{3/2}$ **b.** $-16^{3/4}$ **c.** $(-27)^{2/3}$

    d. $\left(\dfrac{1}{9}\right)^{3/2}$ **e.** $(4x - 1)^{3/5}$

Solution

    a. $4^{3/2} = (\sqrt{4})^3 = 2^3 = 8$ **b.** $-16^{3/4} = -(\sqrt[4]{16})^3 = -(2)^3 = -8$

    c. $(-27)^{2/3} = (\sqrt[3]{-27})^2 = (-3)^2 = 9$ **d.** $\left(\dfrac{1}{9}\right)^{3/2} = \left(\sqrt{\dfrac{1}{9}}\right)^3 = \left(\dfrac{1}{3}\right)^3 = \dfrac{1}{27}$

    e. $(4x - 1)^{3/5} = \sqrt[5]{(4x - 1)^3}$ $\square$

PRACTICE
2   Use radical notation to write the following. Simplify if possible.

    a. $16^{3/2}$ **b.** $-1^{3/5}$ **c.** $-(81)^{3/4}$

    d. $\left(\dfrac{1}{25}\right)^{3/2}$ **e.** $(3x + 2)^{5/9}$ ■

> **Helpful Hint**
>
> The *denominator* of a rational exponent is the index of the corresponding radical. For example, $x^{1/5} = \sqrt[5]{x}$ and $z^{2/3} = \sqrt[3]{z^2}$, or $z^{2/3} = (\sqrt[3]{z})^2$.

OBJECTIVE
3   Understanding the Meaning of $a^{-m/n}$

The rational exponents we have given meaning to exclude negative rational numbers. To complete the set of definitions, we define $a^{-m/n}$.

> **Definition of $a^{-m/n}$**
>
> $$a^{-m/n} = \dfrac{1}{a^{m/n}}$$
>
> as long as $a^{m/n}$ is a nonzero real number.

EXAMPLE 3   Write each expression with a positive exponent, and then simplify.

    a. $16^{-3/4}$ **b.** $(-27)^{-2/3}$

Solution

    a. $16^{-3/4} = \dfrac{1}{16^{3/4}} = \dfrac{1}{(\sqrt[4]{16})^3} = \dfrac{1}{2^3} = \dfrac{1}{8}$

    b. $(-27)^{-2/3} = \dfrac{1}{(-27)^{2/3}} = \dfrac{1}{(\sqrt[3]{-27})^2} = \dfrac{1}{(-3)^2} = \dfrac{1}{9}$ $\square$

(Continued on next page)

PRACTICE
3 Write each expression with a positive exponent; then simplify.

a. $9^{-3/2}$ **b.** $(-64)^{-2/3}$

> **Helpful Hint**
>
> If an expression contains a negative rational exponent, such as $9^{-3/2}$, you may want to first write the expression with a positive exponent and then interpret the rational exponent. Notice that the sign of the base is not affected by the sign of its exponent. For example,
>
> $$9^{-3/2} = \frac{1}{9^{3/2}} = \frac{1}{(\sqrt{9})^3} = \frac{1}{27}$$
>
> Also,
>
> $$(-27)^{-1/3} = \frac{1}{(-27)^{1/3}} = -\frac{1}{3}$$

✔ **CONCEPT CHECK**
Which one is correct?

a. $-8^{2/3} = \frac{1}{4}$ **b.** $8^{-2/3} = -\frac{1}{4}$ **c.** $8^{-2/3} = -4$ **d.** $-8^{-2/3} = -\frac{1}{4}$

OBJECTIVE
4 Using Rules for Exponents to Simplify Expressions

It can be shown that the properties of integer exponents hold for rational exponents. By using these properties and definitions, we can now simplify expressions that contain rational exponents.

These rules are repeated here for review.

Note: For the remainder of this chapter, we will assume that variables represent positive real numbers. Since this is so, we need not insert absolute value bars when we simplify even roots.

> **Summary of Exponent Rules**
>
> If m and n are rational numbers, and a, b, and c are numbers for which the expressions below exist, then
>
> | | |
> |---|---|
> | Product rule for exponents: | $a^m \cdot a^n = a^{m+n}$ |
> | Power rule for exponents: | $(a^m)^n = a^{m \cdot n}$ |
> | Power rules for products and quotients: | $(ab)^n = a^n b^n$ and |
> | | $\left(\dfrac{a}{c}\right)^n = \dfrac{a^n}{c^n}, c \neq 0$ |
> | Quotient rule for exponents: | $\dfrac{a^m}{a^n} = a^{m-n}, a \neq 0$ |
> | Zero exponent: | $a^0 = 1, a \neq 0$ |
> | Negative exponent: | $a^{-n} = \dfrac{1}{a^n}, a \neq 0$ |

EXAMPLE 4 Use properties of exponents to simplify. Write results with only positive exponents.

a. $b^{1/3} \cdot b^{5/3}$ **b.** $x^{1/2} x^{1/3}$ **c.** $\dfrac{7^{1/3}}{7^{4/3}}$

d. $y^{-4/7} \cdot y^{6/7}$ **e.** $\dfrac{(2x^{2/5}y^{-1/3})^5}{x^2 y}$

Solution

a. $b^{1/3} \cdot b^{5/3} = b^{(1/3+5/3)} = b^{6/3} = b^2$ — Use the product rule.

b. $x^{1/2}x^{1/3} = x^{(1/2+1/3)} = x^{3/6+2/6} = x^{5/6}$ — Use the product rule.

c. $\dfrac{7^{1/3}}{7^{4/3}} = 7^{1/3-4/3} = 7^{-3/3} = 7^{-1} = \dfrac{1}{7}$ — Use the quotient rule.

d. $y^{-4/7} \cdot y^{6/7} = y^{-4/7+6/7} = y^{2/7}$ — Use the product rule.

e. We begin by using the power rule $(ab)^m = a^m b^m$ to simplify the numerator.

$$\frac{(2x^{2/5}y^{-1/3})^5}{x^2 y} = \frac{2^5(x^{2/5})^5(y^{-1/3})^5}{x^2 y} = \frac{32x^2 y^{-5/3}}{x^2 y}$$ Use the power rule and simplify

$$= 32x^{2-2}y^{-5/3-3/3}$$ Apply the quotient rule.

$$= 32x^0 y^{-8/3}$$

$$= \frac{32}{y^{8/3}}$$

PRACTICE
4 Use properties of exponents to simplify.

a. $y^{2/3} \cdot y^{8/3}$ **b.** $x^{3/5} \cdot x^{1/4}$ **c.** $\dfrac{9^{2/7}}{9^{9/7}}$

d. $b^{4/9} \cdot b^{-2/9}$ **e.** $\dfrac{(3x^{1/4}y^{-2/3})^4}{x^4 y}$

EXAMPLE 5 Multiply.

a. $z^{2/3}(z^{1/3} - z^5)$ **b.** $(x^{1/3} - 5)(x^{1/3} + 2)$

Solution

a. $z^{2/3}(z^{1/3} - z^5) = z^{2/3}z^{1/3} - z^{2/3}z^5$ — Apply the distributive property.

$$= z^{(2/3+1/3)} - z^{(2/3+5)}$$ Use the product rule.

$$= z^{3/3} - z^{(2/3+15/3)}$$

$$= z - z^{17/3}$$

b. $(x^{1/3} - 5)(x^{1/3} + 2) = x^{2/3} + 2x^{1/3} - 5x^{1/3} - 10$ Think of $(x^{1/3} - 5)$ and $(x^{1/3} + 2)$ as 2 binomials,

$$= x^{2/3} - 3x^{1/3} - 10$$ then multiply using FOIL.

PRACTICE
5 Multiply.

a. $x^{3/5}(x^{1/3} - x^2)$ **b.** $(x^{1/2} + 6)(x^{1/2} - 2)$

EXAMPLE 6 Factor $x^{-1/2}$ from the expression $3x^{-1/2} - 7x^{5/2}$. Assume that all variables represent positive numbers.

Solution

$$3x^{-1/2} - 7x^{5/2} = (x^{-1/2})(3) - (x^{-1/2})(7x^{6/2})$$
$$= x^{-1/2}(3 - 7x^3)$$

To check, multiply $x^{-1/2}(3 - 7x^3)$ to see that the product is $3x^{-1/2} - 7x^{5/2}$.

PRACTICE
6 Factor $x^{-1/5}$ from the expression $2x^{-1/5} - 7x^{4/5}$.

OBJECTIVE

5 Using Rational Exponents to Simplify Radical Expressions

Some radical expressions are easier to simplify when we first write them with rational exponents. Next, use properties of exponents to simplify the expression, and then convert it back to radical notation.

EXAMPLE 7 Use rational exponents to simplify. Assume that variables represent positive numbers.

a. $\sqrt[8]{x^4}$ **b.** $\sqrt[6]{25}$ **c.** $\sqrt[4]{r^2 s^6}$

Solution

a. $\sqrt[8]{x^4} = x^{4/8} = x^{1/2} = \sqrt{x}$

b. $\sqrt[6]{25} = 25^{1/6} = (5^2)^{1/6} = 5^{2/6} = 5^{1/3} = \sqrt[3]{5}$

c. $\sqrt[4]{r^2 s^6} = (r^2 s^6)^{1/4} = r^{2/4} s^{6/4} = r^{1/2} s^{3/2} = (r s^3)^{1/2} = \sqrt{r s^3}$ ☐

PRACTICE

7 Use rational exponents to simplify. Assume that the variables represent positive numbers.

a. $\sqrt[9]{x^3}$ **b.** $\sqrt[4]{36}$ **c.** $\sqrt[8]{a^4 b^2}$ ■

EXAMPLE 8 Use rational exponents to write as a single radical.

a. $\sqrt{x} \cdot \sqrt[4]{x}$ **b.** $\dfrac{\sqrt{x}}{\sqrt[3]{x}}$ **c.** $\sqrt[3]{3} \cdot \sqrt{2}$

Solution

a. $\sqrt{x} \cdot \sqrt[4]{x} = x^{1/2} \cdot x^{1/4} = x^{1/2 + 1/4}$

$\qquad\qquad = x^{3/4} = \sqrt[4]{x^3}$

b. $\dfrac{\sqrt{x}}{\sqrt[3]{x}} = \dfrac{x^{1/2}}{x^{1/3}} = x^{1/2 - 1/3} = x^{3/6 - 2/6}$

$\qquad\qquad = x^{1/6} = \sqrt[6]{x}$

c. $\sqrt[3]{3} \cdot \sqrt{2} = 3^{1/3} \cdot 2^{1/2}$ Write with rational exponents.

$\qquad\quad = 3^{2/6} \cdot 2^{3/6}$ Write the exponents so that they have the same denominator.

$\qquad\quad = (3^2 \cdot 2^3)^{1/6}$ Use $a^n b^n = (ab)^n$

$\qquad\quad = \sqrt[6]{3^2 \cdot 2^3}$ Write with radical notation.

$\qquad\quad = \sqrt[6]{72}$ Multiply $3^2 \cdot 2^3$.   ☐

PRACTICE

8 Use rational exponents to write each of the following as a single radical.

a. $\sqrt[3]{x} \cdot \sqrt[4]{x}$ **b.** $\dfrac{\sqrt[3]{y}}{\sqrt[5]{y}}$ **c.** $\sqrt[3]{5} \cdot \sqrt{3}$ ■

 Vocabulary, Readiness & Video Check

Answer each true or false.

1. $9^{-1/2}$ is a positive number. _____

2. $9^{-1/2}$ is a whole number. _____

3. $\dfrac{1}{a^{-m/n}} = a^{m/n}$ (where $a^{m/n}$ is a nonzero real number). _____

Fill in the blank with the correct choice.

4. To simplify $x^{2/3} \cdot x^{1/5}$, _____ the exponents.

   a. add   **b.** subtract   **c.** multiply   **d.** divide

5. To simplify $(x^{2/3})^{1/5}$, _____ the exponents.

   a. add   **b.** subtract   **c.** multiply   **d.** divide

6. To simplify $\dfrac{x^{2/3}}{x^{1/5}}$, _____ the exponents.

   a. add   **b.** subtract   **c.** multiply   **d.** divide

Martin-Gay Interactive Videos

See Video 7.2

Watch the section lecture video and answer the following questions.

OBJECTIVE 1

7. After studying Example 2, write $-(3x)^{1/5}$ in radical notation.

OBJECTIVE 2

8. From Examples 3 and 4, in a fractional exponent, what do the numerator and denominator each represent in radical form?

OBJECTIVE 3

9. Based on Example 5, complete the following statements. A negative fractional exponent will move a base from the numerator to the _____ with the fractional exponent becoming _____.

OBJECTIVE 4

10. Based on Examples 7–9, complete the following statements. Assume you have an expression with fractional exponents. If applying the product rule of exponents, you _____ the exponents. If applying the quotient rule of exponents, you _____ the exponents. If applying the power rule of exponents, you _____ the exponents.

OBJECTIVE 5

11. From Example 10, describe a way to simplify a radical of a variable raised to a power if the index and the exponent have a common factor.

7.2   Exercise Set   MyMathLab®

Use radical notation to write each expression. Simplify if possible. See Example 1.

1. $49^{1/2}$

2. $64^{1/3}$

3. $27^{1/3}$

4. $8^{1/3}$

5. $\left(\dfrac{1}{16}\right)^{1/4}$

6. $\left(\dfrac{1}{64}\right)^{1/2}$

7. $169^{1/2}$

8. $81^{1/4}$

9. $2m^{1/3}$

10. $(2m)^{1/3}$

11. $(9x^4)^{1/2}$

12. $(16x^8)^{1/2}$

13. $(-27)^{1/3}$

14. $-64^{1/2}$

15. $-16^{1/4}$

16. $(-32)^{1/5}$

Use radical notation to write each expression. Simplify if possible. See Example 2.

17. $16^{3/4}$

18. $4^{5/2}$

19. $(-64)^{2/3}$

20. $(-8)^{4/3}$

21. $(-16)^{3/4}$

22. $(-9)^{3/2}$

23. $(2x)^{3/5}$

24. $2x^{3/5}$

25. $(7x + 2)^{2/3}$

26. $(x - 4)^{3/4}$

27. $\left(\dfrac{16}{9}\right)^{3/2}$

28. $\left(\dfrac{49}{25}\right)^{3/2}$

Write with positive exponents. Simplify if possible. See Example 3.

29. $8^{-4/3}$

30. $64^{-2/3}$

31. $(-64)^{-2/3}$

32. $(-8)^{-4/3}$

33. $(-4)^{-3/2}$

34. $(-16)^{-5/4}$

35. $x^{-1/4}$

36. $y^{-1/6}$

37. $\dfrac{1}{a^{-2/3}}$

38. $\dfrac{1}{n^{-8/9}}$

39. $\dfrac{5}{7x^{-3/4}}$

40. $\dfrac{2}{3y^{-5/7}}$

Use the properties of exponents to simplify each expression. Write with positive exponents. See Example 4.

41. $a^{2/3}a^{5/3}$

42. $b^{9/5}b^{8/5}$

43. $x^{-2/5} \cdot x^{7/5}$

44. $y^{4/3} \cdot y^{-1/3}$

45. $3^{1/4} \cdot 3^{3/8}$

46. $5^{1/2} \cdot 5^{1/6}$

47. $\dfrac{y^{1/3}}{y^{1/6}}$

48. $\dfrac{x^{3/4}}{x^{1/8}}$

49. $(4u^2)^{3/2}$

50. $(32^{1/5}x^{2/3})^3$

51. $\dfrac{b^{1/2}b^{3/4}}{-b^{1/4}}$

52. $\dfrac{a^{1/4}a^{-1/2}}{a^{2/3}}$

53. $\dfrac{(x^3)^{1/2}}{x^{7/2}}$

54. $\dfrac{y^{11/3}}{(y^5)^{1/3}}$

55. $\dfrac{(3x^{1/4})^3}{x^{1/12}}$

56. $\dfrac{(2x^{1/5})^4}{x^{3/10}}$

57. $\dfrac{(y^3z)^{1/6}}{y^{-1/2}z^{1/3}}$

58. $\dfrac{(m^2n)^{1/4}}{m^{-1/2}n^{5/8}}$

59. $\dfrac{(x^3y^2)^{1/4}}{(x^{-5}y^{-1})^{-1/2}}$

60. $\dfrac{(a^{-2}b^3)^{1/8}}{(a^{-3}b)^{-1/4}}$

Multiply. See Example 5.

61. $y^{1/2}(y^{1/2} - y^{2/3})$

62. $x^{1/2}(x^{1/2} + x^{3/2})$

63. $x^{2/3}(x - 2)$

64. $3x^{1/2}(x + y)$

65. $(2x^{1/3} + 3)(2x^{1/3} - 3)$

66. $(y^{1/2} + 5)(y^{1/2} + 5)$

Factor the given factor from the expression. See Example 6.

67. $x^{8/3}; x^{8/3} + x^{10/3}$

68. $x^{3/2}; x^{5/2} - x^{3/2}$

69. $x^{1/5}; x^{2/5} - 3x^{1/5}$

70. $x^{2/7}; x^{3/7} - 2x^{2/7}$

71. $x^{-1/3}; 5x^{-1/3} + x^{2/3}$

72. $x^{-3/4}; x^{-3/4} + 3x^{1/4}$

Use rational exponents to simplify each radical. Assume that all variables represent positive numbers. See Example 7.

73. $\sqrt[6]{x^3}$

74. $\sqrt[9]{a^3}$

75. $\sqrt[6]{4}$

76. $\sqrt[4]{36}$

77. $\sqrt[4]{16x^2}$

78. $\sqrt[8]{4y^2}$

79. $\sqrt[8]{x^4y^4}$

80. $\sqrt[9]{y^6z^3}$

81. $\sqrt[12]{a^8b^4}$

82. $\sqrt[10]{a^5b^5}$

83. $\sqrt[4]{(x + 3)^2}$

84. $\sqrt[8]{(y + 1)^4}$

Use rational exponents to write as a single radical expression. See Example 8.

85. $\sqrt[3]{y} \cdot \sqrt[5]{y^2}$

86. $\sqrt[3]{y^2} \cdot \sqrt[6]{y}$

87. $\dfrac{\sqrt[3]{b^2}}{\sqrt[4]{b}}$

88. $\dfrac{\sqrt[4]{a}}{\sqrt[5]{a}}$

89. $\sqrt[3]{x} \cdot \sqrt[4]{x} \cdot \sqrt[8]{x^3}$

90. $\sqrt[6]{y} \cdot \sqrt[3]{y} \cdot \sqrt[5]{y^2}$

91. $\dfrac{\sqrt[3]{a^2}}{\sqrt[6]{a}}$

92. $\dfrac{\sqrt[5]{b^2}}{\sqrt[10]{b^3}}$

93. $\sqrt{3} \cdot \sqrt[3]{4}$

94. $\sqrt[3]{5} \cdot \sqrt{2}$

95. $\sqrt[5]{7} \cdot \sqrt[3]{y}$

96. $\sqrt[4]{5} \cdot \sqrt[3]{x}$

97. $\sqrt{5r} \cdot \sqrt[3]{s}$

98. $\sqrt[3]{b} \cdot \sqrt[5]{4a}$

REVIEW AND PREVIEW

Write each integer as a product of two integers such that one of the factors is a perfect square. For example, write 18 as 9 · 2 because 9 is a perfect square.

99. 75

100. 20

101. 48

102. 45

Write each integer as a product of two integers such that one of the factors is a perfect cube. For example, write 24 as 8 · 3 because 8 is a perfect cube.

103. 16

104. 56

105. 54

106. 80

CONCEPT EXTENSIONS

Choose the correct letter for each exercise. Letters will be used more than once. No pencil is needed. Just think about the meaning of each expression.

A = 2, B = −2, C = not a real number

107. $4^{1/2}$ _____

108. $-4^{1/2}$ _____

109. $(-4)^{1/2}$ _____

110. $8^{1/3}$ _____

111. $-8^{1/3}$ _____

112. $(-8)^{1/3}$ _____

Basal metabolic rate (BMR) is the number of calories per day a person needs to maintain life. A person's basal metabolic rate $B(w)$ in calories per day can be estimated with the function $B(w) = 70w^{3/4}$, where w is the person's weight in kilograms. Use this information to answer Exercises 113 and 114.

113. Estimate the BMR for a person who weighs 60 kilograms. Round to the nearest calorie. (*Note:* 60 kilograms is approximately 132 pounds.)

114. Estimate the BMR for a person who weighs 90 kilograms. Round to the nearest calorie. (*Note:* 90 kilograms is approximately 198 pounds.)

The number of cellular telephone subscribers in the United States from 2010–2015 can be modeled by $f(x) = 236x^{1/20}$, where $f(x)$ is the number of cellular telephone subscriptions in millions, x years after 2010. (Source: International Telecommunications Union) Use this information to answer Exercises 115 and 116.

115. Use this model to estimate the number of cellular telephone subscriptions in 2015. Round to the nearest tenth of a million.

116. Predict the number of cellular telephone subscriptions in 2020. Round to the nearest tenth of a million.

117. Explain how writing x^{-7} with positive exponents is similar to writing $x^{-1/4}$ with positive exponents.

118. Explain how writing $2x^{-5}$ with positive exponents is similar to writing $2x^{-3/4}$ with positive exponents.

Fill in each box with the correct expression.

119. $\square \cdot a^{2/3} = a^{3/3}$, or a

120. $\square \cdot x^{1/8} = x^{4/8}$, or $x^{1/2}$

121. $\dfrac{\square}{x^{-2/5}} = x^{3/5}$

122. $\dfrac{\square}{y^{-3/4}} = y^{4/4}$, or y

Use a calculator to write a four-decimal-place approximation of each number.

123. $8^{1/4}$

124. $20^{1/5}$

125. $18^{3/5}$

126. $76^{5/7}$

127. In physics, the speed of a wave traveling over a stretched string with tension t and density u is given by the expression $\dfrac{\sqrt{t}}{\sqrt{u}}$. Write this expression with rational exponents.

128. In electronics, the angular frequency of oscillations in a certain type of circuit is given by the expression $(LC)^{-1/2}$. Use radical notation to write this expression.

7.3 Simplifying Radical Expressions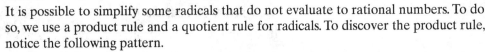

OBJECTIVES

1 Use the Product Rule for Radicals.

2 Use the Quotient Rule for Radicals.

3 Simplify Radicals.

4 Use the Distance and Midpoint Formulas.

OBJECTIVE

1 Using the Product Rule

It is possible to simplify some radicals that do not evaluate to rational numbers. To do so, we use a product rule and a quotient rule for radicals. To discover the product rule, notice the following pattern.

$$\sqrt{9} \cdot \sqrt{4} = 3 \cdot 2 = 6$$
$$\sqrt{9 \cdot 4} = \sqrt{36} = 6$$

Since both expressions simplify to 6, it is true that

$$\sqrt{9} \cdot \sqrt{4} = \sqrt{9 \cdot 4}$$

This pattern suggests the following product rule for radicals.

> **Product Rule for Radicals**
> If $\sqrt[n]{a}$ and $\sqrt[n]{b}$ are real numbers, then
> $$\sqrt[n]{a} \cdot \sqrt[n]{b} = \sqrt[n]{ab}$$

Notice that the product rule is the relationship $a^{1/n} \cdot b^{1/n} = (ab)^{1/n}$ stated in radical notation.

EXAMPLE 1 Multiply.

a. $\sqrt{3} \cdot \sqrt{5}$ **b.** $\sqrt{21} \cdot \sqrt{x}$ **c.** $\sqrt[3]{4} \cdot \sqrt[3]{2}$

d. $\sqrt[4]{5y^2} \cdot \sqrt[4]{2x^3}$ **e.** $\sqrt{\dfrac{2}{a}} \cdot \sqrt{\dfrac{b}{3}}$

Solution

a. $\sqrt{3} \cdot \sqrt{5} = \sqrt{3 \cdot 5} = \sqrt{15}$

b. $\sqrt{21} \cdot \sqrt{x} = \sqrt{21x}$

c. $\sqrt[3]{4} \cdot \sqrt[3]{2} = \sqrt[3]{4 \cdot 2} = \sqrt[3]{8} = 2$

d. $\sqrt[4]{5y^2} \cdot \sqrt[4]{2x^3} = \sqrt[4]{5y^2 \cdot 2x^3} = \sqrt[4]{10y^2x^3}$

e. $\sqrt{\dfrac{2}{a}} \cdot \sqrt{\dfrac{b}{3}} = \sqrt{\dfrac{2}{a} \cdot \dfrac{b}{3}} = \sqrt{\dfrac{2b}{3a}}$

PRACTICE

1 Multiply.

a. $\sqrt{5} \cdot \sqrt{7}$ **b.** $\sqrt{13} \cdot \sqrt{z}$ **c.** $\sqrt[4]{125} \cdot \sqrt[4]{5}$

d. $\sqrt[3]{5y} \cdot \sqrt[3]{3x^2}$ **e.** $\sqrt{\dfrac{5}{m}} \cdot \sqrt{\dfrac{t}{2}}$

OBJECTIVE

2 Using the Quotient Rule

To discover a quotient rule for radicals, notice the following pattern.

$$\sqrt{\frac{4}{9}} = \frac{2}{3}$$

$$\frac{\sqrt{4}}{\sqrt{9}} = \frac{2}{3}$$

Since both expressions simplify to $\frac{2}{3}$, it is true that

$$\sqrt{\frac{4}{9}} = \frac{\sqrt{4}}{\sqrt{9}}$$

This pattern suggests the following quotient rule for radicals.

Quotient Rule for Radicals

If $\sqrt[n]{a}$ and $\sqrt[n]{b}$ are real numbers and $\sqrt[n]{b}$ is not zero, then

$$\sqrt[n]{\frac{a}{b}} = \frac{\sqrt[n]{a}}{\sqrt[n]{b}}$$

Notice that the quotient rule is the relationship $\left(\dfrac{a}{b}\right)^{1/n} = \dfrac{a^{1/n}}{b^{1/n}}$ stated in radical notation. We can use the quotient rule to simplify radical expressions by reading the rule from left to right or to divide radicals by reading the rule from right to left.

For example,

$$\sqrt{\frac{x}{16}} = \frac{\sqrt{x}}{\sqrt{16}} = \frac{\sqrt{x}}{4} \qquad \text{Using } \sqrt[n]{\frac{a}{b}} = \frac{\sqrt[n]{a}}{\sqrt[n]{b}}$$

$$\frac{\sqrt{75}}{\sqrt{3}} = \sqrt{\frac{75}{3}} = \sqrt{25} = 5 \qquad \text{Using } \frac{\sqrt[n]{a}}{\sqrt[n]{b}} = \sqrt[n]{\frac{a}{b}}$$

Note: *Recall that from Section 7.2 on, we assume that variables represent positive real numbers. Since this is so, we need not insert absolute value bars when we simplify even roots.*

EXAMPLE 2 Use the quotient rule to simplify.

a. $\sqrt{\dfrac{25}{49}}$ **b.** $\sqrt{\dfrac{x}{9}}$ **c.** $\sqrt[3]{\dfrac{8}{27}}$ **d.** $\sqrt[4]{\dfrac{3}{16y^4}}$

Solution

a. $\sqrt{\dfrac{25}{49}} = \dfrac{\sqrt{25}}{\sqrt{49}} = \dfrac{5}{7}$ **b.** $\sqrt{\dfrac{x}{9}} = \dfrac{\sqrt{x}}{\sqrt{9}} = \dfrac{\sqrt{x}}{3}$

c. $\sqrt[3]{\dfrac{8}{27}} = \dfrac{\sqrt[3]{8}}{\sqrt[3]{27}} = \dfrac{2}{3}$ **d.** $\sqrt[4]{\dfrac{3}{16y^4}} = \dfrac{\sqrt[4]{3}}{\sqrt[4]{16y^4}} = \dfrac{\sqrt[4]{3}}{2y}$

PRACTICE

2 Use the quotient rule to simplify.

a. $\sqrt{\dfrac{36}{49}}$ **b.** $\sqrt{\dfrac{z}{16}}$ **c.** $\sqrt[3]{\dfrac{125}{8}}$ **d.** $\sqrt[4]{\dfrac{5}{81x^8}}$

OBJECTIVE

3 Simplifying Radicals

Both the product and quotient rules can be used to simplify a radical. If the product rule is read from right to left, we have that

$$\sqrt[n]{ab} = \sqrt[n]{a} \cdot \sqrt[n]{b}.$$

This is used to simplify the following radicals.

EXAMPLE 3 Simplify the following.

  a. $\sqrt{50}$ **b.** $\sqrt[3]{24}$ **c.** $\sqrt{26}$ **d.** $\sqrt[4]{32}$

Solution

a. Factor 50 such that one factor is the largest perfect square that divides 50. The largest perfect square factor of 50 is 25, so we write 50 as $25 \cdot 2$ and use the product rule for radicals to simplify.

$$\sqrt{50} = \sqrt{25 \cdot 2} = \sqrt{25} \cdot \sqrt{2} = 5\sqrt{2}$$

The largest perfect square factor of 50

Helpful Hint
Don't forget that, for example, $5\sqrt{2}$ means $5 \cdot \sqrt{2}$.

b. $\sqrt[3]{24} = \sqrt[3]{8 \cdot 3} = \sqrt[3]{8} \cdot \sqrt[3]{3} = 2\sqrt[3]{3}$

The largest perfect cube factor of 24

c. $\sqrt{26}$ The largest perfect square factor of 26 is 1, so $\sqrt{26}$ cannot be simplified further.

d. $\sqrt[4]{32} = \sqrt[4]{16 \cdot 2} = \sqrt[4]{16} \cdot \sqrt[4]{2} = 2\sqrt[4]{2}$

The largest fourth power factor of 32

PRACTICE

3 Simplify the following.

  a. $\sqrt{98}$ **b.** $\sqrt[3]{54}$ **c.** $\sqrt{35}$ **d.** $\sqrt[4]{243}$

After simplifying a radical such as a square root, always check the radicand to see that it contains no other perfect square factors. It may, if the largest perfect square factor of the radicand was not originally recognized. For example,

$$\sqrt{200} = \sqrt{4 \cdot 50} = \sqrt{4} \cdot \sqrt{50} = 2\sqrt{50}$$

Notice that the radicand 50 still contains the perfect square factor 25. This is because 4 is not the largest perfect square factor of 200. We continue as follows.

$$2\sqrt{50} = 2\sqrt{25 \cdot 2} = 2 \cdot \sqrt{25} \cdot \sqrt{2} = 2 \cdot 5 \cdot \sqrt{2} = 10\sqrt{2}$$

The radical is now simplified since 2 contains no perfect square factors (other than 1).

Helpful Hint

To help you recognize largest perfect power factors of a radicand, it will help if you are familiar with some perfect powers. A few are listed below.

Perfect Squares   1,   4,   9,   16,   25,   36,   49,   64,   81,   100,   121,   144
            1^2 2^2 3^2 4^2 5^2 6^2 7^2 8^2 9^2 10^2 11^2 12^2

Perfect Cubes   1,   8,   27,   64,   125
          1^3 2^3 3^3 4^3 5^3

Perfect Fourth   1,   16,   81,   256
Powers 1^4 2^4 3^4 4^4

In general, we say that a radicand of the form $\sqrt[n]{a}$ is simplified when the radicand a contains no factors that are perfect nth powers (other than 1 or -1).

EXAMPLE 4 Use the product rule to simplify.

  a. $\sqrt{25x^3}$ **b.** $\sqrt[3]{54x^6y^8}$ **c.** $\sqrt[4]{81z^{11}}$

Solution

a. $\sqrt{25x^3} = \sqrt{25x^2 \cdot x}$ Find the largest perfect square factor.

$= \sqrt{25x^2} \cdot \sqrt{x}$ Apply the product rule.

$= 5x\sqrt{x}$ Simplify.

b. $\sqrt[3]{54x^6y^8} = \sqrt[3]{27 \cdot 2 \cdot x^6 \cdot y^6 \cdot y^2}$ Factor the radicand and identify perfect cube factors.

$= \sqrt[3]{27x^6y^6 \cdot 2y^2}$

$= \sqrt[3]{27x^6y^6} \cdot \sqrt[3]{2y^2}$ Apply the product rule.

$= 3x^2y^2\sqrt[3]{2y^2}$ Simplify.

c. $\sqrt[4]{81z^{11}} = \sqrt[4]{81 \cdot z^8 \cdot z^3}$ Factor the radicand and identify perfect fourth power factors.

$= \sqrt[4]{81z^8} \cdot \sqrt[4]{z^3}$ Apply the product rule.

$= 3z^2\sqrt[4]{z^3}$ Simplify.   ☐

PRACTICE

4 Use the product rule to simplify.

  a. $\sqrt{36z^7}$ **b.** $\sqrt[3]{32p^4q^7}$ **c.** $\sqrt[4]{16x^{15}}$

EXAMPLE 5 Use the quotient rule to divide, and simplify if possible.

  a. $\dfrac{\sqrt{20}}{\sqrt{5}}$ **b.** $\dfrac{\sqrt{50x}}{2\sqrt{2}}$ **c.** $\dfrac{7\sqrt[3]{48x^4y^8}}{\sqrt[3]{6y^2}}$ **d.** $\dfrac{2\sqrt[4]{32a^8b^6}}{\sqrt[4]{a^{-1}b^2}}$

Solution

a. $\dfrac{\sqrt{20}}{\sqrt{5}} = \sqrt{\dfrac{20}{5}}$ Apply the quotient rule.

$= \sqrt{4}$ Simplify.

$= 2$ Simplify.

b. $\dfrac{\sqrt{50x}}{2\sqrt{2}} = \dfrac{1}{2} \cdot \sqrt{\dfrac{50x}{2}}$ Apply the quotient rule.

$= \dfrac{1}{2} \cdot \sqrt{25x}$ Simplify.

$= \dfrac{1}{2} \cdot \sqrt{25} \cdot \sqrt{x}$ Factor $25x$.

$= \dfrac{1}{2} \cdot 5 \cdot \sqrt{x}$ Simplify.

$= \dfrac{5}{2}\sqrt{x}$

c. $\dfrac{7\sqrt[3]{48x^4y^8}}{\sqrt[3]{6y^2}} = 7 \cdot \sqrt[3]{\dfrac{48x^4y^8}{6y^2}}$ Apply the quotient rule.

$= 7 \cdot \sqrt[3]{8x^4y^6}$ Simplify.

$= 7\sqrt[3]{8x^3y^6 \cdot x}$ Factor.

$= 7 \cdot \sqrt[3]{8x^3y^6} \cdot \sqrt[3]{x}$ Apply the product rule.

$= 7 \cdot 2xy^2 \cdot \sqrt[3]{x}$ Simplify.

$= 14xy^2\sqrt[3]{x}$

d. $\dfrac{2\sqrt[4]{32a^8b^6}}{\sqrt[4]{a^{-1}b^2}} = 2\sqrt[4]{\dfrac{32a^8b^6}{a^{-1}b^2}} = 2\sqrt[4]{32a^9b^4} = 2\sqrt[4]{16 \cdot a^8 \cdot b^4 \cdot 2 \cdot a}$

$\qquad\qquad = 2\sqrt[4]{16a^8b^4} \cdot \sqrt[4]{2a} = 2 \cdot 2a^2b \cdot \sqrt[4]{2a} = 4a^2b\sqrt[4]{2a}$ ☐

PRACTICE
5   Use the quotient rule to divide and simplify.

a. $\dfrac{\sqrt{80}}{\sqrt{5}}$ **b.** $\dfrac{\sqrt{98z}}{3\sqrt{2}}$ **c.** $\dfrac{5\sqrt[3]{40x^5y^7}}{\sqrt[3]{5y}}$ **d.** $\dfrac{3\sqrt[5]{64x^9y^8}}{\sqrt[5]{x^{-1}y^2}}$ ▪

✔ **CONCEPT CHECK**

Find and correct the error:

$$\dfrac{\sqrt[3]{27}}{\sqrt{9}} = \sqrt[3]{\dfrac{27}{9}} = \sqrt[3]{3}$$

OBJECTIVE
4   **Using the Distance and Midpoint Formulas**

Now that we know how to simplify radicals, we can derive and use the distance formula. The midpoint formula is often confused with the distance formula, so to clarify both, we will also review the midpoint formula.

The Cartesian coordinate system helps us visualize a distance between points. To find the distance between two points, we use the distance formula, which is derived from the Pythagorean theorem.

To find the distance d between two points (x_1, y_1) and (x_2, y_2) as shown to the left, notice that the length of leg a is $x_2 - x_1$ and that the length of leg b is $y_2 - y_1$.

Thus, the Pythagorean theorem tells us that

$$d^2 = a^2 + b^2$$

or

$$d^2 = (x_2 - x_1)^2 + (y_2 - y_1)^2$$

or

$$d = \sqrt{(x_2 - x_1)^2 + (y_2 - y_1)^2}$$

This formula gives us the distance between any two points on the real plane.

> **Distance Formula**
> The distance d between two points (x_1, y_1) and (x_2, y_2) is given by
> $$d = \sqrt{(x_2 - x_1)^2 + (y_2 - y_1)^2}$$

EXAMPLE 6   Find the distance between $(2, -5)$ and $(1, -4)$. Give the exact distance and a three-decimal-place approximation.

Solution To use the distance formula, it makes no difference which point we call (x_1, y_1) and which point we call (x_2, y_2). We will let $(x_1, y_1) = (2, -5)$ and $(x_2, y_2) = (1, -4)$.

Answer to Concept Check:
$\dfrac{\sqrt[3]{27}}{\sqrt{9}} = \dfrac{3}{3} = 1$

(Continued on next page)

$$d = \sqrt{(x_2 - x_1)^2 + (y_2 - y_1)^2}$$
$$= \sqrt{(1 - 2)^2 + [-4 - (-5)]^2}$$
$$= \sqrt{(-1)^2 + (1)^2}$$
$$= \sqrt{1 + 1}$$
$$= \sqrt{2} \approx 1.414$$

The distance between the two points is exactly $\sqrt{2}$ units, or approximately 1.414 units.

PRACTICE

6 Find the distance between $(-3, 7)$ and $(-2, 3)$. Give the exact distance and a three-decimal-place approximation.

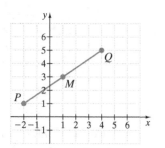

The **midpoint** of a line segment is the **point** located exactly halfway between the two endpoints of the line segment. On the graph to the left, the point M is the midpoint of line segment PQ. Thus, the distance between M and P equals the distance between M and Q.

Note: We usually need no knowledge of roots to calculate the midpoint of a line segment. We review midpoint here only because it is often confused with the distance between two points.

The x-coordinate of M is at half the distance between the x-coordinates of P and Q, and the y-coordinate of M is at half the distance between the y-coordinates of P and Q. That is, the x-coordinate of M is the average of the x-coordinates of P and Q; the y-coordinate of M is the average of the y-coordinates of P and Q.

> **Midpoint Formula**
>
> The midpoint of the line segment whose endpoints are (x_1, y_1) and (x_2, y_2) is the point with coordinates
> $$\left(\frac{x_1 + x_2}{2}, \frac{y_1 + y_2}{2} \right)$$

EXAMPLE 7 Find the midpoint of the line segment that joins points $P(-3, 3)$ and $Q(1, 0)$.

Solution Use the midpoint formula. It makes no difference which point we call (x_1, y_1) or which point we call (x_2, y_2). Let $(x_1, y_1) = (-3, 3)$ and $(x_2, y_2) = (1, 0)$.

$$\text{midpoint} = \left(\frac{x_1 + x_2}{2}, \frac{y_1 + y_2}{2} \right)$$
$$= \left(\frac{-3 + 1}{2}, \frac{3 + 0}{2} \right)$$
$$= \left(\frac{-2}{2}, \frac{3}{2} \right)$$
$$= \left(-1, \frac{3}{2} \right)$$

The midpoint of the segment is $\left(-1, \frac{3}{2} \right)$.

PRACTICE

7 Find the midpoint of the line segment that joins points $P(5, -2)$ and $Q(8, -6)$.

> **Helpful Hint**
>
> The distance between two points is a distance. The midpoint of a line segment is the point halfway between the endpoints of the segment.
>
> distance — measured in units
>
> midpoint — it is a point

✓ Vocabulary, Readiness & Video Check

Use the choices below to fill in each blank. Some choices may be used more than once.

distance   midpoint   point

1. The _____ of a line segment is the _____ exactly halfway between the two endpoints of the line segment.

2. The _____ between two points is a distance, measured in units.

3. The _____ formula is $d = \sqrt{(x_2 - x_1)^2 + (y_2 - y_1)^2}$.

4. The _____ formula is $\left(\dfrac{x_1 + x_2}{2}, \dfrac{y_1 + y_2}{2}\right)$.

Martin-Gay Interactive Videos

See Video 7.3 🌀

Watch the section lecture video and answer the following questions.

OBJECTIVE 1

5. From ▦ Example 1 and the lecture before, in order to apply the product rule for radicals, what must be true about the indexes of the radicals being multiplied?

OBJECTIVE 2

6. From ▦ Examples 2–6, when might you apply the quotient rule (in either direction) in order to simplify a fractional radical expression?

OBJECTIVE 3

7. From ▦ Example 8, we know that an even power of a variable is a perfect square factor of the variable, leaving no factor in the radicand once simplified. Therefore, what must be true about the power of any variable left in the radicand of a simplified square root? Explain.

OBJECTIVE 4

8. From ▦ Example 10, the formula uses the coordinates of two points similar to the slope formula. What caution should you take when replacing values in the formula?

OBJECTIVE 4

9. Based on ▦ Example 11, complete the following statement. The *x*-value of the midpoint is the _____ of the *x*-values of the endpoints and the *y*-value of the midpoint is the _____ of the *y*-values of the endpoints.

7.3 Exercise Set   MyMathLab® ▶

Use the product rule to multiply. See Example 1.

1. $\sqrt{7} \cdot \sqrt{2}$

2. $\sqrt{11} \cdot \sqrt{10}$

3. $\sqrt[4]{8} \cdot \sqrt[4]{2}$

4. $\sqrt[4]{27} \cdot \sqrt[4]{3}$

5. $\sqrt[3]{4} \cdot \sqrt[3]{9}$

6. $\sqrt[3]{10} \cdot \sqrt[3]{5}$

▶ **7.** $\sqrt{2} \cdot \sqrt{3x}$

8. $\sqrt{3y} \cdot \sqrt{5x}$

9. $\sqrt{\dfrac{7}{x}} \cdot \sqrt{\dfrac{2}{y}}$

10. $\sqrt{\dfrac{6}{m}} \cdot \sqrt{\dfrac{n}{5}}$

11. $\sqrt[4]{4x^3} \cdot \sqrt[4]{5}$

12. $\sqrt[4]{ab^2} \cdot \sqrt[4]{27ab}$

Use the quotient rule to simplify. See Examples 2 and 3.

▶ **13.** $\sqrt{\dfrac{6}{49}}$

14. $\sqrt{\dfrac{8}{81}}$

15. $\sqrt{\dfrac{2}{49}}$

16. $\sqrt{\dfrac{5}{121}}$

▶ **17.** $\sqrt[4]{\dfrac{x^3}{16}}$

18. $\sqrt[4]{\dfrac{y}{81x^4}}$

19. $\sqrt[3]{\dfrac{4}{27}}$

20. $\sqrt[3]{\dfrac{3}{64}}$

21. $\sqrt[4]{\dfrac{8}{x^8}}$

22. $\sqrt[4]{\dfrac{a^3}{81}}$

23. $\sqrt[3]{\dfrac{2x}{81y^{12}}}$

24. $\sqrt[3]{\dfrac{3}{8x^6}}$

25. $\sqrt{\dfrac{x^2y}{100}}$

26. $\sqrt{\dfrac{y^2z}{36}}$

27. $\sqrt{\dfrac{5x^2}{4y^2}}$

28. $\sqrt{\dfrac{y^{10}}{9x^6}}$

29. $-\sqrt[3]{\dfrac{z^7}{27x^3}}$

30. $-\sqrt[3]{\dfrac{64a}{b^9}}$

Simplify. See Examples 3 and 4.

31. $\sqrt{32}$

32. $\sqrt{27}$

33. $\sqrt[3]{192}$

34. $\sqrt[3]{108}$

35. $5\sqrt{75}$

36. $3\sqrt{8}$

37. $\sqrt{24}$

38. $\sqrt{20}$

39. $\sqrt{100x^5}$

40. $\sqrt{64y^9}$

41. $\sqrt[3]{16y^7}$

42. $\sqrt[3]{64y^9}$

43. $\sqrt[4]{a^8b^7}$

44. $\sqrt[5]{32z^{12}}$

45. $\sqrt{y^5}$

46. $\sqrt[3]{y^5}$

47. $\sqrt{25a^2b^3}$

48. $\sqrt{9x^5y^7}$

49. $\sqrt[5]{-32x^{10}y}$

50. $\sqrt[5]{-243z^9}$

51. $\sqrt[3]{50x^{14}}$

52. $\sqrt[3]{40y^{10}}$

53. $-\sqrt{32a^8b^7}$

54. $-\sqrt{20ab^6}$

55. $\sqrt{9x^7y^9}$

56. $\sqrt{12r^9s^{12}}$

57. $\sqrt[3]{125r^9s^{12}}$

58. $\sqrt[3]{8a^6b^9}$

59. $\sqrt[4]{32x^{12}y^5}$

60. $\sqrt[4]{162x^7y^{20}}$

Use the quotient rule to divide. Then simplify if possible. See Example 5.

61. $\dfrac{\sqrt{14}}{\sqrt{7}}$

62. $\dfrac{\sqrt{45}}{\sqrt{9}}$

63. $\dfrac{\sqrt[3]{24}}{\sqrt[3]{3}}$

64. $\dfrac{\sqrt[3]{10}}{\sqrt[3]{2}}$

65. $\dfrac{5\sqrt[4]{48}}{\sqrt[4]{3}}$

66. $\dfrac{7\sqrt[4]{162}}{\sqrt[4]{2}}$

67. $\dfrac{\sqrt{x^5y^3}}{\sqrt{xy}}$

68. $\dfrac{\sqrt{a^7b^6}}{\sqrt{a^3b^2}}$

69. $\dfrac{8\sqrt[3]{54m^7}}{\sqrt[3]{2m}}$

70. $\dfrac{\sqrt[3]{128x^3}}{-3\sqrt[3]{2x}}$

71. $\dfrac{3\sqrt{100x^2}}{2\sqrt{2x^{-1}}}$

72. $\dfrac{\sqrt{270y^2}}{5\sqrt{3y^{-4}}}$

73. $\dfrac{\sqrt[4]{96a^{10}b^3}}{\sqrt[4]{3a^2b^3}}$

74. $\dfrac{\sqrt[4]{160x^{10}y^5}}{\sqrt[4]{2x^2y^2}}$

75. $\dfrac{\sqrt[5]{64x^{10}y^3}}{\sqrt[5]{2x^3y^{-7}}}$

76. $\dfrac{\sqrt[5]{192x^6y^{12}}}{\sqrt[5]{2x^{-1}y^{-3}}}$

Find the distance between each pair of points. Give the exact distance and a three-decimal-place approximation. See Example 6.

77. $(5,1)$ and $(8,5)$

78. $(2,3)$ and $(14,8)$

79. $(-3,2)$ and $(1,-3)$

80. $(3,-2)$ and $(-4,1)$

81. $(-9,4)$ and $(-8,1)$

82. $(-5,-2)$ and $(-6,-6)$

83. $(0,-\sqrt{2})$ and $(\sqrt{3},0)$

84. $(-\sqrt{5},0)$ and $(0,\sqrt{7})$

85. $(1.7,-3.6)$ and $(-8.6,5.7)$

86. $(9.6,2.5)$ and $(-1.9,-3.7)$

Find the midpoint of the line segment whose endpoints are given. See Example 7.

87. $(6,-8)$, $(2,4)$

88. $(3,9)$, $(7,11)$

89. $(-2,-1)$, $(-8,6)$

90. $(-3,-4)$, $(6,-8)$

91. $(7,3)$, $(-1,-3)$

92. $(-2,5)$, $(-1,6)$

93. $\left(\dfrac{1}{2},\dfrac{3}{8}\right)$, $\left(-\dfrac{3}{2},\dfrac{5}{8}\right)$

94. $\left(-\dfrac{2}{5},\dfrac{7}{15}\right)$, $\left(-\dfrac{2}{5},-\dfrac{4}{15}\right)$

95. $(\sqrt{2},3\sqrt{5})$, $(\sqrt{2},-2\sqrt{5})$

96. $(\sqrt{8},-\sqrt{12})$, $(3\sqrt{2},7\sqrt{3})$

97. $(4.6,-3.5)$, $(7.8,-9.8)$

98. $(-4.6,2.1)$, $(-6.7,1.9)$

REVIEW AND PREVIEW

Perform each indicated operation. See Sections 1.4 and 5.4.

99. $6x+8x$

100. $(6x)(8x)$

101. $(2x+3)(x-5)$

102. $(2x+3)+(x-5)$

103. $9y^2-8y^2$

104. $(9y^2)(-8y^2)$

105. $-3(x+5)$

106. $-3+x+5$

107. $(x-4)^2$

108. $(2x+1)^2$

CONCEPT EXTENSIONS

Answer true or false. Assume all radicals represent nonzero real numbers.

109. $\sqrt[n]{a}\cdot\sqrt[n]{b}=\sqrt[n]{ab}$, _____

110. $\sqrt[3]{7}\cdot\sqrt[3]{11}=\sqrt[3]{18}$, _____

111. $\sqrt[3]{7}\cdot\sqrt{11}=\sqrt{77}$, _____

112. $\sqrt{x^7y^8}=\sqrt{x^7}\cdot\sqrt{y^8}$, _____

113. $\dfrac{\sqrt[n]{a}}{\sqrt[n]{b}}=\sqrt[n]{\dfrac{a}{b}}$, _____

114. $\dfrac{\sqrt[3]{12}}{\sqrt[3]{4}}=\sqrt[3]{8}$, _____

Find and correct the error. See the Concept Check in this section.

115. $\dfrac{\sqrt[3]{64}}{\sqrt{64}} = \sqrt[3]{\dfrac{64}{64}} = \sqrt[3]{1} = 1$

116. $\dfrac{\sqrt[4]{16}}{\sqrt{4}} = \sqrt[4]{\dfrac{16}{4}} = \sqrt[4]{4}$

Simplify. Assume variables represent positive numbers.

117. $\sqrt[5]{x^{35}}$

118. $\sqrt[6]{y^{48}}$

119. $\sqrt[4]{a^{12}b^4c^{20}}$

120. $\sqrt[3]{a^9b^{21}c^3}$

121. $\sqrt[3]{z^{32}}$

122. $\sqrt[5]{x^{49}}$

123. $\sqrt[7]{q^{17}r^{40}s^7}$

124. $\sqrt[4]{p^{11}q^4r^{45}}$

125. The formula for the radius r of a sphere with surface area A is given by $r = \sqrt{\dfrac{A}{4\pi}}$. Calculate the radius of a standard zorb whose outside surface area is 32.17 square meters. Round to the nearest tenth. (A zorb is a large inflated ball within a ball in which a person, strapped inside, may choose to roll down a hill. *Source:* Zorb, Ltd.)

126. NASA has investigated using a zorb-like Mars explorer, called the tumbleweed rover, to explore the Martian plains using wind power alone. Researchers have determined that the optimal rover would need to be efficient at catching any breeze, light enough to move easily, and large enough to roll over any rocks in its path. (*Source:* NASA)

  a. If scientists determine that the volume of the sphere-shaped tumbleweed rover should be approximately 4200 cubic feet, find the radius for the rover rounded to the nearest tenth. The formula for the radius r of a sphere with volume V is given by $r = \sqrt[3]{\dfrac{3V}{4\pi}}$.

b. One of the designs being considered for further investigation is the so-called box kite drawn below. Here, in addition to a sphere, there are three disks that look like three great circles at right angles to each other with an exoskeleton to protect the "kites." Find the total area of three great circles each with a diameter of 6 meters. Round to the nearest tenth of a square meter.

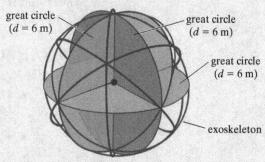

great circle ($d = 6$ m)

great circle ($d = 6$ m)

great circle ($d = 6$ m)

exoskeleton

Box Kite design

c. Do you think the box kite design is better than the sphere-alone design? Why or why not?

127. The formula for the lateral surface area A of a cone with height h and radius r is given by

$$A = \pi r \sqrt{r^2 + h^2}$$

  a. Find the lateral surface area of a cone whose height is 3 centimeters and whose radius is 4 centimeters.

  b. Approximate to two decimal places the lateral surface area of a cone whose height is 7.2 feet and whose radius is 6.8 feet.

128. Before Mount Vesuvius, a volcano in Italy, erupted violently in 79 C.E., its height was 4190 feet. Vesuvius was roughly cone-shaped, and its base had a radius of approximately 25,200 feet. Use the formula for the lateral surface area of a cone, given in Exercise 127, to approximate the surface area this volcano had before it erupted. (*Source:* Global Volcanism Network)

4190 ft

25,200 ft

7.4   Adding, Subtracting, and Multiplying Radical Expressions ▶

OBJECTIVES

1 Add or Subtract Radical Expressions. ▶

2 Multiply Radical Expressions. ▶

OBJECTIVE

1   Adding or Subtracting Radical Expressions ▶

We have learned that sums or differences of like terms can be simplified. To simplify these sums or differences, we use the distributive property. For example,

$$2x + 3x = (2 + 3)x = 5x \quad \text{and} \quad 7x^2y - 4x^2y = (7 - 4)x^2y = 3x^2y$$

The distributive property can also be used to add **like radicals.**

> **Like Radicals**
>
> Radicals with the same index and the same radicand are like radicals.

For example, $2\sqrt{7} + 3\sqrt{7} = (2+3)\sqrt{7} = 5\sqrt{7}$. Also,

Like radicals

$$5\sqrt{3x} - 7\sqrt{3x} = (5-7)\sqrt{3x} = -2\sqrt{3x}$$

The expression $2\sqrt{7} + 2\sqrt[3]{7}$ cannot be simplified further since $2\sqrt{7}$ and $2\sqrt[3]{7}$ are not like radicals.

Unlike radicals

EXAMPLE 1   Add or subtract as indicated. Assume all variables represent positive real numbers.

   a. $4\sqrt{11} + 8\sqrt{11}$ **b.** $5\sqrt[3]{3x} - 7\sqrt[3]{3x}$ **c.** $4\sqrt{5} + 4\sqrt[3]{5}$

Solution

   a. $4\sqrt{11} + 8\sqrt{11} = (4+8)\sqrt{11} = 12\sqrt{11}$
   b. $5\sqrt[3]{3x} - 7\sqrt[3]{3x} = (5-7)\sqrt[3]{3x} = -2\sqrt[3]{3x}$
   c. $4\sqrt{5} + 4\sqrt[3]{5}$

      This expression cannot be simplified since $4\sqrt{5}$ and $4\sqrt[3]{5}$ do not contain like radicals. ☐

PRACTICE
1   Add or subtract as indicated.

   a. $3\sqrt{17} + 5\sqrt{17}$ **b.** $7\sqrt[3]{5z} - 12\sqrt[3]{5z}$ **c.** $3\sqrt{2} + 5\sqrt[3]{2}$ ∎

When adding or subtracting radicals, always check first to see whether any radicals can be simplified.

✔ **CONCEPT CHECK**
True or false?

$$\sqrt{a} + \sqrt{b} = \sqrt{a+b}$$

Explain.

EXAMPLE 2   Add or subtract. Assume that variables represent positive real numbers.

   a. $\sqrt{20} + 2\sqrt{45}$ **b.** $\sqrt[3]{54} - 5\sqrt[3]{16} + \sqrt[3]{2}$ **c.** $\sqrt{27x} - 2\sqrt{9x} + \sqrt{72x}$
   d. $\sqrt[3]{98} + \sqrt{98}$ **e.** $\sqrt[3]{48y^4} + \sqrt[3]{6y^4}$

Solution   First, simplify each radical. Then add or subtract any like radicals.

   a. $\sqrt{20} + 2\sqrt{45} = \sqrt{4 \cdot 5} + 2\sqrt{9 \cdot 5}$ Factor 20 and 45.

                  $= \sqrt{4} \cdot \sqrt{5} + 2 \cdot \sqrt{9} \cdot \sqrt{5}$ Use the product rule.

                  $= 2 \cdot \sqrt{5} + 2 \cdot 3 \cdot \sqrt{5}$ Simplify $\sqrt{4}$ and $\sqrt{9}$.

                  $= 2\sqrt{5} + 6\sqrt{5}$

                  $= 8\sqrt{5}$ Add like radicals.

   b. $\sqrt[3]{54} - 5\sqrt[3]{16} + \sqrt[3]{2}$

        $= \sqrt[3]{27} \cdot \sqrt[3]{2} - 5 \cdot \sqrt[3]{8} \cdot \sqrt[3]{2} + \sqrt[3]{2}$ Factor and use the product rule.

        $= 3 \cdot \sqrt[3]{2} - 5 \cdot 2 \cdot \sqrt[3]{2} + \sqrt[3]{2}$ Simplify $\sqrt[3]{27}$ and $\sqrt[3]{8}$.

        $= 3\sqrt[3]{2} - 10\sqrt[3]{2} + \sqrt[3]{2}$ Write $5 \cdot 2$ as 10.

        $= -6\sqrt[3]{2}$ Combine like radicals.

c. $\sqrt{27x} - 2\sqrt{9x} + \sqrt{72x}$

$= \sqrt{9} \cdot \sqrt{3x} - 2 \cdot \sqrt{9} \cdot \sqrt{x} + \sqrt{36} \cdot \sqrt{2x}$ Factor and use the product rule.

$= 3 \cdot \sqrt{3x} - 2 \cdot 3 \cdot \sqrt{x} + 6 \cdot \sqrt{2x}$ Simplify $\sqrt{9}$ and $\sqrt{36}$.

$= 3\sqrt{3x} - 6\sqrt{x} + 6\sqrt{2x}$ Write $2 \cdot 3$ as 6.

d. $\sqrt[3]{98} + \sqrt{98} = \sqrt[3]{98} + \sqrt{49} \cdot \sqrt{2}$ Factor and use the product rule.

$= \sqrt[3]{98} + 7\sqrt{2}$ No further simplification is possible.

e. $\sqrt[3]{48y^4} + \sqrt[3]{6y^4} = \sqrt[3]{8y^3} \cdot \sqrt[3]{6y} + \sqrt[3]{y^3} \cdot \sqrt[3]{6y}$ Factor and use the product rule.

$= 2y\sqrt[3]{6y} + y\sqrt[3]{6y}$ Simplify $\sqrt[3]{8y^3}$ and $\sqrt[3]{y^3}$.

$= 3y\sqrt[3]{6y}$ Combine like radicals.   □

PRACTICE

2   Add or subtract.

a. $\sqrt{24} + 3\sqrt{54}$ **b.** $\sqrt[3]{24} - 4\sqrt[3]{81} + \sqrt[3]{3}$ **c.** $\sqrt{75x} - 3\sqrt{27x} + \sqrt{12x}$

d. $\sqrt{40} + \sqrt[3]{40}$ **e.** $\sqrt[3]{81x^4} + \sqrt[3]{3x^4}$ ■

Let's continue to assume that variables represent positive real numbers.

EXAMPLE 3   Add or subtract as indicated.

a. $\dfrac{\sqrt{45}}{4} - \dfrac{\sqrt{5}}{3}$ **b.** $\sqrt[3]{\dfrac{7x}{8}} + 2\sqrt[3]{7x}$

Solution

a. $\dfrac{\sqrt{45}}{4} - \dfrac{\sqrt{5}}{3} = \dfrac{3\sqrt{5}}{4} - \dfrac{\sqrt{5}}{3}$ To subtract, notice that the LCD is 12.

$= \dfrac{3\sqrt{5} \cdot 3}{4 \cdot 3} - \dfrac{\sqrt{5} \cdot 4}{3 \cdot 4}$ Write each expression as an equivalent expression with a denominator of 12.

$= \dfrac{9\sqrt{5}}{12} - \dfrac{4\sqrt{5}}{12}$ Multiply factors in the numerator and the denominator.

$= \dfrac{5\sqrt{5}}{12}$ Subtract.

b. $\sqrt[3]{\dfrac{7x}{8}} + 2\sqrt[3]{7x} = \dfrac{\sqrt[3]{7x}}{\sqrt[3]{8}} + 2\sqrt[3]{7x}$ Apply the quotient rule for radicals.

$= \dfrac{\sqrt[3]{7x}}{2} + 2\sqrt[3]{7x}$ Simplify.

$= \dfrac{\sqrt[3]{7x}}{2} + \dfrac{2\sqrt[3]{7x} \cdot 2}{2}$ Write each expression as an equivalent expression with a denominator of 2.

$= \dfrac{\sqrt[3]{7x}}{2} + \dfrac{4\sqrt[3]{7x}}{2}$

$= \dfrac{5\sqrt[3]{7x}}{2}$ Add.   □

PRACTICE

3   Add or subtract as indicated.

a. $\dfrac{\sqrt{28}}{3} - \dfrac{\sqrt{7}}{4}$ **b.** $\sqrt[3]{\dfrac{6y}{64}} + 3\sqrt[3]{6y}$ ■

OBJECTIVE

2 Multiplying Radical Expressions

We can multiply radical expressions by using many of the same properties used to multiply polynomial expressions. For instance, to multiply $\sqrt{2}\left(\sqrt{6} - 3\sqrt{2}\right)$, we use the distributive property and multiply $\sqrt{2}$ by each term inside the parentheses.

$$
\begin{aligned}
\sqrt{2}\left(\sqrt{6} - 3\sqrt{2}\right) &= \sqrt{2}\left(\sqrt{6}\right) - \sqrt{2}\left(3\sqrt{2}\right) && \text{Use the distributive property.} \\
&= \sqrt{2\cdot6} - 3\sqrt{2\cdot2} \\
&= \sqrt{2\cdot2\cdot3} - 3\cdot2 && \text{Use the product rule for radicals.} \\
&= 2\sqrt{3} - 6
\end{aligned}
$$

EXAMPLE 4 Multiply.

a. $\sqrt{3}\left(5 + \sqrt{30}\right)$
b. $\left(\sqrt{5} - \sqrt{6}\right)\left(\sqrt{7} + 1\right)$
c. $\left(7\sqrt{x} + 5\right)\left(3\sqrt{x} - \sqrt{5}\right)$
d. $\left(4\sqrt{3} - 1\right)^2$
e. $\left(\sqrt{2x} - 5\right)\left(\sqrt{2x} + 5\right)$
f. $\left(\sqrt{x-3} + 5\right)^2$

Solution

a.
$$
\begin{aligned}
\sqrt{3}\left(5 + \sqrt{30}\right) &= \sqrt{3}\left(5\right) + \sqrt{3}\left(\sqrt{30}\right) \\
&= 5\sqrt{3} + \sqrt{3\cdot30} \\
&= 5\sqrt{3} + \sqrt{3\cdot3\cdot10} \\
&= 5\sqrt{3} + 3\sqrt{10}
\end{aligned}
$$

b. To multiply, we can use the FOIL method.

$$
\begin{array}{cccc}
& \text{First} & \text{Outer} & \text{Inner} & \text{Last} \\
\left(\sqrt{5} - \sqrt{6}\right)\left(\sqrt{7} + 1\right) &= \sqrt{5}\cdot\sqrt{7} &+ \sqrt{5}\cdot1 &- \sqrt{6}\cdot\sqrt{7} &- \sqrt{6}\cdot1
\end{array}
$$
$$
= \sqrt{35} + \sqrt{5} - \sqrt{42} - \sqrt{6}
$$

c.
$$
\begin{aligned}
\left(7\sqrt{x} + 5\right)\left(3\sqrt{x} - \sqrt{5}\right) &= 7\sqrt{x}\left(3\sqrt{x}\right) - 7\sqrt{x}\left(\sqrt{5}\right) + 5\left(3\sqrt{x}\right) - 5\left(\sqrt{5}\right) \\
&= 21x - 7\sqrt{5x} + 15\sqrt{x} - 5\sqrt{5}
\end{aligned}
$$

d.
$$
\begin{aligned}
\left(4\sqrt{3} - 1\right)^2 &= \left(4\sqrt{3} - 1\right)\left(4\sqrt{3} - 1\right) \\
&= 4\sqrt{3}\left(4\sqrt{3}\right) - 4\sqrt{3}(1) - 1\left(4\sqrt{3}\right) - 1(-1) \\
&= 16\cdot3 - 4\sqrt{3} - 4\sqrt{3} + 1 \\
&= 48 - 8\sqrt{3} + 1 \\
&= 49 - 8\sqrt{3}
\end{aligned}
$$

e.
$$
\begin{aligned}
\left(\sqrt{2x} - 5\right)\left(\sqrt{2x} + 5\right) &= \sqrt{2x}\cdot\sqrt{2x} + 5\sqrt{2x} - 5\sqrt{2x} - 5\cdot5 \\
&= 2x - 25
\end{aligned}
$$

f.
$$
\left(\sqrt{x-3} + 5\right)^2 = \left(\sqrt{x-3}\right)^2 + 2\cdot\sqrt{x-3}\cdot5 + 5^2
$$
$$
\begin{array}{ccccccc}
\uparrow & \uparrow & \uparrow & \uparrow\uparrow & \uparrow & \uparrow & \uparrow \\
a & b & a^2 & +\,2\cdot & a & \cdot b\, + & b^2
\end{array}
$$
$$
\begin{aligned}
&= x - 3 + 10\sqrt{x-3} + 25 && \text{Simplify.} \\
&= x + 22 + 10\sqrt{x-3} && \text{Combine like terms.} \quad \square
\end{aligned}
$$

PRACTICE

4 Multiply.

a. $\sqrt{5}\left(2 + \sqrt{15}\right)$
b. $\left(\sqrt{2} - \sqrt{5}\right)\left(\sqrt{6} + 2\right)$
c. $\left(3\sqrt{z} - 4\right)\left(2\sqrt{z} + 3\right)$
d. $\left(\sqrt{6} - 3\right)^2$
e. $\left(\sqrt{5x} + 3\right)\left(\sqrt{5x} - 3\right)$
f. $\left(\sqrt{x+2} + 3\right)^2$

✔ Vocabulary, Readiness & Video Check

Complete the table with "Like" or "Unlike."

Terms	Like or Unlike Radical Terms?
1. $\sqrt{7}, \sqrt[3]{7}$	
2. $\sqrt[3]{x^2 y}, \sqrt[3]{yx^2}$	
3. $\sqrt[3]{abc}, \sqrt[3]{cba}$	
4. $2x\sqrt{5}, 2x\sqrt{10}$	

Simplify. Assume that all variables represent positive real numbers.

5. $2\sqrt{3} + 4\sqrt{3} =$ _____

6. $5\sqrt{7} + 3\sqrt{7} =$ _____

7. $8\sqrt{x} - \sqrt{x} =$ _____

8. $3\sqrt{y} - \sqrt{y} =$ _____

9. $7\sqrt[3]{x} + \sqrt[3]{x} =$ _____

10. $8\sqrt[3]{z} + \sqrt[3]{z} =$ _____

Martin-Gay Interactive Videos

See Video 7.4

Watch the section lecture video and answer the following questions.

OBJECTIVE 1

11. From Examples 1 and 2, why should you always check to see if all terms in your expression are simplified before attempting to add or subtract radicals?

OBJECTIVE 2

12. In Example 4, what are you told to remember about the square root of a positive number?

7.4 Exercise Set MyMathLab®

Add or subtract. See Examples 1 through 3.

1. $\sqrt{8} - \sqrt{32}$

2. $\sqrt{27} - \sqrt{75}$

3. $2\sqrt{2x^3} + 4x\sqrt{8x}$

4. $3\sqrt{45x^3} + x\sqrt{5x}$

5. $2\sqrt{50} - 3\sqrt{125} + \sqrt{98}$

6. $4\sqrt{32} - \sqrt{18} + 2\sqrt{128}$

7. $\sqrt[3]{16x} - \sqrt[3]{54x}$

8. $2\sqrt[3]{3a^4} - 3a\sqrt[3]{81a}$

9. $\sqrt{9b^3} - \sqrt{25b^3} + \sqrt{49b^3}$

10. $\sqrt{4x^7} + 9x^2\sqrt{x^3} - 5x\sqrt{x^5}$

11. $\dfrac{5\sqrt{2}}{3} + \dfrac{2\sqrt{2}}{5}$

12. $\dfrac{\sqrt{3}}{2} + \dfrac{4\sqrt{3}}{3}$

13. $\sqrt[3]{\dfrac{11}{8}} - \dfrac{\sqrt[3]{11}}{6}$

14. $\dfrac{2\sqrt[3]{4}}{7} - \dfrac{\sqrt[3]{4}}{14}$

15. $\dfrac{\sqrt{20x}}{9} + \sqrt{\dfrac{5x}{9}}$

16. $\dfrac{3x\sqrt{7}}{5} + \sqrt{\dfrac{7x^2}{100}}$

17. $7\sqrt{9} - 7 + \sqrt{3}$

18. $\sqrt{16} - 5\sqrt{10} + 7$

19. $2 + 3\sqrt{y^2} - 6\sqrt{y^2} + 5$

20. $3\sqrt{7} - \sqrt[3]{x} + 4\sqrt{7} - 3\sqrt[3]{x}$

21. $3\sqrt{108} - 2\sqrt{18} - 3\sqrt{48}$

22. $-\sqrt{75} + \sqrt{12} - 3\sqrt{3}$

23. $-5\sqrt[3]{625} + \sqrt[3]{40}$

24. $-2\sqrt[3]{108} - \sqrt[3]{32}$

25. $a^3\sqrt{9ab^3} - \sqrt{25a^7b^3} + \sqrt{16a^7b^3}$

26. $\sqrt{4x^7y^5} + 9x^2\sqrt{x^3y^5} - 5xy\sqrt{x^5y^3}$

27. $5y\sqrt{8y} + 2\sqrt{50y^3}$

28. $3\sqrt{8x^2y^3} - 2x\sqrt{32y^3}$

29. $\sqrt[3]{54xy^3} - 5\sqrt[3]{2xy^3} + y\sqrt[3]{128x}$

30. $2\sqrt[3]{24x^3y^4} + 4x\sqrt[3]{81y^4}$

31. $6\sqrt[3]{11} + 8\sqrt{11} - 12\sqrt{11}$

32. $3\sqrt[3]{5} + 4\sqrt{5} - 8\sqrt{5}$

33. $-2\sqrt[4]{x^7} + 3\sqrt[4]{16x^7} - x\sqrt[4]{x^3}$

34. $6\sqrt[3]{24x^3} - 2\sqrt[3]{81x^3} - x\sqrt[3]{3}$

35. $\dfrac{4\sqrt{3}}{3} - \dfrac{\sqrt{12}}{3}$

36. $\dfrac{\sqrt{45}}{10} + \dfrac{7\sqrt{5}}{10}$

37. $\dfrac{\sqrt[3]{8x^4}}{7} + \dfrac{3x\sqrt[3]{x}}{7}$

38. $\dfrac{\sqrt[4]{48}}{5x} - \dfrac{2\sqrt[4]{3}}{10x}$

39. $\sqrt{\dfrac{28}{x^2}} + \sqrt{\dfrac{7}{4x^2}}$

40. $\dfrac{\sqrt{99}}{5x} - \sqrt{\dfrac{44}{x^2}}$

41. $\sqrt[3]{\dfrac{16}{27}} - \dfrac{\sqrt[3]{54}}{6}$

42. $\dfrac{\sqrt[3]{3}}{10} + \sqrt[3]{\dfrac{24}{125}}$

43. $-\dfrac{\sqrt[3]{2x^4}}{9} + \sqrt[3]{\dfrac{250x^4}{27}}$

44. $\dfrac{\sqrt[3]{y^5}}{8} + \dfrac{5y\sqrt[3]{y^2}}{4}$

△ **45.** Find the perimeter of the trapezoid.

△ **46.** Find the perimeter of the triangle.

Multiply and then simplify if possible. See Example 4.

▶ **47.** $\sqrt{7}(\sqrt{5} + \sqrt{3})$

48. $\sqrt{5}(\sqrt{15} - \sqrt{35})$

49. $(\sqrt{5} - \sqrt{2})^2$

50. $(3x - \sqrt{2})(3x - \sqrt{2})$

51. $\sqrt{3x}(\sqrt{3} - \sqrt{x})$

52. $\sqrt{5y}(\sqrt{y} + \sqrt{5})$

53. $(2\sqrt{x} - 5)(3\sqrt{x} + 1)$

54. $(8\sqrt{y} + z)(4\sqrt{y} - 1)$

55. $(\sqrt[3]{a} - 4)(\sqrt[3]{a} + 5)$

56. $(\sqrt[3]{a} + 2)(\sqrt[3]{a} + 7)$

57. $6(\sqrt{2} - 2)$

58. $\sqrt{5}(6 - \sqrt{5})$

59. $\sqrt{2}(\sqrt{2} + x\sqrt{6})$

60. $\sqrt{3}(\sqrt{3} - 2\sqrt{5x})$

▶ **61.** $(2\sqrt{7} + 3\sqrt{5})(\sqrt{7} - 2\sqrt{5})$

62. $(\sqrt{6} - 4\sqrt{2})(3\sqrt{6} + \sqrt{2})$

63. $(\sqrt{x} - y)(\sqrt{x} + y)$

64. $(\sqrt{3x} + 2)(\sqrt{3x} - 2)$

65. $(\sqrt{3} + x)^2$

66. $(\sqrt{y} - 3x)^2$

67. $(\sqrt{5x} - 2\sqrt{3x})(\sqrt{5x} - 3\sqrt{3x})$

68. $(5\sqrt{7x} - \sqrt{2x})(4\sqrt{7x} + 6\sqrt{2x})$

69. $(\sqrt[3]{4} + 2)(\sqrt[3]{2} - 1)$

70. $(\sqrt[3]{3} + \sqrt[3]{2})(\sqrt[3]{9} - \sqrt[3]{4})$

71. $(\sqrt[3]{x} + 1)(\sqrt[3]{x^2} - \sqrt[3]{x} + 1)$

72. $(\sqrt[3]{3x} + 2)(\sqrt[3]{9x^2} - 2\sqrt[3]{3x} + 4)$

73. $(\sqrt{x - 1} + 5)^2$

74. $(\sqrt{3x + 1} + 2)^2$

75. $(\sqrt{2x + 5} - 1)^2$

76. $(\sqrt{x - 6} - 7)^2$

REVIEW AND PREVIEW

Factor each numerator and denominator. Then simplify if possible. See Section 6.1.

77. $\dfrac{2x - 14}{2}$

78. $\dfrac{8x - 24y}{4}$

79. $\dfrac{7x - 7y}{x^2 - y^2}$

80. $\dfrac{x^3 - 8}{4x - 8}$

81. $\dfrac{6a^2b - 9ab}{3ab}$

82. $\dfrac{14r - 28r^2s^2}{7rs}$

83. $\dfrac{-4 + 2\sqrt{3}}{6}$

84. $\dfrac{-5 + 10\sqrt{7}}{5}$

CONCEPT EXTENSIONS

△ **85.** Find the perimeter and area of the rectangle.

△ **86.** Find the area and perimeter of the trapezoid. (*Hint:* The area of a trapezoid is the product of half the height $6\sqrt{3}$ meters and the sum of the bases $2\sqrt{63}$ and $7\sqrt{7}$ meters.)

$2\sqrt{63}$ m

$2\sqrt{27}$ m

$6\sqrt{3}$ m

$7\sqrt{7}$ m

87. a. Add: $\sqrt{3} + \sqrt{3}$

　　b. Multiply: $\sqrt{3} \cdot \sqrt{3}$

＼ **c.** Describe the differences in parts **a** and **b**.

88. a. Add: $2\sqrt{5} + \sqrt{5}$

　　b. Multiply: $2\sqrt{5} \cdot \sqrt{5}$

＼ **c.** Describe the differences in parts **a** and **b**.

89. Multiply: $(\sqrt{2} + \sqrt{3} - 1)^2$

90. Multiply: $(\sqrt{5} - \sqrt{2} + 1)^2$

＼ **91.** Explain how simplifying $2x + 3x$ is similar to simplifying $2\sqrt{x} + 3\sqrt{x}$.

＼ **92.** Explain how multiplying $(x - 2)(x + 3)$ is similar to multiplying $(\sqrt{x} - \sqrt{2})(\sqrt{x} + \sqrt{3})$.

7.5 Rationalizing Denominators and Numerators of Radical Expressions

OBJECTIVES

1 Rationalize Denominators.

2 Rationalize Denominators Having Two Terms.

3 Rationalize Numerators.

OBJECTIVE

1 Rationalizing Denominators of Radical Expressions

Often in mathematics, it is helpful to write a radical expression such as $\dfrac{\sqrt{3}}{\sqrt{2}}$ either without a radical in the denominator or without a radical in the numerator. The process of writing this expression as an equivalent expression but without a radical in the denominator is called **rationalizing the denominator.** To rationalize the denominator of $\dfrac{\sqrt{3}}{\sqrt{2}}$, we use the fundamental principle of fractions and multiply the numerator and the denominator by $\sqrt{2}$. Recall that this is the same as multiplying by $\dfrac{\sqrt{2}}{\sqrt{2}}$, which simplifies to 1.

$$\frac{\sqrt{3}}{\sqrt{2}} = \frac{\sqrt{3} \cdot \sqrt{2}}{\sqrt{2} \cdot \sqrt{2}} = \frac{\sqrt{6}}{\sqrt{4}} = \frac{\sqrt{6}}{2}$$

In this section, we continue to assume that variables represent positive real numbers.

EXAMPLE 1 Rationalize the denominator of each expression.

a. $\dfrac{2}{\sqrt{5}}$　　　**b.** $\dfrac{2\sqrt{16}}{\sqrt{9x}}$　　　**c.** $\sqrt[3]{\dfrac{1}{2}}$

Solution

a. To rationalize the denominator, we multiply the numerator and denominator by a factor that makes the radicand in the denominator a perfect square.

$$\frac{2}{\sqrt{5}} = \frac{2 \cdot \sqrt{5}}{\sqrt{5} \cdot \sqrt{5}} = \frac{2\sqrt{5}}{5} \quad \text{The denominator is now rationalized.}$$

b. First, we simplify the radicals and then rationalize the denominator.

$$\frac{2\sqrt{16}}{\sqrt{9x}} = \frac{2(4)}{3\sqrt{x}} = \frac{8}{3\sqrt{x}}$$

To rationalize the denominator, multiply the numerator and denominator by $\sqrt{x}$. Then

$$\frac{8}{3\sqrt{x}} = \frac{8 \cdot \sqrt{x}}{3\sqrt{x} \cdot \sqrt{x}} = \frac{8\sqrt{x}}{3x}$$

(Continued on next page)

c. $\sqrt[3]{\dfrac{1}{2}} = \dfrac{\sqrt[3]{1}}{\sqrt[3]{2}} = \dfrac{1}{\sqrt[3]{2}}$. Now we rationalize the denominator. Since $\sqrt[3]{2}$ is a cube root, we want to multiply by a value that will make the radicand 2 a perfect cube. If we multiply $\sqrt[3]{2}$ by $\sqrt[3]{2^2}$, we get $\sqrt[3]{2^3} = \sqrt[3]{8} = 2$.

$$\dfrac{1 \cdot \sqrt[3]{2^2}}{\sqrt[3]{2} \cdot \sqrt[3]{2^2}} = \dfrac{\sqrt[3]{4}}{\sqrt[3]{2^3}} = \dfrac{\sqrt[3]{4}}{2} \qquad \text{Multiply the numerator and}$$
denominator by $\sqrt[3]{2^2}$ and then simplify. □

PRACTICE
1 Rationalize the denominator of each expression.

    a. $\dfrac{5}{\sqrt{3}}$ **b.** $\dfrac{3\sqrt{25}}{\sqrt{4x}}$ **c.** $\sqrt[3]{\dfrac{2}{9}}$

✔ **CONCEPT CHECK**
Determine the smallest number both the numerator and denominator can be multiplied by to rationalize the denominator of the radical expression.

a. $\dfrac{1}{\sqrt[3]{7}}$ **b.** $\dfrac{1}{\sqrt[4]{8}}$

EXAMPLE 2 Rationalize the denominator of $\sqrt{\dfrac{7x}{3y}}$.

Solution $\sqrt{\dfrac{7x}{3y}} = \dfrac{\sqrt{7x}}{\sqrt{3y}}$ Use the quotient rule. No radical may be simplified further.

$\qquad = \dfrac{\sqrt{7x} \cdot \sqrt{3y}}{\sqrt{3y} \cdot \sqrt{3y}}$ Multiply numerator and denominator by $\sqrt{3y}$ so that the radicand in the denominator is a perfect square.

$\qquad = \dfrac{\sqrt{21xy}}{3y}$ Use the product rule in the numerator and denominator. Remember that $\sqrt{3y} \cdot \sqrt{3y} = 3y$. □

PRACTICE
2 Rationalize the denominator of $\sqrt{\dfrac{3z}{5y}}$.

EXAMPLE 3 Rationalize the denominator of $\dfrac{\sqrt[4]{x}}{\sqrt[4]{81y^5}}$.

Solution First, simplify each radical if possible.

$\dfrac{\sqrt[4]{x}}{\sqrt[4]{81y^5}} = \dfrac{\sqrt[4]{x}}{\sqrt[4]{81y^4} \cdot \sqrt[4]{y}}$ Use the product rule in the denominator.

$\qquad = \dfrac{\sqrt[4]{x}}{3y\sqrt[4]{y}}$ Write $\sqrt[4]{81y^4}$ as $3y$.

$\qquad = \dfrac{\sqrt[4]{x} \cdot \sqrt[4]{y^3}}{3y\sqrt[4]{y} \cdot \sqrt[4]{y^3}}$ Multiply numerator and denominator by $\sqrt[4]{y^3}$ so that the radicand in the denominator is a perfect fourth power.

$\qquad = \dfrac{\sqrt[4]{xy^3}}{3y\sqrt[4]{y^4}}$ Use the product rule in the numerator and denominator.

$\qquad = \dfrac{\sqrt[4]{xy^3}}{3y^2}$ In the denominator, $\sqrt[4]{y^4} = y$ and $3y \cdot y = 3y^2$. □

PRACTICE
3 Rationalize the denominator of $\dfrac{\sqrt[3]{z^2}}{\sqrt[3]{27x^4}}$.

Answer to Concept Check:
a. $\sqrt[3]{7^2}$ or $\sqrt[3]{49}$ **b.** $\sqrt[4]{2}$

OBJECTIVE

2 Rationalizing Denominators Having Two Terms

Remember the product of the sum and difference of two terms?

$$(a + b)(a - b) = a^2 - b^2$$

These two expressions are called **conjugates** of each other.

To rationalize a numerator or denominator that is a sum or difference of two terms, we use conjugates. To see how and why this works, let's rationalize the denominator of the expression $\dfrac{5}{\sqrt{3} - 2}$. To do so, we multiply both the numerator and the denominator by $\sqrt{3} + 2$, the **conjugate** of the denominator $\sqrt{3} - 2$, and see what happens.

$$\frac{5}{\sqrt{3} - 2} = \frac{5(\sqrt{3} + 2)}{(\sqrt{3} - 2)(\sqrt{3} + 2)}$$

$$= \frac{5(\sqrt{3} + 2)}{(\sqrt{3})^2 - 2^2} \quad \text{Multiply the sum and difference of two terms: } (a + b)(a - b) = a^2 - b^2.$$

$$= \frac{5(\sqrt{3} + 2)}{3 - 4}$$

$$= \frac{5(\sqrt{3} + 2)}{-1}$$

$$= -5(\sqrt{3} + 2) \quad \text{or} \quad -5\sqrt{3} - 10$$

Notice in the denominator that the product of $(\sqrt{3} - 2)$ and its conjugate, $(\sqrt{3} + 2)$, is -1. In general, the product of an expression and its conjugate will contain no radical terms. This is why, when rationalizing a denominator or a numerator containing two terms, we multiply by its conjugate. Examples of conjugates are

$$\sqrt{a} - \sqrt{b} \quad \text{and} \quad \sqrt{a} + \sqrt{b}$$
$$x + \sqrt{y} \quad \text{and} \quad x - \sqrt{y}$$

EXAMPLE 4   Rationalize each denominator.

a. $\dfrac{2}{3\sqrt{2} + 4}$ **b.** $\dfrac{\sqrt{6} + 2}{\sqrt{5} - \sqrt{3}}$ **c.** $\dfrac{2\sqrt{m}}{3\sqrt{x} + \sqrt{m}}$

Solution

a. Multiply the numerator and denominator by the conjugate of the denominator, $3\sqrt{2} + 4$.

$$\frac{2}{3\sqrt{2} + 4} = \frac{2(3\sqrt{2} - 4)}{(3\sqrt{2} + 4)(3\sqrt{2} - 4)}$$

$$= \frac{2(3\sqrt{2} - 4)}{(3\sqrt{2})^2 - 4^2}$$

$$= \frac{2(3\sqrt{2} - 4)}{18 - 16}$$

$$= \frac{2(3\sqrt{2} - 4)}{2}, \quad \text{or} \quad 3\sqrt{2} - 4$$

It is often useful to leave a numerator in factored form to help determine whether the expression can be simplified.

(Continued on next page)

b. Multiply the numerator and denominator by the conjugate of $\sqrt{5} - \sqrt{3}$.

$$\frac{\sqrt{6} + 2}{\sqrt{5} - \sqrt{3}} = \frac{(\sqrt{6} + 2)(\sqrt{5} + \sqrt{3})}{(\sqrt{5} - \sqrt{3})(\sqrt{5} + \sqrt{3})}$$

$$= \frac{\sqrt{6}\sqrt{5} + \sqrt{6}\sqrt{3} + 2\sqrt{5} + 2\sqrt{3}}{(\sqrt{5})^2 - (\sqrt{3})^2}$$

$$= \frac{\sqrt{30} + \sqrt{18} + 2\sqrt{5} + 2\sqrt{3}}{5 - 3}$$

$$= \frac{\sqrt{30} + 3\sqrt{2} + 2\sqrt{5} + 2\sqrt{3}}{2}$$

c. Multiply by the conjugate of $3\sqrt{x} + \sqrt{m}$ to eliminate the radicals from the denominator.

$$\frac{2\sqrt{m}}{3\sqrt{x} + \sqrt{m}} = \frac{2\sqrt{m}(3\sqrt{x} - \sqrt{m})}{(3\sqrt{x} + \sqrt{m})(3\sqrt{x} - \sqrt{m})} = \frac{6\sqrt{mx} - 2m}{(3\sqrt{x})^2 - (\sqrt{m})^2}$$

$$= \frac{6\sqrt{mx} - 2m}{9x - m}$$

PRACTICE
4   Rationalize each denominator.

a. $\dfrac{5}{3\sqrt{5} + 2}$ **b.** $\dfrac{\sqrt{2} + 5}{\sqrt{3} - \sqrt{5}}$ **c.** $\dfrac{3\sqrt{x}}{2\sqrt{x} + \sqrt{y}}$

OBJECTIVE
3   Rationalizing Numerators

As mentioned earlier, it is also often helpful to write an expression such as $\dfrac{\sqrt{3}}{\sqrt{2}}$ as an equivalent expression without a radical in the numerator. This process is called **rationalizing the numerator.** To rationalize the numerator of $\dfrac{\sqrt{3}}{\sqrt{2}}$, we multiply the numerator and the denominator by $\sqrt{3}$.

$$\frac{\sqrt{3}}{\sqrt{2}} = \frac{\sqrt{3} \cdot \sqrt{3}}{\sqrt{2} \cdot \sqrt{3}} = \frac{\sqrt{9}}{\sqrt{6}} = \frac{3}{\sqrt{6}}$$

EXAMPLE 5   Rationalize the numerator of $\dfrac{\sqrt{7}}{\sqrt{45}}$.

Solution First we simplify $\sqrt{45}$.

$$\frac{\sqrt{7}}{\sqrt{45}} = \frac{\sqrt{7}}{\sqrt{9 \cdot 5}} = \frac{\sqrt{7}}{3\sqrt{5}}$$

Next we rationalize the numerator by multiplying the numerator and the denominator by $\sqrt{7}$.

$$\frac{\sqrt{7}}{3\sqrt{5}} = \frac{\sqrt{7} \cdot \sqrt{7}}{3\sqrt{5} \cdot \sqrt{7}} = \frac{7}{3\sqrt{5 \cdot 7}} = \frac{7}{3\sqrt{35}}$$

PRACTICE
5   Rationalize the numerator of $\dfrac{\sqrt{32}}{\sqrt{80}}$.

EXAMPLE 6 Rationalize the numerator of $\dfrac{\sqrt[3]{2x^2}}{\sqrt[3]{5y}}$.

Solution The numerator and the denominator of this expression are already simplified. To rationalize the numerator, $\sqrt[3]{2x^2}$, we multiply the numerator and denominator by a factor that will make the radicand a perfect cube. If we multiply $\sqrt[3]{2x^2}$ by $\sqrt[3]{4x}$, we get $\sqrt[3]{8x^3} = 2x$.

$$\frac{\sqrt[3]{2x^2}}{\sqrt[3]{5y}} = \frac{\sqrt[3]{2x^2} \cdot \sqrt[3]{4x}}{\sqrt[3]{5y} \cdot \sqrt[3]{4x}} = \frac{\sqrt[3]{8x^3}}{\sqrt[3]{20xy}} = \frac{2x}{\sqrt[3]{20xy}}$$

PRACTICE
6 Rationalize the numerator of $\dfrac{\sqrt[3]{5b}}{\sqrt[3]{2a}}$.

EXAMPLE 7 Rationalize the numerator of $\dfrac{\sqrt{x} + 2}{5}$.

Solution We multiply the numerator and the denominator by the conjugate of the numerator, $\sqrt{x} + 2$.

$$\frac{\sqrt{x} + 2}{5} = \frac{(\sqrt{x} + 2)(\sqrt{x} - 2)}{5(\sqrt{x} - 2)} \qquad \text{Multiply by } \sqrt{x} - 2, \text{ the conjugate of } \sqrt{x} + 2.$$

$$= \frac{(\sqrt{x})^2 - 2^2}{5(\sqrt{x} - 2)} \qquad (a + b)(a - b) = a^2 - b^2$$

$$= \frac{x - 4}{5(\sqrt{x} - 2)}$$

PRACTICE
7 Rationalize the numerator of $\dfrac{\sqrt{x} - 3}{4}$.

✔ Vocabulary, Readiness & Video Check

Use the choices below to fill in each blank. Not all choices will be used.

rationalizing the numerator	conjugate	$\dfrac{\sqrt{3}}{\sqrt{3}}$
rationalizing the denominator	$\dfrac{5}{5}$	

1. The _____ of $a + b$ is $a - b$.

2. The process of writing an equivalent expression, but without a radical in the denominator, is called _____.

3. The process of writing an equivalent expression, but without a radical in the numerator, is called _____.

4. To rationalize the denominator of $\dfrac{5}{\sqrt{3}}$, we multiply by _____.

Martin-Gay Interactive Videos

See Video 7.5

Watch the section lecture video and answer the following questions.

OBJECTIVE 1
5. From Examples 1–3, what is the goal of rationalizing a denominator?

OBJECTIVE 2
6. From Example 4, why will multiplying a denominator by its conjugate always rationalize the denominator?

OBJECTIVE 3
7. From Example 5, is the process of rationalizing a numerator any different from rationalizing a denominator?

7.5   Exercise Set   MyMathLab®

Rationalize each denominator. See Examples 1 through 3.

▶ 1. $\dfrac{\sqrt{2}}{\sqrt{7}}$

2. $\dfrac{\sqrt{3}}{\sqrt{2}}$

3. $\sqrt{\dfrac{1}{5}}$

4. $\sqrt{\dfrac{1}{2}}$

5. $\sqrt{\dfrac{4}{x}}$

6. $\sqrt{\dfrac{25}{y}}$

▶ 7. $\dfrac{4}{\sqrt[3]{3}}$

8. $\dfrac{6}{\sqrt[3]{9}}$

▶ 9. $\dfrac{3}{\sqrt{8x}}$

10. $\dfrac{5}{\sqrt{27a}}$

11. $\dfrac{3}{\sqrt[3]{4x^2}}$

12. $\dfrac{5}{\sqrt[3]{3y}}$

13. $\dfrac{9}{\sqrt{3a}}$

14. $\dfrac{x}{\sqrt{5}}$

15. $\dfrac{3}{\sqrt[3]{2}}$

16. $\dfrac{5}{\sqrt[3]{9}}$

17. $\dfrac{2\sqrt{3}}{\sqrt{7}}$

18. $\dfrac{-5\sqrt{2}}{\sqrt{11}}$

19. $\sqrt{\dfrac{2x}{5y}}$

20. $\sqrt{\dfrac{13a}{2b}}$

21. $\sqrt[3]{\dfrac{3}{5}}$

22. $\sqrt[3]{\dfrac{7}{10}}$

23. $\sqrt{\dfrac{3x}{50}}$

24. $\sqrt{\dfrac{11y}{45}}$

25. $\dfrac{1}{\sqrt{12z}}$

26. $\dfrac{1}{\sqrt{32x}}$

27. $\dfrac{\sqrt[3]{2y^2}}{\sqrt[3]{9x^2}}$

28. $\dfrac{\sqrt[3]{3x}}{\sqrt[3]{4y^4}}$

29. $\sqrt[4]{\dfrac{81}{8}}$

30. $\sqrt[4]{\dfrac{1}{9}}$

31. $\sqrt[4]{\dfrac{16}{9x^7}}$

32. $\sqrt[5]{\dfrac{32}{m^6 n^{13}}}$

33. $\dfrac{5a}{\sqrt[3]{8a^9 b^{11}}}$

34. $\dfrac{9y}{\sqrt[4]{4y^9}}$

Write the conjugate of each expression.

35. $\sqrt{2} + x$

36. $\sqrt{3} + y$

37. $5 - \sqrt{a}$

38. $6 - \sqrt{b}$

39. $-7\sqrt{5} + 8\sqrt{x}$

40. $-9\sqrt{2} - 6\sqrt{y}$

Rationalize each denominator. See Example 4.

41. $\dfrac{6}{2 - \sqrt{7}}$

42. $\dfrac{3}{\sqrt{7} - 4}$

▶ 43. $\dfrac{-7}{\sqrt{x} - 3}$

44. $\dfrac{-8}{\sqrt{y} + 4}$

45. $\dfrac{\sqrt{2} - \sqrt{3}}{\sqrt{2} + \sqrt{3}}$

46. $\dfrac{\sqrt{3} + \sqrt{4}}{\sqrt{2} - \sqrt{3}}$

47. $\dfrac{\sqrt{a} + 1}{2\sqrt{a} - \sqrt{b}}$

48. $\dfrac{2\sqrt{a} - 3}{2\sqrt{a} + \sqrt{b}}$

49. $\dfrac{8}{1 + \sqrt{10}}$

50. $\dfrac{-3}{\sqrt{6} - 2}$

51. $\dfrac{\sqrt{x}}{\sqrt{x} + \sqrt{y}}$

52. $\dfrac{2\sqrt{a}}{2\sqrt{x} - \sqrt{y}}$

53. $\dfrac{2\sqrt{3} + \sqrt{6}}{4\sqrt{3} - \sqrt{6}}$

54. $\dfrac{4\sqrt{5} + \sqrt{2}}{2\sqrt{5} - \sqrt{2}}$

Rationalize each numerator. See Examples 5 and 6.

55. $\sqrt{\dfrac{5}{3}}$

56. $\sqrt{\dfrac{3}{2}}$

▶ 57. $\sqrt{\dfrac{18}{5}}$

58. $\sqrt{\dfrac{12}{7}}$

59. $\dfrac{\sqrt{4x}}{7}$

60. $\dfrac{\sqrt{3x^5}}{6}$

61. $\dfrac{\sqrt[3]{5y^2}}{\sqrt[3]{4x}}$

62. $\dfrac{\sqrt[3]{4x}}{\sqrt[3]{z^4}}$

63. $\sqrt{\dfrac{2}{5}}$

64. $\sqrt{\dfrac{3}{7}}$

65. $\dfrac{\sqrt{2x}}{11}$

66. $\dfrac{\sqrt{y}}{7}$

67. $\sqrt[3]{\dfrac{7}{8}}$

68. $\sqrt[3]{\dfrac{25}{2}}$

69. $\dfrac{\sqrt[3]{3x^5}}{10}$

70. $\sqrt[3]{\dfrac{9y}{7}}$

71. $\sqrt{\dfrac{18x^4 y^6}{3z}}$

72. $\sqrt{\dfrac{8x^5 y}{2z}}$

Rationalize each numerator. See Example 7.

73. $\dfrac{2 - \sqrt{11}}{6}$

74. $\dfrac{\sqrt{15} + 1}{2}$

75. $\dfrac{2 - \sqrt{7}}{-5}$

76. $\dfrac{\sqrt{5} + 2}{\sqrt{2}}$

77. $\dfrac{\sqrt{x} + 3}{\sqrt{x}}$

78. $\dfrac{5 + \sqrt{2}}{\sqrt{2x}}$

79. $\dfrac{\sqrt{2} - 1}{\sqrt{2} + 1}$

80. $\dfrac{\sqrt{8} - \sqrt{3}}{\sqrt{2} + \sqrt{3}}$

81. $\dfrac{\sqrt{x} + 1}{\sqrt{x} - 1}$

82. $\dfrac{\sqrt{x} + \sqrt{y}}{\sqrt{x} - \sqrt{y}}$

REVIEW AND PREVIEW

Solve each equation. See Sections 2.1 and 5.8.

83. $2x - 7 = 3(x - 4)$ **84.** $9x - 4 = 7(x - 2)$

85. $(x - 6)(2x + 1) = 0$ **86.** $(y + 2)(5y + 4) = 0$

87. $x^2 - 8x = -12$ **88.** $x^3 = x$

CONCEPT EXTENSIONS

△ **89.** The formula of the radius r of a sphere with surface area A is

$$r = \sqrt{\frac{A}{4\pi}}$$

Rationalize the denominator of the radical expression in this formula.

△ **90.** The formula for the radius r of a cone with height 7 centimeters and volume V is

$$r = \sqrt{\frac{3V}{7\pi}}$$

Rationalize the numerator of the radical expression in this formula.

7 cm

91. Given $\dfrac{\sqrt{5y^3}}{\sqrt{12x^3}}$, rationalize the denominator by following parts **a** and **b**.

     a. Multiply the numerator and denominator by $\sqrt{12x^3}$.

     b. Multiply the numerator and denominator by $\sqrt{3x}$.

     c. What can you conclude from parts **a** and **b**?

92. Given $\dfrac{\sqrt[3]{5y}}{\sqrt[3]{4}}$, rationalize the denominator by following parts **a** and **b**.

     a. Multiply the numerator and denominator by $\sqrt[3]{16}$.

     b. Multiply the numerator and denominator by $\sqrt[3]{2}$.

     c. What can you conclude from parts **a** and **b**?

Determine the smallest number both the numerator and denominator should be multiplied by to rationalize the denominator of the radical expression. See the Concept Check in this section.

93. $\dfrac{9}{\sqrt[3]{5}}$ **94.** $\dfrac{5}{\sqrt{27}}$

95. When rationalizing the denominator of $\dfrac{\sqrt{5}}{\sqrt{7}}$, explain why both the numerator and the denominator must be multiplied by $\sqrt{7}$.

96. When rationalizing the numerator of $\dfrac{\sqrt{5}}{\sqrt{7}}$, explain why both the numerator and the denominator must be multiplied by $\sqrt{5}$.

97. Explain why rationalizing the denominator does not change the value of the original expression.

98. Explain why rationalizing the numerator does not change the value of the original expression.

Integrated Review Radicals and Rational Exponents

Sections 7.1–7.5

Throughout this review, assume that all variables represent positive real numbers.
Find each root.

1. $\sqrt{81}$ **2.** $\sqrt[3]{-8}$ **3.** $\sqrt[4]{\dfrac{1}{16}}$ **4.** $\sqrt{x^6}$

5. $\sqrt[3]{y^9}$ **6.** $\sqrt{4y^{10}}$ **7.** $\sqrt[5]{-32y^5}$ **8.** $\sqrt[4]{81b^{12}}$

Use radical notation to write each expression. Simplify if possible.

9. $36^{1/2}$ **10.** $(3y)^{1/4}$ **11.** $64^{-2/3}$ **12.** $(x + 1)^{3/5}$

Use the properties of exponents to simplify each expression. Write with positive exponents.

13. $y^{-1/6} \cdot y^{7/6}$ **14.** $\dfrac{(2x^{1/3})^4}{x^{5/6}}$ **15.** $\dfrac{x^{1/4}x^{3/4}}{x^{-1/4}}$ **16.** $4^{1/3} \cdot 4^{2/5}$

Use rational exponents to simplify each radical.

17. $\sqrt[3]{8x^6}$ **18.** $\sqrt[12]{a^9b^6}$

Use rational exponents to write each as a single radical expression.

19. $\sqrt[4]{x} \cdot \sqrt{x}$

20. $\sqrt{5} \cdot \sqrt[3]{2}$

Simplify.

21. $\sqrt{40}$

22. $\sqrt[4]{16x^7y^{10}}$

23. $\sqrt[3]{54x^4}$

24. $\sqrt[5]{-64b^{10}}$

Multiply or divide. Then simplify if possible.

25. $\sqrt{5} \cdot \sqrt{x}$

26. $\sqrt[3]{8x} \cdot \sqrt[3]{8x^2}$

27. $\dfrac{\sqrt{98y^6}}{\sqrt{2y}}$

28. $\dfrac{\sqrt[4]{48a^9b^3}}{\sqrt[4]{ab^3}}$

Perform each indicated operation.

29. $\sqrt{20} - \sqrt{75} + 5\sqrt{7}$

30. $\sqrt[3]{54y^4} - y\sqrt[3]{16y}$

31. $\sqrt{3}(\sqrt{5} - \sqrt{2})$

32. $(\sqrt{7} + \sqrt{3})^2$

33. $(2x - \sqrt{5})(2x + \sqrt{5})$

34. $(\sqrt{x+1} - 1)^2$

Rationalize each denominator.

35. $\sqrt{\dfrac{7}{3}}$

36. $\dfrac{5}{\sqrt[3]{2x^2}}$

37. $\dfrac{\sqrt{3} - \sqrt{7}}{2\sqrt{3} + \sqrt{7}}$

Rationalize each numerator.

38. $\sqrt{\dfrac{7}{3}}$

39. $\sqrt[3]{\dfrac{9y}{11}}$

40. $\dfrac{\sqrt{x} - 2}{\sqrt{x}}$

7.6 Radical Equations and Problem Solving

OBJECTIVES

1 Solve Equations That Contain Radical Expressions. ▶

2 Use the Pythagorean Theorem to Model Problems. ▶

OBJECTIVE

1 Solving Equations That Contain Radical Expressions ▶

In this section, we present techniques to solve equations containing radical expressions such as

$$\sqrt{2x - 3} = 9$$

We use the power rule to help us solve these radical equations.

> **Power Rule**
>
> If both sides of an equation are raised to the same power, **all** solutions of the original equation are **among** the solutions of the new equation.

This property *does not* say that raising both sides of an equation to a power yields an equivalent equation. A solution of the new equation *may or may not* be a solution of the original equation. For example, $(-2)^2 = 2^2$, but $-2 \neq 2$. Thus, *each solution of the new equation must be checked* to make sure it is a solution of the original equation. Recall that a proposed solution that is not a solution of the original equation is called an **extraneous solution**.

EXAMPLE 1 Solve: $\sqrt{2x - 3} = 9$

Solution We use the power rule to square both sides of the equation to eliminate the radical.

$$\sqrt{2x - 3} = 9$$
$$(\sqrt{2x - 3})^2 = 9^2$$
$$2x - 3 = 81$$
$$2x = 84$$
$$x = 42$$

Now we check the solution in the original equation.

Check:

$$\sqrt{2x - 3} = 9$$

$$\sqrt{2(42) - 3} \stackrel{?}{=} 9 \quad \text{Let } x = 42.$$

$$\sqrt{84 - 3} \stackrel{?}{=} 9$$

$$\sqrt{81} \stackrel{?}{=} 9$$

$$9 = 9 \quad \text{True}$$

The solution checks, so we conclude that the solution is 42, or the solution set is $\{42\}$. □

PRACTICE
1   Solve: $\sqrt{3x - 5} = 7$

To solve a radical equation, first isolate a radical on one side of the equation.

EXAMPLE 2   Solve: $\sqrt{-10x - 1} + 3x = 0$

Solution   First, isolate the radical on one side of the equation. To do this, we subtract $3x$ from both sides.

$$\sqrt{-10x - 1} + 3x = 0$$

$$\sqrt{-10x - 1} + 3x - 3x = 0 - 3x$$

$$\sqrt{-10x - 1} = -3x$$

Next we use the power rule to eliminate the radical.

$$(\sqrt{-10x - 1})^2 = (-3x)^2$$

$$-10x - 1 = 9x^2$$

Since this is a quadratic equation, we can set the equation equal to 0 and try to solve by factoring.

$$9x^2 + 10x + 1 = 0$$

$$(9x + 1)(x + 1) = 0 \quad \text{Factor.}$$

$$9x + 1 = 0 \quad \text{or} \quad x + 1 = 0 \quad \text{Set each factor equal to 0.}$$

$$x = -\frac{1}{9} \quad \text{or} \quad x = -1$$

Check: Let $x = -\frac{1}{9}$.   Let $x = -1$.

$$\sqrt{-10x - 1} + 3x = 0 \qquad\qquad \sqrt{-10x - 1} + 3x = 0$$

$$\sqrt{-10\left(-\frac{1}{9}\right) - 1} + 3\left(-\frac{1}{9}\right) \stackrel{?}{=} 0 \qquad \sqrt{-10(-1) - 1} + 3(-1) \stackrel{?}{=} 0$$

$$\sqrt{\frac{10}{9} - \frac{9}{9}} - \frac{3}{9} \stackrel{?}{=} 0 \qquad\qquad \sqrt{10 - 1} - 3 \stackrel{?}{=} 0$$

$$\sqrt{\frac{1}{9}} - \frac{1}{3} \stackrel{?}{=} 0 \qquad\qquad\qquad \sqrt{9} - 3 \stackrel{?}{=} 0$$

$$\frac{1}{3} - \frac{1}{3} = 0 \quad \text{True} \qquad\qquad\qquad 3 - 3 = 0 \quad \text{True}$$

Both solutions check. The solutions are $-\frac{1}{9}$ and -1, or the solution set is $\left\{-\frac{1}{9}, -1\right\}$. □

PRACTICE
2   Solve: $\sqrt{16x - 3} - 4x = 0$

The following steps may be used to solve a radical equation.

Solving a Radical Equation

Step 1. Isolate one radical on one side of the equation.

Step 2. Raise each side of the equation to a power equal to the index of the radical and simplify.

Step 3. If the equation still contains a radical term, repeat Steps 1 and 2. If not, solve the equation.

Step 4. Check all proposed solutions in the original equation.

EXAMPLE 3   Solve: $\sqrt[3]{x + 1} + 5 = 3$

Solution First we isolate the radical by subtracting 5 from both sides of the equation.

$$\sqrt[3]{x + 1} + 5 = 3$$
$$\sqrt[3]{x + 1} = -2$$

Next we raise both sides of the equation to the third power to eliminate the radical.

$$(\sqrt[3]{x + 1})^3 = (-2)^3$$
$$x + 1 = -8$$
$$x = -9$$

The solution checks in the original equation, so the solution is -9. □

PRACTICE
3   Solve: $\sqrt[3]{x - 2} + 1 = 3$ ■

EXAMPLE 4   Solve: $\sqrt{4 - x} = x - 2$

Solution

$$\sqrt{4 - x} = x - 2$$
$$(\sqrt{4 - x})^2 = (x - 2)^2$$
$$4 - x = x^2 - 4x + 4$$

$x^2 - 3x = 0$	Write the quadratic equation in standard form.
$x(x - 3) = 0$	Factor.
$x = 0 \quad \text{or} \quad x - 3 = 0$	Set each factor equal to 0.
$x = 3$	

Check:

$$\sqrt{4 - x} = x - 2 \qquad\qquad \sqrt{4 - x} = x - 2$$
$$\sqrt{4 - 0} \overset{?}{=} 0 - 2 \quad \text{Let } x = 0. \qquad \sqrt{4 - 3} \overset{?}{=} 3 - 2 \quad \text{Let } x = 3.$$
$$2 = -2 \quad \text{False} \qquad\qquad 1 = 1 \quad \text{True}$$

The proposed solution 3 checks, but 0 does not. Since 0 is an extraneous solution, the only solution is 3. □

PRACTICE
4   Solve: $\sqrt{16 + x} = x - 4$ ■

Helpful Hint

In Example 4, notice that $(x - 2)^2 = x^2 - 4x + 4$. Make sure binomials are squared correctly.

✔ **CONCEPT CHECK**

How can you immediately tell that the equation $\sqrt{2y + 3} = -4$ has no real solution?

EXAMPLE 5   Solve: $\sqrt{2x + 5} + \sqrt{2x} = 3$

Solution   We get one radical alone by subtracting $\sqrt{2x}$ from both sides.

$$\sqrt{2x + 5} + \sqrt{2x} = 3$$
$$\sqrt{2x + 5} = 3 - \sqrt{2x}$$

Now we use the power rule to begin eliminating the radicals. First we square both sides.

$$(\sqrt{2x + 5})^2 = (3 - \sqrt{2x})^2$$
$$2x + 5 = 9 - 6\sqrt{2x} + 2x \quad \text{Multiply } (3 - \sqrt{2x})(3 - \sqrt{2x}).$$

There is still a radical in the equation, so we get a radical alone again. Then we square both sides.

$$2x + 5 = 9 - 6\sqrt{2x} + 2x$$

$6\sqrt{2x} = 4$	Get the radical alone.
$36(2x) = 16$	Square both sides of the equation to eliminate the radical.
$72x = 16$	Multiply.
$x = \dfrac{16}{72}$	Solve.
$x = \dfrac{2}{9}$	Simplify.

The proposed solution, $\dfrac{2}{9}$, checks in the original equation. The solution is $\dfrac{2}{9}$.   ☐

PRACTICE

5   Solve: $\sqrt{8x + 1} + \sqrt{3x} = 2$

> **Helpful Hint**
>
> Make sure expressions are squared correctly. In Example 5, we squared $(3 - \sqrt{2x})$ as
>
> $$(3 - \sqrt{2x})^2 = (3 - \sqrt{2x})(3 - \sqrt{2x})$$
> $$= 3 \cdot 3 - 3\sqrt{2x} - 3\sqrt{2x} + \sqrt{2x} \cdot \sqrt{2x}$$
> $$= 9 - 6\sqrt{2x} + 2x$$

✔ **CONCEPT CHECK**

What is wrong with the following solution?

$$\sqrt{2x + 5} + \sqrt{4 - x} = 8$$
$$(\sqrt{2x + 5} + \sqrt{4 - x})^2 = 8^2$$
$$(2x + 5) + (4 - x) = 64$$
$$x + 9 = 64$$
$$x = 55$$

Answers to Concept Checks:
answers may vary;

$(\sqrt{2x + 5} + \sqrt{4 - x})^2$ is not
$(2x + 5) + (4 - x)$.

OBJECTIVE

2   Using the Pythagorean Theorem

Recall that the Pythagorean theorem states that in a right triangle, the length of the hypotenuse squared equals the sum of the lengths of each of the legs squared.

Pythagorean Theorem

If a and b are the lengths of the legs of a right triangle and c is the length of the hypotenuse, then $a^2 + b^2 = c^2$.

⚠️ **EXAMPLE 6**   Find the length of the unknown leg of the right triangle.

Solution In the formula $a^2 + b^2 = c^2$, c is the hypotenuse. Here, $c = 10$, the length of the hypotenuse, and $a = 4$. We solve for b. Then $a^2 + b^2 = c^2$ becomes

$$4^2 + b^2 = 10^2$$
$$16 + b^2 = 100$$
$$b^2 = 84 \qquad \text{Subtract 16 from both sides.}$$
$$b = \pm\sqrt{84} = \pm\sqrt{4 \cdot 21} = \pm 2\sqrt{21}$$

Since b is a length and thus is positive, we will use the positive value only. The unknown leg of the triangle is $2\sqrt{21}$ meters long. ☐

PRACTICE

6   Find the length of the unknown leg of the right triangle.

⚠️ **EXAMPLE 7**   **Calculating Placement of a Wire**

A 50-foot supporting wire is to be attached to a 75-foot antenna. Because of surrounding buildings, sidewalks, and roadways, the wire must be anchored exactly 20 feet from the base of the antenna.

a. How high from the base of the antenna is the wire attached?

b. Local regulations require that a supporting wire be attached at a height no less than $\dfrac{3}{5}$ of the total height of the antenna. From part (a), have local regulations been met?

Solution

1. UNDERSTAND. Read and reread the problem. From the diagram, we notice that a right triangle is formed with hypotenuse 50 feet and one leg 20 feet. Let x be the height from the base of the antenna to the attached wire.

2. TRANSLATE. Use the Pythagorean theorem.

$$a^2 + b^2 = c^2$$
$$20^2 + x^2 = 50^2 \quad a = 20, c = 50$$

3. SOLVE.

$$20^2 + x^2 = 50^2$$
$$400 + x^2 = 2500$$
$$x^2 = 2100 \qquad \text{Subtract 400 from both sides.}$$
$$x = \pm\sqrt{2100}$$
$$= \pm 10\sqrt{21}$$

4. INTERPRET. *Check* the work and *state* the solution.

Check: We will use only the positive value, $x = 10\sqrt{21}$, because x represents length. The wire is attached exactly $10\sqrt{21}$ feet from the base of the pole, or approximately 45.8 feet.

State: The supporting wire must be attached at a height no less than $\frac{3}{5}$ of the total height of the antenna. This height is $\frac{3}{5}$ (75 feet), or 45 feet. Since we know from part (a) that the wire is to be attached at a height of approximately 45.8 feet, local regulations have been met. □

PRACTICE
7

Keith Robinson bought two Siamese fighting fish, but when he got home, he found he only had one rectangular tank that was 12 in. long, 7 in. wide, and 5 in. deep. Since the fish must be kept separated, he needed to insert a plastic divider in the diagonal of the tank. He already has a piece that is 5 in. in one dimension, but how long must it be to fit corner to corner in the tank? ▪

 Graphing Calculator Explorations

We can use a graphing calculator to solve radical equations. For example, to use a graphing calculator to approximate the solutions of the equation solved in Example 4, we graph the following.

$$Y_1 = \sqrt{4 - x} \qquad \text{and} \qquad Y_2 = x - 2$$

The x-value of the point of intersection is the solution. Use the Intersect feature or the Zoom and Trace features of your graphing calculator to see that the solution is 3.

Use a graphing calculator to solve each radical equation. Round all solutions to the nearest hundredth.

1. $\sqrt{x + 7} = x$ **2.** $\sqrt{3x + 5} = 2x$

3. $\sqrt{2x + 1} = \sqrt{2x + 2}$ **4.** $\sqrt{10x - 1} = \sqrt{-10x + 10} - 1$

5. $1.2x = \sqrt{3.1x + 5}$ **6.** $\sqrt{1.9x^2 - 2.2} = -0.8x + 3$

 Vocabulary, Readiness & Video Check

Use the choices below to fill in each blank. Not all choices will be used.

hypotenuse	right	$x^2 + 25$	$16 - 8\sqrt{7x} + 7x$
extraneous solution	legs	$x^2 - 10x + 25$	$16 + 7x$

1. A proposed solution that is not a solution of the original equation is called a(n) _____.

2. The Pythagorean theorem states that $a^2 + b^2 = c^2$ where a and b are the lengths of the _____ of a(n) _____ triangle and c is the length of the _____.

3. The square of $x - 5$, or $(x - 5)^2 = $ _____.

4. The square of $4 - \sqrt{7x}$, or $(4 - \sqrt{7x})^2 = $ _____.

Martin-Gay Interactive Videos

Watch the section lecture video and answer the following questions.

OBJECTIVE 1

5. From Examples 1–4, why must you be careful and check your proposed solution(s) in the original equation?

OBJECTIVE 2

6. From Example 5, when solving problems using the Pythagorean theorem, what two things must you remember?

OBJECTIVE 2

7. What important reminder is given as the final answer to Example 5 is being found?

See Video 7.6

7.6   Exercise Set   MyMathLab®

Solve. See Examples 1 and 2.

1. $\sqrt{2x} = 4$

2. $\sqrt{3x} = 3$

3. $\sqrt{x - 3} = 2$

4. $\sqrt{x + 1} = 5$

5. $\sqrt{2x} = -4$

6. $\sqrt{5x} = -5$

7. $\sqrt{4x - 3} - 5 = 0$

8. $\sqrt{x - 3} - 1 = 0$

9. $\sqrt{2x - 3} - 2 = 1$

10. $\sqrt{3x + 3} - 4 = 8$

Solve. See Example 3.

11. $\sqrt[3]{6x} = -3$

12. $\sqrt[3]{4x} = -2$

13. $\sqrt[3]{x - 2} - 3 = 0$

14. $\sqrt[3]{2x - 6} - 4 = 0$

Solve. See Examples 4 and 5.

15. $\sqrt{13 - x} = x - 1$

16. $\sqrt{2x - 3} = 3 - x$

17. $x - \sqrt{4 - 3x} = -8$

18. $2x + \sqrt{x + 1} = 8$

19. $\sqrt{y + 5} = 2 - \sqrt{y - 4}$

20. $\sqrt{x + 3} + \sqrt{x - 5} = 3$

21. $\sqrt{x - 3} + \sqrt{x + 2} = 5$

22. $\sqrt{2x - 4} - \sqrt{3x + 4} = -2$

MIXED PRACTICE

Solve. See Examples 1 through 5.

23. $\sqrt{3x - 2} = 5$

24. $\sqrt{5x - 4} = 9$

25. $-\sqrt{2x} + 4 = -6$

26. $-\sqrt{3x + 9} = -12$

27. $\sqrt{3x + 1} + 2 = 0$

28. $\sqrt{3x + 1} - 2 = 0$

29. $\sqrt[4]{4x + 1} - 2 = 0$

30. $\sqrt[4]{2x - 9} - 3 = 0$

31. $\sqrt{4x - 3} = 7$

32. $\sqrt{3x + 9} = 6$

33. $\sqrt[3]{6x - 3} - 3 = 0$

34. $\sqrt[3]{3x + 4} = 7$

35. $\sqrt[3]{2x - 3} - 2 = -5$

36. $\sqrt[3]{x - 4} - 5 = -7$

37. $\sqrt{x + 4} = \sqrt{2x - 5}$

38. $\sqrt{3y + 6} = \sqrt{7y - 6}$

39. $x - \sqrt{1 - x} = -5$

40. $x - \sqrt{x - 2} = 4$

41. $\sqrt[3]{-6x - 1} = \sqrt[3]{-2x - 5}$

42. $\sqrt[3]{-4x - 3} = \sqrt[3]{-x - 15}$

43. $\sqrt{5x - 1} - \sqrt{x + 2} = 3$

44. $\sqrt{2x - 1} - 4 = -\sqrt{x - 4}$

45. $\sqrt{2x - 1} = \sqrt{1 - 2x}$

46. $\sqrt{7x - 4} = \sqrt{4 - 7x}$

47. $\sqrt{3x + 4} - 1 = \sqrt{2x + 1}$

48. $\sqrt{x - 2} + 3 = \sqrt{4x + 1}$

49. $\sqrt{y + 3} - \sqrt{y - 3} = 1$

50. $\sqrt{x + 1} - \sqrt{x - 1} = 2$

Find the length of the unknown side of each triangle. See Example 6.

51.

6 ft

3 ft

52.   7 in.

8 in.

53.

3 m

7 m

54.   4 cm

7 cm

Find the length of the unknown side of each triangle. Give the exact length and a one-decimal-place approximation. See Example 6.

55.

9 m

$11\sqrt{5}$ m

56.

$5\sqrt{3}$ cm

10 cm

57.

7 mm

7.2 mm

58.

2.7 in.

2.3 in.

Solve. Give exact answers and two-decimal-place approximations where appropriate. For Exercises 59 and 60, the solutions have been started for you. See Example 7.

59. A wire is needed to support a vertical pole 15 feet tall. The cable will be anchored to a stake 8 feet from the base of the pole. How much cable is needed?

15 ft

8 ft

Start the solution:

1. **UNDERSTAND** the problem. Reread it as many times as needed. Notice that a right triangle is formed with legs of length 8 ft and 15 ft.
   Since we are looking for how much cable is needed, let
   $$x = \text{amount of cable needed.}$$

2. **TRANSLATE** into an equation. We use the Pythagorean theorem. (Fill in the blanks below.)

$$a^2 \quad + \quad b^2 \quad = \quad c^2$$
$$\downarrow \qquad\qquad \downarrow$$
$$\underline{\quad}^2 \quad + \quad \underline{\quad}^2 \quad = \quad \underline{\quad x^2}$$

Finish with:

3. **SOLVE** and **4. INTERPRET**

60. The tallest structure in the United States is a TV tower in Blanchard, North Dakota. Its height is 2063 feet. A 2382-foot length of wire is to be used as a guy wire attached to the top of the tower. Approximate to the nearest foot how far from the base of the tower the guy wire must be anchored. (*Source:* U.S. Geological Survey)

2382 ft   2063 ft

?

Start the solution:

1. **UNDERSTAND** the problem. Reread it as many times as needed. Notice that a right triangle is formed with hypotenuse 2382 feet and one leg 2063 feet.
   Since we are looking for how far from the base of the tower the guy wire is anchored, let
   $$x = \text{distance from base of tower to}$$
   $$\text{where guy wire is anchored.}$$

2. **TRANSLATE** into an equation. We use the Pythagorean theorem. (Fill in the blanks below.)

$$a^2 \quad + \quad b^2 \quad = \quad c^2$$
$$\downarrow \qquad\qquad \downarrow$$
$$\underline{\quad}^2 \quad + \quad \underline{\quad x^2} \quad = \quad \underline{\quad}^2$$

Finish with:

3. **SOLVE** and **4. INTERPRET**

61. A spotlight is mounted on the eaves of a house 12 feet above the ground. A flower bed runs between the house and the sidewalk, so the closest a ladder can be placed to the house is 5 feet. How long of a ladder is needed so that an electrician can reach the place where the light is mounted?

12 ft

5 ft

62. A wire is to be attached to support a telephone pole. Because of surrounding buildings, sidewalks, and roadways, the wire must be anchored exactly 15 feet from the base of the pole. Telephone company workers have only 30 feet of cable, and 2 feet of that must be used to attach the cable to the pole and to the stake on the ground. How high from the base of the pole can the wire be attached?

15 ft

63. The radius of the moon is 1080 miles. Use the formula for the radius r of a sphere given its surface area A,

$$r = \sqrt{\frac{A}{4\pi}}$$

to find the surface area of the moon. Round to the nearest square mile. (*Source:* National Space Science Data Center)

64. Police departments find it very useful to be able to approximate the speed of a car when they are given the distance that the car skidded before it came to a stop. If the road surface is wet concrete, the function $S(x) = \sqrt{10.5x}$ is used, where $S(x)$ is the speed of the car in miles per hour and x is the distance skidded in feet. Find how fast a car was moving if it skidded 280 feet on wet concrete.

65. The formula $v = \sqrt{2gh}$ gives the velocity v, in feet per second, of an object when it falls h feet accelerated by gravity g, in feet per second squared. If g is approximately 32 feet per second squared, find how far an object has fallen if its velocity is 80 feet per second.

66. Two tractors are pulling a tree stump from a field. If two forces A and B pull at right angles (90°) to each other, the size of the resulting force R is given by the formula $R = \sqrt{A^2 + B^2}$. If tractor A is exerting 600 pounds of force and the resulting force is 850 pounds, find how much force tractor B is exerting.

In psychology, it has been suggested that the number S of nonsense syllables that a person can repeat consecutively depends on his or her IQ score I according to the equation $S = 2\sqrt{I} - 9$.

67. Use this relationship to estimate the IQ of a person who can repeat 11 nonsense syllables consecutively.

68. Use this relationship to estimate the IQ of a person who can repeat 15 nonsense syllables consecutively.

*The **period** of a pendulum is the time it takes for the pendulum to make one full back-and-forth swing. The period of a pendulum depends on the length of the pendulum. The formula for the period P, in seconds, is $P = 2\pi\sqrt{\dfrac{l}{32}}$, where l is the length of the pendulum in feet. Use this formula for Exercises 69 through 74.*

69. Find the period of a pendulum whose length is 2 feet. Give the exact answer and a two-decimal-place approximation.

2 feet

70. Klockit sells a 43-inch lyre pendulum. Find the period of this pendulum. Round your answer to two decimal places. (*Hint:* First convert inches to feet.)

71. Find the length of a pendulum whose period is 4 seconds. Round your answer to two decimal places.

72. Find the length of a pendulum whose period is 3 seconds. Round your answer to two decimal places.

73. Study the relationship between period and pendulum length in Exercises 69 through 72 and make a conjecture about this relationship.

74. Galileo experimented with pendulums. He supposedly made conjectures about pendulums of equal length with different bob weights. Try this experiment. Make two pendulums 3 feet long. Attach a heavy weight (lead) to one and a light weight (a cork) to the other. Pull both pendulums back the same angle measure and release. Make a conjecture from your observations.

If the three lengths of the sides of a triangle are known, Heron's formula can be used to find its area. If a, b, and c are the lengths of the three sides, Heron's formula for area is

$$A = \sqrt{s(s - a)(s - b)(s - c)}$$

where s is half the perimeter of the triangle, or $s = \dfrac{1}{2}(a + b + c)$.

Use this formula to find the area of each triangle. Give the exact answer and then a two-decimal-place approximation.

75.

6 mi / 10 mi / 14 mi

76. 2 cm / 3 cm / 3 cm

77. Describe when Heron's formula might be useful.

78. In your own words, explain why you think s in Heron's formula is called the *semiperimeter*.

The maximum distance D(h) in kilometers that a person can see from a height h kilometers above the ground is given by the function $D(h) = 111.7\sqrt{h}$. Use this function for Exercises 79 and 80. Round your answers to two decimal places.

79. Find the height that would allow a person to see 80 kilometers.

80. Find the height that would allow a person to see 40 kilometers.

REVIEW AND PREVIEW

Use the vertical line test to determine whether each graph represents the graph of a function. See Section 3.2.

81.

82.

83.

84.

85.

86.

Simplify. See Section 6.3.

87. $\dfrac{\dfrac{x}{6}}{\dfrac{2x}{3} + \dfrac{1}{2}}$

88. $\dfrac{\dfrac{1}{y} + \dfrac{4}{5}}{-\dfrac{3}{20}}$

89. $\dfrac{\dfrac{z}{5} + \dfrac{1}{10}}{\dfrac{z}{20} - \dfrac{z}{5}}$

90. $\dfrac{\dfrac{1}{y} + \dfrac{1}{x}}{\dfrac{1}{y} - \dfrac{1}{x}}$

CONCEPT EXTENSIONS

Find the error in each solution and correct. See the second Concept Check in this section.

91.
$$\sqrt{5x - 1} + 4 = 7$$
$$(\sqrt{5x - 1} + 4)^2 = 7^2$$
$$5x - 1 + 16 = 49$$
$$5x = 34$$
$$x = \frac{34}{5}$$

92.
$$\sqrt{2x + 3} + 4 = 1$$
$$\sqrt{2x + 3} = 5$$
$$(\sqrt{2x + 3})^2 = 5^2$$
$$2x + 3 = 25$$
$$2x = 22$$
$$x = 11$$

93. Solve: $\sqrt{\sqrt{x + 3}} + \sqrt{x} = \sqrt{3}$

94. The cost $C(x)$ in dollars per day to operate a small delivery service is given by $C(x) = 80\sqrt[3]{x} + 500$, where x is the number of deliveries per day. In July, the manager decides that it is necessary to keep delivery costs below \$1220.00. Find the greatest number of deliveries this company can make per day and still keep overhead below \$1220.00.

95. Consider the equations $\sqrt{2x} = 4$ and $\sqrt[3]{2x} = 4$.

  a. Explain the difference in solving these equations.

  b. Explain the similarity in solving these equations.

96. Explain why proposed solutions of radical equations must be checked in the original equation.

For Exercises 97 through 100, see the example below.

Example

Solve $(t^2 - 3t) - 2\sqrt{t^2 - 3t} = 0$.

Solution

Substitution can be used to make this problem somewhat simpler. Since $t^2 - 3t$ occurs more than once, let $x = t^2 - 3t$.

$$(t^2 - 3t) - 2\sqrt{t^2 - 3t} = 0$$
$$x - 2\sqrt{x} = 0 \quad \text{Let } x = t^2 - 3t.$$
$$x = 2\sqrt{x}$$
$$x^2 = (2\sqrt{x})^2$$
$$x^2 = 4x$$
$$x^2 - 4x = 0$$
$$x(x - 4) = 0$$
$$x = 0 \quad \text{or} \quad x - 4 = 0$$
$$x = 4$$

Now we "undo" the substitution by replacing x with $t^2 - 3t$.

$$x = 0$$
$$t^2 - 3t = 0 \quad \text{Replace } x \text{ with } t^2 - 3t.$$
$$t(t - 3) = 0 \quad \text{Factor.}$$
$$t = 0 \quad \text{or} \quad t - 3 = 0$$
$$t = 3$$

Replace x with $t^2 - 3t$ in $x = 4$.

$$x = 4$$
$$t^2 - 3t = 4 \quad \text{Replace } x \text{ with } t^2 - 3t.$$
$$t^2 - 3t - 4 = 0 \quad \text{Subtract 4.}$$
$$(t - 4)(t + 1) = 0 \quad \text{Factor.}$$
$$t - 4 = 0 \quad \text{or} \quad t + 1 = 0$$
$$t = 4 \quad\quad\quad t = -1$$

In this problem, we have four possible solutions for t: 0, 3, 4, and -1. All four solutions check in the original equation, so the solutions are $-1, 0, 3, 4$.

Solve. See the preceding example.

97. $3\sqrt{x^2 - 8x} = x^2 - 8x$

98. $\sqrt{(x^2 - x) + 7} = 2(x^2 - x) - 1$

99. $7 - (x^2 - 3x) = \sqrt{(x^2 - 3x) + 5}$

100. $x^2 + 6x = 4\sqrt{x^2 + 6x}$

7.7 Complex Numbers

OBJECTIVE

1 Writing Numbers in the Form bi

Our work with radical expressions has excluded expressions such as $\sqrt{-16}$ because $\sqrt{-16}$ is not a real number; there is no real number whose square is -16. In this section, we discuss a number system that includes roots of negative numbers. This number system is the **complex number system,** and it includes the set of real numbers as a subset. The complex number system allows us to solve equations such as $x^2 + 1 = 0$ that have no real number solutions. The set of complex numbers includes the **imaginary unit.**

Imaginary Unit

The imaginary unit, written i, is the number whose square is -1. That is,

$$i^2 = -1 \quad \text{and} \quad i = \sqrt{-1}$$

To write the square root of a negative number in terms of i, use the property that if a is a positive number, then

$$\sqrt{-a} = \sqrt{-1} \cdot \sqrt{a}$$
$$= i \cdot \sqrt{a}$$

Using i, we can write $\sqrt{-16}$ as

$$\sqrt{-16} = \sqrt{-1 \cdot 16} = \sqrt{-1} \cdot \sqrt{16} = i \cdot 4, \text{ or } 4i$$

EXAMPLE 1 Write with i notation.

    a. $\sqrt{-36}$ **b.** $\sqrt{-5}$ **c.** $-\sqrt{-20}$

Solution

    a. $\sqrt{-36} = \sqrt{-1 \cdot 36} = \sqrt{-1} \cdot \sqrt{36} = i \cdot 6, \text{ or } 6i$

    b. $\sqrt{-5} = \sqrt{-1(5)} = \sqrt{-1} \cdot \sqrt{5} = i\sqrt{5}.$

    c. $-\sqrt{-20} = -\sqrt{-1 \cdot 20} = -\sqrt{-1} \cdot \sqrt{4 \cdot 5} = -i \cdot 2\sqrt{5} = -2i\sqrt{5}$

> **Helpful Hint**
>
> Since $\sqrt{5}i$ can easily be confused with $\sqrt{5i}$, we write $\sqrt{5}i$ as $i\sqrt{5}$.

PRACTICE

1 Write with i notation.

    a. $\sqrt{-4}$ **b.** $\sqrt{-7}$ **c.** $-\sqrt{-18}$

The product rule for radicals does not necessarily hold true for imaginary numbers. *To multiply square roots of negative numbers, first we write each number in terms of the imaginary unit i.* For example, to multiply $\sqrt{-4}$ and $\sqrt{-9}$, we first write each number in the form bi.

$$\sqrt{-4}\sqrt{-9} = 2i(3i) = 6i^2 = 6(-1) = -6 \quad \text{Correct}$$

We will also use this method to simplify quotients of square roots of negative numbers. Why? The product rule does not work for this example. In other words,

$$\sout{\sqrt{-4} \cdot \sqrt{-9} = \sqrt{(-4)(-9)} = \sqrt{36} = 6} \quad \text{Incorrect}$$

EXAMPLE 2   Multiply or divide as indicated.

a. $\sqrt{-3} \cdot \sqrt{-5}$ **b.** $\sqrt{-36} \cdot \sqrt{-1}$ **c.** $\sqrt{8} \cdot \sqrt{-2}$ **d.** $\dfrac{\sqrt{-125}}{\sqrt{5}}$

Solution

a. $\sqrt{-3} \cdot \sqrt{-5} = i\sqrt{3}(i\sqrt{5}) = i^2\sqrt{15} = -1\sqrt{15} = -\sqrt{15}$

b. $\sqrt{-36} \cdot \sqrt{-1} = 6i(i) = 6i^2 = 6(-1) = -6$

c. $\sqrt{8} \cdot \sqrt{-2} = 2\sqrt{2}(i\sqrt{2}) = 2i(\sqrt{2}\sqrt{2}) = 2i(2) = 4i$

d. $\dfrac{\sqrt{-125}}{\sqrt{5}} = \dfrac{i\sqrt{125}}{\sqrt{5}} = i\sqrt{25} = 5i$

PRACTICE
2   Multiply or divide as indicated.

a. $\sqrt{-5} \cdot \sqrt{-6}$ **b.** $\sqrt{-9} \cdot \sqrt{-1}$ **c.** $\sqrt{125} \cdot \sqrt{-5}$ **d.** $\dfrac{\sqrt{-27}}{\sqrt{3}}$

Now that we have practiced working with the imaginary unit, we define complex numbers.

Complex Numbers

A **complex number** is a number that can be written in the form $a + bi$, where a and b are real numbers.

Notice that the set of real numbers is a subset of the complex numbers since any real number can be written in the form of a complex number. For example,

$$16 = 16 + 0i$$

In general, a complex number $a + bi$ is a real number if $b = 0$. Also, a complex number is called a **pure imaginary number** or an imaginary number if $a = 0$ and $b \neq 0$. For example,

$$3i = 0 + 3i \quad \text{and} \quad i\sqrt{7} = 0 + i\sqrt{7}$$

are pure imaginary numbers.

The following diagram shows the relationship between complex numbers and their subsets.

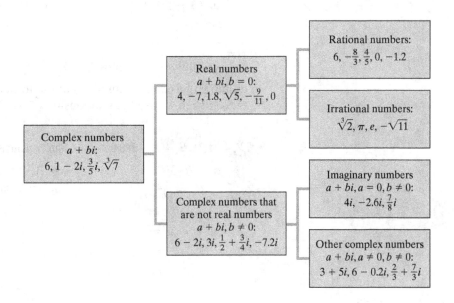

✔ **CONCEPT CHECK**
True or false? Every complex number is also a real number.

OBJECTIVE

2 Adding or Subtracting Complex Numbers

Two complex numbers $a + bi$ and $c + di$ are equal if and only if $a = c$ and $b = d$. Complex numbers can be added or subtracted by adding or subtracting their real parts and then adding or subtracting their imaginary parts.

Sum or Difference of Complex Numbers

If $a + bi$ and $c + di$ are complex numbers, then their sum is

$$(a + bi) + (c + di) = (a + c) + (b + d)i$$

Their difference is

$$(a + bi) - (c + di) = a + bi - c - di = (a - c) + (b - d)i$$

EXAMPLE 3 Add or subtract the complex numbers. Write the sum or difference in the form $a + bi$.

a. $(2 + 3i) + (-3 + 2i)$ **b.** $5i - (1 - i)$ **c.** $(-3 - 7i) - (-6)$

Solution

a. $(2 + 3i) + (-3 + 2i) = (2 - 3) + (3 + 2)i = -1 + 5i$

b. $5i - (1 - i) = 5i - 1 + i$
$$= -1 + (5 + 1)i$$
$$= -1 + 6i$$

c. $(-3 - 7i) - (-6) = -3 - 7i + 6$
$$= (-3 + 6) - 7i$$
$$= 3 - 7i$$ ☐

PRACTICE

3 Add or subtract the complex numbers. Write the sum or difference in the form $a + bi$.

a. $(3 - 5i) + (-4 + i)$ **b.** $4i - (3 - i)$ **c.** $(-5 - 2i) - (-8)$ ▪

OBJECTIVE

3 Multiplying Complex Numbers

To multiply two complex numbers of the form $a + bi$, we multiply as though they are binomials. Then we use the relationship $i^2 = -1$ to simplify.

EXAMPLE 4 Multiply the complex numbers. Write the product in the form $a + bi$.

a. $-7i \cdot 3i$ **b.** $3i(2 - i)$ **c.** $(2 - 5i)(4 + i)$
d. $(2 - i)^2$ **e.** $(7 + 3i)(7 - 3i)$

Solution

a. $-7i \cdot 3i = -21i^2$
$$= -21(-1) \quad \text{Replace } i^2 \text{ with } -1.$$
$$= 21 + 0i$$

b. $3i(2 - i) = 3i \cdot 2 - 3i \cdot i$ Use the distributive property.

$\qquad\qquad = 6i - 3i^2$ Multiply.

$\qquad\qquad = 6i - 3(-1)$ Replace i^2 with -1.

$\qquad\qquad = 6i + 3$

$\qquad\qquad = 3 + 6i$ Use the FOIL order below. (First, Outer, Inner, Last)

c. $(2 - 5i)(4 + i) = 2(4) + 2(i) - 5i(4) - 5i(i)$

$\qquad\qquad\qquad\qquad\quad$ F $\quad$ O $\quad$ I $\quad$ L

$\qquad\qquad\qquad = 8 + 2i - 20i - 5i^2$

$\qquad\qquad\qquad = 8 - 18i - 5(-1)$ $i^2 = -1$

$\qquad\qquad\qquad = 8 - 18i + 5$

$\qquad\qquad\qquad = 13 - 18i$

d. $(2 - i)^2 = (2 - i)(2 - i)$

$\qquad\qquad\quad = 2(2) - 2(i) - 2(i) + i^2$

$\qquad\qquad\quad = 4 - 4i + (-1)$ $i^2 = -1$

$\qquad\qquad\quad = 3 - 4i$

e. $(7 + 3i)(7 - 3i) = 7(7) - 7(3i) + 3i(7) - 3i(3i)$

$\qquad\qquad\qquad = 49 - 21i + 21i - 9i^2$

$\qquad\qquad\qquad = 49 - 9(-1)$ $i^2 = -1$

$\qquad\qquad\qquad = 49 + 9$

$\qquad\qquad\qquad = 58 + 0i$ □

PRACTICE

4   Multiply the complex numbers. Write the product in the form $a + bi$.

$\quad$ **a.** $-4i \cdot 5i$ $\qquad\qquad$ **b.** $5i(2 + i)$ $\qquad\qquad$ **c.** $(2 + 3i)(6 - i)$

$\quad$ **d.** $(3 - i)^2$ $\qquad\qquad$ **e.** $(9 + 2i)(9 - 2i)$ ■

Notice that if you add, subtract, or multiply two complex numbers, just like real numbers, the result is a complex number.

OBJECTIVE

4   Dividing Complex Numbers

From Example 4(e), notice that the product of $7 + 3i$ and $7 - 3i$ is a real number. These two complex numbers are called **complex conjugates** of one another. In general, we have the following definition.

Complex Conjugates

The complex numbers $(a + bi)$ and $(a - bi)$ are called **complex conjugates** of each other, and

$$(a + bi)(a - bi) = a^2 + b^2.$$

To see that the product of a complex number $a + bi$ and its conjugate $a - bi$ is the real number $a^2 + b^2$, we multiply.

$$(a + bi)(a - bi) = a^2 - abi + abi - b^2 i^2$$
$$= a^2 - b^2(-1)$$
$$= a^2 + b^2$$

We use complex conjugates to divide by a complex number.

EXAMPLE 5 Divide. Write in the form $a + bi$.

a. $\dfrac{2 + i}{1 - i}$ **b.** $\dfrac{7}{3i}$

Solution

a. Multiply the numerator and denominator by the complex conjugate of $1 - i$ to eliminate the imaginary number in the denominator.

$$\frac{2 + i}{1 - i} = \frac{(2 + i)(1 + i)}{(1 - i)(1 + i)}$$

$$= \frac{2(1) + 2(i) + 1(i) + i^2}{1^2 - i^2}$$

$$= \frac{2 + 3i - 1}{1 + 1} \qquad \text{Here, } i^2 = -1.$$

$$= \frac{1 + 3i}{2} \quad \text{or} \quad \frac{1}{2} + \frac{3}{2}i$$

b. Multiply the numerator and denominator by the conjugate of $3i$. Note that $3i = 0 + 3i$, so its conjugate is $0 - 3i$ or $-3i$.

$$\frac{7}{3i} = \frac{7(-3i)}{(3i)(-3i)} = \frac{-21i}{-9i^2} = \frac{-21i}{-9(-1)} = \frac{-21i}{9} = \frac{-7i}{3} \quad \text{or} \quad 0 - \frac{7}{3}i \ \square$$

PRACTICE
5 Divide. Write in the form $a + bi$.

a. $\dfrac{4 - i}{3 + i}$ **b.** $\dfrac{5}{2i}$

Helpful Hint

Recall that division can be checked by multiplication.

To check that $\dfrac{2 + i}{1 - i} = \dfrac{1}{2} + \dfrac{3}{2}i$, in Example 5(a), multiply $\left(\dfrac{1}{2} + \dfrac{3}{2}i\right)(1 - i)$ to verify that the product is $2 + i$.

OBJECTIVE

5 Finding Powers of i

We can use the fact that $i^2 = -1$ to find higher powers of i. To find i^3, we rewrite it as the product of i^2 and i.

$$i^3 = i^2 \cdot i = (-1)i = -i$$
$$i^4 = i^2 \cdot i^2 = (-1) \cdot (-1) = 1$$

We continue this process and use the fact that $i^4 = 1$ and $i^2 = -1$ to simplify i^5 and i^6.

$$i^5 = i^4 \cdot i = 1 \cdot i = i$$
$$i^6 = i^4 \cdot i^2 = 1 \cdot (-1) = -1$$

If we continue finding powers of i, we generate the following pattern. Notice that the values i, -1, $-i$, and 1 repeat as i is raised to higher and higher powers.

$i^1 = i$	$i^5 = i$	$i^9 = i$
$i^2 = -1$	$i^6 = -1$	$i^{10} = -1$
$i^3 = -i$	$i^7 = -i$	$i^{11} = -i$
$i^4 = 1$	$i^8 = 1$	$i^{12} = 1$

This pattern allows us to find other powers of i. To do so, we will use the fact that $i^4 = 1$ and rewrite a power of i in terms of i^4. For example,

$$i^{22} = i^{20} \cdot i^2 = (i^4)^5 \cdot i^2 = 1^5 \cdot (-1) = 1 \cdot (-1) = -1.$$

EXAMPLE 6   Find the following powers of i.

    a. i^7 **b.** i^{20} **c.** i^{46} **d.** i^{-12}

Solution

    a. $i^7 = i^4 \cdot i^3 = 1(-i) = -i$

    b. $i^{20} = (i^4)^5 = 1^5 = 1$

    c. $i^{46} = i^{44} \cdot i^2 = (i^4)^{11} \cdot i^2 = 1^{11}(-1) = -1$

    d. $i^{-12} = \dfrac{1}{i^{12}} = \dfrac{1}{(i^4)^3} = \dfrac{1}{(1)^3} = \dfrac{1}{1} = 1$

PRACTICE
6   Find the following powers of i.

    a. i^9 **b.** i^{16} **c.** i^{34} **d.** i^{-24}

 Vocabulary, Readiness & Video Check

Use the choices below to fill in each blank. Not all choices will be used.

-1	$\sqrt{-1}$	real	imaginary unit
1	$\sqrt{1}$	complex	pure imaginary

1. A(n) _____ number is one that can be written in the form $a + bi$, where a and b are real numbers.

2. In the complex number system, i denotes the _____.

3. $i^2 =$ _____

4. $i =$ _____

5. A complex number, $a + bi$, is a(n) _____ number if $b = 0$.

6. A complex number, $a + bi$, is a(n) _____ number if $a = 0$ and $b \neq 0$.

Martin-Gay Interactive Videos

See Video 7.7

Watch the section lecture video and answer the following questions.

OBJECTIVE 1

7. From Example 4, with what rule must you be especially careful when working with imaginary numbers and why?

OBJECTIVE 2

8. In Examples 5 and 6, what is the process of adding and subtracting complex numbers compared to? What important reminder is given about i?

OBJECTIVE 3

9. In Examples 7 and 8, what part of the definition of the imaginary unit i may be used during the multiplication of complex numbers to help simplify products?

OBJECTIVE 4

10. In Example 9, using complex conjugates to divide complex numbers is compared to what process?

OBJECTIVE 5

11. From the lecture before Example 10, what are the first four powers of i whose values keep repeating?

7.7 Exercise Set MyMathLab®

Simplify. See Example 1.

1. $\sqrt{-81}$ **2.** $\sqrt{-49}$ **3.** $\sqrt{-7}$

4. $\sqrt{-3}$ **5.** $-\sqrt{16}$ **6.** $-\sqrt{4}$

7. $\sqrt{-64}$ **8.** $\sqrt{-100}$

Write in terms of i. See Example 1.

9. $\sqrt{-24}$ **10.** $\sqrt{-32}$

11. $-\sqrt{-36}$ **12.** $-\sqrt{-121}$

13. $8\sqrt{-63}$ **14.** $4\sqrt{-20}$

15. $-\sqrt{54}$ **16.** $\sqrt{-63}$

Multiply or divide. See Example 2.

17. $\sqrt{-2}\cdot\sqrt{-7}$ **18.** $\sqrt{-11}\cdot\sqrt{-3}$

19. $\sqrt{-5}\cdot\sqrt{-10}$ **20.** $\sqrt{-2}\cdot\sqrt{-6}$

21. $\sqrt{16}\cdot\sqrt{-1}$ **22.** $\sqrt{3}\cdot\sqrt{-27}$

23. $\dfrac{\sqrt{-9}}{\sqrt{3}}$ **24.** $\dfrac{\sqrt{49}}{\sqrt{-10}}$

25. $\dfrac{\sqrt{-80}}{\sqrt{-10}}$ **26.** $\dfrac{\sqrt{-40}}{\sqrt{-8}}$

Add or subtract. Write the sum or difference in the form a + bi. See Example 3.

27. $(4 - 7i) + (2 + 3i)$ **28.** $(2 - 4i) - (2 - i)$

29. $(6 + 5i) - (8 - i)$ **30.** $(8 - 3i) + (-8 + 3i)$

31. $6 - (8 + 4i)$ **32.** $(9 - 4i) - 9$

Multiply. Write the product in the form a + bi. See Example 4.

33. $-10i\cdot-4i$ **34.** $-2i\cdot-11i$

35. $6i(2 - 3i)$ **36.** $5i(4 - 7i)$

37. $(\sqrt{3} + 2i)(\sqrt{3} - 2i)$ **38.** $(\sqrt{5} - 5i)(\sqrt{5} + 5i)$

39. $(4 - 2i)^2$ **40.** $(6 - 3i)^2$

Write each quotient in the form a + bi. See Example 5.

41. $\dfrac{4}{i}$ **42.** $\dfrac{5}{6i}$

43. $\dfrac{7}{4 + 3i}$ **44.** $\dfrac{9}{1 - 2i}$

45. $\dfrac{3 + 5i}{1 + i}$ **46.** $\dfrac{6 + 2i}{4 - 3i}$

47. $\dfrac{5 - i}{3 - 2i}$ **48.** $\dfrac{6 - i}{2 + i}$

MIXED PRACTICE

Perform each indicated operation. Write the result in the form a + bi.

49. $(7i)(-9i)$ **50.** $(-6i)(-4i)$

51. $(6 - 3i) - (4 - 2i)$ **52.** $(-2 - 4i) - (6 - 8i)$

53. $-3i(-1 + 9i)$ **54.** $-5i(-2 + i)$

55. $\dfrac{4 - 5i}{2i}$ **56.** $\dfrac{6 + 8i}{3i}$

57. $(4 + i)(5 + 2i)$ **58.** $(3 + i)(2 + 4i)$

59. $(6 - 2i)(3 + i)$ **60.** $(2 - 4i)(2 - i)$

61. $(8 - 3i) + (2 + 3i)$ **62.** $(7 + 4i) + (4 - 4i)$

63. $(1 - i)(1 + i)$ **64.** $(6 + 2i)(6 - 2i)$

65. $\dfrac{16 + 15i}{-3i}$ **66.** $\dfrac{2 - 3i}{-7i}$

67. $(9 + 8i)^2$ **68.** $(4 - 7i)^2$

69. $\dfrac{2}{3 + i}$ **70.** $\dfrac{5}{3 - 2i}$

71. $(5 - 6i) - 4i$ **72.** $(6 - 2i) + 7i$

73. $\dfrac{2 - 3i}{2 + i}$ **74.** $\dfrac{6 + 5i}{6 - 5i}$

75. $(2 + 4i) + (6 - 5i)$ **76.** $(5 - 3i) + (7 - 8i)$

77. $(\sqrt{6} + i)(\sqrt{6} - i)$ **78.** $(\sqrt{14} - 4i)(\sqrt{14} + 4i)$

79. $4(2 - i)^2$ **80.** $9(2 - i)^2$

Find each power of i. See Example 6.

81. i^8 **82.** i^{10} **83.** i^{21} **84.** i^{15}

85. i^{11} **86.** i^{40} **87.** i^{-6} **88.** i^{-9}

89. $(2i)^6$ **90.** $(5i)^4$ **91.** $(-3i)^5$ **92.** $(-2i)^7$

REVIEW AND PREVIEW

Recall that the sum of the measures of the angles of a triangle is 180°. Find the unknown angle in each triangle.

93.

94.

Use synthetic division to divide the following. See Section 6.4.

95. $(x^3 - 6x^2 + 3x - 4) \div (x - 1)$

96. $(5x^4 - 3x^2 + 2) \div (x + 2)$

Thirty people were recently polled about the average monthly balance in their checking accounts. The results of this poll are shown in the following histogram. Use this graph to answer Exercises 97 through 102. See Section 1.3.

Average Monthly Checking Account Balance

97. How many people polled reported an average checking balance of $201 to $300?

98. How many people polled reported an average checking balance of $0 to $100?

99. How many people polled reported an average checking balance of $200 or less?

100. How many people polled reported an average checking balance of $301 or more?

101. What percent of people polled reported an average checking balance of $201 to $300? Round to the nearest tenth of a percent.

102. What percent of people polled reported an average checking balance of $0 to $100? Round to the nearest tenth of a percent.

CONCEPT EXTENSIONS

Write in the form a + bi.

103. $i^3 - i^4$

104. $i^8 - i^7$

105. $i^6 + i^8$

106. $i^4 + i^{12}$

107. $2 + \sqrt{-9}$

108. $5 - \sqrt{-16}$

109. $\dfrac{6 + \sqrt{-18}}{3}$

110. $\dfrac{4 - \sqrt{-8}}{2}$

111. $\dfrac{5 - \sqrt{-75}}{10}$

112. $\dfrac{7 + \sqrt{-98}}{14}$

113. Describe how to find the conjugate of a complex number.

114. Explain why the product of a complex number and its complex conjugate is a real number.

Simplify.

115. $(8 - \sqrt{-3}) - (2 + \sqrt{-12})$

116. $(8 - \sqrt{-4}) - (2 + \sqrt{-16})$

117. Determine whether $2i$ is a solution of $x^2 + 4 = 0$.

118. Determine whether $-1 + i$ is a solution of $x^2 + 2x = -2$.

Chapter 7 Vocabulary Check

Fill in each blank with one of the words or phrases listed below.

| index | rationalizing | conjugate | principal square root | cube root | midpoint |
| complex number | like radicals | radicand | imaginary unit | distance | |

1. The _____ of $\sqrt{3} + 2$ is $\sqrt{3} - 2$.

2. The _____ of a positive number a is written as $\sqrt{a}$.

3. The process of writing a radical expression as an equivalent expression but without a radical in the denominator is called _____ the denominator.

4. The _____, written i, is the number whose square is -1.

5. The _____ of a number is written as $\sqrt[3]{a}$.

6. In the notation $\sqrt[n]{a}$, n is called the _____ and a is called the _____.

7. Radicals with the same index and the same radicand are called _____.

8. A(n) _____ is a number that can be written in the form $a + bi$, where a and b are real numbers.

9. The _____ formula is $d = \sqrt{(x_2 - x_1)^2 + (y_2 - y_1)^2}$.

10. The _____ formula is $\left(\dfrac{x_1 + x_2}{2}, \dfrac{y_1 + y_2}{2} \right)$.

Chapter 7 Highlights

DEFINITIONS AND CONCEPTS	EXAMPLES
Section 7.1 Radicals and Radical Functions	
The **positive,** or **principal, square root** of a nonnegative number a is written as $\sqrt{a}$. $$\sqrt{a} = b \text{ only if } b^2 = a \text{ and } b \geq 0$$ The **negative square root of** a is written as $-\sqrt{a}$.	$\sqrt{36} = 6 \qquad \sqrt{\dfrac{9}{100}} = \dfrac{3}{10}$ $-\sqrt{36} = -6 \qquad -\sqrt{0.04} = -0.2$ *(continued)*

DEFINITIONS AND CONCEPTS	EXAMPLES

Section 7.1 Radicals and Radical Functions (continued)

The **cube root** of a real number a is written as $\sqrt[3]{a}$.

$$\sqrt[3]{a} = b \text{ only if } b^3 = a$$

If n is an even positive integer, then $\sqrt[n]{a^n} = |a|$.

If n is an odd positive integer, then $\sqrt[n]{a^n} = a$.

A **radical function** in x is a function defined by an expression containing a root of x.

$$\sqrt[3]{27} = 3 \qquad \sqrt[3]{-\frac{1}{8}} = -\frac{1}{2}$$

$$\sqrt[3]{y^6} = y^2 \qquad \sqrt[3]{64x^9} = 4x^3$$

$$\sqrt{(-3)^2} = |-3| = 3$$

$$\sqrt[3]{(-7)^3} = -7$$

If $f(x) = \sqrt{x} + 2$,

$$f(1) = \sqrt{(1)} + 2 = 1 + 2 = 3$$

$$f(3) = \sqrt{(3)} + 2 \approx 3.73$$

Section 7.2 Rational Exponents

$a^{1/n} = \sqrt[n]{a}$ if $\sqrt[n]{a}$ is a real number.

If m and n are positive integers greater than 1 with $\dfrac{m}{n}$ in lowest terms and $\sqrt[n]{a}$ is a real number, then

$$a^{m/n} = \sqrt[n]{a^m} = \left(\sqrt[n]{a}\right)^m$$

$a^{-m/n} = \dfrac{1}{a^{m/n}}$ as long as $a^{m/n}$ is a nonzero number.

Exponent rules are true for rational exponents.

$$81^{1/2} = \sqrt{81} = 9$$

$$(-8x^3)^{1/3} = \sqrt[3]{-8x^3} = -2x$$

$$4^{5/2} = \left(\sqrt{4}\right)^5 = 2^5 = 32$$

$$27^{2/3} = \left(\sqrt[3]{27}\right)^2 = 3^2 = 9$$

$$16^{-3/4} = \frac{1}{16^{3/4}} = \frac{1}{\left(\sqrt[4]{16}\right)^3} = \frac{1}{2^3} = \frac{1}{8}$$

$$x^{2/3} \cdot x^{-5/6} = x^{2/3-5/6} = x^{-1/6} = \frac{1}{x^{1/6}}$$

$$(8^4)^{1/2} = 8^2 = 64$$

$$\frac{a^{4/5}}{a^{-2/5}} = a^{4/5-(-2/5)} = a^{6/5}$$

Section 7.3 Simplifying Radical Expressions

Product and Quotient Rules

If $\sqrt[n]{a}$ and $\sqrt[n]{b}$ are real numbers,

$$\sqrt[n]{a} \cdot \sqrt[n]{b} = \sqrt[n]{a \cdot b}$$

$$\frac{\sqrt[n]{a}}{\sqrt[n]{b}} = \sqrt[n]{\frac{a}{b}}, \text{ provided } \sqrt[n]{b} \neq 0$$

A radical of the form $\sqrt[n]{a}$ is **simplified** when a contains no factors that are perfect nth powers.

Multiply or divide as indicated:

$$\sqrt{11} \cdot \sqrt{3} = \sqrt{33}$$

$$\frac{\sqrt[3]{40x}}{\sqrt[3]{5x}} = \sqrt[3]{8} = 2$$

$$\sqrt{40} = \sqrt{4 \cdot 10} = 2\sqrt{10}$$

$$\sqrt{36x^5} = \sqrt{36x^4 \cdot x} = 6x^2\sqrt{x}$$

$$\sqrt[3]{24x^7y^3} = \sqrt[3]{8x^6y^3 \cdot 3x} = 2x^2y\sqrt[3]{3x}$$

Distance Formula

The distance d between two points (x_1, y_1) and (x_2, y_2) is given by

$$d = \sqrt{(x_2 - x_1)^2 + (y_2 - y_1)^2}$$

Find the distance between points $(-1, 6)$ and $(-2, -4)$. Let $(x_1, y_1) = (-1, 6)$ and $(x_2, y_2) = (-2, -4)$.

$$d = \sqrt{(x_2 - x_1)^2 + (y_2 - y_1)^2}$$

$$= \sqrt{(-2 - (-1))^2 + (-4 - 6)^2}$$

$$= \sqrt{1 + 100} = \sqrt{101}$$

DEFINITIONS AND CONCEPTS	EXAMPLES

Section 7.3   Simplifying Radical Expressions (continued)

Midpoint Formula

The midpoint of the line segment whose endpoints are (x_1, y_1) and (x_2, y_2) is the point with coordinates

$$\left(\frac{x_1 + x_2}{2}, \frac{y_1 + y_2}{2}\right)$$

Find the midpoint of the line segment whose endpoints are $(-1, 6)$ and $(-2, -4)$.

$$\left(\frac{-1 + (-2)}{2}, \frac{6 + (-4)}{2}\right)$$

The midpoint is $\left(-\frac{3}{2}, 1\right)$.

Section 7.4   Adding, Subtracting, and Multiplying Radical Expressions

Radicals with the same index and the same radicand are **like radicals.**

The distributive property can be used to add like radicals.

$$5\sqrt{6} + 2\sqrt{6} = (5 + 2)\sqrt{6} = 7\sqrt{6}$$

$$-\sqrt[3]{3x} - 10\sqrt[3]{3x} + 3\sqrt[3]{10x}$$
$$= (-1 - 10)\sqrt[3]{3x} + 3\sqrt[3]{10x}$$
$$= -11\sqrt[3]{3x} + 3\sqrt[3]{10x}$$

Radical expressions are multiplied by using many of the same properties used to multiply polynomials.

Multiply.

$$(\sqrt{5} - \sqrt{2x})(\sqrt{2} + \sqrt{2x})$$
$$= \sqrt{10} + \sqrt{10x} - \sqrt{4x} - 2x$$
$$= \sqrt{10} + \sqrt{10x} - 2\sqrt{x} - 2x$$
$$(2\sqrt{3} - \sqrt{8x})(2\sqrt{3} + \sqrt{8x})$$
$$= 4(3) - 8x = 12 - 8x$$

Section 7.5   Rationalizing Denominators and Numerators of Radical Expressions

The **conjugate** of $a + b$ is $a - b$.

The process of writing the denominator of a radical expression without a radical is called **rationalizing the denominator.**

The conjugate of $\sqrt{7} + \sqrt{3}$ is $\sqrt{7} - \sqrt{3}$.

Rationalize each denominator.

$$\frac{\sqrt{5}}{\sqrt{3}} = \frac{\sqrt{5} \cdot \sqrt{3}}{\sqrt{3} \cdot \sqrt{3}} = \frac{\sqrt{15}}{3}$$

$$\frac{6}{\sqrt{7} + \sqrt{3}} = \frac{6(\sqrt{7} - \sqrt{3})}{(\sqrt{7} + \sqrt{3})(\sqrt{7} - \sqrt{3})}$$
$$= \frac{6(\sqrt{7} - \sqrt{3})}{7 - 3}$$
$$= \frac{6(\sqrt{7} - \sqrt{3})}{4} = \frac{3(\sqrt{7} - \sqrt{3})}{2}$$

(continued)

DEFINITIONS AND CONCEPTS	EXAMPLES

Section 7.5 Rationalizing Denominators and Numerators of Radical Expressions (continued)

The process of writing the numerator of a radical expression without a radical is called **rationalizing the numerator.**

Rationalize each numerator.

$$\frac{\sqrt[3]{9}}{\sqrt[3]{5}} = \frac{\sqrt[3]{9} \cdot \sqrt[3]{3}}{\sqrt[3]{5} \cdot \sqrt[3]{3}} = \frac{\sqrt[3]{27}}{\sqrt[3]{15}} = \frac{3}{\sqrt[3]{15}}$$

$$\frac{\sqrt{9} + \sqrt{3x}}{12} = \frac{(\sqrt{9} + \sqrt{3x})(\sqrt{9} - \sqrt{3x})}{12(\sqrt{9} - \sqrt{3x})}$$

$$= \frac{9 - 3x}{12(\sqrt{9} - \sqrt{3x})}$$

$$= \frac{3(3 - x)}{3 \cdot 4(3 - \sqrt{3x})} = \frac{3 - x}{4(3 - \sqrt{3x})}$$

Section 7.6 Radical Equations and Problem Solving

To Solve a Radical Equation

Step 1. Write the equation so that one radical is by itself on one side of the equation.

Step 2. Raise each side of the equation to a power equal to the index of the radical and simplify.

Step 3. If the equation still contains a radical, repeat Steps 1 and 2. If not, solve the equation.

Step 4. Check all proposed solutions in the original equation.

Solve: $x = \sqrt{4x + 9} + 3$

1. $\qquad x - 3 = \sqrt{4x + 9}$

2. $\qquad (x - 3)^2 = (\sqrt{4x + 9})^2$
   $\quad x^2 - 6x + 9 = 4x + 9$

3. $\qquad x^2 - 10x = 0$
   $\qquad x(x - 10) = 0$
   $\qquad\qquad x = 0 \quad \text{or} \quad x = 10$

4. The proposed solution 10 checks, but 0 does not. The solution is 10.

Section 7.7 Complex Numbers

$i^2 = -1$ and $i = \sqrt{-1}$

A **complex number** is a number that can be written in the form $a + bi$, where a and b are real numbers.

Simplify: $\sqrt{-9}$

$$\sqrt{-9} = \sqrt{-1 \cdot 9} = \sqrt{-1} \cdot \sqrt{9} = i \cdot 3 \text{ or } 3i$$

Complex Numbers	**Written in Form $a + bi$**
12	$12 + 0i$
$-5i$	$0 + (-5)i$
$-2 - 3i$	$-2 + (-3)i$

Multiply,

$$\sqrt{-3} \cdot \sqrt{-7} = i\sqrt{3} \cdot i\sqrt{7}$$
$$= i^2 \sqrt{21}$$
$$= -\sqrt{21}$$

To add or subtract complex numbers, add or subtract their real parts and then add or subtract their imaginary parts.

To multiply complex numbers, multiply as though they are binomials.

Perform each indicated operation.

$$(-3 + 2i) - (7 - 4i) = -3 + 2i - 7 + 4i$$
$$= -10 + 6i$$

$$(-7 - 2i)(6 + i) = -42 - 7i - 12i - 2i^2$$
$$= -42 - 19i - 2(-1)$$
$$= -42 - 19i + 2$$
$$= -40 - 19i$$

DEFINITIONS AND CONCEPTS	EXAMPLES
Section 7.7 Complex Numbers (continued)	

The complex numbers $(a + bi)$ and $(a - bi)$ are called **complex conjugates.**

The complex conjugate of $(3 + 6i)$ is $(3 - 6i)$.

Their product is a real number:

$$(3 - 6i)(3 + 6i) = 9 - 36i^2$$
$$= 9 - 36(-1) = 9 + 36 = 45$$

To divide complex numbers, multiply the numerator and the denominator by the conjugate of the denominator.

Divide.

$$\frac{4}{2 - i} = \frac{4(2 + i)}{(2 - i)(2 + i)}$$
$$= \frac{4(2 + i)}{4 - i^2}$$
$$= \frac{4(2 + i)}{5}$$
$$= \frac{8 + 4i}{5} = \frac{8}{5} + \frac{4}{5}i$$

Chapter 7 Review

(7.1) *Find the root. Assume that all variables represent positive numbers.*

1. $\sqrt{81}$

2. $\sqrt[4]{81}$

3. $\sqrt[3]{-8}$

4. $\sqrt[4]{-16}$

5. $-\sqrt{\dfrac{1}{49}}$

6. $\sqrt{x^{64}}$

7. $-\sqrt{36}$

8. $\sqrt[3]{64}$

9. $\sqrt[3]{-a^6 b^9}$

10. $\sqrt{16a^4 b^{12}}$

11. $\sqrt[5]{32a^5 b^{10}}$

12. $\sqrt[5]{-32x^{15}y^{20}}$

13. $\sqrt{\dfrac{x^{12}}{36y^2}}$

14. $\sqrt[3]{\dfrac{27y^3}{z^{12}}}$

Simplify. Use absolute value bars when necessary.

15. $\sqrt{(-x)^2}$

16. $\sqrt[4]{(x^2 - 4)^4}$

17. $\sqrt[3]{(-27)^3}$

18. $\sqrt[5]{(-5)^5}$

19. $-\sqrt[5]{x^5}$

20. $-\sqrt[3]{x^3}$

21. $\sqrt[4]{16(2y + z)^4}$

22. $\sqrt{25(x - y)^2}$

23. $\sqrt[5]{y^5}$

24. $\sqrt[6]{x^6}$

25. Let $f(x) = \sqrt{x} + 3$.
   a. Find $f(0)$ and $f(9)$.
   b. Find the domain of $f(x)$.
   c. Graph $f(x)$.

26. Let $g(x) = \sqrt[3]{x} - 3$.
   a. Find $g(11)$ and $g(20)$.
   b. Find the domain $g(x)$.
   c. Graph $g(x)$.

(7.2) *Evaluate.*

27. $\left(\dfrac{1}{81}\right)^{1/4}$

28. $\left(-\dfrac{1}{27}\right)^{1/3}$

29. $(-27)^{-1/3}$

30. $(-64)^{-1/3}$

31. $-9^{3/2}$

32. $64^{-1/3}$

33. $(-25)^{5/2}$

34. $\left(\dfrac{25}{49}\right)^{-3/2}$

35. $\left(\dfrac{8}{27}\right)^{-2/3}$

36. $\left(-\dfrac{1}{36}\right)^{-1/4}$

Write with rational exponents.

37. $\sqrt[3]{x^2}$

38. $\sqrt[5]{5x^2 y^3}$

Write using radical notation.

39. $y^{4/5}$

40. $5(xy^2 z^5)^{1/3}$

41. $(x + 2)^{-1/3}$

42. $(x + 2y)^{-1/2}$

Simplify each expression. Assume that all variables represent positive real numbers. Write with only positive exponents.

43. $a^{1/3}a^{4/3}a^{1/2}$

44. $\dfrac{b^{1/3}}{b^{4/3}}$

45. $(a^{1/2}a^{-2})^3$

46. $(x^{-3}y^6)^{1/3}$

47. $\left(\dfrac{b^{3/4}}{a^{-1/2}}\right)^8$

48. $\dfrac{x^{1/4}x^{-1/2}}{x^{2/3}}$

49. $\left(\dfrac{49c^{5/3}}{a^{-1/4}b^{5/6}}\right)^{-1}$

50. $a^{-1/4}(a^{5/4} - a^{9/4})$

Use a calculator and write a three-decimal-place approximation of each number.

51. $\sqrt{20}$

52. $\sqrt[3]{-39}$

53. $\sqrt[4]{726}$

54. $56^{1/3}$

55. $-78^{3/4}$

56. $105^{-2/3}$

Use rational exponents to write each as a single radical.

57. $\sqrt[3]{2} \cdot \sqrt{7}$

58. $\sqrt[3]{3} \cdot \sqrt[4]{x}$

(7.3) Perform each indicated operation and then simplify if possible. Assume that all variables represent positive real numbers.

59. $\sqrt{3} \cdot \sqrt{8}$

60. $\sqrt[3]{7y} \cdot \sqrt[3]{x^2z}$

61. $\dfrac{\sqrt{44x^3}}{\sqrt{11x}}$

62. $\dfrac{\sqrt[4]{a^6b^{13}}}{\sqrt[4]{a^2b}}$

Simplify.

63. $\sqrt{60}$

64. $-\sqrt{75}$

65. $\sqrt[3]{162}$

66. $\sqrt[3]{-32}$

67. $\sqrt{36x^7}$

68. $\sqrt[3]{24a^5b^7}$

69. $\sqrt{\dfrac{p^{17}}{121}}$

70. $\sqrt[3]{\dfrac{y^5}{27x^6}}$

71. $\sqrt[4]{\dfrac{xy^6}{81}}$

72. $\sqrt{\dfrac{2x^3}{49y^4}}$

△ *The formula for the radius r of a circle of area A is $r = \sqrt{\dfrac{A}{\pi}}$. Use this for Exercises 73 and 74.*

73. Find the exact radius of a circle whose area is 25 square meters.

74. Approximate to two decimal places the radius of a circle whose area is 104 square inches.

Find the distance between each pair of points. Give the exact value and a three-decimal-place approximation.

75. $(-6, 3)$ and $(8, 4)$

76. $(-4, -6)$ and $(-1, 5)$

77. $(-1, 5)$ and $(2, -3)$

78. $(-\sqrt{2}, 0)$ and $(0, -4\sqrt{6})$

79. $(-\sqrt{5}, -\sqrt{11})$ and $(-\sqrt{5}, -3\sqrt{11})$

80. $(7.4, -8.6)$ and $(-1.2, 5.6)$

Find the midpoint of each line segment whose endpoints are given.

81. $(2, 6); (-12, 4)$

82. $(-6, -5); (-9, 7)$

83. $(4, -6); (-15, 2)$

84. $\left(0, -\dfrac{3}{8}\right); \left(\dfrac{1}{10}, 0\right)$

85. $\left(\dfrac{3}{4}, -\dfrac{1}{7}\right); \left(-\dfrac{1}{4}, -\dfrac{3}{7}\right)$

86. $(\sqrt{3}, -2\sqrt{6}); (\sqrt{3}, -4\sqrt{6})$

(7.4) Perform each indicated operation. Assume that all variables represent positive real numbers.

87. $\sqrt{20} + \sqrt{45} - 7\sqrt{5}$

88. $x\sqrt{75x} - \sqrt{27x^3}$

89. $\sqrt[3]{128} + \sqrt[3]{250}$

90. $3\sqrt[4]{32a^5} - a\sqrt[4]{162a}$

91. $\dfrac{5}{\sqrt{4}} + \dfrac{\sqrt{3}}{3}$

92. $\sqrt{\dfrac{8}{x^2}} - \sqrt{\dfrac{50}{16x^2}}$

93. $2\sqrt{50} - 3\sqrt{125} + \sqrt{98}$

94. $2a\sqrt[4]{32b^5} - 3b\sqrt[4]{162a^4b} + \sqrt[4]{2a^4b^5}$

Multiply and then simplify if possible. Assume that all variables represent positive real numbers.

95. $\sqrt{3}(\sqrt{27} - \sqrt{3})$

96. $(\sqrt{x} - 3)^2$

97. $(\sqrt{5} - 5)(2\sqrt{5} + 2)$

98. $(2\sqrt{x} - 3\sqrt{y})(2\sqrt{x} + 3\sqrt{y})$

99. $(\sqrt{a} + 3)(\sqrt{a} - 3)$

100. $(\sqrt[3]{a} + 2)^2$

101. $(\sqrt[3]{5x} + 9)(\sqrt[3]{5x} - 9)$

102. $(\sqrt[3]{a} + 4)(\sqrt[3]{a^2} - 4\sqrt[3]{a} + 16)$

(7.5) Rationalize each denominator. Assume that all variables represent positive real numbers.

103. $\dfrac{3}{\sqrt{7}}$

104. $\sqrt{\dfrac{x}{12}}$

105. $\dfrac{5}{\sqrt[3]{4}}$

106. $\sqrt{\dfrac{24x^5}{3y}}$

107. $\sqrt[3]{\dfrac{15x^6y^7}{z^2}}$

108. $\sqrt[4]{\dfrac{81}{8x^{10}}}$

109. $\dfrac{3}{\sqrt{y} - 2}$

110. $\dfrac{\sqrt{2} - \sqrt{3}}{\sqrt{2} + \sqrt{3}}$

Rationalize each numerator. Assume that all variables represent positive real numbers.

111. $\dfrac{\sqrt{11}}{3}$

112. $\sqrt{\dfrac{18}{y}}$

113. $\dfrac{\sqrt[3]{9}}{7}$

114. $\sqrt{\dfrac{24x^5}{3y^2}}$

115. $\sqrt[3]{\dfrac{xy^2}{10z}}$

116. $\dfrac{\sqrt{x} + 5}{-3}$

(7.6) Solve each equation.

117. $\sqrt{y - 7} = 5$

118. $\sqrt{2x} + 10 = 4$

119. $\sqrt[3]{2x - 6} = 4$

120. $\sqrt{x + 6} = \sqrt{x + 2}$

121. $2x - 5\sqrt{x} = 3$

122. $\sqrt{x + 9} = 2 + \sqrt{x - 7}$

Find each unknown length.

△ **123.**

△ **124.**

△ **125.** Craig and Daniel Cantwell want to determine the distance *x* across a pond on their property. They are able to measure the distances shown on the following diagram. Find how wide the pond is at the crossing point indicated by the triangle to the nearest tenth of a foot.

△ **126.** Andrea Roberts, a pipefitter, needs to connect two underground pipelines that are offset by 3 feet, as pictured in the diagram. Neglecting the joints needed to join the pipes, find the length of the shortest possible connecting pipe rounded to the nearest hundredth of a foot.

(7.7) *Perform each indicated operation and simplify. Write the results in the form a + bi.*

127. $\sqrt{-8}$

128. $-\sqrt{-6}$

129. $\sqrt{-4} + \sqrt{-16}$

130. $\sqrt{-2} \cdot \sqrt{-5}$

131. $(12 - 6i) + (3 + 2i)$

132. $(-8 - 7i) - (5 - 4i)$

133. $(2i)^6$

134. $(3i)^4$

135. $-3i(6 - 4i)$

136. $(3 + 2i)(1 + i)$

137. $(2 - 3i)^2$

138. $(\sqrt{6} - 9i)(\sqrt{6} + 9i)$

139. $\dfrac{2 + 3i}{2i}$

140. $\dfrac{1 + i}{-3i}$

MIXED REVIEW

Simplify. Use absolute value bars when necessary.

141. $\sqrt[3]{x^3}$

142. $\sqrt{(x + 2)^2}$

Simplify. Assume that all variables represent positive real numbers. If necessary, write answers with positive exponents only.

143. $-\sqrt{100}$

144. $\sqrt[3]{-x^{12}y^3}$

145. $\sqrt[4]{\dfrac{y^{20}}{16x^{12}}}$

146. $9^{1/2}$

147. $64^{-1/2}$

148. $\left(\dfrac{27}{64}\right)^{-2/3}$

149. $\dfrac{(x^{2/3}x^{-3})^3}{x^{-1/2}}$

150. $\sqrt{200x^9}$

151. $\sqrt{\dfrac{3n^3}{121m^{10}}}$

152. $3\sqrt{20} - 7x\sqrt[3]{40} + 3\sqrt[3]{5x^3}$

153. $(2\sqrt{x} - 5)^2$

154. Find the distance between $(-3, 5)$ and $(-8, 9)$.

155. Find the midpoint of the line segment joining $(-3, 8)$ and $(11, 24)$.

Rationalize each denominator.

156. $\dfrac{7}{\sqrt{13}}$

157. $\dfrac{2}{\sqrt{x} + 3}$

Solve.

158. $\sqrt{x} + 2 = x$

159. $\sqrt{2x - 1} + 2 = x$

1c

Chapter 7 Getting Ready for the Test

MULTIPLE CHOICE *Select the correct choice.*

▶ **1.** Which radical simplifies to -4?

    A. $\sqrt{16}$ **B.** $\sqrt{-16}$ **C.** $\sqrt[3]{64}$ **D.** $\sqrt[3]{-64}$

▶ **2.** Which radical does not simplify to a whole number?

    A. $\sqrt{16}$ **B.** $\sqrt[3]{16}$ **C.** $\sqrt{64}$ **D.** $\sqrt[3]{64}$

For Exercises 3–6, identify each as **A.** *a real number or* **B.** *not a real number.*

3. $\sqrt{5}$ **4.** $\sqrt{-11}$ **5.** $\sqrt[3]{-9}$ **6.** $-\sqrt{17}$

MATCHING *Match each expression with its simplified form. Letters may be used more than once or not at all.*

7. $25^{1/2}$ **A.** 5

8. $(-25)^{1/2}$ **B.** -5

9. $(-125)^{1/3}$ **C.** not a real number

10. $-25^{1/2}$

MULTIPLE CHOICE *For Exercises 11–14, identify each statement as* **A.** *true or* **B.** *false.*

11. $\sqrt{5} \cdot \sqrt{10} = \sqrt{15}$ **12.** $\sqrt[3]{4} \cdot \sqrt[3]{9} = \sqrt[3]{36}$ **13.** $\dfrac{\sqrt{12}}{\sqrt{6}} = \sqrt{2}$

14. $\dfrac{\sqrt[3]{10}}{\sqrt[3]{4}} = \sqrt[3]{6}$ **15.** $\sqrt{2} + \sqrt{3} = \sqrt{5}$ **16.** $\sqrt[3]{7} + \sqrt{7} = \sqrt[4]{7}$

MULTIPLE CHOICE *Select the correct choice.*

17. Which expression simplifies to x?

     A. $x^{1/2} + x^{1/2}$ **B.** $x^{1/2} \cdot x^{1/2}$ **C.** $\left(x^{1/2}\right)^2$ **D.** both B and C   **E.** A, B, and C

18. To rationalize the numerator of $\dfrac{\sqrt{x} - 3}{\sqrt{x}}$, we multiply by:

     A. $\dfrac{\sqrt{x}}{\sqrt{x} + 3}$ **B.** $\dfrac{\sqrt{x}}{\sqrt{x}}$ **C.** $\dfrac{\sqrt{x} + 3}{\sqrt{x} + 3}$ **D.** $\dfrac{\sqrt{x} + 3}{\sqrt{x}}$

19. Square both sides of the equation $\sqrt{x + 1} = 3 + \sqrt{x - 1}$. The result is:

     A. $x + 1 = 9 + (x - 1)$ **B.** $x + 1 = 9 + 6\sqrt{x - 1} + (x - 1)$ **C.** $x + 1 = 6 + (x - 1)$

20. $(5 - 2i)^2 =$

     A. $25 + 4i$ **B.** 21   **C.** 29   **D.** $21 - 20i$

21. The expression $\dfrac{3 + \sqrt{-9}}{3}$ simplifies to:

     A. $1 + i$ **B.** $3i$ **C.** $1 + 3i$ **D.** $2i$

Chapter 7 Test   MyMathLab®   You Tube

Raise to the power or find the root. Assume that all variables represent positive numbers. Write with only positive exponents.

1. $\sqrt{216}$ **2.** $-\sqrt[4]{x^{64}}$

3. $\left(\dfrac{1}{125}\right)^{1/3}$ **4.** $\left(\dfrac{1}{125}\right)^{-1/3}$

5. $\left(\dfrac{8x^3}{27}\right)^{2/3}$ **6.** $\sqrt[3]{-a^{18}b^9}$

7. $\left(\dfrac{64c^{4/3}}{a^{-2/3}b^{5/6}}\right)^{1/2}$ **8.** $a^{-2/3}(a^{5/4} - a^3)$

Find the root. Use absolute value bars when necessary.

9. $\sqrt[4]{(4xy)^4}$ **10.** $\sqrt[3]{(-27)^3}$

Rationalize the denominator. Assume that all variables represent positive numbers.

11. $\sqrt{\dfrac{9}{y}}$ **12.** $\dfrac{4 - \sqrt{x}}{4 + 2\sqrt{x}}$ **13.** $\dfrac{\sqrt[3]{ab}}{\sqrt[3]{ab^2}}$

14. Rationalize the numerator of $\dfrac{\sqrt{6} + x}{8}$ and simplify.

Perform the indicated operations. Assume that all variables represent positive numbers.

15. $\sqrt{125x^3} - 3\sqrt{20x^3}$

16. $\sqrt{3}(\sqrt{16} - \sqrt{2})$

17. $(\sqrt{x} + 1)^2$

18. $(\sqrt{2} - 4)(\sqrt{3} + 1)$

19. $(\sqrt{5} + 5)(\sqrt{5} - 5)$

Use a calculator to approximate each to three decimal places.

20. $\sqrt{561}$ **21.** $386^{-2/3}$

Solve.

22. $x = \sqrt{x - 2} + 2$

23. $\sqrt{x^2 - 7} + 3 = 0$

24. $\sqrt[3]{x + 5} = \sqrt[3]{2x - 1}$

Perform the indicated operation and simplify. Write the result in the form $a + bi$.

25. $\sqrt{-2}$ **26.** $-\sqrt{-8}$

27. $(12 - 6i) - (12 - 3i)$ **28.** $(6 - 2i)(6 + 2i)$

29. $(4 + 3i)^2$

30. $\dfrac{1 + 4i}{1 - i}$

31. Find x.

32. Identify the domain of $g(x)$. Then complete the accompanying table and graph $g(x)$.

$$g(x) = \sqrt{x + 2}$$

x	-2	-1	2	7
$g(x)$				

33. Find the distance between the points $(-6, 3)$ and $(-8, -7)$.

34. Find the distance between the points $(-2\sqrt{5}, \sqrt{10})$ and $(-\sqrt{5}, 4\sqrt{10})$.

35. Find the midpoint of the line segment whose endpoints are $(-2, -5)$ and $(-6, 12)$.

36. Find the midpoint of the line segment whose endpoints are $\left(-\dfrac{2}{3}, -\dfrac{1}{5}\right)$ and $\left(-\dfrac{1}{3}, \dfrac{4}{5}\right)$.

Solve.

37. The function $V(r) = \sqrt{2.5r}$ can be used to estimate the maximum safe velocity V in miles per hour at which a car can travel if it is driven along a curved road with a *radius of curvature r* in feet. To the nearest whole number, find the maximum safe speed if a cloverleaf exit on an expressway has a radius of curvature of 300 feet.

38. Use the formula from Exercise 37 to find the radius of curvature if the safe velocity is 30 mph.

Chapter 7 Cumulative Review

1. Simplify each expression.

  a. $3xy - 2xy + 5 - 7 + xy$

  b. $7x^2 + 3 - 5(x^2 - 4)$

  c. $(2.1x - 5.6) - (-x - 5.3)$

  d. $\dfrac{1}{2}(4a - 6b) - \dfrac{1}{3}(9a + 12b - 1) + \dfrac{1}{4}$

2. Simplify each expression.

  a. $2(x - 3) + (5x + 3)$

  b. $4(3x + 2) - 3(5x - 1)$

  c. $7x + 2(x - 7) - 3x$

3. Solve for x: $\dfrac{x + 5}{2} + \dfrac{1}{2} = 2x - \dfrac{x - 3}{8}$

4. Solve for a: $\dfrac{a - 1}{2} + a = 2 - \dfrac{2a + 7}{8}$

5. A salesperson earns \$600 per month plus a commission of 20% of sales. Find the minimum amount of sales needed to receive a total income of at least \$1500 per month.

6. The Smith family owns a lake house 121.5 miles from home. If it takes them $4\dfrac{1}{2}$ hours round-trip to drive from their house to their lake house, find their average speed.

7. Solve: $2|x| + 25 = 23$

8. Solve: $|3x - 2| + 5 = 5$

9. Solve: $\left|\dfrac{x}{3} - 1\right| - 7 \geq -5$

10. Solve: $\left|\dfrac{x}{2} - 1\right| \leq 0$

11. Graph the equation: $y = |x|$

12. Graph: $y = |x - 2|$

13. Determine the domain and range of each relation.

  a. $\{(2, 3), (2, 4), (0, -1), (3, -1)\}$

  b.

  c.

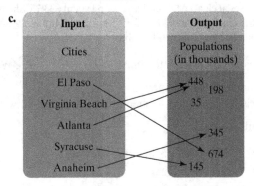

14. Find the domain and the range of each relation. Use the vertical line test to determine whether each graph is the graph of a function.

  a.

b.

c.

15. Graph: $y = -3$

16. Graph: $f(x) = -2$

17. Find the slope of the line $x = -5$.

18. Find the slope of $y = -3$.

19. Use the substitution method to solve the system.

$$\begin{cases} -\dfrac{x}{6} + \dfrac{y}{2} = \dfrac{1}{2} \\ \dfrac{x}{3} - \dfrac{y}{6} = -\dfrac{3}{4} \end{cases}$$

20. Use the substitution method to solve the system.

$$\begin{cases} \dfrac{x}{6} - \dfrac{y}{2} = 1 \\ \dfrac{x}{3} - \dfrac{y}{4} = 2 \end{cases}$$

21. Use the product rule to simplify.

   a. $2^2 \cdot 2^5$

   b. $x^7 x^3$

   c. $y \cdot y^2 \cdot y^4$

22. At a seasonal clearance sale, Nana Long spent $33.75. She paid $3.50 for tee-shirts and $4.25 for shorts. If she bought 9 items, how many of each item did she buy?

23. Use scientific notation to simplify $\dfrac{2000 \times 0.000021}{700}$. Write the result in scientific notation.

24. Use scientific notation to simplify and write the answer in scientific notation $\dfrac{0.0000035 \times 4000}{0.28}$.

25. If $P(x) = 3x^2 - 2x - 5$, find the following.

   a. $P(1)$

   b. $P(-2)$

26. Subtract $(2x - 5)$ from the sum of $(5x^2 - 3x + 6)$ and $(4x^2 + 5x - 3)$.

27. Multiply and simplify the product if possible.

   a. $(x + 3)(2x + 5)$

   b. $(2x - 3)(5x^2 - 6x + 7)$

28. Multiply and simplify the product if possible.

   a. $(y - 2)(3y + 4)$

   b. $(3y - 1)(2y^2 + 3y - 1)$

29. Find the GCF of $20x^3y$, $10x^2y^2$, and $35x^3$.

30. Factor: $x^3 - x^2 + 4x - 4$

31. Simplify each rational expression.

   a. $\dfrac{x^3 + 8}{2 + x}$

   b. $\dfrac{2y^2 + 2}{y^3 - 5y^2 + y - 5}$

32. Simplify each rational expression.

   a. $\dfrac{a^3 - 8}{2 - a}$

   b. $\dfrac{3a^2 - 3}{a^3 + 5a^2 - a - 5}$

33. Perform the indicated operation.

   a. $\dfrac{2}{x^2y} + \dfrac{5}{3x^3y}$

   b. $\dfrac{3}{x + 2} + \dfrac{2x}{x - 2}$

   c. $\dfrac{2x - 6}{x - 1} - \dfrac{4}{1 - x}$

34. Perform the indicated operation.

   a. $\dfrac{3}{xy^2} - \dfrac{2}{3x^2y}$

   b. $\dfrac{5x}{x + 3} - \dfrac{2x}{x - 3}$

   c. $\dfrac{x}{x - 2} - \dfrac{5}{2 - x}$

35. Simplify each complex fraction.

   a. $\dfrac{\dfrac{5x}{x + 2}}{\dfrac{10}{x - 2}}$

   b. $\dfrac{\dfrac{x}{y^2} + \dfrac{1}{y}}{\dfrac{y}{x^2} + \dfrac{1}{x}}$

36. Simplify each complex fraction.

   a. $\dfrac{\dfrac{y - 2}{16}}{\dfrac{2y + 3}{12}}$

   b. $\dfrac{\dfrac{x}{16} - \dfrac{1}{x}}{1 - \dfrac{4}{x}}$

37. Divide $10x^3 - 5x^2 + 20x$ by $5x$.

38. Divide $x^3 - 2x^2 + 3x - 6$ by $x - 2$.

39. Use synthetic division to divide $2x^3 - x^2 - 13x + 1$ by $x - 3$.

40. Use synthetic division to divide $4y^3 - 12y^2 - y + 12$ by $y - 3$.

41. Solve: $\dfrac{x + 6}{x - 2} = \dfrac{2(x + 2)}{x - 2}$

42. Solve: $\dfrac{28}{9 - a^2} = \dfrac{2a}{a - 3} + \dfrac{6}{a + 3}$

43. Solve for x: $\dfrac{1}{x} + \dfrac{1}{y} = \dfrac{1}{z}$

44. Solve for a: $A = \dfrac{h(a + b)}{2}$

45. Suppose that u varies inversely as w. If u is 3 when w is 5, find the constant of variation and the inverse variation equation.

46. Suppose that y varies directly as x. If $y = 0.51$ when $x = 3$, find the constant of variation and the direct variation equation.

47. Write each expression with a positive exponent and then simplify.

   a. $16^{-3/4}$

   b. $(-27)^{-2/3}$

48. Write each expression with a positive exponent and then simplify.

   a. $(81)^{-3/4}$

   b. $(-125)^{-2/3}$

49. Rationalize the numerator of $\dfrac{\sqrt{x} + 2}{5}$.

50. Add or subtract.

   a. $\sqrt{36a^3} - \sqrt{144a^3} + \sqrt{4a^3}$

   b. $\sqrt[3]{128ab^3} - 3\sqrt[3]{2ab^3} + b\sqrt[3]{16a}$

   c. $\dfrac{\sqrt[3]{81}}{10} + \sqrt[3]{\dfrac{192}{125}}$

CHAPTER 8

Quadratic Equations and Functions

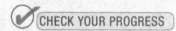
CHECK YOUR PROGRESS

An important part of the study of algebra is learning to model and solve problems. Often, the model of a problem is a quadratic equation or a function containing a second-degree polynomial. In this chapter, we continue the work begun in Chapter 5, when we solved polynomial equations in one variable by factoring. Two additional methods of solving quadratic equations are analyzed as well as methods of solving nonlinear inequalities in one variable.

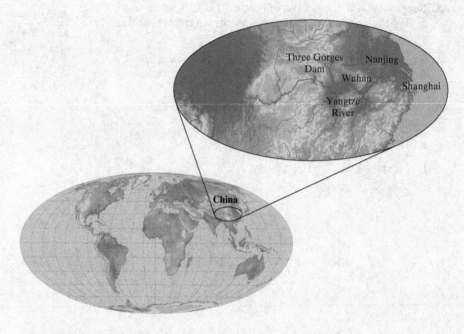

Why Are Dams Built?

One type of a dam is a man-made structure built across a river. Dams are built primarily to control river flow, improve navigation, provide reservoirs for fresh water, or to produce hydroelectric power. The Three Gorges Dam in China is the largest operating hydroelectric facility. While this dam produces the most electricity of any dam in the world, it is only 610 feet in height.

In Section 8.1, Exercises 81 and 82, we will examine the height of some of the great dams.

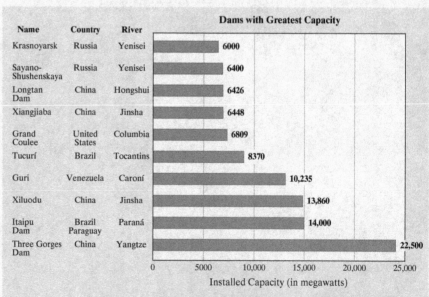

Dams with Greatest Capacity

Name	Country	River	Installed Capacity (in megawatts)
Krasnoyarsk	Russia	Yenisei	6000
Sayano-Shushenskaya	Russia	Yenisei	6400
Longtan Dam	China	Hongshui	6426
Xiangjiaba	China	Jinsha	6448
Grand Coulee	United States	Columbia	6809
Tucuri	Brazil	Tocantins	8370
Guri	Venezuela	Caroní	10,235
Xiluodu	China	Jinsha	13,860
Itaipu Dam	Brazil Paraguay	Paraná	14,000
Three Gorges Dam	China	Yangtze	22,500

Source: U.S. Committee on Large Dams of the International Commission on Large Dams   Note: 1 megawatt = 1,000,000,000

8.1 Solving Quadratic Equations by Completing the Square

OBJECTIVE

1 Using the Square Root Property

In Chapter 5, we solved quadratic equations by factoring. Recall that a **quadratic,** or **second-degree, equation** is an equation that can be written in the form $ax^2 + bx + c = 0$, where a, b, and c are real numbers and a is not 0. To solve a quadratic equation such as $x^2 = 9$ by factoring, we use the zero factor property. To use the zero factor property, the equation must first be written in standard form, $ax^2 + bx + c = 0$.

$$x^2 = 9$$
$$x^2 - 9 = 0 \qquad \text{Subtract 9 from both sides.}$$
$$(x + 3)(x - 3) = 0 \qquad \text{Factor.}$$
$$x + 3 = 0 \quad \text{or} \quad x - 3 = 0 \qquad \text{Set each factor equal to 0.}$$
$$x = -3 \qquad x = 3 \qquad \text{Solve.}$$

The solution set is $\{-3, 3\}$, the positive and negative square roots of 9. Not all quadratic equations can be solved by factoring, so we need to explore other methods. Notice that the solutions of the equation $x^2 = 9$ are two numbers whose square is 9.

$$3^2 = 9 \qquad \text{and} \qquad (-3)^2 = 9$$

Thus, we can solve the equation $x^2 = 9$ by taking the square root of both sides. Be sure to include both $\sqrt{9}$ and $-\sqrt{9}$ as solutions since both $\sqrt{9}$ and $-\sqrt{9}$ are numbers whose square is 9.

$$x^2 = 9$$
$$\sqrt{x^2} = \pm\sqrt{9} \qquad \text{The notation } \pm\sqrt{9} \text{ (read as "plus or minus } \sqrt{9}\text{")}$$
$$x = \pm 3 \qquad \text{indicates the pair of numbers } +\sqrt{9} \text{ and } -\sqrt{9}.$$

This illustrates the square root property.

> **Square Root Property**
>
> If b is a real number and if $a^2 = b$, then $a = \pm\sqrt{b}$.

> **Helpful Hint**
>
> The notation ± 3, for example, is read as "plus or minus 3." It is a shorthand notation for the pair of numbers $+3$ and -3.

EXAMPLE 1   Use the square root property to solve $x^2 = 50$.

Solution

$$x^2 = 50$$
$$x = \pm\sqrt{50} \qquad \text{Use the square root property.}$$
$$x = \pm 5\sqrt{2} \qquad \text{Simplify the radical.}$$

Check:

Let $x = 5\sqrt{2}$.	Let $x = -5\sqrt{2}$.
$x^2 = 50$	$x^2 = 50$
$(5\sqrt{2})^2 \stackrel{?}{=} 50$	$(-5\sqrt{2})^2 \stackrel{?}{=} 50$
$25 \cdot 2 \stackrel{?}{=} 50$	$25 \cdot 2 \stackrel{?}{=} 50$
$50 = 50$ True	$50 = 50$ True

The solutions are $5\sqrt{2}$ and $-5\sqrt{2}$, or the solution set is $\{-5\sqrt{2}, 5\sqrt{2}\}$.   ☐

PRACTICE

1   Use the square root property to solve $x^2 = 32$.   ■

EXAMPLE 2   Use the square root property to solve $2x^2 - 14 = 0$.

Solution First we get the squared variable alone on one side of the equation.

$$2x^2 - 14 = 0$$

$$2x^2 = 14 \qquad \text{Add 14 to both sides.}$$

$$x^2 = 7 \qquad \text{Divide both sides by 2.}$$

$$x = \pm\sqrt{7} \qquad \text{Use the square root property.}$$

Check to see that the solutions are $\sqrt{7}$ and $-\sqrt{7}$, or the solution set is $\{-\sqrt{7}, \sqrt{7}\}$. □

PRACTICE
2   Use the square root property to solve $5x^2 - 50 = 0$. ▪

EXAMPLE 3   Use the square root property to solve $(x + 1)^2 = 12$.

Solution

$$(x + 1)^2 = 12$$

$$x + 1 = \pm\sqrt{12} \qquad \text{Use the square root property.}$$

$$x + 1 = \pm 2\sqrt{3} \qquad \text{Simplify the radical.}$$

$$x = -1 \pm 2\sqrt{3} \qquad \text{Subtract 1 from both sides.}$$

> **Helpful Hint**
>
> Don't forget that $-1 \pm 2\sqrt{3}$, for example, means $-1 + 2\sqrt{3}$ and $-1 - 2\sqrt{3}$. In other words, the equation in Example 3 has two solutions.

Check: Below is a check for $-1 + 2\sqrt{3}$. The check for $-1 - 2\sqrt{3}$ is almost the same and is left for you to do on your own.

$$(x + 1)^2 = 12$$

$$(-1 + 2\sqrt{3} + 1)^2 \stackrel{?}{=} 12$$

$$(2\sqrt{3})^2 \stackrel{?}{=} 12$$

$$4 \cdot 3 \stackrel{?}{=} 12$$

$$12 = 12 \qquad \text{True}$$

The solutions are $-1 + 2\sqrt{3}$ and $-1 - 2\sqrt{3}$. □

PRACTICE
3   Use the square root property to solve $(x + 3)^2 = 20$. ▪

EXAMPLE 4   Use the square root property to solve $(2x - 5)^2 = -16$.

Solution

$$(2x - 5)^2 = -16$$

$$2x - 5 = \pm\sqrt{-16} \qquad \text{Use the square root property.}$$

$$2x - 5 = \pm 4i \qquad \text{Simplify the radical.}$$

$$2x = 5 \pm 4i \qquad \text{Add 5 to both sides.}$$

$$x = \frac{5 \pm 4i}{2} \qquad \text{Divide both sides by 2.}$$

The solutions are $\dfrac{5 + 4i}{2}$ and $\dfrac{5 - 4i}{2}$. □

PRACTICE
4   Use the square root property to solve $(5x - 2)^2 = -9$. ▪

✔ CONCEPT CHECK
How do you know just by looking that $(x - 2)^2 = -4$ has complex but not real solutions?

OBJECTIVE

2 Solving by Completing the Square

Notice from Examples 3 and 4 that, if we write a quadratic equation so that one side is the square of a binomial, we can solve by using the square root property. To write the square of a binomial, we write perfect square trinomials. Recall that a perfect square trinomial is a trinomial that can be factored into two identical binomial factors.

Perfect Square Trinomials	*Factored Form*
$x^2 + 8x + 16$	$(x + 4)^2$
$x^2 - 6x + 9$	$(x - 3)^2$
$x^2 + 3x + \dfrac{9}{4}$	$\left(x + \dfrac{3}{2}\right)^2$

Notice that for each perfect square trinomial in x, **the constant term of the trinomial is the square of half the coefficient of the x-term.** For example,

$$x^2 + 8x + 16 \qquad x^2 - 6x + 9$$

$$\frac{1}{2}(8) = 4 \text{ and } 4^2 = 16 \qquad \frac{1}{2}(-6) = -3 \text{ and } (-3)^2 = 9$$

The process of writing a quadratic equation so that one side is a perfect square trinomial is called **completing the square.**

EXAMPLE 5   Solve $p^2 + 2p = 4$ by completing the square.

Solution   First, add the square of half the coefficient of p to both sides so that the resulting trinomial will be a perfect square trinomial. The coefficient of p is 2.

$$\frac{1}{2}(2) = 1 \quad \text{and} \quad 1^2 = 1$$

Add 1 to both sides of the original equation.

$$p^2 + 2p = 4$$
$$p^2 + 2p + 1 = 4 + 1 \quad \text{Add 1 to both sides.}$$
$$(p + 1)^2 = 5 \qquad \text{Factor the trinomial; simplify the right side.}$$

We may now use the square root property and solve for p.

$$p + 1 = \pm\sqrt{5} \qquad \text{Use the square root property.}$$
$$p = -1 \pm \sqrt{5} \quad \text{Subtract 1 from both sides.}$$

Notice that there are two solutions: $-1 + \sqrt{5}$ and $-1 - \sqrt{5}$.   □

PRACTICE

5   Solve $b^2 + 4b = 3$ by completing the square.   ■

EXAMPLE 6   Solve $m^2 - 7m - 1 = 0$ for m by completing the square.

Solution   First, add 1 to both sides of the equation so that the left side has no constant term.

$$m^2 - 7m - 1 = 0$$
$$m^2 - 7m = 1$$

(Continued on next page)

Now find the constant term that makes the left side a perfect square trinomial by squaring half the coefficient of m. Add this constant to both sides of the equation.

$$\frac{1}{2}(-7) = -\frac{7}{2} \quad \text{and} \quad \left(-\frac{7}{2}\right)^2 = \frac{49}{4}$$

$$m^2 - 7m + \frac{49}{4} = 1 + \frac{49}{4} \qquad \text{Add } \frac{49}{4} \text{ to both sides of the equation.}$$

$$\left(m - \frac{7}{2}\right)^2 = \frac{53}{4} \qquad \text{Factor the perfect square trinomial and simplify the right side.}$$

$$m - \frac{7}{2} = \pm\sqrt{\frac{53}{4}} \qquad \text{Apply the square root property.}$$

$$m = \frac{7}{2} \pm \frac{\sqrt{53}}{2} \qquad \text{Add } \frac{7}{2} \text{ to both sides and simplify } \sqrt{\frac{53}{4}}.$$

$$m = \frac{7 \pm \sqrt{53}}{2} \qquad \text{Simplify.}$$

The solutions are $\dfrac{7 + \sqrt{53}}{2}$ and $\dfrac{7 - \sqrt{53}}{2}$. □

PRACTICE

6 Solve $p^2 - 3p + 1 = 0$ by completing the square. ■

The following steps may be used to solve a quadratic equation such as $ax^2 + bx + c = 0$ by completing the square. This method may be used whether or not the polynomial $ax^2 + bx + c$ is factorable.

Solving a Quadratic Equation in *x* by Completing the Square

Step 1. If the coefficient of x^2 is 1, go to Step 2. Otherwise, divide both sides of the equation by the coefficient of x^2.

Step 2. Isolate all variable terms on one side of the equation.

Step 3. Complete the square for the resulting binomial by adding the square of half of the coefficient of x to both sides of the equation.

Step 4. Factor the resulting perfect square trinomial and write it as the square of a binomial.

Step 5. Use the square root property to solve for x.

EXAMPLE 7 Solve: $2x^2 - 8x + 3 = 0$

Solution Our procedure for finding the constant term to complete the square works only if the coefficient of the squared variable term is 1. Therefore, to solve this equation, the first step is to divide both sides by 2, the coefficient of x^2.

$$2x^2 - 8x + 3 = 0$$

Step 1. $x^2 - 4x + \dfrac{3}{2} = 0$ Divide both sides by 2.

Step 2. $x^2 - 4x = -\dfrac{3}{2}$ Subtract $\dfrac{3}{2}$ from both sides.

Next find the square of half of -4.

$$\frac{1}{2}(-4) = -2 \quad \text{and} \quad (-2)^2 = 4$$

Add 4 to both sides of the equation to complete the square.

Step 3. $x^2 - 4x + 4 = -\dfrac{3}{2} + 4$

Step 4. $(x - 2)^2 = \dfrac{5}{2}$ Factor the perfect square and simplify the right side.

Step 5. $x - 2 = \pm\sqrt{\dfrac{5}{2}}$ Apply the square root property.

$x - 2 = \pm\dfrac{\sqrt{10}}{2}$ Rationalize the denominator.

$x = 2 \pm \dfrac{\sqrt{10}}{2}$ Add 2 to both sides.

$= \dfrac{4}{2} \pm \dfrac{\sqrt{10}}{2}$ Find a common denominator.

$= \dfrac{4 \pm \sqrt{10}}{2}$ Simplify.

The solutions are $\dfrac{4 + \sqrt{10}}{2}$ and $\dfrac{4 - \sqrt{10}}{2}$.   ☐

PRACTICE

7   Solve: $3x^2 - 12x + 1 = 0$ ■

EXAMPLE 8   Solve $3x^2 - 9x + 8 = 0$ by completing the square.

Solution $3x^2 - 9x + 8 = 0$

Step 1. $x^2 - 3x + \dfrac{8}{3} = 0$ Divide both sides of the equation by 3.

Step 2. $x^2 - 3x = -\dfrac{8}{3}$ Subtract $\dfrac{8}{3}$ from both sides.

Since $\dfrac{1}{2}(-3) = -\dfrac{3}{2}$ and $\left(-\dfrac{3}{2}\right)^2 = \dfrac{9}{4}$, we add $\dfrac{9}{4}$ to both sides of the equation.

Step 3. $x^2 - 3x + \dfrac{9}{4} = \underbrace{-\dfrac{8}{3} + \dfrac{9}{4}}$

Step 4. $\left(x - \dfrac{3}{2}\right)^2 = -\dfrac{5}{12}$ Factor the perfect square trinomial.

Step 5. $x - \dfrac{3}{2} = \pm\sqrt{-\dfrac{5}{12}}$ Apply the square root property.

$x - \dfrac{3}{2} = \pm\dfrac{i\sqrt{5}}{2\sqrt{3}}$ Simplify the radical.

$x - \dfrac{3}{2} = \pm\dfrac{i\sqrt{15}}{6}$ Rationalize the denominator.

$x = \dfrac{3}{2} \pm \dfrac{i\sqrt{15}}{6}$ Add $\dfrac{3}{2}$ to both sides.

$= \dfrac{9}{6} \pm \dfrac{i\sqrt{15}}{6}$ Find a common denominator.

$= \dfrac{9 \pm i\sqrt{15}}{6}$ Simplify.

The solutions are $\dfrac{9 + i\sqrt{15}}{6}$ and $\dfrac{9 - i\sqrt{15}}{6}$.   ☐

PRACTICE

8   Solve $2x^2 - 5x + 7 = 0$ by completing the square.   ■

3 Solving Problems Modeled by Quadratic Equations

Recall the **simple interest** formula $I = Prt$, where I is the interest earned, P is the principal, r is the rate of interest, and t is time in years. If $100 is invested at a simple interest rate of 5% annually, at the end of 3 years the total interest I earned is

$$I = P \cdot r \cdot t$$

or

$$I = 100 \cdot 0.05 \cdot 3 = \$15$$

and the new principal is

$$\$100 + \$15 = \$115$$

Most of the time, the interest computed on money borrowed or money deposited is **compound interest.** Compound interest, unlike simple interest, is computed on original principal *and* on interest already earned. To see the difference between simple interest and compound interest, suppose that $100 is invested at a rate of 5% compounded annually. To find the total amount of money at the end of 3 years, we calculate as follows.

$$I = P \cdot r \cdot t$$

First year: Interest = $100 \cdot 0.05 \cdot 1 = $5.00
New principal = $100.00 + $5.00 = $105.00

Second year: Interest = $105.00 \cdot 0.05 \cdot 1 = $5.25
New principal = $105.00 + $5.25 = $110.25

Third year: Interest = $110.25 \cdot 0.05 \cdot 1 \approx $5.51
New principal = $110.25 + $5.51 = $115.76

At the end of the third year, the total compound interest earned is $15.76, whereas the total simple interest earned is $15.

It is tedious to calculate compound interest as we did above, so we use a compound interest formula. The formula for calculating the total amount of money when interest is compounded annually is

$$A = P(1 + r)^t$$

where P is the original investment, r is the interest rate per compounding period, and t is the number of periods. For example, the amount of money A at the end of 3 years if $100 is invested at 5% compounded annually is

$$A = \$100(1 + 0.05)^3 \approx \$100(1.1576) = \$115.76$$

as we previously calculated.

EXAMPLE 9   Finding Interest Rates

Use the formula $A = P(1 + r)^t$ to find the interest rate r if $2000 compounded annually grows to $2420 in 2 years.

Solution

1. UNDERSTAND the problem. Since the $2000 is compounded annually, we use the compound interest formula. For this example, make sure that you understand the formula for compounding interest annually.

2. TRANSLATE. We substitute the given values into the formula.

$$A = P(1 + r)^t$$

$$2420 = 2000(1 + r)^2 \quad \text{Let } A = 2420, P = 2000, \text{ and } t = 2.$$

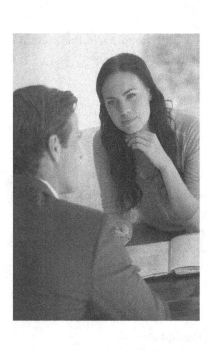

3. SOLVE. Solve the equation for r.

$$2420 = 2000(1 + r)^2$$

$$\frac{2420}{2000} = (1 + r)^2 \qquad \text{Divide both sides by 2000.}$$

$$\frac{121}{100} = (1 + r)^2 \qquad \text{Simplify the fraction.}$$

$$\pm\sqrt{\frac{121}{100}} = 1 + r \qquad \text{Use the square root property.}$$

$$\pm\frac{11}{10} = 1 + r \qquad \text{Simplify.}$$

$$-1 \pm \frac{11}{10} = r$$

$$-\frac{10}{10} \pm \frac{11}{10} = r$$

$$\frac{1}{10} = r \quad \text{or} \quad -\frac{21}{10} = r$$

4. INTERPRET. The rate cannot be negative, so we reject $-\dfrac{21}{10}$.

Check: $\dfrac{1}{10} = 0.10 = 10\%$ per year. If we invest \$2000 at 10% compounded annually, in 2 years the amount in the account would be $2000(1 + 0.10)^2 = 2420$ dollars, the desired amount.

State: The interest rate is 10% compounded annually.   □

PRACTICE

9   Use the formula from Example 9 to find the interest rate r if \$5000 compounded annually grows to \$5618 in 2 years.   ■

Graphing Calculator Explorations

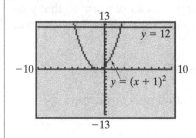

In Section 5.8, we showed how we can use a grapher to approximate real number solutions of a quadratic equation written in standard form. We can also use a grapher to solve a quadratic equation when it is not written in standard form. For example, to solve $(x + 1)^2 = 12$, the quadratic equation in Example 3, we graph the following on the same set of axes. Use Xmin $= -10$, Xmax $= 10$, Ymin $= -13$, and Ymax $= 13$.

$$Y_1 = (x + 1)^2 \quad \text{and} \quad Y_2 = 12$$

Use the Intersect feature or the Zoom and Trace features to locate the points of intersection of the graphs. (See your manuals for specific instructions.) The x-values of these points are the solutions of $(x + 1)^2 = 12$. The solutions, rounded to two decimal places, are 2.46 and -4.46.

Check to see that these numbers are approximations of the exact solutions $-1 \pm 2\sqrt{3}$.

Use a graphing calculator to solve each quadratic equation. Round all solutions to the nearest hundredth.

1. $x(x - 5) = 8$ **2.** $x(x + 2) = 5$

3. $x^2 + 0.5x = 0.3x + 1$ **4.** $x^2 - 2.6x = -2.2x + 3$

5. Use a graphing calculator and solve $(2x - 5)^2 = -16$, Example 4 in this section, using the window

$$Xmin = -20$$
$$Xmax = 20$$
$$Xscl = 1$$
$$Ymin = -20$$
$$Ymax = 20$$
$$Yscl = 1$$

Explain the results. Compare your results with the solution found in Example 4.

6. What are the advantages and disadvantages of using a graphing calculator to solve quadratic equations?

✔ Vocabulary, Readiness & Video Check

Use the choices below to fill in each blank. Not all choices will be used.

binomial	$\sqrt{b}$	$\pm\sqrt{b}$	b^2	9	25	completing the square
quadratic	$-\sqrt{b}$	$\dfrac{b}{2}$	$\left(\dfrac{b}{2}\right)^2$	3	5	

1. By the square root property, if b is a real number, and $a^2 = b$, then $a =$ _____.
2. A _____ equation can be written in the form $ax^2 + bx + c = 0, a \neq 0$.
3. The process of writing a quadratic equation so that one side is a perfect square trinomial is called _____.
4. A perfect square trinomial is one that can be factored as a _____ squared.
5. To solve $x^2 + 6x = 10$ by completing the square, add _____ to both sides.
6. To solve $x^2 + bx = c$ by completing the square, add _____ to both sides.

Martin-Gay Interactive Videos

See Video 8.1

Watch the section lecture video and answer the following questions.

OBJECTIVE
1 7. From ▦ Examples 2 and 3, explain a step you can perform so that you may easily apply the square root property to $2x^2 = 16$. Explain why you perform this step.

OBJECTIVE
2 8. In ▦ Example 5, why is the equation first divided through by 3?

OBJECTIVE
3 9. In ▦ Example 6, why is the negative solution not considered?

8.1 Exercise Set MyMathLab®

Use the square root property to solve each equation. These equations have real number solutions. See Examples 1 through 3.

1. $x^2 = 16$
2. $x^2 = 49$
3. $x^2 - 7 = 0$
4. $x^2 - 11 = 0$
5. $x^2 = 18$
6. $y^2 = 20$
7. $3z^2 - 30 = 0$
8. $2x^2 - 4 = 0$
9. $(x + 5)^2 = 9$
10. $(y - 3)^2 = 4$

11. $(z - 6)^2 = 18$
12. $(y + 4)^2 = 27$
13. $(2x - 3)^2 = 8$
14. $(4x + 9)^2 = 6$

Use the square root property to solve each equation. See Examples 1 through 4.

15. $x^2 + 9 = 0$
16. $x^2 + 4 = 0$
17. $x^2 - 6 = 0$
18. $y^2 - 10 = 0$
19. $2z^2 + 16 = 0$
20. $3p^2 + 36 = 0$

21. $(3x - 1)^2 = -16$

22. $(4y + 2)^2 = -25$

23. $(z + 7)^2 = 5$

24. $(x + 10)^2 = 11$

25. $(x + 3)^2 + 8 = 0$

26. $(y - 4)^2 + 18 = 0$

Add the proper constant to each binomial so that the resulting trinomial is a perfect square trinomial. Then factor the trinomial.

27. $x^2 + 16x +$ _____

28. $y^2 + 2y +$ _____

29. $z^2 - 12z +$ _____

30. $x^2 - 8x +$ _____

31. $p^2 + 9p +$ _____

32. $n^2 + 5n +$ _____

33. $x^2 + x +$ _____

34. $y^2 - y +$ _____

MIXED PRACTICE

Solve each equation by completing the square. These equations have real number solutions. See Examples 5 through 7.

35. $x^2 + 8x = -15$

36. $y^2 + 6y = -8$

▶ **37.** $x^2 + 6x + 2 = 0$

38. $x^2 - 2x - 2 = 0$

39. $x^2 + x - 1 = 0$

40. $x^2 + 3x - 2 = 0$

41. $x^2 + 2x - 5 = 0$

42. $x^2 - 6x + 3 = 0$

43. $y^2 + y - 7 = 0$

44. $x^2 - 7x - 1 = 0$

45. $3p^2 - 12p + 2 = 0$

46. $2x^2 + 14x - 1 = 0$

47. $4y^2 - 2 = 12y$

48. $6x^2 - 3 = 6x$

49. $2x^2 + 7x = 4$

50. $3x^2 - 4x = 4$

51. $x^2 + 8x + 1 = 0$

52. $x^2 - 10x + 2 = 0$

▶ **53.** $3y^2 + 6y - 4 = 0$

54. $2y^2 + 12y + 3 = 0$

55. $2x^2 - 3x - 5 = 0$

56. $5x^2 + 3x - 2 = 0$

Solve each equation by completing the square. See Examples 5 through 8.

57. $y^2 + 2y + 2 = 0$

58. $x^2 + 4x + 6 = 0$

59. $y^2 + 6y - 8 = 0$

60. $y^2 + 10y - 26 = 0$

61. $2a^2 + 8a = -12$

62. $3x^2 + 12x = -14$

63. $5x^2 + 15x - 1 = 0$

64. $16y^2 + 16y - 1 = 0$

65. $2x^2 - x + 6 = 0$

66. $4x^2 - 2x + 5 = 0$

67. $x^2 + 10x + 28 = 0$

68. $y^2 + 8y + 18 = 0$

69. $z^2 + 3z - 4 = 0$

70. $y^2 + y - 2 = 0$

71. $2x^2 - 4x = -3$

72. $9x^2 - 36x = -40$

73. $3x^2 + 3x = 5$

74. $10y^2 - 30y = 2$

Use the formula $A = P(1 + r)^t$ to solve Exercises 75 through 78. See Example 9.

▶ **75.** Find the rate r at which $3000 compounded annually grows to $4320 in 2 years.

76. Find the rate r at which $800 compounded annually grows to $882 in 2 years.

77. Find the rate at which $15,000 compounded annually grows to $16,224 in 2 years.

78. Find the rate at which $2000 compounded annually grows to $2880 in 2 years.

Neglecting air resistance, the distance $s(t)$ in feet traveled by a freely falling object is given by the function $s(t) = 16t^2$, where t is time in seconds. Use this formula to solve Exercises 79 through 82. Round answers to two decimal places.

79. The Petronas Towers in Kuala Lumpur, completed in 1998, are the tallest buildings in Malaysia. Each tower is 1483 feet tall. How long would it take an object to fall to the ground from the top of one of the towers? (*Source:* Council on Tall Buildings and Urban Habitat, Lehigh University)

80. The Burj Khalifa, the tallest building in the world, was completed in 2010 in Dubai. It is estimated to be 2717 feet tall. How long would it take an object to fall to the ground from the top of the building? (*Source:* Council on Tall Buildings and Urban Habitat)

81. The Three Gorges Dam, while producing the most electricity of any dam in the world, is only 610 feet tall. How long would it take an object to fall from the top to the base of the dam? (*Source:* U.S. Committee on Large Dams of the International Commission on Large Dams)

82. The Hoover Dam, located on the Colorado River on the border of Nevada and Arizona near Las Vegas, is 725 feet tall. How long would it take an object to fall from the top to the base of the dam? (*Source:* U.S. Committee on Large Dams of the International Commission on Large Dams)

Solve.

△ **83.** The area of a square room is 225 square feet. Find the dimensions of the room.

△ **84.** The area of a circle is 36π square inches. Find the radius of the circle.

△ **85.** An isosceles right triangle has legs of equal length. If the hypotenuse is 20 centimeters long, find the length of each leg.

△ **86.** The top of a square coffee table has a diagonal that measures 30 inches. Find the length of each side of the top of the coffee table.

Simplify each expression. See Section 7.1.

87. $\dfrac{1}{2} - \sqrt{\dfrac{9}{4}}$

88. $\dfrac{9}{10} - \sqrt{\dfrac{49}{100}}$

Simplify each expression. See Section 7.5.

89. $\dfrac{6 + 4\sqrt{5}}{2}$

90. $\dfrac{10 - 20\sqrt{3}}{2}$

91. $\dfrac{3 - 9\sqrt{2}}{6}$

92. $\dfrac{12 - 8\sqrt{7}}{16}$

Evaluate $\sqrt{b^2 - 4ac}$ for each set of values. See Section 7.3.

93. $a = 2, b = 4, c = -1$

94. $a = 1, b = 6, c = 2$

95. $a = 3, b = -1, c = -2$

96. $a = 1, b = -3, c = -1$

CONCEPT EXTENSIONS

Without solving, determine whether the solutions of each equation are real numbers or complex but not real numbers. See the Concept Check in this section.

97. $(x + 1)^2 = -1$

98. $(y - 5)^2 = -9$

99. $3z^2 = 10$

100. $4x^2 = 17$

101. $(2y - 5)^2 + 7 = 3$

102. $(3m + 2)^2 + 4 = 1$

Find two possible missing terms so that each is a perfect square trinomial.

103. $x^2 + \quad + 16$

104. $y^2 + \quad + 9$

105. $z^2 + \quad + \dfrac{25}{4}$

106. $x^2 + \quad + \dfrac{1}{4}$

107. In your own words, explain how to calculate the number that will complete the square on an expression such as $x^2 - 5x$.

108. In your own words, what is the difference between simple interest and compound interest?

109. If you are depositing money in an account that pays 4%, would you prefer the interest to be simple or compound? Explain your answer.

110. If you are borrowing money at a rate of 10%, would you prefer the interest to be simple or compound? Explain your answer.

A common equation used in business is a demand equation. It expresses the relationship between the unit price of some commodity and the quantity demanded. For Exercises 111 and 112, p represents the unit price and x represents the quantity demanded in thousands.

111. A manufacturing company has found that the demand equation for a certain type of scissors is given by the equation $p = -x^2 + 47$. Find the demand for the scissors if the price is $11 per pair.

112. Acme, Inc., sells desk lamps and has found that the demand equation for a certain style of desk lamp is given by the equation $p = -x^2 + 15$. Find the demand for the desk lamp if the price is $7 per lamp.

8.2 Solving Quadratic Equations by the Quadratic Formula

OBJECTIVE

1 Solving Quadratic Equations by Using the Quadratic Formula

Any quadratic equation can be solved by completing the square. Since the same sequence of steps is repeated each time we complete the square, let's complete the square for a general quadratic equation, $ax^2 + bx + c = 0, a \neq 0$. By doing so, we find a pattern for the solutions of a quadratic equation known as the **quadratic formula.**

Recall that to complete the square for an equation such as $ax^2 + bx + c = 0$, we first divide both sides by the coefficient of x^2.

$$ax^2 + bx + c = 0$$

$$x^2 + \frac{b}{a}x + \frac{c}{a} = 0 \qquad \text{Divide both sides by } a, \text{ the coefficient of } x^2.$$

$$x^2 + \frac{b}{a}x = -\frac{c}{a} \qquad \text{Subtract the constant } \frac{c}{a} \text{ from both sides.}$$

Next, find the square of half $\frac{b}{a}$, the coefficient of x.

$$\frac{1}{2}\left(\frac{b}{a}\right) = \frac{b}{2a} \quad \text{and} \quad \left(\frac{b}{2a}\right)^2 = \frac{b^2}{4a^2}$$

Add this result to both sides of the equation.

$$x^2 + \frac{b}{a}x + \frac{b^2}{4a^2} = -\frac{c}{a} + \frac{b^2}{4a^2} \qquad \text{Add } \frac{b^2}{4a^2} \text{ to both sides.}$$

$$x^2 + \frac{b}{a}x + \frac{b^2}{4a^2} = \frac{-c \cdot 4a}{a \cdot 4a} + \frac{b^2}{4a^2} \qquad \begin{array}{l}\text{Find a common denominator} \\ \text{on the right side.}\end{array}$$

$$x^2 + \frac{b}{a}x + \frac{b^2}{4a^2} = \frac{b^2 - 4ac}{4a^2} \qquad \text{Simplify the right side.}$$

$$\left(x + \frac{b}{2a}\right)^2 = \frac{b^2 - 4ac}{4a^2} \qquad \begin{array}{l}\text{Factor the perfect square} \\ \text{trinomial on the left side.}\end{array}$$

$$x + \frac{b}{2a} = \pm\sqrt{\frac{b^2 - 4ac}{4a^2}} \qquad \text{Apply the square root property.}$$

$$x + \frac{b}{2a} = \pm\frac{\sqrt{b^2 - 4ac}}{2a} \qquad \text{Simplify the radical.}$$

$$x = -\frac{b}{2a} \pm \frac{\sqrt{b^2 - 4ac}}{2a} \qquad \text{Subtract } \frac{b}{2a} \text{ from both sides.}$$

$$x = \frac{-b \pm \sqrt{b^2 - 4ac}}{2a} \qquad \text{Simplify.}$$

This equation identifies the solutions of the general quadratic equation in standard form and is called the quadratic formula. It can be used to solve any equation written in standard form $ax^2 + bx + c = 0$ as long as a is not 0.

Quadratic Formula

A quadratic equation written in the form $ax^2 + bx + c = 0$ has the solutions

$$x = \frac{-b \pm \sqrt{b^2 - 4ac}}{2a}$$

EXAMPLE 1 Solve $3x^2 + 16x + 5 = 0$ for x.

Solution This equation is in standard form, so $a = 3$, $b = 16$, and $c = 5$. Substitute these values into the quadratic formula.

$$x = \frac{-b \pm \sqrt{b^2 - 4ac}}{2a} \qquad \text{Quadratic formula}$$

$$= \frac{-16 \pm \sqrt{16^2 - 4(3)(5)}}{2 \cdot 3} \qquad \text{Use } a = 3, b = 16, \text{ and } c = 5.$$

$$= \frac{-16 \pm \sqrt{256 - 60}}{6}$$

$$= \frac{-16 \pm \sqrt{196}}{6} = \frac{-16 \pm 14}{6}$$

$$x = \frac{-16 + 14}{6} = -\frac{1}{3} \quad \text{or} \quad x = \frac{-16 - 14}{6} = -\frac{30}{6} = -5$$

The solutions are $-\frac{1}{3}$ and -5, or the solution set is $\left\{ -\frac{1}{3}, -5 \right\}$. □

PRACTICE

1 Solve $3x^2 - 5x - 2 = 0$ for x.

Helpful Hint
To replace a, b, and c correctly in the quadratic formula, write the quadratic equation in standard form $ax^2 + bx + c = 0$.

EXAMPLE 2 Solve: $2x^2 - 4x = 3$

Solution First write the equation in standard form by subtracting 3 from both sides.

$$2x^2 - 4x - 3 = 0$$

Now $a = 2$, $b = -4$, and $c = -3$. Substitute these values into the quadratic formula.

$$x = \frac{-b \pm \sqrt{b^2 - 4ac}}{2a}$$

$$= \frac{-(-4) \pm \sqrt{(-4)^2 - 4(2)(-3)}}{2 \cdot 2}$$

$$= \frac{4 \pm \sqrt{16 + 24}}{4}$$

$$= \frac{4 \pm \sqrt{40}}{4} = \frac{4 \pm 2\sqrt{10}}{4}$$

$$= \frac{2(2 \pm \sqrt{10})}{2 \cdot 2} = \frac{2 \pm \sqrt{10}}{2}$$

The solutions are $\dfrac{2 + \sqrt{10}}{2}$ and $\dfrac{2 - \sqrt{10}}{2}$, or the solution set is $\left\{ \dfrac{2 - \sqrt{10}}{2}, \dfrac{2 + \sqrt{10}}{2} \right\}$. □

PRACTICE

2 Solve: $3x^2 - 8x = 2$

Helpful Hint
To simplify the expression $\dfrac{4 \pm 2\sqrt{10}}{4}$ in the preceding example, note that 2 is factored out of both terms of the numerator _before_ simplifying. $$\frac{4 \pm 2\sqrt{10}}{4} = \frac{2(2 \pm \sqrt{10})}{2 \cdot 2} = \frac{2 \pm \sqrt{10}}{2}$$

✔ **CONCEPT CHECK**
For the quadratic equation $x^2 = 7$, choose the correct substitution for a, b, and c in the standard form $ax^2 + bx + c = 0$.
a. $a = 1, b = 0$, and $c = -7$
b. $a = 1, b = 0$, and $c = 7$
c. $a = 0, b = 0$, and $c = 7$
d. $a = 1, b = 1$, and $c = -7$

EXAMPLE 3   Solve: $\dfrac{1}{4} m^2 - m + \dfrac{1}{2} = 0$

Solution We could use the quadratic formula with $a = \dfrac{1}{4}$, $b = -1$, and $c = \dfrac{1}{2}$. Instead, we find a simpler, equivalent standard form equation whose coefficients are not fractions.

Multiply both sides of the equation by the LCD 4 to clear fractions.

$$4\left(\frac{1}{4} m^2 - m + \frac{1}{2}\right) = 4 \cdot 0$$

$$m^2 - 4m + 2 = 0 \qquad \text{Simplify.}$$

Substitute $a = 1$, $b = -4$, and $c = 2$ into the quadratic formula and simplify.

$$m = \frac{-(-4) \pm \sqrt{(-4)^2 - 4(1)(2)}}{2 \cdot 1} = \frac{4 \pm \sqrt{16 - 8}}{2}$$

$$= \frac{4 \pm \sqrt{8}}{2} = \frac{4 \pm 2\sqrt{2}}{2} = \frac{2(2 \pm \sqrt{2})}{2}$$

$$= 2 \pm \sqrt{2}$$

The solutions are $2 + \sqrt{2}$ and $2 - \sqrt{2}$.   □

PRACTICE
3   Solve: $\dfrac{1}{8} x^2 - \dfrac{1}{4} x - 2 = 0$ ■

EXAMPLE 4   Solve: $x = -3x^2 - 3$

Solution The equation in standard form is $3x^2 + x + 3 = 0$. Thus, let $a = 3$, $b = 1$, and $c = 3$ in the quadratic formula.

$$x = \frac{-1 \pm \sqrt{1^2 - 4(3)(3)}}{2 \cdot 3} = \frac{-1 \pm \sqrt{1 - 36}}{6} = \frac{-1 \pm \sqrt{-35}}{6} = \frac{-1 \pm i\sqrt{35}}{6}$$

The solutions are $\dfrac{-1 + i\sqrt{35}}{6}$ and $\dfrac{-1 - i\sqrt{35}}{6}$.   □

PRACTICE
4   Solve: $x = -2x^2 - 2$ ■

✔ **CONCEPT CHECK**
What is the first step in solving $-3x^2 = 5x - 4$ using the quadratic formula?

In Example 1, the equation $3x^2 + 16x + 5 = 0$ had 2 real roots, $-\dfrac{1}{3}$ and -5.

In Example 4, the equation $3x^2 + x + 3 = 0$ (written in standard form) had no real roots. How do their related graphs compare? Recall that the x-intercepts of $f(x) = 3x^2 + 16x + 5$ occur where $f(x) = 0$ or where $3x^2 + 16x + 5 = 0$.

Since this equation has 2 real roots, the graph has 2 x-intercepts. Similarly, since the equation $3x^2 + x + 3 = 0$ has no real roots, the graph of $f(x) = 3x^2 + x + 3$ has no x-intercepts.

OBJECTIVE

2 Using the Discriminant

In the quadratic formula, $x = \dfrac{-b \pm \sqrt{b^2 - 4ac}}{2a}$, the radicand $b^2 - 4ac$ is called the **discriminant** because, by knowing its value, we can **discriminate** among the possible number and type of solutions of a quadratic equation. Possible values of the discriminant and their meanings are summarized next.

Discriminant

The following table corresponds the discriminant $b^2 - 4ac$ of a quadratic equation of the form $ax^2 + bx + c = 0$ with the number and type of solutions of the equation.

$b^2 - 4ac$	Number and Type of Solutions
Positive	Two real solutions
Zero	One real solution
Negative	Two complex but not real solutions

EXAMPLE 5 Use the discriminant to determine the number and type of solutions of each quadratic equation.

a. $x^2 + 2x + 1 = 0$ **b.** $3x^2 + 2 = 0$ **c.** $2x^2 - 7x - 4 = 0$

Solution

a. In $x^2 + 2x + 1 = 0$, $a = 1$, $b = 2$, and $c = 1$. Thus,

$$b^2 - 4ac = 2^2 - 4(1)(1) = 0$$

Since $b^2 - 4ac = 0$, this quadratic equation has one real solution.

b. In this equation, $a = 3$, $b = 0$, $c = 2$. Then $b^2 - 4ac = 0 - 4(3)(2) = -24$. Since $b^2 - 4ac$ is negative, the quadratic equation has two complex but not real solutions.

c. In this equation, $a = 2$, $b = -7$, and $c = -4$. Then

$$b^2 - 4ac = (-7)^2 - 4(2)(-4) = 81$$

Since $b^2 - 4ac$ is positive, the quadratic equation has two real solutions. □

PRACTICE

5 Use the discriminant to determine the number and type of solutions of each quadratic equation.

a. $x^2 - 6x + 9 = 0$ **b.** $x^2 - 3x - 1 = 0$ **c.** $7x^2 + 11 = 0$

The discriminant helps us determine the number and type of solutions of a quadratic equation, $ax^2 + bx + c = 0$. Recall from Section 5.8 that the solutions of this equation are the same as the x-intercepts of its related graph $f(x) = ax^2 + bx + c$. This means that the discriminant of $ax^2 + bx + c = 0$ also tells us the number of x-intercepts for the graph of $f(x) = ax^2 + bx + c$ or, equivalently, $y = ax^2 + bx + c$.

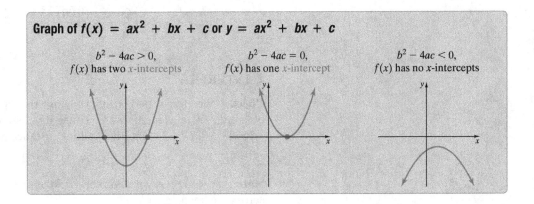

Graph of $f(x) = ax^2 + bx + c$ or $y = ax^2 + bx + c$

$b^2 - 4ac > 0$,
$f(x)$ has two x-intercepts

$b^2 - 4ac = 0$,
$f(x)$ has one x-intercept

$b^2 - 4ac < 0$,
$f(x)$ has no x-intercepts

OBJECTIVE

3   **Solving Problems Modeled by Quadratic Equations**

The quadratic formula is useful in solving problems that are modeled by quadratic equations.

 EXAMPLE 6   **Calculating Distance Saved**

At a local university, students often leave the sidewalk and cut across the lawn to save walking distance. Given the diagram below of a favorite place to cut across the lawn, approximate how many feet of walking distance a student saves by cutting across the lawn instead of walking on the sidewalk.

50 ft

x

$x + 20$

Solution

1. **UNDERSTAND.** Read and reread the problem. In the diagram, notice that a triangle is formed. Since the corner of the block forms a right angle, we use the Pythagorean theorem for right triangles. You may want to review this theorem.

2. **TRANSLATE.** By the Pythagorean theorem, we have

$$\text{In words: } (\text{leg})^2 + (\text{leg})^2 = (\text{hypotenuse})^2$$

$$\text{Translate: } x^2 + (x + 20)^2 = 50^2$$

3. **SOLVE.** Use the quadratic formula to solve.

$$x^2 + x^2 + 40x + 400 = 2500 \quad \text{Square } (x + 20) \text{ and } 50.$$

$$2x^2 + 40x - 2100 = 0 \qquad \text{Set the equation equal to } 0.$$

$$x^2 + 20x - 1050 = 0 \qquad \text{Divide by } 2.$$

(Continued on next page)

Here, $a = 1, b = 20, c = -1050$. By the quadratic formula,

$$x = \frac{-20 \pm \sqrt{20^2 - 4(1)(-1050)}}{2 \cdot 1}$$

$$= \frac{-20 \pm \sqrt{400 + 4200}}{2} = \frac{-20 \pm \sqrt{4600}}{2}$$

$$= \frac{-20 \pm \sqrt{100 \cdot 46}}{2} = \frac{-20 \pm 10\sqrt{46}}{2}$$

$$= -10 \pm 5\sqrt{46} \quad \text{Simplify.}$$

4. INTERPRET.

Check: We have two results using the quadratic formula. The length of a side of a triangle can't be negative, so we reject $-10 - 5\sqrt{46}$. Since $-10 + 5\sqrt{46} \approx 24$ feet, the walking distance along the sidewalk is

$$x + (x + 20) \approx 24 + (24 + 20) = 68 \text{ feet.}$$

State: A student saves about $68 - 50$ or 18 feet of walking distance by cutting across the lawn. □

15 ft

x

x + 3

PRACTICE

6 Given the diagram, approximate to the nearest foot how many feet of walking distance a person can save by cutting across the lawn instead of walking on the sidewalk. ■

EXAMPLE 7 **Calculating Landing Time**

An object is thrown upward from the top of a 200-foot cliff with a velocity of 12 feet per second. The height h in feet of the object after t seconds is

$$h = -16t^2 + 12t + 200$$

How long after the object is thrown will it strike the ground? Round to the nearest tenth of a second.

200 ft

Solution

1. UNDERSTAND. Read and reread the problem.

2. TRANSLATE. Since we want to know when the object strikes the ground, we want to know when the height $h = 0$, or

$$0 = -16t^2 + 12t + 200$$

3. SOLVE. First we divide both sides of the equation by -4.

$$0 = 4t^2 - 3t - 50 \quad \text{Divide both sides by } -4.$$

Here, $a = 4, b = -3$, and $c = -50$. By the quadratic formula,

$$t = \frac{-(-3) \pm \sqrt{(-3)^2 - 4(4)(-50)}}{2 \cdot 4}$$

$$= \frac{3 \pm \sqrt{9 + 800}}{8}$$

$$= \frac{3 \pm \sqrt{809}}{8}$$

4. INTERPRET.

Check: We check our calculations from the quadratic formula. Since the time won't be negative, we reject the proposed solution

$$\frac{3 - \sqrt{809}}{8}.$$

State: The time it takes for the object to strike the ground is exactly

$$\frac{3 + \sqrt{809}}{8} \text{ seconds} \approx 3.9 \text{ seconds.}$$ □

PRACTICE

7   A toy rocket is shot upward from the top of a 45-foot-tall building, with an initial velocity of 20 feet per second. The height h in feet of the rocket after t seconds is

$$h = -16t^2 + 20t + 45$$

How long after the rocket is launched will it strike the ground? Round to the nearest tenth of a second.   ■

✔ Vocabulary, Readiness & Video Check

Fill in each blank.

1. The quadratic formula is _____.

2. For $2x^2 + x + 1 = 0,$ if $a = 2,$ then $b =$ _____ and $c =$ _____ .

3. For $5x^2 - 5x - 7 = 0,$ if $a = 5,$ then $b =$ _____ and $c =$ _____ .

4. For $7x^2 - 4 = 0,$ if $a = 7,$ then $b =$ _____ and $c =$ _____ .

5. For $x^2 + 9 = 0,$ if $c = 9,$ then $a =$ _____ and $b =$ _____ .

6. The correct simplified form of $\dfrac{5 \pm 10\sqrt{2}}{5}$ is _____ .
 a. $1 \pm 10\sqrt{2}$ **b.** $2\sqrt{2}$ **c.** $1 \pm 2\sqrt{2}$ **d.** $\pm 5\sqrt{2}$

Martin-Gay Interactive Videos

See Video 8.2 ◉

Watch the section lecture video and answer the following questions.

OBJECTIVE
1   **7.** Based on ▤ Examples 1–3, answer the following.
 a. Must a quadratic equation be written in standard form in order to use the quadratic formula? Why or why not?
 b. Must fractions be cleared from an equation before using the quadratic formula? Why or why not?

OBJECTIVE
2   **8.** Based on ▤ Example 4 and the lecture before, complete the following statements. The discriminant is the _____ in the quadratic formula and can be used to find the number and type of solutions of a quadratic equation without _____ the equation. To use the discriminant, the quadratic equation needs to be written in _____ form.

OBJECTIVE
3   **9.** In ▤ Example 5, the value of x is found, which is then used to find the dimensions of the triangle. Yet all this work still does not solve the problem. Explain.

8.2 Exercise Set MyMathLab ▷

Use the quadratic formula to solve each equation. These equations have real number solutions only. See Examples 1 through 3.

1. $m^2 + 5m - 6 = 0$

2. $p^2 + 11p - 12 = 0$

3. $2y = 5y^2 - 3$

4. $5x^2 - 3 = 14x$

5. $x^2 - 6x + 9 = 0$

6. $y^2 + 10y + 25 = 0$

▷ **7.** $x^2 + 7x + 4 = 0$

8. $y^2 + 5y + 3 = 0$

9. $8m^2 - 2m = 7$

10. $11n^2 - 9n = 1$

11. $3m^2 - 7m = 3$

12. $x^2 - 13 = 5x$

13. $\frac{1}{2}x^2 - x - 1 = 0$

14. $\frac{1}{6}x^2 + x + \frac{1}{3} = 0$

15. $\frac{2}{5}y^2 + \frac{1}{5}y = \frac{3}{5}$

16. $\frac{1}{8}x^2 + x = \frac{5}{2}$

17. $\frac{1}{3}y^2 = y + \frac{1}{6}$

18. $\frac{1}{2}y^2 = y + \frac{1}{2}$

19. $x^2 + 5x = -2$

20. $y^2 - 8 = 4y$

21. $(m + 2)(2m - 6) = 5(m - 1) - 12$

22. $7p(p - 2) + 2(p + 4) = 3$

MIXED PRACTICE

Use the quadratic formula to solve each equation. These equations have real solutions and complex but not real solutions. See Examples 1 through 4.

23. $x^2 + 6x + 13 = 0$

24. $x^2 + 2x + 2 = 0$

▷ **25.** $(x + 5)(x - 1) = 2$

26. $x(x + 6) = 2$

27. $6 = -4x^2 + 3x$

28. $2 = -9x^2 - x$

29. $\frac{x^2}{3} - x = \frac{5}{3}$

30. $\frac{x^2}{2} - 3 = -\frac{9}{2}x$

31. $10y^2 + 10y + 3 = 0$

32. $3y^2 + 6y + 5 = 0$

33. $x(6x + 2) = 3$

34. $x(7x + 1) = 2$

▷ **35.** $\frac{2}{5}y^2 + \frac{1}{5}y + \frac{3}{5} = 0$

36. $\frac{1}{8}x^2 + x + \frac{5}{2} = 0$

37. $\frac{1}{2}y^2 = y - \frac{1}{2}$

38. $\frac{2}{3}x^2 - \frac{20}{3}x = -\frac{100}{6}$

39. $(n - 2)^2 = 2n$

40. $\left(p - \frac{1}{2}\right)^2 = \frac{p}{2}$

Use the discriminant to determine the number and types of solutions of each equation. See Example 5.

41. $x^2 - 5 = 0$

42. $x^2 - 7 = 0$

43. $4x^2 + 12x = -9$

44. $9x^2 + 1 = 6x$

45. $3x = -2x^2 + 7$

46. $3x^2 = 5 - 7x$

▷ **47.** $6 = 4x - 5x^2$

48. $8x = 3 - 9x^2$

49. $9x - 2x^2 + 5 = 0$

50. $5 - 4x + 12x^2 = 0$

Solve. See Examples 6 and 7.

51. Nancy, Thelma, and John Varner live on a corner lot. Often, neighborhood children cut across their lot to save walking distance. Given the diagram below, approximate to the nearest foot how many feet of walking distance is saved by cutting across their property instead of walking around the lot.

△ **52.** Given the diagram below, approximate to the nearest foot how many feet of walking distance a person saves by cutting across the lawn instead of walking on the sidewalk.

△ **53.** The hypotenuse of an isosceles right triangle is 2 centimeters longer than either of its legs. Find the exact length of each side. (*Hint:* An isosceles right triangle is a right triangle whose legs are the same length.)

△ **54.** The hypotenuse of an isosceles right triangle is one meter longer than either of its legs. Find the length of each side.

△ **55.** Bailey's rectangular dog pen for his Irish setter must have an area of 400 square feet. Also, the length must be 10 feet longer than the width. Find the dimensions of the pen.

△ **56.** An entry in the Peach Festival Poster Contest must be rectangular and have an area of 1200 square inches. Furthermore, its length must be 20 inches longer than its width. Find the dimensions each entry must have.

△ **57.** A holding pen for cattle must be square and have a diagonal length of 100 meters.

a. Find the length of a side of the pen.

b. Find the area of the pen.

△ **58.** A rectangle is three times longer than it is wide. It has a diagonal of length 50 centimeters.

a. Find the dimensions of the rectangle.

b. Find the perimeter of the rectangle.

△ **59.** The heaviest reported door in the world is the 708.6-ton radiation shield door in the National Institute for Fusion Science at Toki, Japan. If the height of the door is 1.1 feet longer than its width, and its front area (neglecting depth) is 1439.9 square feet, find its width and height [Interesting note: the door is 6.6 feet thick.] (*Source: Guinness World Records*)

△ **60.** Christi and Robbie Wegmann are constructing a rectangular stained glass window whose length is 7.3 inches longer than its width. If the area of the window is 569.9 square inches, find its width and length.

△ **61.** The base of a triangle is four more than twice its height. If the area of the triangle is 42 square centimeters, find its base and height.

62. If a point *B* divides a line segment such that the smaller portion is to the larger portion as the larger is to the whole, the whole is the length of the *golden ratio*.

The golden ratio was thought by the Greeks to be the most pleasing to the eye, and many of their buildings contained numerous examples of the golden ratio. The value of the golden ratio is the positive solution of

$$\begin{array}{ll}\text{(smaller)} & \dfrac{x-1}{1} = \dfrac{1}{x} \quad \text{(larger)} \\ \text{(larger)} & \qquad\qquad\qquad \text{(whole)}\end{array}$$

Find this value.

The Wollomombi Falls in Australia have a height of 1100 feet. A pebble is thrown upward from the top of the falls with an initial velocity of 20 feet per second. The height of the pebble h after t seconds is given by the equation $h = -16t^2 + 20t + 1100$. Use this equation for Exercises 63 and 64.

63. How long after the pebble is thrown will it hit the ground? Round to the nearest tenth of a second.

64. How long after the pebble is thrown will it be 550 feet from the ground? Round to the nearest tenth of a second.

A ball is thrown downward from the top of a 180-foot building with an initial velocity of 20 feet per second. The height of the ball h after t seconds is given by the equation $h = -16t^2 - 20t + 180$. Use this equation to answer Exercises 65 and 66.

65. How long after the ball is thrown will it strike the ground? Round the result to the nearest tenth of a second.

66. How long after the ball is thrown will it be 50 feet from the ground? Round the result to the nearest tenth of a second.

REVIEW AND PREVIEW

Solve each equation. See Sections 6.6 and 7.6.

67. $\sqrt{5x - 2} = 3$

68. $\sqrt{y + 2} + 7 = 12$

69. $\dfrac{1}{x} + \dfrac{2}{5} = \dfrac{7}{x}$

70. $\dfrac{10}{z} = \dfrac{5}{z} - \dfrac{1}{3}$

Factor. See Section 5.7.

71. $x^4 + x^2 - 20$

72. $4y^4 + 23y^2 - 6$

73. $z^4 - 13z^2 + 36$

74. $x^4 - 1$

CONCEPT EXTENSIONS

For each quadratic equation, choose the correct substitution for a, b, and c in the standard form $ax^2 + bx + c = 0$.

75. $x^2 = -10$

   a. $a = 1, b = 0, c = -10$

   b. $a = 1, b = 0, c = 10$

   c. $a = 0, b = 1, c = -10$

   d. $a = 1, b = 1, c = 10$

76. $x^2 + 5 = -x$

   a. $a = 1, b = 5, c = -1$

   b. $a = 1, b = -1, c = 5$

   c. $a = 1, b = 5, c = 1$

   d. $a = 1, b = 1, c = 5$

77. Solve Exercise 1 by factoring. Explain the result.

78. Solve Exercise 2 by factoring. Explain the result.

Use the quadratic formula and a calculator to approximate each solution to the nearest tenth.

79. $2x^2 - 6x + 3 = 0$

80. $3.6x^2 + 1.8x - 4.3 = 0$

The accompanying graph shows the daily low temperatures for one week in New Orleans, Louisiana.

81. Between which days of the week was there the greatest decrease in the low temperature?

82. Between which days of the week was there the greatest increase in the low temperature?

83. Which day of the week had the lowest low temperature?

84. Use the graph to estimate the low temperature on Thursday.

Notice that the shape of the temperature graph is similar to the curve drawn. In fact, this graph can be modeled by the quadratic function $f(x) = 3x^2 - 18x + 56$, where $f(x)$ is the temperature in degrees Fahrenheit and x is the number of days from Sunday. (This graph is shown in blue.) Use this function to answer Exercises 85 and 86.

85. Use the quadratic function given to approximate the temperature on Thursday. Does your answer agree with the graph?

86. Use the function given and the quadratic formula to find when the temperature was 35° F. [Hint: Let $f(x) = 35$ and solve for x.] Round your answer to one decimal place and interpret your result. Does your answer agree with the graph?

Solve.

87. The number of Internet users worldwide (in millions) can be modeled by the quadratic equation $f(x) = 5x^2 + 55x + 29$, where $f(x)$ is the number of Internet users worldwide in millions of users, and x is the number of years after 1995. (Source: Data from International Telecommunications Union)

   a. Find the number of Internet users worldwide in 2015.

   b. If the trend described in this model continues, in what year after 1995 will the worldwide users of the Internet reach 4500 million?

88. While the number of farms in the United States was decreasing through the late twentieth century and the early twenty-first century, the average size of farms was increasing. This may be due to consolidation of existing farmlands. The equation $f(x) = -0.5x^2 + 4x + 429$ models the size of the average farm, where $f(x)$ is farm size in acres, and x represents the number of years after 2011. (Source: Based on data from the National Agricultural Statistics Service)

   a. Find the size of the average farm in 2012. Round to the nearest acre.

   b. Find the size of the average farm in 2014. Round to the nearest acre.

89. The amount of money spent in restaurants in the United States x years after 1970 can be modeled by $f(x) = 0.2x^2 + 5.1x + 45.3$, where $f(x)$ is the amount of money spent in restaurants (in billions of dollars), and x is the number of years since 1970.

   a. Find the amount the American public spent in restaurants in 2015. Round to the nearest tenth of a billion.

   b. According to this model, in what year after 1970 was the amount of money spent in restaurants $400 billion?

   c. According to this model, in what year after 1970 will the amount of money spent on restaurants equal $1000 billion?

90. The relationship between body weight and the Recommended Dietary Allowance (RDA) for vitamin A in children up to age 10 is modeled by the quadratic equation $y = 0.149x^2 - 4.475x + 406.478$, where y is the RDA for vitamin A in micrograms for a child whose weight is x pounds. (*Source:* Based on data from the Food and Nutrition Board, National Academy of Sciences–Institute of Medicine, 1989)

   a. Determine the vitamin A requirements of a child who weighs 35 pounds.

   b. What is the weight of a child whose RDA of vitamin A is 600 micrograms? Round your answer to the nearest pound.

The solutions of the quadratic equation $ax^2 + bx + c = 0$ are
$$\frac{-b + \sqrt{b^2 - 4ac}}{2a} \text{ and } \frac{-b - \sqrt{b^2 - 4ac}}{2a}.$$

91. Show that the sum of these solutions is $\dfrac{-b}{a}$.

92. Show that the product of these solutions is $\dfrac{c}{a}$.

Use the quadratic formula to solve each quadratic equation.

93. $3x^2 - \sqrt{12}x + 1 = 0$
   (*Hint:* $a = 3, b = -\sqrt{12}, c = 1$)

94. $5x^2 + \sqrt{20}x + 1 = 0$

95. $x^2 + \sqrt{2}x + 1 = 0$

96. $x^2 - \sqrt{2}x + 1 = 0$

97. $2x^2 - \sqrt{3}x - 1 = 0$

98. $7x^2 + \sqrt{7}x - 2 = 0$

99. Use a graphing calculator to solve Exercises 63 and 65.

100. Use a graphing calculator to solve Exercises 64 and 66.

Recall that the discriminant also tells us the number of x-intercepts of the related function.

101. Check the results of Exercise 49 by graphing $y = 9x - 2x^2 + 5$.

102. Check the results of Exercise 50 by graphing $y = 5 - 4x + 12x^2$.

8.3 Solving Equations by Using Quadratic Methods ▶

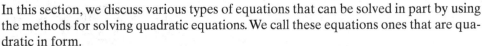

OBJECTIVES

1 Solve Various Equations That Are Quadratic in Form. ▶

2 Solve Problems That Lead to Quadratic Equations. ▶

OBJECTIVE

1 Solving Equations That Are Quadratic in Form ▶

In this section, we discuss various types of equations that can be solved in part by using the methods for solving quadratic equations. We call these equations ones that are quadratic in form.

Once each equation is simplified, you may want to use these steps when deciding which method to use to solve the quadratic equation.

Solving a Quadratic Equation

Step 1. If the equation is in the form $(ax + b)^2 = c$, use the square root property and solve. If not, go to Step 2.

Step 2. Write the equation in standard form: $ax^2 + bx + c = 0$.

Step 3. Try to solve the equation by the factoring method. If not possible, go to Step 4.

Step 4. Solve the equation by the quadratic formula.

The first example is a radical equation that becomes a quadratic equation once we square both sides.

EXAMPLE 1   Solve: $x - \sqrt{x} - 6 = 0$

Solution Recall that to solve a radical equation, first get the radical alone on one side of the equation. Then square both sides.

$$x - 6 = \sqrt{x} \qquad \text{Add } \sqrt{x} \text{ to both sides.}$$
$$(x - 6)^2 = (\sqrt{x})^2 \qquad \text{Square both sides.}$$
$$x^2 - 12x + 36 = x$$
$$x^2 - 13x + 36 = 0 \qquad \text{Set the equation equal to 0.}$$
$$(x - 9)(x - 4) = 0$$
$$x - 9 = 0 \quad \text{or} \quad x - 4 = 0$$
$$x = 9 \qquad\qquad x = 4$$

(Continued on next page)

Check:

Let $x = 9$	Let $x = 4$
$x - \sqrt{x} - 6 = 0$	$x - \sqrt{x} - 6 = 0$
$9 - \sqrt{9} - 6 \overset{?}{=} 0$	$4 - \sqrt{4} - 6 \overset{?}{=} 0$
$9 - 3 - 6 \overset{?}{=} 0$	$4 - 2 - 6 \overset{?}{=} 0$
$0 = 0$ True	$-4 = 0$ False

The solution is 9 or the solution set is {9}.   □

PRACTICE

1   Solve: $x - \sqrt{x + 1} - 5 = 0$ ■

EXAMPLE 2   Solve: $\dfrac{3x}{x - 2} - \dfrac{x + 1}{x} = \dfrac{6}{x(x - 2)}$

Solution In this equation, x cannot be either 2 or 0 because these values cause denominators to equal zero. To solve for x, we first multiply both sides of the equation by $x(x - 2)$ to clear the fractions. By the distributive property, this means that we multiply each term by $x(x - 2)$.

$$x(x - 2)\left(\frac{3x}{x - 2}\right) - x(x - 2)\left(\frac{x + 1}{x}\right) = x(x - 2)\left[\frac{6}{x(x - 2)}\right]$$

$$3x^2 - (x - 2)(x + 1) = 6 \quad \text{Simplify.}$$
$$3x^2 - (x^2 - x - 2) = 6 \quad \text{Multiply.}$$
$$3x^2 - x^2 + x + 2 = 6$$
$$2x^2 + x - 4 = 0 \quad \text{Simplify.}$$

This equation cannot be factored using integers, so we solve by the quadratic formula.

$$x = \frac{-1 \pm \sqrt{1^2 - 4(2)(-4)}}{2 \cdot 2} \quad \begin{array}{l}\text{Use } a = 2, b = 1, \text{ and } c = -4 \\ \text{in the quadratic formula.}\end{array}$$

$$= \frac{-1 \pm \sqrt{1 + 32}}{4} \quad \text{Simplify.}$$

$$= \frac{-1 \pm \sqrt{33}}{4}$$

Neither proposed solution will make the denominators 0.

The solutions are $\dfrac{-1 + \sqrt{33}}{4}$ and $\dfrac{-1 - \sqrt{33}}{4}$ or the solution set is $\left\{\dfrac{-1 + \sqrt{33}}{4}, \dfrac{-1 - \sqrt{33}}{4}\right\}$.   □

PRACTICE

2   Solve: $\dfrac{5x}{x + 1} - \dfrac{x + 4}{x} = \dfrac{3}{x(x + 1)}$ ■

EXAMPLE 3   Solve: $p^4 - 3p^2 - 4 = 0$

Solution First we factor the trinomial.

$$p^4 - 3p^2 - 4 = 0$$
$$(p^2 - 4)(p^2 + 1) = 0 \quad\quad \text{Factor.}$$
$$(p - 2)(p + 2)(p^2 + 1) = 0 \quad\quad \text{Factor further.}$$
$$p - 2 = 0 \quad \text{or} \quad p + 2 = 0 \quad \text{or} \quad p^2 + 1 = 0 \quad \begin{array}{l}\text{Set each factor equal} \\ \text{to 0 and solve.}\end{array}$$
$$p = 2 \quad\quad\quad\quad p = -2 \quad\quad\quad\quad p^2 = -1$$
$$p = \pm\sqrt{-1} = \pm i$$

The solutions are $2, -2, i$ and $-i$. ☐

PRACTICE
3 Solve: $p^4 - 7p^2 - 144 = 0$ ■

Helpful Hint

Example 3 can be solved using substitution also. Think of $p^4 - 3p^2 - 4 = 0$ as

$$(p^2)^2 - 3p^2 - 4 = 0 \quad \text{Then let } x = p^2 \text{ and solve and substitute back.}$$
$$\text{The solutions will be the same.}$$
$$x^2 - 3x - 4 = 0$$

✔ **CONCEPT CHECK**

a. True or false? The maximum number of solutions that a quadratic equation can have is 2.
b. True or false? The maximum number of solutions that an equation in quadratic form can have is 2.

EXAMPLE 4 Solve: $(x - 3)^2 - 3(x - 3) - 4 = 0$

Solution Notice that the quantity $(x - 3)$ is repeated in this equation. Sometimes it is helpful to substitute a variable (in this case other than x) for the repeated quantity. We will let $y = x - 3$. Then

$$(x - 3)^2 - 3(x - 3) - 4 = 0$$

becomes

$$y^2 - 3y - 4 = 0 \quad \text{Let } x - 3 = y.$$
$$(y - 4)(y + 1) = 0 \quad \text{Factor.}$$

To solve, we use the zero factor property.

$$y - 4 = 0 \quad \text{or} \quad y + 1 = 0 \quad \text{Set each factor equal to 0.}$$
$$y = 4 \qquad\qquad y = -1 \quad \text{Solve.}$$

Helpful Hint

When using substitution, don't forget to substitute back to the original variable.

To find values of x, we substitute back. That is, we substitute $x - 3$ for y.

$$x - 3 = 4 \quad \text{or} \quad x - 3 = -1$$
$$x = 7 \qquad\qquad x = 2$$

Both 2 and 7 check. The solutions are 2 and 7. ☐

PRACTICE
4 Solve: $(x + 2)^2 - 2(x + 2) - 3 = 0$ ■

EXAMPLE 5 Solve: $x^{2/3} - 5x^{1/3} + 6 = 0$

Solution The key to solving this equation is recognizing that $x^{2/3} = (x^{1/3})^2$. We replace $x^{1/3}$ with m so that

$$(x^{1/3})^2 - 5x^{1/3} + 6 = 0$$

becomes

$$m^2 - 5m + 6 = 0$$

Now we solve by factoring.

$$m^2 - 5m + 6 = 0$$
$$(m - 3)(m - 2) = 0 \qquad\qquad \text{Factor.}$$
$$m - 3 = 0 \quad \text{or} \quad m - 2 = 0 \quad \text{Set each factor equal to 0.}$$
$$m = 3 \qquad\qquad m = 2$$

(Continued on next page)

Since $m = x^{1/3}$, we have

$$x^{1/3} = 3 \quad \text{or} \quad x^{1/3} = 2$$
$$x = 3^3 = 27 \quad \text{or} \quad x = 2^3 = 8$$

Both 8 and 27 check. The solutions are 8 and 27.

PRACTICE
5 Solve: $x^{2/3} - 5x^{1/3} + 4 = 0$

OBJECTIVE
2 Solving Problems That Lead to Quadratic Equations

The next example is a work problem. This problem is modeled by a rational equation that simplifies to a quadratic equation.

EXAMPLE 6 Finding Work Time

Together, an experienced word processor and an apprentice word processor can create a word document in 6 hours. Alone, the experienced word processor can create the document 2 hours faster than the apprentice word processor can. Find the time in which each person can create the word document alone.

Solution

1. UNDERSTAND. Read and reread the problem. The key idea here is the relationship between the *time* (hours) it takes to complete the job and the *part of the job* completed in one unit of time (hour). For example, because they can complete the job together in 6 hours, the *part of the job* they can complete in 1 hour is $\frac{1}{6}$.

Let

$x =$ the *time* in hours it takes the apprentice word processor to complete the job alone, and

$x - 2 =$ the *time* in hours it takes the experienced word processor to complete the job alone.

We can summarize in a chart the information discussed.

	Total Hours to Complete Job	*Part of Job Completed in 1 Hour*
Apprentice Word Processor	x	$\frac{1}{x}$
Experienced Word Processor	$x - 2$	$\frac{1}{x-2}$
Together	6	$\frac{1}{6}$

2. TRANSLATE.

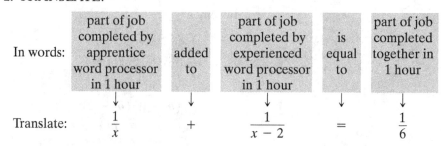

In words: part of job completed by apprentice word processor in 1 hour | added to | part of job completed by experienced word processor in 1 hour | is equal to | part of job completed together in 1 hour

Translate: $\frac{1}{x}$ $+$ $\frac{1}{x-2}$ $=$ $\frac{1}{6}$

3. SOLVE.

$$\frac{1}{x} + \frac{1}{x-2} = \frac{1}{6}$$

$$6x(x-2)\left(\frac{1}{x} + \frac{1}{x-2}\right) = 6x(x-2)\cdot\frac{1}{6}$$ Multiply both sides by the LCD $6x(x-2)$.

$$6x(x-2)\cdot\frac{1}{x} + 6x(x-2)\cdot\frac{1}{x-2} = 6x(x-2)\cdot\frac{1}{6}$$ Use the distributive property.

$$6(x-2) + 6x = x(x-2)$$

$$6x - 12 + 6x = x^2 - 2x$$

$$0 = x^2 - 14x + 12$$

Now we can substitute $a = 1$, $b = -14$, and $c = 12$ into the quadratic formula and simplify.

$$x = \frac{-(-14) \pm \sqrt{(-14)^2 - 4(1)(12)}}{2\cdot 1} = \frac{14 \pm \sqrt{148}^*}{2}$$

Using a calculator or a square root table, we see that $\sqrt{148} \approx 12.2$ rounded to one decimal place. Thus,

$$x \approx \frac{14 \pm 12.2}{2}$$

$$x \approx \frac{14 + 12.2}{2} = 13.1 \quad \text{or} \quad x \approx \frac{14 - 12.2}{2} = 0.9$$

4. INTERPRET.

Check: If the apprentice word processor completes the job alone in 0.9 hours, the experienced word processor completes the job alone in $x - 2 = 0.9 - 2 = -1.1$ hours. Since this is not possible, we reject the solution of 0.9. The approximate solution thus is 13.1 hours.

State: The apprentice word processor can complete the job alone in approximately 13.1 hours, and the experienced word processor can complete the job alone in approximately

$$x - 2 = 13.1 - 2 = 11.1 \text{ hours} \qquad \square$$

PRACTICE

6   Together, Katy and Steve can groom all the dogs at the Barkin' Doggie Day Care in 4 hours. Alone, Katy can groom the dogs 1 hour faster than Steve can groom the dogs alone. Find the time in which each of them can groom the dogs alone.

EXAMPLE 7   **Finding Driving Speeds**

Beach and Fargo are about 400 miles apart. A salesperson travels from Fargo to Beach one day at a certain speed. She returns to Fargo the next day and drives 10 mph faster. Her total travel time was $14\frac{2}{3}$ hours. Find her speed to Beach and the return speed to Fargo.

*This expression can be simplified further, but this will suffice because we are approximating.

(Continued on next page)

Solution

1. UNDERSTAND. Read and reread the problem. Let

$$x = \text{the speed to Beach, so}$$
$$x + 10 = \text{the return speed to Fargo.}$$

Then organize the given information in a table.

Helpful Hint

Since $d = rt, t = \dfrac{d}{r}$. The time column was completed using $\dfrac{d}{r}$.

	distance = rate · time		
To Beach	400	x	$\dfrac{400}{x}$ ← distance ← rate
Return to Fargo	400	$x + 10$	$\dfrac{400}{x + 10}$ ← distance ← rate

2. TRANSLATE.

In words: | time to Beach | + | return time to Fargo | = | $14\dfrac{2}{3}$ hours |

Translate: $\dfrac{400}{x} + \dfrac{400}{x + 10} = \dfrac{44}{3}$

3. SOLVE.

$$\frac{400}{x} + \frac{400}{x + 10} = \frac{44}{3}$$

$$\frac{100}{x} + \frac{100}{x + 10} = \frac{11}{3} \qquad \text{Divide both sides by 4.}$$

$$3x(x + 10)\left(\frac{100}{x} + \frac{100}{x + 10}\right) = 3x(x + 10) \cdot \frac{11}{3} \qquad \begin{array}{l}\text{Multiply both} \\ \text{sides by the LCD} \\ 3x(x + 10).\end{array}$$

$$3x(x + 10) \cdot \frac{100}{x} + 3x(x + 10) \cdot \frac{100}{x + 10} = 3x(x + 10) \cdot \frac{11}{3} \qquad \begin{array}{l}\text{Use the distributive} \\ \text{property.}\end{array}$$

$$3(x + 10) \cdot 100 + 3x \cdot 100 = x(x + 10) \cdot 11$$

$$300x + 3000 + 300x = 11x^2 + 110x$$

$$0 = 11x^2 - 490x - 3000 \qquad \begin{array}{l}\text{Set equation} \\ \text{equal to 0.}\end{array}$$

$$0 = (11x + 60)(x - 50) \qquad \text{Factor.}$$

$$11x + 60 = 0 \quad \text{or} \quad x - 50 = 0 \qquad \begin{array}{l}\text{Set each factor} \\ \text{equal to 0.}\end{array}$$

$$x = -\frac{60}{11} \text{ or } -5\frac{5}{11}; \quad x = 50$$

4. INTERPRET.

Check: The speed is not negative, so it's not $-5\dfrac{5}{11}$. The number 50 does check.

State: The speed to Beach was 50 mph, and her return speed to Fargo was 60 mph. □

PRACTICE

7 The 36-km S-shaped Hangzhou Bay Bridge is the longest cross-sea bridge in the world, linking Ningbo and Shanghai, China. A merchant drives over the bridge one morning from Ningbo to Shanghai in very heavy traffic and returns home that night driving 50 km per hour faster. The total travel time was 1.3 hours. Find the speed to Shanghai and the return speed to Ningbo. ■

✔ **Vocabulary, Readiness & Video Check**

Martin-Gay Interactive Videos

See Video 8.3 ⊚

Watch the section lecture video and answer the following questions.

OBJECTIVE
1

1. From Examples 1 and 2, what's the main thing to remember when using a substitution in order to solve an equation by quadratic methods?

OBJECTIVE
2

2. In ▦ Example 4, the translated equation is actually a rational equation. Explain how we end up solving it using quadratic methods.

8.3 **Exercise Set** MyMathLab® ▶

Solve. See Example 1.

1. $2x = \sqrt{10 + 3x}$

2. $3x = \sqrt{8x + 1}$

3. $x - 2\sqrt{x} = 8$

4. $x - \sqrt{2x} = 4$

5. $\sqrt{9x} = x + 2$

6. $\sqrt{16x} = x + 3$

Solve. See Example 2.

⊚ **7.** $\dfrac{2}{x} + \dfrac{3}{x - 1} = 1$

8. $\dfrac{6}{x^2} = \dfrac{3}{x + 1}$

9. $\dfrac{3}{x} + \dfrac{4}{x + 2} = 2$

10. $\dfrac{5}{x - 2} + \dfrac{4}{x + 2} = 1$

11. $\dfrac{7}{x^2 - 5x + 6} = \dfrac{2x}{x - 3} - \dfrac{x}{x - 2}$

12. $\dfrac{11}{2x^2 + x - 15} = \dfrac{5}{2x - 5} - \dfrac{x}{x + 3}$

Solve. See Example 3.

13. $p^4 - 16 = 0$

14. $x^4 + 2x^2 - 3 = 0$

15. $4x^4 + 11x^2 = 3$

16. $z^4 = 81$

17. $z^4 - 13z^2 + 36 = 0$

18. $9x^4 + 5x^2 - 4 = 0$

Solve. See Examples 4 and 5.

⊚ **19.** $x^{2/3} - 3x^{1/3} - 10 = 0$

20. $x^{2/3} + 2x^{1/3} + 1 = 0$

21. $(5n + 1)^2 + 2(5n + 1) - 3 = 0$

22. $(m - 6)^2 + 5(m - 6) + 4 = 0$

23. $2x^{2/3} - 5x^{1/3} = 3$

24. $3x^{2/3} + 11x^{1/3} = 4$

25. $1 + \dfrac{2}{3t - 2} = \dfrac{8}{(3t - 2)^2}$

26. $2 - \dfrac{7}{x + 6} = \dfrac{15}{(x + 6)^2}$

27. $20x^{2/3} - 6x^{1/3} - 2 = 0$

28. $4x^{2/3} + 16x^{1/3} = -15$

MIXED PRACTICE

Solve. See Examples 1 through 5.

29. $a^4 - 5a^2 + 6 = 0$

30. $x^4 - 12x^2 + 11 = 0$

31. $\dfrac{2x}{x - 2} + \dfrac{x}{x + 3} = -\dfrac{5}{x + 3}$

32. $\dfrac{5}{x - 3} + \dfrac{x}{x + 3} = \dfrac{19}{x^2 - 9}$

⊚ **33.** $(p + 2)^2 = 9(p + 2) - 20$

34. $2(4m - 3)^2 - 9(4m - 3) = 5$

35. $2x = \sqrt{11x + 3}$

36. $4x = \sqrt{2x + 3}$

37. $x^{2/3} - 8x^{1/3} + 15 = 0$

38. $x^{2/3} - 2x^{1/3} - 8 = 0$

39. $y^3 + 9y - y^2 - 9 = 0$

40. $x^3 + x - 3x^2 - 3 = 0$

41. $2x^{2/3} + 3x^{1/3} - 2 = 0$

42. $6x^{2/3} - 25x^{1/3} - 25 = 0$

43. $x^{-2} - x^{-1} - 6 = 0$

44. $y^{-2} - 8y^{-1} + 7 = 0$

45. $x - \sqrt{x} = 2$

46. $x - \sqrt{3x} = 6$

47. $\dfrac{x}{x-1} + \dfrac{1}{x+1} = \dfrac{2}{x^2-1}$

48. $\dfrac{x}{x-5} + \dfrac{5}{x+5} = -\dfrac{1}{x^2-25}$

49. $p^4 - p^2 - 20 = 0$

50. $x^4 - 10x^2 + 9 = 0$

51. $(x+3)(x^2 - 3x + 9) = 0$

52. $(x-6)(x^2 + 6x + 36) = 0$

53. $1 = \dfrac{4}{x-7} + \dfrac{5}{(x-7)^2}$

54. $3 + \dfrac{1}{2p+4} = \dfrac{10}{(2p+4)^2}$

55. $27y^4 + 15y^2 = 2$

56. $8z^4 + 14z^2 = -5$

57. $x - \sqrt{19 - 2x} - 2 = 0$

58. $x - \sqrt{17 - 4x} - 3 = 0$

Solve. For Exercises 59 and 60, the solutions have been started for you. See Examples 6 and 7.

59. Roma Sherry drove 330 miles from her hometown to Tucson. During her return trip, she was able to increase her speed by 11 miles per hour. If her return trip took 1 hour less time, find her original speed and her speed returning home.

Start the solution:

1. UNDERSTAND the problem. Reread it as many times as needed. Let

$$x = \text{original speed, and}$$
$$x + 11 = \text{return-trip speed.}$$

Organize the information in a table.

	distance =	rate ·	time	
To Tucson	330	x	$\dfrac{330}{x}$	← distance ← rate
Return trip	330	___	___	← distance ← rate

2. TRANSLATE into an equation. (Fill in the blanks below.)

time to Tucson	equals	return trip time	plus	1 hour
↓	↓	↓	↓	↓
___	=	___	+	1

Finish with:

3. SOLVE and **4.** INTERPRET

60. A salesperson drove to Portland, a distance of 300 miles. During the last 80 miles of his trip, heavy rainfall forced him to decrease his speed by 15 miles per hour. If his total driving time was 6 hours, find his original speed and his speed during the rainfall.

Start the solution:

1. UNDERSTAND the problem. Reread it as many times as needed. Let

$$x = \text{original speed, and}$$
$$x - 15 = \text{rainfall speed.}$$

Organize the information in a table.

	distance =	rate ·	time	
First part of trip	300 − 80, or 220	x	$\dfrac{220}{x}$	← distance ← rate
Heavy rainfall part of trip	80	$x - 15$	$\dfrac{80}{}$	← distance ← rate

2. TRANSLATE into an equation. (Fill in the blanks below.)

time during first part of trip	plus	time during heavy rainfall	equals	6 hr
↓	↓	↓	↓	↓
___	+	___	=	6

Finish with:

3. SOLVE and **4.** INTERPRET

61. A jogger ran 3 miles, decreased her speed by 1 mile per hour, and then ran another 4 miles. If her total time jogging was $1\dfrac{3}{5}$ hours, find her speed for each part of her run.

62. Mark Keaton's workout consists of jogging for 3 miles and then riding his bike for 5 miles at a speed 4 miles per hour faster than he jogs. If his total workout time is 1 hour, find his jogging speed and his biking speed.

63. A Chinese restaurant in Mandeville, Louisiana, has a large goldfish pond around the restaurant. Suppose that an inlet pipe and a hose together can fill the pond in 8 hours. The inlet pipe alone can complete the job in one hour less time than the hose alone. Find the time that the hose can complete the job alone and the time that the inlet pipe can complete the job alone. Round each to the nearest tenth of an hour.

64. A water tank on a farm in Flatonia, Texas, can be filled with a large inlet pipe and a small inlet pipe in 3 hours. The large inlet pipe alone can fill the tank in 2 hours less time than the small inlet pipe alone. Find the time to the nearest tenth of an hour each pipe can fill the tank alone.

65. Bill Shaughnessy and his son Billy can clean the house together in 4 hours. When the son works alone, it takes him an hour longer to clean than it takes his dad alone. Find how long to the nearest tenth of an hour it takes the son to clean alone.

66. Together, Noodles and Freckles eat a 50-pound bag of dog food in 30 days. Noodles by himself eats a 50-pound bag in 2 weeks less time than Freckles does by himself. How many days to the nearest whole day would a 50-pound bag of dog food last Freckles?

67. The product of a number and 4 less than the number is 96. Find the number.

68. A whole number increased by its square is two more than twice itself. Find the number.

△ **69.** Suppose that an open box is to be made from a square sheet of cardboard by cutting out squares from each corner as shown and then folding along the dotted lines. If the box is to have a volume of 300 cubic inches, find the original dimensions of the sheet of cardboard.

a. The ? in the drawing above will be the length (and the width) of the box as shown. Represent this length in terms of x.

b. Use the formula for volume of a box, $V = l \cdot w \cdot h$, to write an equation in x.

c. Solve the equation for x and give the dimensions of the sheet of cardboard. Check your solution.

△ **70.** Suppose that an open box is to be made from a square sheet of cardboard by cutting out squares from each corner as shown and then folding along the dotted lines. If the box is to have a volume of 128 cubic inches, find the original dimensions of the sheet of cardboard.

a. The ? in the drawing above will be the length (and the width) of the box as shown. Represent this length in terms of x.

b. Use the formula for volume of a box, $V = l \cdot w \cdot h$, to write an equation in x.

c. Solve the equation for x and give the dimensions of the sheet of cardboard. Check your solution.

△ **71.** A sprinkler that sprays water in a circular pattern is to be used to water a square garden. If the area of the garden is 920 square feet, find the smallest whole number *radius* that the sprinkler can be adjusted to so that the entire garden is watered.

△ **72.** Suppose that a square field has an area of 6270 square feet. See Exercise 71 and find the sprinkler radius.

REVIEW AND PREVIEW

Solve each inequality. See Section 2.4.

73. $\dfrac{5x}{3} + 2 \le 7$ **74.** $\dfrac{2x}{3} + \dfrac{1}{6} \ge 2$

75. $\dfrac{y-1}{15} > -\dfrac{2}{5}$ **76.** $\dfrac{z-2}{12} < \dfrac{1}{4}$

Find the domain and range of each graphed relation. Decide which relations are also functions. See Section 3.2.

77.

78.

79.

80.

CONCEPT EXTENSIONS

Solve.

81. $5y^3 + 45y - 5y^2 - 45 = 0$

82. $10x^3 + 10x - 30x^2 - 30 = 0$

83. $3x^{-2} - 3x^{-1} - 18 = 0$

84. $2y^{-2} - 16y^{-1} + 14 = 0$

85. $2x^3 = -54$

86. $y^3 - 216 = 0$

87. Write a polynomial equation that has three solutions: 2, 5, and −7.

88. Write a polynomial equation that has three solutions: 0, $2i$, and $-2i$.

89. In 2015, the Daytona 500 race was extended to 203 laps, which increased the race distance to 507.5 miles. Dale Earnhardt Jr. won the 2014 Daytona 500 race but came in third in the 2015 race. Joey Logano, who won the 2015 race, completed the 203-lap race in 3 hours, 5 minutes, and 15 seconds. Logano's average speed for the race was 1.193 seconds per lap faster than that of Earnhardt. (Source: Nascar)

   a. Find Joey Logano's average race speed (miles per hour) for the 2015 Daytona 500. Round to the nearest hundredth.

   b. Find Joey Logano's average lap time (seconds per lap) for the 2015 Daytona 500. Round to the nearest thousandth.

   c. Find Dale Earnhart Jr.'s average lap time.

   d. Find Dale Earnhardt Jr.'s average race speed (miles per hour).

90. Use a graphing calculator to solve Exercise 29. Compare the solution with the solution from Exercise 29. Explain any differences.

| Integrated Review | Summary on Solving Quadratic Equations |

Sections 8.1–8.3

Use the square root property to solve each equation.

1. $x^2 - 10 = 0$

2. $x^2 - 14 = 0$

3. $(x - 1)^2 = 8$

4. $(x + 5)^2 = 12$

Solve each equation by completing the square.

5. $x^2 + 2x - 12 = 0$

6. $x^2 - 12x + 11 = 0$

7. $3x^2 + 3x = 5$

8. $16y^2 + 16y = 1$

Use the quadratic formula to solve each equation

9. $2x^2 - 4x + 1 = 0$

10. $\frac{1}{2}x^2 + 3x + 2 = 0$

11. $x^2 + 4x = -7$

12. $x^2 + x = -3$

Solve each equation. Use a method of your choice.

13. $x^2 + 3x + 6 = 0$

14. $2x^2 + 18 = 0$

15. $x^2 + 17x = 0$

16. $4x^2 - 2x - 3 = 0$

17. $(x - 2)^2 = 27$

18. $\frac{1}{2}x^2 - 2x + \frac{1}{2} = 0$

19. $3x^2 + 2x = 8$

20. $2x^2 = -5x - 1$

21. $x(x - 2) = 5$

22. $x^2 - 31 = 0$

23. $5x^2 - 55 = 0$

24. $5x^2 + 55 = 0$

25. $x(x + 5) = 66$

26. $5x^2 + 6x - 2 = 0$

27. $2x^2 + 3x = 1$

28. $x - \sqrt{13 - 3x} - 3 = 0$

29. $\dfrac{5x}{x - 2} - \dfrac{x + 1}{x} = \dfrac{3}{x(x - 2)}$

Solve.

△ **30.** The diagonal of a square room measures 20 feet. Find the exact length of a side of the room. Then approximate the length to the nearest tenth of a foot.

31. Together, Jack and Lucy Hoag can prepare a crawfish boil for a large party in 4 hours. Lucy alone can complete the job in 2 hours less time than Jack alone. Find the time that each person can prepare the crawfish boil alone. Round each time to the nearest tenth of an hour.

32. Diane Gray exercises at Total Body Gym. On the treadmill, she runs 5 miles, then increases her speed by 1 mile per hour and runs an additional 2 miles. If her total time on the treadmill is $1\frac{1}{3}$ hours, find her speed during each part of her run.

8.4 Nonlinear Inequalities in One Variable

OBJECTIVES

1 Solve Polynomial Inequalities of Degree 2 or Greater.

2 Solve Inequalities That Contain Rational Expressions with Variables in the Denominator.

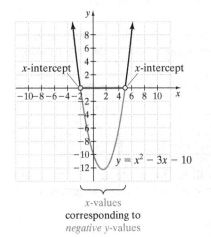

x-values corresponding to *negative y*-values

Helpful Hint

The related equation is found by replacing the inequality symbol with "=".

OBJECTIVE

1 Solving Polynomial Inequalities

Just as we can solve linear inequalities in one variable, so can we also solve quadratic inequalities in one variable. A **quadratic inequality** is an inequality that can be written so that one side is a quadratic expression and the other side is 0. Here are examples of quadratic inequalities in one variable. Each is written in **standard form**.

$$x^2 - 10x + 7 \le 0 \qquad 3x^2 + 2x - 6 > 0$$
$$2x^2 + 9x - 2 < 0 \qquad x^2 - 3x + 11 \ge 0$$

A solution of a quadratic inequality in one variable is a value of the variable that makes the inequality a true statement.

The value of an expression such as $x^2 - 3x - 10$ will sometimes be positive, sometimes negative, and sometimes 0, depending on the value substituted for x. To solve the inequality $x^2 - 3x - 10 < 0$, we are looking for all values of x that make the expression $x^2 - 3x - 10$ **less than 0**, or **negative.** To understand how we find these values, we'll study the graph of the quadratic function $y = x^2 - 3x - 10$.

Notice that the x-values for which y is positive are separated from the x values for which y is negative by the x-intercepts. (Recall that the x-intercepts correspond to values of x for which $y = 0$.) Thus, the solution set of $x^2 - 3x - 10 < 0$ consists of all real numbers from -2 to 5 or, in interval notation, $(-2, 5)$.

It is not necessary to graph $y = x^2 - 3x - 10$ to solve the related inequality $x^2 - 3x - 10 < 0$. Instead, we can draw a number line representing the x-axis and keep the following in mind: *A region on the number line for which the value of* $x^2 - 3x - 10$ *is positive is separated from a region on the number line for which the value of* $x^2 - 3x - 10$ *is negative by a value for which the expression is 0.*

Let's find these values for which the expression is 0 by solving the related equation:

$$x^2 - 3x - 10 = 0$$
$$(x - 5)(x + 2) = 0 \qquad \text{Factor.}$$
$$x - 5 = 0 \quad \text{or} \quad x + 2 = 0 \qquad \text{Set each factor equal to 0.}$$
$$x = 5 \qquad\qquad x = -2 \qquad \text{Solve.}$$

These two numbers, -2 and 5, divide the number line into three regions. We will call the regions A, B, and C. These regions are important because, if the value of $x^2 - 3x - 10$ is negative when a number from a region is substituted for x, then $x^2 - 3x - 10$ is negative when any number in that region is substituted for x. The same is true if the value of $x^2 - 3x - 10$ is positive for a particular value of x in a region.

To see whether the inequality $x^2 - 3x - 10 < 0$ is true or false in each region, we choose a test point from each region and substitute its value for x in the inequality $x^2 - 3x - 10 < 0$. If the resulting inequality is true, the region containing the test point is a solution region.

Region	Test Point Value	$(x - 5)(x + 2) < 0$	Result
A	-3	$(-8)(-1) < 0$	False
B	0	$(-5)(2) < 0$	True
C	6	$(1)(8) < 0$	False

The values in region B satisfy the inequality. The numbers -2 and 5 are not included in the solution set since the inequality symbol is $<$. The solution set is $(-2, 5)$, and its graph is shown.

$$\begin{array}{ccccc} & A & B & C & \\ & & & & \\ \text{F} & -2 & \text{T} & 5 & \text{F} \end{array}$$

EXAMPLE 1   Solve: $(x + 3)(x - 3) > 0$

Solution First we solve the related equation, $(x + 3)(x - 3) = 0$.

$$(x + 3)(x - 3) = 0$$
$$x + 3 = 0 \quad \text{or} \quad x - 3 = 0$$
$$x = -3 \qquad\qquad x = 3$$

> **Helpful Hint**
>
> Inequality: $(x + 3)(x - 3) > 0$
> Related equation:
> $(x + 3)(x - 3) = 0$

The two numbers -3 and 3 separate the number line into three regions, A, B, and C.

$$\begin{array}{ccc} A & B & C \\ & & \\ -3 & & 3 \end{array}$$

Now we substitute the value of a test point from each region. If the test value satisfies the inequality, every value in the region containing the test value is a solution.

Region	Test Point Value	$(x + 3)(x - 3) > 0$	Result
A	-4	$(-1)(-7) > 0$	True
B	0	$(3)(-3) > 0$	False
C	4	$(7)(1) > 0$	True

The points in regions A and C satisfy the inequality. The numbers -3 and 3 are not included in the solution since the inequality symbol is $>$. The solution set is $(-\infty, -3) \cup (3, \infty)$, and its graph is shown.

$$\begin{array}{ccccc} & A & B & C & \\ & & & & \\ \text{T} & -3 & \text{F} & 3 & \text{T} \end{array}$$

PRACTICE

1   Solve: $(x - 4)(x + 3) > 0$

The following steps may be used to solve a polynomial inequality.

> **Solving a Polynomial Inequality**
>
> **Step 1.** Solve the related equation.
>
> **Step 2.** Separate the number line into regions with the solutions from Step 1.
>
> **Step 3.** For each region, choose a test point and determine whether its value satisfies the *original inequality*.
>
> **Step 4.** The solution set includes the regions whose test point value is a solution. If the inequality symbol is $\leq$ or $\geq$, the values from Step 1 are solutions; if $<$ or $>$, they are not.

✔ **CONCEPT CHECK**

When choosing a test point in Step 3, why would the solutions from Step 2 not make good choices for test points?

EXAMPLE 2   Solve: $x^2 - 4x \leq 0$

Solution First we solve the related equation, $x^2 - 4x = 0$.

$$x^2 - 4x = 0$$
$$x(x - 4) = 0$$
$$x = 0 \quad \text{or} \quad x = 4$$

The numbers 0 and 4 separate the number line into three regions, A, B, and C.

We check a test value in each region in the original inequality. Values in region B satisfy the inequality. The numbers 0 and 4 are included in the solution since the inequality symbol is $\leq$. The solution set is $[0, 4]$, and its graph is shown.

PRACTICE

2 Solve: $x^2 - 8x \leq 0$

EXAMPLE 3   Solve: $(x + 2)(x - 1)(x - 5) \leq 0$

Solution First we solve $(x + 2)(x - 1)(x - 5) = 0$. By inspection, we see that the solutions are -2, 1, and 5. They separate the number line into four regions, A, B, C, and D. Next we check test points from each region.

Region	Test Point Value	$(x + 2)(x - 1)(x - 5) \leq 0$	Result
A	-3	$(-1)(-4)(-8) \leq 0$	True
B	0	$(2)(-1)(-5) \leq 0$	False
C	2	$(4)(1)(-3) \leq 0$	True
D	6	$(8)(5)(1) \leq 0$	False

Answer to Concept Check:
The solutions found in Step 2 have a value of 0 in the original inequality.

(Continued on next page)

The solution set is $(-\infty, -2] \cup [1, 5]$, and its graph is shown. We include the numbers -2, 1, and 5 because the inequality symbol is $\leq$.

$$
\begin{array}{c}
\quad A \quad\quad B \quad C \quad\quad D \\
\xleftarrow{\qquad\underset{\text{T } -2 \text{ F } 1 \text{ T } 5 \text{ F}}{\rule{0pt}{0pt}}\qquad} \\
\end{array}
$$

□

PRACTICE
3 Solve: $(x + 3)(x - 2)(x + 1) \leq 0$

■

OBJECTIVE

2 Solving Rational Inequalities

Inequalities containing rational expressions with variables in the denominator are solved by using a similar procedure.

EXAMPLE 4 Solve: $\dfrac{x + 2}{x - 3} \leq 0$

Solution First we find all values that make the denominator equal to 0. To do this, we solve $x - 3 = 0$ and find that $x = 3$.

Next, we solve the related equation $\dfrac{x + 2}{x - 3} = 0$.

$$\frac{x + 2}{x - 3} = 0$$

$$x + 2 = 0 \qquad \text{Multiply both sides by the LCD, } x - 3.$$

$$x = -2$$

Now we place these numbers on a number line and proceed as before, checking test point values in the original inequality.

$$
\begin{array}{c}
\quad A \quad\quad B \quad\quad C \\
\xleftarrow{\qquad\underset{-2 \qquad\quad 3}{\rule{0pt}{0pt}}\qquad} \\
\end{array}
$$

Choose -3 from region A.

$$\frac{x + 2}{x - 3} \leq 0$$

$$\frac{-3 + 2}{-3 - 3} \leq 0$$

$$\frac{-1}{-6} \leq 0$$

$$\frac{1}{6} \leq 0 \quad \text{False}$$

Choose 0 from region B.

$$\frac{x + 2}{x - 3} \leq 0$$

$$\frac{0 + 2}{0 - 3} \leq 0$$

$$-\frac{2}{3} \leq 0 \quad \text{True}$$

Choose 4 from region C.

$$\frac{x + 2}{x - 3} \leq 0$$

$$\frac{4 + 2}{4 - 3} \leq 0$$

$$6 \leq 0 \quad \text{False}$$

The solution set is $[-2, 3)$. This interval includes -2 because -2 satisfies the original inequality. This interval does not include 3 because 3 would make the denominator 0.

$$
\begin{array}{c}
\quad A \quad\quad B \quad\quad C \\
\xleftarrow{\qquad\underset{\text{F } -2 \text{ T } 3 \text{ F}}{\rule{0pt}{0pt}}\qquad} \\
\end{array}
$$

□

PRACTICE
4 Solve: $\dfrac{x - 5}{x + 4} \leq 0$

■

The following steps may be used to solve a rational inequality with variables in the denominator.

Solving a Rational Inequality

Step 1. Solve for values that make all denominators 0.

Step 2. Solve the related equation.

Step 3. Separate the number line into regions with the solutions from Steps 1 and 2.

Step 4. For each region, choose a test point and determine whether its value satisfies the *original inequality*.

Step 5. The solution set includes the regions whose test point value is a solution. Check whether to include values from Step 2. Be sure *not* to include values that make any denominator 0.

EXAMPLE 5   Solve: $\dfrac{5}{x+1} < -2$

Solution First we find values for x that make the denominator equal to 0.

$$x + 1 = 0$$
$$x = -1$$

Next we solve $\dfrac{5}{x+1} = -2$.

$$(x+1) \cdot \frac{5}{x+1} = (x+1) \cdot -2 \quad \text{Multiply both sides by the LCD, } x+1.$$
$$5 = -2x - 2 \qquad \text{Simplify.}$$
$$7 = -2x$$
$$-\frac{7}{2} = x$$

We use these two solutions to divide a number line into three regions and choose test points. Only a test point value from region B satisfies the *original inequality*. The solution set is $\left(-\dfrac{7}{2}, -1 \right)$, and its graph is shown.

PRACTICE
5   Solve: $\dfrac{7}{x+3} < 5$

Vocabulary, Readiness & Video Check

Write the graphed solution set in interval notation.

1.

_____

2.

_____

3.

_____

4.

_____

5.

_____

6.

_____

Martin-Gay Interactive Videos

See Video 8.4 🌀

Watch the section lecture video and answer the following questions.

OBJECTIVE
1

7. From ▦ Examples 1–3, how does solving a related equation help you solve a polynomial inequality? Are the solutions to the related equation ever solutions to the inequality?

OBJECTIVE
2

8. In ▦ Example 4, one of the values that separates the number line into regions is 4. The inequality is ≥, so why isn't 4 included in the solution set?

8.4 Exercise Set MyMathLab® ▶

Solve each polynomial inequality. Write the solution set in interval notation. See Examples 1 through 3.

1. $(x + 1)(x + 5) > 0$

2. $(x + 1)(x + 5) \le 0$

▶ **3.** $(x - 3)(x + 4) \le 0$

4. $(x + 4)(x - 1) > 0$

5. $x^2 - 7x + 10 \le 0$

6. $x^2 + 8x + 15 \ge 0$

7. $3x^2 + 16x < -5$

8. $2x^2 - 5x < 7$

9. $(x - 6)(x - 4)(x - 2) > 0$

10. $(x - 6)(x - 4)(x - 2) \le 0$

11. $x(x - 1)(x + 4) \le 0$

12. $x(x - 6)(x + 2) > 0$

13. $(x^2 - 9)(x^2 - 4) > 0$

14. $(x^2 - 16)(x^2 - 1) \le 0$

Solve each inequality. Write the solution set in interval notation. See Example 4.

15. $\dfrac{x + 7}{x - 2} < 0$

16. $\dfrac{x - 5}{x - 6} > 0$

17. $\dfrac{5}{x + 1} > 0$

18. $\dfrac{3}{y - 5} < 0$

▶ **19.** $\dfrac{x + 1}{x - 4} \ge 0$

20. $\dfrac{x + 1}{x - 4} \le 0$

Solve each inequality. Write the solution set in interval notation. See Example 5.

21. $\dfrac{3}{x - 2} < 4$

22. $\dfrac{-2}{y + 3} > 2$

23. $\dfrac{x^2 + 6}{5x} \ge 1$

24. $\dfrac{y^2 + 15}{8y} \le 1$

25. $\dfrac{x + 2}{x - 3} < 1$

26. $\dfrac{x - 1}{x + 4} > 2$

MIXED PRACTICE

Solve each inequality. Write the solution set in interval notation.

27. $(2x - 3)(4x + 5) \le 0$

28. $(6x + 7)(7x - 12) > 0$

▶ **29.** $x^2 > x$

30. $x^2 < 25$

31. $(2x - 8)(x + 4)(x - 6) \le 0$

32. $(3x - 12)(x + 5)(2x - 3) \ge 0$

33. $6x^2 - 5x \ge 6$

34. $12x^2 + 11x \le 15$

35. $4x^3 + 16x^2 - 9x - 36 > 0$

36. $x^3 + 2x^2 - 4x - 8 < 0$

▶ **37.** $x^4 - 26x^2 + 25 \ge 0$

38. $16x^4 - 40x^2 + 9 \le 0$

39. $(2x - 7)(3x + 5) > 0$

40. $(4x - 9)(2x + 5) < 0$

41. $\dfrac{x}{x - 10} < 0$

42. $\dfrac{x + 10}{x - 10} > 0$

43. $\dfrac{x - 5}{x + 4} \geq 0$

44. $\dfrac{x - 3}{x + 2} \leq 0$

45. $\dfrac{x(x + 6)}{(x - 7)(x + 1)} \geq 0$

46. $\dfrac{(x - 2)(x + 2)}{(x + 1)(x - 4)} \leq 0$

47. $\dfrac{-1}{x - 1} > -1$

48. $\dfrac{4}{y + 2} < -2$

49. $\dfrac{x}{x + 4} \leq 2$

50. $\dfrac{4x}{x - 3} \geq 5$

51. $\dfrac{z}{z - 5} \geq 2z$

52. $\dfrac{p}{p + 4} \leq 3p$

53. $\dfrac{(x + 1)^2}{5x} > 0$

54. $\dfrac{(2x - 3)^2}{x} < 0$

REVIEW AND PREVIEW

Recall that the graph of $f(x) + K$ is the same as the graph of $f(x)$ shifted K units upward if $K > 0$ and $|K|$ units downward if $K < 0$. Use the graph of $f(x) = |x|$ below to sketch the graph of each function. See Section 3.6.

55. $g(x) = |x| + 2$

56. $H(x) = |x| - 2$

57. $G(x) = |x| - 1$

58. $h(x) = |x| + 5$

Use the graph of $f(x) = x^2$ below to sketch the graph of each function.

59. $F(x) = x^2 - 3$

60. $h(x) = x^2 - 4$

61. $H(x) = x^2 + 1$

62. $g(x) = x^2 + 3$

CONCEPT EXTENSIONS

63. Explain why $\dfrac{x + 2}{x - 3} > 0$ and $(x + 2)(x - 3) > 0$ have the same solutions.

64. Explain why $\dfrac{x + 2}{x - 3} \geq 0$ and $(x + 2)(x - 3) \geq 0$ do not have the same solutions.

Find all numbers that satisfy each of the following.

65. A number minus its reciprocal is less than zero. Find the numbers.

66. Twice a number added to its reciprocal is nonnegative. Find the numbers.

67. The total profit function $P(x)$ for a company producing x thousand units is given by

$$P(x) = -2x^2 + 26x - 44$$

Find the values of x for which the company makes a profit. (*Hint:* The company makes a profit when $P(x) > 0$.)

68. A projectile is fired straight up from the ground with an initial velocity of 80 feet per second. Its height $s(t)$ in feet at any time t is given by the function

$$s(t) = -16t^2 + 80t$$

Find the interval of time for which the height of the projectile is greater than 96 feet.

Use a graphing calculator to check each exercise.

69. Exercise 37

70. Exercise 38

71. Exercise 39

72. Exercise 40

8.5 Quadratic Functions and Their Graphs

OBJECTIVE

1 Graphing $f(x) = x^2 + k$

We first graphed the quadratic equation $y = x^2$ in Section 3.1. In Section 3.2, we learned that this graph defines a function, and we wrote $y = x^2$ as $f(x) = x^2$. In those sections, we discovered that the graph of a quadratic function is a parabola opening upward or downward. In this section, we continue our study of quadratic functions and their graphs. (Much of the contents of this section is a review of shifting and reflecting techniques from Section 3.6, but specific to quadratic functions.)

First, let's recall the definition of a quadratic function.

> **Quadratic Function**
>
> A quadratic function is a function that can be written in the form $f(x) = ax^2 + bx + c$, where a, b, and c are real numbers and $a \neq 0$.

Notice that equations of the form $y = ax^2 + bx + c$, where $a \neq 0$, define quadratic functions, since y is a function of x or $y = f(x)$.

Recall that if $a > 0$, the parabola opens upward and if $a < 0$, the parabola opens downward. Also, the vertex of a parabola is the lowest point if the parabola opens upward and the highest point if the parabola opens downward. The axis of symmetry is the vertical line that passes through the vertex.

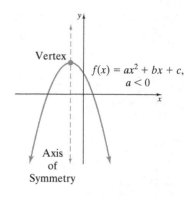

EXAMPLE 1 Graph $f(x) = x^2$ and $g(x) = x^2 + 6$ on the same set of axes.

Solution First we construct a table of values for $f(x)$ and plot the points. Notice that for each x-value, the corresponding value of $g(x)$ must be 6 more than the corresponding value of $f(x)$ since $f(x) = x^2$ and $g(x) = x^2 + 6$. In other words, the graph of $g(x) = x^2 + 6$ is the same as the graph of $f(x) = x^2$ shifted upward 6 units. The axis of symmetry for both graphs is the y-axis.

x	$f(x) = x^2$	$g(x) = x^2 + 6$
-2	4	10
-1	1	7
0	0	6
1	1	7
2	4	10

Each y-value is increased by 6.

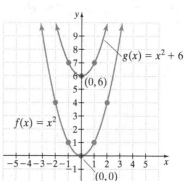

PRACTICE

1 Graph $f(x) = x^2$ and $g(x) = x^2 - 4$ on the same set of axes.

In general, we have the following properties.

Graphing the Parabola Defined by $f(x) = x^2 + k$

If k is positive, the graph of $f(x) = x^2 + k$ is the graph of $y = x^2$ shifted upward k units.

If k is negative, the graph of $f(x) = x^2 + k$ is the graph of $y = x^2$ shifted downward $|k|$ units.

The vertex is $(0, k)$, and the axis of symmetry is the y-axis.

EXAMPLE 2   Graph each function.

    a. $F(x) = x^2 + 2$ **b.** $g(x) = x^2 - 3$

Solution

a. $F(x) = x^2 + 2$

The graph of $F(x) = x^2 + 2$ is obtained by shifting the graph of $y = x^2$ upward 2 units.

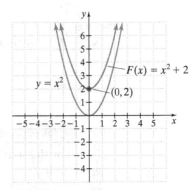

b. $g(x) = x^2 - 3$

The graph of $g(x) = x^2 - 3$ is obtained by shifting the graph of $y = x^2$ downward 3 units.

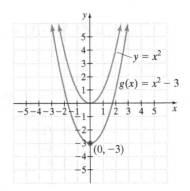

PRACTICE

2   Graph each function.

    a. $f(x) = x^2 - 5$ **b.** $g(x) = x^2 + 3$

OBJECTIVE

2   Graphing $f(x) = (x - h)^2$

Now we will graph functions of the form $f(x) = (x - h)^2$.

EXAMPLE 3   Graph $f(x) = x^2$ and $g(x) = (x - 2)^2$ on the same set of axes.

Solution By plotting points, we see that for each x-value, the corresponding value of $g(x)$ is the same as the value of $f(x)$ when the x-value is increased by 2. Thus, the graph of $g(x) = (x - 2)^2$ is the graph of $f(x) = x^2$ shifted to the right 2 units. The axis of symmetry for the graph of $g(x) = (x - 2)^2$ is also shifted 2 units to the right and is the line $x = 2$.

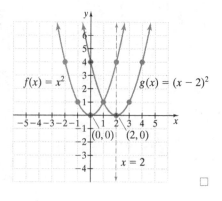

x	$f(x) = x^2$	x	$g(x) = (x - 2)^2$
−2	4	0	4
−1	1	1	1
0	0	2	0
1	1	3	1
2	4	4	4

Each x-value increased by 2 corresponds to same y-value.

PRACTICE
3   Graph $f(x) = x^2$ and $g(x) = (x + 6)^2$ on the same set of axes.

In general, we have the following properties.

Graphing the Parabola Defined by $f(x) = (x - h)^2$

If h is positive, the graph of $f(x) = (x - h)^2$ is the graph of $y = x^2$ shifted to the right h units.
If h is negative, the graph of $f(x) = (x - h)^2$ is the graph of $y = x^2$ shifted to the left $|h|$ units.
The vertex is $(h, 0)$, and the axis of symmetry is the vertical line $x = h$.

EXAMPLE 4   Graph each function.

a. $G(x) = (x - 3)^2$ **b.** $F(x) = (x + 1)^2$

Solution

a. The graph of $G(x) = (x - 3)^2$ is obtained by shifting the graph of $y = x^2$ to the right 3 units. The graph of $G(x)$ is below on the left.

b. The equation $F(x) = (x + 1)^2$ can be written as $F(x) = [x - (-1)]^2$. The graph of $F(x) = [x - (-1)]^2$ is obtained by shifting the graph of $y = x^2$ to the left 1 unit. The graph of $F(x)$ is below on the right.

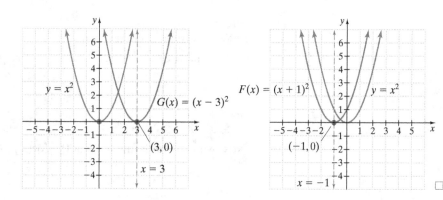

PRACTICE
4   Graph each function.
 a. $G(x) = (x + 4)^2$ **b.** $H(x) = (x - 7)^2$

OBJECTIVE
3   Graphing $f(x) = (x - h)^2 + k$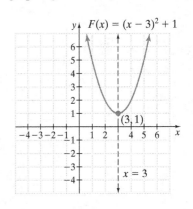

As we will see in graphing functions of the form $f(x) = (x - h)^2 + k$, it is possible to combine vertical and horizontal shifts.

> **Graphing the Parabola Defined by $f(x) = (x - h)^2 + k$**
>
> The parabola has the same shape as $y = x^2$.
> The vertex is (h, k), and the axis of symmetry is the vertical line $x = h$.

EXAMPLE 5   Graph: $F(x) = (x - 3)^2 + 1$

Solution The graph of $F(x) = (x - 3)^2 + 1$ is the graph of $y = x^2$ shifted 3 units to the right and 1 unit up. The vertex is then $(3, 1)$, and the axis of symmetry is $x = 3$. A few ordered pair solutions are plotted to aid in graphing.

x	$F(x) = (x - 3)^2 + 1$
1	5
2	2
4	2
5	5

PRACTICE
5   Graph: $f(x) = (x + 2)^2 + 2$

OBJECTIVE
4   Graphing $f(x) = ax^2$

Next, we discover the change in the shape of the graph when the coefficient of x^2 is not 1.

EXAMPLE 6   Graph $f(x) = x^2$, $g(x) = 3x^2$, and $h(x) = \frac{1}{2}x^2$ on the same set of axes.

Solution Comparing the tables of values, we see that for each x-value, the corresponding value of $g(x)$ is triple the corresponding value of $f(x)$. Similarly, the value of $h(x)$ is half the value of $f(x)$.

x	$f(x) = x^2$
-2	4
-1	1
0	0
1	1
2	4

x	$g(x) = 3x^2$
-2	12
-1	3
0	0
1	3
2	12

x	$h(x) = \frac{1}{2}x^2$
-2	2
-1	$\frac{1}{2}$
0	0
1	$\frac{1}{2}$
2	2

(Continued on next page)

The result is that the graph of $g(x) = 3x^2$ is narrower than the graph of $f(x) = x^2$, and the graph of $h(x) = \frac{1}{2}x^2$ is wider. The vertex for each graph is $(0, 0)$, and the axis of symmetry is the y-axis.

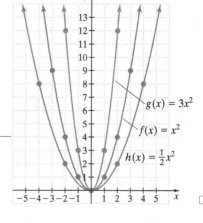

Additional ordered-pair solutions are shown on the graph.

PRACTICE
6 Graph $f(x) = x^2$, $g(x) = 4x^2$, and $h(x) = \frac{1}{4}x^2$ on the same set of axes.

Graphing the Parabola Defined by $f(x) = ax^2$

If a is positive, the parabola opens upward, and if a is negative, the parabola opens downward.
If $|a| > 1$, the graph of the parabola is narrower than the graph of $y = x^2$.
If $|a| < 1$, the graph of the parabola is wider than the graph of $y = x^2$.

EXAMPLE 7   Graph: $f(x) = -2x^2$

Solution Because $a = -2$, a negative value, this parabola opens downward. Since $|-2| = 2$ and $2 > 1$, the parabola is narrower than the graph of $y = x^2$. The vertex is $(0, 0)$, and the axis of symmetry is the y-axis. We verify this by plotting a few points.

x	$f(x) = -2x^2$
-2	-8
-1	-2
0	0
1	-2
2	-8

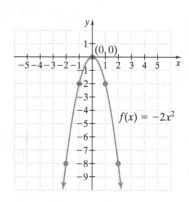

PRACTICE
7   Graph: $f(x) = -\frac{1}{2}x^2$

OBJECTIVE
5   Graphing $f(x) = a(x - h)^2 + k$

Now we will see the shape of the graph of a quadratic function of the form $f(x) = a(x - h)^2 + k$.

EXAMPLE 8   Graph $g(x) = \frac{1}{2}(x + 2)^2 + 5$. Find the vertex and the axis of symmetry.

Solution   The function $g(x) = \frac{1}{2}(x + 2)^2 + 5$ may be written as $g(x) = \frac{1}{2}[x - (-2)]^2 + 5$. Thus, this graph is the same as the graph of $y = x^2$ shifted 2 units to the left and 5 units up, and it is wider because a is $\frac{1}{2}$. The vertex is $(-2, 5)$, and the axis of symmetry is $x = -2$. We plot a few points to verify.

x	$g(x) = \dfrac{1}{2}(x + 2)^2 + 5$
-4	7
-3	$5\dfrac{1}{2}$
-2	5
-1	$5\dfrac{1}{2}$
0	7

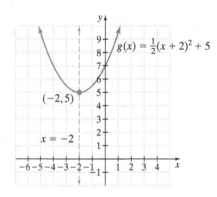

PRACTICE
8   Graph $h(x) = \frac{1}{3}(x - 4)^2 - 3$.

In general, the following holds.

Graph of a Quadratic Function

The graph of a quadratic function written in the form $f(x) = a(x - h)^2 + k$ is a parabola with vertex (h, k).

If $a > 0$, the parabola opens upward.
If $a < 0$, the parabola opens downward.

The axis of symmetry is the line whose equation is $x = h$.

Graphing Calculator Explorations

Use a graphing calculator to graph the first function of each pair that follows. Then use its graph to predict the graph of the second function. Check your prediction by graphing both on the same set of axes.

1. $F(x) = \sqrt{x}; G(x) = \sqrt{x} + 1$

2. $g(x) = x^3; H(x) = x^3 - 2$

3. $H(x) = |x|; f(x) = |x - 5|$

4. $h(x) = x^3 + 2; g(x) = (x - 3)^3 + 2$

5. $f(x) = |x + 4|; F(x) = |x + 4| + 3$

6. $G(x) = \sqrt{x} - 2; g(x) = \sqrt{x - 4} - 2$

✔ **Vocabulary, Readiness & Video Check**

Use the choices below to fill in each blank. Some choices will be used more than once.

| upward | highest | parabola | downward | lowest | quadratic |

1. A(n) _____ function is one that can be written in the form $f(x) = ax^2 + bx + c, a \neq 0$.

2. The graph of a quadratic function is a(n) _____ opening _____ or _____.

3. If $a > 0$, the graph of the quadratic function opens _____.

4. If $a < 0$, the graph of the quadratic function opens _____.

5. The vertex of a parabola is the _____ point if $a > 0$.

6. The vertex of a parabola is the _____ point if $a < 0$.

State the vertex of the graph of each quadratic function.

7. $f(x) = x^2$

8. $f(x) = -5x^2$

9. $g(x) = (x - 2)^2$

10. $g(x) = (x + 5)^2$

11. $f(x) = 2x^2 + 3$

12. $h(x) = x^2 - 1$

13. $g(x) = (x + 1)^2 + 5$

14. $h(x) = (x - 10)^2 - 7$

Martin-Gay Interactive Videos

See Video 8.5

Watch the section lecture video and answer the following questions.

OBJECTIVE 1

15. From Examples 1 and 2 and the lecture before, how do graphs of the form $f(x) = x^2 + k$ differ from $y = x^2$? Consider the location of the vertex $(0, k)$ on these graphs of the form $f(x) = x^2 + k$—by what other name do we call this point on a graph?

OBJECTIVE 2

16. From Example 3 and the lecture before, how do graphs of the form $f(x) = (x - h)^2$ differ from $y = x^2$? Consider the location of the vertex $(h, 0)$ on these graphs of the form $f(x) = (x - h)^2$—by what other name do we call this point on a graph?

OBJECTIVE 3

17. From Example 4 and the lecture before, what general information does the equation $f(x) = (x - h)^2 + k$ tell us about its graph?

OBJECTIVE 4

18. From the lecture before ▦ Example 5, besides the direction a parabola opens, what other graphing information can the value of a tell us?

OBJECTIVE 5

19. In ▦ Examples 6 and 7, what four properties of the graph did we learn from the equation that helped us locate and draw the general shape of the parabola?

8.5   Exercise Set   MyMathLab® ▶

MIXED PRACTICE

Sketch the graph of each quadratic function. Label the vertex and sketch and label the axis of symmetry. See Examples 1 through 5.

1. $f(x) = x^2 - 1$
2. $g(x) = x^2 + 3$

3. $h(x) = x^2 + 5$
4. $h(x) = x^2 - 4$

5. $g(x) = x^2 + 7$
6. $f(x) = x^2 - 2$

7. $f(x) = (x - 5)^2$
8. $g(x) = (x + 5)^2$

9. $h(x) = (x + 2)^2$
10. $H(x) = (x - 1)^2$

11. $G(x) = (x + 3)^2$
12. $f(x) = (x - 6)^2$

13. $f(x) = (x - 2)^2 + 5$
14. $g(x) = (x - 6)^2 + 1$

15. $h(x) = (x + 1)^2 + 4$
16. $G(x) = (x + 3)^2 + 3$

17. $g(x) = (x + 2)^2 - 5$
18. $h(x) = (x + 4)^2 - 6$

Sketch the graph of each quadratic function. Label the vertex, and sketch and label the axis of symmetry. See Examples 6 and 7.

19. $H(x) = 2x^2$
20. $f(x) = 5x^2$

21. $h(x) = \dfrac{1}{3}x^2$
22. $f(x) = -\dfrac{1}{4}x^2$

23. $g(x) = -x^2$
24. $g(x) = -3x^2$

Sketch the graph of each quadratic function. Label the vertex and sketch and label the axis of symmetry. See Example 8.

25. $f(x) = 2(x - 1)^2 + 3$
26. $g(x) = 4(x - 4)^2 + 2$

27. $h(x) = -3(x + 3)^2 + 1$
28. $f(x) = -(x - 2)^2 - 6$

29. $H(x) = \dfrac{1}{2}(x - 6)^2 - 3$
30. $G(x) = \dfrac{1}{5}(x + 4)^2 + 3$

MIXED PRACTICE

Sketch the graph of each quadratic function. Label the vertex and sketch and label the axis of symmetry.

31. $f(x) = -(x - 2)^2$
32. $g(x) = -(x + 6)^2$

33. $F(x) = -x^2 + 4$
34. $H(x) = -x^2 + 10$

35. $F(x) = 2x^2 - 5$
36. $g(x) = \dfrac{1}{2}x^2 - 2$

37. $h(x) = (x - 6)^2 + 4$
38. $f(x) = (x - 5)^2 + 2$

39. $F(x) = \left(x + \dfrac{1}{2}\right)^2 - 2$
40. $H(x) = \left(x + \dfrac{1}{2}\right)^2 - 3$

41. $F(x) = \dfrac{3}{2}(x + 7)^2 + 1$
42. $g(x) = -\dfrac{3}{2}(x - 1)^2 - 5$

43. $f(x) = \dfrac{1}{4}x^2 - 9$
44. $H(x) = \dfrac{3}{4}x^2 - 2$

45. $G(x) = 5\left(x + \dfrac{1}{2}\right)^2$
46. $F(x) = 3\left(x - \dfrac{3}{2}\right)^2$

47. $h(x) = -(x - 1)^2 - 1$
48. $f(x) = -3(x + 2)^2 + 2$

49. $g(x) = \sqrt{3}(x + 5)^2 + \dfrac{3}{4}$
50. $G(x) = \sqrt{5}(x - 7)^2 - \dfrac{1}{2}$

51. $h(x) = 10(x + 4)^2 - 6$
52. $h(x) = 8(x + 1)^2 + 9$

53. $f(x) = -2(x - 4)^2 + 5$
54. $G(x) = -4(x + 9)^2 - 1$

REVIEW AND PREVIEW

Add the proper constant to each binomial so that the resulting trinomial is a perfect square trinomial. See Section 8.1.

55. $x^2 + 8x$
56. $y^2 + 4y$

57. $z^2 - 16z$
58. $x^2 - 10x$

59. $y^2 + y$
60. $z^2 - 3z$

Solve by completing the square. See Section 8.1.

61. $x^2 + 4x = 12$
62. $y^2 + 6y = -5$

63. $z^2 + 10z - 1 = 0$
64. $x^2 + 14x + 20 = 0$

65. $z^2 - 8z = 2$
66. $y^2 - 10y = 3$

CONCEPT EXTENSIONS

Solve. See the Concept Check in this section.

67. Which description of $f(x) = -213(x - 0.1)^2 + 3.6$ is correct?

Graph Opens	Vertex
a. upward	$(0.1, 3.6)$
b. upward	$(-213, 3.6)$
c. downward	$(0.1, 3.6)$
d. downward	$(-0.1, 3.6)$

68. Which description of $f(x) = 5\left(x + \dfrac{1}{2}\right)^2 + \dfrac{1}{2}$ is correct?

Graph Opens	Vertex
a. upward	$\left(\dfrac{1}{2}, \dfrac{1}{2}\right)$
b. upward	$\left(-\dfrac{1}{2}, \dfrac{1}{2}\right)$
c. downward	$\left(\dfrac{1}{2}, -\dfrac{1}{2}\right)$
d. downward	$\left(-\dfrac{1}{2}, -\dfrac{1}{2}\right)$

Write the equation of the parabola that has the same shape as $f(x) = 5x^2$ but with the following vertex.

69. $(2, 3)$
70. $(1, 6)$

71. $(-3, 6)$
72. $(4, -1)$

The shifting properties covered in this section apply to the graphs of all functions. Given the graph of $y = f(x)$ below, sketch the graph of each of the following.

73. $y = f(x) + 1$

74. $y = f(x) - 2$

75. $y = f(x - 3)$

76. $y = f(x + 3)$

77. $y = f(x + 2) + 2$

78. $y = f(x - 1) + 1$

79. The quadratic function $f(x) = 12.5x^2 - 64x + 135$ approximates the annual retail sales from online shopping in the United States from 2005 through 2014, where x is the number of years past 2005 and $f(x)$ is the annual retail sales in billions of dollars. (*Source:* Based on data from the U.S. Census Bureau and the Retail Association of America)

a. Use this function to find the online retail sales in the United States for 2013.

b. Use this function to predict the online retail sales in the United States for 2020.

80. Use the function in Exercise 79.

a. Use this function to predict the online retail sales in the United States for 2018.

b. Look up the annual online retail sales for the United States for the current year.

c. Based on your answers for parts **a** and **b**, discuss some possible limitations of using this quadratic function to predict data.

8.6 Further Graphing of Quadratic Functions

OBJECTIVES

1 Write Quadratic Functions in the Form $y = a(x - h)^2 + k$.

2 Derive a Formula for Finding the Vertex of a Parabola.

3 Find the Minimum or Maximum Value of a Quadratic Function.

OBJECTIVE

1 Writing Quadratic Functions in the Form $y = a(x - h)^2 + k$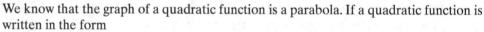

We know that the graph of a quadratic function is a parabola. If a quadratic function is written in the form

$$f(x) = a(x - h)^2 + k$$

we can easily find the vertex (h, k) and graph the parabola. To write a quadratic function in this form, complete the square. (See Section 8.1. for a review of completing the square.)

EXAMPLE 1 Graph $f(x) = x^2 - 4x - 12$. Find the vertex and any intercepts.

Solution The graph of this quadratic function is a parabola. To find the vertex of the parabola, we will write the function in the form $y = (x - h)^2 + k$. To do this, we complete the square on the binomial $x^2 - 4x$. To simplify our work, we let $f(x) = y$.

$$y = x^2 - 4x - 12 \quad \text{Let } f(x) = y.$$
$$y + 12 = x^2 - 4x \quad \text{Add 12 to both sides to get the } x\text{-variable terms alone.}$$

Now we add the square of half of -4 to both sides.

$$\frac{1}{2}(-4) = -2 \quad \text{and} \quad (-2)^2 = 4$$

$$y + 12 + 4 = x^2 - 4x + 4 \quad \text{Add 4 to both sides.}$$
$$y + 16 = (x - 2)^2 \quad \text{Factor the trinomial.}$$
$$y = (x - 2)^2 - 16 \quad \text{Subtract 16 from both sides.}$$
$$f(x) = (x - 2)^2 - 16 \quad \text{Replace } y \text{ with } f(x).$$

From this equation, we can see that the vertex of the parabola is $(2, -16)$, a point in quadrant IV, and the axis of symmetry is the line $x = 2$.

Notice that $a = 1$. Since $a > 0$, the parabola opens upward. This parabola opening upward with vertex $(2, -16)$ will have two x-intercepts and one y-intercept. (See the Helpful Hint after this example.)

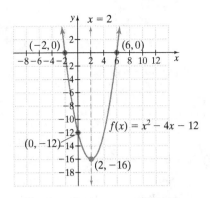

x-intercepts: let y or $f(x) = 0$

$$f(x) = x^2 - 4x - 12$$
$$0 = x^2 - 4x - 12$$
$$0 = (x - 6)(x + 2)$$
$$0 = x - 6 \quad \text{or} \quad 0 = x + 2$$
$$6 = x \qquad\qquad -2 = x$$

y-intercept: let $x = 0$

$$f(x) = x^2 - 4x - 12$$
$$f(0) = 0^2 - 4 \cdot 0 - 12$$
$$= -12$$

The two x-intercepts are $(6, 0)$ and $(-2, 0)$. The y-intercept is $(0, -12)$. The sketch of $f(x) = x^2 - 4x - 12$ is shown.

Notice that the axis of symmetry is always halfway between the x-intercepts. For this example, halfway between -2 and 6 is $\dfrac{-2 + 6}{2} = 2$, and the axis of symmetry is $x = 2$. ☐

PRACTICE
1 Graph $g(x) = x^2 - 2x - 3$. Find the vertex and any intercepts. ■

Helpful Hint

Parabola Opens Upward
Vertex in I or II: no x-intercept
Vertex in III or IV: 2 x-intercepts

Parabola Opens Downward
Vertex in I or II: 2 x-intercepts
Vertex in III or IV: no x-intercept.

EXAMPLE 2   Graph $f(x) = 3x^2 + 3x + 1$. Find the vertex and any intercepts.

Solution Replace $f(x)$ with y and complete the square on x to write the equation in the form $y = a(x - h)^2 + k$.

$$y = 3x^2 + 3x + 1 \qquad \text{Replace } f(x) \text{ with } y.$$
$$y - 1 = 3x^2 + 3x \qquad \text{Isolate } x\text{-variable terms.}$$

Factor 3 from the terms $3x^2 + 3x$ so that the coefficient of x^2 is 1.

$$y - 1 = 3(x^2 + x) \qquad \text{Factor out 3.}$$

The coefficient of x in the parentheses above is 1. Then $\dfrac{1}{2}(1) = \dfrac{1}{2}$ and $\left(\dfrac{1}{2}\right)^2 = \dfrac{1}{4}$.

Since we are adding $\dfrac{1}{4}$ inside the parentheses, we are really adding $3\left(\dfrac{1}{4}\right)$, so we *must* add $3\left(\dfrac{1}{4}\right)$ to the left side.

(Continued on next page)

$$y - 1 + 3\left(\frac{1}{4}\right) = 3\left(x^2 + x + \frac{1}{4}\right)$$

$$y - \frac{1}{4} = 3\left(x + \frac{1}{2}\right)^2 \qquad \text{Simplify the left side and factor the right side.}$$

$$y = 3\left(x + \frac{1}{2}\right)^2 + \frac{1}{4} \qquad \text{Add } \frac{1}{4} \text{ to both sides.}$$

$$f(x) = 3\left(x + \frac{1}{2}\right)^2 + \frac{1}{4} \qquad \text{Replace } y \text{ with } f(x).$$

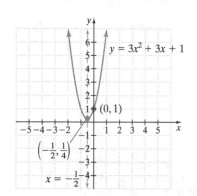

Then $a = 3, h = -\dfrac{1}{2}$, and $k = \dfrac{1}{4}$. This means that the parabola opens upward with vertex $\left(-\dfrac{1}{2}, \dfrac{1}{4}\right)$ and that the axis of symmetry is the line $x = -\dfrac{1}{2}$.

To find the y-intercept, let $x = 0$. Then

$$f(0) = 3(0)^2 + 3(0) + 1 = 1$$

Thus, the y-intercept is $(0, 1)$.

This parabola has no x-intercepts since the vertex is in the second quadrant and the parabola opens upward. Use the vertex, axis of symmetry, and y-intercept to sketch the parabola. □

PRACTICE

2 Graph $g(x) = 4x^2 + 4x + 3$. Find the vertex and any intercepts.

EXAMPLE 3 Graph $f(x) = -x^2 - 2x + 3$. Find the vertex and any intercepts.

Solution We write $f(x)$ in the form $a(x - h)^2 + k$ by completing the square. First we replace $f(x)$ with y.

$$f(x) = -x^2 - 2x + 3$$
$$y = -x^2 - 2x + 3$$
$$y - 3 = -x^2 - 2x \qquad \begin{array}{l}\text{Subtract 3 from both sides to get}\\ \text{the } x\text{-variable terms alone.}\end{array}$$
$$y - 3 = -1(x^2 + 2x) \qquad \text{Factor } -1 \text{ from the terms } -x^2 - 2x.$$

The coefficient of x is 2. Then $\dfrac{1}{2}(2) = 1$ and $1^2 = 1$. We add 1 to the right side inside the parentheses and add $-1(1)$ to the left side.

$$y - 3 - 1(1) = -1(x^2 + 2x + 1)$$
$$y - 4 = -1(x + 1)^2 \qquad \begin{array}{l}\text{Simplify the left side and}\\ \text{factor the right side.}\end{array}$$
$$y = -1(x + 1)^2 + 4 \qquad \text{Add 4 to both sides.}$$
$$f(x) = -1(x + 1)^2 + 4 \qquad \text{Replace } y \text{ with } f(x).$$

Helpful Hint

This can be written as
$f(x) = -1[x - (-1)]^2 + 4$.
Notice that the vertex is $(-1, 4)$.

Since $a = -1$, the parabola opens downward with vertex $(-1, 4)$ and axis of symmetry $x = -1$.

To find the y-intercept, we let $x = 0$. Then

$$f(0) = -0^2 - 2(0) + 3 = 3$$

Thus, $(0, 3)$ is the y-intercept.

To find the x-intercepts, we let y or $f(x) = 0$ and solve for x.

$$f(x) = -x^2 - 2x + 3$$
$$0 = -x^2 - 2x + 3 \qquad \text{Let } f(x) = 0.$$

$f(x) = -x^2 - 2x + 3$

$x = -1$

Now we divide both sides by -1 so that the coefficient of x^2 is 1.

$$\frac{0}{-1} = \frac{-x^2}{-1} - \frac{2x}{-1} + \frac{3}{-1} \qquad \text{Divide both sides by } -1.$$

$$0 = x^2 + 2x - 3 \qquad \text{Simplify.}$$

$$0 = (x + 3)(x - 1) \qquad \text{Factor.}$$

$$x + 3 = 0 \quad \text{or} \quad x - 1 = 0 \qquad \text{Set each factor equal to 0.}$$

$$x = -3 \qquad\qquad x = 1 \qquad \text{Solve.}$$

The x-intercepts are $(-3, 0)$ and $(1, 0)$. Use these points to sketch the parabola. □

PRACTICE

3   Graph $g(x) = -x^2 + 5x + 6$. Find the vertex and any intercepts. ▪

OBJECTIVE

2   Deriving a Formula for Finding the Vertex

There is also a formula that may be used to find the vertex of a parabola. Now that we have practiced completing the square, we will show that the x-coordinate of the vertex of the graph of $f(x)$ or $y = ax^2 + bx + c$ can be found by the formula $x = \dfrac{-b}{2a}$. To do so, we complete the square on x and write the equation in the form $y = a(x - h)^2 + k$.

First, isolate the x-variable terms by subtracting c from both sides.

$$y = ax^2 + bx + c$$

$$y - c = ax^2 + bx$$

Next, factor a from the terms $ax^2 + bx$.

$$y - c = a\left(x^2 + \frac{b}{a}x\right)$$

Next, add the square of half of $\dfrac{b}{a}$, or $\left(\dfrac{b}{2a}\right)^2 = \dfrac{b^2}{4a^2}$, to the right side inside the parentheses. Because of the factor a, what we really added was $a\left(\dfrac{b^2}{4a^2}\right)$, and this must be added to the left side.

$$y - c + a\left(\frac{b^2}{4a^2}\right) = a\left(x^2 + \frac{b}{a}x + \frac{b^2}{4a^2}\right)$$

$$y - c + \frac{b^2}{4a} = a\left(x + \frac{b}{2a}\right)^2 \qquad \begin{array}{l}\text{Simplify the left side and}\\ \text{factor the right side.}\end{array}$$

$$y = a\left(x + \frac{b}{2a}\right)^2 + c - \frac{b^2}{4a} \qquad \begin{array}{l}\text{Add } c \text{ to both sides and subtract } \dfrac{b^2}{4a}\\ \text{from both sides.}\end{array}$$

Compare this form with $f(x)$ or $y = a(x - h)^2 + k$ and see that h is $\dfrac{-b}{2a}$, which means that the x-coordinate of the vertex of the graph of $f(x) = ax^2 + bx + c$ is $\dfrac{-b}{2a}$.

Vertex Formula

The graph of $f(x) = ax^2 + bx + c$, when $a \neq 0$, is a parabola with vertex

$$\left(\frac{-b}{2a}, f\left(\frac{-b}{2a}\right)\right)$$

Let's use this formula to find the vertex of the parabola we graphed in Example 1.

EXAMPLE 4   Find the vertex of the graph of $f(x) = x^2 - 4x - 12$.

Solution To find the vertex (h, k), notice that for $f(x) = x^2 - 4x - 12$, we have $a = 1, b = -4$, and $c = -12$. Then

$$h = \frac{-b}{2a} = \frac{-(-4)}{2(1)} = 2$$

The x-value of the vertex is 2. To find the corresponding $f(x)$ or y-value, find $f(2)$. Then

$$f(2) = 2^2 - 4(2) - 12 = 4 - 8 - 12 = -16$$

The vertex is $(2, -16)$. These results agree with our findings in Example 1.   □

PRACTICE
4   Find the vertex of the graph of $g(x) = x^2 - 2x - 3$.   ■

OBJECTIVE
3   Finding Minimum and Maximum Values

The vertex of a parabola gives us some important information about its corresponding quadratic function. The quadratic function whose graph is a parabola that opens upward has a minimum value, and the quadratic function whose graph is a parabola that opens downward has a maximum value. The $f(x)$ or y-value of the vertex is the minimum or maximum value of the function.

✔ **CONCEPT CHECK**

Without making any calculations, tell whether the graph of $f(x) = 7 - x - 0.3x^2$ has a maximum value or a minimum value. Explain your reasoning.

EXAMPLE 5   Finding Maximum Height

A rock is thrown upward from the ground. Its height in feet above ground after t seconds is given by the function $f(t) = -16t^2 + 20t$. Find the maximum height of the rock and the number of seconds it took for the rock to reach its maximum height.

Solution

1. UNDERSTAND. The maximum height of the rock is the largest value of $f(t)$. Since the function $f(t) = -16t^2 + 20t$ is a quadratic function, its graph is a parabola. It opens downward since $-16 < 0$. Thus, the maximum value of $f(t)$ is the $f(t)$ or y-value of the vertex of its graph.

Answer to Concept Check:
$f(x)$ has a maximum value since it opens downward.

2. TRANSLATE. To find the vertex (h, k), notice that for $f(t) = -16t^2 + 20t$, $a = -16, b = 20$, and $c = 0$. We will use these values and the vertex formula

$$\left(\frac{-b}{2a}, f\left(\frac{-b}{2a}\right)\right)$$

3. SOLVE.

$$h = \frac{-b}{2a} = \frac{-20}{-32} = \frac{5}{8}$$

$$f\left(\frac{5}{8}\right) = -16\left(\frac{5}{8}\right)^2 + 20\left(\frac{5}{8}\right)$$

$$= -16\left(\frac{25}{64}\right) + \frac{25}{2}$$

$$= -\frac{25}{4} + \frac{50}{4} = \frac{25}{4}$$

4. INTERPRET. The graph of $f(t)$ is a parabola opening downward with vertex $\left(\frac{5}{8}, \frac{25}{4}\right)$. This means that the rock's maximum height is $\frac{25}{4}$ feet, or $6\frac{1}{4}$ feet, which was reached in $\frac{5}{8}$ second.   □

PRACTICE
5   A ball is tossed upward from the ground. Its height in feet above ground after t seconds is given by the function $h(t) = -16t^2 + 24t$. Find the maximum height of the ball and the number of seconds it took for the ball to reach the maximum height.   ■

✔ Vocabulary, Readiness & Video Check

Fill in each blank.

1. If a quadratic function is in the form $f(x) = a(x - h)^2 + k$, the vertex of its graph is _____ .

2. The graph of $f(x) = ax^2 + bx + c, a \neq 0$, is a parabola whose vertex has x-value _____ .

See Video 8.6

Watch the section lecture video and answer the following questions.

OBJECTIVE 1
3. From 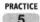 Example 1, how does writing a quadratic function in the form $f(x) = a(x - h)^2 + k$ help us graph the function? What procedure can we use to write a quadratic function in this form?

OBJECTIVE 2
4. From Example 2, how can locating the vertex and knowing whether the parabola opens upward or downward potentially help save unnecessary work? Explain.

OBJECTIVE 3
5. From Example 4, when an application involving a quadratic function asks for the maximum or minimum, what part of a parabola should we find?

8.6 Exercise Set MyMathLab®

Fill in each blank.

	Parabola Opens	*Vertex Location*	*Number of x-intercept(s)*	*Number of y-intercept(s)*
1.	up	Q I		
2.	up	Q III		
3.	down	Q II		
4.	down	Q IV		
5.	up	x-axis		
6.	down	x-axis		
7.		Q III	0	
8.		Q I	2	
9.		Q IV	2	
10.		Q II	0	

Find the vertex of the graph of each quadratic function. See Examples 1 through 4.

11. $f(x) = x^2 + 8x + 7$

12. $f(x) = x^2 + 6x + 5$

13. $f(x) = -x^2 + 10x + 5$

14. $f(x) = -x^2 - 8x + 2$

15. $f(x) = 5x^2 - 10x + 3$

16. $f(x) = -3x^2 + 6x + 4$

17. $f(x) = -x^2 + x + 1$

18. $f(x) = x^2 - 9x + 8$

Match each function with its graph. See Examples 1 through 4.

19. $f(x) = x^2 - 4x + 3$ **20.** $f(x) = x^2 + 2x - 3$

21. $f(x) = x^2 - 2x - 3$ **22.** $f(x) = x^2 + 4x + 3$

A.

$(-1, -4)$

B.

$(1, -4)$

C.

$(-2, -1)$

D.

$(2, -1)$

MIXED PRACTICE

Find the vertex of the graph of each quadratic function. Determine whether the graph opens upward or downward, find any intercepts, and sketch the graph. See Examples 1 through 4.

23. $f(x) = x^2 + 4x - 5$ **24.** $f(x) = x^2 + 2x - 3$

 25. $f(x) = -x^2 + 2x - 1$ **26.** $f(x) = -x^2 + 4x - 4$

27. $f(x) = x^2 - 4$ **28.** $f(x) = x^2 - 1$

29. $f(x) = 4x^2 + 4x - 3$ **30.** $f(x) = 2x^2 - x - 3$

31. $f(x) = \frac{1}{2}x^2 + 4x + \frac{15}{2}$ **32.** $f(x) = \frac{1}{5}x^2 + 2x + \frac{9}{5}$

33. $f(x) = x^2 - 6x + 5$ **34.** $f(x) = x^2 - 4x + 3$

35. $f(x) = x^2 - 4x + 5$ **36.** $f(x) = x^2 - 6x + 11$

37. $f(x) = 2x^2 + 4x + 5$ **38.** $f(x) = 3x^2 + 12x + 16$

39. $f(x) = -2x^2 + 12x$ **40.** $f(x) = -4x^2 + 8x$

41. $f(x) = x^2 + 1$ **42.** $f(x) = x^2 + 4$

43. $f(x) = x^2 - 2x - 15$ **44.** $f(x) = x^2 - x - 12$

45. $f(x) = -5x^2 + 5x$ **46.** $f(x) = 3x^2 - 12x$

47. $f(x) = -x^2 + 2x - 12$ **48.** $f(x) = -x^2 + 8x - 17$

49. $f(x) = 3x^2 - 12x + 15$ **50.** $f(x) = 2x^2 - 8x + 11$

51. $f(x) = x^2 + x - 6$ **52.** $f(x) = x^2 + 3x - 18$

53. $f(x) = -2x^2 - 3x + 35$ **54.** $f(x) = 3x^2 - 13x - 10$

Solve. See Example 5.

55. If a projectile is fired straight upward from the ground with an initial speed of 96 feet per second, then its height h in feet after t seconds is given by the equation

$$h(t) = -16t^2 + 96t$$

Find the maximum height of the projectile.

56. If Rheam Gaspar throws a ball upward with an initial speed of 32 feet per second, then its height h in feet after t seconds is given by the equation

$$h(t) = -16t^2 + 32t$$

Find the maximum height of the ball.

57. The cost C in dollars of manufacturing x bicycles at Holladay's Production Plant is given by the function

$$C(x) = 2x^2 - 800x + 92{,}000.$$

  a. Find the number of bicycles that must be manufactured to minimize the cost.

  b. Find the minimum cost.

58. The Utah Ski Club sells calendars to raise money. The profit P, in cents, from selling x calendars is given by the equation $P(x) = 360x - x^2$.

  a. Find how many calendars must be sold to maximize profit.

  b. Find the maximum profit in dollars.

59. Find two numbers whose sum is 60 and whose product is as large as possible. [*Hint:* Let x and $60 - x$ be the two positive numbers. Their product can be described by the function $f(x) = x(60 - x).$]

60. Find two numbers whose sum is 11 and whose product is as large as possible. (Use the hint for Exercise 59.)

61. Find two numbers whose difference is 10 and whose product is as small as possible. (Use the hint for Exercise 59.)

62. Find two numbers whose difference is 8 and whose product is as small as possible. (Use the hint for Exercise 59.)

△ **63.** The length and width of a rectangle must have a sum of 40. Find the dimensions of the rectangle that will have the maximum area. (Use the hint for Exercise 59.)

△ **64.** The length and width of a rectangle must have a sum of 50. Find the dimensions of the rectangle that will have maximum area. (Use the hint for Exercise 59.)

REVIEW AND PREVIEW

Sketch the graph of each function. See Sections 3.3 and 8.5.

65. $f(x) = x^2 + 2$ **66.** $f(x) = (x - 3)^2$

67. $g(x) = x + 2$ **68.** $h(x) = x - 3$

69. $f(x) = (x + 5)^2 + 2$ **70.** $f(x) = 2(x - 3)^2 + 2$

71. $f(x) = 3(x - 4)^2 + 1$ **72.** $f(x) = (x + 1)^2 + 4$

73. $f(x) = -(x - 4)^2 + \dfrac{3}{2}$ **74.** $f(x) = -2(x + 7)^2 + \dfrac{1}{2}$

CONCEPT EXTENSIONS

Without calculating, tell whether each graph has a minimum value or a maximum value. See the Concept Check in the section.

75. $f(x) = 2x^2 - 5$

76. $g(x) = -7x^2 + x + 1$

77. $f(x) = 3 - \dfrac{1}{2}x^2$

78. $G(x) = 3 - \dfrac{1}{2}x + 0.8x^2$

Find the vertex of the graph of each quadratic function. Determine whether the graph opens upward or downward, find the y-intercept, approximate the x-intercepts to one decimal place, and sketch the graph.

79. $f(x) = x^2 + 10x + 15$ **80.** $f(x) = x^2 - 6x + 4$

81. $f(x) = 3x^2 - 6x + 7$ **82.** $f(x) = 2x^2 + 4x - 1$

Find the maximum or minimum value of each function. Approximate to two decimal places.

83. $f(x) = 2.3x^2 - 6.1x + 3.2$

84. $f(x) = 7.6x^2 + 9.8x - 2.1$

85. $f(x) = -1.9x^2 + 5.6x - 2.7$

86. $f(x) = -5.2x^2 - 3.8x + 5.1$

87. The projected number of Wi-Fi-enabled cell phones in the United States can be modeled by the quadratic function $c(x) = -0.4x^2 + 21x + 35$, where $c(x)$ is the projected number of Wi-Fi-enabled cell phones in millions and x is the number of years after 2009. (*Source:* Techcrunch)

  a. Will this function have a maximum or a minimum? How can you tell?

  b. According to this model, in what year will the number of Wi-Fi-enabled cell phones in the United States be at its maximum or minimum?

  c. What is the maximum/minimum number of Wi-Fi-enabled cell phones predicted? Round to the nearest whole million.

88. Methane is a gas produced by landfills, natural gas systems, and coal mining that contributes to the greenhouse effect and global warming. Projected methane emissions in the United States can be modeled by the quadratic function

$$f(x) = -0.072x^2 + 1.93x + 173.9$$

where $f(x)$ is the amount of methane produced in million metric tons and x is the number of years after 2000. (*Source:* Based on data from the U.S. Environmental Protection Agency, 2000–2020)

  a. According to this model, what will U.S. emissions of methane be in 2018? Round to 2 decimal places.

  b. Will this function have a maximum or a minimum? How can you tell?

  c. In what year will methane emissions in the United States be at their maximum/minimum? Round to the nearest whole year.

d. What is the level of methane emissions for that year? (Use your rounded answer from part **c.** Round this answer to 2 decimals places.)

Use a graphing calculator to check each exercise.

89. Exercise 37   **90.** Exercise 38

91. Exercise 47   **92.** Exercise 48

Chapter 8 Vocabulary Check

Fill in each blank with one of the words or phrases listed below.

quadratic formula	quadratic	discriminant	$\pm \sqrt{b}$
completing the square	quadratic inequality	(h, k)	$(0, k)$
$(h, 0)$	$\dfrac{-b}{2a}$		

1. The _____ helps us find the number and type of solutions of a quadratic equation.

2. If $a^2 = b$, then $a =$ _____.

3. The graph of $f(x) = ax^2 + bx + c$, where a is not 0, is a parabola whose vertex has x-value _____.

4. A _____ is an inequality that can be written so that one side is a quadratic expression and the other side is 0.

5. The process of writing a quadratic equation so that one side is a perfect square trinomial is called _____.

6. The graph of $f(x) = x^2 + k$ has vertex _____.

7. The graph of $f(x) = (x - h)^2$ has vertex _____.

8. The graph of $f(x) = (x - h)^2 + k$ has vertex _____.

9. The formula $x = \dfrac{-b \pm \sqrt{b^2 - 4ac}}{2a}$ is called the _____.

10. A _____ equation is one that can be written in the form $ax^2 + bx + c = 0$ where $a, b,$ and c are real numbers and a is not 0.

Chapter 8 Highlights

DEFINITIONS AND CONCEPTS	EXAMPLES

Section 8.1   Solving Quadratic Equations by Completing the Square

DEFINITIONS AND CONCEPTS	EXAMPLES
Square Root Property If b is a real number and if $a^2 = b$, then $a = \pm \sqrt{b}$.	Solve: $(x + 3)^2 = 14$ $\qquad x + 3 = \pm \sqrt{14}$ $\qquad\qquad x = -3 \pm \sqrt{14}$
To Solve a Quadratic Equation in x by Completing the Square	Solve: $3x^2 - 12x - 18 = 0$
Step 1. If the coefficient of x^2 is not 1, divide both sides of the equation by the coefficient of x^2.	**1.** $x^2 - 4x - 6 = 0$
Step 2. Isolate the variable terms.	**2.** $\qquad x^2 - 4x = 6$
Step 3. Complete the square by adding the square of half of the coefficient of x to both sides.	**3.** $\dfrac{1}{2}(-4) = -2$ and $(-2)^2 = 4$ $x^2 - 4x + 4 = 6 + 4$
Step 4. Write the resulting trinomial as the square of a binomial.	**4.** $\quad (x - 2)^2 = 10$
Step 5. Apply the square root property and solve for x.	**5.** $\qquad x - 2 = \pm \sqrt{10}$ $\qquad\qquad x = 2 \pm \sqrt{10}$

DEFINITIONS AND CONCEPTS	EXAMPLES

Section 8.2   Solving Quadratic Equations by the Quadratic Formula

A quadratic equation written in the form $ax^2 + bx + c = 0$ has solutions $$x = \frac{-b \pm \sqrt{b^2 - 4ac}}{2a}$$	Solve: $x^2 - x - 3 = 0$ $$a = 1, b = -1, c = -3$$ $$x = \frac{-(-1) \pm \sqrt{(-1)^2 - 4(1)(-3)}}{2 \cdot 1}$$ $$x = \frac{1 \pm \sqrt{13}}{2}$$

Section 8.3   Solving Equations by Using Quadratic Methods

Substitution is often helpful in solving an equation that contains a repeated variable expression.	Solve: $(2x + 1)^2 - 5(2x + 1) + 6 = 0$ Let $m = 2x + 1$. Then $$m^2 - 5m + 6 = 0 \qquad \text{Let } m = 2x + 1.$$ $$(m - 3)(m - 2) = 0$$ $$m = 3 \quad \text{or} \quad m = 2$$ $$2x + 1 = 3 \quad \text{or} \quad 2x + 1 = 2 \quad \text{Substitute back.}$$ $$x = 1 \quad \text{or} \quad x = \frac{1}{2}$$

Section 8.4   Nonlinear Inequalities in One Variable

To Solve a Polynomial Inequality

Step 1. Write the inequality in standard form.

Step 2. Solve the related equation.

Step 3. Use solutions from Step 2 to separate the number line into regions.

Step 4. Use test points to determine whether values in each region satisfy the original inequality.

Step 5. Write the solution set as the union of regions whose test point value is a solution.

Solve: $x^2 \geq 6x$

1. $x^2 - 6x \geq 0$

2. $x^2 - 6x = 0$
$$x(x - 6) = 0$$
$$x = 0 \quad \text{or} \quad x = 6$$

3.
$$
\begin{array}{ccccc}
A & & B & & C \\
\hline
& 0 & & 6 &
\end{array}
$$

4.

Region	Test Point Value	$x^2 \geq 6x$	Result
A	-2	$(-2)^2 \geq 6(-2)$	True
B	1	$1^2 \geq 6(1)$	False
C	7	$7^2 \geq 6(7)$	True

5.
$$
\begin{array}{ccc}
\bullet & & \bullet \\
\hline
0 & & 6
\end{array}
$$

The solution set is $(-\infty, 0] \cup [6, \infty)$.

To Solve a Rational Inequality

Step 1. Solve for values that make all denominators 0.

Step 2. Solve the related equation.

Step 3. Use solutions from Steps 1 and 2 to separate the number line into regions.

Step 4. Use test points to determine whether values in each region satisfy the original inequality.

Step 5. Write the solution set as the union of regions whose test point value is a solution. Do not include values from step 1.

Solve: $\dfrac{6}{x - 1} < -2$

1. $x - 1 = 0$ Set denominator equal to 0.
$$x = 1$$

2. $\dfrac{6}{x - 1} = -2$
$$6 = -2(x - 1) \quad \text{Multiply by } (x - 1).$$
$$6 = -2x + 2$$
$$4 = -2x$$
$$-2 = x$$

(continued)

DEFINITIONS AND CONCEPTS	EXAMPLES

Section 8.4 Nonlinear Inequalities in One Variable (continued)

3.

4. Only a test value from region B satisfies the original inequality.

5.

The solution set is $(-2, 1)$.

Section 8.5 Quadratic Functions and Their Graphs

Graph of a Quadratic Function

The graph of a quadratic function written in the form $f(x) = a(x - h)^2 + k$ is a parabola with vertex (h, k). If $a > 0$, the parabola opens upward; if $a < 0$, the parabola opens downward. The axis of symmetry is the line whose equation is $x = h$.

Graph: $g(x) = 3(x - 1)^2 + 4$

The graph is a parabola with vertex $(1, 4)$ and axis of symmetry $x = 1$. Since $a = 3$ is positive, the graph opens upward.

Section 8.6 Further Graphing of Quadratic Functions

The graph of $f(x) = ax^2 + bx + c$, where $a \neq 0$, is a parabola with vertex

$$\left(\frac{-b}{2a}, f\left(\frac{-b}{2a} \right) \right)$$

Graph $f(x) = x^2 - 2x - 8$. Find the vertex and x- and y-intercepts.

$$\frac{-b}{2a} = \frac{-(-2)}{2 \cdot 1} = 1$$
$$f(1) = 1^2 - 2(1) - 8 = -9$$

The vertex is $(1, -9)$.

$$0 = x^2 - 2x - 8$$
$$0 = (x - 4)(x + 2)$$
$$x = 4 \quad \text{or} \quad x = -2$$

The x-intercepts are $(4, 0)$ and $(-2, 0)$.

$$f(0) = 0^2 - 2 \cdot 0 - 8 = -8$$

The y-intercept is $(0, -8)$.

Chapter 8 Review

(8.1) *Solve by factoring.*

1. $x^2 - 15x + 14 = 0$

2. $7a^2 = 29a + 30$

Solve by using the square root property.

3. $4m^2 = 196$

4. $(5x - 2)^2 = 2$

Solve by completing the square.

5. $z^2 + 3z + 1 = 0$

6. $(2x + 1)^2 = x$

7. If P dollars are originally invested, the formula $A = P(1 + r)^2$ gives the amount A in an account paying interest rate r compounded annually after 2 years. Find the interest rate r such that \$2500 increases to \$2717 in 2 years. Round the result to the nearest hundredth of a percent.

△ **8.** Two ships leave a port at the same time and travel at the same speed. One ship is traveling due north and the other due east. In a few hours, the ships are 150 miles apart. How many miles has each ship traveled? Give the exact answer and a one-decimal-place approximation.

(8.2) *If the discriminant of a quadratic equation has the given value, determine the number and type of solutions of the equation.*

9. -8

10. 48

11. 100

12. 0

Solve by using the quadratic formula.

13. $x^2 - 16x + 64 = 0$

14. $x^2 + 5x = 0$

15. $2x^2 + 3x = 5$

16. $9x^2 + 4 = 2x$

17. $6x^2 + 7 = 5x$

18. $(2x - 3)^2 = x$

19. Cadets graduating from military school usually toss their hats high into the air at the end of the ceremony. One cadet threw his hat so that its distance $d(t)$ in feet above the ground t seconds after it was thrown was $d(t) = -16t^2 + 30t + 6$.
 a. Find the distance above the ground of the hat 1 second after it was thrown.
 b. Find the time it takes the hat to hit the ground. Give the exact time and a one-decimal-place approximation.

△ **20.** The hypotenuse of an isosceles right triangle is 6 centimeters longer than either of the legs. Find the length of the legs.

(8.3) *Solve each equation for the variable.*

21. $x^3 = 27$

22. $y^3 = -64$

23. $\dfrac{5}{x} + \dfrac{6}{x - 2} = 3$

24. $x^4 - 21x^2 - 100 = 0$

25. $x^{2/3} - 6x^{1/3} + 5 = 0$

26. $5(x + 3)^2 - 19(x + 3) = 4$

27. $a^6 - a^2 = a^4 - 1$

28. $y^{-2} + y^{-1} = 20$

29. Two postal workers, Jerome Grant and Tim Bozik, can sort a stack of mail in 5 hours. Working alone, Tim can sort the mail in 1 hour less time than Jerome can. Find the time that each postal worker can sort the mail alone. Round the result to one decimal place.

30. A negative number decreased by its reciprocal is $-\dfrac{24}{5}$. Find the number.

(8.4) *Solve each inequality for x. Write each solution set in interval notation.*

31. $2x^2 - 50 \le 0$

32. $\dfrac{1}{4}x^2 < \dfrac{1}{16}$

33. $(x^2 - 4)(x^2 - 25) \le 0$

34. $(x^2 - 16)(x^2 - 1) > 0$

35. $\dfrac{x - 5}{x - 6} < 0$

36. $\dfrac{(4x + 3)(x - 5)}{x(x + 6)} > 0$

37. $(x + 5)(x - 6)(x + 2) \le 0$

38. $x^3 + 3x^2 - 25x - 75 > 0$

39. $\dfrac{x^2 + 4}{3x} \le 1$

40. $\dfrac{3}{x - 2} > 2$

(8.5) *Sketch the graph of each function. Label the vertex and the axis of symmetry.*

41. $f(x) = x^2 - 4$

42. $g(x) = x^2 + 7$

43. $H(x) = 2x^2$

44. $h(x) = -\dfrac{1}{3}x^2$

45. $F(x) = (x - 1)^2$

46. $G(x) = (x + 5)^2$

47. $f(x) = (x - 4)^2 - 2$

48. $f(x) = -3(x - 1)^2 + 1$

(8.6) *Sketch the graph of each function. Find the vertex and the intercepts.*

49. $f(x) = x^2 + 10x + 25$

50. $f(x) = -x^2 + 6x - 9$

51. $f(x) = 4x^2 - 1$

52. $f(x) = -5x^2 + 5$

53. Find the vertex of the graph of $f(x) = -3x^2 - 5x + 4$. Determine whether the graph opens upward or downward, find the y-intercept, approximate the x-intercepts to one decimal place, and sketch the graph.

54. The function $h(t) = -16t^2 + 120t + 300$ gives the height in feet of a projectile fired from the top of a building after t seconds.
 a. When will the object reach a height of 350 feet? Round your answer to one decimal place.
 b. Explain why part **a** has two answers.

55. Find two numbers whose product is as large as possible, given that their sum is 420.

56. Write an equation of a quadratic function whose graph is a parabola that has vertex $(-3, 7)$. Let the value of a be $-\dfrac{7}{9}$.

MIXED REVIEW

Solve each equation or inequality.

57. $x^2 - x - 30 = 0$

58. $10x^2 = 3x + 4$

59. $9y^2 = 36$

60. $(9n + 1)^2 = 9$

61. $x^2 + x + 7 = 0$

62. $(3x - 4)^2 = 10x$

63. $x^2 + 11 = 0$

64. $x^2 + 7 = 0$

65. $(5a - 2)^2 - a = 0$

66. $\dfrac{7}{8} = \dfrac{8}{x^2}$

67. $x^{2/3} - 6x^{1/3} = -8$

68. $(2x - 3)(4x + 5) \geq 0$

69. $\dfrac{x(x + 5)}{4x - 3} \geq 0$

70. $\dfrac{3}{x - 2} > 2$

71. The busiest airport in the world is the Hartsfield-Jackson International Airport in Atlanta, Georgia. The total amount of passenger traffic through Atlanta during the period 2005 through 2014 can be modeled by the equation $y = -111x^2 + 1960x + 85{,}907$, where y is the number of passengers enplaned and deplaned in thousands, and x is the number of years after 2005. (*Source:* Based on data from Airports Council International)
 a. Estimate the passenger traffic at Atlanta's Hartsfield-Jackson International Airport in 2020.
 b. According to this model, will the passenger traffic at Atlanta's Hartsfield-Jackson International Airport continue to grow? Why or why not?

Chapter 8 Getting Ready for the Test

MULTIPLE CHOICE *For each quadratic equation in Exercises 1 and 2, choose the correct substitution for a, b, and c in the standard form* $ax^2 + bx + c = 0$.

1. $x^2 = 8$

 A. $a = 1, b = 0, c = 8$ **B.** $a = 1, b = 8, c = 0$ **C.** $a = 1, b = 0, c = -8$

2. $\dfrac{1}{9}x^2 + \dfrac{1}{3} = x$ One correct substitution is $a = \dfrac{1}{9}, b = -1, c = \dfrac{1}{3}$. Find another.

 A. $a = 1, b = -1, c = 3$ **B.** $a = 1, b = -9, c = 3$ **C.** $a = 1, b = 9, c = 3$ **D.** $a = 1, b = -1, c = 1$.

MULTIPLE CHOICE *Select the correct choice.*

3. $\dfrac{-4 \pm \sqrt{-4}}{2}$ simplifies to

   A. $-2 \pm i$ **B.** $-2 \pm 2i$ **C.** $\pm 4i$ **D.** $-2 \pm i\sqrt{2}$

4. $\dfrac{9 \pm \sqrt{27}}{3}$ simplifies to

   A. $3 \pm \sqrt{27}$ **B.** $3 \pm 3\sqrt{3}$ **C.** $9 \pm \sqrt{3}$ **D.** $3 \pm \sqrt{3}$

5. To solve $2x^2 + 16x = 5$ by completing the square, choose the next correct step.

   A. $x^2 + 8x = 5$ **B.** $x^2 + 8x = \dfrac{5}{2}$ **C.** $2x^2 + 16x + 16 = 5$ **D.** $2x^2 + 16x + 64 = 5$

6. To solve $x^2 - 7x = 5$ by completing the square, choose the next correct step.

   A. $x^2 - 7x + 49 = 5$ **B.** $x^2 - 7x + 49 = 5 + 49$ **C.** $x^2 - 7x + \dfrac{49}{4} = 5$ **D.** $x^2 - 7x + \dfrac{49}{4} = 5 + \dfrac{49}{4}$

7. The solution set of $(x + 5)(x - 1) \le 0$ is $[-5, 1]$. Use this to select the solution set of $\dfrac{x + 5}{x - 1} \le 0$.

   A. $[-5, 1]$ **B.** $(-5, 1]$ **C.** $[-5, 1)$ **D.** $(-5, 1)$

8. Choose the correct description of the graph of $f(x) = -103(x - 20)^2 + 5.6$.

   A. opens up; vertex $(20, 5.6)$ **B.** opens up; vertex $(-20, 5.6)$
   C. opens down; vertex $(20, 5.6)$ **D.** opens down; vertex $(20, -5.6)$

9. Choose the correct description of the graph of $f(x) = 0.5(x + 1)^2 - 3$.
   A. opens up; vertex $(-1, -3)$ **B.** opens up; vertex $(1, -3)$
   C. opens down; vertex $(-1, -3)$ **D.** opens down; vertex $(-3, -1)$

10. Select the vertex of the graph of $f(x) = 3x^2 + 12x - 7$.

   A. $(-2, -7)$ **B.** $(-2, -19)$ **C.** $\left(-\dfrac{1}{2}, -12\dfrac{1}{4}\right)$ **D.** $(-12, 281)$

11. Select the x-intercept(s) of the graph of $f(x) = 2x^2 - x - 10$.

   A. $(0, 0)$ **B.** $(5, 0), (-2, 0)$ **C.** $\left(\dfrac{5}{2}, 0\right), (-2, 0)$ **D.** $\left(-\dfrac{5}{2}, 0\right), (2, 0)$

Chapter 8 Test   MyMathLab®   You Tube

Solve each equation.

1. $5x^2 - 2x = 7$

2. $(x + 1)^2 = 10$

3. $m^2 - m + 8 = 0$

4. $u^2 - 6u + 2 = 0$

5. $7x^2 + 8x + 1 = 0$

6. $y^2 - 3y = 5$

7. $\dfrac{4}{x + 2} + \dfrac{2x}{x - 2} = \dfrac{6}{x^2 - 4}$

8. $x^5 + 3x^4 = x + 3$

9. $x^6 + 1 = x^4 + x^2$

10. $(x + 1)^2 - 15(x + 1) + 56 = 0$

Solve by completing the square.

11. $x^2 - 6x = -2$

12. $2a^2 + 5 = 4a$

Solve each inequality for x. Write the solution set in interval notation.

13. $2x^2 - 7x > 15$

14. $(x^2 - 16)(x^2 - 25) \ge 0$

15. $\dfrac{5}{x + 3} < 1$

16. $\dfrac{7x - 14}{x^2 - 9} \le 0$

Graph each function. Label the vertex.

17. $f(x) = 3x^2$

18. $G(x) = -2(x - 1)^2 + 5$

Graph each function. Find and label the vertex, y-intercept, and x-intercepts (if any).

19. $h(x) = x^2 - 4x + 4$

20. $F(x) = 2x^2 - 8x + 9$

21. Dave and Sandy Hartranft can paint a room together in 4 hours. Working alone, Dave can paint the room in 2 hours less time than Sandy can. Find how long it takes Sandy to paint the room alone.

22. A stone is thrown upward from a bridge. The stone's height in feet, $s(t)$, above the water t seconds after the stone is thrown is a function given by the equation $s(t) = -16t^2 + 32t + 256$.

   a. Find the maximum height of the stone.

   b. Find the time it takes the stone to hit the water. Round the answer to two decimal places.

256 ft

23. Given the diagram shown, approximate to the nearest tenth of a foot how many feet of walking distance a person saves by cutting across the lawn instead of walking on the sidewalk.

20 ft
$x + 8$
x

Chapter 8 Cumulative Review

1. Write each sentence using mathematical symbols.

   a. The sum of 5 and y is greater than or equal to 7.

   b. 11 is not equal to z.

   c. 20 is less than the difference of 5 and twice x.

2. Solve: $|3x - 2| = -5$

3. Find the slope of the line containing the points $(0, 3)$ and $(2, 5)$. Graph the line.

4. Use the elimination method to solve the system.

$$\begin{cases} -6x + y = 5 \\ 4x - 2y = 6 \end{cases}$$

5. Use the elimination method to solve the system:

$$\begin{cases} x - 5y = -12 \\ -x + y = 4 \end{cases}$$

6. Simplify. Use positive exponents to write each answer.

   a. $(a^{-2}bc^3)^{-3}$

   b. $\left(\dfrac{a^{-4}b^2}{c^3}\right)^{-2}$

   c. $\left(\dfrac{3a^8b^2}{12a^5b^5}\right)^{-2}$

7. Multiply.

   a. $(2x - 7)(3x - 4)$

   b. $(3x^2 + y)(5x^2 - 2y)$

8. Multiply.

   a. $(4a - 3)(7a - 2)$

   b. $(2a + b)(3a - 5b)$

9. Factor.

   a. $8x^2 + 4$

   b. $5y - 2z^4$

   c. $6x^2 - 3x^3 + 12x^4$

10. Factor.

   a. $9x^3 + 27x^2 - 15x$

   b. $2x(3y - 2) - 5(3y - 2)$

   c. $2xy + 6x - y - 3$

Factor the polynomials in Exercises 11 through 14.

11. $x^2 - 12x + 35$

12. $x^2 - 2x - 48$

13. $12a^2x - 12abx + 3b^2x$

14. Factor: $2ax^2 - 12axy + 18ay^2$

15. Solve: $3(x^2 + 4) + 5 = -6(x^2 + 2x) + 13$

16. Solve: $2(a^2 + 2) - 8 = -2a(a - 2) - 5$

17. Solve: $x^3 = 4x$

18. Find the vertex and any intercepts of $f(x) = x^2 + x - 12$.

19. Simplify: $\dfrac{2x^2}{10x^3 - 2x^2}$

20. Simplify: $\dfrac{x^2 - 4x + 4}{2 - x}$

21. Add: $\dfrac{2x - 1}{2x^2 - 9x - 5} + \dfrac{x + 3}{6x^2 - x - 2}$.

22. Subtract: $\dfrac{a + 1}{a^2 - 6a + 8} - \dfrac{3}{16 - a^2}$

23. Simplify: $\dfrac{x^{-1} + 2xy^{-1}}{x^{-2} - x^{-2}y^{-1}}$

24. Simplify: $\dfrac{(2a)^{-1} + b^{-1}}{a^{-1} + (2b)^{-1}}$

25. Divide: $\dfrac{3x^5y^2 - 15x^3y - x^2y - 6x}{x^2y}$

26. Divide $x^3 - 3x^2 - 10x + 24$ by $x + 3$.

27. If $P(x) = 2x^3 - 4x^2 + 5$,
    a. Find $P(2)$ by substitution.
    b. Use synthetic division to find the remainder when $P(x)$ is divided by $x - 2$.

28. If $P(x) = 4x^3 - 2x^2 + 3$,
    a. Find $P(-2)$ by substitution.
    b. Use synthetic division to find the remainder when $P(x)$ is divided by $x + 2$.

29. Solve: $\dfrac{4x}{5} + \dfrac{3}{2} = \dfrac{3x}{10}$

30. Solve: $\dfrac{x + 3}{x^2 + 5x + 6} = \dfrac{3}{2x + 4} - \dfrac{1}{x + 3}$

31. If a certain number is subtracted from the numerator and added to the denominator of $\dfrac{9}{19}$, the new fraction is equivalent to $\dfrac{1}{3}$. Find the number.

32. Mr. Briley can roof his house in 24 hours. His son can roof the same house in 40 hours. If they work together, how long will it take to roof the house?

33. Suppose that y varies directly as x. If y is 5 when x is 30, find the constant of variation and the direct variation equation.

34. Suppose that y varies inversely as x. If y is 8 when x is 14, find the constant of variation and the inverse variation equation.

35. Simplify.
    a. $\sqrt{(-3)^2}$
    b. $\sqrt{x^2}$
    c. $\sqrt[4]{(x - 2)^4}$
    d. $\sqrt[3]{(-5)^3}$
    e. $\sqrt[5]{(2x - 7)^5}$
    f. $\sqrt{25x^2}$
    g. $\sqrt{x^2 + 2x + 1}$

36. Simplify.
    a. $\sqrt{(-2)^2}$
    b. $\sqrt{y^2}$
    c. $\sqrt[4]{(a - 3)^4}$
    d. $\sqrt[3]{(-6)^3}$
    e. $\sqrt[5]{(3x - 1)^5}$

37. Use rational exponents to simplify. Assume that variables represent positive numbers.
    a. $\sqrt[8]{x^4}$
    b. $\sqrt[6]{25}$
    c. $\sqrt[4]{r^2 s^6}$

38. Use rational exponents to simplify. Assume that variables represent positive numbers.
    a. $\sqrt[4]{5^2}$
    b. $\sqrt[12]{x^3}$
    c. $\sqrt[6]{x^2 y^4}$

39. Use the product rule to simplify.
    a. $\sqrt{25x^3}$
    b. $\sqrt[3]{54x^6 y^8}$
    c. $\sqrt[4]{81z^{11}}$

40. Use the product rule to simplify. Assume that variables represent positive numbers.
    a. $\sqrt{64a^5}$
    b. $\sqrt[3]{24a^7 b^9}$
    c. $\sqrt[4]{48x^9}$

41. Rationalize the denominator of each expression.
    a. $\dfrac{2}{\sqrt{5}}$
    b. $\dfrac{2\sqrt{16}}{\sqrt{9x}}$
    c. $\sqrt[3]{\dfrac{1}{2}}$

42. Multiply. Simplify if possible.
    a. $(\sqrt{3} - 4)(2\sqrt{3} + 2)$
    b. $(\sqrt{5} - x)^2$
    c. $(\sqrt{a} + b)(\sqrt{a} - b)$

43. Solve: $\sqrt{2x + 5} + \sqrt{2x} = 3$

44. Solve: $\sqrt{x - 2} = \sqrt{4x + 1} - 3$

45. Divide. Write in the form $a + bi$.
    a. $\dfrac{2 + i}{1 - i}$
    b. $\dfrac{7}{3i}$

46. Write each product in the form of $a + bi$.
    a. $3i(5 - 2i)$
    b. $(6 - 5i)^2$
    c. $(\sqrt{3} + 2i)(\sqrt{3} - 2i)$

47. Use the square root property to solve: $(x + 1)^2 = 12$

48. Use the square root property to solve: $(y - 1)^2 = 24$

49. Solve: $x - \sqrt{x} - 6 = 0$.

50. Use the quadratic formula to solve: $m^2 = 4m + 8$

Appendix A

Geometry

A.1 Geometric Formulas

Rectangle

Perimeter: $P = 2l + 2w$
Area: $A = lw$

Square

Perimeter: $P = 4s$
Area: $A = s^2$

Triangle

Perimeter: $P = a + b + c$
Area: $A = \frac{1}{2}bh$

Sum of Angles of Triangle

$A + B + C = 180°$

The sum of the measures of the three angles is 180°.

Right Triangles

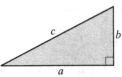

Perimeter: $P = a + b + c$
Area: $A = \frac{1}{2}ab$

One 90° (right) angle

Pythagorean Theorem (for right triangles)

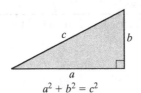

$a^2 + b^2 = c^2$

Isosceles Triangle

Triangle has:
two equal sides and
two equal angles.

Equilateral Triangle

Triangle has:
three equal sides and
three equal angles.
Measure of each angle is 60°.

Trapezoid

Perimeter: $P = a + b + c + B$
Area: $A = \frac{1}{2}h(B + b)$

Parallelogram

Perimeter: $P = 2a + 2b$
Area: $A = bh$

Circle

Circumference: $C = \pi d$
$C = 2\pi r$
Area: $A = \pi r^2$

Rectangular Solid

Volume: $V = LWH$
Surface Area:
$S = 2LW + 2HL + 2HW$

Cube

Volume: $V = s^3$
Surface Area: $S = 6s^2$

Cone

Volume: $V = \frac{1}{3}\pi r^2 h$
Lateral Surface Area:
$S = \pi r\sqrt{r^2 + h^2}$

Right Circular Cylinder

Volume: $V = \pi r^2 h$
Surface Area: $S = 2\pi r^2 + 2\pi rh$

Sphere

Volume: $V = \frac{4}{3}\pi r^3$
Surface Area: $S = 4\pi r^2$

Other Formulas

Distance: $d = rt$ (r = rate, t = time)

Percent: $p = br$ (p = percentage, b = base, r = rate)

Compound Interest: $A = P\left(1 + \dfrac{r}{n}\right)^{nt}$

(P = principal, r = annual interest rate, t = time in years, n = number of compoundings per year)

Temperature: $F = \dfrac{9}{5}C + 32 \quad C = \dfrac{5}{9}(F - 32)$

Simple Interest: $I = Prt$

(P = principal, r = annual interest rate, t = time in years)

A.2 Review of Geometric Figures

Plane figures have length and width but no thickness or depth		
Name	**Description**	**Figure**
Polygon	Union of three or more coplanar line segments that intersect with each other only at each endpoint, with each endpoint shared by two segments.	
Triangle	Polygon with three sides (sum of measures of three angles is 180°).	
Scalene Triangle	Triangle with no sides of equal length.	
Isosceles Triangle	Triangle with two sides of equal length.	
Equilateral Triangle	Triangle with all sides of equal length.	
Right Triangle	Triangle that contains a right angle.	leg, hypotenuse, leg
Quadrilateral	Polygon with four sides (sum of measures of four angles is 360°).	
Trapezoid	Quadrilateral with exactly one pair of opposite sides parallel.	base, leg, parallel sides, leg, base
Isosceles Trapezoid	Trapezoid with legs of equal length.	
Parallelogram	Quadrilateral with both pairs of opposite sides parallel and equal in length.	

Plane figures have length and width but no thickness or depth		
Name	*Description*	*Figure*
Rhombus	Parallelogram with all sides of equal length.	
Rectangle	Parallelogram with four right angles.	
Square	Rectangle with all sides of equal length.	
Circle	All points in a plane the same distance from a fixed point called the **center.**	

Solids have length, width, and depth		
Rectangular Solid	A solid with six sides, all of which are rectangles.	
Cube	A rectangular solid whose six sides are squares.	
Sphere	All points the same distance from a fixed point called the center.	
Right Circular Cylinder	A cylinder with two circular bases that are perpendicular to their altitude.	
Right Circular Cone	A cone with a circular base that is perpendicular to its altitude.	

A.3 Review of Volume and Surface Area

A **convex solid** is a set of points, S, not all in one plane, such that for any two points A and B in S, all points between A and B are also in S. In this appendix, we will find the volume and surface area of special types of solids called polyhedrons. A solid formed by the intersection of a finite number of planes is called a **polyhedron.** The box below is an example of a polyhedron.

Polyhedron

Each of the plane regions of the polyhedron is called a **face** of the polyhedron. If the intersection of two faces is a line segment, this line segment is an **edge** of the polyhedron. The intersections of the edges are the **vertices** of the polyhedron.

Volume is a measure of the space of a solid. The volume of a box or can, for example, is the amount of space inside. Volume can be used to describe the amount of juice in a pitcher or the amount of concrete needed to pour a foundation for a house.

The volume of a solid is the number of **cubic units** in the solid. A cubic centimeter and a cubic inch are illustrated.

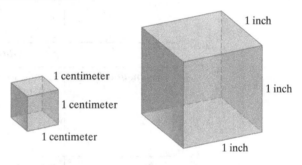

1 cubic centimeter   **1 cubic inch**

The **surface area** of a polyhedron is the sum of the areas of the faces of the polyhedron. For example, each face of the cube to the left above has an area of 1 square centimeter. Since there are 6 faces of the cube, the sum of the areas of the faces is 6 square centimeters. Surface area can be used to describe the amount of material needed to cover or form a solid. Surface area is measured in square units.

Formulas for finding the volumes, V, and surface areas, SA, of some common solids are given next.

Volume and Surface Area Formulas of Common Solids	
Solid	*Formulas*
RECTANGULAR SOLID	$V = lwh$ $SA = 2lh + 2wh + 2lw$ where h = height, w = width, l = length
CUBE	$V = s^3$ $SA = 6s^2$ where s = side

Volume and Surface Area Formulas of Common Solids

Solid	Formulas
SPHERE radius	$V = \dfrac{4}{3}\pi r^3$ $SA = 4\pi r^2$ where r = radius
CIRCULAR CYLINDER height radius	$V = \pi r^2 h$ $SA = 2\pi rh + 2\pi r^2$ where h = height, r = radius
CONE height radius	$V = \dfrac{1}{3}\pi r^2 h$ $SA = \pi r\sqrt{r^2 + h^2} + \pi r^2$ where h = height, r = radius
SQUARE-BASED PYRAMID height · slant height · side	$V = \dfrac{1}{3}s^2 h$ $SA = B + \dfrac{1}{2}pl$ where B = area of base; p = perimeter of base, h = height, s = side, l = slant height

> **Helpful Hint**
>
> Volume is measured in cubic units. Surface area is measured in square units.

EXAMPLE 1   Find the volume and surface area of a rectangular box that is 12 inches long, 6 inches wide, and 3 inches high.

3 in.

6 in.   12 in.

Solution Let $h = 3$ in., $l = 12$ in., and $w = 6$ in.

$$V = lwh$$
$$V = 12 \text{ inches} \cdot 6 \text{ inches} \cdot 3 \text{ inches} = 216 \text{ cubic inches}$$

The volume of the rectangular box is 216 cubic inches.

$$SA = 2lh + 2wh + 2lw$$
$$= 2(12 \text{ in.})(3 \text{ in.}) + 2(6 \text{ in.})(3 \text{ in.}) + 2(12 \text{ in.})(6 \text{ in.})$$
$$= 72 \text{ sq in.} + 36 \text{ sq in.} + 144 \text{ sq in.}$$
$$= 252 \text{ sq in.}$$

The surface area of the rectangular box is 252 square inches.

EXAMPLE 2   Find the volume and surface area of a ball of radius 2 inches. Give the exact volume and surface area and then use the approximation $\frac{22}{7}$ for π.

Solution

$$V = \frac{4}{3}\pi r^3 \qquad \text{Formula for volume of a sphere}$$

$$V = \frac{4}{3}\pi (2 \text{ in.})^3 \qquad \text{Let } r = 2 \text{ inches.}$$

$$= \frac{32}{3}\pi \text{ cu in.} \qquad \text{Simplify.}$$

$$\approx \frac{32}{3} \cdot \frac{22}{7} \text{ cu in.} \qquad \text{Approximate } \pi \text{ with } \frac{22}{7}.$$

$$= \frac{704}{21} \text{ or } 33\frac{11}{21} \text{ cu in.}$$

The volume of the sphere is exactly $\frac{32}{3}\pi$ cubic inches or approximately $33\frac{11}{21}$ cubic inches.

$$SA = 4\pi r^2 \qquad \text{Formula for surface area}$$

$$SA = 4\pi (2 \text{ in.})^2 \qquad \text{Let } r = 2 \text{ inches.}$$

$$= 16\pi \text{ sq in.} \qquad \text{Simplify.}$$

$$\approx 16 \cdot \frac{22}{7} \text{ sq in.} \qquad \text{Approximate } \pi \text{ with } \frac{22}{7}.$$

$$= \frac{352}{7} \text{ or } 50\frac{2}{7} \text{ sq in.}$$

The surface area of the sphere is exactly 16π square inches or approximately $50\frac{2}{7}$ square inches.   □

A.3   Exercise Set   MyMathLab ▶

Find the volume and surface area of each solid. See Examples 1 and 2. For formulas that contain π, give the exact answer and then approximate using $\frac{22}{7}$ for π.

5. (For surface area, use 3.14 to approximate π and round to two decimal places.)

1.

4 in.
3 in.
6 in.

2.

3 mi

3 yd
2 yd

6.

10 ft
6 ft

7.

10 in.

3.

8 cm
8 cm
8 cm

4.

4 cm
4 cm
8 cm

8. Find the volume only.

1¾ in.

9 in.

9.

4 cm

5 cm

6 cm

10.

1 ft

Solve.

11. Find the volume of a cube with edges of $1\frac{1}{3}$ inches.

$1\frac{1}{3}$ in.

12. A water storage tank is in the shape of a cone with the pointed end down. If the radius is 14 ft and the depth of the tank is 15 ft, approximate the volume of the tank in cubic feet. Use $\frac{22}{7}$ for π.

14 ft

15 ft

13. Find the surface area of a rectangular box 2 ft by 1.4 ft by 3 ft.

14. Find the surface area of a box in the shape of a cube that is 5 ft on each side.

15. Find the volume of a pyramid with a square base 5 in. on a side and a height of 1.3 in.

16. Approximate to the nearest hundredth the volume of a sphere with a radius of 2 cm. Use 3.14 for π.

17. A paperweight is in the shape of a square-based pyramid 20 cm tall. If an edge of the base is 12 cm, find the volume of the paperweight.

18. A bird bath is made in the shape of a hemisphere (half-sphere). If its radius is 10 in., approximate the volume. Use $\frac{22}{7}$ for π.

10 in.

19. Find the exact surface area of a sphere with a radius of 7 in.

20. A tank is in the shape of a cylinder 8 ft tall and 3 ft in radius. Find the exact surface area of the tank.

21. Find the volume of a rectangular block of ice 2 ft by $2\frac{1}{2}$ ft by $1\frac{1}{2}$ ft.

22. Find the capacity (volume in cubic feet) of a rectangular ice chest with inside measurements of 3 ft by $1\frac{1}{2}$ ft by $1\frac{3}{4}$ ft.

23. An ice cream cone with a 4-cm diameter and 3-cm depth is filled exactly level with the top of the cone. Approximate how much ice cream (in cubic centimeters) is in the cone. Use $\frac{22}{7}$ for π.

24. A child's toy is in the shape of a square-based pyramid 10 in. tall. If an edge of the base is 7 in., find the volume of the toy.

Appendix B

Stretching and Compressing Graphs of Absolute Value Functions

In Section 3.6, we learned to shift and reflect graphs of common functions: $f(x) = x$, $f(x) = x^2$, $f(x) = |x|$, and $f(x) = \sqrt{x}$. Since other common functions are studied throughout this text, in this appendix we concentrate on the absolute value function.

Recall that the graph of $h(x) = -|x - 1| + 2$, for example, is the same as the graph of $f(x) = |x|$ reflected about the x-axis, moved 1 unit to the right and 2 units upward. In other words,

$$h(x) = -|x - 1| + 2$$

opens downward $(1, 2)$ location of vertex of V-shape

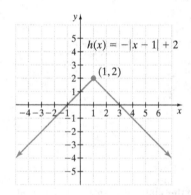

Let's now study the graphs of a few other absolute value functions.

EXAMPLE I Graph $h(x) = 2|x|$, and $g(x) = \dfrac{1}{2}|x|$.

<u>Solution</u> Let's find and plot ordered pair solutions for the functions.

x	$h(x)$	$g(x)$
-2	4	1
-1	2	$\dfrac{1}{2}$
0	0	0
1	2	$\dfrac{1}{2}$
2	4	2

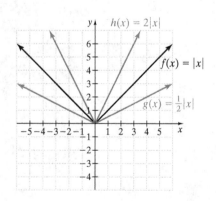

Notice that the graph of $h(x) = 2|x|$ is narrower than the graph of $f(x) = |x|$ and the graph of $g(x) = \dfrac{1}{2}|x|$ is wider than the graph of $f(x) = |x|$. ☐

690

In general, for the absolute value function, we have the following:

> ### The Graph of the Absolute Value Function
>
> The graph of $f(x) = a|x - h| + k$
> - Has vertex (h, k) and is V-shaped.
> - Opens up if $a > 0$ and down if $a < 0$.
> - If $|a| < 1$, the graph is wider than the graph of $y = |x|$.
> - If $|a| > 1$, the graph is narrower than the graph of $y = |x|$.

EXAMPLE 2   Graph $f(x) = -\dfrac{1}{3}|x + 2| + 4$.

Solution   Let's write this function in the form $f(x) = a|x - h| + k$. For our function, we have $f(x) = -\dfrac{1}{3}|x - (-2)| + 4$. Thus,

- vertex is $(-2, 4)$
- since $a < 0$, V-shape opens down
- since $|a| = \left|-\dfrac{1}{3}\right| = \dfrac{1}{3} < 1$, the graph is wider than $y = |x|$

We will also find and plot ordered pair solutions.

If $x = -5, f(-5) = -\dfrac{1}{3}|-5 + 2| + 4$, or 3

If $x = 1, f(1) = -\dfrac{1}{3}|1 + 2| + 4$, or 3

If $x = 3, f(3) = -\dfrac{1}{3}|3 + 2| + 4$, or $\dfrac{7}{3}$, or $2\dfrac{1}{3}$

x	$f(x)$
-5	3
1	3
3	$2\dfrac{1}{3}$

 Exercise Set MyMathLab®

Sketch the graph of each function. Label the vertex of the V-shape.

1. $f(x) = 3|x|$

2. $f(x) = 5|x|$

3. $f(x) = \dfrac{1}{4}|x|$

4. $f(x) = \dfrac{1}{3}|x|$

5. $g(x) = 2|x| + 3$

6. $g(x) = 3|x| + 2$

7. $h(x) = -\dfrac{1}{2}|x|$

8. $h(x) = -\dfrac{1}{3}|x|$

9. $f(x) = 4|x - 1|$

10. $f(x) = 3|x - 2|$

11. $g(x) = -\dfrac{1}{3}|x| - 2$

12. $g(x) = -\dfrac{1}{2}|x| - 3$

13. $f(x) = -2|x - 3| + 4$

14. $f(x) = -3|x - 1| + 5$

15. $f(x) = \dfrac{2}{3}|x + 2| - 5$

16. $f(x) = \dfrac{3}{4}|x + 1| - 4$

Appendix C

Solving Systems of Equations Using Determinants

We have solved systems of two linear equations in two variables in four ways: graphically, by substitution, by elimination, and by matrices. Now we analyze another method, called **Cramer's rule.**

OBJECTIVE

1 Evaluating 2 × 2 Determinants

Recall that a matrix is a rectangular array of numbers. If a matrix has the same number of rows and columns, it is called a **square matrix.** Examples of square matrices are

$$\begin{bmatrix} 1 & 6 \\ 5 & 2 \end{bmatrix} \qquad \begin{bmatrix} 2 & 4 & 1 \\ 0 & 5 & 2 \\ 3 & 6 & 9 \end{bmatrix}$$

A **determinant** is a real number associated with a square matrix. The determinant of a square matrix is denoted by placing vertical bars about the array of numbers. Thus,

The determinant of the square matrix $\begin{bmatrix} 1 & 6 \\ 5 & 2 \end{bmatrix}$ is $\begin{vmatrix} 1 & 6 \\ 5 & 2 \end{vmatrix}$.

The determinant of the square matrix $\begin{bmatrix} 2 & 4 & 1 \\ 0 & 5 & 2 \\ 3 & 6 & 9 \end{bmatrix}$ is $\begin{vmatrix} 2 & 4 & 1 \\ 0 & 5 & 2 \\ 3 & 6 & 9 \end{vmatrix}$.

We define the determinant of a 2 × 2 matrix first. (Recall that 2 × 2 is read "two by two." It means that the matrix has 2 rows and 2 columns.)

Determinant of a 2 × 2 Matrix

$$\begin{vmatrix} a & b \\ c & d \end{vmatrix} = ad - bc$$

EXAMPLE 1 Evaluate each determinant

a. $\begin{vmatrix} -1 & 2 \\ 3 & -4 \end{vmatrix}$ **b.** $\begin{vmatrix} 2 & 0 \\ 7 & -5 \end{vmatrix}$

Solution First we identify the values of $a, b, c,$ and d. Then we perform the evaluation.

a. Here $a = -1, b = 2, c = 3,$ and $d = -4$.

$$\begin{vmatrix} -1 & 2 \\ 3 & -4 \end{vmatrix} = ad - bc = (-1)(-4) - (2)(3) = -2$$

b. In this example, $a = 2, b = 0, c = 7,$ and $d = -5$.

$$\begin{vmatrix} 2 & 0 \\ 7 & -5 \end{vmatrix} = ad - bc = 2(-5) - (0)(7) = -10$$

OBJECTIVE

2   Using Cramer's Rule to Solve a System of Two Linear Equations

To develop Cramer's rule, we solve the system $\begin{cases} ax + by = h \\ cx + dy = k \end{cases}$ using elimination. First, we eliminate y by multiplying both sides of the first equation by d and both sides of the second equation by $-b$ so that the coefficients of y are opposites. The result is that

$$\begin{cases} d(ax + by) = d \cdot h \\ -b(cx + dy) = -b \cdot k \end{cases} \quad \text{simplifies to} \quad \begin{cases} adx + bdy = hd \\ -bcx - bdy = -kb \end{cases}$$

We now add the two equations and solve for x.

$$adx + bdy = hd$$
$$\underline{-bcx - bdy = -kb}$$
$$adx - bcx = hd - kb \quad \text{Add the equations.}$$
$$(ad - bc)x = hd - kb$$
$$x = \frac{hd - kb}{ad - bc} \quad \text{Solve for } x.$$

When we replace x with $\dfrac{hd - kb}{ad - bc}$ in the equation $ax + by = h$ and solve for y, we find that $y = \dfrac{ak - ch}{ad - bc}$.

Notice that the numerator of the value of x is the determinant of

$$\begin{vmatrix} h & b \\ k & d \end{vmatrix} = hd - kb$$

Also, the numerator of the value of y is the determinant of

$$\begin{vmatrix} a & h \\ c & k \end{vmatrix} = ak - hc$$

Finally, the denominators of the values of x and y are the same and are the determinant of

$$\begin{vmatrix} a & b \\ c & d \end{vmatrix} = ad - bc$$

This means that the values of x and y can be written in determinant notation:

$$x = \frac{\begin{vmatrix} h & b \\ k & d \end{vmatrix}}{\begin{vmatrix} a & b \\ c & d \end{vmatrix}} \quad \text{and} \quad y = \frac{\begin{vmatrix} a & h \\ c & k \end{vmatrix}}{\begin{vmatrix} a & b \\ c & d \end{vmatrix}}$$

For convenience, we label the determinants D, D_x, and D_y.

x-coefficients

y-coefficients

$$\begin{vmatrix} a & b \\ c & d \end{vmatrix} = D \qquad \begin{vmatrix} h & b \\ k & d \end{vmatrix} = D_x \qquad \begin{vmatrix} a & h \\ c & k \end{vmatrix} = D_y$$

x-column replaced y-column replaced
by constants   by constants

These determinant formulas for the coordinates of the solution of a system are known as **Cramer's rule.**

Cramer's Rule for Two Linear Equations in Two Variables

The solution of the system $\begin{cases} ax + by = h \\ cx + dy = k \end{cases}$ is given by

$$x = \frac{\begin{vmatrix} h & b \\ k & d \end{vmatrix}}{\begin{vmatrix} a & b \\ c & d \end{vmatrix}} = \frac{D_x}{D} \qquad y = \frac{\begin{vmatrix} a & h \\ c & k \end{vmatrix}}{\begin{vmatrix} a & b \\ c & d \end{vmatrix}} = \frac{D_y}{D}$$

as long as $D = ad - bc$ is not 0.

When $D = 0$, the system is either inconsistent or the equations are dependent. When this happens, we need to use another method to see which is the case.

EXAMPLE 2   Use Cramer's rule to solve the system

$$\begin{cases} 3x + 4y = -7 \\ x - 2y = -9 \end{cases}$$

Solution   First we find D, D_x, and D_y.

$$\begin{array}{ccc} a & b & h \\ \downarrow & \downarrow & \downarrow \end{array}$$
$$\begin{cases} 3x + 4y = -7 \\ x - 2y = -9 \end{cases}$$
$$\begin{array}{ccc} \uparrow & \uparrow & \uparrow \\ c & d & k \end{array}$$

$$D = \begin{vmatrix} a & b \\ c & d \end{vmatrix} = \begin{vmatrix} 3 & 4 \\ 1 & -2 \end{vmatrix} = 3(-2) - 4(1) = -10$$

$$D_x = \begin{vmatrix} h & b \\ k & d \end{vmatrix} = \begin{vmatrix} -7 & 4 \\ -9 & -2 \end{vmatrix} = (-7)(-2) - 4(-9) = 50$$

$$D_y = \begin{vmatrix} a & h \\ c & d \end{vmatrix} = \begin{vmatrix} 3 & -7 \\ 1 & -9 \end{vmatrix} = 3(-9) - (-7)(1) = -20$$

Then $x = \dfrac{D_x}{D} = \dfrac{50}{-10} = -5$ and $y = \dfrac{D_y}{D} = \dfrac{-20}{-10} = 2$.

The ordered pair solution is $(-5, 2)$.

As always, check the solution in both original equations.   □

EXAMPLE 3   Use Cramer's rule to solve the system

$$\begin{cases} 5x + y = 5 \\ -7x - 2y = -7 \end{cases}$$

Solution   First we find D, D_x, and D_y.

$$D = \begin{vmatrix} 5 & 1 \\ -7 & -2 \end{vmatrix} = 5(-2) - (-7)(1) = -3$$

$$D_x = \begin{vmatrix} 5 & 1 \\ -7 & -2 \end{vmatrix} = 5(-2) - (-7)(1) = -3$$

$$D_y = \begin{vmatrix} 5 & 5 \\ -7 & -7 \end{vmatrix} = 5(-7) - 5(-7) = 0$$

Then

$$x = \frac{D_x}{D} = \frac{-3}{-3} = 1 \qquad y = \frac{D_y}{D} = \frac{0}{-3} = 0$$

The ordered pair solution is $(1, 0)$.

OBJECTIVE

3 Evaluating 3 × 3 Determinants

A 3×3 determinant can be used to solve a system of three equations in three variables. The determinant of a 3×3 matrix, however, is considerably more complex than a 2×2 one.

Determinant of a 3 × 3 Matrix

$$\begin{vmatrix} a_1 & b_1 & c_1 \\ a_2 & b_2 & c_2 \\ a_3 & b_3 & c_3 \end{vmatrix} = a_1 \cdot \begin{vmatrix} b_2 & c_2 \\ b_3 & c_3 \end{vmatrix} - a_2 \cdot \begin{vmatrix} b_1 & c_1 \\ b_3 & c_3 \end{vmatrix} + a_3 \cdot \begin{vmatrix} b_1 & c_1 \\ b_2 & c_2 \end{vmatrix}$$

Notice that the determinant of a 3×3 matrix is related to the determinants of three 2×2 matrices. Each determinant of these 2×2 matrices is called a **minor,** and every element of a 3×3 matrix has a minor associated with it. For example, the minor of c_2 is the determinant of the 2×2 matrix found by deleting the row and column containing c_2.

$$\begin{matrix} a_1 & b_1 & c_1 \\ a_2 & b_2 & c_2 \\ a_3 & b_3 & c_3 \end{matrix} \qquad \text{The minor of } c_2 \text{ is} \qquad \begin{vmatrix} a_1 & b_1 \\ a_3 & b_3 \end{vmatrix}$$

Also, the minor of element a_1 is the determinant of the 2×2 matrix that has no row or column containing a_1.

$$\begin{matrix} a_1 & b_1 & c_1 \\ a_2 & b_2 & c_2 \\ a_3 & b_3 & c_3 \end{matrix} \qquad \text{The minor of } a_1 \text{ is} \qquad \begin{vmatrix} b_2 & c_2 \\ b_3 & c_3 \end{vmatrix}$$

So the determinant of a 3×3 matrix can be written as

$$a_1 \cdot (\text{minor of } a_1) - a_2 \cdot (\text{minor of } a_2) + a_3 \cdot (\text{minor of } a_3)$$

Finding the determinant by using minors of elements in the first column is called **expanding** by the minors of the first column. *The value of a determinant can be found by expanding by the minors of any row or column.* The following **array of signs** is helpful in determining whether to add or subtract the product of an element and its minor.

Answer to Concept Check (below):

$$\begin{matrix} + & - & + & - \\ - & + & - & + \\ + & - & + & - \\ - & + & - & + \end{matrix}$$

$$\begin{matrix} + & - & + \\ - & + & - \\ + & - & + \end{matrix}$$

If an element is in a position marked $+$, we add. If marked $-$, we subtract.

✔ **CONCEPT CHECK**
Suppose you are interested in finding the determinant of a 4×4 matrix. Study the pattern shown in the array of signs for a 3×3 matrix. Use the pattern to expand the array of signs for use with a 4×4 matrix.

EXAMPLE 4 Evaluate by expanding by the minors of the given row or column.

$$\begin{vmatrix} 0 & 5 & 1 \\ 1 & 3 & -1 \\ -2 & 2 & 4 \end{vmatrix}$$

a. First column   **b.** Second row

Solution

a. The elements of the first column are 0, 1, and −2. The first column of the array of signs is +, −, +.

$$\begin{vmatrix} 0 & 5 & 1 \\ 1 & 3 & -1 \\ -2 & 2 & 4 \end{vmatrix} = 0 \cdot \begin{vmatrix} 3 & -1 \\ 2 & 4 \end{vmatrix} - 1 \cdot \begin{vmatrix} 5 & 1 \\ 2 & 4 \end{vmatrix} + (-2) \cdot \begin{vmatrix} 5 & 1 \\ 3 & -1 \end{vmatrix}$$

$$= 0(12 - (-2)) - 1(20 - 2) + (-2)(-5 - 3)$$

$$= 0 - 18 + 16 = -2$$

b. The elements of the second row are 1, 3, and −1. This time, the signs begin with − and again alternate.

$$\begin{vmatrix} 0 & 5 & 1 \\ 1 & 3 & -1 \\ -2 & 2 & 4 \end{vmatrix} = -1 \cdot \begin{vmatrix} 5 & 1 \\ 2 & 4 \end{vmatrix} + 3 \cdot \begin{vmatrix} 0 & 1 \\ -2 & 4 \end{vmatrix} - (-1) \cdot \begin{vmatrix} 0 & 5 \\ -2 & 2 \end{vmatrix}$$

$$= -1(20 - 2) + 3(0 - (-2)) - (-1)(0 - (-10))$$

$$= -18 + 6 + 10 = -2$$

Notice that the determinant of the 3 × 3 matrix is the same regardless of the row or column you select to expand by. □

✔ CONCEPT CHECK

Why would expanding by minors of the second row be a good choice for the determinant $\begin{vmatrix} 3 & 4 & -2 \\ 5 & 0 & 0 \\ 6 & -3 & 7 \end{vmatrix}$?

OBJECTIVE

4 Using Cramer's Rule to Solve a System of Three Linear Equations

A system of three equations in three variables may be solved with Cramer's rule also. Using the elimination process to solve a system with unknown constants as coefficients leads to the following.

Cramer's Rule for Three Equations in Three Variables

The solution of the system $\begin{cases} a_1x + b_1y + c_1z = k_1 \\ a_2x + b_2y + c_2z = k_2 \\ a_3x + b_3y + c_3z = k_3 \end{cases}$ is given by

$$x = \frac{D_x}{D} \quad\quad y = \frac{D_y}{D} \quad \text{and} \quad z = \frac{D_z}{D}$$

where

$$D = \begin{vmatrix} a_1 & b_1 & c_1 \\ a_2 & b_2 & c_2 \\ a_3 & b_3 & c_3 \end{vmatrix} \quad\quad D_x = \begin{vmatrix} k_1 & b_1 & c_1 \\ k_2 & b_2 & c_2 \\ k_3 & b_3 & c_3 \end{vmatrix}$$

$$D_y = \begin{vmatrix} a_1 & k_1 & c_1 \\ a_2 & k_2 & c_2 \\ a_3 & k_3 & c_3 \end{vmatrix} \quad\quad D_z = \begin{vmatrix} a_1 & b_1 & k_1 \\ a_2 & b_2 & k_2 \\ a_3 & b_3 & k_3 \end{vmatrix}$$

as long as D is not 0.

Answer to Concept Check:
Two elements of the second row are 0, which makes calculations easier.

EXAMPLE 5   Use Cramer's rule to solve the system

$$\begin{cases} x - 2y + z = 4 \\ 3x + y - 2z = 3 \\ 5x + 5y + 3z = -8 \end{cases}$$

Solution   First we find $D, D_x, D_y,$ and D_z. Beginning with D, we expand by the minors of the first column.

$$D = \begin{vmatrix} 1 & -2 & 1 \\ 3 & 1 & -2 \\ 5 & 5 & 3 \end{vmatrix} = 1 \cdot \begin{vmatrix} 1 & -2 \\ 5 & 3 \end{vmatrix} - 3 \cdot \begin{vmatrix} -2 & 1 \\ 5 & 3 \end{vmatrix} + 5 \cdot \begin{vmatrix} -2 & 1 \\ 1 & -2 \end{vmatrix}$$

$$= 1(3 - (-10)) - 3(-6 - 5) + 5(4 - 1)$$

$$= 13 + 33 + 15 = 61$$

$$D_x = \begin{vmatrix} 4 & -2 & 1 \\ 3 & 1 & -2 \\ -8 & 5 & 3 \end{vmatrix} = 4 \cdot \begin{vmatrix} 1 & -2 \\ 5 & 3 \end{vmatrix} - 3 \cdot \begin{vmatrix} -2 & 1 \\ 5 & 3 \end{vmatrix} + (-8) \cdot \begin{vmatrix} -2 & 1 \\ 1 & -2 \end{vmatrix}$$

$$= 4(3 - (-10)) - 3(-6 - 5) + (-8)(4 - 1)$$

$$= 52 + 33 - 24 = 61$$

$$D_y = \begin{vmatrix} 1 & 4 & 1 \\ 3 & 3 & -2 \\ 5 & -8 & 3 \end{vmatrix} = 1 \cdot \begin{vmatrix} 3 & -2 \\ -8 & 3 \end{vmatrix} - 3 \cdot \begin{vmatrix} 4 & 1 \\ -8 & 3 \end{vmatrix} + 5 \cdot \begin{vmatrix} 4 & 1 \\ 3 & -2 \end{vmatrix}$$

$$= 1(9 - 16) - 3(12 - (-8)) + 5(-8 - 3)$$

$$= -7 - 60 - 55 = -122$$

$$D_z = \begin{vmatrix} 1 & -2 & 4 \\ 3 & 1 & 3 \\ 5 & 5 & -8 \end{vmatrix} = 1 \cdot \begin{vmatrix} 1 & 3 \\ 5 & -8 \end{vmatrix} - 3 \cdot \begin{vmatrix} -2 & 4 \\ 5 & -8 \end{vmatrix} + 5 \cdot \begin{vmatrix} -2 & 4 \\ 1 & 3 \end{vmatrix}$$

$$= 1(-8 - 15) - 3(16 - 20) + 5(-6 - 4)$$

$$= -23 + 12 - 50 = -61$$

From these determinants, we calculate the solution:

$$x = \frac{D_x}{D} = \frac{61}{61} = 1 \quad y = \frac{D_y}{D} = \frac{-122}{61} = -2 \quad z = \frac{D_z}{D} = \frac{-61}{61} = -1$$

The ordered triple solution is $(1, -2, -1)$. Check this solution by verifying that it satisfies each equation of the system.   □

Vocabulary and Readiness Check

Evaluate each determinant mentally.

1. $\begin{vmatrix} 7 & 2 \\ 0 & 8 \end{vmatrix}$

2. $\begin{vmatrix} 6 & 0 \\ 1 & 2 \end{vmatrix}$

3. $\begin{vmatrix} -4 & 2 \\ 0 & 8 \end{vmatrix}$

4. $\begin{vmatrix} 5 & 0 \\ 3 & -5 \end{vmatrix}$

5. $\begin{vmatrix} -2 & 0 \\ 3 & -10 \end{vmatrix}$

6. $\begin{vmatrix} -1 & 4 \\ 0 & -18 \end{vmatrix}$

C Exercise Set MyMathLab®

Evaluate each determinant. See Example 1.

1. $\begin{vmatrix} 3 & 5 \\ -1 & 7 \end{vmatrix}$ 　　　 **2.** $\begin{vmatrix} -5 & 1 \\ 1 & -4 \end{vmatrix}$

3. $\begin{vmatrix} 9 & -2 \\ 4 & -3 \end{vmatrix}$ 　　　 **4.** $\begin{vmatrix} 4 & -1 \\ 9 & 8 \end{vmatrix}$

5. $\begin{vmatrix} -2 & 9 \\ 4 & -18 \end{vmatrix}$ 　　　 **6.** $\begin{vmatrix} -40 & 8 \\ 70 & -14 \end{vmatrix}$

7. $\begin{vmatrix} \frac{3}{4} & \frac{5}{2} \\ -\frac{1}{6} & \frac{7}{3} \end{vmatrix}$ 　　　 **8.** $\begin{vmatrix} \frac{5}{7} & \frac{1}{3} \\ \frac{6}{7} & \frac{2}{3} \end{vmatrix}$

Use Cramer's rule, if possible, to solve each system of linear equations. See Examples 2 and 3.

9. $\begin{cases} 2y - 4 = 0 \\ x + 2y = 5 \end{cases}$ 　　 **10.** $\begin{cases} 4x - y = 5 \\ 3x - 3 = 0 \end{cases}$

11. $\begin{cases} 3x + y = 1 \\ 2y = 2 - 6x \end{cases}$ 　　 **12.** $\begin{cases} y = 2x - 5 \\ 8x - 4y = 20 \end{cases}$

13. $\begin{cases} 5x - 2y = 27 \\ -3x + 5y = 18 \end{cases}$ 　　 **14.** $\begin{cases} 4x - y = 9 \\ 2x + 3y = -27 \end{cases}$

15. $\begin{cases} 2x - 5y = 4 \\ x + 2y = -7 \end{cases}$ 　　 **16.** $\begin{cases} 3x - y = 2 \\ -5x + 2y = 0 \end{cases}$

17. $\begin{cases} \frac{2}{3}x - \frac{3}{4}y = -1 \\ -\frac{1}{6}x + \frac{3}{4}y = \frac{5}{2} \end{cases}$ 　 **18.** $\begin{cases} \frac{1}{2}x - \frac{1}{3}y = -3 \\ \frac{1}{8}x + \frac{1}{6}y = 0 \end{cases}$

Evaluate. See Example 4.

19. $\begin{vmatrix} 2 & 1 & 0 \\ 0 & 5 & -3 \\ 4 & 0 & 2 \end{vmatrix}$ 　　 **20.** $\begin{vmatrix} -6 & 4 & 2 \\ 1 & 0 & 5 \\ 0 & 3 & 1 \end{vmatrix}$

21. $\begin{vmatrix} 4 & -6 & 0 \\ -2 & 3 & 0 \\ 4 & -6 & 1 \end{vmatrix}$ 　　 **22.** $\begin{vmatrix} 5 & 2 & 1 \\ 3 & -6 & 0 \\ -2 & 8 & 0 \end{vmatrix}$

23. $\begin{vmatrix} 1 & 0 & 4 \\ 1 & -1 & 2 \\ 3 & 2 & 1 \end{vmatrix}$ 　　 **24.** $\begin{vmatrix} 0 & 1 & 2 \\ 3 & -1 & 2 \\ 3 & 2 & -2 \end{vmatrix}$

25. $\begin{vmatrix} 3 & 6 & -3 \\ -1 & -2 & 3 \\ 4 & -1 & 6 \end{vmatrix}$ 　　 **26.** $\begin{vmatrix} 2 & -2 & 1 \\ 4 & 1 & 3 \\ 3 & 1 & 2 \end{vmatrix}$

Use Cramer's rule, if possible, to solve each system of linear equations. See Example 5.

27. $\begin{cases} 3x + z = -1 \\ -x - 3y + z = 7 \\ 3y + z = 5 \end{cases}$

28. $\begin{cases} 4y - 3z = -2 \\ 8x - 4y \phantom{{}+ z} = 4 \\ -8x + 4y + z = -2 \end{cases}$

29. $\begin{cases} x + y + z = 8 \\ 2x - y - z = 10 \\ x - 2y + 3z = 22 \end{cases}$

30. $\begin{cases} 5x + y + 3z = 1 \\ x - y - 3z = -7 \\ -x + y \phantom{{}- 3z} = 1 \end{cases}$

31. $\begin{cases} 2x + 2y + z = 1 \\ -x + y + 2z = 3 \\ x + 2y + 4z = 0 \end{cases}$

32. $\begin{cases} 2x - 3y + z = 5 \\ x + y + z = 0 \\ 4x + 2y + 4z = 4 \end{cases}$

33. $\begin{cases} x - 2y + z = -5 \\ 3y + 2z = 4 \\ 3x - y \phantom{{}+ 2z} = -2 \end{cases}$

34. $\begin{cases} 4x + 5y \phantom{{}+ 2z} = 10 \\ 3y + 2z = -6 \\ x + y + z = 3 \end{cases}$

CONCEPT EXTENSIONS

Find the value of x that will make each a true statement.

35. $\begin{vmatrix} 1 & x \\ 2 & 7 \end{vmatrix} = -3$

36. $\begin{vmatrix} 6 & 1 \\ -2 & x \end{vmatrix} = 26$

37. If all the elements in a single row of a determinant are zero, what is the value of the determinant? Explain your answer.

38. If all the elements in a single column of a determinant are 0, what is the value of the determinant? Explain your answer.

Appendix D

An Introduction to Using a Graphing Utility

The Viewing Window and Interpreting Window Settings

In this appendix, we will use the term **graphing utility** to mean a graphing calculator or a computer software graphing package. All graphing utilities graph equations by plotting points on a screen. Although plotting several points can be slow and sometimes tedious, a graphing utility can quickly and accurately plot hundreds of points. How does a graphing utility show plotted points? A computer or calculator screen is made up of a grid of small rectangular areas called **pixels.** If a pixel contains a point to be plotted, the pixel is turned "on"; otherwise, the pixel remains "off." The graph of an equation is then a collection of pixels turned "on." The graph of $y = 3x + 1$ from a graphing calculator is shown in Figure A-1. Notice the irregular shape of the line caused by the rectangular pixels.

Figure A-1

The portion of the coordinate plane shown on the screen in Figure A-1 is called the **viewing window** or the **viewing rectangle.** Notice the x-axis and the y-axis on the graph. Tick marks are shown on the axes, but they are not labeled. This means that from this screen alone, we do not know how many units each tick mark represents. To see what each tick mark represents and the minimum and maximum values on the axes, check the window setting of the graphing utility. It defines the viewing window. The window of the graph of $y = 3x + 1$ shown in Figure A-1 has the following setting (Figure A-2):

Figure A-2

$$\text{Xmin} = -10 \quad \text{The minimum } x\text{-value is } -10.$$
$$\text{Xmax} = 10 \quad \text{The maximum } x\text{-value is } 10.$$
$$\text{Xscl} = 1 \quad \text{The } x\text{-axis scale is 1 unit per tick mark.}$$
$$\text{Ymin} = -10 \quad \text{The minimum } y\text{-value is } -10.$$
$$\text{Ymax} = 10 \quad \text{The maximum } y\text{-value is 10.}$$
$$\text{Yscl} = 1 \quad \text{The } y\text{-axis scale is 1 unit per tick mark.}$$

By knowing the scale, we can find the minimum and the maximum values on the axes simply by counting tick marks. For example, if both the Xscl (x-axis scale) and the Yscl are 1 unit per tick mark on the graph in Figure A-3, we can count the tick marks and find that the minimum x-value is -10 and the maximum x-value is 10. Also, the minimum y-value is -10 and the maximum y-value is 10. If the Xscl (x-axis scale) changes to 2 units per tick mark (shown in Figure A-4), by counting tick marks, we see that the minimum x-value is now -20 and the maximum x-value is now 20.

Xscl = 1   Yscl = 1

Figure A-3

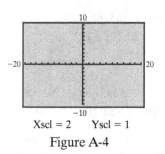

Xscl = 2   Yscl = 1

Figure A-4

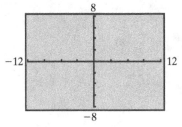

Figure A-5

It is also true that if we know the Xmin and the Xmax values, we can calculate the Xscl by the displayed axes. For example, the Xscl of the graph in Figure A-5 must be 3 units per tick mark for the maximum and minimum x-values to be as shown. Also, the Yscl of that graph must be 2 units per tick mark for the maximum and minimum y-values to be as shown.

We will call the viewing window in Figure A-3 a *standard* viewing window or rectangle. Although a standard viewing window is sufficient for much of this text, special care must be taken to ensure that all key features of a graph are shown. Figures A-6, A-7, and A-8 show the graph of $y = x^2 + 11x - 1$ on three viewing windows. Note that certain viewing windows for this equation are misleading.

Figure A-6

Figure A-7

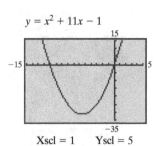

Figure A-8

How do we ensure that all distinguishing features of the graph of an equation are shown? It helps to know about the equation that is being graphed. For example, the equation $y = x^2 + 11x - 1$ is not a linear equation and its graph is not a line. This equation is a quadratic equation and, therefore, its graph is a parabola. By knowing this information, we know that the graph shown in Figure A-6, although correct, is misleading. Of the three viewing rectangles shown, the graph in Figure A-8 is best because it shows more of the distinguishing features of the parabola. Properties of equations needed for graphing will be studied in this text.

Viewing Window and Interpreting Window Settings Exercise Set

In Exercises 1–4, determine whether all ordered pairs listed will lie within a standard viewing rectangle.

1. $(-9, 0), (5, 8), (1, -8)$
2. $(4, 7), (0, 0), (-8, 9)$
3. $(-11, 0), (2, 2), (7, -5)$
4. $(3, 5), (-3, -5), (15, 0)$

In Exercises 5–10, choose an Xmin, Xmax, Ymin, and Ymax so that all ordered pairs listed will lie within the viewing rectangle.

5. $(-90, 0), (55, 80), (0, -80)$
6. $(4, 70), (20, 20), (-18, 90)$
7. $(-11, 0), (2, 2), (7, -5)$
8. $(3, 5), (-3, -5), (15, 0)$
9. $(200, 200), (50, -50), (70, -50)$
10. $(40, 800), (-30, 500), (15, 0)$

Write the window setting for each viewing window shown. Use the following format:

11.

12.

13.

14.

15.

16.

17.
Xscl = 1, Yscl = 3

18.
Xscl = 10, Yscl = 2

19.
Xscl = 5, Yscl = 10

20.
Xscl = 100, Yscl = 200

Graphing Equations and Square Viewing Window

In general, the following steps may be used to graph an equation on a standard viewing window.

Graphing an Equation in *X* and *Y* with a Graphing Utility on a Standard Viewing Window

Step 1: Solve the equation for y.

Step 2: Using your graphing utility, enter the equation in the form
$Y = expression\ involving\ x$.

Step 3: Activate the graphing utility.

Special care must be taken when entering the *expression involving x* in Step 2. You must be sure that the graphing utility you are using interprets the expression as you want it to. For example, let's graph $3y = 4x$. To do so,

Step 1: Solve the equation for y.

$$3y = 4x$$

$$\frac{3y}{3} = \frac{4x}{3}$$

$$y = \frac{4}{3}x$$

Step 2: Using your graphing utility, enter the expression $\frac{4}{3}x$ after the $Y =$ prompt.

For your graphing utility to interpret the expression correctly, you may need to enter $(4/3)x$ or $(4 \div 3)x$.

Step 3: Activate the graphing utility. The graph should appear as in Figure A-9.

Figure A-9

Distinguishing features of the graph of a line include showing all the intercepts of the line. For example, the window of the graph of the line in Figure A-10 does not show both intercepts of the line, but the window of the graph of the same line in Figure A-11 does show both intercepts.

Figure A-10

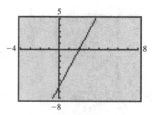

Figure A-11

On a standard viewing window, the tick marks on the *y*-axis are closer together than the tick marks on the *x*-axis. This happens because the viewing window is a rectangle, so 10 equally spaced tick marks on the positive *y*-axis will be closer together than 10 equally spaced tick marks on the positive *x*-axis. This causes the appearance of graphs to be distorted.

For example, notice the different appearances of the same line graphed using different viewing windows. The line in Figure A-12 is distorted because the tick marks along the *x*-axis are farther apart than the tick marks along the *y*-axis. The graph of the same line in Figure A-13 is not distorted because the viewing rectangle has been selected so that there is equal spacing between tick marks on both axes.

Figure A-12

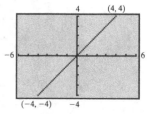

Figure A-13

We say that the line in Figure A-13 is graphed on a *square* setting. Some graphing utilities have a built-in program that, if activated, will automatically provide a square setting. A square setting is especially helpful when we are graphing perpendicular lines, circles, or when a true geometric perspective is desired. Some examples of square screens are shown in Figures A-14 and A-15.

Figure A-14

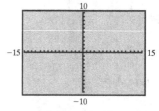

Figure A-15

Other features of a graphing utility such as Trace, Zoom, Intersect, and Table are discussed in appropriate Graphing Calculator Explorations in this text.

Graphing Equations and Square Viewing Window Exercise Set

Graph each linear equation in two variables, using the different range settings given. Determine which setting shows all intercepts of a line.

1. $y = 2x + 12$
  Setting A: $[-10, 10]$ by $[-10, 10]$
  Setting B: $[-10, 10]$ by $[-10, 15]$

2. $y = -3x + 25$
  Setting A: $[-5, 5]$ by $[-30, 10]$
  Setting B: $[-10, 10]$ by $[-10, 30]$

3. $y = -x - 41$
  Setting A: $[-50, 10]$ by $[-10, 10]$
  Setting B: $[-50, 10]$ by $[-50, 15]$

4. $y = 6x - 18$
  Setting A: $[-10, 10]$ by $[-20, 10]$
  Setting B: $[-10, 10]$ by $[-10, 10]$

5. $y = \dfrac{1}{2}x - 15$
  Setting A: $[-10, 10]$ by $[-20, 10]$
  Setting B: $[-10, 35]$ by $[-20, 15]$

6. $y = -\dfrac{2}{3}x - \dfrac{29}{3}$
  Setting A: $[-10, 10]$ by $[-10, 10]$
  Setting B: $[-15, 5]$ by $[-15, 5]$

The graph of each equation is a line. Use a graphing utility and a standard viewing window to graph each equation.

7. $3x = 5y$ **8.** $7y = -3x$ **9.** $9x - 5y = 30$

10. $4x + 6y = 20$ **11.** $y = -7$ **12.** $y = 2$

13. $x + 10y = -5$ **14.** $x - 5y = 9$

Graph the following equations using the square setting given. Some keystrokes that may be helpful are given.

15. $y = \sqrt{x}$ $[-12, 12]$ by $[-8, 8]$
  Suggested keystrokes: $\sqrt{\ }\, x$

16. $y = \sqrt{2x}$ $[-12, 12]$ by $[-8, 8]$
  Suggested keystrokes: $\sqrt{\ }\,(2x)$

17. $y = x^2 + 2x + 1$ $[-15, 15]$ by $[-10, 10]$
  Suggested keystrokes: $x\verb|^|2 + 2x + 1$

18. $y = x^2 - 5$ $[-15, 15]$ by $[-10, 10]$
  Suggested keystrokes: $x\verb|^|2 - 5$

19. $y = |x|$ $[-9, 9]$ by $[-6, 6]$
  Suggested keystrokes: ABS (x)

20. $y = |x - 2|$ $[-9, 9]$ by $[-6, 6]$
  Suggested keystrokes: ABS$(x - 2)$

Graph each line. Use a standard viewing window; then, if necessary, change the viewing window so that all intercepts of each line show.

21. $x + 2y = 30$ **22.** $1.5x - 3.7y = 40.3$

Contents of Student Resources

Student Resources

Study Skills Builders

Attitude and Study Tips

Study Skills Builder 1

Have You Decided to Complete This Course Successfully?

Ask yourself if one of your current goals is to complete this course successfully.

If it is not a goal of yours, ask yourself why. One common reason is fear of failure. Amazingly enough, fear of failure alone can be strong enough to keep many of us from doing our best in any endeavor.

Another common reason is that you simply haven't taken the time to think about or write down your goals for this course. To help accomplish this, answer the exercises below.

Exercises

1. Write down your goal(s) for this course.

2. Now list steps you will take to make sure your goal(s) in Exercise 1 are accomplished.

3. Rate your commitment to this course with a number between 1 and 5. Use the diagram below to help.

High Commitment		Average Commitment		Not Commited at All
5	4	3	2	1

4. If you have rated your personal commitment level (from the exercise above) as a 1, 2, or 3, list the reasons why this is so. Then determine whether it is possible to increase your commitment level to a 4 or 5.

Good luck, and don't forget that a positive attitude will make a big difference.

Study Skills Builder 2

Tips for Studying for an Exam

To prepare for an exam, try the following study techniques:

- Start the study process days before your exam.
- Make sure that you are up to date on your assignments.
- If there is a topic that you are unsure of, use one of the many resources that are available to you. For example,

    See your instructor.

    View a lecture video on the topic.

    Visit a learning resource center on campus.

    Read the textbook material and examples on the topic.

- Reread your notes and carefully review the Chapter Highlights at the end of any chapter.
- Work the review exercises at the end of the chapter.
- Find a quiet place to take the Chapter Test found at the end of the chapter. Do not use any resources when taking this sample test. This way, you will have a clear indication of how prepared you are for your exam. Check your answers and use the Chapter Test Prep Videos to make sure that you correct any missed exercises.

Good luck, and keep a positive attitude.

Exercises

Let's see how you did on your last exam.

1. How many days before your last exam did you start studying for that exam?

2. Were you up to date on your assignments at that time, or did you need to catch up on assignments?

3. List the most helpful text supplement (if you used one).

4. List the most helpful campus supplement (if you used one).

5. List your process for preparing for a mathematics test.

6. Was this process helpful? In other words, were you satisfied with your performance on your exam?

7. If not, what changes can you make in your process that will make it more helpful to you?

Study Skills Builder 3

What to Do the Day of an Exam

Your first exam may be soon. On the day of an exam, don't forget to try the following:

- Allow yourself plenty of time to arrive.
- Read the directions on the test carefully.
- Read each problem carefully as you take your test. Make sure that you answer the question asked.
- Watch your time and pace yourself so that you may attempt each problem on your test.
- Check your work and answers.
- **Do not turn your test in early.** If you have extra time, spend it double-checking your work.

Good luck!

Exercises

Answer the following questions based on your most recent mathematics exam, whenever that was.

1. How soon before class did you arrive?
2. Did you read the directions on the test carefully?
3. Did you make sure you answered the question asked for each problem on the exam?
4. Were you able to attempt each problem on your exam?
5. If your answer to Exercise 4 is no, list reasons why.
6. Did you have extra time on your exam?
7. If your answer to Exercise 6 is yes, describe how you spent that extra time.

Study Skills Builder 4

Are You Satisfied with Your Performance on a Particular Quiz or Exam?

If not, don't forget to analyze your quiz or exam and look for common errors. Were most of your errors a result of:

- *Carelessness?* Did you turn in your quiz or exam before the allotted time expired? If so, resolve to use any extra time to check your work.
- *Running out of time?* Answer the questions you are sure of first. Then attempt the questions you are unsure of and delay checking your work until all questions have been answered.
- *Not understanding a concept?* If so, review that concept and correct your work so that you make sure you understand it before the next quiz or the final exam.
- *Test conditions?* When studying for a quiz or exam, make sure you place yourself in conditions similar to test conditions. For example, before your next quiz or exam, take a sample test without the aid of your notes or text.

  (For a sample test, see your instructor or use the Chapter Test at the end of each chapter.)

Exercises

1. Have you corrected all your previous quizzes and exams?
2. List any errors you have found common to two or more of your graded papers.
3. Is one of your common errors not understanding a concept? If so, are you making sure you understand all the concepts for the next quiz or exam?
4. Is one of your common errors making careless mistakes? If so, are you now taking all the time allotted to check over your work so that you can minimize the number of careless mistakes?
5. Are you satisfied with your grades thus far on quizzes and tests?
6. If your answer to Exercise 5 is no, are there any more suggestions you can make to your instructor or yourself to help? If so, list them here and share these with your instructor.

Study Skills Builder 5

How Are You Doing?

If you haven't done so yet, take a few moments to think about how you are doing in this course. Are you working toward your goal of successfully completing this course? Is your performance on homework, quizzes, and tests satisfactory? If not, you might want to see your instructor to see whether he/she has any suggestions on how you can improve your performance. Reread Section 1.1 for ideas on places to get help with your mathematics course.

Exercises

Answer the following.

1. List any textbook supplements you are using to help you through this course.

2. List any campus resources you are using to help you through this course.

3. Write a short paragraph describing how you are doing in your mathematics course.

4. If improvement is needed, list ways that you can work toward improving your situation as described in Exercise 3.

Study Skills Builder 6

Are You Preparing for Your Final Exam?

To prepare for your final exam, try the following study techniques:

- Review the material that you will be responsible for on your exam. This includes material from your textbook, your notebook, and any handouts from your instructor.
- Review any formulas that you may need to memorize.
- Check to see if your instructor or mathematics department will be conducting a final exam review.
- Check with your instructor to see whether final exams from previous semesters/quarters are available to students for review.

- Use your previously taken exams as a practice final exam. To do so, rewrite the test questions in mixed order on blank sheets of paper. This will help you prepare for exam conditions.
- If you are unsure of a few concepts, see your instructor or visit a learning lab for assistance. Also, view the video segment of any troublesome sections.
- If you need further exercises to work, try the Cumulative Reviews at the end of the chapters.

Once again, good luck! I hope you are enjoying this textbook and your mathematics course.

Organizing Your Work

Study Skills Builder 7

Learning New Terms

Many of the terms used in this text may be new to you. It will be helpful to make a list of new mathematical terms and symbols as you encounter them and to review them frequently. Placing these new terms (including page references) on 3×5 index cards might help you later when you're preparing for a quiz.

Exercises

1. Name one way you might place a word and its definition on a 3×5 card.

2. How do new terms stand out in this text so that they can be found?

Study Skills Builder 8

Are You Organized?

Have you ever had trouble finding a completed assignment? When it's time to study for a test, are your notes neat and organized? Have you ever had trouble reading your own mathematics handwriting? (Be honest—I have.)

When any of these things happens, it's time to get organized. Here are a few suggestions:

- Write your notes and complete your homework assignments in a notebook with pockets (spiral or ring binder).
- Take class notes in this notebook and then follow the notes with your completed homework assignment.
- When you receive graded papers or handouts, place them in the notebook pocket so that you will not lose them.
- Mark (possibly with an exclamation point) any note(s) that seem extra important to you.
- Mark (possibly with a question mark) any notes or homework that you are having trouble with.
- See your instructor or a math tutor to help you with the concepts or exercises that you are having trouble understanding.

- If you are having trouble reading your own handwriting, *slow down* and write your mathematics work clearly!

Exercises

1. Have you been completing your assignments on time?

2. Have you been correcting any exercises you may be having difficulty with?

3. If you are having trouble with a mathematical concept or correcting any homework exercises, have you visited your instructor, a tutor, or your campus math lab?

4. Are you taking lecture notes in your mathematics course? (By the way, these notes should include worked-out examples solved by your instructor.)

5. Is your mathematics course material (handouts, graded papers, lecture notes) organized?

6. If your answer to Exercise 5 is no, take a moment to review your course material. List at least two ways that you might organize it better.

Study Skills Builder 9

Organizing a Notebook

It's never too late to get organized. If you need ideas about organizing a notebook for your mathematics course, try some of these:

- Use a spiral or ring binder notebook with pockets and use it for mathematics only.
- Start each page by writing the book's section number you are working on at the top.
- When your instructor is lecturing, take notes. *Always* include any examples your instructor works for you.
- Place your worked-out homework exercises in your notebook immediately after the lecture notes from that section. This way, a section's worth of material is together.
- Homework exercises: Attempt and check all assigned homework.
- Place graded quizzes in the pockets of your notebook or a special section of your binder.

Exercises

Check your notebook organization by answering the following questions.

1. Do you have a spiral or ring binder notebook for your mathematics course only?

2. Have you ever had to flip through several sheets of notes and work in your mathematics notebook to determine what section's work you are in?

3. Are you now writing the textbook's section number at the top of each notebook page?

4. Have you ever lost or had trouble finding a graded quiz or test?

5. Are you now placing all your graded work in a dedicated place in your notebook?

6. Are you attempting all of your homework and placing all of your work in your notebook?

7. Are you checking and correcting your homework in your notebook? If not, why not?

8. Are you writing in your notebook the examples your instructor works for you in class?

Study Skills Builder 10

How Are Your Homework Assignments Going?

It is very important in mathematics to keep up with homework. Why? Many concepts build on each other. Often your understanding of a day's concepts depends on an understanding of the previous day's material.

Remember that completing your homework assignment involves a lot more than attempting a few of the problems assigned.

To complete a homework assignment, remember these four things:

● Attempt all of it.
● Check it.
● Correct it.
● If needed, ask questions about it.

Exercises

Take a moment to review your completed homework assignments. Answer the questions below based on this review.

1. Approximate the fraction of your homework you have attempted.

2. Approximate the fraction of your homework you have checked (if possible).

3. If you are able to check your homework, have you corrected it when errors have been found?

4. When working homework, if you do not understand a concept, what do you do?

MyMathLab and MathXL

Study Skills Builder 11

Tips for Turning in Your Homework on Time

It is very important to keep up with your mathematics homework assignments. Why? Many concepts in mathematics build upon each other.

Remember these four tips to help ensure that your work is completed on time:

● Know the assignments and due dates set by your instructor.
● Do not wait until the last minute to submit your homework.
● Set a goal to submit your homework 6–8 hours before the scheduled due date in case you have unexpected technology trouble.
● Schedule enough time to complete each assignment.

Following these tips will also help you avoid losing points for late or missed assignments.

Exercises

Take a moment to consider your work on your homework assignments to date and answer the following questions:

1. What percentage of your assignments have you turned in on time?

2. Why might it be a good idea to submit your homework 6–8 hours before the scheduled deadline?

3. If you have missed submitting any homework by the due date, list some of the reasons this occurred.

4. What steps do you plan to take in the future to ensure that your homework is submitted on time?

Study Skills Builder 12

Tips for Doing Your Homework Online

Practice is one of the main keys to success in any mathematics course. Did you know that MyMathLab/MathXL provides you with **immediate feedback** for each exercise? If you are incorrect, you are given hints to work the exercise correctly. You have **unlimited practice opportunities** and can rework any exercises you have trouble with until you master them and submit homework assignments unlimited times before the deadline.

Remember these success tips when doing your homework online:

- Attempt all assigned exercises.
- Write down (neatly) your step-by-step work for each exercise before entering your answer.
- Use the immediate feedback provided by the program to help you check and correct your work for each exercise.
- Rework any exercises you have trouble with until you master them.
- Work through your homework assignment as many times as necessary until you are satisfied.

Exercises

Take a moment to think about your homework assignments to date and answer the following:

1. Have you attempted all assigned exercises?

2. Of the exercises attempted, have you also written out your work before entering your answer so that you can check it?

3. Are you familiar with how to enter answers using the MathXL player so that you avoid answer entry type errors?

4. List some ways the immediate feedback and practice supports have helped you with your homework. If you have not used these supports, how do you plan to use them with the given success tips on your next assignment?

Study Skills Builder 13

Organizing Your Work

Have you ever used any readily available paper (such as the back of a flyer, another course assignment, post-it notes, etc.) to work out homework exercises before entering the answer in MathXL? To save time, have you ever entered answers directly into MathXL without working the exercises on paper? When it's time to study, have you ever been unable to find your completed work or read and follow your own mathematics handwriting?

When any of these things happen, it's time to get organized. Here are some suggestions:

- Write your step-by-step work for each homework exercise (neatly) on lined, loose-leaf paper and keep this in a 3-ring binder.
- Refer to your step-by-step work when you receive feedback that your answer is incorrect in MathXL. Double-check against the steps and hints provided by the program and correct your work accordingly.
- Keep your written homework with your class notes for that section.
- Identify any exercises you are having trouble with and ask questions about them.
- Keep all graded quizzes and tests in this binder as well to study later.

If you follow these suggestions, you and your instructor or tutor will be able to follow your steps and correct any mistakes. You will have a written copy of your work to refer to later to ask questions and study for tests.

Exercises

1. Why is it important to write out your step-by-step work to homework exercises and keep a hard copy of all work submitted online?

2. If you have gotten an incorrect answer, are you able to follow your steps and find your error?

3. If you were asked today to review your previous homework assignments and first test, could you find them? If not, list some ways you might organize your work better.

Study Skills Builder 14
Getting Help with Your Homework Assignments

Many helpful resources are available to you through MathXL to help you work through any homework exercises you may have trouble with. It is important for you to know what these resources are and when and how to use them.

Let's review these features, found in the homework exercises:

- **Help Me Solve This**—provides step-by-step help for the exercise you are working. You must work an additional exercise of the same type (without this help) before you can get credit for having worked it correctly.
- **View an Example**—allows you to view a correctly worked exercise similar to the one you are having trouble with. You can go back to your original exercise and work it on your own.
- **E-Book**—allows you to read examples from your text and find similar exercises.
- **Video****—your text author, Elayn Martin-Gay, works an exercise similar to the one you need help with. **Not all exercises have an accompanying video clip.
- **Ask My Instructor**—allows you to email your instructor for help with an exercise.

Exercises

1. How does the "Help Me Solve This" feature work?
2. If the "View an Example" feature is used, is it necessary to work an additional problem before continuing the assignment?
3. When might be a good time to use the "Video" feature? Do all exercises have an accompanying video clip?
4. Which of the features have you used? List those you found the most helpful to you.
5. If you haven't used the features discussed, list those you plan to try on your next homework assignment.

Study Skills Builder 15
Tips for Preparing for an Exam

Did you know that you can rework your previous homework assignments in MyMathLab and MathXL? This is a great way to prepare for tests. To do this, open a previous homework assignment and click "similar exercise." This will generate new exercises similar to the homework you have submitted. You can then rework the exercises and assignments until you feel confident that you understand them.

To prepare for an exam, follow these tips:

- Review your written work for your previous homework assignments along with your class notes.
- Identify any exercises or topics that you have questions on or have difficulty understanding.
- Rework your previous assignments in MyMathLab and MathXL until you fully understand them and can do them without help.
- Get help for any topics you feel unsure of or for which you have questions.

Exercises

1. Are your current homework assignments up to date and is your written work for them organized in a binder or notebook? If the answer is no, it's time to get organized. For tips on this, see Study Skills Builder 13—Organizing Your Work.
2. How many days in advance of an exam do you usually start studying?
3. List some ways you think that practicing previous homework assignments can help you prepare for your test.
4. List two or three resources you can use to get help for any topics you are unsure of or have questions on.

Good luck!

Study Skills Builder 16

How Well Do You Know the Resources Available to You in MyMathLab?

Many helpful resources are available to you in MyMathLab. Let's take a moment to locate and explore a few of them now. Go into your MyMathLab course and visit the multimedia library, tools for success, and E-book.

Let's see what you found.

Exercises

1. List the resources available to you in the Multimedia Library.

2. List the resources available to you in the Tools for Success folder.

3. Where did you find the English/Spanish Audio Glossary?

4. Can you view videos from the E-book?

5. Did you find any resources you did not know about? If so, which ones?

6. Which resources have you used most often or found most helpful?

Additional Help Inside and Outside Your Textbook

Study Skills Builder 17

How Well Do You Know Your Textbook?

The following questions will help determine whether you are familiar with your textbook. For additional information, see Section 1.1 in this text.

1. What does the ▶ icon mean?

2. What does the ╲ icon mean?

3. What does the △ icon mean?

4. Where can you find a review for each chapter? What answers to this review can be found in the back of your text?

5. Each chapter contains an overview of the chapter along with examples. What is this feature called?

6. Each chapter contains a review of vocabulary. What is this feature called?

7. Practice exercises are contained in this text. What are they and how can they be used?

8. This text contains a student section in the back entitled Student Resources. List the contents of this section and how they might be helpful.

9. What exercise answers are available in this text? Where are they located?

Study Skills Builder 18

Are You Familiar with Your Textbook Supplements?

Below is a review of some of the student supplements available for additional study. Check to see whether you are using the ones most helpful to you.

- Chapter Test Prep Videos. These videos provide video clip solutions to the Chapter Test exercises in this text. You will find this extremely useful when studying for tests or exams.

- Interactive DVD Lecture Series. These are keyed to each section of the text. The material is presented by me, Elayn Martin-Gay, and I have placed a ▶ by the exercises in the text that I have worked on the video.

- The *Student Solutions Manual*. This contains worked-out solutions to odd-numbered exercises as well as every exercise in the Integrated Reviews, Chapter Reviews, Chapter Tests, and Cumulative Reviews and every Practice exercise.

- Pearson Tutor Center. Mathematics questions may be phoned, faxed, or emailed to this center.

- MyMathLab is a text-specific online course. MathXL is an online homework, tutorial, and assessment system. Take a moment to determine whether these are available to you.

As usual, your instructor is your best source of information.

Exercises

Let's see how you are doing with textbook supplements.

1. Name one way the Lecture Videos can be helpful to you.

2. Name one way the Chapter Test Prep Video can help you prepare for a chapter test.

3. List any textbook supplements that you have found useful.

4. Have you located and visited a learning resource lab located on your campus?

5. List the textbook supplements that are currently housed in your campus's learning resource lab.

Study Skills Builder 19

Are You Getting All the Mathematics Help That You Need?

Remember that, in addition to your instructor, there are many places to get help with your mathematics course. For example:

- This text has an accompanying video lesson by the author for every section. There are also worked-out video solutions by the author to every Chapter Test exercise.

- The back of the book contains answers to odd-numbered exercises.

- A *Student Solutions Manual* is available that contains worked-out solutions to odd-numbered exercises as well as solutions to every exercise in the Integrated Reviews, Chapter Reviews, Chapter Tests, and Cumulative Reviews and every Practice exercise.

- Don't forget to check with your instructor for other local resources available to you, such as a tutor center.

Exercises

1. List items you find helpful in the text and all student supplements to this text.

2. List all the campus help that is available to you for this course.

3. List any help (besides the textbook) from Exercises 1 and 2 above that you are using.

4. List any help (besides the textbook) that you feel you should try.

5. Write a goal for yourself that includes trying everything you listed in Exercise 4 during the next week.

Bigger Picture—Study Guide Outline

I. Equations

  A. Linear Equations (Sec. 2.1)

  $$5(x - 2) = \frac{4(2x + 1)}{3}$$

  $$3 \cdot 5(x - 2) = \cancel{3} \cdot \frac{4(2x + 1)}{\cancel{3}}$$

  $$15x - 30 = 8x + 4$$

  $$7x = 34$$

  $$x = \frac{34}{7}$$

  B. Absolute Value Equations (Sec. 2.6)

  $|3x - 1| = 8$

  $3x - 1 = 8$ or $3x - 1 = -8$

  $3x = 9$ or $3x = -7$

  $x = 3$ or $x = -\dfrac{7}{3}$

  $|x - 5| = |x + 1|$

  $x - 5 = x + 1$ or $x - 5 = -(x + 1)$

  $\underline{-5 = 1}$ or $x - 5 = -x - 1$

  No solution or $2x = 4$

  $x = 2$

  C. Quadratic and Higher-Degree Equations (Secs. 5.8, 8.1, 8.2, 8.3)

  $2x^2 - 7x = 9$

  $2x^2 - 7x - 9 = 0$

  $(2x - 9)(x + 1) = 0$

  $2x - 9 = 0$ or $x + 1 = 0$

  $x = \dfrac{9}{2}$ or $x = -1$

  $2x^2 + x - 2 = 0$

  $a = 2,\ b = 1,\ c = -2$

  $$x = \frac{-1 \pm \sqrt{1^2 - 4(2)(-2)}}{2 \cdot 2}$$

  $$x = \frac{-1 \pm \sqrt{17}}{4}$$

  D. Equations with Rational Expressions (Sec. 6.5)

  $$\frac{7}{x - 1} + \frac{3}{x + 1} = \frac{x + 3}{x^2 - 1}$$

  $$\cancel{(x - 1)}(x + 1) \cdot \frac{7}{\cancel{x - 1}} + (x - 1)\cancel{(x + 1)} \cdot \frac{3}{\cancel{x + 1}}$$

  $$= \cancel{(x - 1)}\cancel{(x + 1)} \cdot \frac{x + 3}{\cancel{(x - 1)}\cancel{(x + 1)}}$$

  $$7(x + 1) + 3(x - 1) = x + 3$$

  $$7x + 7 + 3x - 3 = x + 3$$

  $$9x = -1$$

  $$x = -\frac{1}{9}$$

E. Equations with Radicals (Sec. 7.6)

$$\sqrt{5x + 10} - 2 = x$$
$$\sqrt{5x + 10} = x + 2$$
$$(\sqrt{5x + 10})^2 = (x + 2)^2$$
$$5x + 10 = x^2 + 4x + 4$$
$$0 = x^2 - x - 6$$
$$0 = (x - 3)(x + 2)$$
$$x - 3 = 0 \quad \text{or} \quad x + 2 = 0$$
$$x = 3 \quad \text{or} \qquad x = -2$$

Both solutions check.

F. Exponential Equations (Secs. 9.3, 9.8)

$$9^x = 27^{x+1} \qquad\qquad 5^x = 7$$
$$(3^2)^x = (3^3)^{x+1} \qquad \log 5^x = \log 7$$
$$3^{2x} = 3^{3x+3} \qquad\quad x \log 5 = \log 7$$
$$2x = 3x + 3$$
$$-3 = x \qquad\qquad\quad x = \frac{\log 7}{\log 5}$$

G. Logarithmic Equations (Sec. 9.8)

$$\log 7 + \log(x + 3) = \log 5$$
$$\log 7(x + 3) = \log 5$$
$$7(x + 3) = 5$$
$$7x + 21 = 5$$
$$7x = -16$$
$$x = -\frac{16}{7}$$

II. Inequalities

A. Linear Inequalities (Sec. 2.4)

$$-3(x + 2) \geq 6$$
$$-3x - 6 \geq 6$$
$$-3x \geq 12$$
$$\frac{-3x}{-3} \leq \frac{12}{-3}$$
$$x \leq -4 \quad \text{or} \quad (-\infty, -4]$$

B. Compound Inequalities (Sec. 2.5)

$$x \leq 3 \quad \textit{and} \quad x < -7$$

$\{x \mid x \leq 3\}$ $(-\infty, 3]$

$\{x \mid x < -7\}$ $(-\infty, -7)$

$\{x \mid x \leq 3 \text{ and } x < -7\}$ $(-\infty, -7)$

$$x \le 3 \quad or \quad x < -7$$

$\{x \mid x \le 3\}$ $(-\infty, 3]$

$\{x \mid x < -7\}$ $(-\infty, -7)$

$\{x \mid x \le 3 \text{ or } x < -7\}$ $(-\infty, 3]$

C. Absolute Value Inequalities (Sec. 2.7)

$$|x - 5| - 8 < -2$$
$$|x - 5| < 6$$
$$-6 < x - 5 < 6$$
$$-1 < x < 11$$
$$(-1, 11)$$

$$|2x + 1| \ge 17$$
$$2x + 1 \ge 17 \quad or \quad 2x + 1 \le -17$$
$$2x \ge 16 \quad or \quad 2x \le -18$$
$$x \ge 8 \quad or \quad x \le -9$$
$$(-\infty, -9] \cup [8, \infty)$$

D. Nonlinear Inequalities (Sec. 8.4)

$$x^2 - x < 6$$
$$x^2 - x - 6 < 0$$
$$(x - 3)(x + 2) < 0$$

     ✗   ✓   ✗
     -2 3

$$(-2, 3)$$

$$\frac{x - 5}{x + 1} \ge 0$$

     ✓   ✗   ✓
     -1 5

$$(-\infty, -1) \cup [5, \infty)$$

Simplify. If needed, write answers with positive exponents only.

1. $\sqrt{216}$

2. $\dfrac{(4 - \sqrt{16}) - (-7 - 20)}{-2(1 - 4)^2}$

3. $\left(\dfrac{1}{125}\right)^{-1/3}$

4. $(-9x)^{-2}$

5. $\dfrac{\dfrac{5}{x} - \dfrac{7}{3x}}{\dfrac{9}{8x} - \dfrac{1}{x}}$

6. $\dfrac{6^{-1}a^2b^{-3}}{3^{-2}a^{-5}b^2}$

7. $\left(\dfrac{64c^{4/3}}{a^{-2/3}b^{5/6}}\right)^{1/2}$

Factor completely.

8. $3x^2y - 27y^3$

9. $16y^3 - 2$

10. $x^2y - 9y - 3x^2 + 27$

Perform the indicated operations and simplify if possible.

11. $(4x^3y - 3x - 4) - (9x^3y + 8x + 5)$

12. $(6m + n)^2$

13. $(2x - 1)(x^2 - 6x + 4)$

14. $\dfrac{3x^2 - 12}{x^2 + 2x - 8} \div \dfrac{6x + 18}{x + 4}$

15. $\dfrac{2x^2 + 7}{2x^4 - 18x^2} - \dfrac{6x + 7}{2x^4 - 18x^2}$

16. $\dfrac{3}{x^2 - x - 6} + \dfrac{2}{x^2 - 5x + 6}$

17. $\sqrt{125x^3} - 3\sqrt{20x^3}$

18. $(\sqrt{5} + 5)(\sqrt{5} - 5)$

19. $(4x^3 - 5x) \div (2x + 1)$ [Use long division.]

Solve each equation or inequality. Write inequality solutions using interval notation.

20. $9(x + 2) = 5[11 - 2(2 - x) + 3]$

21. $|6x - 5| - 3 = -2$

22. $3n(7n - 20) = 96$

23. $-3 < 2(x - 3) \le 4$

24. $|3x + 1| > 5$

25. $\dfrac{x^2 + 8}{x} - 1 = \dfrac{2(x + 4)}{x}$

26. $y^2 - 3y = 5$

27. $x = \sqrt{x - 2} + 2$

28. $2x^2 - 7x > 15$

29. Solve the system: $\begin{cases} \dfrac{x}{2} + \dfrac{y}{4} = -\dfrac{3}{4} \\ x + \dfrac{3}{4}y = -4 \end{cases}$

Graph the following.

30. $4x + 6y = 7$

31. $2x - y > 5$

32. $y = -3$

33. $g(x) = -|x + 2| - 1$. Also, find the domain and range of this function.

34. $h(x) = x^2 - 4x + 4$. Label the vertex and any intercepts.

35. $f(x) = \begin{cases} -\dfrac{1}{2}x & \text{if } x \le 0 \\ 2x - 3 & \text{if } x > 0 \end{cases}$. Also, find the domain and range of this function.

Write equations of the following lines. Write each equation using function notation.

36. through $(4, -2)$ and $(6, -3)$

37. through $(-1, 2)$ and perpendicular to $3x - y = 4$

Find the distance or midpoint.

38. Find the distance between the points $(-6, 3)$ and $(-8, -7)$.

39. Find the midpoint of the line segment whose endpoints are $(-2, -5)$ and $(-6, 12)$.

Rationalize each denominator. Assume that variables represent positive numbers.

40. $\sqrt{\dfrac{9}{y}}$

41. $\dfrac{4 - \sqrt{x}}{4 + 2\sqrt{x}}$

Solve.

42. In 2022, the number of people employed as registered nurses in the United States is expected to be 3,240,000. This represents a 19% increase over the number of people employed as registered nurses in 2012. Find the number of registered nurses employed in 2012. Round to the nearest thousand. (*Source:* Bureau of Labor Statistics)

43. Write the area of the shaded region as a factored polynomial.

44. The product of one more than a number and twice the reciprocal of the number is $\frac{12}{5}$. Find the number.

45. Suppose that W is inversely proportional to V. If $W = 20$ when $V = 12$, find W when $V = 15$.

46. Given the diagram shown, approximate to the nearest tenth of a foot how many feet of walking distance a person saves by cutting across the lawn instead of walking on the sidewalk.

47. A stone is thrown upward from a bridge. The stone's height in feet, $s(t)$, above the water t seconds after the stone is thrown is a function given by the equation

$$s(t) = -16t^2 + 32t + 256$$

   a. Find the maximum height of the stone.
   b. Find the time it takes the stone to hit the water. Round the answer to two decimal places.

48. The research department of a company that manufactures children's fruit drinks is experimenting with a new flavor. A 17.5% fructose solution is needed, but only 10% and 20% solutions are available. How many gallons of the 10% fructose solution should be mixed with the 20% fructose solution to obtain 20 gallons of a 17.5% fructose solution?

COMPLEX NUMBERS: CHAPTER 7

Perform the indicated operation and simplify. Write the result in the form $a + bi$.

49. $-\sqrt{-8}$

50. $(12 - 6i) - (12 - 3i)$

51. $(4 + 3i)^2$

52. $\dfrac{1 + 4i}{1 - i}$

INVERSE, EXPONENTIAL, AND LOGARITHMIC FUNCTIONS: CHAPTER 9

53. If $g(x) = x - 7$ and $h(x) = x^2 - 6x + 5$, find $(g \circ h)(x)$.

54. Decide whether $f(x) = 6 - 2x$ is a one-to-one function. If it is, find its inverse.

55. Use properties of logarithms to write the expression as a single logarithm.

$$\log_5 x + 3\log_5 x - \log_5(x + 1)$$

Solve. Give exact solutions.

56. $8^{x-1} = \dfrac{1}{64}$

57. $3^{2x+5} = 4$ Give the exact solution and a 4-decimal-place approximation.

58. $\log_8(3x - 2) = 2$

59. $\log_4(x + 1) - \log_4(x - 2) = 3$

60. $\ln\sqrt{e} = x$

61. Graph $y = \left(\dfrac{1}{2}\right)^x + 1$

62. The prairie dog population of the Grand Forks area now stands at 57,000 animals. If the population is growing at a rate of 2.6% annually, how many prairie dogs there will be in that area 5 years from now?

CONIC SECTIONS: CHAPTER 10

Sketch the graph of each equation.

63. $x^2 - y^2 = 36$

64. $16x^2 + 9y^2 = 144$

65. $x^2 + y^2 + 6x = 16$

66. Solve the system:
$$\begin{cases} x^2 + y^2 = 26 \\ x^2 - 2y^2 = 23 \end{cases}$$

SEQUENCES, SERIES, AND THE BINOMIAL THEOREM: CHAPTER 11

67. Find the first five terms of the sequence $a_n = \dfrac{(-1)^n}{n + 4}$.

68. Find the partial sum, S_5, of the sequence $a_n = 5(2)^{n-1}$.

69. Find S_∞ of the sequence $\dfrac{3}{2}, -\dfrac{3}{4}, \dfrac{3}{8}, \ldots$

70. Find $\sum_{i=1}^{4} i(i - 2)$

71. Expand: $(2x + y)^5$

Answers to Selected Exercises

CHAPTER 1 REAL NUMBERS AND ALGEBRAIC EXPRESSIONS

Section 1.2
Practice Exercises
1. 14 sq cm　**2.** 31　**3. a.** $\{6, 7, 8, 9\}$　**b.** $\{41, 42, 43, \ldots\}$　**4. a.** true　**b.** true　**5. a.** true　**b.** false　**c.** true　**d.** false
6. a. 4　**b.** $\frac{1}{2}$　**c.** 1　**d.** -6.8　**e.** -4　**7. a.** -5.4　**b.** $\frac{3}{5}$　**c.** -18　**8. a.** $3x$　**b.** $2x - 5$　**c.** $3\frac{5}{8} + x$　**d.** $x \div 2$ or $\frac{x}{2}$
e. $x - 14$　**f.** $5(x + 10)$

Vocabulary, Readiness and Video Check 1.2
1. variables　**3.** absolute value　**5.** natural numbers　**7.** integers　**9.** rational number　**11.** This is an application, so the answer needs to be put in context. The decimal actually represents money.　**13.** distance; 0; positive; negative　**15.** Order is important in subtraction so you must read the phrase carefully to determine the order of subtraction in your algebraic expression.

Exercise Set 1.2
1. 35　**3.** 30.38　**5.** $\frac{3}{8}$　**7.** 22　**9.** 2000 mi　**11.** 20.4 sq ft　**13.** \$10,612.80　**15.** $\{1, 2, 3, 4, 5\}$　**17.** $\{11, 12, 13, 14, 15, 16\}$

19. $\{0\}$　**21.** $\{0, 2, 4, 6, 8\}$　**23.** ⟵•┼•┼•┼•⟶ 0 2 4 6　**25.** ⟵┼┼┼┼••┼⟶ 0 $\frac{1\,2}{2\,3}$ 1　**27.** ⟵•┼┼┼•┼┼•⟶ -10 -6 -2　**29.** ⟵┼┼•┼•┼┼⟶ -2 $-1\frac{1}{3}$ $-\frac{1}{3}$ -1 0　**31.** $\{3, 0, \sqrt{36}\}$

33. $\{3, \sqrt{36}\}$　**35.** $\{\sqrt{7}\}$　**37.** $\in$　**39.** $\notin$　**41.** $\notin$　**43.** $\notin$　**45.** true　**47.** true　**49.** false　**51.** false　**53.** true

55. false　**57.** -2　**59.** 4　**61.** 0　**63.** -3　**65.** 6.2　**67.** $-\frac{4}{7}$　**69.** $\frac{2}{3}$　**71.** 0　**73.** $2x$　**75.** $2x + 5$　**77.** $x - 10$

79. $x + 2$　**81.** $\frac{x}{11}$　**83.** $12 - 3x$　**85.** $x + 2.3$ or $x + 2\frac{3}{10}$　**87.** $1\frac{1}{3} - x$　**89.** $\frac{5}{4 - x}$　**91.** $2(x + 3)$　**93.** 137　**95.** 69
97. answers may vary　**99.** answers may vary　**101.** answers may vary

Section 1.3
Practice Exercises
1. a. -8　**b.** -3　**c.** 5　**d.** -8.1　**e.** $\frac{1}{15}$　**f.** $-\frac{7}{22}$　**2. a.** -8　**b.** -3　**c.** -12　**d.** 7.7　**e.** $-\frac{22}{21}$　**f.** 1.8　**g.** -7

3. a. 12　**b.** -4　**4. a.** -15　**b.** $\frac{1}{2}$　**c.** -10.2　**d.** 0　**e.** $-\frac{2}{13}$　**f.** 36　**g.** -11.5　**5. a.** -2　**b.** 5　**c.** $-\frac{1}{6}$　**d.** -6

e. $\frac{1}{9}$　**f.** 0　**6. a.** 8　**b.** $\frac{1}{9}$　**c.** -144　**d.** 144　**e.** -64　**f.** -64　**7. a.** 7　**b.** $\frac{1}{4}$　**c.** -8　**d.** not a real number　**e.** 10

8. a. 4　**b.** -1　**c.** 10　**9. a.** 2　**b.** 27　**c.** -29　**10.** 19　**11.** $-\frac{17}{44}$　**12. a.** 67　**b.** -100　**c.** $-\frac{39}{80}$　**13.** 23; 50; 77

Vocabulary, Readiness and Video Check 1.3
1. 0　**3.** reciprocal　**5.** exponent　**7.** square root　**9.** addition　**11.** The parentheses, or lack of them, determine the base of the expression. In Example 7, -7^2, the base is 7 and only 7 is squared. In Example 8, $(-7)^2$, the base is -7 and all of -7 is squared.　**13.** It allows each expression to evaluate to a single number.

Exercise Set 1.3
1. 5　**3.** -24　**5.** -11　**7.** -4　**9.** $\frac{4}{3}$　**11.** -2　**13.** $-\frac{1}{2}$　**15.** -6　**17.** -60　**19.** 0　**21.** 0　**23.** -3　**25.** 3　**27.** $-\frac{1}{6}$

29. 0.56　**31.** -7　**33.** -8　**35.** -49　**37.** 36　**39.** -8　**41.** $-\frac{1}{27}$　**43.** 7　**45.** $-\frac{2}{3}$　**47.** 4　**49.** 3　**51.** not a real number

53. 48　**55.** -1　**57.** -9　**59.** 17　**61.** -4　**63.** -2　**65.** 11　**67.** $-\frac{3}{4}$　**69.** 7　**71.** -11　**73.** -2.1　**75.** $-\frac{1}{3}$　**77.** $-\frac{79}{15}$

79. $-\frac{4}{5}$　**81.** -81　**83.** $-\frac{20}{33}$　**85.** 93　**87.** -12　**89.** $-\frac{23}{18}$　**91.** 5　**93.** $-\frac{3}{19}$　**95. a.** 18; 22; 28; 208　**b.** increase; answers may vary

97. a. 600; 150; 105　**b.** decrease; answers may vary　**99.** b, c　**101.** b, d　**103.** b　**105.** $\frac{5}{2}$　**107.** $\frac{13}{35}$　**109.** 4205 m　**111.** $(2 + 7) \cdot (1 + 3)$
113. 20 million　**115.** 70 million　**117.** increasing; answers may vary　**119.** answers may vary　**121.** 3.1623　**123.** 2.8107　**125.** -0.5876

Integrated Review
1. 16　**2.** -16　**3.** 0　**4.** -11　**5.** -5　**6.** $-\frac{1}{60}$　**7.** undefined　**8.** -2.97　**9.** 4　**10.** -50　**11.** 35　**12.** 92

13. $-15 - 2x$　**14.** $3x + 5$　**15.** 0　**16.** true

Section 1.4
Practice Exercises

1. $-4x = 20$ **2.** $3(z - 3) = 9$ **3.** $x + 5 = 2x - 3$ **4.** $y + 2 = 4 + \dfrac{z}{8}$ **5. a.** $<$ **b.** $=$ **c.** $>$ **d.** $<$ **e.** $>$ **f.** $<$

6. a. $x - 3 \le 5$ **b.** $y \ne -4$ **c.** $2 < 4 + \dfrac{1}{2}z$ **7. a.** 7 **b.** -4.7 **c.** $\dfrac{3}{8}$ **8. a.** $-\dfrac{3}{5}$ **b.** $\dfrac{1}{14}$ **c.** $-\dfrac{1}{2}$ **9.** $13x + 8$ **10.** $(3 \cdot 11)b = 33b$

11. a. $4x + 20y$ **b.** $-3 + 2z$ **c.** $0.3xy - 0.9x$ **12. a.** $0.10x$ **b.** $26y$ **c.** $1.75z$ **d.** $0.15t$ **13. a.** $16 - x$ **b.** $180 - x$

c. $x + 2$ **d.** $x + 9$ **14. a.** $5ab$ **b.** $10x - 5$ **c.** $17p - 9$ **15. a.** $-pq + 7$ **b.** $x^2 + 19$ **c.** $5.8x + 3.8$ **d.** $-c - 8d + \dfrac{1}{4}$

Vocabulary, Readiness and Video Check 1.4

1. $<$ **3.** $\ne$ **5.** $\ge$ **7.** $-a$ **9.** commutative **11.** distributive **13.** $=, \ne, <, \le, >, \ge$ **15.** order; grouping **17.** by combining like terms; distributive property

Exercise Set 1.4

1. $10 + x = -12$ **3.** $2x + 5 = -14$ **5.** $\dfrac{n}{5} = 4n$ **7.** $z - \dfrac{1}{2} = \dfrac{1}{2}z$ **9.** $7x \le -21$ **11.** $2(x - 6) > \dfrac{1}{11}$ **13.** $2(x - 6) = -27$ **15.** $>$

17. $=$ **19.** $<$ **21.** $<$ **23.** $<$ **25.** $-5; \dfrac{1}{5}$ **27.** $-8; -\dfrac{1}{8}$ **29.** $\dfrac{1}{7}; -7$ **31.** 0; undefined **33.** $\dfrac{7}{8}; -\dfrac{7}{8}$ **35.** $y + 7x$ **37.** $w \cdot z$

39. $\dfrac{x}{5} \cdot \dfrac{1}{3}$ **41.** $(5 \cdot 7)x$ **43.** $x + (1.2 + y)$ **45.** $14(z \cdot y)$ **47.** $3x + 15$ **49.** $-2a - b$ **51.** $12x + 10y + 4z$ **53.** $-4x + 8y - 28$

55. $3xy - 1.5x$ **57.** $6 + 3x$ **59.** 0 **61.** 7 **63.** $(10 \cdot 2)y$ **65.** $0.1d$ **67.** $112 - x$ **69.** $180 - x$ **71.** $\$6.49x$ **73.** $x + 2$

75. $-6x + 9$ **77.** $2k + 10$ **79.** $-3x + 5$ **81.** $-x^2 + 4xy + 9$ **83.** $4n - 8$ **85.** -24 **87.** $2x + 10$ **89.** $0.8x - 3.6$

91. $\dfrac{11}{12}b - \dfrac{7}{6}$ **93.** $6x + 14$ **95.** $-5x + \dfrac{5}{6}y - 1$ **97.** $3a + \dfrac{3}{35}$ **99.** $3x + 12$ **101.** $(5 \cdot 7)y$ **103.** $a(b + c) = ab + ac$

105. zero; answers may vary **107.** no; answers may vary **109.** answers may vary **111.** $15.4z + 31.11$

Chapter 1 Vocabulary Check

1. algebraic expression **2.** opposite **3.** distributive **4.** absolute value **5.** exponent **6.** variable **7.** inequality **8.** reciprocals
9. commutative **10.** associative **11.** whole **12.** real

Chapter 1 Review

1. 21 **3.** 4200 **5.** $\{-1, 1, 3\}$ **7.** $\varnothing$ **9.** $\{6, 7, 8, \dots\}$ **11.** true **13.** true **15.** false **17.** false **19.** true **21.** false

23. $\left\{5, \dfrac{8}{2}, \sqrt{9}\right\}$ **25.** $\left\{5, -\dfrac{2}{3}, \dfrac{8}{2}, \sqrt{9}, 0.3, 1\dfrac{5}{8}, -1\right\}$ **27.** $\left\{5, -\dfrac{2}{3}, \dfrac{8}{2}, \sqrt{9}, 0.3, \sqrt{7}, 1\dfrac{5}{8}, -1, \pi\right\}$ **29.** $\dfrac{3}{4}$ **31.** 0 **33.** $-\dfrac{4}{3}$ **35.** undefined

37. -4 **39.** -2 **41.** 8 **43.** 0 **45.** undefined **47.** 4 **49.** $-\dfrac{2}{15}$ **51.** $\dfrac{5}{12}$ **53.** 9 **55.** 3 **57.** $-\dfrac{32}{135}$ **59.** $-\dfrac{5}{4}$ **61.** $\dfrac{5}{8}$

63. -1 **65.** 1 **67.** -4 **69.** $\dfrac{5}{7}$ **71.** $\dfrac{1}{5}$ **73.** -5 **75.** 5 **77.** 6.28; 62.8; 628 **79.** $-xy + 1$ **81.** $2x^2 - 2$ **83.** $-1.1x - 0.3$

85. $12 = -4x$ **87.** $4(y + 3) = -1$ **89.** $z - 7 = 6$ **91.** $x - 5 \ge 12$ **93.** $\dfrac{2}{3} \ne 2\left(n + \dfrac{1}{4}\right)$ **95.** associative property of addition

97. additive inverse property **99.** associative and commutative properties of multiplication **101.** multiplication property of zero
103. additive identity property **105.** $5(x - 3z)$ **107.** $2 + (-2)$, for example **109.** $3.4[(0.7)5]$ **111.** $>$ **113.** $<$ **115.** $<$

117. $\dfrac{3}{4}; -\dfrac{4}{3}$ **119.** $-10x + 6.1$ **121.** $-\dfrac{6}{11}$ **123.** $-\dfrac{4}{15}$ **125.** $-x + 3y + 1$ **127.** 2.2 **129.** 2.3 **131.** 1.4

Chapter 1 Getting Ready for the Test

1. A **2.** C **3.** B **4.** A **5.** C **6.** B **7.** B and D **8.** A and B **9.** B **10.** C **11.** A **12.** E **13.** B **14.** D **15.** B **16.** C

Chapter 1 Test

1. true **2.** false **3.** false **4.** false **5.** true **6.** false **7.** -3 **8.** -56 **9.** -225 **10.** 3 **11.** 1 **12.** $-\dfrac{3}{2}$ **13.** 12

14. 1 **15. a.** 8.75; 26.25; 87.50; 175.00 **b.** increase **16.** $2(x + 5) = 30$ **17.** $\dfrac{(6 - y)^2}{7} < -2$ **18.** $\dfrac{9z}{|-12|} \ne 10$ **19.** $3\left(\dfrac{n}{5}\right) = -n$

20. $20 = 2x - 6$ **21.** $-2 = \dfrac{x}{x + 5}$ **22.** distributive property **23.** associative property of addition **24.** additive inverse property

25. multiplication property of zero **26.** $0.05n + 0.1d$ **27.** reciprocal: $-\dfrac{11}{7}$; opposite: $\dfrac{7}{11}$ **28.** $\dfrac{1}{2}a - \dfrac{9}{8}$ **29.** $2y - 10$ **30.** $-1.3x + 1.9$

CHAPTER 2 EQUATIONS, INEQUALITIES, AND PROBLEM SOLVING

Section 2.1
Practice Exercises

1. 5 **2.** 0.2 **3.** -5 **4.** -4 **5.** $\dfrac{5}{6}$ **6.** $\dfrac{5}{4}$ **7.** -3 **8.** $\{\,\}$ or $\varnothing$ **9.** all real numbers or $\{x \mid x \text{ is a real number}\}$

Vocabulary, Readiness & Video Check 2.1

1. equivalent **3.** addition **5.** expression **7.** equation **9.** both sides; same **11.** to make the calculations less tedious

Exercise Set 2.1

1. 6   **3.** −22   **5.** 4.7   **7.** 10   **9.** −1.1   **11.** −5   **13.** −2   **15.** 0   **17.** 2   **19.** −9   **21.** $-\dfrac{10}{7}$ **23.** $\dfrac{9}{10}$ **25.** 4   **27.** 1
29. 5   **31.** $\dfrac{40}{3}$ **33.** 17   **35.** all real numbers   **37.** ∅   **39.** all real numbers   **41.** ∅   **43.** $\dfrac{1}{8}$ **45.** 0   **47.** all real numbers
49. 4   **51.** $\dfrac{4}{5}$ **53.** 8   **55.** ∅   **57.** −8   **59.** $-\dfrac{5}{4}$ **61.** −2   **63.** 23   **65.** $-\dfrac{2}{9}$ **67.** $\dfrac{8}{x}$ **69.** $8x$ **71.** $2x - 5$ **73.** subtract 19
instead of adding; −3   **75.** $0.4 - 1.6 = -1.2$, not 1.2; −0.24   **77.** all real numbers   **79.** no solution   **81. a.** $4x + 5$ **b.** −3   **c.** answers
may vary   **83.** answers may vary   **85.** $K = -11$ **87.** $K = -23$ **89.** answers may vary   **91.** 1   **93.** 3   **95.** −4.86   **97.** 1.53

Section 2.2
Practice Exercises
1. a. $3x + 6$ **b.** $6x - 1$ **2.** $4x - 28.8$ **3.** 14, 34, 70   **4.** \$450   **5.** width: 32 in.; length: 48 in.   **6.** 25, 27, 29

Vocabulary, Readiness & Video Check 2.2
1. >   **3.** =   **5.** 31, 32, 33, 34   **7.** 18, 20, 22   **9.** $y, y + 1, y + 2$ **11.** $p, p + 1, p + 2, p + 3$ **13.** distributive property

Exercise Set 2.2
1. $4y$ **3.** $3z + 3$ **5.** $(65x + 30)$ cents   **7.** $10x + 3$ **9.** $2x + 14$ **11.** −5   **13.** 45, 225, 145   **15.** approximately 1612.41 million acres
17. 14,940 earthquakes   **19.** 1275 shoppers   **21.** 61%   **23.** 14%   **25.** 29°, 35°, 116°   **27.** 28 m, 36 m, 38 m   **29.** 18 in., 18 in., 27 in., 36 in.
31. 75, 76, 77   **33.** Fallon's ZIP code is 89406; Fernley's ZIP code is 89408; Gardnerville Ranchos' ZIP code is 89410   **35.** 1960 million; 2130 million;
2290 million   **37.** nurse: 527 thousand; food service: 422 thousand; customer service: 299 thousand   **39.** B767-300ER: 207 seats; B737-200: 119 seats;
F-100: 87 seats   **41.** \$430.00   **43.** \$496,244   **45.** 83,328,000   **47.** 40°, 140°   **49.** 64°, 32°, 84°   **51.** square: 18 cm; triangle: 24 cm
53. 76, 78, 80   **55.** Darlington: 61,000; Daytona: 159,000   **57.** New York: 20.6 million; Delhi: 25.2 million; Tokyo-Yokohama: 37.8 million   **59.** 40.5 ft;
202.5 ft; 240 ft   **61.** incandescent: 1500 bulb hours; fluorescent: 100,000 bulb hours; halogen: 4000 bulb hours   **63.** Yankees: 84; Blue Jays: 83;
Brewers: 82   **65.** Guy's Tower: 469 ft; Queen Mary Hospital: 449 ft; Galter Pavilion: 402 ft   **67.** 208   **69.** −55   **71.** 3195   **73.** yes; answers
may vary   **75.** 80°   **77.** 2025   **79.** 442   **81.** any three consecutive integers   **83.** 25 skateboards   **85.** company loses money

Section 2.3
Practice Exercises
1. $T = \dfrac{I}{PR}$ **2.** $y = \dfrac{7}{2}x - \dfrac{5}{2}$ **3.** $r = \dfrac{A - P}{Pt}$ **4.** \$10, 134.16   **5.** $25\dfrac{1}{3}$ hours; 25 hours 20 minutes

Vocabulary, Readiness & Video Check 2.3
1. $y = 5 - 2x$ **3.** $a = 5b + 8$ **5.** $k = h - 5j + 6$ **7.** That the specified variable will equal some expression and that this expression should
not contain the specified variable.

Exercise Set 2.3
1. $t = \dfrac{d}{r}$ **3.** $R = \dfrac{I}{PT}$ **5.** $y = \dfrac{9x - 16}{4}$ **7.** $W = \dfrac{P - 2L}{2}$ **9.** $A = \dfrac{J + 3}{C}$ **11.** $g = \dfrac{W}{h - 3t^2}$ **13.** $B = \dfrac{T - 2C}{AC}$ **15.** $r = \dfrac{C}{2\pi}$
17. $r = \dfrac{E - IR}{I}$ **19.** $L = \dfrac{2s - na}{n}$ **21.** $v = \dfrac{3st^4 - N}{5s}$ **23.** $H = \dfrac{S - 2LW}{2L + 2W}$ **25.** \$4703.71; \$4713.99; \$4719.22; \$4722.74; \$4724.45
27. a. \$7313.97   **b.** \$7321.14   **c.** \$7325.98   **29.** 3.6 hr or 3 hr 36 min   **31.** 40°C   **33.** 171 packages   **35.** 9 ft   **37.** 2 gal   **39.** 20 m
41. a. 288π cu mm   **b.** 904.78 cu mm   **43. a.** 1174.86 cu m   **b.** 310.34 cu m   **c.** 1485.20 cu m   **45.** 128.3 mph   **47.** 0.42 ft
49. 41.125π ft ≈ 129.198 ft   **51.** \$1831.96   **53.** $f = \dfrac{C - 4h - 4p}{9}$ **55.** 178 cal   **57.** 1.5 g   **59.** −3, −2, −1   **61.** −3, −2, −1, 0, 1
63. answers may vary   **65.** 0.723   **67.** 1.523   **69.** 9.538   **71.** 30.065   **73.** answers may vary   **75.** answers may vary; $g = \dfrac{W}{h - 3t^2}$
77. $\dfrac{1}{8}$ **79.** $\dfrac{1}{8}$ **81.** $\dfrac{1}{2}$ **83.** $\dfrac{3}{8}$ **85.** 0   **87.** 0

Section 2.4
Practice Exercises
1. a. $(-\infty, 3.5)$ **b.** $[-3, \infty)$ **c.** $[-1, 4)$ **2.** $(4, \infty)$
3. $(-\infty, -4]$ **4. a.** $\left[\dfrac{2}{3}, \infty\right)$ **b.** $(-4, \infty)$ **5.** $\left[-\dfrac{3}{2}, \infty\right)$
6. $(-\infty, 13]$ **7.** $(-\infty, \infty)$ **8.** Sales must be ≥ \$10,000 per month.   **9.** the year 2022 and after

Vocabulary, Readiness & Video Check 2.4
1. d   **3.** b   **5.** $[-0.4, \infty)$ **7.** $(-\infty, -0.4]$ **9.** The graph of Example 1 is shaded from $-\infty$ to, but not including, −3, as indicated by a parenthesis. To write interval notation, write down what is shaded for the inequality from left to right. A parenthesis is always used with $-\infty$, so from the
graph, the interval notation is $(-\infty, -3)$.   **11.** same; reverse

Exercise Set 2.4

1. $(-\infty, -3)$ **3.** $[0.3, \infty)$ **5.** $[-7, \infty)$ **7.** $(-2, 5)$

9. $(-1, 5]$ **11.** $[-2, \infty)$ **13.** $(-\infty, 1)$ **15.** $(-\infty, 2]$

17. $[8, \infty)$ **19.** $(-\infty, -4.7)$ **21.** $(-\infty, -3]$ **23.** $(-\infty, -1]$ **25.** $(-\infty, 11]$ **27.** $(0, \infty)$

29. $(-13, \infty)$ **31.** $\left[-\dfrac{79}{3}, \infty\right)$ **33.** $\left(-\infty, -\dfrac{35}{6}\right)$ **35.** $(-\infty, -6)$ **37.** $(4, \infty)$ **39.** $[-0.5, \infty)$ **41.** $(-\infty, 7]$ **43.** $[0, \infty)$

45. $(-\infty, -29]$ **47.** $[3, \infty)$ **49.** $(-\infty, -1]$ **51.** $[-31, \infty)$ **53.** $(-\infty, \infty)$ **55.** $\varnothing$ **57.** $(-\infty, 9)$ **59.** $\left(-\infty, -\dfrac{11}{2}\right]$

61. $(-\infty, -2]$ **63.** $(-\infty, -15)$ **65.** $\left[-\dfrac{37}{3}, \infty\right)$ **67.** $(-\infty, 5)$ **69. a.** $\{x \mid x \geq 81\}$ **b.** A final exam grade of 81 or higher will result in an average of 77 or higher.   **71. a.** $\{x \mid x \leq 20.5\}$ **b.** She can move at most 20 whole boxes at one time.   **73. a.** $\{x \mid x \leq 1040\}$ **b.** The luggage and cargo must weigh 1040 pounds or less.   **75. a.** $\{x \mid x > 80\}$ **b.** If you drive more than 80 miles per day, plan A is more economical.   **77.** $\{F \mid F \geq 932°\}$ **79. a.** 2024   **b.** answers may vary   **81.** decreasing; answers may vary   **83.** 21 lb   **85.** during 2016   **87.** answers may vary

89. a. $\{t \mid t > 18.8\}$ **b.** 2023   **91.** 2, 3, 4   **93.** 2, 3, 4, …   **95.** 5   **97.** $\dfrac{13}{6}$ **99.** $\{x \mid x \geq 2\}$; $[2, \infty)$ **101.** $(-\infty, 0)$

103. $\{x \mid -2 < x \leq 1.5\}$;   **105.** yes   **107.** yes   **109.** $\{4\}$ **111.** $(-\infty, 4)$ **113.** answers may vary   **115.** answers may vary

Integrated Review

1. -5 **2.** $(-5, \infty)$ **3.** $\left[\dfrac{8}{3}, \infty\right)$ **4.** $[-1, \infty)$ **5.** 0   **6.** $\left[-\dfrac{1}{10}, \infty\right)$ **7.** $\left(-\infty, -\dfrac{1}{6}\right]$ **8.** 0   **9.** $\varnothing$ **10.** $\left[-\dfrac{3}{5}, \infty\right)$ **11.** 4.2

12. 6   **13.** -8 **14.** $(-\infty, -16)$ **15.** $\dfrac{20}{11}$ **16.** 1   **17.** $(38, \infty)$ **18.** -5.5 **19.** $\dfrac{3}{5}$ **20.** $(-\infty, \infty)$ **21.** 29   **22.** all real numbers

23. $(-\infty, 1)$ **24.** $\dfrac{9}{13}$ **25.** $(23, \infty)$ **26.** $(-\infty, 6]$ **27.** $\left(-\infty, \dfrac{3}{5}\right]$ **28.** $\left(-\infty, -\dfrac{19}{32}\right)$

Section 2.5
Practice Exercises

1. $\{1, 3\}$ **2.** $(-\infty, 2)$ **3.** $\{\ \}$ or $\varnothing$ **4.** $(-4, 2)$ **5.** $[-6, 8]$ **6.** $\{1, 2, 3, 4, 5, 6, 7, 9\}$ **7.** $\left(-\infty, \dfrac{3}{8}\right] \cup [3, \infty)$ **8.** $(-\infty, \infty)$

Vocabulary, Readiness & Video Check 2.5

1. compound   **3.** or   **5.** $\cup$ **7.** and   **9.** or

Exercise Set 2.5

1. $\{2, 3, 4, 5, 6, 7\}$ **3.** $\{4, 6\}$ **5.** $\{\ldots, -2, -1, 0, 1, \ldots\}$ **7.** $\{5, 7\}$ **9.** $\{x \mid x \text{ is an odd integer or } x = 2 \text{ or } x = 4\}$ **11.** $\{2, 4\}$ **13.** $(-3, 1)$ **15.** $\varnothing$ **17.** $(-\infty, -1)$ **19.** $[6, \infty)$ **21.** $(-\infty, -3]$ **23.** $(4, 10)$

25. $(11, 17)$ **27.** $[1, 4]$ **29.** $\left[-3, \dfrac{3}{2}\right]$ **31.** $\left[-\dfrac{7}{3}, 7\right]$ **33.** $(-\infty, 5)$ **35.** $(-\infty, -4] \cup [1, \infty)$

37. $(-\infty, \infty)$ **39.** $[2, \infty)$ **41.** $(-\infty, -4) \cup (-2, \infty)$ **43.** $(-\infty, \infty)$ **45.** $\left(-\dfrac{1}{2}, \dfrac{2}{3}\right)$ **47.** $(-\infty, \infty)$ **49.** $\left[\dfrac{3}{2}, 6\right]$

51. $\left(\dfrac{5}{4}, \dfrac{11}{4}\right)$ **53.** $\varnothing$ **55.** $\left(-\infty, -\dfrac{56}{5}\right) \cup \left(\dfrac{5}{3}, \infty\right)$ **57.** $\left(-5, \dfrac{5}{2}\right)$ **59.** $\left(0, \dfrac{14}{3}\right]$ **61.** $(-\infty, -3]$ **63.** $(-\infty, 1] \cup \left(\dfrac{29}{7}, \infty\right)$ **65.** $\varnothing$

67. $\left[-\dfrac{1}{2}, \dfrac{3}{2}\right)$ **69.** $\left(-\dfrac{4}{3}, \dfrac{7}{3}\right)$ **71.** $(6, 12)$ **73.** -12 **75.** -4 **77.** $-7, 7$ **79.** 0   **81.** 2004, 2005   **83.** answers may vary

85. $(6, \infty)$ **87.** $[3, 7]$ **89.** $(-\infty, -1)$ **91.** $-20.2° \leq F \leq 95°$ **93.** $67 \leq \text{final score} \leq 94$

Section 2.6
Practice Exercises

1. $-13, 13$ **2.** $-1, 4$ **3.** $-80, 70$ **4.** $-2, 2$ **5.** 0   **6.** $\{\ \}$ or $\varnothing$ **7.** $\{\ \}$ or $\varnothing$ **8.** $-\dfrac{3}{5}, 5$ **9.** 5

Vocabulary, Readiness & Video Check 2.6

1. C   **3.** B   **5.** D

Exercise Set 2.6

1. $-7, 7$ **3.** $4.2, -4.2$ **5.** $7, -2$ **7.** $8, 4$ **9.** $5, -5$ **11.** $3, -3$ **13.** 0   **15.** $\varnothing$ **17.** $\dfrac{1}{5}$ **19.** $9, -\dfrac{1}{2}$ **21.** $-\dfrac{5}{2}$ **23.** $4, -4$

25. 0   **27.** $\varnothing$ **29.** $0, \dfrac{14}{3}$ **31.** $2, -2$ **33.** $\varnothing$ **35.** $7, -1$ **37.** $\varnothing$ **39.** $\varnothing$ **41.** $-\dfrac{1}{8}$ **43.** $\dfrac{1}{2}, -\dfrac{5}{6}$ **45.** $2, -\dfrac{12}{5}$ **47.** $3, -2$

49. $-8, \dfrac{2}{3}$ **51.** $\varnothing$ **53.** 4   **55.** $13, -8$ **57.** $3, -3$ **59.** $8, -7$ **61.** $2, 3$ **63.** $2, -\dfrac{10}{3}$ **65.** $\dfrac{3}{2}$ **67.** $\varnothing$ **69.** 29.1%

71. $33.12°$ **73.** answers may vary   **75.** answers may vary   **77.** $\varnothing$ **79.** $|x| = 5$ **81.** answers may vary   **83.** $|x-1| = 5$ **85.** answers may vary   **87.** $|x| = 6$ **89.** $|x - 2| = |3x - 4|$

Section 2.7
Practice Exercises

1. $(-5, 5)$ **2.** $(-4, 2)$ **3.** $\left[-\frac{2}{3}, 2\right]$ **4.** { } or $\varnothing$ **5.** {2}

6. $(-\infty, -10] \cup [2, \infty)$ **7.** $(-\infty, \infty)$ **8.** $(-\infty, 0) \cup (12, \infty)$

Vocabulary, Readiness & Video Check 2.7

1. D **3.** C **5.** A **7.** The solution set involves "or" and "or" means "union."

Exercise Set 2.7

1. $[-4, 4]$ **3.** $(1, 5)$ **5.** $(-5, -1)$ **7.** $[-10, 3]$

9. $[-5, 5]$ **11.** $\varnothing$ **13.** $[0, 12]$ **15.** $(-\infty, -3) \cup (3, \infty)$

17. $(-\infty, -24] \cup [4, \infty)$ **19.** $(-\infty, -4) \cup (4, \infty)$ **21.** $(-\infty, \infty)$

23. $\left(-\infty, \frac{2}{3}\right) \cup (2, \infty)$ **25.** $\{0\}$ **27.** $\left(-\infty, -\frac{3}{8}\right) \cup \left(-\frac{3}{8}, \infty\right)$ **29.** $[-2, 2]$

31. $(-\infty, -1) \cup (1, \infty)$ **33.** $(-5, 11)$ **35.** $(-\infty, 4) \cup (6, \infty)$ **37.** $\varnothing$

39. $(-\infty, \infty)$ **41.** $[-2, 9]$ **43.** $(-\infty, -11] \cup [1, \infty)$ **45.** $(-\infty, 0) \cup (0, \infty)$

47. $(-\infty, \infty)$ **49.** $\left[-\frac{1}{2}, 1\right]$ **51.** $(-\infty, -3) \cup (0, \infty)$ **53.** $\varnothing$

55. $\left\{\frac{3}{8}\right\}$ **57.** $\left(-\frac{2}{3}, 0\right)$ **59.** $(-\infty, -12) \cup (0, \infty)$ **61.** $[-1, 8]$

63. $\left[-\frac{23}{8}, \frac{17}{8}\right]$ **65.** $(-2, 5)$ **67.** $5, -2$ **69.** $(-\infty, -7] \cup [17, \infty)$ **71.** $-\frac{9}{4}$ **73.** $(-2, 1)$ **75.** $2, \frac{4}{3}$ **77.** $\varnothing$

79. $\frac{19}{2}, -\frac{17}{2}$ **81.** $\left(-\infty, -\frac{25}{3}\right) \cup \left(\frac{35}{3}, \infty\right)$ **83.** $\frac{1}{6}$ **85.** 0 **87.** $\frac{1}{3}$ **89.** -1.5 **91.** 0 **93.** $|x| < 7$ **95.** $|x| \leq 5$ **97.** answers may vary **99.** $3.45 < x < 3.55$

Chapter 2 Vocabulary Check

1. compound inequality **2.** contradiction **3.** intersection **4.** union **5.** identity **6.** formula **7.** absolute value **8.** solution **9.** consecutive integers **10.** linear inequality in one variable **11.** linear equation in one variable

Chapter 2 Review

1. 3 **3.** $-\frac{45}{14}$ **5.** 0 **7.** 6 **9.** all real numbers **11.** $\varnothing$ **13.** -3 **15.** $\frac{96}{5}$ **17.** 32 **19.** 8 **21.** $\varnothing$ **23.** -7 **25.** 52

27. width: 40 m; length: 75 m **29.** 10, 11, 12, 13 **31.** 258 mi **33.** $w = \frac{V}{lh}$ **35.** $y = \frac{5x + 12}{4}$ **37.** $m = \frac{y - y_1}{x - x_1}$ **39.** $r = \frac{E - IR}{I}$

41. $g = \frac{T}{r + vt}$ **43. a.** $3695.27 **b.** $3700.81 **45.** length: 10 in.; width: 8 in. **47.** $(3, \infty)$ **49.** $(-4, \infty)$ **51.** $(-\infty, 7]$ **53.** $(-\infty, 1)$

55. more than 35 pounds per week **57.** $\left[2, \frac{5}{2}\right]$ **59.** $\left(\frac{1}{8}, 2\right)$ **61.** $\left(\frac{7}{8}, \frac{27}{20}\right]$ **63.** $\left(\frac{11}{3}, \infty\right)$ **65.** $1750 \leq x \leq 3750$ **67.** 5, 11

69. $-1, \frac{11}{3}$ **71.** $-\frac{1}{6}$ **73.** $\varnothing$ **75.** $5, -\frac{1}{3}$ **77.** $\left(-\frac{8}{5}, 2\right)$ **79.** $(-\infty, -3) \cup (3, \infty)$

81. $\varnothing$ **83.** $(-\infty, -27) \cup (-9, \infty)$ **85.** 2 **87.** $B = \frac{2A - hb}{h}$ **89.** China: 137 million; United States: 102 million; France: 93 million **91.** cylinder holds more ice cream **93.** $(2, \infty)$ **95.** $(-\infty, \infty)$ **97.** 3, -3 **99.** $-10, -\frac{4}{3}$ **101.** $\left(-\frac{1}{2}, 2\right)$

Chapter 2 Getting Ready for the Test

1. C **2.** C **3.** A **4.** B **5.** A **6.** B **7.** D **8.** C **9.** A **10.** E **11.** B **12.** A **13.** A **14.** B

Chapter 2 Test

1. 10 **2.** -32 **3.** $\varnothing$ **4.** all real numbers **5.** $-\frac{80}{29}$ **6.** $\frac{29}{4}$ **7.** $1, \frac{2}{3}$ **8.** $\varnothing$ **9.** $-4, -\frac{1}{3}$ **10.** $\frac{3}{2}$ **11.** $y = \frac{3x - 8}{4}$

12. $g = \frac{S}{t^2 + vt}$ **13.** $C = \frac{5}{9}(F - 32)$ or $C = \frac{5F - 160}{9}$ **14.** $(5, \infty)$ **15.** $\left(-\infty, -\frac{11}{3}\right]$ **16.** $\left(\frac{3}{2}, 5\right]$ **17.** $(-\infty, -2) \cup \left(\frac{4}{3}, \infty\right)$ **18.** $(3, 7)$

19. $[5, \infty)$ **20.** $[4, \infty)$ **21.** $\left[1, \frac{11}{2}\right)$ **22.** $(-\infty, \infty)$ **23.** 9.6 **24.** 1,922,000 vehicles **25.** at most 8 hunting dogs

26. 2,723,000 **27.** $3542.27 **28.** Florida: $17 billion; California: $13 billion; New York: $9 billion

Chapter 2 Cumulative Review

1. a. $\{101, 102, 103, \ldots\}$ **b.** $\{2, 3, 4, 5\}$; Sec. 1.2, Ex. 3 **3. a.** 3 **b.** $\frac{1}{7}$ **c.** -2.7 **d.** -8 **e.** 0; Sec. 1.2, Ex. 6 **5. a.** -14 **b.** -4

c. 5 **d.** -10.2 **e.** $\frac{1}{4}$ **f.** $-\frac{5}{21}$; Sec. 1.3, Ex. 1 **7. a.** 3 **b.** 5 **c.** $\frac{1}{2}$ **d.** -6 **e.** not a real number; Sec. 1.3, Ex. 7 **9. a.** 33

b. -18 **c.** $\frac{1}{12}$; Sec. 1.3, Ex. 12 **11. a.** $x + 5 = 20$ **b.** $2(3 + y) = 4$ **c.** $x - 8 = 2x$ **d.** $\frac{z}{9} = 9 + z$; Sec. 1.4, Ex. 1 **13.** $5 + 7x$;

Sec. 1.4, Ex. 9 **15.** 2; Sec. 2.1, Ex. 1 **17.** all real numbers; Sec. 2.1, Ex. 9 **19. a.** $3x + 3$ **b.** $12x - 3$; Sec. 2.2, Ex. 1 **21.** 23, 49, 92;

Sec. 2.2, Ex. 3 **23.** $y = \frac{2x + 7}{3}$ or $y = \frac{2x}{3} + \frac{7}{3}$; Sec. 2.3, Ex. 2 **25.** $b = \frac{2A - Bh}{h}$; Sec. 2.3, Ex. 3 **27. a.** ; $[2, \infty)$

b. ; $(-\infty, -1)$ **c.** ; $(0.5, 3]$; Sec. 2.4, Ex. 1 **29.** $\left[\frac{5}{2}, \infty\right)$; Sec. 2.4, Ex. 5 **31.** $(-\infty, \infty)$; Sec. 2.4, Ex. 7

33. $\{4, 6\}$; Sec. 2.5, Ex. 1 **35.** $(-\infty, 4)$; Sec. 2.5, Ex. 2 **37.** $\{2, 3, 4, 5, 6, 8\}$; Sec. 2.5, Ex. 6 **39.** $(-\infty, \infty)$; Sec. 2.5, Ex. 8

41. 2, -2; Sec. 2.6, Ex. 1 **43.** 24, -20; Sec. 2.6, Ex. 3 **45.** 4; Sec. 2.6, Ex. 9 **47.** $[-3, 3]$; Sec. 2.7, Ex. 1 **49.** $(-\infty, \infty)$; Sec. 2.7, Ex. 7

CHAPTER 3 GRAPHS AND FUNCTIONS

Section 3.1

Practice Exercises

1.

a. quadrant IV **b.** y-axis **c.** quadrant II **d.** x-axis **e.** quadrant III **f.** quadrant I
2. yes, no, yes **3. a.** $4200 **b.** more than $9000

4. $y = -3x - 2$ **5.** $y = -\frac{1}{2}x$ **6.** $y = 4x^2$ **7.** $y = -|x|$

Graphing Calculator Explorations 3.1

1. **3.** **5.** **7.**

Vocabulary, Readiness & Video Check 3.1

1. origin **3.** 1 **5.** V-shaped **7.** origin; left (if negative) or right (if positive); up (if positive) or down (if negative) **9.** The graph of an equation is a picture of its ordered pair solutions; a third point is found as a check to make sure the points line up and a mistake hasn't been made.

Exercise Set 3.1

1. quadrant I **3.** quadrant II **5.** quadrant IV **7.** y-axis **9.** quadrant III

11. $(-5, -2)$ **13.** $(-1, 0)$ **15.** $(3, 0)$ **17.** no; yes **19.** yes; yes **21.** yes; yes **23.** yes; no **25.** yes; yes
27. linear **29.** linear **31.** linear **33.** not linear **35.** linear **37.** not linear

39. not linear   **41.** linear   **43.** linear   **45.** not linear   **47.** not linear   **49.** not linear

51. linear   **53.** linear   **55.** -5 **57.** $-\dfrac{1}{10}$ **59.** $(-\infty, -5]$ **61.** $(-\infty, -4)$ **63.** quadrant IV   **65.** y-axis

67. quadrant III   **69.** quadrant IV   **71.** x-axis   **73.** quadrant III   **75.** b   **77.** B
79. C   **81.** 1997   **83.** answers may vary

85.   **87. a.**   **b.** 14 in.   **89.** $7000   **91.** $500   **93.** Depreciation is the same from year to year.   **95.** ; answers may vary

97. $y = 3x + 5$ **99.** $y = x^2 + 2$ **101.**   **103.**

Section 3.2
Practice Exercises
1. a. Domain: $\{4, 5\}$; Range: $\{1, -3, -2, 6\}$ **b.** Domain: $\{3\}$; Range: $\{-4, -3, -2, -1, 0, 1, 2, 3, 4\}$ **c.** domain: {Accountant, Computer Programmer, Engineer, Social Worker, Paralegal}; range: $\{51, 73, 92, 81, 48\}$ **2. a.** function   **b.** not a function   **c.** function
3. yes   **4.** yes   **5. a.** function   **b.** function   **c.** not a function   **d.** function   **e.** not a function   **6. a.** Domain: $[-1, 2]$;
Range: $[-2, 9]$; function   **b.** Domain: $[-1, 1]$; Range: $[-4, 4]$; not a function   **c.** Domain: $(-\infty, \infty)$; Range: $(-\infty, 4]$; function   **d.** Domain:
$(-\infty, \infty)$; Range: $(-\infty, \infty)$; function   **7. a.** 1   **b.** 6   **c.** -2 **d.** 15   **8. a.** -3 **b.** -2 **c.** 3   **d.** 1   **e.** -1 and 3   **f.** -3
9. 7.6 million or 7,600,000 students   **10.** 7.45 million or 7,450,000 students

Graphing Calculator Explorations 3.2

1.   **3.**   **5.**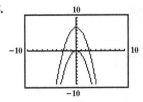

Vocabulary, Readiness & Video Check 3.2
1. relation   **3.** domain   **5.** vertical   **7.** An equation is one way of writing down a correspondence that produces ordered pair solutions; a relation between two sets of coordinates, x's and y's.   **9.** If a vertical line intersects a graph two (or more) times, then there's an x-value corresponding to two (or more) different y-values and is thus not a function.   **11.** Using function notation, the replacement value for x and the resulting $f(x)$ or y-value corresponds to an ordered pair (x, y) solution of the function.

Exercise Set 3.2
1. domain: $\{-1, 0, -2, 5\}$; range: $\{7, 6, 2\}$; function   **3.** domain: $\{-2, 6, -7\}$; range: $\{4, -3, -8\}$; not a function   **5.** domain: $\{1\}$; range:
$\{1, 2, 3, 4\}$; not a function   **7.** domain: $\left\{\dfrac{3}{2}, 0\right\}$; range: $\left\{\dfrac{1}{2}, -7, \dfrac{4}{5}\right\}$; not a function   **9.** domain: $\{-3, 0, 3\}$; range: $\{-3, 0, 3\}$; function
11. domain: $\{-1, 1, 2, 3\}$; range: $\{2, 1\}$; function   **13.** domain: $\{1994, 1998, 2002, 2006, 2010, 2014\}$; range: $\{6, 9, 10\}$; function   **15.** domain:
$\{32°, 104°, 212°, 50°\}$; range: $\{0°, 40°, 10°, 100°\}$; function   **17.** domain: $\{0\}$; range: $\{2, -1, 5, 100\}$; not a function   **19.** function
21. not a function   **23.** function   **25.** not a function   **27.** function   **29.** domain: $[0, \infty)$; range: $(-\infty, \infty)$; not a function   **31.** domain: $[-1, 1]$;
range: $(-\infty, \infty)$; not a function   **33.** domain: $(-\infty, \infty)$; range: $(-\infty, -3] \cup [3, \infty)$; not a function   **35.** domain: $[2, 7]$; range $[1, 6]$; not a function
37. domain: $\{-2\}$; range: $(-\infty, \infty)$; not a function   **39.** domain: $(-\infty, \infty)$; range: $(-\infty, 3]$; function   **41.** yes   **43.** no   **45.** yes   **47.** yes

49. yes   **51.** no   **53.** 15   **55.** 38   **57.** 7   **59.** 3   **61. a.** 0   **b.** 1   **c.** -1 **63. a.** 246   **b.** 6   **c.** $\dfrac{9}{2}$ **65. a.** -5 **b.** -5

c. -5 **67. a.** 5.1   **b.** 15.5   **c.** 9.533   **69.** $(1, -10)$ **71.** $(4, 56)$ **73.** $f(-1) = -2$ **75.** $g(2) = 0$ **77.** $-4, 0$ **79.** 3
81. 90.68; In 2014, about 90.68% of Americans age 25 and older had completed at least high school.   **83.** 94.112; In 2020, we predict that 94.112% of
Americans age 25 and older will have completed at least high school.   **85.** answers may vary   **87.** $15.54 billion   **89.** $f(x) = x + 7$ **91.** 25π sq cm
93. 2744 cu in.   **95.** 166.38 cm   **97.** 163.2 mg   **99. a.** 54.68; per capita consumption of beef was 54.68 lb in 2014   **b.** 48.83 lb

101. 5, −5, 6   **103.** 2, $\dfrac{8}{7}$, $\dfrac{12}{7}$ **105.** 0, 0, −6   **107.** yes; 170 m   **109.** true   **111.** true

113. a. 16   **b.** $a^2 + 7$ **115. a.** 0   **b.** $3a − 12$ **c.** $−3x − 12$ **d.** $3x + 3h − 12$ **117.** infinitely many   **119.** answers may vary
121. answers may vary

Section 3.3
Practice Exercises

1. $g(x) = 4x − 3$, $f(x) = 4x$ **2.** $g(x) = −2x + 5$, $f(x) = −2x$ **3. a.** $\left(0, −\dfrac{2}{5}\right)$ **b.** $(0, 4.1)$ **4.** $4x − 5y = −20$, $(0, 4)$, $(−5, 0)$ **5.** $y = −3x$ $(−1, 3)$, $(0, 0)$, $(1, −3)$

6. $x = −4$ **7.** $y = 4$

Graphing Calculator Explorations 3.3

1. $y = \dfrac{x}{3.5}$ **3.** $y = −\dfrac{5.78}{2.31}x + \dfrac{10.98}{2.31}$

5. $y = |x| + 3.78$ **7.** $y = 5.6x^2 + 7.7x + 1.5$

Vocabulary, Readiness & Video Check 3.3

1. linear   **3.** vertical; $(c, 0)$ **5.** $y; f(x); x$ **7.** $f(x) = mx + b$ **9.** For a horizontal line, the coefficient of x is 0 for a vertical line, the coefficient of y is 0.

Exercise Set 3.3

1. $f(x) = −2x$ $(−1, 2)$, $(0, 0)$, $(1, −2)$ **3.** $(−1, 5)$, $f(x) = −2x + 3$, $(0, 3)$, $(1, 1)$ **5.** $f(x) = \dfrac{1}{2}x$, $(2, 1)$, $(0, 0)$, $(−2, −1)$ **7.** $f(x) = \dfrac{1}{2}x − 4$, $(4, −2)$, $(2, −3)$, $(0, −4)$ **9.** C   **11.** D   **13.** $f(x) = x − 3$

15. $f(x) = \dfrac{x}{5}$ **17.** $f(x) = \dfrac{1}{2}x + 3$ **19.** $f(x) = \dfrac{1}{2}x − 2$ **21.**   **23.**   **25.**

27. C   **29.** A   **31.** $x + 2y = 8$ **33.** $3x + 5y = 7$ **35.** $x + 8y = 8$ **37.** $5 = 6x − y$ **39.** $−x + 10y = 11$

41. $y = \frac{3}{2}$

43. $2x + 3y = 6$

45. $x + 3 = 0$

47. $f(x) = \frac{3}{4}x + 2$

49. $f(x) = x$

51. $f(x) = \frac{1}{2}x$

53. $f(x) = 4x - \frac{1}{3}$

55. $x = -3$

57. $9, -3$ **59.** $(-\infty, -4) \cup (-1, \infty)$ **61.** $\left[\frac{2}{3}, 2\right]$ **63.** $\frac{3}{2}$ **65.** 6 **67.** $-\frac{6}{5}$

69. no; answers may vary **71.** yes; answers may vary **73. a.** $(0, 500)$; if no tables are produced, 500 chairs can be produced **b.** $(750, 0)$; if no chairs are produced, 750 tables can be produced **c.** 466 chairs

75. a. $64 **b.**

c. The line moves upward from left to right. **77. a.** $13,706 **b.** 2023 **c.** answers may vary **79.** answers may vary **81.** The vertical line $x = 0$ has y-intercepts. **83.** a line parallel to $y = -4x$ but with y-intercept $(0, 2)$ **85.** D **87.** C **89.** **91.**

Section 3.4

Practice Exercises

1. $m = -\frac{1}{2}$;

2. $m = \frac{3}{5}$;

3. $m = -4$ **4.** $m = \frac{2}{3}$; y-intercept: $(0, -3)$ **5. a.** 6,216,550

b. The number of people age 85 or older in the United States increases at a rate of 269,370 per year. **c.** At year $x = 0$, or 2010, there were 4,869,700 people age 85 or older in the United States. **6.** undefined **7.** $m = 0$

8. a. perpendicular **b.** parallel

Graphing Calculator Explorations 3.4

1. 18.4   **3.** -1.5

5. $14.0; 4.3, -9.4$

Vocabulary, Readiness & Video Check 3.4

1. slope **3.** $m; (0, b)$ **5.** horizontal **7.** -1 **9.** increases; decreases **11.** Slope–intercept form allows us to see the slope and y-intercept so we can discuss them in the context of the application. Slope is a rate of change and tells us the rate of increase of registered nurses (52.7 thousand per year). The y-intercept tells us the number of registered nurses at "zero" year (2711 thousand in 2012). **13.** The slopes of vertical lines are undefined and we can't mathematically work with undefined slopes.

Exercise Set 3.4

1. $\frac{9}{5}$ **3.** $-\frac{7}{2}$ **5.** $-\frac{5}{6}$ **7.** $\frac{1}{3}$ **9.** $-\frac{4}{3}$ **11.** 0 **13.** undefined **15.** 2 **17.** -1 **19.** upward **21.** horizontal **23.** l_2

25. l_2 **27.** l_2 **29.** $m = 5; (0, -2)$ **31.** $m = -2; (0, 7)$ **33.** $m = \frac{2}{3}; \left(0, -\frac{10}{3}\right)$ **35.** $m = \frac{1}{2}; (0, 0)$ **37.** A **39.** B

41. undefined **43.** 0 **45.** undefined **47.** $m = -1; (0, 5)$ **49.** $m = \frac{6}{5}; (0, 6)$ **51.** $m = 3; (0, 9)$ **53.** $m = 0; (0, 4)$

55. $m = 7; (0, 0)$ **57.** $m = 0; (0, -6)$ **59.** slope is undefined, no y-intercept **61.** parallel **63.** neither **65.** perpendicular

67. parallel **69.** perpendicular **71.** $\frac{3}{2}$ **73.** $-\frac{1}{2}$ **75.** $\frac{2}{3}$ **77.** approximately -0.12 **79. a.** 77.5 yr **b.** $m = 0.15$; The life expectancy of a female born in the United States is approximately 0.15 year more than a female born the year before. **c.** $(0, 71.5)$: In year 0, or in 1950, the life expectancy of an American female born that year was 71.5 years. **81. a.** $m = 52.7$; $(0, 2711)$ **b.** The number of people employed as registered nurses increases 52.7 thousand for every 1 year. **c.** There were 2711 thousand registered nurses in 2012.

83. a. \$1.67 billion **b.** 2015 **c.** answers may vary **85.** $y = 5x + 32$ **87.** $y = 2x - 1$ **89.** $m = \dfrac{-14 - 6}{7 - (-2)} = \dfrac{-20}{9}$ or $-\dfrac{20}{9}$

91. $m = \dfrac{-10 - (-5)}{-8 - (-11)} = \dfrac{-5}{3}$ or $-\dfrac{5}{3}$ **93.** $-\dfrac{7}{2}$ **95.** $\dfrac{2}{7}$ **97.** $\dfrac{5}{2}$ **99.** $-\dfrac{2}{5}$ **101.** l_1: -2, l_2: -1, l_3: $-\dfrac{2}{3}$ **103.** $(6, 20)$ **105.** $-\dfrac{7}{4}$

or -1.75 yd per sec **107.** answers may vary **109.** answers may vary **111.** $\dfrac{1}{48}$ **113.**

Section 3.5
Practice Exercises

1. **2.** **3.** $y = -\dfrac{3}{4}x + 4$ **4.** $y = -4x - 3$ **5.** $f(x) = -\dfrac{2}{3}x + \dfrac{4}{3}$ **6.** $2x + 3y = 5$

7. 9044 home sales **8.** $y = -2$ **9.** $x = 6$ **10.** $3x + 4y = 12$ **11.** $f(x) = \dfrac{4}{3}x - \dfrac{41}{3}$

Vocabulary, Readiness & Video Check 3.5

1. $m = -4$, y-intercept: $(0, 12)$ **3.** $m = 5$, y-intercept: $(0, 0)$ **5.** $m = \dfrac{1}{2}$, y-intercept: $(0, 6)$ **7.** parallel **9.** neither **11.** slope-intercept; y-intercept; slope **13.** if one of the two given points is the y-intercept **15.** $f(x) = \dfrac{1}{3}x - \dfrac{17}{3}$

Exercise Set 3.5

1. **3.** **5.** **7.** $y = -x + 1$ **9.** $y = 2x + \dfrac{3}{4}$ **11.** $y = \dfrac{2}{7}x$ **13.** $y = 3x - 1$

15. $y = -2x - 1$ **17.** $y = \dfrac{1}{2}x + 5$ **19.** $y = -\dfrac{9}{10}x - \dfrac{27}{10}$ **21.** $f(x) = 3x - 6$ **23.** $f(x) = -2x + 1$ **25.** $f(x) = -\dfrac{1}{2}x - 5$

27. $f(x) = \dfrac{1}{3}x - 7$ **29.** $f(x) = -\dfrac{3}{8}x + \dfrac{5}{8}$ **31.** $2x + y = 3$ **33.** $2x - 3y = -7$ **35.** -2 **37.** 2 **39.** -2 **41.** $y = -4$

43. $x = 4$ **45.** $y = 5$ **47.** $f(x) = 4x - 4$ **49.** $f(x) = -3x + 1$ **51.** $f(x) = -\dfrac{3}{2}x - 6$ **53.** $2x - y = -7$ **55.** $f(x) = -x + 7$

57. $x + 2y = 22$ **59.** $2x + 7y = -42$ **61.** $4x + 3y = -20$ **63.** $x = -2$ **65.** $x + 2y = 2$ **67.** $y = 12$ **69.** $8x - y = 47$

71. $x = 5$ **73.** $f(x) = -\dfrac{3}{8}x - \dfrac{29}{4}$ **75. a.** $y = 32x$ **b.** 128 ft per sec **77. a.** $y = -250x + 3500$ **b.** 1625 Frisbees

79. a. $y = 52.7x + 2711$ **b.** 2974.5 thousand or 2,974,500 **81. a.** $y = 14{,}920x + 268{,}200$ **b.** \$402,480 **83.** $(-\infty, 14]$ **85.** $\left[\dfrac{7}{2}, \infty\right)$

87. $\left(-\infty, -\dfrac{1}{4}\right)$ **89.** true **91.** $-4x + y = 4$ **93.** $2x + y = -23$ **95.** $3x - 2y = -13$ **97.** answers may vary

99. **101.** **103.**

Integrated Review

1. **2.** **3.** **4.** **5.** 0 **6.** $-\dfrac{3}{5}$ **7.** $m = 3$; $(0, -5)$ **8.** $m = \dfrac{5}{2}$; $\left(0, -\dfrac{7}{2}\right)$

9. parallel **10.** perpendicular **11.** $y = -x + 7$

12. $x = -2$ **13.** $y = 0$ **14.** $f(x) = -\dfrac{1}{2}x - 8$

15. $f(x) = -5x - 6$ **16.** $f(x) = -4x + \dfrac{1}{3}$ **17.** $f(x) = \dfrac{1}{2}x - 1$ **18.** $y = 3x - \dfrac{3}{2}$ **19.** $y = 3x - 2$ **20.** $y = -\dfrac{5}{4}x + 4$

21. $y = \dfrac{1}{4}x - \dfrac{7}{2}$ **22.** $y = -\dfrac{5}{2}x - \dfrac{5}{2}$ **23.** $x = -1$ **24.** $y = 3$

Section 3.6
Practice Exercises
1. $f(4) = 5; f(-2) = 6; f(0) = -2$

2.   **3.**   **4.**   **5.**   **6.**   **7.**

Vocabulary, Readiness & Video Check 3.6
1. C   **3.** D   **5.** Although $f(x) = x + 3$ isn't defined for $x = -1$, we need to clearly indicate the point where this piece of the graph ends. Therefore, we find this point and graph it as an open circle.   **7.** x-axis

Exercise Set 3.6
1.   **3.**   **5.**   **7.**   **9.** domain: $(-\infty, \infty)$; range: $[0, \infty)$

11. domain: $(-\infty, \infty)$; range: $(-\infty, 5)$ **13.** domain: $(-\infty, \infty)$; range: $(-\infty, 6]$ **15.** domain: $(-\infty, 0] \cup [1, \infty)$; range: $\{-4, -2\}$

17.   **19.**   **21.**   **23.**   **25.**   **27.**

29.   **31.**   **33.**   **35.**   **37.**   **39.**

41.   **43.**   **45.**   **47.**   **49.** A   **51.** D   **53.** answers may vary
55.   **57.** domain: $[2, \infty)$; range: $[3, \infty)$

59. domain: $(-\infty, \infty)$; range: $(-\infty, 3]$ **61.** $[20, \infty)$ **63.** $(-\infty, \infty)$ **65.** $[-103, \infty)$
67. domain: $(-\infty, \infty)$; range: $[0, \infty)$ **69.** domain: $(-\infty, \infty)$; range: $(-\infty, 0] \cup (2, \infty)$

Section 3.7
Practice Exercises
1.   **2.**   **3.**   **4.**

Vocabulary, Readiness & Video Check 3.7

1. We find the boundary line equation by replacing the inequality symbol with =. The points on this line are solutions (line is solid) if the inequality is ≥ or ≤; the points on this line are not solutions (line is dashed) if the inequality is > or <.

Exercise Set 3.7

1. $x < 2$ **3.**   **5.** $3x + y > 6$ **7.** $y \le -2x$ **9.** $2x + 4y \ge 8$ **11.** $5x + 3y > -15$

13.   **15.**   **17.**   **19.**   **21.**   **23.**

25.   **27.**   **29.**   **31.**   **33.**   **35.**

37.   **39.**   **41.**   **43.**   **45.** D **47.** A **49.** $x \ge 2$ **51.** $y \le -3$ **53.** $y > 4$ **55.** $x < 1$ **57.** 8 **59.** -25 **61.** 16 **63.** $\dfrac{27}{125}$ **65.** domain: [1, 5]; range: [1, 3]; no **67.** with < or > **69.**

Chapter 3 Vocabulary Check

1. relation **2.** line **3.** linear inequality **4.** Standard **5.** range **6.** Parallel **7.** Slope–intercept **8.** function **9.** slope **10.** perpendicular **11.** y **12.** domain **13.** linear function **14.** x **15.** point–slope

Chapter 3 Review

1.   A: quadrant IV; B: quadrant II; C: y-axis; D: quadrant III **3.** no, yes **5.** yes, yes **7.** linear   **9.** linear

11. nonlinear   **13.** linear   **15.** linear   **17.** linear

19. domain: $\left\{-\dfrac{1}{2}, 6, 0, 25\right\}$; range: $\left\{\dfrac{3}{4} \text{ (or 0.75)}, -12, 25\right\}$; function **21.** domain: $\{2, 4, 6, 8\}$; range: $\{2, 4, 5, 6\}$; not a function

23. domain: $(-\infty, \infty)$; range: $(-\infty, -1] \cup [1, \infty)$; not a function **25.** domain: $(-\infty, \infty)$; range: $\{4\}$; function **27.** -3 **29.** 18

31. -3 **33.** 381 lb **35.** 0 **37.** $-2, 4$ **39.**   **41.**   **43.** C **45.** B **47.**

49.   **51.**   **53.**   **55.** -3 **57.** $\dfrac{5}{2}$ **59.** $m = -3; \left(0, \dfrac{1}{2}\right)$

61. $m = \dfrac{2}{5}, \left(0, -\dfrac{4}{3}\right)$ **63.** 0 **65.** l_2 **67.** l_2 **69. a.** $87 **b.** $m = 0.3$; cost increases by $0.30 for each additional mile driven **c.** $(0, 42)$; cost for 0 miles driven is $42 **71.** neither **73.** parallel

75.   **77.**   **79.**   **81.** $y = -1$ **83.** $x = -4$ **85.** $3x - y = -14$ **87.** $x + 2y = -8$

89. $y = 3$ **91.** $f(x) = -\dfrac{2}{3}x + 4$ **93.** $f(x) = -2x - 2$

95. $f(x) = \dfrac{3}{4}x + \dfrac{7}{2}$ **97. a.** $y = 12{,}000x + 126{,}000$ **b.** $342{,}000

99. **101.** **103.** **105.** **107.**

109. **111.** **113.** **115.**   **117.** $x = -7$ **119.** $y = \frac{3}{4}x + 2$ **121.** $y = -\frac{3}{2}x - 8$

123. **125.**

Getting Ready for the Test

1. A **2.** C **3.** F **4.** E **5.** B **6.** D **7.** A **8.** B **9.** D **10.** C **11.** B **12.** C **13.** A **14.** A **15.** B **16.** A **17.** B **18.** D **19.** C or E;
C or E **20.** D **21.** G **22.** I **23.** D **24.** A

Chapter 3 Test

1. A: quadrant IV; B: x-axis; C: quadrant II **2.** **3.** **4.** $f(x) = \frac{2}{3}x$

5. **6.** $-\frac{3}{2}$ **7.** $m = -\frac{1}{4}, \left(0, \frac{2}{3}\right)$ **8.** $f(x) = (x-1)^2$ **9.** $g(x) = |x| + 2$ **10.** $y = -8$ **11.** $x = -4$

12. $y = -2$ **13.** $3x + y = 11$ **14.** $5x - y = 2$ **15.** $f(x) = -\frac{1}{2}x$ **16.** $f(x) = -\frac{1}{3}x + \frac{5}{3}$ **17.** $f(x) = -\frac{1}{2}x - \frac{1}{2}$ **18.** neither

19. $x \le -4$ **20.** $2x - y > 5$ **21.**

22. domain: $(-\infty, \infty)$; range: $\{5\}$; function
23. domain: $\{-2\}$; range: $(-\infty, \infty)$; not a function
24. domain: $(-\infty, \infty)$; range: $[0, \infty)$; function
25. domain: $(-\infty, \infty)$; range: $(-\infty, \infty)$; function
26. a. 82 games **b.** 84 games **c.** $648 million **d.** $m = 0.024$;
Every million dollars spent on payroll increases winnings by 0.024 games.

27. domain: $(-\infty, \infty)$;
range: $(-3, \infty)$ **28.** **29.** domain: $(-\infty, \infty)$;
range: $(-\infty, -1]$ **30.**

Chapter 3 Cumulative Review

1. 41; Sec. 1.2, Ex. 2 **3. a.** true **b.** false **c.** false **d.** false; Sec. 1.2, Ex. 5 **5. a.** -6 **b.** -7 **c.** -16 **d.** 20.5 **e.** $-\frac{7}{6}$
f. 0.94 **g.** -3; Sec. 1.3, Ex. 2 **7. a.** 9 **b.** $\frac{1}{16}$ **c.** -25 **d.** 25 **e.** -125 **f.** -125; Sec. 1.3, Ex. 6 **9. a.** > **b.** =
c. < **d.** < **e.** > **f.** <; Sec. 1.4, Ex. 5 **11. a.** $\frac{1}{11}$ **b.** $-\frac{1}{9}$ **c.** $\frac{4}{7}$; Sec. 1.4, Ex. 8 **13.** 0.4; Sec. 2.1, Ex. 2 **15.** { } or $\varnothing$;
Sec. 2.1, Ex. 8 **17. a.** $3x + 3$ **b.** $12x - 3$; Sec. 2.2, Ex. 1 **19.** 86, 88, and 90; Sec. 2.2, Ex. 6 **21.** $\frac{V}{lw} = h$; Sec. 2.3, Ex. 1

23. $\{x \mid x < 7\}$ or $(-\infty, 7)$; Sec. 2.4, Ex. 2 **25.** $\left(-\infty, -\frac{7}{3}\right]$; Sec. 2.4, Ex. 6 **27.** $\varnothing$; Sec. 2.5, Ex. 3 **29.** $\left(-\infty, \frac{13}{5}\right] \cup [4, \infty)$; Sec. 2.5, Ex. 7

31. $-2, \frac{4}{5}$; Sec. 2.6, Ex. 2 **33.** $\frac{3}{4}, 5$; Sec. 2.6, Ex. 8 **35.** $\left[-2, \frac{8}{5}\right]$; Sec. 2.7, Ex. 3 **37.** $(-\infty, -4) \cup (10, \infty)$; Sec. 2.7, Ex. 6

39. solutions: $(0, -12)$, $(2, -6)$; not a solution $(1, 9)$; Sec. 3.1, Ex. 2   **41.** yes; Sec. 3.2, Ex. 3   **43. a.** $\left(0, \dfrac{3}{7}\right)$ **b.** $(0, -3.2)$; Sec. 3.3, Ex. 3

45. $\dfrac{2}{3}$; Sec. 3.4, Ex. 3   **47.** $y = \dfrac{1}{4}x - 3$; Sec. 3.5 Ex. 3   **49.**   Sec. 3.7; Ex. 1

CHAPTER 4 SYSTEMS OF EQUATIONS

Section 4.1

Practice Exercises

1. a. yes   **b.** no
2. solution: $(1, 5)$ **3.** no solution   **4.** $\{(x, y) \mid 3x - 2y = 4\}$ or $\{(x, y) \mid -9x + 6y = -12\}$

5. $\left(-\dfrac{1}{2}, 5\right)$ **6.** $\left(-\dfrac{9}{5}, -\dfrac{2}{5}\right)$ **7.** $(2, 1)$ **8.** $(-2, 0)$ **9.** $\varnothing$ or $\{\ \}$ **10.** $\{(x, y) \mid -3x + 2y = -1\}$ or $\{(x, y) \mid 9x - 6y = 3\}$

Graphing Calculator Explorations 4.1

1. $(2.11, 0.17)$ **3.** $(0.57, -1.97)$

Vocabulary, Readiness & Video Check 4.1

1. B   **3.** A   **5.** The ordered pair must be a solution of *both* equations of the system in order to be a solution of the system.   **7.** Solve one equation for a variable. Next be sure to substitute this expression for the variable into the *other* equation.

Exercise Set 4.1

1. yes   **3.** no   **5.** yes   **7.** no   **9.** $(2, -1)$ **11.** $(1, 2)$ **13.** $\varnothing$

15. $(2, 8)$ **17.** $(0, -9)$ **19.** $(1, -1)$ **21.** $(-5, 3)$ **23.** $\left(\dfrac{5}{2}, \dfrac{5}{4}\right)$ **25.** $(1, -2)$ **27.** $(8, 2)$ **29.** $(7, 2)$ **31.** $\varnothing$

33. $\{(x, y) \mid 3x + y = 1\}$ **35.** $\left(\dfrac{3}{2}, 1\right)$ **37.** $(2, -1)$ **39.** $(-5, 3)$ **41.** $\{(x, y) \mid 3x + 9y = 12\}$ **43.** $\varnothing$ **45.** $\left(\dfrac{1}{2}, \dfrac{1}{5}\right)$ **47.** $(9, 9)$

49. $\{(x, y) \mid x = 3y + 2\}$ **51.** $\left(-\dfrac{1}{4}, \dfrac{1}{2}\right)$ **53.** $(3, 2)$ **55.** $(7, -3)$ **57.** $\varnothing$ **59.** $(3, 4)$ **61.** $(-2, 1)$ **63.** $(1.2, -3.6)$ **65.** true

67. false   **69.** $6y - 4z = 25$ **71.** $x + 10y = 2$ **73.** no solution   **75.** infinite number of solutions   **77.** no; answers may vary
79. 5000 DVDs; $21   **81.** supply greater than demand   **83.** $(1875, 4687.5)$ **85.** makes money   **87.** for x-values greater than 1875
89. answers may vary; One possibility: $\begin{cases} -2x + y = 1 \\ x - 2y = -8 \end{cases}$ **91. a.** Mobile phone subscriptions are growing, while landline subscriptions are decreasing.

b. $(4, 60)$ **c.** In the year 2004, the number of mobile phone subscriptions was about the same as the number of landline subscriptions.

93. $\left(\dfrac{1}{4}, 8\right)$ **95.** $\left(\dfrac{1}{3}, \dfrac{1}{2}\right)$ **97.** $\varnothing$ **99.** $\left(-\dfrac{1}{4}, \dfrac{1}{3}\right)$

Section 4.2

Practice Exercises

1. $(-1, 2, 1)$ **2.** $\{\ \}$ or $\varnothing$ **3.** $\left(\dfrac{2}{3}, -\dfrac{1}{2}, 0\right)$ **4.** $\{(x, y, z) \mid 2x + y - 3z = 6\}$ **5.** $(6, 15, -5)$

Vocabulary, Readiness & Video Check 4.2

1. a, b, d   **3.** yes; answers may vary   **5.** Once we have one equation in two variables, we need to get another equation in the *same* two variables, giving us a system of two equations in two variables. We solve this new system to find the value of two variables. We then substitute these values into an original equation to find the value of the third.

Exercise Set 4.2

1. $(-1, 5, 2)$ **3.** $(-2, 5, 1)$ **5.** $(-2, 3, -1)$ **7.** $\{(x, y, z) \mid x - 2y + z = -5\}$ **9.** $\varnothing$ **11.** $(0, 0, 0)$ **13.** $(-3, -35, -7)$

15. $(6, 22, -20)$ **17.** $\varnothing$ **19.** $(3, 2, 2)$ **21.** $\{(x, y, z) \mid x + 2y - 3z = 4\}$ **23.** $(-3, -4, -5)$ **25.** $\left(0, \dfrac{1}{2}, -4\right)$ **27.** $(12, 6, 4)$

29. 15 and 30   **31.** 5   **33.** $-\dfrac{5}{3}$ **35.** answers may vary   **37.** answers may vary   **39.** $(1, 1, -1)$ **41.** $(1, 1, 0, 2)$

43. $(1, -1, 2, 3)$ **45.** answers may vary

Section 4.3

Practice Exercises

1. a. 2017   **b.** yes; answers may vary   **2.** 17 and 12   **3.** Atlantique: 500 kph; V150: 575 kph   **4.** 0.95 liter of water; 0.05 liter of 99% HCl
5. 1500 packages   **6.** 40°, 60°, 80°

Vocabulary, Readiness & Video Check 4.3

1. Up to now we've been choosing one variable/unknown and translating into one equation. To solve by a system of equations, we'll choose two variables to represent two unknowns and translate into two equations.   **3.** The ordered triple still needs to be interpreted in the context of the application. Each value actually represents the angle measure of a triangle, in degrees.

Exercise Set 4.3

1. 10 and 8   **3. a.** Enterprise class: 1101 ft; Nimitz class: 1092 ft   **b.** 3.67 football fields   **5.** plane: 520 mph; wind: 40 mph
7. 20 qt of 4%; 40 qt of 1%   **9.** United Kingdom: 37,623; Italy: 28,941   **11.** 9 large frames; 13 small frames   **13.** -10 and -8
15. a. answers may vary   **b.** 2008   **17.** tablets: $0.80; pens: $0.20   **19.** speed of plane: 630 mph; speed of wind: 90 mph   **21. a.** 2012
b. answers may vary   **23.** 28 cm; 28 cm; 37 cm   **25.** 600 mi   **27.** $x = 75; y = 105$ **29.** 625 units   **31.** 3000 units   **33.** 1280 units
35. a. $R(x) = 450x$ **b.** $C(x) = 200x + 6000$ **c.** 24 desks   **37.** 2 units of Mix A; 3 units of Mix B; 1 unit of Mix C
39. 5 in.; 7 in.; 7 in.; 10 in.   **41.** 18, 13, and 9   **43.** free throws: 703; 2-pt field goals: 657; 3-pt fields goals: 192   **45.** $x = 60; y = 55; z = 65$
47. $5x + 5z = 10$ **49.** $-5y + 2z = 2$ **51.** 2007: 780,000; 2014: 936,800   **53.** $a = 3, b = 4, c = -1$ **55.** $a = 0.5, b = 24.5, c = 849; 2015$:
1774 thousand students   **57.** $(10, 13)$

Integrated Review

1. C   **2.** D   **3.** A   **4.** B   **5.** $(1, 3)$ **6.** $\left(\dfrac{4}{3}, \dfrac{16}{3}\right)$ **7.** $(2, -1)$ **8.** $(5, 2)$ **9.** $\left(\dfrac{3}{2}, 1\right)$ **10.** $\left(-2, \dfrac{3}{4}\right)$ **11.** $\varnothing$

12. $\{(x, y) \mid 2x - 5y = 3\}$ **13.** $\left(1, \dfrac{1}{3}\right)$ **14.** $\left(3, \dfrac{3}{4}\right)$ **15.** $(-1, 3, 2)$ **16.** $(1, -3, 0)$ **17.** $\varnothing$ **18.** $\{(x, y, z) \mid x - y + 3z = 2\}$

19. $\left(2, 5, \dfrac{1}{2}\right)$ **20.** $\left(1, 1, \dfrac{1}{3}\right)$ **21.** 19 and 27   **22.** 70°; 70°; 100°; 120°

Section 4.4

Practice Exercises

1. $(2, -1)$ **2.** $\varnothing$ **3.** $(-1, 1, 2)$

Vocabulary, Readiness & Video Check 4.4

1. matrix   **3.** row   **5.** false   **7.** true   **9.** Two rows may be interchanged, the elements of any row may be multiplied/divided by the same nonzero number, the elements of any row may be multiplied/divided by the same nonzero number and added to their corresponding elements in any other row; rows were not interchanged in Example 1.

Exercise Set 4.4

1. $(2, -1)$ **3.** $(-4, 2)$ **5.** $\varnothing$ **7.** $\{(x, y) \mid 3x - 3y = 9\}$ **9.** $(-2, 5, -2)$ **11.** $(1, -2, 3)$ **13.** $(4, -3)$ **15.** $(2, 1, -1)$
17. $(9, 9)$ **19.** $\varnothing$ **21.** $\varnothing$ **23.** $(1, -4, 3)$ **25.** function   **27.** not a function   **29.** -13 **31.** -36 **33.** 0   **35.** c
37. a. in 2005   **b.** no; answers may vary   **c.** no; it has a positive slope   **d.** answers may vary   **39.** answers may vary

Section 4.5

Practice Exercises

Vocabulary, Readiness & Video Check 4.5

1. system   **3.** corner   **5.** No; we can choose any test point except a point on the second inequality's own boundary line.

Exercise Set 4.5

1. **3.** **5.** **7.** **9.** **11.**

13. **15.** **17.** **19.** **21.** C **23.** D **25.** 9 **27.** $\dfrac{4}{9}$ **29.** 5 **31.** 59

33. the line $y = 3$ **35.** answers may vary

Chapter 4 Vocabulary Check

1. system of equations **2.** solution **3.** consistent **4.** triple **5.** inconsistent **6.** matrix **7.** element **8.** row **9.** column

Chapter 4 Review

1. $(-3, 1)$ **3.** $\varnothing$ **5.** $\left(3, \dfrac{8}{3}\right)$ **7.** $(2, 0, 2)$ **9.** $\left(-\dfrac{1}{2}, \dfrac{3}{4}, 1\right)$ **11.** $\varnothing$ **13.** $(1, 1, -2)$

15. 10, 40, and 48 **17.** 58 mph; 65 mph **19.** 20 L of 10% solution; 30 L of 60% solution **21.** 17 pennies; 20 nickels; 16 dimes

23. two sides: 22 cm each; third side; 29 cm **25.** $(-3, 1)$ **27.** $\left(-\dfrac{2}{3}, 3\right)$ **29.** $\left(\dfrac{5}{4}, \dfrac{5}{8}\right)$ **31.** $(1, 3)$ **33.** $(1, 2, 3)$ **35.** $(3, -2, 5)$

37. $(1, 1, -2)$ **39.** **41.** **43.** **45.** **47.** $\left(\dfrac{7}{3}, -\dfrac{8}{3}\right)$

49. $\{(x, y) \mid 5x - 2y = 10\}$ **51.** $(-1, 3, 5)$ **53.** 28 units, 42 units, 56 units **55.** 2000

Chapter 4 Getting Ready for the Test

1. C **2.** B **3.** C **4.** B **5.** A **6.** C **7.** C **8.** D **9.** B **10.** A

Chapter 4 Test

1. $(1, 3)$ **2.** $\varnothing$ **3.** $(2, -3)$ **4.** $\{(x, y) \mid 10x + 4y = 10\}$ **5.** $(-1, -2, 4)$ **6.** $\varnothing$ **7.** $\left(\dfrac{7}{2}, -10\right)$

8. $\{(x, y) \mid x - y = -2\}$ **9.** $(5, -3)$ **10.** $(-1, -1, 0)$ **11.** 53 double rooms; 27 single rooms **12.** 5 gal of 10%; 15 gal of 20% **13.** 800 packages **14.** 23°, 45°, 112°

15.

Chapter 4 Cumulative Review

1. a. true **b.** true; Sec. 1.2, Ex. 4 **3. a.** 6 **b.** -7; Sec. 1.3, Ex. 3 **5. a.** -4 **b.** $-\dfrac{3}{7}$ **c.** 11.2; Sec. 1.4, Ex. 7 **7. a.** $6x + 3y$

b. $-3x + 1$ **c.** $0.7ab - 1.4a$; Sec. 1.4, Ex. 11 **9. a.** $-2x + 4$ **b.** $8yz$ **c.** $4z + 6.1$; Sec. 1.4, Ex. 14 **11.** -4; Sec. 2.1, Ex. 3

13. -4; Sec. 2.1, Ex. 7 **15.** 25 cm, 62 cm, 62 cm; Sec. 2.2, Ex. 5 **17.** $[-10, \infty)$; Sec. 2.4, Ex. 3 **19.** $(-3, 2)$; Sec. 2.5, Ex. 4

21. $1, -1$; Sec. 2.6, Ex. 4 **23.** $(4, 8)$; Sec. 2.7, Ex. 2 **25. a.** quadrant IV **b.** y-axis **c.** quadrant II **d.** x-axis **e.** quadrant III **f.** quadrant I; **27.** no; Sec. 3.2, Ex. 4 **29. a.** 5 **b.** 6 **c.** 35 **d.** -2; Sec. 3.2, Ex. 7

31. ; Sec. 3.3, Ex. 1 **33.** slope: $\dfrac{3}{4}$; y-intercept: $(0, -1)$; Sec. 3.4, Ex. 4

35. a. parallel **b.** neither; Sec. 3.4, Ex. 8 **37.** $f(x) = \frac{5}{8}x - \frac{5}{2}$; Sec. 3.5, Ex. 5 **39.** ; Sec. 3.7, Ex. 2

41. a. yes **b.** no; Sec. 4.1, Ex. 1 **43.** $(-4, 2, -1)$; Sec. 4.2, Ex. 1 **45.** $(-1, 2)$; Sec. 4.4, Ex. 1

CHAPTER 5 EXPONENTS, POLYNOMIALS, AND POLYNOMIAL FUNCTIONS

Section 5.1
Practice Exercises

1. a. 3^6 **b.** x^7 **c.** y^9 **2. a.** $35z^4$ **b.** $-20.5t^6q^8$ **3. a.** 1 **b.** -1 **c.** 1 **d.** 3 **4. a.** z^5 **b.** 3^6 **c.** $9x^4$ **d.** $\frac{4}{3}a^7$ or $\frac{4a^7}{3}$
5. a. $\frac{1}{36}$ **b.** $\frac{1}{64}$ **c.** $\frac{3}{x^5}$ **d.** $\frac{1}{5y}$ **e.** $\frac{1}{k^7}$ **f.** $\frac{1}{25}$ **g.** $\frac{9}{20}$ **h.** z^8 **6. a.** $\frac{1}{z^{11}}$ **b.** $7t^8$ **c.** 9 **d.** $\frac{b^7}{3a^7}$ **e.** $\frac{2}{x^4}$ **7. a.** x^{3a+4}
b. x^{2t+1} **8. a.** 6.5×10^4 **b.** 3.8×10^{-5} **9. a.** 620,000 **b.** 0.03109

Scientific Calculator Explorations 5.1
1. 6×10^{43} **3.** 3.796×10^{28}

Vocabulary, Readiness & Video Check 5.1
1. x **3.** 3 **5.** y^7 **7.** These properties allow us to reorder and regroup factors to put those with the same bases together so that we may apply the product rule. **9.** Subtract the exponents on like bases when applying the quotient rule. **11.** When you move the decimal point to the left, the sign of the exponent is positive; when you move the decimal point to the right, the sign of the exponent is negative.

Exercise Set 5.1

1. $\frac{5}{xy^2}$ **3.** $\frac{a^2}{bc^5}$ **5.** $\frac{x^4}{y^2}$ **7.** 4^5 **9.** x^8 **11.** m^{14} **13.** $-20x^2y$ **15.** $-16x^6y^3p^2$ **17.** -1 **19.** 1 **21.** -1 **23.** 9 **25.** a^3
27. $-13z^4$ **29.** x **31.** $\frac{4}{3}x^3y^2$ **33.** $-6a^4b^4c^6$ **35.** $\frac{1}{16}$ **37.** $-\frac{1}{27}$ **39.** $\frac{1}{x^8}$ **41.** $\frac{5}{a^4}$ **43.** $\frac{y^2}{x^7}$ **45.** $\frac{1}{x^7}$ **47.** $4r^8$ **49.** 1
51. $\frac{b^7}{9a^7}$ **53.** $\frac{6x^{16}}{5}$ **55.** $-140x^{12}$ **57.** x^{16} **59.** $10x^{10}$ **61.** 6 **63.** $\frac{1}{z^3}$ **65.** -2 **67.** y^4 **69.** $\frac{13}{36}$ **71.** $\frac{3}{x}$ **73.** r^8 **75.** $\frac{1}{x^9y^4}$
77. $24x^7y^6$ **79.** $\frac{x}{16}$ **81.** 625 **83.** $\frac{1}{8}$ **85.** $\frac{a^5}{81}$ **87.** $\frac{7}{x^3z^5}$ **89.** x^{7a+5} **91.** x^{2t-1} **93.** y^{11p} **95.** z^{6x-7} **97.** x^{6t-1}
99. 3.125×10^7 **101.** 1.6×10^{-2} **103.** 6.7413×10^4 **105.** 1.25×10^{-2} **107.** 5.3×10^{-5} **109.** 7.783×10^8 **111.** 1.6773×10^{13}
113. 1.24×10^{11} **115.** 1.0×10^{-3} **117.** 0.0000000036 **119.** 93,000,000 **121.** 1,278,000 **123.** 7,350,000,000,000 **125.** 0.000000403
127. 300,000,000 **129.** 0.0095 **131.** \$66,683,000,000 **133.** 100 **135.** $\frac{27}{64}$ **137.** 64 **139.** answers may vary **141.** answers may vary
143. a. x^{2a} **b.** $2x^a$ **c.** x^{a-b} **d.** x^{a+b} **e.** $x^a + x^b$ **145.** 7^{13} **147.** 7^{-11}

Section 5.2
Practice Exercises

1. a. z^{15} **b.** 625 **c.** $\frac{1}{27}$ **d.** x^{24} **2. a.** $32x^{15}$ **b.** $\frac{9}{25}$ **c.** $\frac{16a^{20}}{b^{28}}$ **d.** $9x$ **e.** $\frac{a^4b^{10}}{c^8}$ **3. a.** $\frac{b^{15}}{27a^3}$ **b.** y^{15} **c.** $\frac{64}{9}$ **d.** $\frac{b^8}{81a^6}$
4. a. $\frac{c^3}{125a^{36}b^3}$ **b.** $\frac{16x^{16}y^4}{25}$ **5. a.** $27x^a$ **b.** y^{5b+3} **6. a.** 1.7×10^{-2} **b.** 4×10^9 **7.** 4.2×10^{-6}

Vocabulary, Readiness & Video Check 5.2
1. x^{20} **3.** x^9 **5.** y^{42} **7.** z^{36} **9.** z^{18} **11.** The power rule involves a power of a base raised to a power and exponents are multiplied; the product rule involves a product and exponents are added. **13.** We are asked to write the answer in scientific notation. The first product isn't because the number multiplied by the power of 10 is not between 1 and 10.

Exercise Set 5.2

1. $\frac{1}{9}$ **3.** $\frac{1}{x^{36}}$ **5.** $9x^4y^6$ **7.** $16x^{20}y^{12}$ **9.** $\frac{c^{18}}{64a^{12}b^6}$ **11.** $\frac{y^{15}}{x^{35}z^{20}}$ **13.** $-64y^3$ **15.** $\frac{1}{a^2}$ **17.** $\frac{36}{p^{12}}$ **19.** $-\frac{a^6}{512x^3y^9}$ **21.** $\frac{64}{27}$
23. $4a^8b^4$ **25.** $\frac{x^{14}y^{14}}{a^{21}}$ **27.** $\frac{1}{y^{10}}$ **29.** $\frac{1}{125}$ **31.** $\frac{1}{x^{63}}$ **33.** $\frac{1}{x^{20}y^{15}}$ **35.** $16x^4$ **37.** $4^8x^2y^6$ **39.** $\frac{x^9}{8y^3}$ **41.** $\frac{x^4}{4z^2}$ **43.** $\frac{x^4}{16}$
45. $\frac{1}{y^{15}}$ **47.** $\frac{16a^2b^9}{9}$ **49.** $\frac{3}{8x^8y^7}$ **51.** $\frac{1}{x^{30}b^6c^6}$ **53.** $\frac{25}{8x^5y^4}$ **55.** $\frac{2}{x^4y^{10}}$ **57.** x^{9a+18} **59.** x^{12a+2} **61.** b^{10x-4} **63.** y^{15a+3}
65. $16x^{4t+4}$ **67.** $5x^{-a}y^{-a+2}$ **69.** 1.45×10^9 **71.** 8×10^{15} **73.** 4×10^{-7} **75.** 3×10^{-1} **77.** 2×10^1 **79.** 1×10^1

81. 8×10^{-5} **83.** 1.1×10^7 **85.** 3.5×10^{22} **87.** 2.5808×10^{-5} sq m **89.** $-2y - 18$ **91.** $-7x + 2$ **93.** $-3z - 14$
95. $\dfrac{8}{x^6 y^3}$ cu m **97.** 2×10^3 lb/ft^3 **99.** yes; $a = \pm 1$ **101.** no; answers may vary **103.** 90 people per sq mi **105.** 1.6

Section 5.3

Practice Exercises

1. a. 5 **b.** 3 **c.** 1 **d.** 11 **e.** 0 **2. a.** degree 4; trinomial **b.** degree 5; monomial **c.** degree 5; binomial **3.** 5
4. a. -15 **b.** -47 **5.** 290 feet; 226 feet **6. a.** $3x^4 - 5x$ **b.** $7ab - 3b$ **7.** $6x^3 + 6x^2 - 7x - 8$ **8. a.** $3a^4b + 4ab^2 - 5$
b. $2x^5 + y - x - 9$ **9.** $15a^4 - 15a^3 + 3$ **10.** $6x^2y^2 - 4xy^2 - 5y^3$ **11.** C

Graphing Calculator Explorations 5.3

1. $x^3 - 4x^2 + 7x - 8$ **3.** $-2.1x^2 - 3.2x - 1.7$ **5.** $7.69x^2 - 1.26x + 5.3$

Vocabulary, Readiness & Video Check 5.3

1. coefficient **3.** binomial **5.** trinomial **7.** degree **9.** We are finding the degree of the polynomial, which is the greatest degree of any of its terms, so we find the degree of each term first. **11.** by combining like terms **13.** Change the operation from subtraction to addition and add the opposite of the polynomial that is being subtracted—that is, change the signs of all terms of the polynomial being subtracted and add.

Exercise Set 5.3

1. 0 **3.** 2 **5.** 3 **7.** 3 **9.** 9 **11.** degree 1; binomial **13.** degree 2; trinomial **15.** degree 3; monomial **17.** degree 4; none of these
19. 57 **21.** 499 **23.** $-\dfrac{11}{16}$ **25.** 1061 ft **27.** 549 ft **29.** $-7y^2 + 6y$ **31.** $x^2y - 5x - \dfrac{1}{2}$ **33.** $6x^2 - xy + 16y^2$
35. $18y^2 - 17$ **37.** $3x^2 - 3xy + 6y^2$ **39.** $x^2 - 4x + 8$ **41.** $12x^3y + 8x + 8$ **43.** $4.5x^3 + 0.2x^2 - 3.8x + 9.1$ **45.** $y^2 + 3$
47. $-2x^2 + 5x$ **49.** $7y^2 - 12y - 3$ **51.** $7x^3 + 4x^2 + 8x - 10$ **53.** $-20y^2 + 3yx$ **55.** $-3x^2 + 3$ **57.** $2y^4 - 5y^2 + x^2 + 1$
59. $5x^2 - 9x - 3$ **61.** $3x^2 + x + 18$ **63.** $4x - 13$ **65.** $-x^3 + 8a - 12$ **67.** $14ab + 10a^2b + 12b^2 - 18a^2$ **69.** $5x^2 + 22x + 16$
71. 0 **73.** $8xy^2 + 2x^3 + 3x^2 - 3$ **75.** $3x^2 - 9x + 15$ **77.** $15x^2 + 8x - 6$ **79.** $\dfrac{1}{3}x^2 - x + 1$ **81.** 202 sq in. **83. a.** 284 ft **b.** 536 ft
c. 1400 ft **d.** 1064 ft **e.** answers may vary **f.** 19 sec **85.** \$80,000 **87.** \$16,500 **89.** A **91.** D **93.** $15x - 10$
95. $-2x^2 + 10x - 12$ **97.** a and c **99.** $(12x - 1.7) - (15x + 6.2) = 12x - 1.7 - 15x - 6.2 = -3x - 7.9$ **101.** answers may vary
103. answers may vary **105.** $3x^{2a} + 2x^a + 0.7$ **107.** $4x^{2y} + 2x^y - 11$ **109.** $(6x^2 + 14y)$ units **111.** $4x^2 - 3x + 6$ **113.** $-x^2 - 6x + 10$
115. $3x^2 - 12x + 13$ **117.** $15x^2 + 12x - 9$ **119. a.** $2a - 3$ **b.** $-2x - 3$ **c.** $2x + 2h - 3$ **121. a.** $4a$ **b.** $-4x$ **c.** $4x + 4h$
123. a. $4a - 1$ **b.** $-4x - 1$ **c.** $4x + 4h - 1$ **125. a.** \$483.05 billion **b.** \$591.1 billion **c.** \$843.2 billion **d.** answers may vary

Section 5.4

Practice Exercises

1. a. $6x^6$ **b.** $40m^5n^2p^8$ **2. a.** $21x^2 - 3x$ **b.** $-15a^4 + 30a^3 - 25a^2$ **c.** $-5m^3n^5 - 2m^2n^4 + 5m^2n^3$ **3. a.** $2x^2 + 13x + 15$
b. $3x^3 - 19x^2 + 12x - 2$ **4.** $3x^4 - 12x^3 - 13x^2 - 8x - 10$ **5.** $x^2 - 2x - 15$ **6. a.** $6x^2 - 31x + 35$ **b.** $8x^4 - 10x^2y - 3y^2$
7. a. $x^2 + 12x + 36$ **b.** $x^2 - 4x + 4$ **c.** $9x^2 + 30xy + 25y^2$ **d.** $9x^4 - 48x^2b + 64b^2$ **8. a.** $x^2 - 49$ **b.** $4a^2 - 25$ **c.** $25x^4 - \dfrac{1}{16}$
d. $a^6 - 16b^4$ **9.** $4 + 12x - 4y + 9x^2 - 6xy + y^2$ **10.** $9x^2 - 6xy + y^2 - 25$ **11.** $x^4 - 32x^2 + 256$ **12.** $h^2 - h + 3$

Graphing Calculator Explorations 5.4

1. $x^2 - 16$ **3.** $9x^2 - 42x + 49$ **5.** $5x^3 - 14x^2 - 13x - 2$

Vocabulary, Readiness & Video Check 5.4

1. b. $3x^6$ **3. b.** $x^2 - 49$ **5. d.** $(a + 1)^2 + 1$ **7.** distributive property, product rule **9.** FOIL order or distributive property **11.** Multiply two at a time and multiply as usual, using patterns if you recognize them. Keep multiplying until you are through.

Exercise Set 5.4

1. $-12x^5$ **3.** $86a^5b^8c^3$ **5.** $12x^2 + 21x$ **7.** $-24x^2y - 6xy^2$ **9.** $-4a^3bx - 4a^3by + 12ab$ **11.** $2x^2 - 2x - 12$
13. $2x^4 + 3x^3 - 2x^2 + x + 6$ **15.** $15x^2 - 7x - 2$ **17.** $15m^3 + 16m^2 - m - 2$ **19.** $-30a^2b^4 + 36a^3b^2 + 36a^2b^3$ **21.** $x^2 + x - 12$
23. $10x^2 - 21xy + 8y^2$ **25.** $16x^2 - \dfrac{2}{3}x - \dfrac{1}{6}$ **27.** $5x^4 - 17x^2y^2 + 6y^4$ **29.** $x^2 + 8x + 16$ **31.** $36y^2 - 1$ **33.** $9x^2 - 6xy + y^2$
35. $49a^2b^2 - 9c^2$ **37.** $9x^2 - \dfrac{1}{4}$ **39.** $9 + 24b + 6a + 16b^2 + 8ab + a^2$ **41.** $4s^2 - 12s + 8$ **43.** $x^4 + 8x^3 + 4x^2 - 48x + 36$
45. $x^4 - 2x^2y^2 + y^4$ **47.** $x^4 - 8x^3 + 24x^2 - 32x + 16$ **49.** $x^4 - 625$ **51.** $-24a^2b^3 + 40a^2b^2 - 160a^2b$ **53.** $36x^2 + 12x + 1$
55. $25x^6 - 4y^2$ **57.** $10x^5 + 8x^4 + 2x^3 + 25x^2 + 20x + 5$ **59.** $9x^4 + 12x^3 - 2x^2 - 4x + 1$ **61.** $3x^2 + 8x - 3$ **63.** $9x^6 + 15x^4 + 3x^2 + 5$
65. $9x^2 + 6x + 1$ **67.** $9b^2 - 36y^2$ **69.** $49x^2 - 9$ **71.** $9x^3 + 30x^2 + 12x - 24$ **73.** $12x^3 - 2x^2 + 13x + 5$
75. $x^2 + 2xy + y^2 - 14x - 14y + 49$ **77.** $22a^3 + 11a^2 + 2a + 1$ **79.** $\dfrac{1}{3}n^2 - 7n + 18$ **81.** $45x^3 + 18x^2y - 5x - 2y$ **83.** $a^2 - 3a$
85. $a^2 + 2ah + h^2 - 3a - 3h$ **87.** $b^2 - 7b + 10$ **89.** -2 **91.** $\dfrac{3}{5}$ **93.** function **95.** $7y(3z - 2) + 1 = 21yz - 14y + 1$
97. answers may vary **99. a.** $a^2 + 2ah + h^2 + 3a + 3h + 2$ **b.** $a^2 + 3a + 2$ **c.** $2ah + h^2 + 3h$ **101.** $30x^2y^{2n+1} - 10x^2y^n$

103. $x^{3a} + 5x^{2a} - 3x^a - 15$ **105.** $\pi(25x^2 - 20x + 4)$ sq km or $(25\pi x^2 - 20\pi x + 4\pi)$ sq km   **107.** $(8x^2 - 12x + 4)$ sq in.   **109. a.** $6x + 12$
b. $9x^2 + 36x + 35$; one operation is addition, the other is multiplication.   **111.** $5x^2 + 25x$ **113.** $x^4 - 4x^2 + 4$ **115.** $x^3 + 5x^2 - 2x - 10$

Section 5.5

Practice Exercises

1. $8y$ **2. a.** $3(4x^2 + 3 + 5x)$ **b.** no common factor other than 1   **c.** $2a^3(4a - 1)$ **3.** $8x^3y^2(8x^2 - 1)$
4. $-xy^2(9x^3 - 5x - 7)$ or $xy^2(-9x^3 + 5x + 7)$ **5.** $(x + 4)(3 + 5b)$ **6.** $(a^3 + 2y)(8b - 1)$ **7.** $(x + 2)(y - 5)$ **8.** $(a + 2)(a^2 + 5)$
9. $(x^2 + 3)(y^2 - 5)$ **10.** $(q + 3)(p - 1)$

Vocabulary, Readiness & Video Check 5.5

1. factoring   **3.** least   **5.** false   **7.** false   **9.** The GCF is that common variable raised to the smallest exponent in the list.   **11.** Look for a
GCF other than 1 or -1; if you have a four-term polynomial

Exercise Set 5.5

1. a^3 **3.** y^2z^2 **5.** $3x^2y$ **7.** $5xz^3$ **9.** $6(3x - 2)$ **11.** $4y^2(1 - 4xy)$ **13.** $2x^3(3x^2 - 4x + 1)$ **15.** $4ab(2a^2b^2 - ab + 1 + 4b)$
17. $(x + 3)(6 + 5a)$ **19.** $(z + 7)(2x + 1)$ **21.** $(6x^2 + 5)(3x - 2)$ **23.** no common factor other than 1   **25.** $13x^2y^3(3x - 2)$
27. $(a + 2)(b + 3)$ **29.** $(a - 2)(c + 4)$ **31.** $(x - 2)(2y - 3)$ **33.** $(4x - 1)(3y - 2)$ **35.** $3(2x^3 + 3)$ **37.** $x^2(x + 3)$
39. $4a(2a^2 - 1)$ **41.** no common factor other than 1   **43.** $-4xy(5x - 4y^2)$ or $4xy(-5x + 4y^2)$ **45.** $5ab^2(2ab + 1 - 3b)$
47. $3b(3ac^2 + 2a^2c - 2a + c)$ **49.** $(y - 2)(4x - 3)$ **51.** $(2x + 3)(3y + 5)$ **53.** $(x + 3)(y - 5)$ **55.** $(2a - 3)(3b - 1)$
57. $(6x + 1)(2y + 3)$ **59.** $(n - 8)(2m - 1)$ **61.** $3x^2y^2(5x - 6)$ **63.** $(2x + 3y)(x + 2)$ **65.** $(5x - 3)(x + y)$
67. $(x^2 + 4)(x + 3)$ **69.** $(x^2 - 2)(x - 1)$ **71.** $55x^7$ **73.** $125x^6$ **75.** $x^2 - 3x - 10$ **77.** $x^2 + 5x + 6$ **79.** $y^2 - 4y + 3$
81. d   **83.** $2\pi r(r + h)$ **85.** $A = 5600(1 + RT)$ **87.** answers may vary   **89.** none   **91.** answers may vary   **93.** $I(R_1 + R_2) = E$
95. $x^n(x^{2n} - 2x^n + 5)$ **97.** $2x^{3a}(3x^{5a} - x^{2a} - 2)$ **99. a.** $h(t) = -16t(t - 4)$ **b.** 48 ft   **c.** answers may vary
101. $f(x) = 4(16x^3 - 186x^2 + 3363x + 18{,}946)$

Section 5.6

Practice Exercises

1. $(x + 3)(x + 2)$ **2.** $(x - 3)(x - 8)$ **3.** $3x(x - 5)(x + 2)$ **4.** $2(b^2 - 9b - 11)$ **5.** $(2x + 1)(x + 6)$ **6.** $(4x - 3)(x + 2)$
7. $3b^2(2b - 5)(3b - 2)$ **8.** $(5x + 2y)^2$ **9.** $(5x + 2)(4x + 3)$ **10.** $(5x + 3)(3x - 1)$ **11.** $(x - 3)(3x + 8)$ **12.** $(3x^2 + 2)(2x^2 - 5)$

Vocabulary, Readiness & Video Check 5.6

1. 5 and 2   **3.** 8 and 3   **5.** Check by multiplying. If you get a middle term of $2x$, not $-2x$, switch the signs of your factors of -24.   **7.** Write down
the factors of the first and last terms. Try various combinations of these factors and look at the sum of the outer and inner products to see if you get the
middle term of the trinomial. If not, try another combination of factors.   **9.** Our factoring involves a substitution from the original expression, so we
need to substitute back in order to get a factorization in terms of the original variable/expression, and simplify if necessary.

Exercise Set 5.6

1. $(x + 3)(x + 6)$ **3.** $(x - 8)(x - 4)$ **5.** $(x + 12)(x - 2)$ **7.** $(x - 6)(x + 4)$ **9.** $3(x - 2)(x - 4)$ **11.** $4z(x + 2)(x + 5)$
13. $2(x^2 - 12x - 32)$ **15.** $(5x + 1)(x + 3)$ **17.** $(2x - 3)(x - 4)$ **19.** prime polynomial   **21.** $(2x - 3)^2$ **23.** $2(3x - 5)(2x + 5)$
25. $y^2(3y + 5)(y - 2)$ **27.** $2x(3x^2 + 4x + 12)$ **29.** $(2x + y)(x - 3y)$ **31.** $2(7y + 2)(2y + 1)$ **33.** $(2x - 3)(x + 9)$
35. $(x^2 + 3)(x^2 - 2)$ **37.** $(5x + 8)(5x + 2)$ **39.** $(x^3 - 4)(x^3 - 3)$ **41.** $(a - 3)(a + 8)$ **43.** $(x - 27)(x + 3)$
45. $(x - 18)(x + 3)$ **47.** $3(x - 1)^2$ **49.** $(3x + 1)(x - 2)$ **51.** $(4x - 3)(2x - 5)$ **53.** $3x^2(2x + 1)(3x + 2)$ **55.** $(x + 7z)(x + z)$
57. $(x - 4)(x + 3)$ **59.** $3(a + 2b)^2$ **61.** prime polynomial   **63.** $(2x + 13)(x + 3)$ **65.** $(3x - 2)(2x - 15)$ **67.** $(x^2 - 6)(x^2 + 1)$
69. $x(3x + 1)(2x - 1)$ **71.** $(4a - 3b)(3a - 5b)$ **73.** $(3x + 5)^2$ **75.** $y(3x - 8)(x - 1)$ **77.** $2(x + 3)(x - 2)$ **79.** $(x + 2)(x - 7)$
81. $(2x^3 - 3)(x^3 + 3)$ **83.** $2x(6y^2 - z)^2$ **85.** $2xy(x + 3)(x - 2)$ **87.** $(x + 5y)(x + y)$ **89.** $x^2 - 9$ **91.** $4x^2 + 4x + 1$ **93.** $x^3 - 8$
95. $\pm 5, \pm 7$ **97.** $x(x + 4)(x - 2)$ **99. a.** 576 ft; 672 ft; 640 ft; 480 ft   **b.** answers may vary   **c.** $-16(t + 4)(t - 9)$ **101.** $(x^n + 2)(x^n + 8)$
103. $(x^n - 6)(x^n + 3)$ **105.** $(2x^n + 1)(x^n + 5)$ **107.** $(2x^n - 3)^2$ **109.** $x^2(x + 5)(x + 1)$ **111.** $3x(5x - 1)(2x + 1)$

Section 5.7

Practice Exercises

1. $(b + 8)^2$ **2.** $5b(3x - 1)^2$ **3. a.** $(x + 4)(x - 4)$ **b.** $(5b - 7)(5b + 7)$ **c.** $5(3 - 2x)(3 + 2x)$ **d.** $\left(y - \dfrac{1}{9}\right)\left(y + \dfrac{1}{9}\right)$
4. a. $(x^2 + 100)(x + 10)(x - 10)$ **b.** $(x + 9)(x - 5)$ **5.** $(m + 3 + n)(m + 3 - n)$ **6.** $(x + 4)(x^2 - 4x + 16)$
7. $(a + 2b)(a^2 - 2ab + 4b^2)$ **8.** $(3 - y)(9 + 3y + y^2)$ **9.** $x^2(b - 2)(b^2 + 2b + 4)$

Vocabulary, Readiness & Video Check 5.7

1. $(9y)^2$ **3.** $(8x^3)^2$ **5.** $(2x)^3$ **7.** $(4x^2)^3$ **9.** See if the first term is a square, say a^2, and the last term is a square, say b^2. Check to see if
the middle term is $2 \cdot a \cdot b$ or $-2 \cdot a \cdot b$.   **11.** First rewrite the original binomial so that each term is some quantity cubed. Your answers will then vary
depending on your interpretation.

Exercise Set 5.7

1. $(x + 3)^2$ **3.** $(2x - 3)^2$ **5.** $(5x + 1)^2$ **7.** $3(x - 4)^2$ **9.** $x^2(3y + 2)^2$ **11.** $(4x - 7y)^2$ **13.** $(x + 5)(x - 5)$
15. $\left(\dfrac{1}{3} + 2z\right)\left(\dfrac{1}{3} - 2z\right)$ **17.** $(y + 9)(y - 5)$ **19.** $4(4x + 5)(4x - 5)$ **21.** $(x + 2y + 3)(x + 2y - 3)$ **23.** $(x + 3 + y)(x + 3 - y)$

25. $(x + 8 + x^2)(x + 8 - x^2)$ **27.** $(x + 3)(x^2 - 3x + 9)$ **29.** $(z - 1)(z^2 + z + 1)$ **31.** $(m + n)(m^2 - mn + n^2)$
33. $y^2(3 - x)(9 + 3x + x^2)$ **35.** $a(2b + 3a)(4b^2 - 6ab + 9a^2)$ **37.** $2(5y - 2x)(25y^2 + 10xy + 4x^2)$ **39.** $(x - 6)^2$
41. $2y(3x + 1)(3x - 1)$ **43.** $(3x + 7)(3x - 7)$ **45.** $(x^2 + 1)(x + 1)(x - 1)$ **47.** $(x^2 - y)(x^4 + x^2y + y^2)$
49. $(2x + 3y)(4x^2 - 6xy + 9y^2)$ **51.** $(2x + 1 + z)(2x + 1 - z)$ **53.** $3y^2(x^2 + 3)(x^4 - 3x^2 + 9)$ **55.** $\left(n - \dfrac{1}{3}\right)\left(n^2 + \dfrac{1}{3}n + \dfrac{1}{9}\right)$
57. $-16(y + 2)(y - 2)$ **59.** $(x - 5 + y)(x - 5 - y)$ **61.** $(ab + 5)(a^2b^2 - 5ab + 25)$ **63.** $\left(\dfrac{x}{5} + \dfrac{y}{3}\right)\left(\dfrac{x}{5} - \dfrac{y}{3}\right)$
65. $(x + y + 5)(x^2 + 2xy + y^2 - 5x - 5y + 25)$ **67.** 5   **69.** $-\dfrac{1}{3}$ **71.** 0   **73.** 5   **75.** no; $x^2 - 4$ can be factored further
77. yes   **79.** $\pi R^2 - \pi r^2 = \pi(R + r)(R - r)$ **81.** $x^3 - y^2x; x(x + y)(x - y)$ **83.** $c = 9$ **85.** $c = 49$ **87.** $c = \pm 8$
89. a. $(x + 1)(x^2 - x + 1)(x - 1)(x^2 + x + 1)$ **b.** $(x + 1)(x - 1)(x^4 + x^2 + 1)$ **c.** answers may vary   **91.** $(x^n + 5)(x^n - 5)$
93. $(6x^n + 7)(6x^n - 7)$ **95.** $(x^{2n} + 4)(x^n + 2)(x^n - 2)$

Integrated Review Practice Exercises

1. a. $3xy(4x - 1)$ **b.** $(7x + 2)(7x - 2)$ **c.** $(5x - 3)(x + 1)$ **d.** $(3 + x)(x^2 + 2)$ **e.** $(2x + 5)^2$ **f.** cannot be factored
2. a. $(4x + y)(16x^2 - 4xy + y^2)$ **b.** $7y^2(x - 3y)(x + 3y)$ **c.** $3(x + 2 + b)(x + 2 - b)$ **d.** $x^2y(xy + 3)(x^2y^2 - 3xy + 9)$
e. $(x + 7 + 9y)(x + 7 - 9y)$

Integrated Review

1. $2y^2 + 2y - 11$ **2.** $-2z^4 - 6z^2 + 3z$ **3.** $x^2 - 7x + 7$ **4.** $7x^2 - 4x - 5$ **5.** $25x^2 - 30x + 9$ **6.** $5x^2 - 19x - 4$
7. $2x^3 - 3x + 4$ **8.** $4x^3 - 13x^2 - 5x + 2$ **9.** $(x - 4 + y)(x - 4 - y)$ **10.** $2(3x + 2)(2x - 5)$ **11.** $x(x - 1)(x^2 + x + 1)$
12. $2x(2x - 1)$ **13.** $2xy(7x - 1)$ **14.** $6ab(4b - 1)$ **15.** $4(x + 2)(x - 2)$ **16.** $9(x + 3)(x - 3)$ **17.** $(3x - 11)(x + 1)$
18. $(5x + 3)(x - 1)$ **19.** $4(x + 3)(x - 1)$ **20.** $6(x + 1)(x - 2)$ **21.** $(2x + 9)^2$ **22.** $(5x + 4)^2$ **23.** $(2x + 5y)(4x^2 - 10xy + 25y^2)$
24. $(3x - 4y)(9x^2 + 12xy + 16y^2)$ **25.** $8x^2(2y - 1)(4y^2 + 2y + 1)$ **26.** $27x^2y(xy - 2)(x^2y^2 + 2xy + 4)$
27. $(x + 5 + y)(x^2 + 10x + 25 - xy - 5y + y^2)$ **28.** $(y - 1 + 3x)(y^2 - 2y + 1 - 3xy + 3x + 9x^2)$ **29.** $(5a - 6)^2$ **30.** $(4r + 5)^2$
31. $7x(x - 9)$ **32.** $(4x + 3)(5x + 2)$ **33.** $(a + 7)(b - 6)$ **34.** $20(x - 6)(x - 5)$ **35.** $(x^2 + 1)(x - 1)(x + 1)$ **36.** $5x(3x - 4)$
37. $(5x - 11)(2x + 3)$ **38.** $9m^2n^2(5mn - 3)$ **39.** $5a^3b(b^2 - 10)$ **40.** $x(x + 1)(x^2 - x + 1)$ **41.** prime   **42.** $20(x + y)(x^2 - xy + y^2)$
43. $10x(x - 10)(x - 11)$ **44.** $(3y - 7)^2$ **45.** $a^3b(4b - 3)(16b^2 + 12b + 9)$ **46.** $(y^2 + 4)(y + 2)(y - 2)$ **47.** $2(x - 3)(x^2 + 3x + 9)$
48. $(2s - 1)(r + 5)$ **49.** $(y^4 + 2)(3y - 5)$ **50.** prime   **51.** $100(z + 1)(z^2 - z + 1)$ **52.** $2x(5x - 2)(25x^2 + 10x + 4)$
53. $(2b - 9)^2$ **54.** $(a^4 + 3)(2a - 1)$ **55.** $(y - 4)(y - 5)$ **56.** $(c - 3)(c + 1)$ **57.** $A = 9 - 4x^2 = (3 + 2x)(3 - 2x)$

Section 5.8

Practice Exercises

1. $-8, 5$ **2.** $-4, \dfrac{2}{3}$ **3.** $-4, -\dfrac{2}{3}$ **4.** $-\dfrac{3}{4}$ **5.** $-\dfrac{1}{8}, 2$ **6.** $0, 3, -1$ **7.** $3, -3, -2$ **8.** 6 seconds   **9.** 6, 8, 10 units
10. $f(x):C; g(x):A; h(x):B$

Graphing Calculator Explorations 5.8

1. $-3.562, 0.562$ **3.** $-0.874, 2.787$ **5.** $-0.465, 1.910$

Vocabulary, Readiness & Video Check 5.8

1. $3, -5$ **3.** $3, -7$ **5.** $0, 9$ **7.** One side of the equation must be a factored polynomial and the other side must be zero.   **9.** Finding the x-intercepts of any equation in two variables means you let $y = 0$ and solve for x. Doing this with a quadratic equation gives us an equation $= 0$, which may be solved by factoring.

Exercise Set 5.8

1. $-3, \dfrac{4}{3}$ **3.** $\dfrac{5}{2}, -\dfrac{3}{4}$ **5.** $-3, -8$ **7.** $\dfrac{1}{4}, -\dfrac{2}{3}$ **9.** $1, 9$ **11.** $\dfrac{3}{5}, -1$ **13.** 0   **15.** $6, -3$ **17.** $\dfrac{2}{5}, -\dfrac{1}{2}$ **19.** $\dfrac{3}{4}, -\dfrac{1}{2}$ **21.** $-2, 7, \dfrac{8}{3}$
23. $-1, 1, -\dfrac{1}{6}$ **25.** $0, 3, -3$ **27.** $2, 1, -1$ **29.** $-\dfrac{7}{2}, 10$ **31.** $0, 5$ **33.** $-3, 5$ **35.** $-\dfrac{1}{2}, \dfrac{1}{3}$ **37.** $-4, 9$ **39.** $\dfrac{4}{5}$
41. $-5, 0, 2$ **43.** $-3, 0, \dfrac{4}{5}$ **45.** $\varnothing$ **47.** $-7, 4$ **49.** $4, 6$ **51.** $-\dfrac{1}{2}$ **53.** $-4, -3, 3$ **55.** $-5, 0, 5$ **57.** $-6, 5$ **59.** $-\dfrac{1}{3}, 0, 1$
61. $-\dfrac{1}{3}, 0$ **63.** $-\dfrac{7}{8}$ **65.** $\dfrac{31}{4}$ **67.** 1   **69.** -11 and -6 or 6 and 11   **71.** 75 ft   **73.** 105 units   **75.** 12 cm and 9 cm   **77.** 2 in.
79. 10 sec   **81.** width: $7\dfrac{1}{2}$ ft; length: 12 ft   **83.** 10-in. square tier   **85.** 9 sec   **87.** E   **89.** F   **91.** B   **93.** $(-3, 0), (0, 2)$; function
95. $(-4, 0), (4, 0), (0, 2), (0, -2)$; not a function   **97.** $x - 5 = 0$ or $x + 2 = 0$ **99.**
$$x = 5 \quad \text{or} \quad x = -2$$

$$
\begin{aligned}
y(y - 5) &= -6\\
y^2 - 5y + 6 &= 0\\
(y - 2)(y - 3) &= 0\\
y - 2 = 0 \quad &\text{or} \quad y - 3 = 0\\
y = 2 \quad &\text{or} \quad y = 3
\end{aligned}
$$

101. $-3, -\dfrac{1}{3}, 2, 5$ **103.** $x = 4$ or $x = -11$ **105.** answers may vary   **107.** no; answers may vary   **109.** answers may vary
111. answers may vary   **113.** answers may vary

Chapter 5 Vocabulary Check

1. polynomial   **2.** Factoring   **3.** Exponents   **4.** degree of a term   **5.** monomial   **6.** 1   **7.** trinomial   **8.** quadratic equation
9. scientific notation   **10.** degree of a polynomial   **11.** binomial   **12.** 0

Chapter 5 Review

1. 4   **3.** -4 **5.** 1   **7.** $-\dfrac{1}{16}$ **9.** $-x^2y^7z$ **11.** $\dfrac{1}{a^9}$ **13.** $\dfrac{1}{x^{11}}$ **15.** $\dfrac{1}{y^5}$ **17.** 3.689×10^7 **19.** 0.000001678   **21.** 8^{15} **23.** $27x^3$
25. $\dfrac{36x^2}{25}$ **27.** $\dfrac{9}{16}$ **29.** $\dfrac{1}{4p^4}$ **31.** $x^{25}y^{15}z^{15}$ **33.** $\dfrac{x^2}{625y^4z^4}$ **35.** $27x^{19a}$ **37.** 5.76×10^4 **39.** $\dfrac{3x^7}{2y^2}$ **41.** 5   **43.** $12x - 6x^2 - 6x^2y$
45. $4x^2 + 8y + 6$ **47.** $8x^2 + 2b - 22$ **49.** $-x + 5$ **51.** $x^2 - 6x + 3$ **53.** 290   **55.** 58   **57.** $x^2 + 4x - 6$
59. $(6x^2y - 12x + 12)\,\text{cm}$ **61.** $-24x^3 + 36x^2 - 6x$ **63.** $2x^2 + x - 36$ **65.** $36x^3 - 11x^2 - 8x - 3$ **67.** $15x^2 + 18xy - 81y^2$
69. $x^4 + 18x^3 + 83x^2 + 18x + 1$ **71.** $9x^2 - 6xy + y^2$ **73.** $x^2 - 9y^2$ **75.** $(9y^2 - 49z^2)$ sq units   **77.** $12a^{2b+2} - 28a^b$
79. $8x^2(2x - 3)$ **81.** $2ab(3b + 4 - 2ab)$ **83.** $(a + 3b)(6a - 5)$ **85.** $(x - 6)(y + 3)$ **87.** $(p - 5)(q - 3)$
89. $x(2y - x)$ **91.** $(x - 18)(x + 4)$ **93.** $2(x - 2)(x - 7)$ **95.** $x(2x - 9)(x + 1)$ **97.** $(6x + 5)(x + 2)$ **99.** $2(2x - 3)(x + 2)$
101. $(x + 6)^2(y - 3)(y + 1)$ **103.** $(x^2 - 8)(x^2 + 2)$ **105.** $(x + 10)(x - 10)$ **107.** $2(x + 4)(x - 4)$ **109.** $(9 + x^2)(3 + x)(3 - x)$
111. $(y + 7)(y - 3)$ **113.** $(x + 6)(x^2 - 6x + 36)$ **115.** $(2 - 3y)(4 + 6y + 9y^2)$ **117.** $6xy(x + 2)(x^2 - 2x + 4)$
119. $(x - 1 - y)(x - 1 + y)$ **121.** $(2x + 3)^2$ **123.** $\pi h(R - r)(R + r)$ cu units   **125.** $\dfrac{1}{3}, -7$ **127.** $0, 4, \dfrac{9}{2}$ **129.** $0, 6$ **131.** $-\dfrac{1}{3}, 2$
133. $-4, 1$ **135.** $0, 6, -3$ **137.** $0, -2, 1$ **139.** $-\dfrac{15}{2}$ or 7   **141.** 5 sec   **143.** $3x^3 + 13x^2 - 9x + 5$ **145.** $8x^2 + 3x + 4.5$ **147.** -24
149. $6y^4(2y - 1)$ **151.** $2(3x + 1)(x - 6)$ **153.** $z^5(2z + 7)(2z - 7)$ **155.** $0, 3$

Chapter 5 Getting Ready for the Test

1. C   **2.** D   **3.** F   **4.** G   **5.** A   **6.** E   **7.** C   **8.** B   **9.** C   **10.** C   **11.** D   **12.** B   **13.** C   **14.** A   **15.** B
16. B   **17.** A

Chapter 5 Test

1. $\dfrac{1}{81x^2}$ **2.** $-12x^2z$ **3.** $\dfrac{3a^7}{2b^5}$ **4.** $-\dfrac{y^{40}}{z^5}$ **5.** 6.3×10^8 **6.** 1.2×10^{-2} **7.** 0.000005   **8.** 0.0009   **9.** $-5x^3y - 11x - 9$
10. $-12x^2y - 3xy^2$ **11.** $12x^2 - 5x - 28$ **12.** $25a^2 - 4b^2$ **13.** $36m^2 + 12mn + n^2$ **14.** $2x^3 - 13x^2 + 14x - 4$
15. $4x^2y(4x - 3y^3)$ **16.** $(x - 15)(x + 2)$ **17.** $(2y + 5)^2$ **18.** $3(2x + 1)(x - 3)$ **19.** $(2x + 5)(2x - 5)$
20. $(x + 4)(x^2 - 4x + 16)$ **21.** $3y(x + 3y)(x - 3y)$ **22.** $6(x^2 + 4)$ **23.** $2(2y - 1)(4y^2 + 2y + 1)$ **24.** $(x + 3)(x - 3)(y - 3)$
25. $4, -\dfrac{8}{7}$ **26.** $-3, 8$ **27.** $-\dfrac{5}{2}, -2, 2$ **28.** $(x + 2y)(x - 2y)$ **29. a.** 960 ft   **b.** 953.44 ft   **c.** $-16(t - 11)(t + 5)$ **d.** 11 sec

Chapter 5 Cumulative Review

1. a. -3 **b.** 1   **c.** 2; Sec. 1.3, Ex. 8   **3.** 1; Sec. 2.1, Ex. 4   **5.** \$11,607.55; Sec. 2.3, Ex. 4   **7. a.** $\left(-\infty, \dfrac{3}{2}\right]$

b. $(-3, \infty)$; Sec. 2.4, Ex. 4   **9.** $\left[-9, -\dfrac{9}{2}\right]$; Sec. 2.5, Ex. 5   **11.** 0; Sec. 2.6, Ex. 5   **13.** { } or $\varnothing$; Sec. 2.7, Ex. 4

15. ; Sec. 3.1, Ex. 5   **17.** $(2, -3)$, $(-6, -9)$, $(0, 3)$; Sec. 3.6, Ex. 1   **19.** ; Sec. 3.3, Ex. 6   **21.** 0; Sec. 3.4, Ex. 7

23. $y = 3$; Sec. 3.5, Ex. 8   **25.** ; Sec. 3.7, Ex. 4   **27.** $\left(-4, \dfrac{1}{2}\right)$; Sec. 4.1, Ex. 5   **29.** $\left(\dfrac{1}{2}, 0, \dfrac{3}{4}\right)$; Sec. 4.2, Ex. 3

31. 7 and 11; Sec. 4.3, Ex. 2   **33.** no solution; Sec. 4.4, Ex. 2   **35.** $30°, 40°, 110°$; Sec. 4.3, Ex. 6   **37. a.** 7.3×10^5 **b.** 1.04×10^{-6}; Sec. 5.1, Ex. 8
39. a. $\dfrac{y^6}{4}$ **b.** x^9 **c.** $\dfrac{49}{4}$ **d.** $\dfrac{y^{16}}{25x^5}$; Sec. 5.2, Ex. 3   **41.** 4; Sec. 5.3, Ex. 3   **43. a.** $10x^9$ **b.** $-7xy^{15}z^9$; Sec. 5.4, Ex. 1
45. $17x^3y^2(1 - 2x)$; Sec. 5.5, Ex. 3   **47.** $(x + 2)(x + 8)$; Sec. 5.6, Ex. 1   **49.** $-5, \dfrac{1}{2}$; Sec. 5.8, Ex. 2

CHAPTER 6 RATIONAL EXPRESSIONS

Section 6.1

Practice Exercises

1. a. $\{x \mid x \text{ is a real number}\}$ **b.** $\{x \mid x \text{ is a real number and } x \neq -3\}$ **c.** $\{x \mid x \text{ is a real number and } x \neq 2, x \neq 3\}$ **2. a.** $\dfrac{1}{2z - 1}$

b. $\dfrac{5x + 3}{6x - 5}$ **3. a.** 1 **b.** -1 **4.** $-\dfrac{5(2 + x)}{x + 3}$ **5. a.** $x^2 - 4x + 16$ **b.** $\dfrac{5}{z - 3}$ **6. a.** $\dfrac{2n + 1}{n(n - 1)}$ **b.** $-x^2$ **7. a.** $-\dfrac{y^3}{21(y + 3)}$

b. $\dfrac{7x + 2}{x + 2}$ **8.** $\dfrac{5}{3(x - 3)}$ **9. a.** \$7.20 **b.** \$3.60

Graphing Calculator Explorations 6.1

1. $\{x \mid x \text{ is a real number and } x \neq -2, x \neq 2\}$

3. $\left\{ x \mid x \text{ is a real number and } x \neq -4, x \neq \dfrac{1}{2} \right\}$

Vocabulary, Readiness & Video Check 6.1

1. rational **3.** domain **5.** 1 **7.** $\dfrac{-a}{b}; \dfrac{a}{-b}$ **9.** Rational expressions are fractions and are therefore undefined if the denominator is zero; the domain of a rational function consists of all real numbers except those for which the rational expression is undefined. **11.** Yes, multiplying and also simplifying rational expressions often require polynomial factoring. Example 6 involves factoring out a GCF and factoring a difference of squares. **13.** Since the domain consists of all allowable x-values and x is defined as the number of years since the book was published, we do not allow x to be negative for the context of this application.

Exercise Set 6.1

1. $\{x \mid x \text{ is a real number}\}$ **3.** $\{t \mid t \text{ is a real number and } t \neq 0\}$ **5.** $\{x \mid x \text{ is a real number and } x \neq 7\}$ **7.** $\left\{ x \mid x \text{ is a real number and } x \neq \dfrac{1}{3} \right\}$

9. $\{x \mid x \text{ is a real number and } x \neq -2, x \neq 0, x \neq 1\}$ **11.** $\{x \mid x \text{ is a real number and } x \neq 2, x \neq -2\}$ **13.** $1 - 2x$ **15.** $x - 3$ **17.** $\dfrac{9}{7}$

19. $x - 4$ **21.** -1 **23.** $-(x + 7)$ **25.** $\dfrac{2x + 1}{x - 1}$ **27.** $\dfrac{x^2 + 5x + 25}{2}$ **29.** $\dfrac{x - 2}{2x^2 + 1}$ **31.** $\dfrac{1}{3x + 5}$ **33.** $-\dfrac{4}{5}$ **35.** $-\dfrac{6a}{2a + 1}$

37. $\dfrac{3}{2(x - 1)}$ **39.** $\dfrac{x + 2}{x + 3}$ **41.** $\dfrac{3a}{5(a - b)}$ **43.** $\dfrac{1}{6}$ **45.** $\dfrac{x}{3}$ **47.** $\dfrac{4a^2}{a - b}$ **49.** $\dfrac{4}{(x + 2)(x + 3)}$ **51.** $\dfrac{1}{2}$ **53.** -1 **55.** $\dfrac{8(a - 2)}{3(a + 2)}$

57. $\dfrac{(x + 2)(x + 3)}{4}$ **59.** $\dfrac{2(x + 3)(x - 3)}{5(x^2 - 8x - 15)}$ **61.** $r^2 - rs + s^2$ **63.** $\dfrac{8}{x^2 y}$ **65.** $\dfrac{(y + 5)(2x - 1)}{(y + 2)(5x + 1)}$ **67.** $\dfrac{5(3a + 2)}{a}$ **69.** $\dfrac{5x^2 - 2}{(x - 1)^2}$

71. $\dfrac{10}{3}, -8, -\dfrac{7}{3}$ **73.** $-\dfrac{17}{48}, \dfrac{2}{7}, -\dfrac{3}{8}$ **75. a.** \$200 million **b.** \$500 million **c.** \$300 million **d.** $\{x \mid x \text{ is a real number}\}$ **77.** $\dfrac{7}{5}$ **79.** $\dfrac{1}{12}$

81. $\dfrac{11}{16}$ **83.** b and d **85.** no; answers may vary **87.** $\dfrac{5}{x - 2}$ sq m **89.** $\dfrac{(x + 2)(x - 1)^2}{x^5}$ ft **91.** answers may vary

93. a. 1 **b.** -1 **c.** neither **d.** -1 **e.** -1 **f.** 1 **95.** answers may vary **97.** $0, \dfrac{20}{9}, \dfrac{60}{7}, 20, \dfrac{140}{3}, 180, 380, 1980;$

99. -1 **101.** $\dfrac{1}{x^n - 4}$ **103.** $2x^2(x^n + 2)$ **105.** $\dfrac{1}{10y(y^n + 3)}$ **107.** $\dfrac{y^n + 1}{2(y^n - 1)}$

Section 6.2

Practice Exercises

1. a. $\dfrac{9 + x}{11z^2}$ **b.** $\dfrac{3x}{4}$ **c.** $x - 4$ **d.** $-\dfrac{3}{2a^2}$ **2. a.** $18x^3 y^5$ **b.** $(x - 2)(x + 3)$ **c.** $(b - 4)^2(b + 4)(2b + 3)$ **d.** $-4(y - 3)(y + 3)$

3. a. $\dfrac{20p + 3}{5p^4 q}$ **b.** $\dfrac{5y^2 + 19y - 12}{(y + 3)(y - 3)}$ **c.** 3 **4.** $\dfrac{t^2 - t - 15}{(t + 5)(t - 5)(t + 2)}$ **5.** $\dfrac{5x^2 - 12x - 3}{(3x + 1)(x - 2)(2x - 5)}$ **6.** $\dfrac{4}{x - 2}$

Vocabulary, Readiness & Video Check 6.2

1. a, b **3.** c **5.** $\dfrac{12}{y}$ **7.** $\dfrac{35}{y^2}$ **9.** We need to be sure we subtract the entire second numerator — that is, make sure we "distribute" the subtraction to each term in the second numerator. **11.** numerator; one; value

Exercise Set 6.2

1. $\dfrac{-x+4}{2x}$ **3.** $\dfrac{16}{y-2}$ **5.** $-\dfrac{3}{xz^2}$ **7.** $\dfrac{x+2}{x-2}$ **9.** $x-2$ **11.** $-\dfrac{1}{x-2}$ or $\dfrac{1}{2-x}$ **13.** $-\dfrac{5}{x}$ **15.** $35x$ **17.** $x(x+1)$

19. $(x+7)(x-7)$ **21.** $6(x+2)(x-2)$ **23.** $(a+b)(a-b)^2$ **25.** $-4x(x+3)(x-3)$ **27.** $\dfrac{17}{6x}$ **29.** $\dfrac{35-4y}{14y^2}$

31. $\dfrac{-13x+4}{(x+4)(x-4)}$ **33.** $\dfrac{3}{x+4}$ **35.** 0 **37.** $-\dfrac{x}{x-1}$ **39.** $\dfrac{-x+1}{x-2}$ **41.** $\dfrac{y^2+2y+10}{(y+4)(y-4)(y-2)}$ **43.** $\dfrac{5(x^2+x-4)}{(3x+2)(x+3)(2x-5)}$

45. $\dfrac{-x^2+10x+19}{(x-2)(x+1)(x+3)}$ **47.** $\dfrac{x^2+4x+2}{(2x+5)(x-7)(x-1)}$ **49.** $\dfrac{5a+1}{(a+1)^2(a-1)}$ **51.** $\dfrac{3}{x^2y^3}$ **53.** $-\dfrac{5}{x}$ **55.** $\dfrac{25}{6(x+5)}$ **57.** $\dfrac{-2x-1}{x^2(x-3)}$

59. $\dfrac{b(2a-b)}{(a+b)(a-b)}$ **61.** $\dfrac{2(x+8)}{(x+2)^2(x-2)}$ **63.** $\dfrac{3x^2+23x-7}{(2x-1)(x-5)(x+3)}$ **65.** $\dfrac{5-2x}{2(x+1)}$ **67.** $\dfrac{2(x^2+x-21)}{(x+3)^2(x-3)}$ **69.** $\dfrac{6x}{(x+3)(x-3)^2}$

71. $\dfrac{4}{3}$ **73.** $\dfrac{2x^2+9x-18}{6x^2}$ or $\dfrac{(x+6)(2x-3)}{6x^2}$ **75.** $\dfrac{4a^2}{9(a-1)}$ **77.** 4 **79.** $-\dfrac{4}{x-1}$ **81.** $-\dfrac{32}{x(x+2)(x-2)}$ **83.** 10 **85.** $4+x^2$

87. 10 **89.** 2 **91.** 3 **93.** $5m$ **95.** $\dfrac{2x-3}{x^2+1}-\dfrac{x-6}{x^2+1}=\dfrac{2x-3-x+6}{x^2+1}=\dfrac{x+3}{x^2+1}$ **97.** $\dfrac{4x}{x+5}$ ft; $\dfrac{x^2}{(x+5)^2}$ sq ft **99.** answers may vary

101. answers may vary **103.** answers may vary **105.** $\dfrac{3}{2x}$ **107.** $\dfrac{4-3x}{x^2}$ **109.**

Section 6.3
Practice Exercises

1. a. $\dfrac{1}{12m}$ **b.** $\dfrac{8x(x+4)}{3(x-4)}$ **c.** $\dfrac{b^2}{a^2}$ **2. a.** $\dfrac{8x(x+4)}{3(x-4)}$ **b.** $\dfrac{b^2}{a^2}$ **3.** $\dfrac{y(3xy+1)}{x^2(1+xy)}$ **4.** $\dfrac{1-6x}{15+6x}$ or $\dfrac{1-6x}{3(5+2x)}$

Vocabulary, Readiness & Video Check 6.3

1. $\dfrac{7}{1+z}$ **3.** $\dfrac{1}{x^2}$ **5.** $\dfrac{2}{x}$ **7.** $\dfrac{1}{9y}$ **9.** a single fraction in the numerator and in the denominator **11.** Since a negative exponent moves its base from a numerator to a denominator of the expression, a rational expression containing negative exponents can become a complex fraction when rewritten with positive exponents.

Exercise Set 6.3

1. 4 **3.** $\dfrac{7}{13}$ **5.** $\dfrac{4}{x}$ **7.** $\dfrac{9(x-2)}{9x^2+4}$ **9.** $2x+y$ **11.** $\dfrac{2(x+1)}{2x-1}$ **13.** $\dfrac{2x+3}{4-9x}$ **15.** $\dfrac{1}{x^2-2x+4}$ **17.** $\dfrac{x}{5(x-2)}$ **19.** $\dfrac{x-2}{2x-1}$

21. $\dfrac{x}{2-3x}$ **23.** $-\dfrac{y}{x+y}$ **25.** $-\dfrac{2x^3}{y(x-y)}$ **27.** $\dfrac{2x+1}{y}$ **29.** $\dfrac{x-3}{9}$ **31.** $\dfrac{1}{x+2}$ **33.** 2 **35.** $\dfrac{xy^2}{x^2+y^2}$ **37.** $\dfrac{2b^2+3a}{b(b-a)}$

39. $\dfrac{x}{(x+1)(x-1)}$ **41.** $\dfrac{1+a}{1-a}$ **43.** $\dfrac{x(x+6y)}{2y}$ **45.** $\dfrac{5a}{2(a+2)}$ **47.** $xy(5y+2x)$ **49.** $\dfrac{xy}{2x+5y}$ **51.** $\dfrac{x^2y^2}{4}$ **53.** $-9x^3y^4$

55. $-4, 14$ **57.** a and c **59.** $\dfrac{770a}{770-s}$ **61.** a, b **63.** answers may vary **65.** $\dfrac{1+x}{2+x}$ **67.** $x(x+1)$ **69.** $\dfrac{x-3y}{x+3y}$ **71.** $3a^2+4a+4$

73. a. $\dfrac{1}{a+h}$ **b.** $\dfrac{1}{a}$ **c.** $\dfrac{\dfrac{1}{a+h}-\dfrac{1}{a}}{h}$ **d.** $-\dfrac{1}{a(a+h)}$ **75. a.** $\dfrac{3}{a+h+1}$ **b.** $\dfrac{3}{a+1}$ **c.** $\dfrac{\dfrac{3}{a+h+1}-\dfrac{3}{a+1}}{h}$ **d.** $-\dfrac{3}{(a+h+1)(a+1)}$

Section 6.4
Practice Exercises

1. $3a^2-2a+5$ **2.** $5a^2b^2-8ab+1-\dfrac{8}{ab}$ **3.** $3x-2$ **4.** $3x-2+\dfrac{6}{2x-1}$ **5.** $5x^2-6x+8+\dfrac{6}{x+3}$ **6.** $2x^2+3x-2+\dfrac{-8x+4}{x^2+1}$

7. $16x^2+20x+25$ **8.** $4x^2+x+7+\dfrac{12}{x-1}$ **9.** $x^3-5x+15-\dfrac{33}{x+3}$ **10. a.** -4 **b.** -4 **11.** 15

Vocabulary, Readiness & Video Check 6.4

1. the common denominator **3.** The last number is the remainder and the other numbers are the coefficients of the variables in the quotient; the degree of the quotient is one less than the degree of the dividend.

Exercise Set 6.4

1. $2a+4$ **3.** $3ab+4$ **5.** $2y+\dfrac{3y}{x}-\dfrac{2y}{x^2}$ **7.** $x+1$ **9.** $2x-8$ **11.** $x-\dfrac{1}{2}$ **13.** $2x^2-\dfrac{1}{2}x+5$ **15.** $2x^2-6$

17. $3x^3+5x+4-\dfrac{2x}{x^2-2}$ **19.** $2x^3+\dfrac{9}{2}x^2+10x+21+\dfrac{42}{x-2}$ **21.** $x+8$ **23.** $x-1$ **25.** $x^2-5x-23-\dfrac{41}{x-2}$

27. $4x + 8 + \dfrac{7}{x - 2}$ **29.** $x^6 y + \dfrac{2}{y} + 1$ **31.** $5x^2 - 6 - \dfrac{5}{2x - 1}$ **33.** $2x^2 + 2x + 8 + \dfrac{28}{x - 4}$ **35.** $2x^3 - 3x^2 + x - 4$

37. $3x^2 + 4x - 8 + \dfrac{20}{x + 1}$ **39.** $3x^2 + 3x - 3$ **41.** $x^2 + x + 1$ **43.** $-\dfrac{5y}{x} - \dfrac{15z}{x} - 25z$ **45.** $3x^4 - 2x$ **47.** 1   **49.** -133 **51.** 3

53. $-\dfrac{187}{81}$ **55.** $\dfrac{95}{32}$ **57.** $-\dfrac{5}{6}$ **59.** 2   **61.** 54   **63.** $(x - 1)(x^2 + x + 1)$ **65.** $(5z + 2)(25z^2 - 10z + 4)$ **67.** $(y + 2)(x + 3)$

69. $x(x + 3)(x - 3)$ **71.** yes   **73.** no   **75.** a or d   **77.** $(x^4 + 2x^2 - 6)$ m   **79.** $(3x - 7)$ in.   **81.** $(x^3 - 5x^2 + 2x - 1)$cm

83. $x^3 + \dfrac{5}{3}x^2 + \dfrac{5}{3}x + \dfrac{8}{3} + \dfrac{8}{3(x - 1)}$ **85.** $\dfrac{3}{2}x^3 + \dfrac{1}{4}x^2 + \dfrac{1}{8}x - \dfrac{7}{16} + \dfrac{1}{16(2x - 1)}$ **87.** $x^3 - \dfrac{2}{5}x$ **89.** $5x - 1 + \dfrac{6}{x}; x \neq 0$

91. $7x^3 + 14x^2 + 25x + 50 + \dfrac{102}{x - 2}; x \neq 2$ **93.** answers may vary   **95.** answers may vary   **97.** $(x + 3)(x^2 + 4) = x^3 + 3x^2 + 4x + 12$

99. $2x^3 - 5x^2 - 31x + 33$ **101. a.** $m(x) = \dfrac{-0.08x^3 - 0.04x^2 + 1.06x + 1.9}{2.2x + 9.38}$ **b.** -1.23 **103.** 0

Section 6.5

Practice Exercises

1. 4   **2.** 7   **3.** { } or $\varnothing$ **4.** -1 **5.** 1   **6.** $12, -1$

Vocabulary, Readiness & Video Check 6.5

1. equation   **3.** expression   **5.** equation   **7.** 14; c   **9.** $(x + 4)(x - 4)$; a   **11.** Linear and quadratic equations are solved in very different ways, so you need to determine the next correct move to make.

Exercise Set 6.5

1. 72   **3.** 2   **5.** 6   **7.** 2, -2 **9.** $\varnothing$ **11.** $-\dfrac{28}{3}$ **13.** 3   **15.** -8 **17.** 3   **19.** $\varnothing$ **21.** 1   **23.** 3   **25.** -1 **27.** 6   **29.** $\dfrac{1}{3}$

31. $-5, 5$ **33.** 3   **35.** 7   **37.** $\varnothing$ **39.** $\dfrac{4}{3}$ **41.** -12 **43.** $1, \dfrac{11}{4}$ **45.** $-5, -1$ **47.** $-\dfrac{7}{5}$ **49.** 5   **51.** length: 15 in.; width: 10 in.

53. 19.2%   **55.** 30–34   **57.** 240,936 inmates   **59.** answers may vary   **61.** 3000 game disks   **63.** $\dfrac{1}{16}, \dfrac{1}{3}$ **65.** $-\dfrac{1}{5}, 1$ **67.** -0.17

69. 0.42   **71.** $-1, 0$ **73.** -2 **75.**   **77.**

Integrated Review

1. $\dfrac{1}{2}$ **2.** 10   **3.** $\dfrac{1 + 2x}{8}$ **4.** $\dfrac{15 + x}{10}$ **5.** $\dfrac{2(x - 4)}{(x + 2)(x - 1)}$ **6.** $-\dfrac{5(x - 8)}{(x - 2)(x + 4)}$ **7.** 4   **8.** 8   **9.** -5 **10.** $-\dfrac{2}{3}$ **11.** $\dfrac{2x + 5}{x(x - 3)}$

12. $\dfrac{5}{2x}$ **13.** -2 **14.** $-\dfrac{y}{x}$ **15.** $\dfrac{(a + 3)(a + 1)}{a + 2}$ **16.** $\dfrac{-a^2 + 31a + 10}{5(a - 6)(a + 1)}$ **17.** $-\dfrac{1}{5}$ **18.** $-\dfrac{3}{13}$ **19.** $\dfrac{4a + 1}{(3a + 1)(3a - 1)}$

20. $\dfrac{-a - 8}{4a(a - 2)}$ or $-\dfrac{a + 8}{4a(a - 2)}$ **21.** $-1, \dfrac{3}{2}$ **22.** $\dfrac{x^2 - 3x + 10}{2(x + 3)(x - 3)}$ **23.** $\dfrac{3}{x + 1}$ **24.** $\{x \mid x \text{ is a real number and } x \neq 2, x \neq -1\}$ **25.** -1

26. $\dfrac{22z - 45}{3z(z - 3)}$ **27. a.** $\dfrac{x}{5} - \dfrac{x}{4} + \dfrac{1}{10}$ **b.** Write each rational expression term so that the denominator is the LCD, 20.   **c.** $\dfrac{-x + 2}{20}$

28. a. $\dfrac{x}{5} - \dfrac{x}{4} = \dfrac{1}{10}$ **b.** Clear the equation of fractions by multiplying each term by the LCD, 20.   **c.** -2 **29.** b   **30.** d   **31.** d   **32.** a   **33.** d

Section 6.6

Practice Exercises

1. $a = \dfrac{bc}{b + c}$ **2.** 7   **3.** 14,400 homes   **4.** $1\dfrac{1}{5}$ hr   **5.** 8 mph

Vocabulary, Readiness & Video Check 6.6

1. After we multiply through by the LCD, we factor the specified variable out so that we can divide and get the specified variable alone.   **3.** We write the same units in the numerators and the same units in the denominators.   **5.** $x + y$ (or $y + x$)

Exercise Set 6.6

1. $C = \dfrac{5}{9}(F - 32)$ **3.** $I = A - QL$ **5.** $R = \dfrac{R_1 R_2}{R_1 + R_2}$ **7.** $n = \dfrac{2S}{a + L}$ **9.** $b = \dfrac{2A - ah}{h}$ **11.** $T_2 = \dfrac{P_2 V_2 T_1}{P_1 V_1}$ **13.** $f_2 = \dfrac{f_1 f}{f_1 - f}$

15. $L = \dfrac{n\lambda}{2}$ **17.** $c = \dfrac{2L\omega}{\theta}$ **19.** 1 or 5   **21.** 5   **23.** 4.5 gal   **25.** 87,265 women   **27.** 15.6 hr   **29.** 10 min   **31.** 200 mph

33. 15 mph   **35.** -8 and -7 **37.** 36 min   **39.** 45 mph; 60 mph   **41.** 5.9 hr   **43.** 2 hr   **45.** 135 mph   **47.** 12 mi   **49.** $\dfrac{7}{8}$

51. $1\frac{1}{2}$ min   **53.** 1 hr   **55.** $2\frac{2}{9}$ hr   **57.** 2 hr   **59.** 415 movies   **61.** -5 **63.** 2   **65.** 164 lb   **67.** higher; F   **69.** 6 ohms

71. $\frac{1}{R} = \frac{1}{R_1} + \frac{1}{R_2} + \frac{1}{R_3}$; $R = \frac{15}{13}$ ohms

Section 6.7
Practice Exercises

1. $k = \frac{4}{3}$; $y = \frac{4}{3}x$ **2.** $18\frac{3}{4}$ in.   **3.** $k = 45$; $b = \frac{45}{a}$ **4.** $653\frac{1}{3}$ kilopascals   **5.** $A = kpa$ **6.** $k = 4$; $y = \frac{4}{x^3}$ **7.** $k = 81$; $y = \frac{81z}{x^3}$

Vocabulary, Readiness & Video Check 6.7

1. direct   **3.** joint   **5.** inverse   **7.** direct   **9.** linear; slope   **11.** $y = ka^2b^5$

Exercise Set 6.7

1. $k = \frac{1}{5}$; $y = \frac{1}{5}x$ **3.** $k = \frac{3}{2}$; $y = \frac{3}{2}x$ **5.** $k = 14$; $y = 14x$ **7.** $k = 0.25$; $y = 0.25x$ **9.** 4.05 lb   **11.** 12.5 billion gal   **13.** $k = 30$; $y = \frac{30}{x}$

15. $k = 700$; $y = \frac{700}{x}$ **17.** $k = 2$; $y = \frac{2}{x}$ **19.** $k = 0.14$; $y = \frac{0.14}{x}$ **21.** 54 mph   **23.** 72 amps   **25.** divided by 4   **27.** $x = kyz$

29. $r = kst^3$ **31.** $k = \frac{1}{3}$; $y = \frac{1}{3}x^3$ **33.** $k = 0.2$; $y = 0.2\sqrt{x}$ **35.** $k = 1.3$; $y = \frac{1.3}{x^2}$ **37.** $k = 3$; $y = 3xz^3$ **39.** 22.5 tons   **41.** 15π cu in.

43. 8 ft   **45.** $y = kx$ **47.** $a = \frac{k}{b}$ **49.** $y = kxz$ **51.** $y = \frac{k}{x^3}$ **53.** $y = \frac{kx}{p^2}$ **55.** $C = 8\pi$ in.; $A = 16\pi$ sq in.

57. $C = 18\pi$ cm; $A = 81\pi$ sq cm   **59.** 9   **61.** 1   **63.** $\frac{1}{2}$ **65.** $\frac{2}{3}$ **67.** a   **69.** c   **71.** multiplied by 8   **73.** multiplied by 2

75.   **77.**

Chapter 6 Vocabulary Check

1. complex fraction   **2.** long division   **3.** directly   **4.** inversely   **5.** least common denominator   **6.** synthetic division   **7.** jointly
8. opposites   **9.** rational expression   **10.** equation; expression

Chapter 6 Review

1. $\{x \mid x$ is a real number$\}$ **3.** $\{x \mid x$ is a real number and $x \neq 5\}$ **5.** $\{x \mid x$ is a real number and $x \neq 0, x \neq -8\}$ **7.** -1 **9.** $\frac{1}{x-1}$

11. $\frac{2(x-3)}{x-4}$ **13.** $-\frac{3}{2}$ **15.** $\frac{a-b}{2a}$ **17.** $\frac{12}{5}$ **19.** $\frac{a-b}{5a}$ **21.** $-\frac{1}{x}$ **23.** $60x^2y^5$ **25.** $5x(x-5)$ **27.** $\frac{4+x}{x-4}$ **29.** $\frac{3}{2(x-2)}$

31. $\frac{-7x-6}{5(x-3)(x+3)}$ **33.** $\frac{5a-1}{(a-1)^2(a+1)}$ **35.** $\frac{5-2x}{2(x-1)}$ **37.** $\frac{4-3x}{8+x}$ **39.** $\frac{5(4x-3)}{2(5x^2-2)}$ **41.** $\frac{x(5y+1)}{3y}$ **43.** $\frac{1+x}{1-x}$ **45.** $\frac{3}{a+h}$

47. $\frac{\frac{3}{a+h} - \frac{3}{a}}{h}$ **49.** $1 + \frac{x}{2y} - \frac{9}{4xy}$ **51.** $3x^3 + 9x^2 + 2x + 6 - \frac{2}{x-3}$ **53.** $x^2 - 1 + \frac{5}{2x+3}$ **55.** $3x^2 + 6x + 24 + \frac{44}{x-2}$

57. $x^2 + 3x + 9 - \frac{54}{x-3}$ **59.** 3043   **61.** $\frac{365}{32}$ **63.** 6   **65.** $\frac{3}{2}$ **67.** $\frac{2x+5}{x(x-7)}$ **69.** $-\frac{1}{3}, 2$ **71.** $a = \frac{2A}{h} - b$ **73.** $R = \frac{E}{I} - r$

75. $x = \frac{yz}{z-y}$ **77.** 1, 2   **79.** $1\frac{23}{37}$ hr   **81.** 8 mph   **83.** 9   **85.** 2   **87.** $\frac{3}{5x}$ **89.** $\frac{5(a-2)}{7}$ **91.** $\frac{13}{3x}$ **93.** $\frac{1}{x-2}$ **95.** $\frac{2}{15-2x}$

97. $\frac{2(x-1)}{x+6}$ **99.** 2   **101.** $\frac{23}{25}$ **103.** 10 hr   **105.** $63\frac{2}{3}$ mph; 45 mph   **107.** 25,265   **109.** $3x^3 + 13x^2 + 51x + 204 + \frac{814}{x-4}$

Chapter 6 Getting Ready for the Test

1. D   **2.** B   **3.** E   **4.** B   **5.** A   **6.** A   **7.** C   **8.** B   **9.** C   **10.** D   **11.** A   **12.** C   **13.** D   **14.** D   **15.** B
16. C   **17.** A   **18.** E

Chapter 6 Test

1. $\{x \mid x$ is a real number and $x \neq 1\}$ **2.** $\{x \mid x$ is a real number and $x \neq -3, x \neq -1\}$ **3.** $-\frac{7}{8}$ **4.** $\frac{x}{x+9}$ **5.** $x^2 + 2x + 4$ **6.** $\frac{5}{3x}$

7. $\frac{3}{x^3}$ **8.** $\frac{x+2}{2(x+3)}$ **9.** $-\frac{4(2x+9)}{5}$ **10.** -1 **11.** $\frac{1}{x(x+3)}$ **12.** $\frac{5x-2}{(x-3)(x+2)(x-2)}$ **13.** $\frac{-x+30}{6(x-7)}$ **14.** $\frac{3}{2}$ **15.** $\frac{64}{3}$

16. $\dfrac{(x-3)^2}{x-2}$ **17.** $\dfrac{4xy}{3z}+\dfrac{3}{z}+1$ **18.** $2x^2-x-2+\dfrac{2}{2x+1}$ **19.** $4x^3-15x^2+45x-136+\dfrac{407}{x+3}$ **20.** 91 **21.** 7 **22.** 8 **23.** $\dfrac{2}{7}$

24. 3 **25.** $x=\dfrac{7a^2+b^2}{4a-b}$ **26.** 5 **27.** $\dfrac{6}{7}$ hr **28.** 16 **29.** 9 **30.** 256 ft

Chapter 6 Cumulative Review

1. a. $8x$ **b.** $8x+3$ **c.** $x\div-7$ or $\dfrac{x}{-7}$ **d.** $2x-1.6$ **e.** $x-6$ **f.** $2(4+x)$; Sec. 1.2, Ex. 8 **3.** 2; Sec. 2.1, Ex. 5

5. 2020 and all years after; Sec. 2.4, Ex. 9 **7.** $\varnothing$; Sec. 2.6, Ex. 7 **9.** -1; Sec. 2.7, Ex. 5 **11.** ; Sec. 3.1, Ex. 4

13. a. function **b.** not a function **c.** function; Sec. 3.2, Ex. 2 **15.** ; Sec. 3.3, Ex. 4 **17.** $y=-3x-2$; Sec. 3.5, Ex. 4

19. ; Sec. 3.7, Ex. 3 **21.** $(0,-5)$; Sec. 4.1, Ex. 8 **23.** $\varnothing$; Sec. 4.2, Ex. 2 **25.** $30°,110°,40°$; Sec. 4.3, Ex. 6

27. $(1,-1,3)$; Sec. 4.4, Ex. 3 **29. a.** 1 **b.** -1 **c.** 1 **d.** 2; Sec. 5.1, Ex. 3 **31. a.** $4x^b$ **b.** y^{5a+6}; Sec 5.2, Ex. 5 **33. a.** 2 **b.** 5

c. 1 **d.** 6 **e.** 0; Sec. 5.3, Ex. 1 **35.** $9+12a+6b+4a^2+4ab+b^2$; Sec. 5.4, Ex. 9 **37.** $(b-6)(a+2)$; Sec 5.5, Ex. 7

39. $2(n^2-19n+40)$; Sec. 5.6, Ex. 4 **41.** $(x+2+y)(x+2-y)$; Sec. 5.7, Ex. 5 **43.** $-2,6$; Sec. 5.8, Ex. 1 **45. a.** $\dfrac{1}{5x-1}$

b. $\dfrac{9x+4}{8x-7}$; Sec. 6.1, Ex. 2 **47.** $\dfrac{5k^2-7k+4}{(k+2)(k-2)(k-1)}$; Sec. 6.2, Ex. 4 **49.** -2; Sec. 6.5, Ex. 2

CHAPTER 7 RATIONAL EXPONENTS, RADICALS, AND COMPLEX NUMBERS

Section 7.1

Practice Exercises

1. a. 7 **b.** 0 **c.** $\dfrac{4}{9}$ **d.** 0.8 **e.** z^4 **f.** $4b^2$ **g.** -6 **h.** not a real number **2.** 6.708 **3. a.** -1 **b.** 3 **c.** $\dfrac{3}{4}$ **d.** x^4

e. $-2x$ **4. a.** 10 **b.** -1 **c.** -9 **d.** not a real number **e.** $3x^3$ **5. a.** 4 **b.** $|x^7|$ **c.** $|x+7|$ **d.** -7 **e.** $3x-5$

f. $7|x|$ **g.** $|x+8|$ **6. a.** 4 **b.** 2 **c.** 2 **d.** $\sqrt[3]{-9}$ **7.** **8.**

Vocabulary, Readiness & Video Check 7.1

1. index; radical sign; radicand **3.** is not **5.** $[0,\infty)$ **7.** $(16,4)$ **9.** Divide the index into each exponent in the radicand. **11.** The square root of a negative number is not a real number, but the cube root of a negative number is a real number. **13.** For odd roots, there's only one root/answer whether the radicand is positive or negative, so absolute value bars aren't needed.

Exercise Set 7.1

1. 10 **3.** $\dfrac{1}{2}$ **5.** 0.01 **7.** -6 **9.** x^5 **11.** $4y^3$ **13.** 2.646 **15.** 6.164 **17.** 14.142 **19.** 4 **21.** $\dfrac{1}{2}$ **23.** -1 **25.** x^4 **27.** $-3x^3$

29. -2 **31.** not a real number **33.** -2 **35.** x^4 **37.** $2x^2$ **39.** $9x^2$ **41.** $4x^2$ **43.** 8 **45.** -8 **47.** $2|x|$ **49.** x **51.** $|x-5|$

53. $|x+2|$ **55.** -11 **57.** $2x$ **59.** y^6 **61.** $5ab^{10}$ **63.** $-3x^4y^3$ **65.** a^4b **67.** $-2x^2y$ **69.** $\dfrac{5}{7}$ **71.** $\dfrac{x^{10}}{2y}$ **73.** $-\dfrac{z^7}{3x}$ **75.** $\dfrac{x}{2}$

77. $\sqrt{3}$ **79.** -1 **81.** -3 **83.** $\sqrt[4]{7}$ **85.** $[0,\infty)$; **87.** $[3,\infty)$; $0,1,2,3$ **89.** $(-\infty,\infty)$; **91.** $(-\infty,\infty)$; $0,1,-1,2,-2$

93. $-32x^{15}y^{10}$ **95.** $-60x^7y^{10}z^5$ **97.** $\dfrac{x^9y^5}{2}$ **99.** not a real number   **101.** not a real number   **103.** d   **105.** d   **107.** b   **109.** b

111. answers may vary   **113.** 1.69 sq m   **115.** 11,181 m per sec   **117.** answers may vary   **119.**

121.

Section 7.2
Practice Exercises

1. a. 6   **b.** 10   **c.** $\sqrt[3]{x}$ **d.** 1   **e.** -8 **f.** $5x^3$ **g.** $3\sqrt[4]{x}$ **2. a.** 64   **b.** -1 **c.** -27 **d.** $\dfrac{1}{125}$ **e.** $\sqrt[9]{(3x+2)^5}$

3. a. $\dfrac{1}{27}$ **b.** $\dfrac{1}{16}$ **4. a.** $y^{10/3}$ **b.** $x^{17/20}$ **c.** $\dfrac{1}{9}$ **d.** $b^{2/9}$ **e.** $\dfrac{81}{x^3y^{11/3}}$ **5. a.** $x^{14/15}-x^{13/5}$ **b.** $x+4x^{1/2}-12$ **6.** $x^{-1/5}(2-7x)$

7. a. $\sqrt[3]{x}$ **b.** $\sqrt{6}$ **c.** $\sqrt[4]{a^2b}$ **8. a.** $\sqrt[12]{x^7}$ **b.** $\sqrt[15]{y^2}$ **c.** $\sqrt[6]{675}$

Vocabulary, Readiness & Video Check 7.2

1. true   **3.** true   **5.** multiply, c   **7.** $-\sqrt[5]{3x}$ **9.** denominator; positive   **11.** Write the radical using an equivalent fractional exponent form, simplify the fraction, then write as a radical again.

Exercise Set 7.2

1. 7   **3.** 3   **5.** $\dfrac{1}{2}$ **7.** 13   **9.** $2\sqrt[3]{m}$ **11.** $3x^2$ **13.** -3 **15.** -2 **17.** 8   **19.** 16   **21.** not a real number   **23.** $\sqrt[5]{(2x)^3}$

25. $\sqrt[3]{(7x+2)^2}$ **27.** $\dfrac{64}{27}$ **29.** $\dfrac{1}{16}$ **31.** $\dfrac{1}{16}$ **33.** not a real number   **35.** $\dfrac{1}{x^{1/4}}$ **37.** $a^{2/3}$ **39.** $\dfrac{5x^{3/4}}{7}$ **41.** $a^{7/3}$ **43.** x **45.** $3^{5/8}$

47. $y^{1/6}$ **49.** $8u^3$ **51.** $-b$ **53.** $\dfrac{1}{x^2}$ **55.** $27x^{2/3}$ **57.** $\dfrac{y}{z^{1/6}}$ **59.** $\dfrac{1}{x^{7/4}}$ **61.** $y-y^{7/6}$ **63.** $x^{5/3}-2x^{2/3}$ **65.** $4x^{2/3}-9$

67. $x^{8/3}(1+x^{2/3})$ **69.** $x^{1/5}(x^{1/5}-3)$ **71.** $x^{-1/3}(5+x)$ **73.** $\sqrt{x}$ **75.** $\sqrt[3]{2}$ **77.** $2\sqrt{x}$ **79.** $\sqrt{xy}$ **81.** $\sqrt[3]{a^2b}$ **83.** $\sqrt{x+3}$

85. $\sqrt[15]{y^{11}}$ **87.** $\sqrt[12]{b^5}$ **89.** $\sqrt[24]{x^{23}}$ **91.** $\sqrt{a}$ **93.** $\sqrt[6]{432}$ **95.** $\sqrt[15]{343y^5}$ **97.** $\sqrt[6]{125r^3s^2}$ **99.** $25\cdot3$ **101.** $16\cdot3$ or $4\cdot12$

103. $8\cdot2$ **105.** $27\cdot2$ **107.** A   **109.** C   **111.** B   **113.** 1509 calories   **115.** 255.8 million   **117.** answers may vary   **119.** $a^{1/3}$

121. $x^{1/5}$ **123.** 1.6818   **125.** 5.6645   **127.** $\dfrac{t^{1/2}}{u^{1/2}}$

Section 7.3
Practice Exercises

1. a. $\sqrt{35}$ **b.** $\sqrt{13z}$ **c.** 5   **d.** $\sqrt[3]{15x^2y}$ **e.** $\sqrt{\dfrac{5t}{2m}}$ **2. a.** $\dfrac{6}{7}$ **b.** $\dfrac{\sqrt{z}}{4}$ **c.** $\dfrac{5}{2}$ **d.** $\dfrac{\sqrt[4]{5}}{3x^2}$ **3. a.** $7\sqrt{2}$ **b.** $3\sqrt[3]{2}$

c. $\sqrt{35}$ **d.** $3\sqrt[4]{3}$ **4. a.** $6z^3\sqrt{z}$ **b.** $2pq^2\sqrt[3]{4pq}$ **c.** $2x^3\sqrt[4]{x^3}$ **5. a.** 4   **b.** $\dfrac{7}{3}\sqrt{z}$ **c.** $10xy^2\sqrt[3]{x^2}$ **d.** $6x^2y\sqrt[5]{2y}$

6. $\sqrt{17}$ units ≈ 4.123 units   **7.** $\left(\dfrac{13}{2},-4\right)$

Vocabulary, Readiness & Video Check 7.3

1. midpoint; point   **3.** distance   **5.** the indexes must be the same   **7.** The power must be 1. Any even power is a perfect square and will leave no factor in the radicand; any higher odd power can have an even power factored from it, leaving one factor remaining in the radicand.   **9.** average; average

Exercise Set 7.3

1. $\sqrt{14}$ **3.** 2   **5.** $\sqrt[3]{36}$ **7.** $\sqrt{6x}$ **9.** $\sqrt{\dfrac{14}{xy}}$ **11.** $\sqrt[4]{20x^3}$ **13.** $\dfrac{\sqrt{6}}{7}$ **15.** $\dfrac{\sqrt{2}}{7}$ **17.** $\dfrac{\sqrt[4]{x^3}}{2}$ **19.** $\dfrac{\sqrt[3]{4}}{3}$ **21.** $\dfrac{\sqrt[4]{8}}{x^2}$

23. $\dfrac{\sqrt[3]{2x}}{3y^4\sqrt[3]{3}}$ **25.** $\dfrac{x\sqrt{y}}{10}$ **27.** $\dfrac{x\sqrt{5}}{2y}$ **29.** $-\dfrac{z^2\sqrt[3]{z}}{3x}$ **31.** $4\sqrt{2}$ **33.** $4\sqrt[3]{3}$ **35.** $25\sqrt{3}$ **37.** $2\sqrt{6}$ **39.** $10x^2\sqrt{x}$ **41.** $2y^2\sqrt[3]{2y}$

43. $a^2b\sqrt[4]{b^3}$ **45.** $y^2\sqrt{y}$ **47.** $5ab\sqrt{b}$ **49.** $-2x^2\sqrt[5]{y}$ **51.** $x^4\sqrt[3]{50x^2}$ **53.** $-4a^4b^3\sqrt{2b}$ **55.** $3x^3y^4\sqrt{xy}$ **57.** $5r^3s^4$

59. $2x^3y\sqrt[4]{2y}$ **61.** $\sqrt{2}$ **63.** 2   **65.** 10   **67.** x^2y **69.** $24m^2$ **71.** $\dfrac{15x\sqrt{2x}}{2}$ or $\dfrac{15x}{2}\sqrt{2x}$ **73.** $2a^2\sqrt[4]{2}$ **75.** $2xy^2\sqrt[5]{x^2}$ **77.** 5 units

79. $\sqrt{41}$ units ≈ 6.403 units   **81.** $\sqrt{10}$ units ≈ 3.162 units   **83.** $\sqrt{5}$ units ≈ 2.236 units   **85.** $\sqrt{192.58}$ units ≈ 13.877 units   **87.** $(4,-2)$

89. $\left(-5,\dfrac{5}{2}\right)$ **91.** $(3,0)$ **93.** $\left(-\dfrac{1}{2},\dfrac{1}{2}\right)$ **95.** $\left(\sqrt{2},\dfrac{\sqrt{5}}{2}\right)$ **97.** $(6.2,-6.65)$ **99.** $14x$ **101.** $2x^2-7x-15$ **103.** y^2

105. $-3x - 15$ **107.** $x^2 - 8x + 16$ **109.** true   **111.** false   **113.** true   **115.** $\dfrac{\sqrt[3]{64}}{\sqrt{64}} = \dfrac{4}{8} = \dfrac{1}{2}$ **117.** x^7 **119.** a^3bc^5 **121.** $z^{10}\sqrt[3]{z^2}$

123. $q^2r^5s\sqrt[4]{q^3r^5}$ **125.** 1.6 m   **127. a.** 20π sq cm   **b.** 211.57 sq ft

Section 7.4

Practice Exercises

1. a. $8\sqrt{17}$ **b.** $-5\sqrt[3]{5z}$ **c.** $3\sqrt{2} + 5\sqrt[3]{2}$ **2. a.** $11\sqrt{6}$ **b.** $-9\sqrt[3]{3}$ **c.** $-2\sqrt{3x}$ **d.** $2\sqrt{10} + 2\sqrt[3]{5}$ **e.** $4x\sqrt[3]{3x}$

3. a. $\dfrac{5\sqrt{7}}{12}$ **b.** $\dfrac{13\sqrt[3]{6y}}{4}$ **4. a.** $2\sqrt{5} + 5\sqrt{3}$ **b.** $2\sqrt{3} + 2\sqrt{2} - \sqrt{30} - 2\sqrt{5}$ **c.** $6z + \sqrt{z} - 12$ **d.** $-6\sqrt{6} + 15$

e. $5x - 9$ **f.** $6\sqrt{x + 2} + x + 11$

Vocabulary, Readiness & Video Check 7.4

1. Unlike   **3.** Like   **5.** $6\sqrt{3}$ **7.** $7\sqrt{x}$ **9.** $8\sqrt[3]{x}$ **11.** Sometimes you can't see that there are like radicals until you simplify, so you may incorrectly think you cannot add or subtract if you don't simplify first.

Exercise Set 7.4

1. $-2\sqrt{2}$ **3.** $10x\sqrt{2x}$ **5.** $17\sqrt{2} - 15\sqrt{5}$ **7.** $-\sqrt[3]{2x}$ **9.** $5b\sqrt{b}$ **11.** $\dfrac{31\sqrt{2}}{15}$ **13.** $\dfrac{\sqrt[3]{11}}{3}$ **15.** $\dfrac{5\sqrt{5x}}{9}$ **17.** $14 + \sqrt{3}$

19. $7 - 3y$ **21.** $6\sqrt{3} - 6\sqrt{2}$ **23.** $-23\sqrt[3]{5}$ **25.** $2a^3b\sqrt{ab}$ **27.** $20y\sqrt{2y}$ **29.** $2y\sqrt[3]{2x}$ **31.** $6\sqrt[3]{11} - 4\sqrt{11}$ **33.** $3x\sqrt[4]{x^3}$ **35.** $\dfrac{2\sqrt{3}}{3}$

37. $\dfrac{5x\sqrt[3]{x}}{7}$ **39.** $\dfrac{5\sqrt{7}}{2x}$ **41.** $\dfrac{\sqrt[3]{2}}{6}$ **43.** $\dfrac{14x\sqrt[3]{2x}}{9}$ **45.** $15\sqrt{3}$ in.   **47.** $\sqrt{35} + \sqrt{21}$ **49.** $7 - 2\sqrt{10}$ **51.** $3\sqrt{x} - x\sqrt{3}$

53. $6x - 13\sqrt{x} - 5$ **55.** $\sqrt[3]{a^2} + \sqrt[3]{a} - 20$ **57.** $6\sqrt{2} - 12$ **59.** $2 + 2x\sqrt{3}$ **61.** $-16 - \sqrt{35}$ **63.** $x - y^2$ **65.** $3 + 2x\sqrt{3} + x^2$

67. $23x - 5x\sqrt{15}$ **69.** $2\sqrt[3]{2} - \sqrt[3]{4}$ **71.** $x + 1$ **73.** $x + 24 + 10\sqrt{x - 1}$ **75.** $2x + 6 - 2\sqrt{2x + 5}$ **77.** $x - 7$ **79.** $\dfrac{7}{x + y}$

81. $2a - 3$ **83.** $\dfrac{-2 + \sqrt{3}}{3}$ **85.** $22\sqrt{5}$ ft; 150 sq ft   **87. a.** $2\sqrt{3}$ **b.** 3   **c.** answers may vary   **89.** $2\sqrt{6} - 2\sqrt{2} - 2\sqrt{3} + 6$

91. answers may vary

Section 7.5

Practice Exercises

1. a. $\dfrac{5\sqrt{3}}{3}$ **b.** $\dfrac{15\sqrt{x}}{2x}$ **c.** $\dfrac{\sqrt[3]{6}}{3}$ **2.** $\dfrac{\sqrt{15yz}}{5y}$ **3.** $\dfrac{\sqrt[3]{z^2x^2}}{3x^2}$ **4. a.** $\dfrac{5(3\sqrt{5} - 2)}{41}$ **b.** $\dfrac{\sqrt{6} + \sqrt{10} + 5\sqrt{3} + 5\sqrt{5}}{-2}$ **c.** $\dfrac{6x - 3\sqrt{xy}}{4x - y}$

5. $\dfrac{2}{\sqrt{10}}$ **6.** $\dfrac{5b}{\sqrt[3]{50ab^2}}$ **7.** $\dfrac{x - 9}{4(\sqrt{x} + 3)}$

Vocabulary, Readiness & Video Check 7.5

1. conjugate   **3.** rationalizing the numerator   **5.** To write an equivalent expression without a radical in the denominator.   **7.** No, except for the fact you're working with numerators, the process is the same.

Exercise Set 7.5

1. $\dfrac{\sqrt{14}}{7}$ **3.** $\dfrac{\sqrt{5}}{5}$ **5.** $\dfrac{2\sqrt{x}}{x}$ **7.** $\dfrac{4\sqrt[3]{9}}{3}$ **9.** $\dfrac{3\sqrt{2x}}{4x}$ **11.** $\dfrac{3\sqrt[3]{2x}}{2x}$ **13.** $\dfrac{3\sqrt{3a}}{a}$ **15.** $\dfrac{3\sqrt[3]{4}}{2}$ **17.** $\dfrac{2\sqrt{21}}{7}$ **19.** $\dfrac{\sqrt{10xy}}{5y}$ **21.** $\dfrac{\sqrt[3]{75}}{5}$

23. $\dfrac{\sqrt{6x}}{10}$ **25.** $\dfrac{\sqrt{3z}}{6z}$ **27.** $\dfrac{\sqrt[3]{6xy^2}}{3x}$ **29.** $\dfrac{3\sqrt[3]{2}}{2}$ **31.** $\dfrac{2\sqrt[3]{9x}}{3x^2}$ **33.** $\dfrac{5\sqrt[3]{4ab^4}}{2ab^3}$ **35.** $\sqrt{2} - x$ **37.** $5 + \sqrt{a}$ **39.** $-7\sqrt{5} - 8\sqrt{x}$

41. $-2(2 + \sqrt{7})$ **43.** $\dfrac{7(3 + \sqrt{x})}{9 - x}$ **45.** $-5 + 2\sqrt{6}$ **47.** $\dfrac{2a + 2\sqrt{a} + \sqrt{ab} + \sqrt{b}}{4a - b}$ **49.** $-\dfrac{8(1 - \sqrt{10})}{9}$ **51.** $\dfrac{x - \sqrt{xy}}{x - y}$

53. $\dfrac{5 + 3\sqrt{2}}{7}$ **55.** $\dfrac{5}{\sqrt{15}}$ **57.** $\dfrac{6}{\sqrt{10}}$ **59.** $\dfrac{2x}{7\sqrt{x}}$ **61.** $\dfrac{5y}{\sqrt[3]{100xy}}$ **63.** $\dfrac{2}{\sqrt{10}}$ **65.** $\dfrac{2x}{11\sqrt{2x}}$ **67.** $\dfrac{7}{2\sqrt[3]{49}}$ **69.** $\dfrac{3x^2}{10\sqrt[3]{9x}}$ **71.** $\dfrac{6x^2y^3}{\sqrt{6z}}$

73. $\dfrac{-7}{12 + 6\sqrt{11}}$ **75.** $\dfrac{3}{10 + 5\sqrt{7}}$ **77.** $\dfrac{x - 9}{x - 3\sqrt{x}}$ **79.** $\dfrac{1}{3 + 2\sqrt{2}}$ **81.** $\dfrac{x - 1}{x - 2\sqrt{x} + 1}$ **83.** 5   **85.** $-\dfrac{1}{2}, 6$ **87.** 2, 6   **89.** $r = \dfrac{\sqrt{A\pi}}{2\pi}$

91. a. $\dfrac{y\sqrt{15xy}}{6x^2}$ **b.** $\dfrac{y\sqrt{15xy}}{6x^2}$ **c.** answers may vary   **93.** $\sqrt[3]{25}$ **95.** answers may vary   **97.** answers may vary

Integrated Review

1. 9   **2.** -2 **3.** $\dfrac{1}{2}$ **4.** x^3 **5.** y^3 **6.** $2y^5$ **7.** $-2y$ **8.** $3b^3$ **9.** 6   **10.** $\sqrt[4]{3y}$ **11.** $\dfrac{1}{16}$ **12.** $\sqrt[5]{(x + 1)^3}$ **13.** y

14. $16x^{1/2}$ **15.** $x^{5/4}$ **16.** $4^{11/15}$ **17.** $2x^2$ **18.** $\sqrt[4]{a^3b^2}$ **19.** $\sqrt[4]{x^3}$ **20.** $\sqrt[6]{500}$ **21.** $2\sqrt{10}$ **22.** $2xy^2\sqrt[4]{x^3y^2}$ **23.** $3x\sqrt[3]{2x}$

24. $-2b^2\sqrt[5]{2}$ **25.** $\sqrt{5x}$ **26.** $4x$ **27.** $7y^2\sqrt{y}$ **28.** $2a^2\sqrt[4]{3}$ **29.** $2\sqrt{5} - 5\sqrt{3} + 5\sqrt{7}$ **30.** $y\sqrt[3]{2y}$ **31.** $\sqrt{15} - \sqrt{6}$ **32.** $10 + 2\sqrt{21}$
33. $4x^2 - 5$ **34.** $x + 2 - 2\sqrt{x + 1}$ **35.** $\dfrac{\sqrt{21}}{3}$ **36.** $\dfrac{5\sqrt[3]{4x}}{2x}$ **37.** $\dfrac{13 - 3\sqrt{21}}{5}$ **38.** $\dfrac{7}{\sqrt{21}}$ **39.** $\dfrac{3y}{\sqrt[3]{33y^2}}$ **40.** $\dfrac{x - 4}{x + 2\sqrt{x}}$

Section 7.6
Practice Exercises

1. 18 **2.** $\dfrac{1}{4}, \dfrac{3}{4}$ **3.** 10 **4.** 9 **5.** $\dfrac{3}{25}$ **6.** $6\sqrt{3}$ m **7.** $\sqrt{193}$ in. ≈ 13.89 in.

Graphing Calculator Explorations 7.6

1. 3.19 **3.** $\varnothing$ **5.** 3.23

Vocabulary, Readiness & Video Check 7.6

1. extraneous solution **3.** $x^2 - 10x + 25$ **5.** Applying the power rule can result in an equation with more solutions than the original equation, so you need to check all proposed solutions in the original equation. **7.** Our answer is either a positive square root of a value or a negative square root of a value. We're looking for a length, which must be positive, so our answer must be the positive square root.

Exercise Set 7.6

1. 8 **3.** 7 **5.** $\varnothing$ **7.** 7 **9.** 6 **11.** $-\dfrac{9}{2}$ **13.** 29 **15.** 4 **17.** -4 **19.** $\varnothing$ **21.** 7 **23.** 9 **25.** 50 **27.** $\varnothing$
29. $\dfrac{15}{4}$ **31.** 13 **33.** 5 **35.** -12 **37.** 9 **39.** -3 **41.** 1 **43.** 1 **45.** $\dfrac{1}{2}$ **47.** 0, 4 **49.** $\dfrac{37}{4}$ **51.** $3\sqrt{5}$ ft
53. $2\sqrt{10}$ m **55.** $2\sqrt{131}$ m ≈ 22.9 m **57.** $\sqrt{100.84}$ mm ≈ 10.0 mm **59.** 17 ft **61.** 13 ft **63.** 14,657,415 sq mi **65.** 100 ft
67. 100 **69.** $\dfrac{\pi}{2}$ sec ≈ 1.57 sec **71.** 12.97 ft **73.** answers may vary **75.** $15\sqrt{3}$ sq mi ≈ 25.98 sq mi **77.** answers may vary
79. 0.51 km **81.** function **83.** function **85.** not a function **87.** $\dfrac{x}{4x + 3}$ **89.** $-\dfrac{4z + 2}{3z}$
91. $\sqrt{5x - 1} + 4 = 7$ **93.** 1 **95. a.–b.** answers may vary **97.** $-1, 0, 8, 9$ **99.** $-1, 4$
$\quad\quad \sqrt{5x - 1} = 3$
$\quad\quad (\sqrt{5x - 1})^2 = 3^2$
$\quad\quad\quad 5x - 1 = 9$
$\quad\quad\quad\quad 5x = 10$
$\quad\quad\quad\quad\ x = 2$

Section 7.7
Practice Exercises

1. a. $2i$ **b.** $i\sqrt{7}$ **c.** $-3i\sqrt{2}$ **2. a.** $-\sqrt{30}$ **b.** -3 **c.** $25i$ **d.** $3i$ **3. a.** $-1 - 4i$ **b.** $-3 + 5i$ **c.** $3 - 2i$
4. a. $20 + 0i$ **b.** $-5 + 10i$ **c.** $15 + 16i$ **d.** $8 - 6i$ **e.** $85 + 0i$ **5. a.** $\dfrac{11}{10} - \dfrac{7}{10}i$ **b.** $0 - \dfrac{5}{2}i$ **6. a.** i **b.** 1 **c.** -1 **d.** 1

Vocabulary, Readiness & Video Check 7.7

1. complex **3.** -1 **5.** real **7.** The product rule for radicals; you need to first simplify each separate radical and have nonnegative radicands before applying the product rule. **9.** The fact that $i^2 = -1$. **11.** $i, i^2 = -1, i^3 = -i, i^4 = 1$

Exercise Set 7.7

1. $9i$ **3.** $i\sqrt{7}$ **5.** -4 **7.** $8i$ **9.** $2i\sqrt{6}$ **11.** $-6i$ **13.** $24i\sqrt{7}$ **15.** $-3\sqrt{6}$ **17.** $-\sqrt{14}$ **19.** $-5\sqrt{2}$ **21.** $4i$ **23.** $i\sqrt{3}$
25. $2\sqrt{2}$ **27.** $6 - 4i$ **29.** $-2 + 6i$ **31.** $-2 - 4i$ **33.** $-40 + 0i$ **35.** $18 + 12i$ **37.** $7 + 0i$ **39.** $12 - 16i$ **41.** $0 - 4i$
43. $\dfrac{28}{25} - \dfrac{21}{25}i$ **45.** $4 + i$ **47.** $\dfrac{17}{13} + \dfrac{7}{13}i$ **49.** $63 + 0i$ **51.** $2 - i$ **53.** $27 + 3i$ **55.** $-\dfrac{5}{2} - 2i$ **57.** $18 + 13i$ **59.** $20 + 0i$
61. $10 + 0i$ **63.** $2 + 0i$ **65.** $-5 + \dfrac{16}{3}i$ **67.** $17 + 144i$ **69.** $\dfrac{3}{5} - \dfrac{1}{5}i$ **71.** $5 - 10i$ **73.** $\dfrac{1}{5} - \dfrac{8}{5}i$ **75.** $8 - i$ **77.** $7 + 0i$
79. $12 - 16i$ **81.** 1 **83.** i **85.** $-i$ **87.** -1 **89.** -64 **91.** $-243i$ **93.** $40°$ **95.** $x^2 - 5x - 2 - \dfrac{6}{x - 1}$ **97.** 5 people
99. 14 people **101.** 16.7% **103.** $-1 - i$ **105.** $0 + 0i$ **107.** $2 + 3i$ **109.** $2 + i\sqrt{2}$ **111.** $\dfrac{1}{2} - \dfrac{\sqrt{3}}{2}i$ **113.** answers may vary
115. $6 - 3i\sqrt{3}$ **117.** yes

Chapter 7 Vocabulary Check

1. conjugate **2.** principal square root **3.** rationalizing **4.** imaginary unit **5.** cube root **6.** index; radicand **7.** like radicals
8. complex number **9.** distance **10.** midpoint

Chapter 7 Review

1. 9 **3.** -2 **5.** $-\dfrac{1}{7}$ **7.** -6 **9.** $-a^2b^3$ **11.** $2ab^2$ **13.** $\dfrac{x^6}{6y}$ **15.** $|-x|$ **17.** -27 **19.** $-x$ **21.** $2|2y + z|$ **23.** y **25. a.** 3, 6

b. $[0, \infty)$ **c.**

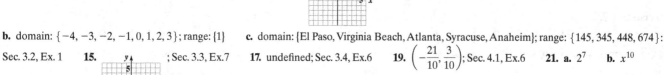

(graph of $f(x) = \sqrt{x} + 3$)

27. $\dfrac{1}{3}$ **29.** $-\dfrac{1}{3}$ **31.** -27 **33.** not a real number   **35.** $\dfrac{9}{4}$ **37.** $x^{2/3}$ **39.** $\sqrt[5]{y^4}$ **41.** $\dfrac{1}{\sqrt[3]{x+2}}$

43. $a^{13/6}$ **45.** $\dfrac{1}{a^{9/2}}$ **47.** $a^4 b^6$ **49.** $\dfrac{b^{5/6}}{49a^{1/4}c^{5/3}}$ **51.** 4.472   **53.** 5.191   **55.** -26.246 **57.** $\sqrt[6]{1372}$

59. $2\sqrt{6}$ **61.** $2x$ **63.** $2\sqrt{15}$ **65.** $3\sqrt[3]{6}$ **67.** $6x^3\sqrt{x}$ **69.** $\dfrac{p^8\sqrt{p}}{11}$ **71.** $\dfrac{y\sqrt[4]{xy^2}}{3}$

73. $\dfrac{5}{\sqrt{\pi}}$ m or $\dfrac{5\sqrt{\pi}}{\pi}$ m   **75.** $\sqrt{197}$ units ≈ 14.036 units   **77.** $\sqrt{73}$ units ≈ 8.544 units   **79.** $2\sqrt{11}$ units ≈ 6.633 units   **81.** $(-5, 5)$

83. $\left(-\dfrac{11}{2}, -2\right)$ **85.** $\left(\dfrac{1}{4}, -\dfrac{2}{7}\right)$ **87.** $-2\sqrt{5}$ **89.** $9\sqrt[3]{2}$ **91.** $\dfrac{15 + 2\sqrt{3}}{6}$ **93.** $17\sqrt{2} - 15\sqrt{5}$ **95.** 6   **97.** $-8\sqrt{5}$

99. $a - 9$ **101.** $\sqrt[3]{25x^2} - 81$ **103.** $\dfrac{3\sqrt{7}}{7}$ **105.** $\dfrac{5\sqrt[3]{2}}{2}$ **107.** $\dfrac{x^2 y^2\sqrt[3]{15yz}}{z}$ **109.** $\dfrac{3\sqrt{y} + 6}{y - 4}$ **111.** $\dfrac{11}{3\sqrt{11}}$ **113.** $\dfrac{3}{7\sqrt[3]{3}}$ **115.** $\dfrac{xy}{\sqrt[3]{10x^2 yz}}$

117. 32   **119.** 35   **121.** 9   **123.** $3\sqrt{2}$ cm   **125.** 51.2 ft   **127.** $0 + 2i\sqrt{2}$ **129.** $0 + 6i$ **131.** $15 - 4i$ **133.** -64

135. $-12 - 18i$ **137.** $-5 - 12i$ **139.** $\dfrac{3}{2} - i$ **141.** x **143.** -10 **145.** $\dfrac{y^5}{2x^3}$ **147.** $\dfrac{1}{8}$ **149.** $\dfrac{1}{x^{13/2}}$ **151.** $\dfrac{n\sqrt{3n}}{11m^5}$

153. $4x - 20\sqrt{x} + 25$ **155.** $(4, 16)$ **157.** $\dfrac{2\sqrt{x} - 6}{x - 9}$ **159.** 5

Chapter 7 Getting Ready for the Test

1. D   **2.** B   **3.** A   **4.** B   **5.** A   **6.** A   **7.** A   **8.** C   **9.** B   **10.** B   **11.** B   **12.** A   **13.** A   **14.** B   **15.** B
16. B   **17.** D   **18.** C   **19.** B   **20.** D   **21.** A

Chapter 7 Test

1. $6\sqrt{6}$ **2.** $-x^{16}$ **3.** $\dfrac{1}{5}$ **4.** 5   **5.** $\dfrac{4x^2}{9}$ **6.** $-a^6 b^3$ **7.** $\dfrac{8a^{1/3}c^{2/3}}{b^{5/12}}$ **8.** $a^{7/12} - a^{7/3}$ **9.** $|4xy|$ or $4|xy|$ **10.** -27 **11.** $\dfrac{3\sqrt{y}}{y}$

12. $\dfrac{8 - 6\sqrt{x} + x}{8 - 2x}$ **13.** $\dfrac{\sqrt[3]{b^2}}{b}$ **14.** $\dfrac{6 - x^2}{8(\sqrt{6} - x)}$ **15.** $-x\sqrt{5x}$ **16.** $4\sqrt{3} - \sqrt{6}$ **17.** $x + 2\sqrt{x} + 1$ **18.** $\sqrt{6} + \sqrt{2} - 4\sqrt{3} - 4$

19. -20 **20.** 23.685   **21.** 0.019   **22.** 2, 3   **23.** $\varnothing$ **24.** 6   **25.** $0 + i\sqrt{2}$ **26.** $0 - 2i\sqrt{2}$ **27.** $0 - 3i$ **28.** $40 + 0i$ **29.** $7 + 24i$

30. $-\dfrac{3}{2} + \dfrac{5}{2}i$ **31.** $\dfrac{5\sqrt{2}}{2}$ **32.** $[-2, \infty)$; 0, 1, 2, 3;   **33.** $2\sqrt{26}$ units   **34.** $\sqrt{95}$ units   **35.** $\left(-4, \dfrac{7}{2}\right)$ **36.** $\left(-\dfrac{1}{2}, \dfrac{3}{10}\right)$

(graph of $g(x) = \sqrt{x} + 2$)   **37.** 27 mph   **38.** 360 ft

Chapter 7 Cumulative Review

1. a. $2xy - 2$ **b.** $2x^2 + 23$ **c.** $3.1x - 0.3$ **d.** $-a - 7b + \dfrac{7}{12}$; Sec. 1.4 Ex. 15   **3.** $\dfrac{21}{11}$; Sec. 2.1 Ex. 6   **5.** \$4500 per month; Sec. 2.4 Ex. 8
7. $\varnothing$; Sec. 2.6, Ex. 6   **9.** $(-\infty, -3] \cup [9, \infty)$; Sec. 2.7, Ex. 8   **11.** *(graph $y = |x|$)*; Sec. 3.1 Ex. 7   **13. a.** domain: $\{2, 0, 3\}$; range: $\{3, 4, -1\}$

b. domain: $\{-4, -3, -2, -1, 0, 1, 2, 3\}$; range: $\{1\}$ **c.** domain: {El Paso, Virginia Beach, Atlanta, Syracuse, Anaheim}; range: $\{145, 345, 448, 674\}$:
Sec. 3.2, Ex. 1   **15.** *(graph $y = -3$)*; Sec. 3.3, Ex. 7   **17.** undefined; Sec. 3.4, Ex. 6   **19.** $\left(-\dfrac{21}{10}, \dfrac{3}{10}\right)$; Sec. 4.1, Ex. 6   **21. a.** 2^7 **b.** x^{10}

c. y^7; Sec. 5.1; Ex. 1   **23.** 6×10^{-5}; Sec. 5.2, Ex. 7   **25. a.** -4 **b.** 11; Sec. 5.3, Ex. 4   **27. a.** $2x^2 + 11x + 15$ **b.** $10x^3 - 27x^2 + 32x - 21$;
Sec. 5.4, Ex. 3   **29.** $5x^2$; Sec. 5.5, Ex. 1   **31. a.** $x^2 - 2x + 4$ **b.** $\dfrac{2}{y - 5}$; Sec. 6.1, Ex. 5   **33. a.** $\dfrac{6x + 5}{3x^3 y}$ **b.** $\dfrac{2x^2 + 7x - 6}{(x + 2)(x - 2)}$

c. 2; Sec. 6.2, Ex. 3   **35. a.** $\dfrac{x(x - 2)}{2(x + 2)}$ **b.** $\dfrac{x^2}{y^2}$; Sec. 6.3, Ex. 2   **37.** $2x^2 - x + 4$; Sec. 6.4, Ex. 1   **39.** $2x^2 + 5x + 2 + \dfrac{7}{x - 3}$; Sec. 6.4, Ex. 8

41. $\varnothing$; Sec. 6.5, Ex. 3   **43.** $x = \dfrac{yz}{y - z}$; Sec. 6.6, Ex. 1   **45.** constant of variation: 15; $u = \dfrac{15}{w}$; Sec. 6.7, Ex. 3   **47. a.** $\dfrac{1}{8}$ **b.** $\dfrac{1}{9}$; Sec. 7.2, Ex. 3

49. $\dfrac{x - 4}{5(\sqrt{x} - 2)}$; Sec. 7.5, Ex. 7

CHAPTER 8 QUADRATIC EQUATIONS AND FUNCTIONS

Section 8.1
Practice Exercises

1. $-4\sqrt{2}, 4\sqrt{2}$ **2.** $-\sqrt{10}, \sqrt{10}$ **3.** $-3 - 2\sqrt{5}, -3 + 2\sqrt{5}$ **4.** $\dfrac{2 + 3i}{5}, \dfrac{2 - 3i}{5}$ **5.** $-2 - \sqrt{7}, -2 + \sqrt{7}$ **6.** $\dfrac{3 - \sqrt{5}}{2}, \dfrac{3 + \sqrt{5}}{2}$
7. $\dfrac{6 - \sqrt{33}}{3}, \dfrac{6 + \sqrt{33}}{3}$ **8.** $\dfrac{5 - i\sqrt{31}}{4}, \dfrac{5 + i\sqrt{31}}{4}$ **9.** 6%

Graphing Calculator Explorations 8.1

1. $-1.27, 6.27$ **3.** $-1.10, 0.90$ **5.** no real solutions

Vocabulary, Readiness & Video Check 8.1

1. $\pm\sqrt{b}$ **3.** completing the square   **5.** 9   **7.** We need a quantity squared by itself on one side of the equation. The only quantity squared is x, so we need to divide both sides by 2 before applying the square root property.   **9.** We're looking for an interest rate so a negative value does not make sense.

Exercise Set 8.1

1. $-4, 4$ **3.** $-\sqrt{7}, \sqrt{7}$ **5.** $-3\sqrt{2}, 3\sqrt{2}$ **7.** $-\sqrt{10}, \sqrt{10}$ **9.** $-8, -2$ **11.** $6 - 3\sqrt{2}, 6 + 3\sqrt{2}$ **13.** $\dfrac{3 - 2\sqrt{2}}{2}, \dfrac{3 + 2\sqrt{2}}{2}$

15. $-3i, 3i$ **17.** $-\sqrt{6}, \sqrt{6}$ **19.** $-2i\sqrt{2}, 2i\sqrt{2}$ **21.** $\dfrac{1 - 4i}{3}, \dfrac{1 + 4i}{3}$ **23.** $-7 - \sqrt{5}, -7 + \sqrt{5}$ **25.** $-3 - 2i\sqrt{2}, -3 + 2i\sqrt{2}$

27. $x^2 + 16x + 64 = (x + 8)^2$ **29.** $z^2 - 12z + 36 = (z - 6)^2$ **31.** $p^2 + 9p + \dfrac{81}{4} = \left(p + \dfrac{9}{2}\right)^2$ **33.** $x^2 + x + \dfrac{1}{4} = \left(x + \dfrac{1}{2}\right)^2$

35. $-5, -3$ **37.** $-3 - \sqrt{7}, -3 + \sqrt{7}$ **39.** $\dfrac{-1 - \sqrt{5}}{2}, \dfrac{-1 + \sqrt{5}}{2}$ **41.** $-1 - \sqrt{6}, -1 + \sqrt{6}$ **43.** $\dfrac{-1 - \sqrt{29}}{2}, \dfrac{-1 + \sqrt{29}}{2}$

45. $\dfrac{6 - \sqrt{30}}{3}, \dfrac{6 + \sqrt{30}}{3}$ **47.** $\dfrac{3 - \sqrt{11}}{2}, \dfrac{3 + \sqrt{11}}{2}$ **49.** $-4, \dfrac{1}{2}$ **51.** $-4 - \sqrt{15}, -4 + \sqrt{15}$ **53.** $\dfrac{-3 - \sqrt{21}}{3}, \dfrac{-3 + \sqrt{21}}{3}$ **55.** $-1, \dfrac{5}{2}$

57. $-1 - i, -1 + i$ **59.** $3 - \sqrt{17}, 3 + \sqrt{17}$ **61.** $-2 - i\sqrt{2}, -2 + i\sqrt{2}$ **63.** $\dfrac{-15 - 7\sqrt{5}}{10}, \dfrac{-15 + 7\sqrt{5}}{10}$ **65.** $\dfrac{1 - i\sqrt{47}}{4}, \dfrac{1 + i\sqrt{47}}{4}$

67. $-5 - i\sqrt{3}, -5 + i\sqrt{3}$ **69.** $-4, 1$ **71.** $\dfrac{2 - i\sqrt{2}}{2}, \dfrac{2 + i\sqrt{2}}{2}$ **73.** $\dfrac{-3 - \sqrt{69}}{6}, \dfrac{-3 + \sqrt{69}}{6}$ **75.** 20%   **77.** 4%   **79.** 9.63 sec

81. 6.17 sec   **83.** 15 ft by 15 ft   **85.** $10\sqrt{2}$ cm   **87.** -1 **89.** $3 + 2\sqrt{5}$ **91.** $\dfrac{1 - 3\sqrt{2}}{2}$ **93.** $2\sqrt{6}$ **95.** 5   **97.** complex, but not

real numbers   **99.** real numbers   **101.** complex, but not real numbers   **103.** $-8x, 8x$ **105.** $-5z, 5z$ **107.** answers may vary
109. compound; answers may vary   **111.** 6 thousand scissors

Section 8.2
Practice Exercises

1. $2, -\dfrac{1}{3}$ **2.** $\dfrac{4 - \sqrt{22}}{3}, \dfrac{4 + \sqrt{22}}{3}$ **3.** $1 - \sqrt{17}, 1 + \sqrt{17}$ **4.** $\dfrac{-1 - i\sqrt{15}}{4}, \dfrac{1 + i\sqrt{15}}{4}$ **5. a.** one real solution   **b.** two real solutions
c. two complex but not real solutions   **6.** 6 ft   **7.** 2.4 sec

Vocabulary, Readiness & Video Check 8.2

1. $x = \dfrac{-b \pm \sqrt{b^2 - 4ac}}{2a}$ **3.** $-5; -7$ **5.** $1; 0$ **7. a.** Yes, in order to make sure we have correct values for a, b, and c.   **b.** No; clearing fractions makes the work less tedious, but it's not a necessary step.   **9.** With applications, we need to make sure we answer the question(s) asked. Here we're asked how much distance is saved, so once the dimensions of the triangle are known, further calculations are needed to answer this question and solve the problem.

Exercise Set 8.2

1. $-6, 1$ **3.** $-\dfrac{3}{5}, 1$ **5.** 3   **7.** $\dfrac{-7 - \sqrt{33}}{2}, \dfrac{-7 + \sqrt{33}}{2}$ **9.** $\dfrac{1 - \sqrt{57}}{8}, \dfrac{1 + \sqrt{57}}{8}$ **11.** $\dfrac{7 - \sqrt{85}}{6}, \dfrac{7 + \sqrt{85}}{6}$ **13.** $1 - \sqrt{3}, 1 + \sqrt{3}$

15. $-\dfrac{3}{2}, 1$ **17.** $\dfrac{3 - \sqrt{11}}{2}, \dfrac{3 + \sqrt{11}}{2}$ **19.** $\dfrac{-5 - \sqrt{17}}{2}, \dfrac{-5 + \sqrt{17}}{2}$ **21.** $\dfrac{5}{2}, 1$ **23.** $-3 - 2i, -3 + 2i$ **25.** $-2 - \sqrt{11}, -2 + \sqrt{11}$

27. $\dfrac{3 - i\sqrt{87}}{8}, \dfrac{3 + i\sqrt{87}}{8}$ **29.** $\dfrac{3 - \sqrt{29}}{2}, \dfrac{3 + \sqrt{29}}{2}$ **31.** $\dfrac{-5 - i\sqrt{5}}{10}, \dfrac{-5 + i\sqrt{5}}{10}$ **33.** $\dfrac{-1 - \sqrt{19}}{6}, \dfrac{-1 + \sqrt{19}}{6}$

35. $\dfrac{-1 - i\sqrt{23}}{4}, \dfrac{-1 + i\sqrt{23}}{4}$ **37.** 1   **39.** $3 - \sqrt{5}, 3 + \sqrt{5}$ **41.** two real solutions   **43.** one real solution   **45.** two real solutions

47. two complex but not real solutions   **49.** two real solutions   **51.** 14 ft   **53.** $(2 + 2\sqrt{2})$ cm, $(2 + 2\sqrt{2})$ cm, $(4 + 2\sqrt{2})$ cm

55. width: $(-5 + 5\sqrt{17})$ ft; length: $(5 + 5\sqrt{17})$ ft   **57. a.** $50\sqrt{2}$ m   **b.** 5000 sq m   **59.** 37.4 ft by 38.5 ft   **61.** base: $(2 + 2\sqrt{43})$ cm; height:

$(-1 + \sqrt{43})$ cm   **63.** 8.9 sec   **65.** 2.8 sec   **67.** $\dfrac{11}{5}$ **69.** 15   **71.** $(x^2 + 5)(x + 2)(x - 2)$ **73.** $(z + 3)(z - 3)(z + 2)(z - 2)$

75. b   **77.** answers may vary   **79.** 0.6, 2.4   **81.** Sunday to Monday   **83.** Wednesday   **85.** $f(4) = 32$; yes   **87. a.** 3129 million

b. 2019   **89. a.** \$679.8 billion   **b.** 2001   **c.** 2027   **91.** answers may vary   **93.** $\dfrac{\sqrt{3}}{3}$ **95.** $\dfrac{-\sqrt{2} - i\sqrt{2}}{2}, \dfrac{-\sqrt{2} + i\sqrt{2}}{2}$

97. $\dfrac{\sqrt{3} - \sqrt{11}}{4}, \dfrac{\sqrt{3} + \sqrt{11}}{4}$ **99.** 8.9 sec: 2.8 sec: **101.** two real solutions

Section 8.3
Practice Exercises

1. 8   **2.** $\dfrac{5 \pm \sqrt{137}}{8}$ **3.** 4, -4, $3i$, $-3i$ **4.** 1, -3 **5.** 1, 64   **6.** Katy: $\dfrac{7 + \sqrt{65}}{2} \approx 7.5$ hr; Steve: $\dfrac{9 + \sqrt{65}}{2} \approx 8.5$ hr

7. to Shanghai: 40 km/hr; to Ningbo: 90 km/hr

Vocabulary, Readiness & Video Check 8.3

1. The values we get for the substituted variable are *not* our final answers. Remember to always substitute back to the original variable and solve for it if necessary.

Exercise Set 8.3

1. 2   **3.** 16   **5.** 1, 4   **7.** $3 - \sqrt{7}, 3 + \sqrt{7}$ **9.** $\dfrac{3 - \sqrt{57}}{4}, \dfrac{3 + \sqrt{57}}{4}$ **11.** $\dfrac{1 - \sqrt{29}}{2}, \dfrac{1 + \sqrt{29}}{2}$ **13.** $-2, 2, -2i, 2i$

15. $-\dfrac{1}{2}, \dfrac{1}{2}, -i\sqrt{3}, i\sqrt{3}$ **17.** $-3, 3, -2, 2$ **19.** $125, -8$ **21.** $-\dfrac{4}{5}, 0$ **23.** $-\dfrac{1}{8}, 27$ **25.** $-\dfrac{2}{3}, \dfrac{4}{3}$ **27.** $-\dfrac{1}{125}, \dfrac{1}{8}$ **29.** $-\sqrt{2}, \sqrt{2}, -\sqrt{3}, \sqrt{3}$

31. $\dfrac{-9 - \sqrt{201}}{6}, \dfrac{-9 + \sqrt{201}}{6}$ **33.** 2, 3   **35.** 3   **37.** 27, 125   **39.** 1, $-3i$, $3i$ **41.** $\dfrac{1}{8}, -8$ **43.** $-\dfrac{1}{2}, \dfrac{1}{3}$ **45.** 4   **47.** -3

49. $-\sqrt{5}, \sqrt{5}, -2i, 2i$ **51.** $-3, \dfrac{3 - 3i\sqrt{3}}{2}, \dfrac{3 + 3i\sqrt{3}}{2}$ **53.** 6, 12   **55.** $-\dfrac{1}{3}, \dfrac{1}{3}, -\dfrac{i\sqrt{6}}{3}, \dfrac{i\sqrt{6}}{3}$ **57.** 5   **59.** 55 mph: 66 mph

61. 5 mph, then 4 mph   **63.** inlet pipe: 15.5 hr; hose: 16.5 hr   **65.** 8.5 hr   **67.** 12 or -8 **69. a.** $(x - 6)$ in.   **b.** $300 = (x - 6) \cdot (x - 6) \cdot 3$
c. 16 in. by 16 in.   **71.** 22 feet   **73.** $(-\infty, 3]$ **75.** $(-5, \infty)$ **77.** domain: $(-\infty, \infty)$; range: $(-\infty, \infty)$; function   **79.** domain: $(-\infty, \infty)$;

range: $[-1, \infty)$; function   **81.** 1, $-3i$, $3i$ **83.** $-\dfrac{1}{2}, \dfrac{1}{3}$ **85.** $-3, \dfrac{3 - 3i\sqrt{3}}{2}, \dfrac{3 + 3i\sqrt{3}}{2}$ **87.** answers may vary   **89. a.** approximately 164.37 mph

b. 54.754 sec/lap   **c.** 55.947 sec/lap   **d.** 160.87 mph

Integrated Review

1. $-\sqrt{10}, \sqrt{10}$ **2.** $-\sqrt{14}, \sqrt{14}$ **3.** $1 - 2\sqrt{2}, 1 + 2\sqrt{2}$ **4.** $-5 - 2\sqrt{3}, -5 + 2\sqrt{3}$ **5.** $-1 - \sqrt{13}, -1 + \sqrt{13}$ **6.** 1, 11

7. $\dfrac{-3 - \sqrt{69}}{6}, \dfrac{-3 + \sqrt{69}}{6}$ **8.** $\dfrac{-2 - \sqrt{5}}{4}, \dfrac{-2 + \sqrt{5}}{4}$ **9.** $\dfrac{2 - \sqrt{2}}{2}, \dfrac{2 + \sqrt{2}}{2}$ **10.** $-3 - \sqrt{5}, -3 + \sqrt{5}$ **11.** $-2 - i\sqrt{3}, -2 + i\sqrt{3}$

12. $\dfrac{-1 - i\sqrt{11}}{2}, \dfrac{-1 + i\sqrt{11}}{2}$ **13.** $\dfrac{-3 - i\sqrt{15}}{2}, \dfrac{-3 + i\sqrt{15}}{2}$ **14.** $-3i, 3i$ **15.** $-17, 0$ **16.** $\dfrac{1 - \sqrt{13}}{4}, \dfrac{1 + \sqrt{13}}{4}$ **17.** $2 - 3\sqrt{3}, 2 + 3\sqrt{3}$

18. $2 - \sqrt{3}, 2 + \sqrt{3}$ **19.** $-2, \dfrac{4}{3}$ **20.** $\dfrac{-5 - \sqrt{17}}{4}, \dfrac{-5 + \sqrt{17}}{4}$ **21.** $1 - \sqrt{6}, 1 + \sqrt{6}$ **22.** $-\sqrt{31}, \sqrt{31}$ **23.** $-\sqrt{11}, \sqrt{11}$

24. $-i\sqrt{11}, i\sqrt{11}$ **25.** $-11, 6$ **26.** $\dfrac{-3 - \sqrt{19}}{5}, \dfrac{-3 + \sqrt{19}}{5}$ **27.** $\dfrac{-3 - \sqrt{17}}{4}, \dfrac{-3 + \sqrt{17}}{4}$ **28.** 4   **29.** $\dfrac{-1 - \sqrt{17}}{8}, \dfrac{-1 + \sqrt{17}}{8}$

30. $10\sqrt{2}$ ft ≈ 14.1 ft   **31.** Jack: 9.1 hr; Lucy: 7.1 hr   **32.** 5 mph during the first part, then 6 mph

Section 8.4
Practice Exercises

1. $(-\infty, -3) \cup (4, \infty)$ **2.** $[0, 8]$ **3.** $(-\infty, -3] \cup [-1, 2]$ **4.** $(-4, 5]$ **5.** $(-\infty, -3) \cup \left(-\dfrac{8}{5}, \infty\right)$

Vocabulary, Readiness & Video Check 8.4

1. $[-7, 3)$ **3.** $(-\infty, 0]$ **5.** $(-\infty, -12) \cup [-10, \infty)$ **7.** We use the solutions to the related equation to divide the number line into regions that either entirely are or entirely are not solution regions; the solutions to the related equation are solutions to the inequality only if the inequality symbol is $\le$ or $\ge$.

Exercise Set 8.4

1. $(-\infty, -5) \cup (-1, \infty)$ **3.** $[-4, 3]$ **5.** $[2, 5]$ **7.** $\left(-5, -\frac{1}{3}\right)$ **9.** $(2, 4) \cup (6, \infty)$ **11.** $(-\infty, -4] \cup [0, 1]$

13. $(-\infty, -3) \cup (-2, 2) \cup (3, \infty)$ **15.** $(-7, 2)$ **17.** $(-1, \infty)$ **19.** $(-\infty, -1] \cup (4, \infty)$ **21.** $(-\infty, 2) \cup \left(\frac{11}{4}, \infty\right)$ **23.** $(0, 2] \cup [3, \infty)$

25. $(-\infty, 3)$ **27.** $\left[-\frac{5}{4}, \frac{3}{2}\right]$ **29.** $(-\infty, 0) \cup (1, \infty)$ **31.** $(-\infty, -4] \cup [4, 6]$ **33.** $\left(-\infty, -\frac{2}{3}\right] \cup \left[\frac{3}{2}, \infty\right)$

35. $\left(-4, -\frac{3}{2}\right) \cup \left(\frac{3}{2}, \infty\right)$ **37.** $(-\infty, -5] \cup [-1, 1] \cup [5, \infty)$ **39.** $\left(-\infty, -\frac{5}{3}\right) \cup \left(\frac{7}{2}, \infty\right)$ **41.** $(0, 10)$ **43.** $(-\infty, -4) \cup [5, \infty)$

45. $(-\infty, -6] \cup (-1, 0] \cup (7, \infty)$ **47.** $(-\infty, 1) \cup (2, \infty)$ **49.** $(-\infty, -8] \cup (-4, \infty)$ **51.** $(-\infty, 0] \cup \left(5, \frac{11}{2}\right]$ **53.** $(0, \infty)$

55.   **57.**   **59.**   **61.**   **63.** answers may vary
65. $(-\infty, -1) \cup (0, 1)$, or any number less than -1 or between 0 and 1

67. x is between 2 and 11   **69.**   **71.**

Section 8.5
Practice Exercises

1. $f(x) = x^2$ **2. a.**   **b.**   **3.**   **4. a.**   **b.**

5.   **6.** $f(x) = x^2$ $g(x) = 4x^2$ **7.**   **8.**

Graphing Calculator Explorations 8.5

1.   **3.**   **5.**

Vocabulary, Readiness & Video Check 8.5

1. quadratic   **3.** upward   **5.** lowest   **7.** $(0, 0)$ **9.** $(2, 0)$ **11.** $(0, 3)$ **13.** $(-1, 5)$ **15.** Graphs of the form $f(x) = x^2 + k$ shift up or down the y-axis k units from $y = x^2$; the y-intercept.   **17.** The vertex, (h, k), and the axis of symmetry, $x = h$; the basic shape of $y = x^2$ does not change.   **19.** the coordinates of the vertex, whether the graph opens upward or downward, whether the graph is narrower or wider than $y = x^2$, and the graph's axis of symmetry

Exercise Set 8.5

1. $x = 0$

3. $V(0,5)$ $x = 0$

5. $V(0,7)$ $x = 0$

7. $V(5,0)$ $x = 5$

9. $V(-2,0)$ $x = -2$

11. $V(-3,0)$ $x = -3$

13. $V(2,5)$ $x = 2$

15. $V(-1,4)$ $x = -1$

17. $V(-2,-5)$ $x = -2$

19. $V(0,0)$ $x = 0$

21. $V(0,0)$ $x = 0$

23. $V(0,0)$ $x = 0$

25. $V(1,3)$ $x = 1$

27. $V(-3,1)$ $x = -3$

29. $V(6,-3)$ $x = 6$

31. $x = 2$ $V(2,0)$ $f(x) = -(x-2)^2$

33. $x = 0$ $V(0,4)$ $F(x) = -x^2 + 4$

35. $V(0,-5)$ $F(x) = 2x^2 - 5$ $x = 0$

37. $h(x) = (x-6)^2 + 4$ $V(6,4)$ $x = 6$

39. $F(x) = \left(x + \frac{1}{2}\right)^2 - 2$ $V\left(-\frac{1}{2}, -2\right)$ $x = -\frac{1}{2}$

41. $F(x) = \frac{3}{2}(x+7)^2 + 1$ $V(-7,1)$ $x = -7$

43. $f(x) = \frac{1}{4}x^2 - 9$ $V(0,-9)$ $x = 0$

45. $G(x) = 5\left(x + \frac{1}{2}\right)^2$ $V\left(-\frac{1}{2}, 0\right)$ $x = -\frac{1}{2}$

47. $x = 1$ $V(1,-1)$ $h(x) = -(x-1)^2 - 1$

49. $g(x) = \sqrt{3}(x+5)^2 + \frac{3}{4}$ $V\left(-5, \frac{3}{4}\right)$ $x = -5$

51. $h(x) = 10(x+4)^2 - 6$ $V(-4,-6)$ $x = -4$

53. $x = 4$ $V(4,5)$ $f(x) = -2(x-4)^2 + 5$

55. $x^2 + 8x + 16$ **57.** $z^2 - 16z + 64$ **59.** $y^2 + y + \frac{1}{4}$ **61.** $-6, 2$ **63.** $-5 - \sqrt{26}, -5 + \sqrt{26}$

65. $4 - 3\sqrt{2}, 4 + 3\sqrt{2}$ **67.** c   **69.** $f(x) = 5(x-2)^2 + 3$ **71.** $f(x) = 5(x+3)^2 + 6$

73.

75.

77.

79. a. \$423 billion   **b.** \$1987.5 billion

Section 8.6
Practice Exercises

1. $(-1,0)$ $(3,0)$ $(0,-3)$ $(1,-4)$

2. $\left(-\frac{1}{2}, 2\right)$ $(0,3)$

3. $(2.5, 12.25)$ $(0,6)$ $(6,0)$ $(-1,0)$

4. $(1,-4)$ **5.** Maximum height 9 feet in $\frac{3}{4}$ second

Vocabulary, Readiness & Video Check 8.6

1. (h, k) **3.** We can immediately identify the vertex (h, k), whether the parabola opens upward or downward, and know its axis of symmetry; completing the square.   **5.** the vertex

Exercise Set 8.6

1. $0; 1$ **3.** $2; 1$ **5.** $1; 1$ **7.** down   **9.** up   **11.** $(-4, -9)$ **13.** $(5, 30)$ **15.** $(1, -2)$ **17.** $\left(\frac{1}{2}, \frac{5}{4}\right)$ **19.** D   **21.** B

23. $f(x) = x^2 + 4x - 5$ $(-5,0)$ $(1,0)$ $(0,-5)$ $(-2,-9)$

25. $(1,0)$ $(0,-1)$ $f(x) = -x^2 + 2x - 1$

27. $f(x) = x^2 - 4$ $(2,0)$ $(-2,0)$ $(0,-4)$

29. $f(x) = 4x^2 + 4x - 3$ $\left(-\frac{3}{2}, 0\right)$ $\left(\frac{1}{2}, 0\right)$ $\left(-\frac{1}{2}, -4\right)$ $(0,-3)$

31. $f(x) = \frac{1}{2}x^2 + 4x + \frac{15}{2}$ $\left(0, \frac{15}{2}\right)$ $(-5,0)$ $(-3,0)$ $\left(-4, -\frac{1}{2}\right)$

33. $f(x) = x^2 - 6x + 5$; (0, 5); (1, 0); (5, 0); (3, -4)

35. $f(x) = x^2 - 4x + 5$; (0, 5); (2, 1)

37. $f(x) = 2x^2 + 4x + 5$; (0, 5); (-1, 3)

39. $f(x) = -2x^2 + 12x$; (3, 18); (0, 0); (6, 0)

41. $f(x) = x^2 + 1$; (0, 1)

43. $f(x) = x^2 - 2x - 15$; (-3, 0); (5, 0); (0, -15); (1, -16)

45. $f(x) = -5x^2 + 5x$; (0, 0); (1, 0); $\left(\frac{1}{2}, \frac{5}{4}\right)$

47. $f(x) = -x^2 + 2x - 12$; (0, -12); (1, -11)

49. $f(x) = 3x^2 - 12x + 15$; (0, 15); (2, 3)

51. $f(x) = x^2 + x - 6$; (-3, 0); (2, 0); (0, -6); $\left(-\frac{1}{2}, -\frac{25}{4}\right)$

53. $f(x) = -2x^2 - 3x + 35$; $\left(-\frac{3}{4}, \frac{289}{8}\right)$; (0, 35); (-5, 0); $\left(\frac{7}{2}, 0\right)$

55. 144 ft   **57. a.** 200 bicycles   **b.** \$12,000   **59.** 30 and 30   **61.** 5, -5   **63.** length: 20 units; width: 20 units

65. $f(x) = x^2 + 2$; (0, 2)

67. $g(x) = x + 2$

69. $f(x) = (x + 5)^2 + 2$; (-5, 2)

71. $f(x) = 3(x - 4)^2 + 1$; (4, 1)

73. $\left(4, \frac{3}{2}\right)$; $f(x) = -(x - 4)^2 + \frac{3}{2}$

75. minimum value   **77.** maximum value   **79.** $f(x) = x^2 + 10x + 15$; (-8.2, 0); (0, 15); (-1.8, 0); (-5, -10)

81. (0, 7); (1, 4); $f(x) = 3x^2 - 6x + 7$

83. -0.84   **85.** 1.43

87. a. maximum; answers may vary   **b.** 2035   **c.** 311 million

89.

91.

Chapter 8 Vocabulary Check

1. discriminant   **2.** $\pm\sqrt{b}$ **3.** $\dfrac{-b}{2a}$ **4.** quadratic inequality   **5.** completing the square   **6.** $(0, k)$ **7.** $(h, 0)$ **8.** (h, k)

9. quadratic formula   **10.** quadratic

Chapter 8 Review

1. 14, 1   **3.** -7, 7   **5.** $\dfrac{-3 - \sqrt{5}}{2}, \dfrac{-3 + \sqrt{5}}{2}$ **7.** 4.25%   **9.** two complex but not real solutions   **11.** two real solutions   **13.** 8

15. $-\dfrac{5}{2}, 1$ **17.** $\dfrac{5 - i\sqrt{143}}{12}, \dfrac{5 + i\sqrt{143}}{12}$ **19. a.** 20 ft   **b.** $\dfrac{15 + \sqrt{321}}{16}$ sec; 2.1 sec   **21.** 3, $\dfrac{-3 - 3i\sqrt{3}}{2}, \dfrac{-3 + 3i\sqrt{3}}{2}$ **23.** $\dfrac{2}{3}, 5$ **25.** 1, 125

27. -1, 1, -i, i   **29.** Jerome: 10.5 hr; Tim: 9.5 hr   **31.** $[-5, 5]$ **33.** $[-5, -2] \cup [2, 5]$ **35.** (5, 6)   **37.** $(-, -5] \cup [-2, 6]$ **39.** $(-\infty, 0)$

41. (0, -4); $x = 0$

43. (0, 0); $x = 0$

45. (1, 0); $x = 1$

47. (4, -2); $x = 4$

49. (-5, 0); (0, 25)

51. $\left(-\dfrac{1}{2}, 0\right)$; $\left(\dfrac{1}{2}, 0\right)$; (0, -1)

53. $\left(-\frac{5}{6}, \frac{73}{12}\right)$

55. 210 and 210   **57.** $-5, 6$ **59.** $-2, 2$ **61.** $\dfrac{-1 - 3i\sqrt{3}}{2}, \dfrac{-1 + 3i\sqrt{3}}{2}$ **63.** $-i\sqrt{11}, i\sqrt{11}$

65. $\dfrac{21 - \sqrt{41}}{50}, \dfrac{21 + \sqrt{41}}{50}$ **67.** 8, 64   **69.** $[-5, 0] \cup \left(\dfrac{3}{4}, \infty\right)$ **71. a.** 90,332 thousand passengers   **b.** no; answers may vary

Chapter 8 Getting Ready for the Test

1. C   **2.** B   **3.** A   **4.** D   **5.** B   **6.** D   **7.** C   **8.** C   **9.** A   **10.** B   **11.** C

Chapter 8 Test

1. $\dfrac{7}{5}, -1$ **2.** $-1 - \sqrt{10}, -1 + \sqrt{10}$ **3.** $\dfrac{1 - i\sqrt{31}}{2}, \dfrac{1 + i\sqrt{31}}{2}$ **4.** $3 - \sqrt{7}, 3 + \sqrt{7}$ **5.** $-\dfrac{1}{7}, -1$ **6.** $\dfrac{3 - \sqrt{29}}{2}, \dfrac{3 + \sqrt{29}}{2}$

7. $-2 - \sqrt{11}, -2 + \sqrt{11}$ **8.** $-1, 1, -i, i, -3$ **9.** $-1, 1, -i, i$ **10.** $6, 7$ **11.** $3 - \sqrt{7}, 3 + \sqrt{7}$ **12.** $\dfrac{2 - i\sqrt{6}}{2}, \dfrac{2 + i\sqrt{6}}{2}$

13. $\left(-\infty, -\dfrac{3}{2}\right) \cup (5, \infty)$ **14.** $(-\infty, -5] \cup [-4, 4] \cup [5, \infty)$ **15.** $(-\infty, -3) \cup (2, \infty)$ **16.** $(-\infty, -3) \cup [2, 3)$

17.   **18.**   **19.**   **20.**   **21.** $(5 + \sqrt{17})\,\text{hr} \approx 9.12\,\text{hr}$ **22. a.** 272 ft
b. 5.12 sec   **23.** 7.2 ft

Chapter 8 Cumulative Review

1. a. $5 + y \geq 7$ **b.** $11 \neq z$ **c.** $20 < 5 - 2x$; Sec. 1.4, Ex. 6   **3.** $m = 1$; ; Sec. 3.4, Ex. 1   **5.** $(-2, 2)$; Sec. 4.1, Ex. 7

7. a. $6x^2 - 29x + 28$ **b.** $15x^4 - x^2y - 2y^2$; Sec. 5.4, Ex. 6   **9. a.** $4(2x^2 + 1)$ **b.** prime polynomial   **c.** $3x^2(2 - x + 4x^2)$; Sec. 5.5, Ex. 2

11. $(x - 5)(x - 7)$; Sec. 5.6, Ex. 2   **13.** $3x(a - 2b)^2$; Sec. 5.7, Ex. 2   **15.** $-\dfrac{2}{3}$; Sec. 5.8, Ex. 4   **17.** $-2, 0, 2$; Sec. 5.8, Ex. 6   **19.** $\dfrac{1}{5x - 1}$;

Sec. 6.1, Ex. 2a   **21.** $\dfrac{7x^2 - 9x - 13}{(2x + 1)(x - 5)(3x - 2)}$; Sec. 6.2, Ex. 5   **23.** $\dfrac{xy + 2x^3}{y - 1}$ or $\dfrac{x(y + 2x^2)}{y - 1}$; Sec. 6.3, Ex. 3   **25.** $3x^3y - 15x - 1 - \dfrac{6}{xy}$; Sec. 6.4, Ex. 2

27. a. 5   **b.** 5; Sec. 6.4, Ex. 10   **29.** -3; Sec. 6.5, Ex. 1   **31.** 2; Sec. 6.6, Ex. 2   **33.** $k = \dfrac{1}{6}; y = \dfrac{1}{6}x$; Sec. 6.7, Ex. 1   **35. a.** 3   **b.** $|x|$

c. $|x - 2|$ **d.** -5 **e.** $2x - 7$ **f.** $5|x|$ **g.** $|x + 1|$; Sec. 7.1, Ex. 5   **37. a.** $\sqrt{x}$ **b.** $\sqrt[3]{5}$ **c.** $\sqrt{rs^3}$; Sec. 7.2, Ex. 7   **39. a.** $5x\sqrt{x}$

b. $3x^2y^2\sqrt[3]{2y^2}$ **c.** $3z^2\sqrt[3]{z^3}$; Sec. 7.3, Ex. 4   **41. a.** $\dfrac{2\sqrt{5}}{5}$ **b.** $\dfrac{8\sqrt{x}}{3x}$ **c.** $\dfrac{\sqrt[3]{4}}{2}$; Sec. 7.5, Ex. 1   **43.** $\dfrac{2}{9}$; Sec. 7.6, Ex. 5   **45. a.** $\dfrac{1}{2} + \dfrac{3}{2}i$

b. $0 - \dfrac{7}{3}i$; Sec. 7.7, Ex. 5   **47.** $-1 + 2\sqrt{3}, -1 - 2\sqrt{3}$; Sec. 8.1, Ex. 3   **49.** 9; Sec. 8.3, Ex. 1

APPENDIX A GEOMETRY

Exercise Set Appendix A

1. $V = 72$ cu in.; $SA = 108$ sq in.   **3.** $V = 512$ cu cm; $SA = 384$ sq cm   **5.** $V = 4\pi$ cu yd $\approx 12\frac{4}{7}$ cu yd; $SA = \left(2\pi\sqrt{13} + 4\pi\right)$ sq yd ≈ 35.20 sq yd

7. $V = \dfrac{500}{3}\pi$ cu in. $\approx 523\frac{17}{21}$ cu in.; $SA = 100\pi$ sq in. $\approx 314\frac{2}{7}$ sq in.   **9.** $V = 48$ cu cm; $SA = 96$ sq cm   **11.** $2\frac{10}{27}$ cu in.   **13.** 26 sq ft

15. $10\frac{5}{6}$ cu in.   **17.** 960 cu cm   **19.** 196π sq in.   **21.** $7\frac{1}{2}$ cu ft   **23.** $12\frac{4}{7}$ cu cm

APPENDIX B STRETCHING AND COMPRESSING GRAPHS OF ABSOLUTE VALUE FUNCTIONS

Exercise Set Appendix B

1.   **3.**   **5.**   **7.**   **9.**

11.   **13.**   **15.**

APPENDIX C SOLVING SYSTEMS OF EQUATIONS USING DETERMINANTS

Vocabulary, Readiness & Video Check Appendix C

1. 56   **3.** −32   **5.** 20

Exercise Set Appendix C

1. 26   **3.** −19   **5.** 0   **7.** $\dfrac{13}{6}$ **9.** $(1, 2)$ **11.** $\{(x, y) \mid 3x + y = 1\}$ **13.** $(9, 9)$ **15.** $(-3, -2)$ **17.** $(3, 4)$ **19.** 8   **21.** 0

23. 15   **25.** 54   **27.** $(-2, 0, 5)$ **29.** $(6, -2, 4)$ **31.** $(-2, 3, -1)$ **33.** $(0, 2, -1)$ **35.** 5   **37.** 0; answers may vary

APPENDIX D AN INTRODUCTION TO USING A GRAPHING UTILITY

Viewing Window and Interpreting Window Settings Exercise Set

1. yes   **3.** no   **5.** answers may vary   **7.** answers may vary   **9.** answers may vary

11. Xmin = −12 Ymin = −12   **13.** Xmin = −9 Ymin = −12   **15.** Xmin = −10 Ymin = −25   **17.** Xmin = −10 Ymin = −30
  Xmax = 12 Ymax = 12   Xmax = 9 Ymax = 12   Xmax = 10 Ymax = 25   Xmax = 10 Ymax = 30
  Xscl = 3 Yscl = 3   Xscl = 1 Yscl = 2   Xscl = 2 Yscl = 5   Xscl = 1 Yscl = 3

19. Xmin = −20 Ymin = −30
  Xmax = 30 Ymax = 50
  Xscl = 5 Yscl = 10

Graphing Equations and Square Viewing Window Exercise Set

1. Setting B   **3.** Setting B   **5.** Setting B

7.   **9.**   **11.**   **13.**

15.   **17.**   **19.**   **21.**

PRACTICE FINAL EXAM

1. $6\sqrt{6}$ **2.** $-\dfrac{3}{2}$ **3.** 5 **4.** $\dfrac{1}{81x^2}$ **5.** $\dfrac{64}{3}$ **6.** $\dfrac{3a^7}{2b^5}$ **7.** $\dfrac{8a^{1/3}c^{2/3}}{b^{5/12}}$ **8.** $3y(x+3y)(x-3y)$ **9.** $2(2y-1)(4y^2+2y+1)$

10. $(x+3)(x-3)(y-3)$ **11.** $-5x^3y-11x-9$ **12.** $36m^2+12mn+n^2$ **13.** $2x^3-13x^2+14x-4$ **14.** $\dfrac{x+2}{2(x+3)}$ **15.** $\dfrac{1}{x(x+3)}$

16. $\dfrac{5x-2}{(x-3)(x+2)(x-2)}$ **17.** $-x\sqrt{5x}$ **18.** -20 **19.** $2x^2-x-2+\dfrac{2}{2x+1}$ **20.** -32 **21.** $1,\dfrac{2}{3}$ **22.** $4,-\dfrac{8}{7}$

23. $\left(\dfrac{3}{2},5\right]$ **24.** $(-\infty,-2)\cup\left(\dfrac{4}{3},\infty\right)$ **25.** 3 **26.** $\dfrac{3\pm\sqrt{29}}{2}$ **27.** $2,3$ **28.** $\left(-\infty,-\dfrac{3}{2}\right)\cup(5,\infty)$ **29.** $\left(\dfrac{7}{2},-10\right)$

30. $4x+6y=7$ **31.** $2x-y>5$ **32.** $y=-3$ **33.** $(-2,-1)$; domain: $(-\infty,\infty)$; range: $(-\infty,-1]$

34. $(0,4)$ $(2,0)$ **35.** ; domain: $(-\infty,\infty)$; range: $(-3,\infty)$ **36.** $f(x)=-\dfrac{1}{2}x$ **37.** $f(x)=-\dfrac{1}{3}x+\dfrac{5}{3}$ **38.** $2\sqrt{26}$ units

39. $\left(-4,\dfrac{7}{2}\right)$ **40.** $\dfrac{3\sqrt{y}}{y}$ **41.** $\dfrac{8-6\sqrt{x}+x}{8-2x}$ **42.** $2{,}723{,}000$ **43.** $(x+2y)(x-2y)$ **44.** 5 **45.** 16 **46.** 7.2 ft   **47. a.** 272 ft

b. 5.12 sec   **48.** 5 gal of 10%; 15 gal of 20%   **49.** $0-2i\sqrt{2}$ **50.** $0-3i$ **51.** $7+24i$ **52.** $-\dfrac{3}{2}+\dfrac{5}{2}i$ **53.** $(g\circ h)(x)=x^2-6x-2$

54. $f^{-1}(x)=\dfrac{-x+6}{2}$ **55.** $\log_5\dfrac{x^4}{x+1}$ **56.** -1 **57.** $\dfrac{1}{2}\left(\dfrac{\log 4}{\log 3}-5\right);-1.8691$ **58.** 22 **59.** $\dfrac{43}{21}$ **60.** $\dfrac{1}{2}$

61.   **62.** 64,805 prairie dogs   **63.** $(-6,0)$ $(6,0)$ **64.** $(0,4)$ $(3,0)$ $(-3,0)$ $(0,-4)$ **65.** $r=5$ $C(-3,0)$

66. $(-5,-1),(-5,1),(5,-1),(5,1)$ **67.** $-\dfrac{1}{5},\dfrac{1}{6},-\dfrac{1}{7},\dfrac{1}{8},-\dfrac{1}{9}$ **68.** 155 **69.** 1 **70.** 10 **71.** $32x^5+80x^4y+80x^3y^2+40x^2y^3+10xy^4+y^5$

Index

Photo Credits